1-05-167   (05-1801)

THE CIVILIZATION OF THE AMERICAN INDIAN SERIES
(*Complete list on pages* 388–91)

The Kickapoos: Lords of the Middle Border

THE KICKAPOOS

Lords of the Middle Border

BY A. M. GIBSON

UNIVERSITY OF OKLAHOMA PRESS : NORMAN

Library of Congress Catalog Card Number: 63–18071

Copyright 1963 by the University of Oklahoma Press, Publishing Division of the University. Composed and printed at Norman, Oklahoma, U.S.A., by the University of Oklahoma Press. First edition.

*To the memory of
my father*
ARRELL MORGAN GIBSON

Preface

PROBABLY NO INDIAN TRIBAL NAME has been used as often for non-Indian purposes as "Kickapoo." Because of its appealing sound, "Kickapoo" has been appropriated by geographers, border raiders, politicians, and patent-medicine makers. As one might expect, "Kickapoo" appears most commonly in place geography. These remarkable people have left a legacy of place names in at least eight of the states over which they roamed in earlier times. "Kickapoo" is a popular name for rivers, creeks, towns, and geological configurations such as Kickapoo Gap in south Texas. Fraternal orders, lodges, and even western border raiders during the Civil War, including the famed Kickapoo Rangers, used this tribe's name. Nor did "Kickapoo" escape political appropriation, for splinter parties in Oklahoma Territory often adopted this name, one example being the Kickapoo faction in early Oklahoma City politics.

"Kickapoo" became a common household word throughout America during the late nineteenth century when Healy and Bigelow of New Haven, Connecticut, organized the Kickapoo Medicine Company and peddled Kickapoo Indian Cough Cure, Kickapoo Indian Salve, and Kickapoo Indian Sagwa (a panacea guaranteed to cure symptoms of dyspepsia including neuralgia, headache, constipation, kidney disease, various stomach and liver ailments, and female disorders) through the peripatetic medicine show.

The Kickapoos were known by name only, and many features of their folklore, internal organization, and native religion remain a deep mystery even today. A few names stand out conspicuously among the several hundred Indian tribes of North America. The Cherokees merit special note for their sophistication and remarkable advancement in the arts of western civilization; the Comanches for their barbarity; and the Delawares for friendly service as guides and interpreters. The Kickapoos deserve special recognition also and if one adjective could characterize a tribe, "unconquerable" would best fit these people.

Appropriately named Kickapoo from the Algonquian *Kiwigapawa,* which means "he moves about," and first discovered in the Great Lakes region, this restless people traveled to Wisconsin, Illinois, Indiana, parts of Ohio, Michigan, New York, Pennsylvania, eastern Iowa, Missouri, Kansas, Oklahoma, Texas, and northern Mexico. The Kickapoos ranged south of the Ohio River into Kentucky, Tennessee, Georgia, and Alabama to the Gulf. A substantial Kickapoo community still resides in the north Mexican state of Coahuila.

The Kickapoos were extremely successful warriors. Skilled in warrior craft and inventive strategy, they were much in demand as frontier shock troops, and successively served as mercenaries for the French, Spanish, British, and Mexicans.

Few tribes can match the Kickapoos for vindictiveness. The Kickapoos regarded the United States as the epitome of evil and resisted the Anglo advance with calculated and passionate hostility. While many tribes accepted reservation life, the Kickapoos seemed to become stronger and more determined to resist with each new overture by the United States. The Kickapoos eventually came as prisoners of war from Mexico, sullen and planning new mischief for the agents assigned to watch over them.

On the reservation the Kickapoos carried on an extended cold war against the government's attempts to lead the warriors and their families along the white man's road. In this struggle they were remarkably successful, and in the twentieth century the Kickapoos remain unconquered—a haughty, proud, and courageous people faithful to the ordinances of the Great Spirit.

In assembling the story of the Kickapoos, old friends were called upon for help, and new friends were made. A special word of gratitude must be expressed to Rella Looney, Oklahoma Historical Society; Margaret Blaker, Bureau of American Ethnology; Dorothy Brockhoff, Missouri Historical Society (St. Louis); William B. Miller, Presbyterian Historical Society; Dorothy Libby, Great Lakes Indian Archives Project; and Opal Carr and Mary Webb, University of Oklahoma Library. Also a word of thanks is due the staffs of the National Archives (Washington, D.C. and regional depositories at Kansas City, Missouri, and Fort Worth, Texas), the Library of Congress, Indiana Historical Society, Kansas Historical Society, Wisconsin Historical Society, and the University of Texas Library. I am indebted to Duane Roller and the University of Oklahoma Faculty Research Committee for various grants which made possible the collection of scattered material, and to Arthur McAnally, director of the University of Oklahoma libraries, for enduring interest and encouragement.

A. M. Gibson

Norman, Oklahoma
August 20, 1963

Contents

Illustrations

MAP

The Kickapoos: Lords of the Middle Border

1

Introducing the Kickapoos

THE INDIAN TRIBES OF NORTH AMERICA possessed many common physical and cultural traits which make it difficult to distinguish one tribe from another. Language has been found to be the most reliable basis for separation and classification, yet even the language stocks are broad in their groupings and, in most cases, include a number of tribes. One of the largest language stocks is the Algonquian.

Tribes of this association were widely dispersed at the time of European contact, ranging from the Delawares and Shawnees of the Atlantic seaboard to the Cheyennes and Arapahoes of the western Great Plains. The Algonquian heartland, however, was located in the Old Northwest, and extended from the triangle point of the eastern Great Lakes westward to the Mississippi, flanked on the north by the lake chain and on the south by the Ohio River. Within this range some twenty-odd tribes of the Algonquian linguistic brotherhood were situated, all possessing a common culture.

Generally speaking, an aboriginal history for this entire Algonquian community could be written in rather specific terms, for the culture traits of one tribe were fairly common to all. Each tribe had achieved the approximate cultural level of neighboring tribes. The Algonquians were quasi-sedentary, with fixed villages where crops were planted and tribal affairs were conducted. Autumn and winter were spent in hunting, away from these fixed areas. Their weapons, their methods of raising war parties and conducting warfare, and their marriage and family customs were quite similar. These tribes produced the same crops, had a common method of preparing food, and their clothing and implements were fairly similar.

These Algonquians were hospitable toward visitors, worshiped the same gods, and exhibited a childish curiosity about the goods and manners of Europeans. Their dances, ceremonials, feasts, fasts, and rituals followed a common pattern. These tribes were for the most part self-sufficient, and they operated in an economic and social equilibrium which had existed for a time beyond memory and tradition.

From the seventeenth century until well into the nineteenth, the Algonquian heartland was subjected to a series of invasions which destroyed not only the indigenous culture but entire tribes as well. The French, ardent disciples of mercantilism, were the first invaders. From their St. Lawrence settlements they moved west and south by the Great Lakes and along the Fox, Wisconsin, Illinois, and Wabash rivers into the Algonquian range.

Beginning with Samuel de Champlain in 1608, an increasing number of ambitious French administrators selected strategic sites for military and commercial depots in the Algonquian heartland, and within a century the area had been marked by a complex grid of river routes, portages, and commercial highways connecting distant Quebec and Montreal with Green Bay, Detroit, Fort St. Louis, Cahokia, Kaskaskia, Fort Beauharnois, and Ouiatanon.

The native peoples and resources were gradually integrated into the commercial structure of New France. Ouiatanon, Cahokia, and Green Bay—all of these posts—came to serve as depots for trade goods and furs. Merchants flooded the Algonquians with French trade goods, obligated them by credit purchases, and persuaded them to liquidate their debts by ranging through the forests and prairies for furs. Tribes were encouraged to settle near the posts, abandon their historic self-sufficiency, and become fur hunters. The *coureurs de bois*, or bushrangers, developed new fur sources by trading with those tribes on the periphery of New France.

Missionaries, chiefly the Jesuits, built mission stations near the

4

posts and taught the Algonquians, attempting to civilize them and thereby making them more amenable to French exploitation. These emissaries—political, commercial, and religious—claimed authority in the name of the "Great Chief" at Quebec, and the Algonquians, emulating the Frenchmen's respect for the governor-general, called him Ononthio. Intrigued by the knives, hatchets, and guns; impressed by the blankets, fabrics, and baubles; and warmed by Ononthio's "milk" (fiery brandy dispensed by the French in council in little cups), most of the Algonquians acceded docilely to the French plan.

The Kickapoos were a notable exception. Almost from the beginning of European contact, this tribe exhibited a remarkably independent spirit and a studied hostility toward acculturation. They refused to accept the economic, political, and religious doctrines which the French, the British, and later the Americans sought to impose.

When the French became aware of this reluctance and attempted to force the tribe to accept the new order, the Kickapoos resisted only mildly. Successive mutual insults committed the Kickapoos to an unremitting offensive against French interests. Forming a confederacy with their Algonquian neighbors, the Mascoutens and the Foxes, the Kickapoos became the leaders of a combination which produced constant trouble for New France. In effect, the Kickapoos and their allies became outlaws in the western French territory, a rugged team of bandits who plundered French supply trains, shot down messengers and isolated *coureurs de bois,* massacred Indians friendly to the French, paralyzed communications in the Northwest, and, in general, seriously threatened the dream of French empire in America.

When in 1634 the Kickapoos and their confederates were brought to the attention of the French in a report by Jean Nicolet on the tribes of the Green Bay area, there was every indication that they, like other Algonquian tribes, would conform passively to the emerging French system.[1] Radisson, Groseillers, Allouez, Marquette,

[1] "Tribes and Tribal Wars about Green Bay," Wisconsin Historical Society *Collections,* XVI, 3–10; *Jesuit Relations,* V, 280.

Hennepin, Tonti, LaSalle, and Perrot—all important figures in the development of New France—visited the Kickapoos at various times before 1700 at their villages on the Fox River or in their hunting camps southward on the Illinois.

Although these observers were impressed by the hardiness and endurance of the tribe, they noted the Kickapoo tendency to withdraw and mistakenly attributed it to timidity and shyness, never considering that it might indicate calculated aloofness and contempt. Kickapoo opposition to French intrusion and to the projected consolidation of the Algonquian tribes was suppressed until about 1680, when two additional invasions of Algonquian territory occurred. From the West came the Sioux and from the East, the Iroquois, and the Kickapoos blamed the French for these incursions.

French merchants, in developing the fur trade among the Sioux, had swapped guns and ammunition for skins. Thus armed, the Sioux were encouraged to attempt a conquest they had often ventured but had always failed to accomplish in the pre-European era of Stone Age weapons.

The French could also be considered responsible for the Iroquois activity. Algonquian tradition related that in the early days of French settlements in the St. Lawrence valley, Samuel de Champlain undertook to clear the region of Indian hazards. In so doing he had irritated the Iroquois, and provided them with an historic grudge.

Dutch and English mercantile interests, anxious to delay French development of the Algonquian region, refreshed the Iroquois memory, armed the Senecas, Cayugas, Onondagas, and Oneidas—member tribes of the Iroquois combination—and sent them west. These invasions halted development of the French fur empire in New France. Communications with Montreal and Quebec were cut, French fur depots in the west were abandoned, and the Indians who had been induced to settle near them were left to shift for themselves. Algonquians from the Ohio River country moved north, where they were joined by the Kickapoos and Mascoutens, who had abandoned their villages on Fox River and fled for safety to the forests around Green Bay.

6

As they reached this sanctuary, the Sioux overwhelmed them, and the Algonquian suffering knew no limit. It was bad enough that the self-sufficiency and self-reliance of the entire Algonquian community had been destroyed by Ononthio, his sub-chiefs, the black gowns, and the traders. Now two new furies were loosed on them, and mere survival became a clear and constant question.

The Iroquois, massively poised, seemed to augur sure destruction. The Sioux threat was so awesome it could hardly be conceived. And the subtle schemes of Ononthio threatened annihilation of the entire culture.

After cowering for three years in the dark forests of Green Bay, the Kickapoos and their Algonquian brothers petitioned the French for arms and aid in repelling the Sioux and Iroquois invaders. Thus in 1683 the French undertook a hesitant policy of reconquest. Tonti and La Salle relocated the southern tribes and organized a series of defenses on the Illinois River along the path of the Iroquois invasion. Perrot moved to the Mississippi and stationed the central and western tribes at strategic points in an attempt to thwart the Sioux.[2]

These were defensive measures, however, and the Algonquian pattern of warfare required revenge for the scalps and women carried off by the Iroquois and Sioux. When the Kickapoos had sought French aid, Ononthio had warned the chiefs to be on their guard against the Iroquois, but not to carry the offensive to the enemy. They were instructed rather, to "guard their cabins and repel attacks." The far-flung French defenses against the Iroquois failed, however, and for their pains in following French instructions the Kickapoos and Mascoutens were caught unaware. In a surprise Iroquois raid in 1683, sixty Kickapoos were slain. All the French could offer for this loss was sympathy, guns and tobacco intended to persuade the tribes to remain in their villages, and assurances of improved French protection.

In the west, a Kickapoo band under Pawashee was attempting to contain the Sioux. There also the Kickapoos repeatedly sought a

[2] Emma H. Blair (ed.), *The Indian Tribes of the Upper Mississippi Valley and Region of the Great Lakes*, I, 245–46.

direct policy of attack, but Perrot counseled caution. While stationed on the Mississippi with Perrot, defending French interests in the west and exposed to the threat of daily attack by the Sioux, Pawashee's warriors discovered that French traders were supplying firearms to the enemy. Thus, added to French hesitancy and weakness was hypocrisy.

Finally in 1684 the Kickapoos threw off the net of French control that constrained their natural impulse and began to meet the Sioux and Iroquois on their own terms. Forming an independent confederacy with the Mascoutens and the Foxes, the Kickapoos, contemptuous of French inertia, carried on their own offensive against the Iroquois, bringing in many scalps and prisoners. At the same time they succeeded in seriously harassing the Sioux.[3]

By 1685 the Kickapoo confederacy had become notorious throughout the Algonquian range, and soon its power equaled that of the Iroquois and Sioux. Its members "seemed to have been seized with an excess of homicidal fury. Their hand was against every man, and for twenty years or more they were the firebrands of the West, and a ceaseless peril to French interests."[4]

Kickapoo strategy involved organizing small bands under war chiefs and living in scattered villages, close enough to render mutual aid yet at a distance sufficient to prevent mass casualties in case of attack. While this pattern of group living effectively safeguarded life and property (and accounts in part for the substantial population of the tribe in the twentieth century) it also had several negative effects. Central tribal authority broke down as the various chiefs became autonomous, and by the nineteenth century the Kickapoo tribe consisted of a number of bands organized during the period of peril.

The Kickapoos, famous for their tactics and endurance, were also well known for the wide range of their depredations. During 1684, Kickapoo bands crossed the Mississippi, burned Santee Da-

---

[3] "Perrot's Dealings with the Wisconsin Tribes," *Wisconsin Historical Society Collections*, XVI, 157.

[4] Francis Parkman, *A Half Century of Conflict*, I, 278.

kota villages, and returned with scalps and plunder. Between 1685 and 1690, Kickapoo chiefs led at least eight forays into the country of the Osage and Kanza Indians. In the east, Kickapoo bands carried the tomahawk and scalping knife as far as Niagara in 1688, burning several Iroquois villages and returning with scalps and satisfied vengeance. Their exploits caught the notice of Ononthio, and during the 1690's units of the Kickapoo confederacy formed the vanguard of French expeditions against the Iroquois, although the Kickapoos refused the French attempts to integrate their confederacy into a formal unit for the defense of the French empire.

The Kickapoo resistance to French assimilation also extended to religion, and their hostility toward the black gowns was a continuing mark of their opposition to conversion. While the Jesuits had remarkable success among the Potawatomies, Ottawas, Peorias, and most of the other Algonquian tribes, the Kickapoos remained aloof—the champions of the Algonquian manito.

In 1672 the Jesuits established the mission of St. Jacques near Green Bay for the Kickapoos and Mascoutens.[5] Jean Allouez, a Jesuit official, visited this mission in 1674 and regretted that it was not as well advanced as the others, largely because of lack of interest on the part of the Kickapoos. Aside from their deep-seated loyalty to their ancient gods, the Kickapoos were too mobile to develop a continuing interest in the Jesuit mission program. A ghoulish incident which occurred in 1680 typifies their attitude toward the black robes. A Kickapoo war party, scouting for Iroquois raiders near Creve Coeur on Lake Peoria, chanced upon Father Gabriel, a Recollect friar. The cleric, in the midst of his daily devotions, was laid upon, scalped, and mutilated, and his effects were plundered.[6]

The period of 1690 to 1700 was a busy one for the Kickapoos. Besides burning, looting, and scalping in Iroquois villages in the east and Sioux camps in the west, these tribesmen also plundered

[5] *Jesuit Relations,* LVIII, 21–23.
[6] Louis Hennepin, *A New Discovery of a Vast Country in America* (ed. by Reuben G. Thwaites), I, 343.

French convoys. Most of the forays during this period took place in the west, and the Kickapoos explained that the goods they took were bound for their ancient enemies, the Sioux.[7]

Indians friendly to the French suffered from the scarcity of trade goods caused by the Kickapoo raids, and Algonquian leaders began to petition for relief from a new menace, the Kickapoo confederacy. In August, 1695, a Potawatomi chief, in the presence of the French governor-general and the intendant, denounced the Kickapoos and their allies as having false hearts, charging that they wished to upset the earth and deceive the French.

In an attempt to establish a lasting peace with the Iroquois and quiet the fury of the Kickapoo confederacy, Governor General Callieres called a general Indian congress at Montreal in August, 1701.[8] With Kickapoo delegates there were Iroquois, Mascouten, Sac, Fox, Potawatomi, Miami, and Illinois representatives. Callieres admonished the tribes to return all prisoners and to bury their hatchets with his own in a trench so deep that no one could take them up again to disturb the peace that was being established that day. After smoking the calumet of peace, Callieres asked that his children, the Iroquois and the French Indians, eat of the meat and broth he had prepared for them, so that, like a good father, he might "have the satisfaction [of seeing his] children united together."[9]

Callieres' peace encouraged French reoccupation of the Illinois country. Between 1701 and 1720, old posts at Green Bay and points south were re-established and new ones erected. The old practice of collecting friendly tribes was resumed, and even an affiliated Mascouten-Fox band joined the Ottawas and Potawatomis at Detroit. The Kickapoos, however, took no part in the French organization.

With the Iroquois and Sioux at least temporarily out of the way, the Kickapoos concentrated their dreadful energies upon French

[7] "Narrative of the Most Remarkable Occurrences in Canada, 1692–1693," in E. B. O'Callaghan ed.(ed.), *New York Colonial Documents*, IX, 570.

[8] Pierre F. Charlevoix, *Histoire et description generale de la nouvelle France*, V, 142.

[9] "Ratification of the Peace Between the French and the Indians, August 4, 1701," O'Callaghan (ed.), *op. cit.*, IX, 722.

traders and those Indians friendly to the French. Before 1712 the Kickapoos had acted as a renegade force, looting and plundering French supply trains and fur convoys, and cutting communications among French outposts. In 1712 they launched an all out war which comprised a menace to French interests every bit as deadly as the Iroquois campaign had been. The shift from nuisance activity to full-scale war grew out of the siege of Detroit.

In the spring of 1712, a combined Mascouten and Fox band established a camp not over fifty paces from the entry to Fort Detroit. Commandant Dubuisson protested, but since he had a garrison of only thirty Frenchmen, his protests were mild. Ottawa and Potawatomi bands, also camped near the fort, took up the quarrel for the French, and the altercation resulted in the deaths of a Mascouten and a Fox.

The slayers fled to the fort, and the Fox-Mascouten band set up a siege, sending messengers for the Kickapoos before making an attack. While waiting for the Kickapoos, the Mascoutens amused themselves by killing the fowls, pigeons, and livestock belonging to the French, and small parties crept in each night attempting to set fire to the outer walls of the fort. These marauders were driven off with cannon fire, the barrages made up of slugs from the blacksmith shop. Each day Dubuisson was exposed to a thousand insults from the besiegers.[10]

Finally on May 13, 1712, after eighteen days of siege, a force of Illinois, Missouri, Osage, Ottawa, and Potawatomi warriors moved in and freed the fort, promising to "eat those miserable nations who have troubled all the country."[11] Despairing of their couriers' finding the Kickapoos, the Mascouten-Fox party, consisting of over one thousand men, women, and children, retreated to nearby Presque Island. There the warriors dug trenches to defend their women and children and drove back attack after attack.[12]

The French and their Indian allies, instructed by Dubuisson to

[10] "Report of the Siege of Detroit," Wisconsin Historical Society *Collections,* XVI, 267–85.
[11] *Ibid.*
[12] Hiram W. Beckwith, *The Illinois and Indiana Indians,* 119–20.

show these members of the Kickapoo confederacy no mercy on the grounds that they had been encouraged by British agents to burn Detroit, set up a blockade of the Mascouten defenses and prevented messengers from slipping out to rally help. For nineteen days the French poured cannon fire into the island. Mascouten insolence persisted in their darkest hour, for they spread scarlet blankets on the ground and "sent word that they hoped all the earth would be covered" with French blood, claiming that they "had no father but the English."

On the nineteenth day, Pemoussa, the Mascouten chief, asked for a two-day truce so that he could provide water and food for his old people and children. Dubuisson, pressured by his Indian allies for a fight to the end, refused the request, and the siege continued. After four more days of cannonading, the Mascoutens surrendered. Dubuisson's Ottawas and Potawatomis showed no mercy. Those few who survived the slaughter were brought into the fort as slaves, and three or four were shot each day to amuse the post Indians. Only about one hundred Mascouten warriors escaped this carnage.[13]

Dubuisson, encouraged by the Mascouten defeat, sent detachments out to strike at the surviving Mascoutens and their Kickapoo allies. A party of his mercenaries captured a group of Kickapoos on the Miami River, slew the warriors, and carried their heads to Detroit, where they were paraded before the garrison.[14] After this last insult the Kickapoos welcomed the Mascouten survivors, tightened their confederacy, and began a total war on New France.

In retaliation for the Miami River massacre, the Kickapoos, during the early summer of 1712, looted every fur train on the Detroit periphery and cut communications among French posts and missions in the Illinois country. That the French had proclaimed their intent to destroy the Kickapoos and their partisans or humiliate them so that they would be unable to cause further trouble drove the tribe to a frenzy of vengeance.

During 1713 the Kickapoos, with their Mascouten and Fox allies,

[13] "Report of the Seige of Detroit," *loc. cit.*
[14] Beckwith, *op. cit.*, 119.

12

pushed their attacks to the northern reaches of New France. Kickapoo envoys spent considerable time in the Iroquois country seeking an alliance, and the entire northwest country was in a panic.
Frenchmen were warned not to travel except with armed escort,
for the Kickapoos were found everywhere and were "a people without pity or without reason."[15] All Indian nations allied with the
French took to flight; they dared not venture from their cabins
and they were dying of hunger. Business leaders warned that "the
merchants will have a gloomy confirmation of this . . . on seeing
how little peltry has come down to Michilimakinac."[16]

The Kickapoo revenge was so complete that economic ruin faced
the traders, merchants, and supply houses of New France. Pressured by these interests, French administrators turned to the task
of reconquest. During the winter of 1715 and spring of 1716, Louvigny organized a massive campaign against the Kickapoo confederacy. His forces, besides French troops, consisted of Huron,
Potawatomi, and Illinois warriors. One column under Louis de la
Porte discovered and attacked a fortified village on Fox River defended by Kickapoos, Mascoutens, and Foxes, forcing them to
terms. The agreement included a pledge of peace with the French
and all tribes allied with the French, restoration of prisoners, replacement of allied Indian dead by going "to war in distant regions to get slaves to replace all the dead who have been slain"
in the war, and reparations for the cost of the expedition to be made
with furs gathered during the next winter.[17]

From 1716 until 1729, the Kickapoos, restive under Louvigny's
peace, maintained a hostile attitude toward the French. They returned to their old bandit pattern, seldom missing an opportunity
to loot a fur train or to kill and scalp isolated *coureurs de bois.* During most of this period, however, these fierce people turned their

15 Marest to Vaudreuil, June 21, 1712, Wisconsin Historical Society *Collections,*
VI, 289.

16 Ramezay to the Minister, September 18, 1714, Wisconsin Historical Society
Collections, XVI, 301.

17 Vaudreuil to Council of the Marine, October 14, 1716, Wisconsin Historical
Society *Collections,* XVI, 341–43.

attention south of their old home in lower Wisconsin toward the country of the Illinois. The Illinois tribes had been primarily responsible for the humiliation suffered by the Kickapoos during Louvigny's 1716 campaign. Kickapoo warriors smarted under the shame of their defeat, the extortionate treaty terms, the memory of Kickapoo women and children taken as hostages, and the warriors' scalps in the lodges of the Illinois. This move to the Illinois country not only satisfied Kickapoo desire for vengeance, but also took them farther from the scrutiny of the French. Moreover, concentrated hunting had destroyed game in their northern home, and the Illinois prairies still abounded in buffalo and other wild creatures. By 1718 the Kickapoos, having absorbed the remaining Mascoutens, were building villages on Rock River, and were described by French travelers as a "clever people and brave warriors."[18]

The impressionable Illinois fled before the Kickapoo invaders, pleading to Ononthio for deliverance from this terror. The French complained of the Kickapoos' incessant hostility, claiming that "all would be peaceful on the continent, but for the war which still continues between the Illinois and Kickapoo and Mascoutin," but they did little to improve the situation. Interestingly, the Kickapoos excused their forays on the grounds that the Illinois persisted in attacking them, and they stated that the Illinois started the war.[19]

In the course of their southern migration, the Kickapoos gradually split into two large communities, and by 1765 one group, concentrated near Peoria and south to the Sangamon River, had become known as the Prairie band. The other, settling east on the Wabash and Vermilion rivers, came to be called the Vermilion band.[20] After carving out a new homeland, the Kickapoos con-

[18] "Memoir on the Indians Between Lake Erie and The Mississippi, 1718," O'Callaghan (ed.), *op. cit.*, IX, 889.

[19] Vaudreuil to Council, October 28, 1719, Wisconsin Historical Society *Collections*, XVI, 380–81; Paris Documents, O'Callaghan (ed.), *op. cit.*, IX, 893.

[20] Robert E. Ritzenthaler and Frederick A. Peterson, *The Mexican Kickapoo Indians*, Milwaukee Public Museum *Publications in Anthropology*, No. 2, p. 17; Emily J. Blasingame, "The Illinois Indians, A Study in Depopulation," *Ethnohistory*, Vol. III (Summer, 1956), 193–217.

tinued their raids against the Illinois, extending their war of extermination along the Illinois River to the Mississippi and lower Ohio Valley, so that, by 1750, the Illinois survivors were taking refuge in Kaskaskia and other French settlements.[21]

That the Illinois would be annihilated was assured after an Illinois Indian, reportedly a member of the Kaskaskia tribe, assassinated Pontiac in 1769. The Kickapoos, members of the inner circle of Pontiac's Conspiracy, turned on the Illinois with a new vengeance, their persecution continuing well into the nineteenth century. During 1800 the Kickapoos "made a great slaughter" of the surviving Kaskaskias (Illinois) at their camp near Cahokia.[22] This massacre, which according to the Kickapoos settled historic grievances, prompted the United States to extend special protection, "that which is enjoyed by its own citizens," to the surviving Illinois.[23] Even this did not insure the safety of the one hundred survivors of a tribe which in 1650 may have numbered as many as twenty thousand, for in 1807 a Kickapoo war party ambushed a Kaskaskia Indian seven miles from the town of Kaskaskia, scalped the victim, "cut his skull in two with three tomahawk strokes," carried off his belongings, and left "a Kickapoo war sign on the corpse."[24] When Governor William H. Harrison demanded that the Kickapoo chiefs send the murderers to him, he was refused. The Kickapoos claimed that they planned to destroy all Kaskaskia Indians because of their favored treatment by the United States.[25]

Onontphio was not as concerned about the Kickapoo-Illinois vendetta as he was over the attacks small bands of Kickapoo raiders were making on the fur lines of New France. The number of casualties among French traders was increasing by the year. Five traders

---

[21] Albert Gallatin, "A Synopsis of the Indian Tribes," *Transactions and Collections* of the American Antiquarian Society, II, 62.

[22] Wallace A. Brice, *History of Fort Wayne,* 122.

[23] Harrison to the Secretary of War, Vincennes, July 11, 1807, in Logan Esarey (ed.), *Messages and Letters of William Henry Harrison,* I, 222.

[24] Jones to Harrison, Kaskaskia, May 4, 1807, in Esarey (ed.), *op. cit.,* I, 211.

[25] Harrison to Secretary of War, Vincennes, July 11, 1807, in Esarey (ed.), *op. cit.,* I, 222.

were scalped and robbed by the Kickapoos in 1723; two met the same fate in 1724; and five others died in 1725.[26] After this last raid, which occurred on the Wabash, French officials planned countermeasures, lamenting the fact that these forays were becoming more daring by the year and stating that the colony faced ruin if the Kickapoos were not stopped.

The French, noting the deep concern of Kickapoo warriors for the safety and welfare of their women and children, began in 1726 to scout Kickapoo villages on the Illinois and Wabash. When the warriors were away on a foray or hunt, the French struck. Kickapoo women and children were taken as prisoners to the French towns and held as hostages to insure the future good conduct of the Kickapoo warriors. This strategem drove the entire tribe into the trans-Mississippi West. By 1727 the Kickapoos had reunited with their old allies, the Fox Indians, and established villages on the Skunk River in present Iowa. Although removed from the threat of further French retribution, the Kickapoos did not forget their captured relatives, and their chiefs and headmen spent much time in council seeking a way to recover the prisoners.[27]

The Kickapoos had spent a year in the West, living as of old, free from the contamination of Ononthio's "milk" and the wheedling of his traders, when an answer to their problem suddenly presented itself. This came in the form of a French prisoner taken by a Kickapoo war party on the Mississippi. Of the many captives taken by the Kickapoos, none received better treatment than this one. The Kickapoos' clever exploitation of this man's captive status not only brought about the return of the Kickapoo hostages and put the tribe in better standing with the French, but more significantly, it also produced an amazing metamorphosis in Kickapoo-French relations.[28]

[26] Longueil to the Minister of the Navy, October 31, 1725, Great Lakes Indian Archives Project, Kickapoo File, 1725–39.

[27] "Narrative of Boucher," Wisconsin Historical Society *Collections*, XVII, 36–37.

[28] *Jesuit Relations*, LXVIII, 329–30.

2

Ononthio's Children

THE HISTORIC CHANGE IN KICKAPOO RELATIONS with the French was the result of the abandonment of Fort Beauharnois on Lake Pepin in 1728. A year earlier, Pierre Boucher had led an expedition to the Sioux country in what is now Minnesota. His instructions were to construct a military post and commercial depot on Lake Pepin, and to labor to develop among the Sioux a fur trade like that which already was in operation among the Algonquians east of the Mississippi. The Jesuit Michel Guignas, hoping to establish a mission among the Sioux, accompanied Boucher's party.

Scarcely had the post been completed and preliminary contacts made with the Sioux, when Fox pressure on Boucher's supply line forced him to evacuate the Sioux country. Boucher, Guignas, and fifteen post employees embarked for the Illinois country in early October, 1728.[1]

As the Frenchmen passed the mouth of Skunk River, their boats were intercepted and surrounded by a party of Kickapoos in pirogues, and they were forced to the west bank of the Mississippi. From there the Indians conducted their prisoners to the main Kickapoo village situated three leagues inland. The captives were treated in an unusually polite fashion. Kickapoo warriors carried

[1] Letter of Father le Titit to Father d'Avongour, New Orleans, July 12, 1730, Great Lakes Indian Archives Project, Kickapoo File, 1725–39.

their baggage to the village, and they were not abused, nor were they bound as was the common treatment for captives.[2]

Boucher's party was courteously received, and all manner of hospitality was bestowed upon them. They were assigned to various Kickapoo lodges. Boucher and Guignas, guests in the abode of Chief Ouiskouba, were placed on bearskins, a position of honor, and fed venison and corn by the women of Ouiskouba's household.

Throughout the first night the curious thronged the lodges assigned the captives. Many of the younger Kickapoos had never seen a Frenchman, and excited comments and observations were whispered around the circle of viewers. Next day the chiefs and headmen gathered to examine the captives. Suspicious and probing in their questions, the council members charged that Kickapoo scouts had seen black gowns leading Ononthio's armies against the Indians. Guignas assured them that it must have been a chaplain in Desliettes' French army they had seen. Still suspicious, the Indians watched Guignas as he read from his breviary. Noting that the rubrics were printed in red ink, a chief decided these were drops of blood, and warned that Guignas must be a dangerous man. To silence this charge Guignas put the controversial booklet aside. Since there were no other charges against Guignas and Boucher, the council decided to assign them to Ouiskouba to replace one of his wives and several children who had been slain by the French.[3]

Through the succeeding days, Ouiskouba's council convinced Guignas and Boucher that they had nothing to fear from the Kickapoos. The chiefs explained that the French, angry with the Kickapoos and their allies, the Mascouten and Fox Indians, had turned other tribes against them, so that to escape the French they had fled beyond the Mississippi. The Kickapoo elders made it clear that the Frenchmen were being held to assure the safety and restoration of the captive women and children. Meanwhile, Guignas and Boucher were promised protection from the Fox and other enemies, and they were informed that the entire French party was to winter in the Kickapoo village.[4]

2 A French league measured 2.76 miles.
3 "Narrative of Boucher," Wisconsin Historical Society *Collections*, XVII, 38–39.
4 *Ibid.*, 42–43.

During the winter Fox bands visited the Kickapoo village seeking to persuade the chiefs to produce the prisoners and burn them at the stake. The Kickapoos, aware of the value of their French guests to the safety of the nation, remained adamant. Their desires frustrated, Fox warriors prowled the woods about Ouiskouba's village uttering threats and insults to the Kickapoos and trying to win over the younger warriors.

The Fox interference in Kickapoo affairs and their growing insolence provoked the wrath of the Kickapoos, and an intertribal friendship which had existed for nearly a century soon became a mutual enmity. Guignas played on this growing rift with presents from Boucher's stores, and pledged to use his influence to place the Kickapoos in the good graces of the French whenever his captors were ready to journey with him to the Illinois settlements. Guignas constantly reminded the Kickapoos that the change in tribal policy he recommended would insure the safety and quick return of their women and children.

As the ice cleared from the creeks and rivers near Ouiskouba's village in the spring of 1729, a Kickapoo escort traveled to the Illinois settlements with the Boucher party, delivering the Frenchmen to the commandant at Fort Chartres in early April, 1729.[5] Through the intercession of Father Guignas, the Kickapoo captives were restored, peace was made with the French, and the Kickapoos formally renounced their affiliation with the Foxes.[6]

Governor General Beauharnois praised the Kickapoos for the good treatment accorded the Boucher party, congratulated the tribe on the peace which had been made, and, in an elated report to the crown, advised that the French now had a formidable ally against the Fox tribe.[7] A new era was emerging for the French in the west. Up to this time the Kickapoo confederacy had been a deadly threat to French interests. Its wide-ranging partisans had

[5] Letter of Company of the Indies to Terrior de Solvert, New Orleans, April 22, 1729, Great Lakes Indian Archives Project, Kickapoo File, 1725–39.

[6] *Jesuit Relations,* LXVIII, 207–209.

[7] Beauharnois to French Minister, May 16, 1729, Wisconsin Historical Society *Collections,* XVII, 59–61.

19

destroyed French detachments, killed traders and looted their goods, terrified Indian allies of the French, and, on several occasions, completely paralyzed French communications and trade in the West. Father Guignas' success with the Kickapoos augured well for French hopes to destroy the remaining menace—the Foxes.

In 1730 the Fox Indians having lost their former partners in violence, turned to the Iroquois and the English for support against the French. The Kickapoos learned of the Fox plan, alerted the French, and kept watch on the Foxes. During the summer of 1730 this tribe migrated eastward to effect a union with the Iroquois. Kickapoo scouts discovered their encampment near Le Rocher on the Illinois River, and Chief Ouiskouba's entire warrior force quickly formed a ring of siege around the place. After sealing off all avenues of escape, Ouiskouba sent messengers to Fort Chartres with news of the Fox predicament, and soon the Kickapoo force was augmented by Saint-Ange's army of one hundred Frenchmen and fourteen hundred Indians.

So devastating was the fire of the besiegers that the Fox warriors dug burrows to escape immediate annihilation. After a month of remarkable resistance, suddenly desperate from lack of food and water, the entrenched braves began a series of suicidal charges on the rim of the blockade. Wave after wave of desperate Fox warriors probed at the human wall about their palisade, and each time were turned back in frightful carnage.

On September 7, 1730, a Fox charge nearly cracked a salient on the south slope. This portion, assigned to the timorous Illinois, was abandoned when two hundred fighters of this group fled before the onrushing warriors. Quick action by the Kickapoos filled the gap, and their deadly barrage turned the attackers into the palisade for cover. The Foxes attempted one final assault on the night of September 8. After this was checked, Saint-Ange ordered his besieging force to the attack. On the morning of September 9, it was evident that the last Algonquian threat to French western expansion had been destroyed. Over three hundred Fox warriors and countless women and children had been slain during the night. Not over sixty members of the tribe escaped, and even these were pursued by the Kickapoos. The French were lavish in their praise of the role played by the Kickapoos, and they exulted in the Fox destruction.[8]

Thereafter the Kickapoos became the most reliable defenders of the interests of France in the New World. While their wars on the Illinois tribes continued, they were unswerving in their loyalty to the French, seeming satisfied to vent their hostility on the hapless Illinois. When a Fox band was discovered on the Mississippi in early 1735, the de Noyelle expedition was dispatched to drive the offenders beyond the borders of New France. A Kickapoo party accompanied this French army, serving as guides and assault troops. The Kickapoos made a number of daring raids into the camps of the enemy, while their scouts hunted buffalo to feed the expedition.[9]

Between 1735 and 1763 a new menace appeared in the Algonquian heartland. British agents were moving up the Tennessee toward the Ohio Valley in an attempt to cut the Wabash-Maumee trade route, the most direct communication between New France and Louisiana.[10] These envoys used a variety of tactics to achieve their objective.

One stratagem was to alienate French Indians by offering cheaper British goods at secret rendezvous in the Illinois country. That the French were guilty of unfair trade practices—and thereby vulnerable to the encroaching British competition—is evidenced by French exchange on brandy, a popular trade item. At Chartres, Ouiatanon, or Detroit, "a cask of brandy worth forty dollars fetched $3,000 worth of furs."[11]

British agents also used force to imperil French interests in the Illinois country. French expansion in the Gulf area between 1701

[8] DeVilliers to Beauharnois, September 23, 1730, Wisconsin Historical Society *Collections,* XVII, 109–18.

[9] "Relation of the Journey of Sieur de Noyelle," Wisconsin Historical Society *Collections,* XVII, 231.

[10] Albert T. Volwiler, *George Croghan and the Westward Movement,* 1741–1782, 22.

[11] Blair (ed.), *op. cit.,* I, 209. Blair's figures show that a cask of brandy worth two hundred livres bought fifteen thousand livres worth of skins. The livre was worth about twenty cents.

and 1735 had irritated the Chickasaw and Natchez Indians, who persisted in raiding convoys on the lower Mississippi and land parties east of Biloxi. To put an end to this nuisance, a French army was sent against the Chickasaw towns in 1736. Surprisingly, the invaders met a sharp defeat. British envoys exploited this Chickasaw victory as an indication of French weakness, and they supplied Chickasaw and Natchez warriors with presents, guns, and ammunition, offering bounties for raids north of the Ohio.

The French countered by turning their new mercenaries, the Kickapoos, on the Chickasaws and Natchez. Kickapoo defenses on the Ohio repulsed a number of Chickasaw and Natchez raiders in late 1736, delivering scalps and prisoners to the French post at Ouiatanon on the Wabash.[12] In 1737 the Kickapoos began to depredate in the Chickasaw country, sending four separate expeditions between April 24 and November 15. Each party returned with a substantial quantity of plunder, scalps, and prisoners from the Chickasaw towns. The Kickapoos were fairly well acquainted with the country south of the Ohio, for, while their movements were generally west of the Mississippi, they had also ventured south to the Gulf. Creek tradition relates that before 1700 the Kickapoos often crossed the Ohio River into present Kentucky and beyond to wage war on the Lower Creeks and the Chickasaws.[13]

The Kickapoo offensive against the Chickasaws, carried on throughout the 1740's, significantly reduced the British threat to French interests north of the Ohio. Kickapoo raids during this period, implemented by small, wide-ranging, fast-moving bands of warriors, terrorized the Chickasaw towns, for a Kickapoo foray inevitably resulted in scalped warriors, burned lodges, women prisoners, and deep mourning. These Kickapoo tactics caught the notice of high officials in French Canada and Louisiana, and both administrations sought the use of various Kickapoo bands as mer-

[12] Bienville to Marepas, New Orleans, September 5, 1736, in Dunbar Rowland and A. G. Sanders (eds.), *Mississippi Provincial Archives, 1729–1740*, I, 327–28.

[13] McGillivray Documents, Great Lakes Indian Archives Project, Kickapoo File, before 1700.

cenaries. Vaudreuil for the Canadian interests and Bienville for New Orleans gave special status to the Kickapoos as a first line of defense against the British, both acknowledging that the Kickapoos were "sufficient to cover us" on the lower Wabash and the mouth of the Tennessee.[14]

Thwarted in the attempt to cut French communications north of the Ohio, British agents turned to provoking a conspiracy among the French-allied Indians. The impressionable Miamis were especially active as couriers, circulating the underground war belts of the British among the Algonquian tribes. During 1750 secret councils were conducted by British agents in the Miami camps with the Weas, Piankashaws, Ottawas, and the host Miami warriors in attendance. Presents and promises were showered on the delegates, while inflammatory speeches encouraged them to revolt against the French.[15]

Anxious French officials, noting the growing spirit of revolt among the Algonquian tribes during 1750, took considerable comfort from reports that the Kickapoos had remained loyal to the French, refusing the British belts and ignoring the Miami councils.[16] The well-known fighting ability of the Kickapoos and their loyalty to the French temporarily arrested British designs in the west. The immediate result of British intrigue was a series of murders perpetrated by British-allied Indians at Fort Chartres, Kaskaskia, and Vincennes during 1751. The Miamis and their confederates, annoyed by Kickapoo aloofness, punished these French loyalists by reviling them and attacking small parties far from the settlements. Although their losses were small, the Kickapoos ascribed these murders to British meddling, and this explains in

---

[14] Bienville to Minister, June 21, 1737, Indiana Historical Society *Collections,* III, 311–12; Vaudreuil to Minister, May 24, 1748, Illinois Historical Society *Collections,* XXIX, 71.

[15] Roy to Raymond, March–April, 1750, Illinois Historical Society *Collections,* XXIX, 166–68.

[16] Chaperon to Raymond, May, 1750, Illinois Historical Society *Collections,* XXIX, 194–97; Raymond to La Jonquiere, May 22, 1750, Illinois Historical Society *Collections,* XXIX, 201–206.

part their extended resistance to British occupation of the Algonquian range after 1763.[17]

Throughout the French and Indian War which followed the Miami uprising, the Kickapoos defended the Ohio-Mississippi perimeter of New France, successfully repelling Chickasaw attacks from the valley of the Tennessee. By 1759 the French were on the retreat in America and were hard pressed to defend even the old settlements of Montreal and Quebec. French troops were pulled from the Illinois country as the crisis extended. This left the Kickapoos and other tribes south of the Lakes largely on their own.

British envoys, noting the evacuation of the Illinois country, used gifts and promises to attract the tribes of this area to eastern councils. From November, 1759, to August of 1760, the Kickapoos sent deputies to four of these councils held at Pittsburgh. While the Pittsburgh conference of September 15, 1760, was not attended by the Kickapoos, the tribe did send a belt to the British acknowledging that they had heard of the peace with the British, that they were pleased with it, and that they joined their hands heartily to it.[18]

Apparently these contacts with the British made no enduring impression upon the Kickapoos, for in a 1764 report on the Western tribes friendly to the British and trading with them, the Kickapoos were described as "unacquainted with the English."[19] The future of the Algonquian range was decided in Europe in 1763 by the Treaty of Paris. By this agreement, vanquished France transferred to Great Britain title to Canada and the lands of New France south to the Ohio River. This event, and the transfer of French

[17] D'Organ to Vaudreuil, October 7, 1752, Illinois Historical Society *Collections,* XXIX, 735–40.

[18] "List of Nations at Pittsburgh Council, November 5, 1769," British Museum Manuscripts, Great Lakes Indian Archives Project, Kickapoo File; "Minutes of Pittsburgh Conference, August 12, 1760," Pennsylvania Archives, 1st series, III, 744–52; and "Council of Proceedings, September 15, 1760," Pennsylvania *Colonial Records,* VIII, 497–500.

[19] Morris to Bradstreet, Roche de Bout, August 31, 1764, Gage Papers, American Series, William L. Clements Library, Great Lakes Indian Archives Project, Kickapoo File.

Louisiana to Spain, would have far-reaching effects on Kickapoo tribal history.

When news of the Treaty of Paris reached the Algonquian country, there was general alarm. Around Fort Detroit, in the north, an Ottawa chieftain, Pontiac, became the nucleus of a resistance movement against British occupation of the west. Pontiac's Conspiracy, so called because of the subterfuge the chief contrived to attempt the capture of Fort Detroit, actually was a widespread popular movement among the Algonquians. It encouraged a spirit of resistance to British control which survived the death of Pontiac in 1769.

Because of their long-standing grudge against the British for inciting the Chickasaws to make war on them, and because of recent British intrigue among the Miamis and their confederates, the Kickapoos were eager partisans of Pontiac. Quite early in 1764 Kickapoo bands were camped on the southern routes to Detroit, assuring Pontiac, whose Indian army had taken the fort, that no British aid would pass their defenses.

Saint-Ange, the experienced French administrator in the Illinois country, visited these Kickapoo camps and reminded the warriors that they were obliged by the recent treaty to lay down their arms and council with their new Father, the British. Saint-Ange found that "they all preferred dying to making peace with the British," that they still claimed an attachment to the French and a hatred of the British, and that they were "much offended when one speaks to them about making peace with the British. It is quite certain that they have a deadly hatred" for the British.[20]

While this Kickapoo force was operating in liaison with Pontiac in the north, another was active in the south, forcing the British to evacuate Forts Ouiatanon, Chartres, and Miami. Reluctant to venture a conquest of the Illinois country, the British decided upon an attempt at conciliation. A great council to be held at Niagara late in 1764 was planned, and Captain Thomas Morris was sent into the Illinois country with a message of invitation to the Algonquians.

[20] Saint-Ange to Deboddie, July 15, 1764, Illinois Historical Society *Collections*, X, 289.

Arriving at Fort Miami in the summer of 1764, Morris found the fort and its environs occupied by French traders and a large Kickapoo force. When Morris stated his purpose, the Kickapoo council refused him permission to proceed farther west and promised certain death if he attempted to complete his mission. Intimidated, Morris returned to Detroit.[21]

Sir William Johnson, Indian superintendent for the British in the west, attributed the resistance to British occupation of the Illinois posts to the influence of French traders. He charged that they were persuading the Kickapoos and other tribes to move west of the Mississippi and "practicing so many artifices to obstruct our interests in the Country, that it is likely to become a very Expensive and troublesome Affair."[22]

A crisis now faced the British in the west. Pontiac's eloquence had inspired the Kickapoos and other tribes to solid resistance to British occupation of the old Algonquian range. In the two years following the Peace of Paris, two thousand British soldiers, traders, and settlers had been reported slain or captured, "thousands of . . . settlers driven to beggary, and traders and troops plundered of goods valued at nearly £100,000" by Pontiac's partisans. By 1765, however, British prestige rose as her armies managed to reoccupy all the western towns and forts except those in the Illinois country. Even the redoubtable Pontiac had been forced to flee to the Wabash.[23]

The tribes led by the Kickapoos in the Illinois country possessed formidable power. In dealing with this menace to British consolidation, conciliation seemed preferable to conquest. Johnson therefore organized a special mission, with his chief deputy, George Croghan, at its head, and ordered it to the west.

Setting out from Pittsburgh on May 17, 1765, with an escort of fourteen, Croghan had an uneventful water journey on the Ohio

21 Captain Thomas Morris, *Morris Journals*, in Reuben G. Thwaites (ed.), *Early Western Travels*, I, 314; Francis Parkman, *The Conspiracy of Pontiac*, III, 61.

22 "Review of Trade and Affairs in the Northern District," Illinois Historical Society *Collections*, XVI, 46.

23 Albert T. Volwiler, "The Imperial Indian Department and the Occupation of the Great West," *Transactions* of the Illinois State Historical Society, XXXII, 103.

until he neared the mouth of the Wabash. On June 7 a small Kickapoo force scouting on the north bank discovered Croghan's convoy. Sending a messenger to the Kickapoo village at Ouiatanon for reinforcements, the Kickapoo scouts observed Croghan's movements. The unsuspecting Croghan saw no sign of danger until that evening, when his servant, while gathering wood for the camp, disappeared.

After a search of several hours the man was presumed lost, and at daybreak Croghan resumed his journey. In mid-morning, as Croghan's boats turned into the Wabash, sudden terror struck. Firing from the dense cover of the north bank, Kickapoo sharpshooters succeeded in wounding every member of Croghan's party, killing several. When the eddying current beached the boats, the attackers savagely tomahawked the survivors, killing five on the spot. Even Croghan, suffering from a bullet in the thigh, was laid upon, but as he facetiously reported later, "my skull being pretty thick, the hatchet would not enter, so you may see a thick skull is of service on some occasions."[24]

After looting the goods stowed in the boats, the Kickapoos conducted Croghan and the other survivors to their village at Ouiatanon. Croghan related that the people at this place, besides the Kickapoos, consisted of eighty French families, an "idle, lazy people, a parcel of renegadoes from Canada and much worse than the Indians. They took secret pleasure at my misfortune and enriched themselves by securing my gold and silver specie from the Indians for mere trifles." Croghan explained the purpose of his mission to his captors and tried to impress upon them the importance of his sending out messages. This the Kickapoos refused.

Croghan was held incommunicado for thirty-five days. Finally it became apparent to the Kickapoos that Croghan was indeed a prize, and perhaps sensing the inevitability of British occupation of the west, they decided to use him to place the tribe on somewhat favorable terms with the British. Such political acumen belies the claim made by many observers that they were crude barbarians,

---

[24] Volwiler, *George Croghan,* 184–87.

incapable of appreciating and applying a single art of civilization. Their exploitation of this prisoner resembled their treatment of Father Guignas.

Just as the Guignas captivity produced a pervasive change in Kickapoo relations with the French, so did the Croghan captivity begin a new era in Kickapoo relations with the British. Both captivities had important effects on Kickapoo history, the only difference being the time element. In the case of the French, the move from hostility to unqualified support was immediate. The development of good relations between the Kickapoos and the British was slower, for the Kickapoos continued to depredate on the British in the west until the American War of Independence. The rapid encroachment upon the Algonquian range by American politicians and land speculators after 1783 produced a Kickapoo loyalty for the British which lasted until 1832, and it is significant that the Croghan captivity set this change in motion.

3

Serving Two Masters

THE AWESOME IMPERIAL MACHINE OF THE BRITISH, which Sir William Johnson set in motion by sending the Croghan Mission to the west in the spring of 1765, ran aground on the banks of the Wabash. For thirty-five days George Croghan, deputy chief for Indian affairs in the west, languished in the lodge of Wahpesah, a war chief of the Kickapoos. Broken and bruised by the ferocity of the Kickapoo attack, Croghan recovered slowly.

Robbed of his valuables and at first refused the privilege of sending out messages, Croghan confided his frustration to his journal. The French traders exerted a great influence over these Indians, he noted, "and never fail in telling them many lies to the prejudice of his majesty's interest, by making the English nation odious and hateful to them. I had the greatest difficulties in removing these prejudices. As these Indians are a weak, foolish, and credulous people, they are easily imposed on by a designing people, who have led them hitherto as they pleased."[1]

Finally, by the intercession of the esteemed Pontiac, the Kickapoo council decided on July 12, 1765, to release Croghan and to

---

[1] George Croghan, *Croghan's Journals,* in Reuben G. Thwaites (ed.), *Early Western Travels,* I, 144–45. Croghan's report on the Kickapoo attack is found in O'Callaghan (ed.), *op. cit.,* VII, 779. On p. 765 of the same volume is Johnson's account of Croghan's capture. In Croghan Papers, Draper Manuscript Collection, Wisconsin Historical Society is a sketch of Croghan and the story of his Kickapoo captivity.

permit him to resume his mission.[2] Johnson's deputy spent a month gathering presents for tribal delegations and sending invitations to the tribes of the region. Croghan then conducted two grand councils between August 17 and August 25, 1765, the first at Fort Chartres, the second at Detroit. The Kickapoos were present at both councils and agreed to the terms Croghan set forth.

The British peace for the Illinois country required that the tribes acknowledge the British King as their Father, promise to keep the communications between Pittsburgh, Detroit, and the Illinois country open, and agree to surrender all captives and stolen horses. They were not to oppose the peaceful occupation of existing posts in the Illinois territory, nor the establishment of new ones. Curiously, Indian title to the Illinois country was recognized; the British acknowledged that they were tenants, and each tribe was to receive an annual rental in presents for British use of the land.[3]

Sir William Johnson, pleased with the outcome of the Croghan mission, ventured west himself in 1766. Stopping at Detroit, he spent the month of July attending a general Indian congress. Commenting on Croghan's harrowing adventure with the Kickapoos and the victory of his deputy in spite of the hazards and personal danger, he noted that the Illinois country was quiet and that the breach with the Kickapoos had been healed. He claimed that the tribe had expressed friendship for the British and sought forgiveness for the attack on Croghan.[4]

Johnson, with all his wisdom in handling Indian affairs, misunderstood the Kickapoos. While their old antipathy toward the British had abated, another fifteen years would pass before the Kickapoos really accepted the British king as the tribal Father. In the interim the British had to face an alternating policy of peace and minor war, periods of quiet interspersed with orgies of horse stealing, attacks on supply trains, and raids on settlements.

[2] Volwiler, *George Croghan,* 184–87.

[3] *Ibid.,* 188, 196–97.

[4] "Proceedings of General Indian Congress, July, 1766," in O'Callaghan (ed.), *op. cit.,* VII, 860.

The assassination of the venerable Pontiac by a Kaskaskia Indian near Cahokia in 1769 produced a new turbulence in the Illinois country. The Kickapoos especially seemed driven to avenge his death a thousand times on the hapless Illinois. But after several months of wanton slaughter, with a surfeit of scalps and plunder in their lodges, the Kickapoos turned to conjuring up new mischief for the British. On the night of June 27 an indication of fresh trouble appeared near Fort Chartres. A Kickapoo band ranged through a settlement within sight of the fort, surprised a soldier and a woman in bed, scalped them both, and escaped unscathed.[5]

The hostile activity increased through 1770, and when the tribe ignored repeated British attempts at negotiation, the warriors were accused of being more interested in stealing horses than in reaching an agreement. British settlements around Cahokia, Kaskaskia, and Chartres were terrorized by their forays. Englishmen were slain and scalped, their women and children carried away into captivity, and their slaves mutilated. British intelligence reports for 1771 noted that Kickapoo war parties of about forty warriors each were operating on the Ohio, using boats to intercept travelers on the river. All British troops in the Illinois country were readied against this menace, and if army reprisals failed to stop the Kickapoos, the British planned to bring in the Chickasaws and Cherokees.[6]

The Kickapoo vendetta against the British slowed down suddenly in 1771. The reason for this abrupt reduction was probably not fear of the British, however, but a shift in tribal interest west of the Mississippi. France had ceded Louisiana to Spain in November, 1762, and in the spring of 1765, Spain officially took over the upper portion of this province by sending Antonio de Ulloa of the Royal Spanish Navy as first governor and captain general. Among Ulloa's first acts was the establishment of new posts and settlements along the Mississippi as a defensive move against Brit-

[5] Butricke to Barnesley, Fort Chartres, June 27, 1769, Illinois Historical Society *Collections,* XVI, 566.

[6] Gage to Johnson, September 24, 1771, in James Sullivan (ed.), *The Papers of Sir William Johnson,* VIII, 277–79.

ish extension. Ulloa also sought to become the patron of the Indians of the Illinois country by inviting them to council with him and to receive annual presents.

Some bands of Indians from the Illinois country moved permanently into Spanish Louisiana. Besides Ulloa's inducements, many French traders moved to the west after 1763, and undoubtedly they influenced various bands to accompany them. Serena, a Kickapoo subchief, led his band of seventy-five warriors and their families to Spanish Louisiana in 1765, selecting a village site on the Missouri River about twelve leagues beyond the new post of St. Louis.

Thereafter, three distinct segments of the tribe appear in Kickapoo history. Besides Serena's band, permanently domiciled in the west, there were two larger bands of about three hundred warriors each, one established on the lower Illinois, the other on the Wabash.[7] The three Kickapoo communities continued to council together, and a common tribal policy was apparent—pro-Spanish and anti-British. Kickapoo bands from the east hunted with the western band; they visited one another's camps, held general council on matters of common interest, and traveled together to St. Louis each year for council and presents from the Spanish. All three bands defended Spanish interests much as the Kickapoos had served the French in earlier times.[8]

The Kickapoos knew the country west of the Mississippi well. Warriors from this tribe had roamed the upper Mississippi country with Perrot in the 1690's, and the entire tribe had lived in present Iowa during the late 1720's, until the Guignas captivity made it possible to return safely to their old villages on the Wabash and Illinois. Thereafter various bands had scouted for French armies operating in the west. Kickapoo hunters ventured as far south as the Arkansas in 1725, and, by 1750, had extended their hunting range to the rim of Red River. During this period the Kickapoos

---

[7] "Recopilacion de las naciones," Houck Transcripts, Wisconsin Historical Society; and Louis Houck (ed.), The Spanish Regime in Missouri, I, 141–48.

[8] Gage to Haldimand, June 3, 1773, British Museum MS 21665, Great Lakes Indian Archives Project, Kickapoo File.

were joining in the Arkansas trade and, at the same time, beginning a bitter war with the Osages which extended into the first third of the nineteenth century.

Soon after the outbreak of the American War of Independence in 1775, the British made elaborate efforts to organize the tribes of the Illinois country. British strategy for the west was threefold: build a defense on the Ohio against any American venture in the Northwest; muster a native force sufficient to turn back a possible Spanish offensive from upper Louisiana; and organize raiding parties to terrorize American frontier settlements.

The fighting prowess of the Kickapoos, an acknowledged factor in the power situation of the Illinois country, was courted by both the British and American agents. During 1777, as the focus of the war turned to the west and as the pressure on the tribes of the Illinois country for a decision as to their allegiance increased, Pacana, successor to Wahpesah as one of the leading Kickapoo chiefs, came from his Wabash village to St. Louis for council. Gabriel Cerré, long prominent in Mississippi Valley Indian affairs, was in St. Louis when Pacana and his escort of subchiefs and headmen arrived. Cerré, reporting the Pacana visit to George Rogers Clark, related that the chief drank with his Spanish Father who "promised him a medal, a chiefs coat, a hat," and that Pacana was warned not to mix in the troubles of the Bostonians with the English.[9]

Two exceedingly capable agents were at work on the Kickapoos in the battle for the tribe's allegiance—Henry Hamilton for the British, and George Rogers Clark for the Americans. Both were aware of the importance of winning the Kickapoos. Hamilton, quite anxious about Kickapoo loyalty as a factor in his plan of defense in the Northwest, wrote late in 1778 that it was most important to win the Kickapoos to the British cause since the Indians of the Wabash region would "follow implicitly the example of the Kickapoos, the most warlike and cruel of them all."[10]

[9] A. P. Nasatir, "The Anglo-Spanish Frontier in the Illinois Country During the American Revolution," Historical Society *Journal*, Vol. XXI (October, 1928), 297.

[10] Hamilton to Haldimand, Vincennes, December 18, 1778, Illinois Historical Society *Collections*, I, 233.

George Rogers Clark was equally concerned about Kickapoo allegiance, and went to considerable length to draw them into the American camp. Clark had extensive land interests in the Kentucky settlements, so that even before the outbreak of the American War of Independence he had witnessed the results of Kickapoo depredations south of the Ohio. In 1776 the citizens of Kentucky had petitioned the Virginia Assembly for relief from Kickapoo incursions, since their settlements close to the Ohio River were directly exposed, and since citizens in the west were already abandoning their homes. Clark carried this petition to the Virginia Assembly and made a personal appeal for relief.[11]

The Virginia government decided that the most effective way to protect the Kentucky settlements from British and Indian attacks was to carry an offensive into the Illinois country. A frontier army was raised for this purpose in 1777, and Clark was named to lead it. Knowing his force was too small and too poorly equipped to strike directly at Detroit, the British nerve center in the Northwest, Clark decided to enter on the lower Ohio and attempt to move progressively through Kaskaskia, Cahokia, and Vincennes, thence north to Detroit. He hoped also to gain the allegiance of certain Indian tribes, notably the Kickapoos.

Landing his ragged, homespun army near Fort Massac on the lower Ohio on June 28, 1778, Clark marched northwest and took Kaskaskia six days later. From there his army moved east, and before the summer was over, all of the lower Northwest had capitulated. The Illinois Kickapoos were intrigued by the dress, equipment, and talk of the "Long Knives." Certainly General Clark's direct manner and the forceful, impressive fashion in which he conducted his councils won the tribe's admiration and overcame their uncertainties. The Kickapoos accompanied Clark's army as scouts, and various Kickapoo bands moved to the Ohio to patrol the area around the mouth of the Tennessee. British intrigue in the southeast had excited the Chickasaws and Cherokees, and war parties of these tribes lurked on the south bank of the Ohio in hopes of

11 "Petition of John Jones and George Rogers Clark, October 1, 1776," Illinois Historical Society *Collections,* VIII, 19.

raiding American traffic on the river. During late 1778 Kickapoo patrols made a number of successful attacks on these southern Indians, thereby guarding Clark's rear guard from assault.[12]

With the Illinois Kickapoos already committed to Clark, Henry Hamilton, British lieutenant governor, attempted to win over the Wabash Kickapoos, calculating that half a loaf was better than none. If he could win the three hundred Wabash Kickapoos, he reasoned, tribal loyalty might bring over the three hundred Kickapoo warriors on the Illinois who had joined Clark's camp. Also, it was a known fact that the direction of the Kickapoos would determine the course taken by the other tribes of the region.

On June 29, 1778, at his Detroit headquarters, Hamilton entertained Kickapoo chiefs and headmen from the Wabash. A round of presents and British promises won pledges from this segment of the tribe to go to war for the British and to "spare the aged, women, and children" in the settlements.[13] Additional conferences in July, 1778, attracted various Wabash Kickapoo delegations. During July, Mahinamba, a Kickapoo village chief, returned the pipe Hamilton had sent to the Wabash in the spring, saying it had made the rounds, each had smoked it, and that their "hearts and minds were at rest." Mahinamba also gave Hamilton a pipe painted green, saying that it indicated the sincerity of his nation in their dealings with their Father, the British monarch. He further assured Hamilton that his people had "no will but that of their British Father, who would take pity on them and assist them."[14]

Believing the pledges of the Wabash Kickapoos to be sufficient to control the center of the Illinois country, Hamilton was surprised to learn in September, 1778, that a party of Long Knives had been on the Wabash during late summer seeking to induce the Kickapoos to adopt the American cause as had their fellow tribesmen on the

---

[12] Norman W. Caldwell, "Fort Massac: The American Frontier Post, 1778–1805," Illinois Historical Society *Journal*, Vol. XLIII (Winter, 1950), 272.

[13] John D. Barnhart, *Henry Hamilton and George Clark in the American Revolution*, 33.

[14] "Hamilton's Councils, June and July, 1778," Illinois Historical Society *Collections*, I, 319.

Illinois.[15] Concerned over this development, Hamilton decided to give his personal attention to preventing the defection of the Wabash Kickapoos.

In early December he arrived at the Kickapoo village near Ouiatanon. After sponsoring a great feast well spiced with rum, Hamilton showed in council the green pipe presented him by the Kickapoos during the July meeting. This clever reminder of Kickapoo allegiance to the British cause sobered the chiefs and headmen and increased Hamilton's prestige. He provided more drama when Quaquapoqua, a village chief, displayed an American flag left by Clark's soldiers during the summer visit of the Long Knives to the Wabash. Hamilton took the flag, stamped it into the ground, and berated the Kickapoos for being so susceptible to American influences.[16] Impressed by Hamilton's display, Mohinamba, speaking for the tribe, explained that many of the warriors were in the west hunting, but that when they returned in the spring, the Kickapoos "would appear like mosquitoes and infest the Ohio, and all the rebel frontiers."[17]

From the Kickapoo village Hamilton moved on to Vincennes, and on December 17, 1778, took the fort easily, its garrison consisting of an American officer and a private. In spite of their promises, the Wabash Kickapoos failed to support the British cause with any marked enthusiasm. Kickapoo scouts reconnoitered Fort Vincennes for Hamilton and formed a defensive cordon of one hundred warriors about the post after its capitulation to the British. Thus, when General Clark made a surprise return to Vincennes in February, 1779, the unsuspecting Hamilton, warmly ensconced for the winter, was confident that the Kickapoo army camped on Vincennes' environs would make Clark's position untenable.

The Kickapoos guarding the perimeter, however, suddenly joined the American ranks, making the British position in Vincennes impossible, and thirty-six hours after Clark's arrival, Hamilton capitu-

---

[15] Chevallier to De Peyster, St. Joseph, September 15, 1778, *Michigan Pioneer and Historical Collections,* XIX, 353.

[16] Barnhart, *op. cit.,* 54.

[17] *Ibid.,* 136–37.

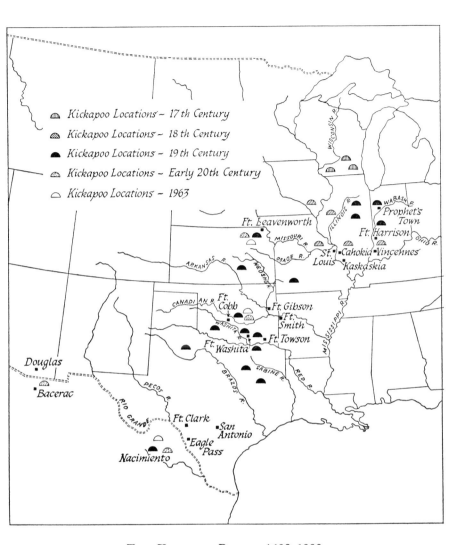

THE KICKAPOO RANGE, 1600–1900

lated. Thereafter the lower Northwest was securely attached to the United States, and Clark's victories were due in no small measure to Kickapoo assistance. Undoubtedly the Kickapoos at Vincennes, whom Hamilton relied upon so heavily for defense of his position, were influenced to desert the British and assist Clark at least in part by historic tribal antipathy for the British.[18]

More important, however, was the fact that Clark, from the beginning, had received active support from the Illinois Kickapoos. And the Wabash Kickapoos, by sustaining their pledges to Hamilton, would have been waging war on fellow tribesmen. Also, both the Illinois and Wabash bands depended on the Spanish officials at St. Louis for advice. Although the Spaniards had early in the war advised both the Illinois and Wabash Kickapoos to avoid involvement in the "troubles of the Long Knives and the English," Spanish support of the American cause had developed, and as the British retaliated against the Spanish, the advice from St. Louis became encouragement of direct assistance to the Americans.

General Clark had high praise for the Kickapoos, giving the tribe due credit for the role it played in American victories in the Northwest. In April, 1779, recounting to Patrick Henry his successes culminating in the recent reconquest of Vincennes, Clark noted that while the Iroquois, Potawatomis, Ottawas, Chippewas, Iowas, and most of the Shawnees were "active" in defending British interests, the Kickapoos and their Wabash allies, notably the Weas and Piankashaws, had treated with him and behaved very well.[19]

After the capitulation of Vincennes and the capture of Hamilton, Clark held a council with the Kickapoos to express appreciation for the tribe's services at Vincennes and in other expeditions in the Northwest. The pledges made to the Kickapoos by Clark, as a spokesman for the United States, set their minds at ease concerning the intentions of the new nation. It is easy to understand the admiration and awe the Kickapoos felt for the forceful Clark, the faith they placed in his speeches before the tribal council, and their

[18] Reuben G. Thwaites, *How George Rogers Clark Won the Northwest*, 57.

[19] Clark to Henry, Kaskaskia, April 28, 1779, Illinois Historical Society *Collections*, VIII, 169–74.

favorable attitude toward the United States as the new patron and Father of the tribe. Clark's report on this council, included in a letter to George Mason, reveals the reason for Kickapoo faith in American intentions. Concerning their fears of American expansion, he wrote that the tribe had been assured that "we were so far from having any design on their lands, that I looked upon it that we were on their land . . . that we claim no land in their country; that the first man to take their lands by violence must strike the tomahawk in my head"; and that he was in their land only long enough to drive out the enemy, promising to leave when this was accomplished.[20]

The composure that Clark's promises produced among the Kickapoos was soon shaken. The acquisitiveness of that "great land animal," the American settler, an eternal force on the frontier and an infernal one to the American Indian, began to assert itself in the Northwest even before Clark's forces left Fort Massac in June of 1778. Twenty families of settlers from Kentucky followed Clark's army from Corn Island to the Illinois country. After Clark's victories in the Northwest had made settlement somewhat safe in 1779, this vanguard was followed by other pioneer families from Virginia and Kentucky.

Armed with land warrants from Revolutionary War service, the settlers established claims around Vincennes. Other settlements followed, and in less than a decade the new government of the United States had passed a series of ordinances regulating settlement and land titles in the area conquered by Clark, providing for civil government, and setting conditions for achieving statehood in the American union. Kickapoo policy toward the Long Knives changed in steady proportion to the advance of settlement. The settlers around Vincennes alarmed the tribe, and Kickapoo delegates began to beat a path to Detroit in 1780 seeking British counsel.[21]

This path widened into a thoroughfare as the Kickapoos, dis-

---

[20] Clark to Mason, Kaskaskia, November 19, 1779, *Illinois Historical Society Collections*, VIII, 140–47.

[21] De Peyster to Haldimand, Detroit, March 8, 1780, *Michigan Pioneer and Historical Collections*, X, 378–79.

claiming their trust in the Americans, joined the Miamis, Pota-watomis, Weas, and other tribes in accepting the British as their Father. For the Kickapoos this comprised double paternity, since they also claimed the Spanish at St. Louis as their Father, and they thereby occupied the curious and at times difficult position of serving two masters.

As allies of the British, the Kickapoos became reliable and trust-ed defenders of British interests, not for the sake of the British per se, but because the objective of the British, the Kickapoos, and the other Indian tribes of the Northwest was the same—namely, stemming the flood of American settlement.

4

The Chickasaw-Osage Campaigns

WITH THE TREATY OF PARIS, 1783, officially ending the American War of Independence, title to the old Algonquian range presumably passed to the United States. American settlers had begun to move north of the Ohio as early as 1778, and the war's end sent an increasing number of homeseekers into the Northwest. Land companies, formed by speculators and former Continental Army officers, were organized to promote the development of this area. One of the enterprises, called the American Settlements Association, was composed of former officers and soldiers who had been members of the Clark expedition.

The hunting grounds of the Algonquians were endangered by this white migration, and Indian resistance to American encroachment set off a series of wars which were of greater duration and more destructive to life and property than all of the Northwest campaigns in the War of Independence. A thread of continuity can be traced through these wars for control of the Algonquian range. The battle began in earnest in 1783 and extended through 1815, and even the Blackhawk outbreaks of 1828–31 on the Upper Mississippi represent a belated reassertion of Indian claim to ownership of these lands.

Throughout this period British agents worked among the Indians of the Northwest, supplying them with arms and presents and inciting them to attack the new American settlements. A loose Algonquian confederacy, with the Kickapoos as the nominal leaders, had been organized with British encouragement by 1784. The common bond of this association was the threat of engulfment by the Long Knives.

While British concern for keeping the Northwest free of American control was based on several considerations, the chief reason was economic, as is illustrated by a petition prepared by the merchants of Montreal and submitted to the Governor-General of Canada in 1790.

To his Excellency . . . the memorial and petition of the merchants of Montreal trading to the Indian, or upper country humbly showeth that your memorialists being ardently engaged in the Indian or upper country trade of the province are not a little alarmed for the safety of the property which they have trusted to the Indian country by reason of the late attempt of the Americans to establish by force a post or posts on the frontiers of the province near Detroit. That should such attempt be attended by success, it is evident that the Indian trade to the south of Lake Erie must fall into their hands to the loss and prejudice of the province in the sum not short of 30,000 pounds sterling. That from so near a vicinity to Detroit your memorialists cannot help suspecting that the views of obtaining that key to the west or the northwest are strongly entertained by our rival neighbors; and they consider with much pain that should they possess themselves of Detroit, they will have in their power the means of commanding the whole western and northwestern trade, which your memorialists esteem to produce returns for British manufactures, chiefly in furs, to the value of 150,000 pounds sterling. Your memorialists might remark on the bad consequences which would follow in particular to the new settlement should our neighbors become masters of the post of Detroit, but knowing that your Lordship can better discern than they can point out, the political injuries which the province would sustain in such an event, they confine themselves solely to the Indian trade, of which from long expense and extensive dealings they can speak with certainty and precision. Your memorialists are aware that by the Treaty of Peace of 1783 a great part of the Indian country was ceded to the American states, but having carried on the trade of that country as was usual before and during the war under the protection and safeguard of government; your memorialists not having since the peace encountered any difficulty from the subjects of the American states, have been led to extend the Indian trade farther west than formerly, from which circumstances their property and connections in that country being greater and more widely extended, any sudden check to their commercial pursuits would occasion their ruin.[1]

British Indian agents encouraged the policy makers at Montreal to intensify their efforts to stop the American advance in the Northwest, advising that those persons "interested in the trade of that country ought to use their interest with the government to put a stop to any further encroachments into the Indian country." This could be accomplished, according to officials in the field, by establishing "a line of division from the Pennsylvania northern and western boundary line as established in 1768 to the southward between the Americans and Indians." This was regarded as the only means of providing security for British trade.[2]

Mercantile pressure on the Canadian politicians resulted in an increase of British intrigue among the tribes of the Northwest after 1790. The Indians were given arms and presents calculated to produce substantial Indian armies poised to strike at the American advance. This was a significant change in strategy, for although the Algonquians had been active between 1783 and 1790, their depredations had been carried out by small bands striking individual families or small settlements. Even this nuisance activity, however, had produced a sizable list of atrocities. The resurgent Algonquians, roaming north and south of the Ohio during this seven-year period, massacred an estimated fifteen hundred American settlers and ran off twenty thousand horses. The Kickapoos could claim more than their share of these outrages.[3] They had concentrated on the lower Ohio, raiding the Kentucky and lower Wabash settlements, waylay-

[1] "Memorial and Petition of the Merchants of Montreal Trading to the Indian Country, Montreal, December 20, 1790," Great Lakes Indian Archives Project, Kickapoo File, 1786–90.

[2] "Sir William Johnson Relative to Indians in the Neighborhood of Detroit, Montreal, December 11, 1790," Great Lakes Indian Archives Project, Kickapoo File, 1786–90.

[3] William McNamara, *The Catholic Church on the Northern Indiana Frontier, 1789–1844,* 4–5.

ing boats on the Ohio, looting and burning the cargo, and mutilating the passengers.

Before 1790 the United States made repeated attempts to negotiate treaties of peace, including acknowledgment of American settlement rights in the Northwest, with the Kickapoos and other tribes, but these efforts met with little success. Learning that the British planned to intensify their activities among the Algonquians in 1790, Arthur St. Clair, governor of the Northwest Territory, made one last attempt at negotiation. Since the balance of power in the Northwest was held by the Kickapoos, St. Clair reasoned that this tribe should be contacted first, hoping that a treaty which separated them from the British-sponsored Algonquian confederacy would cause a serious weakening, possibly the collapse, of the conspiracy.

Governor St. Clair selected for the Kickapoo mission Antoine Gamelin, descendant of one of the early French trader families and by all reports a man well acquainted with the problems of an Indian council. Significantly, even before Gamelin reached the Kickapoo towns, he was met by a Kickapoo war party bound for the Kentucky settlements. Gamelin arrived at the upper Wabash Kickapoo towns on April 11, 1790. Coldly received by the chiefs and headmen, Gamelin delivered the Governor's messages of good will and peace to the council and encouraged negotiations.

The council grumbled at Gamelin for failing to bring the tribe a draught of "milk" (brandy) from the Great White Chief of the Long Knives. The members complained of his lack of presents and instructed St. Clair's envoy on Indian protocol, pointing out that Gamelin "should know a bearer of speeches should never be with empty hands." After hours of abuse, Gamelin departed with the Kickapoo answer to St. Clair's message of peace—the council could not talk peace, for the young men continued to leave for war, and the tribe could not stop them.[4]

The failure of the Gamelin mission indicated the futility of attempting peaceful settlement with the Kickapoos, and when Gov-

---

[4] Antoine Gamelin, "Journal," *American State Papers, Indian Affairs,* I, 93–94.

ernor St. Clair learned of continued Kickapoo hostility, he began preparations for an offensive against the towns on the Wabash. Two years earlier St. Clair had regarded war with the Kickapoos as inevitable and had recommended to the secretary of war that at the proper time a simultaneous strike at Kickapoo and Miami towns would "demoralize the Indian confederacy."[5]

In the autumn of 1790, Governor St. Clair, authorized by the secretary of war to carry out his strategy, launched a series of expeditions against the Algonquian confederacy. Each offensive had two prongs—one American column would strike north and east at the Miami towns located at the head of the Maumee, while the other moved along the Wabash attacking the Kickapoo towns. Kickapoo warriors regularly raced north to assist the Miami, leaving their Wabash towns undefended, and consistently they returned to find their villages desolated.

This sequence of Kickapoo devastation began late in 1790 when Major John F. Hamtramck led an army north from Vincennes and burned an undefended Kickapoo village on the Wabash.[6] Then, during the early summer of 1791, General Charles Scott, at the head of seven hundred mounted militia from Kentucky, paused on the Wabash while planted rumors of an American movement toward the Maumee spread through the Kickapoo towns.

After his scouts reported that Kickapoo warriors had moved in great numbers to intercept the American force supposed to be marching on the Miami towns, leaving the villages with only women, children, and old men, Scott struck. His principal target was the great Kickapoo town near Kithtippecanoe. The Kentucky troopers looted and burned every lodge in the town, destroyed several acres of green corn and a considerable quantity of dried corn in storage, and took several bales of furs. Scott's army climaxed its triumph with the round-up of fifty-eight women and children as captives.[7]

---

[5] St. Clair to Secretary of War, Fort Harmar, September 14, 1788, in Clarence E. Carter (ed.), *Territorial Papers, of the United States,* II, 158.

[6] Beckwith, *The Illinois and Indiana Indians,* 124–25.

[7] Scott to Secretary of War, Lexington, June 28, 1791, *American State Papers, Indian Affairs,* I, 131.

When the Maumee-bound Kickapoo warriors learned of St. Clair's decoy, they quickly returned to their smouldering town, picked up the invaders' trail, and attempted to intercept them and recover the captives. Although the Kickapoos were unsuccessful, the British report on the Wabash attack observed that the Indians were not cast down and were "determined to defend their country to the last" against the Americans.[8]

A third expedition was authorized by St. Clair during August of 1791 against the Wabash Kickapoo towns. General James Wilkinson was chosen to lead a mounted force of five hundred soldiers up from Kentucky. In his orders to Wilkinson, St. Clair pointed out that the time was auspicious for a strike, since most of the Kickapoo families were hunting in the west. If Wilkinson was successful on the Wabash, St. Clair ordered, he would then move against the Kickapoo towns on the Illinois prairie.

Wilkinson arrived in the Kickapoo country early in August, and his first attack was made on the village of Kikiah, situated at the Eel River–Wabash junction. There he found a few women, several old men, and a number of white prisoners digging near the village for a root "they substitute for a potato." Taking thirty-four captives, burning the village, and cutting down a huge cornfield "scarcely in the milk," he moved toward the Illinois Kickapoos. Trouble in the ranks caused Wilkinson to abandon the Illinois venture and return to the Wabash, where he found the Kickapoo village near Kithtippecanoe, leveled by Scott's earlier attack, completely rebuilt. After reducing the village to rubble, Wilkinson turned south to Kentucky.[9]

The destruction of their villages by American armies on three separate occasions persuaded most of the Wabash Kickapoos to abandon their homeland. While a small band continued to reside on the Wabash, the major portion of the eastern Kickapoos, between

[8] "Report to Colonel McKee re The Kickapoo, Grand Glaize, June 15, 1791," *Michigan Pioneer and Historical Collections*, XXIV, 261–62.

[9] Wilkinson to St. Clair, Frankfort, August 24, 1791, *American State Papers, Indian Affairs*, I, 133–35.

1791 and 1808, were lodged in various places. Some moved to the villages of the Illinois branch of the tribe, while others joined Serena's band on the Missouri. The story of the tribe's return to the Wabash in force after 1800 is related to the rise of Elskwatawa (the Prophet) and Tecumseh.

St. Clair's broad strategy reduced the Kickapoos' interest in and support of the Algonquian confederacy. Although both Wabash and Illinois Kickapoos assisted Little Turtle and the Miamis in turning back St. Clair's armies in 1791 and 1792, the tribe took only a casual interest in the prelude to Fallen Timbers. And after General Anthony Wayne's smashing victory over the northwestern tribes in 1794, Kickapoo chiefs joined half-heartedly in the great Indian congress held at Greenville the following year, receiving a five-hundred-dollar annuity for the tribe.[10]

While their chiefs were talking peace, Kickapoo warriors were practicing their primary occupation—gathering scalps and plunder. Most of the tribe's activity between 1795 and 1808 was centered in the Spanish provinces beyond the Mississippi, but before leaving en masse for the West, the Kickapoos raised one last reign of terror in the American settlements around Kaskaskia.

This outbreak occurred during the spring of 1795 and was especially costly in life and property for the pioneer communities. Riley's Mill, a settlement which produced flour for the gulf markets, was terrorized by Kickapoo bandits in early April. The marauders, after killing and scalping the mill owner and several of his Negroes, threw the victims' heads into the mill hopper.[11]

Terror spread through the settlements when on the last day of April, 1795, reports came in that Samuel Chew and his party of five had been attacked by the Kickapoos near Fort Massac on the Ohio. A search party found Chew's baggage looted and his papers and books strewn along the beach. One member of the party was literally butchered—his body cut transversely, his bowels taken

[10] "Treaty of Grenville," *American State Papers, Indian Affairs,* I, 562–53.

[11] Maude C. French, "The Last Years of Kaskaskia," Illinois Historical Society, *Journal,* Vol. XXXVII (September, 1944), 228–41.

out, his head scalped. Four Negroes also were scalped. Chew was found in the river, scalped, and mangled, his body mutilated.[12] The last episode occurred in May when Kickapoo raiders massacred a white family and thirteen Negroes near the mouth of the Ohio.[13]

While these forays show that the Kickapoos were still interested in arresting the advance of American settlements, the tribe turned more and more west of the Mississippi. The entire tribe probably would have moved permanently to the Missouri and Arkansas rivers had not the Indian confederation movement, begun in 1805 and propagated by the Prophet and Tecumseh, caused them to pause in their westward march and return to the Northwest. For the time being, however, many Kickapoos were active in the western provinces, fighting for Spain in the Chickasaw and Osage wars.

For some time Kickapoo bands had assisted the Spaniards, and their services were highly esteemed by Spanish officials. As early as 1784 a Kickapoo delegation was received in New Orleans by the Spanish governor-general and presented with a silver medal in appreciation for the tribe's assistance in defending the empire against the Chickasaws and other enemies.[14]

Just as the Chickasaws in earlier times had attacked French supply lines on the Mississippi, so did they continue to trouble the Spaniards after Spain had succeeded to the control of Louisiana. Every year the Spanish caravan sent from New Orleans to St. Louis with trade goods and presents for the Indian tribes was attacked by Chickasaw bands. Crewmen were slain, cargoes looted, and the boats were burned.

So damaging were Chickasaw raids in 1772 that Governor Cruzat called in the Kickapoos and turned them on the river pirates. "Their enmity for the Chickasaw fired their spirits and without the slightest delay they set out to attack the Chickasaw, spurred on by the desire for revenge which always animates them." When

[12] Hammill to Doyle, Fort Massac, April 30, 1795, Wayne Papers, Pennsylvania Historical Society, Great Lakes Indian Project, Kickapoo File.

[13] St. Clair to Wayne, Cahokia, May 12, 1795, Wayne Papers, Pennsylvania Historical Society, Great Lakes Indian Archives Project, Kickapoo File.

[14] Alfonso Fabila, *La Tribu Kickapoo de Coahuila,* 25.

KEE-AN-NE-KUK (KENNEKUK), the Prophet, in an attitude of prayer.
From a painting by George Catlin.

A typical Kickapoo bark house and storage platform.

the Chickasaws learned that the Kickapoos were invading their country, runners carried the tidings of danger to all the villages. The Chickasaws would not even move out to hunt for food for their families, and the great Chickasaw chief, Panimataja journeyed all the way to St. Louis to plead with Cruzat to call off the Kickapoo avengers.[15]

Cruzat used his control of Kickapoo fighting power to intimidate the Chickasaws into an agreement of peace with the Spanish. This was an uneasy arrangement at best, for Chickasaw raids continued intermittently. But a new menace faced the Spanish in the west, and every available resource had to be mustered to bring it under control. The Osages, with a range extending virtually from the environs of St. Louis to the edge of the Plains and south to the Arkansas, maintained a consistently hostile attitude toward the Spanish and refused to submit to the new rulers of Louisiana.

Becoming more brazen during the 1780's in their flaunting of Spanish control, by 1790 the Osages had made their range unsafe for any Spaniard or agent of the Spanish. Spanish horse and cattle herds were raided within sight of the Missouri and Mississippi settlements, and farmers dared not venture out even to plow their fields or harvest crops.[16]

Even the post of Natchitoches, far to the south, felt the effects of Osage recrimination. Post Commandant DeBlanc complained in January 1790 that the "Osage have been the cause of the ruin of this post. . . . At the present time there is no other crop here to look forward to except tobacco. If it had not been for the Osage, we should have had a quantity of tongues, skins of different sorts, bear oil, tallow, and salted buffalo meat."[17]

By 1792 Spanish officials had armed and organized the Kickapoos, Sacs, Foxes, and Shawnees into an ominous striking force, and they set the Indians loose in small bands in the Osage country.

[15] Cruzat to Miro, St. Louis, August 8, 1782, in Lawrence Kinnaird (ed.), *Spain in the Mississippi Valley 1765–1794,* II, 53–54.

[16] "Secret Report of Baron Carondolet, New Orleans, May 31, 1794," Clark Papers, Draper Manuscript Collection, Wisconsin Historical Society.

[17] DeBlanc to Miro, Natchitoches, January 20, 1790, in Kinnaird (ed.), *op. cit.,* II, 295–97.

Bounties were offered for Osage scalps, and presents were assured for successful raids against Osage villages. To isolate the Osages from all sources of arms, powder, and shot, the governor-general of Louisiana forbade all trade with the Osages "under penalty of three hundred pesos fine, or, in case of insolence, the offender to be sent as a prisoner" to New Orleans. Spanish officers throughout Louisiana were directed to "proclaim that any subject of His Majesty, or individual of any other nations, white or red, may overrun the . . . Osages, kill them and destroy their families, as they are disturbers of the prosperity of all the nations. . . . It is extremely important to humiliate or destroy those barbarians, which can only be done by using severity."[18]

As Spanish mercenaries the Kickapoos roamed over Louisiana northwest up the Missouri, south to the Arkansas, and as far east as Natchitoches. Small mobile bands, well supplied with Spanish powder and shot, ranged widely in search of isolated Osage camps. Striking swiftly, the warriors reaped a harvest of scalps, prisoners, and plunder. After each foray, warriors delivered their trophies to the nearest Spanish scalp buyer, at St. Louis, San Esteban de Arkansas, or Natchitoches. At these places each party collected a barrel of *aguardiente* (brandy), two rolls of tobacco per warrior, and a new supply of powder and shot.[19]

In the spring of 1800 a large Kickapoo force struck an Osage encampment situated on the lower Neosho with remarkable success. The fruits of victory—feather bonnets, scalps, five prisoners, and a large horseherd—were exchanged at St. Louis for the customary bounty.[20]

Even before 1800, however, the Osages, harried at every turn by the imported Spanish mercenaries, were suing for peace. Finally convinced of the Osages' good intentions, Pierre Chouteau

[18] Carondolet to Trudeau, New Orleans, December 22, 1792, Kinnaird (ed.), *op. cit.,* III, 107.

[19] Journal of Lorimier, Cape Girardeau, December 27, 1792, *Archivo General de las Indias Sevilla, Papeles Precedentes de la Isla de Cuba,* Houck Transcripts, Wisconsin Historical Society.

[20] Casa Calvo to Dehault Delassus, New Orleans, June 9, 1800, Pierre Chouteau Papers, Missouri Historical Society.

and other Spanish agents began in 1800 to arrange for peace conferences between the Osages and the Spanish Indian tribes.[21]

The machinery for the destruction of the Osages, once set in motion by the Spanish, was not easily turned to other pursuits. The Kickapoos were especially difficult to restrain. The tribal tradition of conflict, seemingly stultified by the gradually stiffening American defense east of the Mississippi, had been satisfied by the excitement and substantial bounty derived from hunting scalps for the Spaniards. As late as March 14, 1803, long after the Spanish-Osage reconciliation, the Spanish governor at St. Louis reported that only after considerable persuasion had he been able to stop a party of sixty Kickapoos from mounting a surprise attack against the Osages. To satisfy them he had had to give a number of presents, and even then he watched closely to see that they did not carry out their design, as "many white men . . . might have been victims of their voracity."[22]

[21] Great Council Between Delassus and the Osages, 1800. Houck (ed.), *The Spanish Regime in Missouri,* II, 306.

[22] Lisa to Delassus, St. Louis, March 14, 1803, in A. P. Nasatir (ed.), *Before Lewis and Clark,* II, 717.

5

Tecumseh's Minions

As THE KICKAPOOS eliminated the Osage menace in the western provinces and brought this enemy to terms with the Spaniards, Spanish support for the mercenary bands was reduced. The termination of bounty payments for scalps and the cutback of Spanish rations, arms, and presents after 1800 forced the Kickapoo fighting men to shift for themselves. Since the recent war had driven the Osages from the region southwest of St. Louis, Serena, chief of the Missouri Kickapoos, moved part of his band to the Osage and Gasconade River country. A number of eastern Kickapoo warriors who had served in the Osage war settled with their families in the Gasconade villages.

Most of the eastern Kickapoos, however, returned to their old homes on the Illinois and Wabash. These warriors found that many changes had occurred during their sojourn in the west. Most of the old confederacy tribes, smashed by General Wayne's army at Fallen Timbers in 1794, were adrift, divided, and confused. A new American state—Ohio—was evolving within the area of General Wayne's conquest. White settlements were extending beyond the treaty line of Greenville, and the central and western sections of the Algonquian range had been organized into Indiana Territory with William Henry Harrison as governor.

Curiously, most of the Northwest tribes were accepting this engulfment quietly. Probably many were intimidated by American military strength and feared another Fallen Timbers. The moral fiber of the tribes was degenerating, too. If in earlier times French brandy and British rum had won some adherents in each tribe, the cheap whisky pandered by American traders and store-keepers had become a pervasive curse among the Algonquians. This firewater, which sapped tribal honor and struck down the "valor of men and the virtue of women,"[1] did more to emasculate Algonquian resistance and tame the tribesmen than fear of the growing American military power.

Tribal unity was deteriorating and schisms were emerging, largely over the issue of dealing with the American advance. Two groups were fairly evident in each tribe—a pro-American party and an anti-American party. The pro-American group based its stand not on esteem for the United States but on the inevitability of the ultimate white overthrow of Indian culture and, therefore, the futility of resistance. The anti-American party was determined and constant in its animosity, but because of tribal division it lacked sufficient strength to muster an extended and effective resistance. This faction could only carry on nuisance activity against the American settlements.

Governor Harrison and other American officials exploited the tribal disagreement by plying the susceptible faction in each tribe with presents and recognition, officially denouncing the renegade group. Petty chiefs, presuming to speak for the entire tribe, were consulted by government agents whenever a new land cession was required.

Governor Harrison, directed by President Jefferson to extinguish Indian title to lands in Indiana Territory so that a clear public domain would exist ahead of the line of settlement, began soon after his appointment as governor to hold councils with the Kickapoos and other tribes under his jurisdiction. Through these councils the Governor became acquainted with the tribal leaders, noted those chiefs who would yield to his purposes, and sought cession treaties when auspicious.

Disturbed at a growing list of Kickapoo depredations in the Illinois and Wabash settlements during 1802, Harrison held a council

[1] Elmore Barce and Robert A. Swan, *History of Benton County, Indiana,* I, 15–16.

in September with the chiefs and headmen of the tribe. He admonished them to "bury the tomahawk" and fire their "arrows at the buffaloe, the bear, and the deer, which are provided for your use, but spare your brother man." Criticizing the tribe's belligerent attitude, the Governor reminded the members present that it was the wish of their Father, the President, that the chiefs assemble their "scattered warriors . . . form towns and villages, in situations best adapted to cultivation." When this was done, Harrison continued, the tribe would be "furnished with horses, cattle, hogs, and implements." Harrison pointed out that "the game which afforded you subsistence is yearly becoming more scarce, and in a short time you will be left without resource, and your wives and children will in vain ask you for food. . . . There is nothing so pleasing to God as to see his children employed in the cultivation of the earth. . . . The experiment has been fairly tried with your brothers the Creeks and Cherokees. . . . This has had a most happy effect on their population and all their wigwams are filled with children. . . . Let me entreat you to make the experiment, for the sake of the rising generation."[2]

Harrison's proposal that the Kickapoos abandon their exciting and dangerous ways and accept the prosaic life of the farm was coolly received by the tribe, especially by those warriors fresh from wars in the west. A basic Kickapoo trait was intense personal and group pride, and this could be maintained only by a ready redress of grievances according to the Kickapoo formula. The revolutionary pattern of life Harrison sought to impose upon the tribe would mean surrendering the outlet for tribal ego—revenge.

Since their return the Kickapoos had been exposed regularly to insults and injuries from the settlers, and the tribe sought revenge by the only means its custom would permit—violence. Kickapoo horses were stolen by settlers, and the warriors returned the deed in kind, adding plunder and often scalps since the white owners generally resisted such raids, allegedly conceived for the purpose of recovering property already stolen. Incidents continued to occur.

2 Harrison's Speech, Vincennes, September 2, 1802, in Esarey (ed.), *op. cit.,* I, 52.

A single irritation, provoked by either settlers or Kickapoos, often developed into a local vendetta with disastrous results.

A serious example of this began in 1802 in the Illinois settlements over a charge that Kickapoo hunters were "shooting deer with bells on their necks." By 1805, after a series of mutual recriminations, relations between the Kickapoos and the settlers had deteriorated to the point of each group watching the other for an excuse to depredate. Matters reached a climax in December when the son of the Chief Pawatomo of the Illinois Kickapoos, out hunting alone, was caught by an American party, roughly handled, and threatened with death. During the same month some Kickapoo women gathering persimmons were accosted by a group of white men, insulted, and nearly assaulted.[3]

By Christmas Eve, 1805, there was great alarm throughout the Illinois country, for the Kickapoos returned in kind the insults and injuries their men, women, and children had suffered from the settlers. No horseherd was safe; cattle and hogs were butchered; haystacks and barns were burned; and scalps were taken when the settlers resisted.[4]

Each year brought an increase in turmoil in the Indiana Territory. Harrison repeatedly called Pawatomo of the Illinois Kickapoos and Oulawau of the Wabash Kickapoos to task for the conflicts and disorders their warriors caused. Proud Pawatomo, after a series of harassing summons, responded to Harrison: "At the time we lived with the French, our first Father, we were happy, they never said anything to us; since we have known our Father the Long Knife, there are always some complaints."[5]

By 1807 even the conciliatory Harrison was tiring of the outrages committed by the Kickapoos. During May of that year, one of the few surviving Kaskaskia Indians was slain and mutilated by Kickapoo highwaymen on the Massac Road. The crime was particularly brutal (the victim was scalped, his skull cut in pieces

---

[3] Perry to Bond, Cahokia, December 10, 1805, in Esarey (ed.), *op. cit.*, I, 176–77.

[4] Harrison to Secretary of War, Vincennes, December 24, 1805, National Archives, Record Group 107, Secretary of War, Letters Received.

[5] Speech of Pawatomo, Esarey (ed.), *op. cit.*, I, 178–79.

by three tomahawk strokes, and his body was perforated with bullet holes; his rifle, saddle, and accoutrements were taken; to compound their arrogance, the assassins left their tribal sign on the corpse),[6] and the Kickapoos evidently intended the murder to intimidate Indians friendly to the Americans. The Kaskaskia tribe had only recently come under the special care of the United States government, and they were to receive "that protection which is enjoyed by its own citizens." The Kickapoos had further opportunity to exhibit their contempt when American authorities demanded the surrender of the murderers. Harrison's impatience with the Kickapoos was shown in his message to the tribe concerning the Kaskaskia murder: "My Children, Why does it happen that I am so often obliged to address you in the language of complaint?"[7]

The British, still interested in the Northwest, noted the Kickapoo defection and were sympathetic. Beginning in 1804, British-sponsored councils were regularly held at Montreal. The Kickapoos sent delegations to each council, and these representatives aired their grievances against the Americans in the presence of attentive British agents. When Governor Harrison reported that the Kickapoos were turning to the British, President Jefferson directed Harrison to be "particularly friendly" to the Kickapoos and to seek to divert the growing British attachment through such favors as paying the Kickapoos higher prices for their furs and selling them goods at cheaper prices than the British.[8]

Harrison's gestures had little effect upon the anti-American faction among the Kickapoos, largely because the British were giving substantial quantities of goods customarily purchased from American traders. Liaison with the British quickened during 1806, and the Kickapoos became more brazen. With encouragement from Montreal, Kickapoo runners began circulating war belts among the neighboring tribes, inviting them to join in the British-sponsored councils and to prepare for war on the United States. Governor

[6] Jones to Harrison, Kaskaskia, May 4, 1807, in Esarey (ed.), *op. cit.*, I, 211.

[7] Harrison to the Kickapoo, Vincennes, May 19, 1807, in Esarey (ed.), *op. cit.*, I, 215.

[8] Jefferson to Harrison, Washington, January 16, 1806, in Esarey (ed.), *op. cit.*, I, 185–86.

Harrison, watching this conspiracy take shape, reported to President Jefferson that he was perplexed by the Kickapoos' determination to sustain the hope of an Indian overthrow of American rule, even though the tribe knew full well that the United States could mount a force strong enough to destroy all Indians in a very short time. He offered as an explanation the fact that apparently the Kickapoos "had received so many injuries from the Americans that they were determined to perish to a man rather than not revenge them."[9]

The Kickapoo crusade against the American advance was having some effect, for American officials noted a growing belligerence among the tribes of the Northwest during 1806. British agents were reported active in supplying the Kickapoos with gifts and more war belts for distribution throughout the Indian community. Alarm and anxiety in the American settlements increased to such an extent that the secretary of war instructed Governor Harrison to summon the Kickapoo chiefs in council and to "seek to overcome this deception."[10]

Harrison's efforts had little effect, and the anti-American movement which the Kickapoos had initiated and carried forward with angry fanaticism won supporters among the Potawatomis, Miamis, and Piankashaws. Although none of these shared the zeal of the Kickapoos, and for the time being no faction of any tribe was willing to participate in the overt acts which the Kickapoos sought to inspire, yet they were receptive and interested, and subscribed at least in principle.

Then out of the East came an integrating force which fused the tribes into an active, awesome union. The brothers Tecumseh and Elskwatawa, the Prophet, endowed by Shawnee-Creek parentage with a rare combination of powerful personality, perception, and rich eloquence, combined their remarkable talents to forge a common brotherhood among the Indians of the Northwest.

---

[9] Harrison to Jefferson, Vincennes, July 5, 1806, in Esarey (ed.), *op. cit.,* I, 195–96.

[10] Secretary of War to Harrison, Washington, August 10, 1806, National Archives, Secretary of War, Letters Sent Relating to Indian Affairs, Microcopy 15, Roll 2.

Kickapoo war belts had reached Tecumseh and the Prophet at a small Shawnee settlement near Greenville, and after a visit to the Wabash villages in 1806, the pair decided to move to the territory of the Kickapoos and begin the establishment of their Indian utopia. Both favored the Kickapoos because of the tribe's fighting ability. Also, the Kickapoos had been promoting substantially the same ideals taught by Tecumseh and the Prophet, with the only difference a matter of approach; the hardy Kickapoos simply lacked the refinement and poise which this pair's talents had given the dream of generating a "mystic sense of Indian nationality."[11]

By 1808 a cosmopolitan village was rising on the ruins of the old Indian town of Kithtippecanoe. Known as Prophetstown, it became the center for the Indian tribes of the Northwest. Beginning with 140 followers,[12] the Prophet and Tecumseh initiated an evangelistic crusade which inspired the periodic migration of thousands of Indian families to the council grounds on the edge of Prophetstown. There the listeners were entranced with the oratorical brilliance of Tecumseh and the mystical aberrations of the Prophet, each focusing his specialty on the theme of Indian nationalism.

The popular teachings of the Prophet and Tecumseh interpreted and accounted for the woes of the Indian. Both pointed to rampant drunkenness and degeneracy among the nations, the reduction of tribal hunting grounds, internal divisions, and the abandonment of certain old customs which were the source of Indian strength. The debauchery and poverty of the tribes, in fact every torment of the moment, was attributed to the American advance in the Northwest.

The Prophet, more of an exhibitionist than Tecumseh, used mystical seizures to render messages from the Great Spirit. Through the Prophet, the Great Spirit promised his children that soon they would have the means to destroy every American. The Prophet assured his audiences that he had been endowed with the power to cure all disease, confound his enemies, and stay the arm of death in sickness or on the battlefield.[13] The Great Spirit, he claimed, had ordained a new way of life for his children, and all must purify

11 McNamara, *op. cit.,* 6.
12 John B. Dillon, *A History of Indiana,* 426.

themselves and adopt it. Each warrior was to have but one wife; if a married woman misbehaved, her husband might chastise her with a rod as of old, but then she was to look him in the face and both must laugh and forget what happened; the medicine bags were to be destroyed; no follower was to have intercourse with the the whites; the French, Spanish, and English were to be considered the friends of the Indians, the Americans, enemies; each must pray that the earth be bountiful, the fish be plenty, the sun shine, and the rains fall; and all were to confess their sins to the Great Spirit, and sin no more.[14]

The stability of Tecumseh complemented his volatile brother perfectly. Generally avoiding the emotional and dramatic technique of the Prophet, Tecumseh maintained a rational approach to the Indians' problems. His legalism was persuasive. Claiming no special access to the Great Spirit, he taught with direction—drunkenness and vice were condemned; the white man's ways were to be shunned; each warrior must return to certain old customs. As a symbol of Indian rejection of white culture, textile clothing should be abolished and the Indian should wear skins as of old, and each warrior was to reform his personal conduct in order to reconstruct his physical, moral, and spiritual strength.

Since most of the Indian-American friction grew out of land tenure, Tecumseh directed his attention, first, to holding the remaining Indian lands, and, second, to the recovery of those lands in the possession of the Americans. The basis for Tecumseh's argument was that the Great Spirit had provided the land in the beginning for the use of all his children. No single tribe was intended to be the sole proprietor of a given area, contended Tecumseh, and all land was ordained to be held in common. Therefore no tribe or faction in a tribe could presume to transfer title of land to the United States without the common consent of all the Indians.[15]

Most of the communicants returned to their home villages to

[13] Wallace A. Brice, *History of Fort Wayne,* 170.

[14] The Prophet, Tecumseh Papers, Draper Manuscript Collection, Wisconsin Historical Society.

[15] Benjamin Drake, *Life of Tecumseh,* 160–63.

ponder the teachings of Tecumseh and the Prophet and to tell them to their fellow tribesmen. They went back from time to time to receive an interpretation of the most recent revelation by the perceptive Elkswatawa, or an exposition from the eloquent Tecumseh. Many, however, accepted Indian nationalism so completely that they separated from their respective tribes, built lodges for their families at Prophetstown, and settled there permanently. By 1811 the community could boast nearly one thousand warriors from the various tribes.

The sudden consolidation of the Indian nations by Tecumseh and the Prophet made Governor Harrison's task of extinguishing tribal title most dangerous. Pressured by a constantly increasing number of settlers who demanded more and more land, the Governor, in spite of the risks, continued to seek cession treaties from various tribes. A climax in his negotiations came in 1809. Between September and December of that year, councils with the Delawares, Potawatomis, Miamis, and the pro-American party in the Kickapoo tribe produced treaties clearing tribal title from nearly three million acres of land in Indiana Territory.

The Kickapoos were divided on Harrison's request. While the Prophet's partisans boycotted the council, the peace party, carefully cultivated by the Governor, finally signed a cession treaty in December of 1809.[16] The reaction from Prophetstown was immediate. The Prophet warned that he "smelled the Americans too strongly." His aggressive Kickapoo minions drove surveyors from the ceded lands and promised that they would bathe the land in American blood if settlement were attempted there. Then on August 12, 1810, Tecumseh, accompanied by a sizable delegation of warriors from the various tribes, came to Vincennes to hold a stormy ten-day council of protest with Harrison.[17]

Harrison refused to consider Tecumseh's argument that since the land was community property, owned jointly by all the tribes,

[16] "Harrison's Treaties, 1809," *American State Papers, Indian Affairs,* I, 760–63.
[17] Homer J. Webster, "William Henry Harrison's Administration of Indiana Territory," Indiana Historical Society *Publications,* IV, 266–71.

no cession by one tribe would be valid, that the piecemeal cession by petty chiefs must stop, and that the ceded lands would never be surrendered. After several days of heated debate on these issues, tempers became short, Tecumseh called Harrison a liar, and little was accomplished except to further irritate the leadership at Prophetstown.

Alarmed at the possible effects of Tecumseh's argument concerning common tribal title, Harrison requested of the President, soon after the Vincennes meeting, authority to negotiate for additional land before more tribes were converted to Tecumseh's view. Without such purchases Indiana would remain a territory, the Governor observed, and he confided, "I am heartily tired of living in a Territory."[18]

Matters quickly came to a head in Indiana Territory. The strength of the Indian confederation increased daily as warriors from the various tribes moved to Prophetstown. British agents frequently traveled from Montreal to the Wabash, and large tribal delegations passed each month to Canada. Substantial stores of British arms, blankets, hatchets, and rations were building up at Prophetstown, and a horseherd of two thousand animals, most of them stolen, was carefully guarded in the Wabash pastures. American traders complained of their destitute condition, brought about by the Indian boycott of their goods and the flood of free British supplies.[19]

Heavily armed bands of Kickapoos, Potawatomis, and Shawnees roamed over Indiana Territory, intimidating Indians friendly to the United States, stealing horses, and plundering isolated settlements.[20] Travel on the roads between the settlements was hazardous, for ambushes were common, especially for persons in Amer-

[18] Dorothy B. Goebel, *William Henry Harrison, A Political Biography,* Vol. XIV of Indiana Historical Society *Collections,* 117.

[19] Harrison to Secretary of War, Vincennes, April 25, 1810, in Esarey (ed.), *op. cit,* I, 417.

[20] Harrison to Secretary of War, Vincennes, July 11, 1810, in Esarey (ed.), *op. cit.,* I, 444; Edwards to Secretary of War, Elvirade, Illinois Territory, May, 1812; in Ninian W. Edwards, *History of Illinois,* 316.

ican dress. Those who found it necessary to travel came to affect French attire.[21]

During the summer of 1811 a British envoy delivered a talk to the Prophet, declaring that the time had arrived for his Indian armies to take up the tomahawk against the United States.[22] Harrison's Indian informers brought him intelligence of this visit. Faced with the inevitability of war and fearing most the Kickapoos, the Governor sought to remove as many of this tribe as possible from the Prophet's influence. In reporting his preparations to defend the territory against the expected outbreak, Harrison wrote that the "Kickapoo warriors are better than those of any other tribe, the remnant of the Wyandottes excepted," and emphasized the importance of wooing as many Kickapoo warriors as possible away from the Prophet.

About half the tribe, those from the Illinois branch of the tribe under Little Deer who had a reputation for co-operating with Harrison, were opposed to the Prophet and wished "to continue on friendly terms with the white people." These dissenters went to both Harrison at Vincennes and William Clark at St. Louis for guidance as the threat of a general Indian war became more apparent. Clark advised them to return to their villages, "tend their crops, and remain quietly at home."[23]

After the British war talk, Tecumseh, accompanied by a bodyguard of six Kickapoos and an equal number of Shawnees, departed south to attempt to win military support among the Cherokees, Creeks, Choctaws, and Chickasaws. Arriving in the Creek Nation during the late summer of 1811, Tecumseh sent the Kickapoos ahead as envoys to the Chickasaws and Choctaws, while he remained to solicit Creek assistance.[24]

[21] Edmund Flagg, *The Far West,* in Reuben G. Thwaites (ed.), *Early Western Travels,* XXVII, 71.

[22] Harrison to Secretary of War, Vincennes, September 25, 1811, in Esarey (ed.), *op. cit.,* I, 591–92.

[23] Clark to Secretary of War, St. Louis, July 3, 1811, National Archives, Record Group 107, Secretary of War, Letters Received.

[24] "Extracts of Letters to the War Department, Nashville, September 10, 1811," *American State Papers, Indian Affairs,* I, 801.

Tecumseh's departure was the signal for Harrison to act. First he sent messages to the Prophet demanding renunciation of the British alliance, restoration of stolen property, and "true declaration of intentions of the Prophet's party." Then, in late September, he mustered an army, an estimated one thousand from the Kentucky and Indiana territorial milita, and marched toward Prophetstown with the avowed intention of forcing the belligerent Indian community to disperse.

En route from Vincennes the Governor paused to construct a military depot and fortification which he modestly named Fort Harrison. During this pause he awaited an answer to his ultimatum. When by early November no response had been received, Harrison proceeded north to Tippecanoe Creek, the site of Prophetstown. Reaching the edge of the village on November 6, 1811, Harrison deployed his men in battle positions. On November 7 a force of four hundred angry warriors began a series of suicidal assaults on Harrison's lines. The frightened troops finally rallied, the charge was turned, and the warriors retreated. Surprisingly, the Prophet's followers abandoned the village. The American army, collecting its 188 dead and countless wounded, lingered at Prophetstown long enough to burn every lodge, including the vast military stores that had been built up with British assistance.[25] The Indian losses, numbering 38, fell heaviest on the Kickapoos, for 11 warriors of this tribe were slain during the assaults on Harrison's lines.[26]

The Battle of Tippecanoe, hailed by Governor Harrison as a smashing American victory over the Indian menace and an assurance of peace in the Northwest, was actually less than he claimed, if not completely the opposite. Kickapoo, Potawatomi, and Shawnee bands, scattered by Harrison's army over Indiana Territory and destitute of supplies, struck with a fresh fury, for now the necessity for survival was added to vengeance, and the granaries and smokehouses of the settlers could satisfy this need.

[25] Goebel, *op. cit.*, 119–20.

[26] Harrison to the Secretary of War, Vincennes, November 18, 1811, *American State Papers, Indian Affairs*, I, 776–78.

6

Massacre at Pigeon Roost

FOR NEARLY A YEAR before citizens in the eastern United States felt the effects of conflict brought on by the War of 1812, American settlers in the Northwest had been exposed to a British-inspired campaign of calculated extermination. Kickapoo, Potawatomi, and Shawnee predators, dispersed by the American victory at Tippecanoe, roamed the forests and prairies in savage wolf packs, and no settlement was safe. Harrison's destruction of Prophetstown, the sacred village of the new Indian confederacy and the burning of their blankets, food, and military stores drove the followers of Tecumseh and the Prophet into a new frenzy.

As had been expected, the Kickapoos threw themselves into an orgy of depredations, barbarity, and destructiveness. Throughout the winter these warriors, their food stores destroyed, lived off the settlers. Pioneer-farm larders supplied bacon, pork, and corn for the raiders, and even quilts and blankets were gathered up in their forays, so complete was their destitution. While many settler families suffered from Kickapoo reprisals during the winter and early spring of 1812, the worst episode was the O'Neal massacre. The O'Neal family homestead, situated near Peoria in Illinois Territory, was desolated by a Kickapoo war party in February. After looting the smokehouse and corncrib, the raiders burned every structure on the place. A platoon of Illinois rangers found in the ruins the bodies of ten persons "shockingly mangled."[1]

[1] "Relief to Citizens . . . for Indian Depredations," 22 Cong., 1 sess., *House Exec. Doc. No. 38*, 5–7.

Although operating in small scattered bands, the Kickapoos maintained contact with the Prophet, who ventured from his Canadian headquarters at Amherstberg from time to time into the Northwest to rendezvous with his partisans. Tecumseh, who had returned from the southern conferences in December, sojourned among the various camps, lending encouragement and teaching his ideal of Indian nationalism. Large quantities of arms, hatchets, and powder furnished by their "Father, the British," were delivered to these renegade communities by Kickapoo supply parties.[2]

Governors Ninian Edwards of Illinois Territory and William Henry Harrison of Indiana Territory were apprehensive about the activities of the Kickapoos and other tribes in their jurisdictions. Not only were communications cut and commerce and travel virtually impossible, but many settlers were abandoning their homesteads and returning to the East.

Governor Edwards warned that the Kickapoos, far from being repentant after the chastisement Harrison gave them at Prophetstown, were daily becoming more dangerous, since even the American party in the tribe was defecting and British emissaries were more active than ever among them. Edwards warned "we need not flatter ourselves with safety," and he urged the Secretary of War that only "by waging war against them and perpetually harassing them, can we convince them that it is in their interest to sue for peace."[3]

Both Harrison and Edwards attempted several times to hold councils and resolve differences with the Kickapoos. Harrison found such action fruitless, for the Prophet's influence was so strong that the young men were ignoring the older Kickapoo chiefs, the warriors were out of control, and "each man does as he pleases."[4] Harrison believed that no promises made in council by those "scoun-

[2] "Wells Report, Fort Wayne, March 1, 1812," *American State Papers, Indian Affairs,* I, 806.

[3] Edwards to Secretary of War, Elvirade, Illinois Territory, February 10, 1812, in Edwards, *History of Illinois,* 300–302.

[4] Harrison to Secretary of War, April 4, 1812, Vincennes, Harrison Papers, Draper Manuscript Collection, Wisconsin Historical Society.

drels," the Kickapoos, could be trusted, so that the only course "left for us to pursue" is "a war of extirpation upon them. If some offensive operations are not soon commenced against them we shall lose more of our citizens than the most bloody battle would cost us."[5]

An appeal was made to the secretary of war by Governor Edwards in May, 1812, for mounted troops ready to attack, for he declared it was time to expect action from the Kickapoos. The women, he noted, were collected at the Kickapoo villages near Peoria preparing to make corn; the spring hunt was over; and the tribe had finished making maple sugar. The men had nothing to do but make war, and Edwards pointed out that the thick foliage of the season favored their mode of warfare. In estimating Kickapoo strength, the Governor estimated that there were about fifteen hundred warriors scattered in bands throughout his territory, and that several of these "desperate fellows and great plunderers." In addition he believed that there were about one hundred Kickapoos with the Prophet at Amherstberg. "We have no security from these Indians, but by carrying the war into the Indian country we can check them. Otherwise in a few weeks we'll be unable to do so for then the fly season comes on and during its continuance it is utterly impossible to carry on an expedition on horseback through the prairies. Unless checked now, they will continue to depredate until the corn ripens, then I have no doubt they will collect and try to strike some decisive blow."[6]

News of the O'Neal Massacre caused panic in the settlements and set off a new exodus of pioneer families to the safety of the East. Governor Edwards' census revealed that in the spring of 1812 he had only two thousand male citizens above the age of twenty-one upon whom he could call for militia duty, and this number was being daily reduced by the departure of the faint-hearted.[7]

[5] Harrison to Secretary of War, Vincennes, April 22, 1812, in Esarey (ed.), *op. cit.,* II, 41.

[6] Edwards to Secretary of War, Elvirade, Illinois Territory, May 12, 1812, National Archives, Record Group 107, Secretary of War, Letters Received.

[7] Edwards to Secretary of War, Elvirade, Illinois Territory, June 2, 1812, in Edwards, *History of Illinois,* 325–26.

A growing public indignation in the East over the O'Neal murders led the government to order Governor Edwards to demand the surrender of the assassins. Edwards advised the secretary of war that, far from denying the massacre, the Kickapoo chiefs publicly acknowledged the deed and claimed full credit for it, going to considerable lengths to make certain that the Governor was informed of the fact. Edwards pointed to this insolence as a sign of danger and recommended that the government's demand wait, for if it were pushed at this time it might aggravate hostilities and hasten a war "when we are totally unprepared to meet it—no troops of any description" had as yet arrived to strengthen his thin line of militia defenders.[8]

When hostilities were declared by the United States, officially opening the War of 1812, the news reached Tecumseh while he was at Malden en route for Montreal. Two members of his Kickapoo bodyguard were detailed as couriers to carry messages to the Prophet. The message included instructions that the scattered partisans be collected for a major offensive against American posts in the Northwest. The Kickapoo messengers discharged their mission within three days, covering the first one hundred miles in twenty-four hours, appropriately enough, on stolen horses.[9]

In Tecumseh's master plot, the various tribes were assigned particular military posts; for example, the Potawatomis were sent against Fort Wayne, while the Kickapoos were directed to take Fort Harrison. Pakoisheecan, a village chief for the Wabash Kickapoos, and his warrior council drew up a plan of attack and moved toward Fort Harrison in late August. This post, erected in 1811 on the east bank of the Wabash near present Terre Haute, was commanded by Zachary Taylor.

Pakoisheecan's warriors, with their women and children, arrived at Fort Harrison on September 3, 1812. Hoping the women and children would allay Taylor's suspicions concerning their intentions, Pakoisheecan kept them in view of the fort while he ap-

8 Edwards to Secretary of War, Elvirade, Illinois Territory, May 16, 1812, Edwards, *History of Illinois*, 321.

9 Wells to Harrison, Fort Wayne, July 22, 1812, in Esarey (ed.), *op. cit.*, II, 77.

proached the pallisade. There he called up his request for a council and for food for the hungry children. Since two of his pickets had disappeared the day before, Taylor was wary, and he refused Pakoisheecan and his party entrance. Taylor did order up rations for the band, however.

Under cover of night Pakoisheecan sent the women and children a safe distance from the fort and moved his warriors up close. Then, tying a bag of tinder and flint to his side and shrouding a blanket over his shoulders, Pakoisheecan, with a long knife in each hand, slipped slowly through the grass toward the fort, alternating arms to drive the knives into the ground and drawing his body forward noiselessly. Upon reaching the lower blockhouse wall, and after waiting for the sentry to make his turn, Pakoisheecan heaped tinder against the log wall, struck the flint, and covered the rising flame with his blanket.

At Pakoisheecan's signal his warriors noisily rushed the far corner of the fort, drawing the attention of the garrison away as Pakoisheecan's fire climbed the walls of the blockhouse. Just as the heavy corner structure was about to collapse, Taylor discovered the ruse and drew a company from the rifle stand. The headquarters building was quickly dismantled, and its logs were thrown into a breastwork around the burned out blockhouse.

Thwarted at the last moment, Pakoisheecan and his angry warriors set up a siege of Fort Harrison. Since the charred blockhouse had served as a commissary, the food stores were destroyed. Taylor's hungry troops, to survive, were forced to feed on the corn stored in the post stable for livestock. After eight days of siege one of Taylor's couriers managed to slip through the Kickapoo lines and return with a relief force.[10]

Angered by their failure to take Fort Harrison, Pakoisheecan's Kickapoos turned to the settlements on White River. Cutting a course of plundered farms and scalped settlers, they achieved their most notable success in the Pigeon Roost Massacre. With "inventive brutality" the Kickapoos nearly wiped out this settlement.

[10] Beckwith, *The Illinois and Indiana Indians*, 133–35.

Twenty-one scalps were taken, and a relief column of militia found homes looted and burned, and the entire village presented "a mournful scene of desolation, carnage, and death." The Pigeon Roost affair, where children "had their brains knocked out against trees," exceeded the O'Neal Massacre in savagery, and for years to come observers averred that "no other part of the frontier during the war exhibited such a scene of slaughter."[11]

The Pigeon Roost Massacre galvanized frontier defenses in the Northwest. Governor Edwards promptly received an assignment of three companies of United States regulars to serve as a cadre for his militia army. In Kentucky, General Samuel Hopkins raised an army of two thousand mounted riflemen. Highly optimistic at the prospect of their combined forces exterminating this perennial scourge—the Kickapoos—Edwards and Hopkins planned a concerted movement on the principal towns of the Illinois Kickapoos situated at the head of Peoria Lake.

General Hopkins crossed the Ohio at the mouth of the Wabash during the first week in October, 1812, at the head of a troop of Kentuckians high in anticipation of the vengeance they would wreak on their ancient foe. Turning from the valley of the Wabash, Hopkins pushed his two-thousand-man army toward the Illinois for his rendezvous with Edwards' army.

Kickapoo scouts ranging from their villages on the middle Wabash discovered the invading host, and within 24 hours, 150 mounted warriors, dispersed in small bands on the periphery of Hopkins' army, began a campaign of harassment. Kickapoo sharpshooters took their toll daily among Hopkins' mounted columns. At night quick terror struck around the Kentuckians' campfires; their horseherds were spooked by daring nocturnal raiders; and two days beyond the Wabash several companies were afoot.

Hopkins' anxious troops began to complain; his guides were bewildered and lost; and his entire force was discouraged and disheartened. After five days of torment, the Kickapoo persecution

---

[11] Brice, *op. cit.,* 234; "Pigeon Roost Massacre," Indiana Historical Society *Publications,* II, 128–34; and David Thomas, "Travels Through the Western Country in the Summer of 1816," Indiana Historical Society *Collections,* III, 42–135.

reached a climax as Hopkins' army moved across a prairie flat padded with thick tinder-dry grass. Simultaneously, Kickapoo outriders fired the prairie at points calculated to enclose the army within a circle of smoke and flame. Panic hit the ranks, and the men and horses nearly perished. Their baggage destroyed and many of their arms lost, the Kentuckians refused to proceed, and Hopkins abandoned the Kickapoo country, turning south for the safety of Kentucky.[12]

Governor Edwards, unaware of General Hopkins' difficulties and despairing of the Kentuckians' reaching the rendezvous, moved his small army of 360 men toward the Illinois Kickapoo towns at the head of Peoria Lake. Colonel Russell, a troop commander with the Edwards force, related that Hopkins' failure to arrive as planned "prevented us from doing as much mischief to the enemy as we would otherwise have done; as our force was too weak to make any stay in that quarter, and this was farther than any army has as yet gone." Yet on October 18, 1812, the Illinois territorial militia having covered four hundred miles by forced marches, caught the village of Chief Pawatomo totally unprepared for the daring attack Edwards mounted. At the first warning of Edwards' approach, the Kickapoos fled into a "dismal swamp" situated back of the village. The militia's initial charge took a toll of twenty-four Indians, but as the troops pursued the Kickapoos through the swamp, "up to their waists in mud," the Indians separated into small bands and managed to elude the pursuers. Edwards ordered the troops back to the abandoned village where, in the substantial lodges, they found an immense quantity of plunder, large stores of winter provisions, blankets, arms, and powder. In one lodge alone six white scalps were discovered. After rounding up the village horseherd of eighty animals, Edwards' men put the village to the torch.[13]

The northwestern frontier was heartened by this victory, and

[12] Shelby to Harrison, Frankfort, November 1, 1812, in Esarey (ed.), *op. cit.*, II, 192.

[13] Russell to Gibson, Camp Russell, October 31, 1812, Harrison Miscellaneous Collections, Indiana Historical Society; and *Niles' Register*, February 27, 1813.

within a month Edwards' army had increased to fifteen hundred mounted riflemen. Sufficiently strong now to move openly, the Governor managed to frighten the remaining tribes of the territory into an uneasy truce. Mid-November brought his army to Fort Harrison for a strike at the Wabash Kickapoos. A village captured on November 11, 1812, yielded 120 lodges and large quantities of corn and winter provisions. Although Kickapoo warriors harassed his army into and out of their country, the tribe could not mount an offensive strong enough to face Edwards' increasingly formidable army.

For the remainder of the War of 1812, most of the Illinois and Wabash Kickapoos dispersed themselves in small bands across the upper rim of the Northwest. From time to time slipping through the defensive net of ranger patrols organized by Governor Edwards, Kickapoo marauders continued to harass settlements in Illinois Territory. Little Deer, a Kickapoo village chief of the Illinois band, made his way through the American defenses during the spring of 1813 as far south as the Kaskaskia River. While his warriors carried out an active looting and scalping campaign, Little Deer promised his British Father he would never bury his war club until he had expelled "those troubles of the earth, the Americans."[14]

While most of the tribe remained in the Northwest, well over 150 Kickapoos with their families joined Tecumseh and the Prophet in Canada at Amherstberg, where a great inter-tribal village with 2,000 warriors had been established.[15] During January, 1813, these Kickapoos were active in the defeat of General James Winchester's American army, and participated in the famous Raisin River Massacre where five hundred American prisoners-of-war were put to death with brutal and calculated precision. Also, Kickapoo warriors, serving as scouts, reconnoitered American defenses for the British commander, General Proctor.[16]

[14] Forsyth to Clark, St. Louis, July 20, 1813, Clark Papers, Kansas Historical Society.

[15] "War of 1812," Harrison Papers, Draper Manuscript Collection, Wisconsin Historical Society.

[16] DeWar to McDonnell, Amherstburg, October 19, 1812, *Michigan Pioneer Historical Collections*, XV, 170.

During the summer of 1813, the Kickapoo scouts furnished intelligence of an American build-up south of Detroit. General William Henry Harrison, aided by a surprising American navy which cleared Lake Erie of British gunboats, moved on the British at Malden and Detroit. Retreating to the Thames, General Proctor, buttressed by Tecumseh's Indian army, made a fateful stand on October 5, 1813. There Harrison's American forces administered a stunning defeat not only to British ambitions in the American Northwest, but to the cause of Indian nationalism as well, for the venerable Tecumseh was slain in this engagement. After Tecumseh's death bands of Wyandot, Chippewa, Delaware, and Miami warriors defected from the British and met with General Harrison near Detroit on October 10, 1813, to discuss peace terms. A "diehard band" of Kickapoos, however, remained in Canada.[17]

While military operations in the Detroit-Malden sector were brought to a close by Harrison's victory at the Thames, the Canadian Kickapoos, still strong in their attachment to the Prophet, who sojourned at Amherstberg, continued their private war on the United States. American military patrols south of Detroit were frequently cut off by these warriors, houses were looted and burned in the American settlements, and horses were stolen. Throughout 1815, General Harrison and Lewis Cass attempted to placate this Kickapoo band and other tribal remnants yet in Canada with presents and favorable treaty terms. During the Mill Springs' Council held by Cass during 1815, the Prophet and his Kickapoo cohorts left Amherstberg presumably to treat with the American commissioners. After a few days of negotiation, they "left quickly for the British side before anything was concluded, and in a hostile manner to the United States."[18] As late as August, 1816, a year and a half after the end of the War, over 150 Kickapoos were still living at Amherstberg. Of these, thirty-four were reported to be

[17] "Aftermath of the Thames," Tecumseh Papers, Draper Manuscript Collection, Wisconsin Historical Society.

[18] Cass to Crawford, Detroit, April 24, 1816, National Archives, Michigan Superintendency, Letters Received and Sent File; and Parke to Posey, Vincennes, February 19, 1816, in Esarey (ed.), *op. cit.*, II, 719.

"going home."[19] Not until 1819, however, did the entire Canadian band return to the United States.

Thwarted by Harrison's strength in the Lake Erie sector, the British sent the experienced and capable Robert Dickson to the west for the purpose of organizing the Indian tribes and striking a salient into the American settlements on the Mississippi. Dickson, informed that a concentration of anti-American Indians had gathered at the mouth of Rock River, established an arms depot at Prairie du Chien in early 1814. In company with Robert McKay, another British agent, Dickson visited the Rock River camps and found that the largest warrior force was in Chief Pawatomo's Kickapoo village.

Still smarting from Governor Edwards' surprise attack and the devastation of his great town at Peoria Lake, Pawatomo had led his four hundred warriors and their families north beyond the range of Illinois militia patrols. Sending only small bands of marauders on lightning raids into the northern Illinois settlements, Pawatomo and his warriors had languished in their Rock River village since the winter of 1812.

With the Kickapoos, Dickson and McKay found several hundred Sac and Fox warriors, who, like the Kickapoos, were eager for war on the Long Knives. American agents at St. Louis and Kaskaskia, learning of British activities in the Rock River villages, conspired to gain the neutrality of the Kickapoo, Sac, and Fox warriors. This plan was foiled by British councils at which large quantities of presents, shot, and powder were lavished upon the Indians. At one session alone Dickson and McKay dispensed one hundred kegs of gunpowder (fifty pounds each) and several bales of goods to the Kickapoos, Sacs, and Foxes. The buildup of a hostile Indian army of nearly one thousand warriors terrified the Mississippi and Illinois settlements and seemed to promise that soon the frontier would "again be drenched with the blood" of Americans.[20]

---

[19] "Return of Indians Dependent on Amherstburg, August, 1816," *Michigan Pioneer and Historical Collections,* XVI, 524.

[20] Forsyth to Clark, St. Louis, March 31, 1814, Forsyth Papers, Missouri Historical Society.

By late spring, 1814, Dickson and McKay had organized the Kickapoos and their allies into a well-armed striking force. Operating in small, mobile bands of twenty to thirty warriors, the tribesmen roamed south into Illinois and west up the Missouri. One raid at Boone's Lick, a pioneer Missouri community, yielded a load of plunder, three American scalps, and a horseherd.[21] Such raids into the Illinois and trans-Mississippi settlements were of minor consequence, however, compared to the river assault made on an American barge armada on July 21, 1814.

The slow-moving barges, bringing arms and supplies to the upper Mississippi posts, had anchored for the night near the mouth of Rock River. Dickson's Indians discovered the barges and attacked in force. The Kickapoos, Sacs, and Foxes were so "desperate" that even the women boarded the boats with hoes, "some breaking heads, others breaking casks, some trying to cut holes" in the barge bottoms to sink them, "others setting fire" to the decks. Losing only two warriors and one woman, the Indians captured five cannons, killed one hundred Americans, burned one barge, and forced the others downstream. Dickson and McKay were elated over the spirited performance of their followers and estimated that the barge assault was "one of the most brilliant actions fought by Indians . . . since the commencement of the war."[22]

At the council celebrating the barge victory, Dickson distributed a new round of gifts, the Kickapoos receiving as their share twenty kegs of powder and fourteen bales of goods. Climaxing the festivities, twelve Sac women who had been living with American traders were put to death as a symbol of the warriors' contempt for the Long Knives. Dickson's Indians resumed their activities soon after the barge victory, striking the settlements with renewed vigor. One party of ten Kickapoos raided the Whiteside community on the upper Illinois late in July, 1814, looting the dwellings

[21] Forsyth to Edwards, Fort Clark, July 6, 1814, Wisconsin Historical Society Collections, XI, 323–24.

[22] McKay to McDougall, Fort McKay, July 29, 1814. Wisconsin Historical Society Collections, XI, 269–70.

and returning to Rock River with seven American scalps.[23] In the early autumn Kickapoo and Sac bands moved up the Missouri again, raiding, burning, and looting. One Kickapoo force, returning to Rock River, attacked an American gunboat thirty leagues below Des Moines. Unable to capture it, the warriors had to be satisfied with two American scalps.[24]

While the attacks on the American settlements by British Indians from Rock River were potentially far reaching in effect, the fact that the British were unable to spare troops from the East to consolidate and occupy the salient carved out by the Kickapoos and their allies nullified the strategy planned by Dickson and McKay. Before the British could grasp the advantage in the west provided by the Rock River warriors, hostilities between the United States and Great Britain had ended.

The termination of the War of 1812 brought no respite for the American settlements in the west, for Dickson's Indians continued their forays.[25] Throughout the spring of 1815 the Kickapoos were active in Missouri, killing settlers and stealing their livestock. William Clark, United States Indian superintendent at St. Louis, repeatedly sent news of the British-American peace treaty to Rock River. His messengers of peace were regularly decoyed ashore and scalped by Pawatomo's Kickapoo braves. The chief, sullen and surly as ever, sent word to Clark that he intended "to continue the war."[26]

Just as British agents had organized the Kickapoo force in the west, so were they required to contain it. Clark, despairing of communicating directly with the Kickapoo, Sac, and Fox chiefs on Rock River, called upon the British to persuade these tribes to

[23] Forsyth to Edwards, Fort Clark, July 31, 1814, Wisconsin Historical Society *Collections,* XI, 324–27.

[24] Anderson Journal, Entry for October 11, 1814, Wisconsin Historical Society *Collections,* IX, 245.

[25] Forsyth to Clark, St. Louis, April 13, 1815, Forsyth Papers, Missouri Historical Society.

[26] Clark to Secretary of War, St. Louis, May 22, 1815, Indian Papers, Missouri Historical Society.

meet in council with the Americans and talk peace. At Clark's insistence, British agents convoked an Indian congress at Michilimackinac during June, 1815. There the Kickapoos and their allies were informed that their Great Father the King had made peace with the Big Knives and all his red brothers. It was the desire and command of their Great Father the King that his children bury the tomahawk, and it was his wish that they come once each year to their Father at Montreal to receive "that bounty which he is ever ready to bestow upon his good and obedient children."[27]

Subsequent British councils were held at Prairie du Chien during 1815 to encourage the Kickapoos to talk peace with the American commissioners. The Kickapoos continued to suspect American intentions and were especially worried that a treaty with the Big Knives would mean the surrender of more land. Pawatomo and his warriors had been ardent supporters of Tecumseh and had taken seriously his teachings concerning Indian land tenure, believing Tecumseh's dogma to be a supernatural ordinance. This feeling had been expressed by a Kickapoo spokesman as early as October, 1814. During a British council at Michilimackinac, the Indian declared that he wanted to "let those evil spirits the Big Knives know that we hold our lands sacred."[28]

Kickapoo reluctance to negotiate with the Americans and the tribal preference for a British Father were expressed in a speech by Barbouiller, a subchief of Pawatomo's band, during the Prairie du Chien council of August 3, 1814. Addressing Captain Anderson, the British officer presiding over the conference, Barbouiller affirmed: "My chief and warriors sent me to listen to your words, as the voice of our great Father at Michilimackinac. I hear the news from below [St. Louis] and from you. From below I hear, but do not retain it; from you I hear with satisfaction, and my ears and heart are open, and retain what they say. . . . The great Spirit hears us talk today under a clear sky, and we must tell the

[27] "The Michilimackinac Council, June 14, 1815," *Michigan Pioneer and Historical Collections*, XVI, 192–93.

[28] "Minutes of Indian Council, Michilimackinac, October 28, 1814," *Michigan Pioneer Historical Collections*, XXIII, 454.

truth. I squeeze my Father's hand—am obedient to his word, and will not forget the charity he now bestows upon us."[29]

Finally persuaded that the Americans wanted not land, but an affirmation of peace, the Kickapoos met with United States Commissioners William Clark, Ninian Edwards, and Auguste Chouteau at Portage des Sioux in early September, 1815. The treaty that resulted from this council returned matters to the same arrangement as before the outbreak of hostilities. Every injury or act of hostility by one or either party towards the other was "mutually forgiven and forgotten," and each party pledged "perpetual peace and friendship" and vowed to reciprocally deliver up all prisoners.[30] By November, 1815, Pawatomo's band had returned to the old Kickapoo range on the Illinois and its tributaries, and at last— nearly a year after the end of the War of 1812—there was peace in the western settlements.[31]

[29] "Speech of Barbouiller, Prairie du Chien, August 3, 1815," Wisconsin Historical Society *Collections,* IX, 279.

[30] "Portage Treaty of Portage des Sioux, September 1, 1815," *American State Papers, Indian Affairs,* II, 2.

[31] Parke to Posey, Vincennes, November 1, 1815, in Esarey (ed.), *op. cit.,* II, 696.

7

A Home in Missouri

AFTER SIGNING PEACE TREATIES with the United States late in 1815, the Kickapoos returned to their old villages on the Wabash and Illinois to find that American settlement in the Northwest, delayed for three years by the War of 1812, was moving forward rapidly. Well over two million acres in the area between the Illinois and Mississippi rivers had been reserved by Congress for war bounties, and surveys were begun in 1815.[1]

The hunting grounds of the Kickapoos, Potawatomis, and Miamis were quickly girdled by the expanding American settlements, and the more daring pioneers even began to move beyond the treaty lines, claiming rights on Indian lands. Pressured by economic and political interests in Indiana and Illinois, the United States began negotiations in 1816 to extinguish all Indian land title in the Northwest and to remove the tribes west of the Mississippi. Between 1816 and 1818, government commissioners gained cession treaties from the Peorias, Kaskaskias, and other small tribes, thereby acquiring most of central and southern Illinois.

The most important barrier to settlement, however, was the Kickapoos, for extinguishing this tribe's title was a difficult matter. Along with the small landed enclaves on the Wabash in Indiana, the Kickapoos held the rich Illinois and Sangamon river country in north central Illinois. Covetous squatters were cautiously moving into both areas, and territorial as well as federal offi-

[1] R. Carlyle Buley, *The Old Northwest*, I, 48–49.

78

cials feared that these intrusions would set off a new war of resistance.

These fears were not groundless, for the old warrior Chief Pawatomo, newly settled in his village near Peoria Lake and exasperated by the violation of his tribal domain by white intruders, summoned Kickapoo warriors scattered on the upper Sangamon and Wabash rivers to council. Little Otter, a prominent war chief, composed messages during this week-long council, and these were sent by courier, with a pipe and assorted war belts, to the Potawatomis and other tribes of the region.

Little Otter's messages called attention to the survey of military lands between the Illinois and Mississippi rivers, the threat to Indian hunting lands posed by this activity, and the growing insolence of the Long Knives. On behalf of the Kickapoos, he invited the Potawatomis, Miamis, and others to join the Kickapoos in making war on the Americans in the spring. He added that Pawatomo's council hoped that a few American scalps would be taken during the coming winter. Pawatomo was disappointed, for the Potawatomis and other tribes refused Little Otter's war belts.[2]

All through the winter and early spring of 1816, Kickapoo envoys sought to organize among the tribes of the Northwest a united front against the American advance. The Potawatomis, Miamis, and others, fearful of American reprisals, publicly refused the Kickapoo belts and boycotted the councils Little Otter attempted to arrange.[3]

Unable to win followers in their anti-American crusade, the Kickapoos began their own campaign against the Long Knife intruders. Cattle and horses were stolen, settlers' homes were looted, and haystacks and barns were burned by fast-riding Kickapoo raiders. Kickapoo bands lurked near the edges of surveyors' camps, stealing horses and plundering provisions. Surveyors at work in the field were interrupted, their equipment was damaged, and field notes were destroyed. Kickapoo warriors busily hacked at survey marks

2 Parke to Posey, Vincennes, February 6, 1816, in Esarey (ed.), *op. cit.*, II, 716.

3 Chumm to Parke, Fort Harrison, March 29, 1817, National Archives, Record Group 107, Secretary of War, Letters Received.

on trees and pulled up field stakes. As a last resort, the Indian marauders threatened the surveyors with death, forcing them to flee in terror to the protection of the American settlements.[4]

While these tactics temporarily halted the line of settlement, they were of little more than nuisance value. Companies of heavily armed rangers were soon patrolling the boundaries of settlements; United States troops guarded the survey camps; and it became more and more risky for the Kickapoos to attack. Unable to raise a warrior force strong enough to block American settlement, and noting that other tribes were signing away their lands and moving west of the Mississippi, Pawatomo, Little Otter, and other chiefs began to consider removal. During 1817 and 1818 tribal leaders spent much time west of the Mississippi with the Missouri Kickapoos discussing the subject of withdrawal to the West.

For over three years United States Commissioners Benjamin Parke, August Chouteau, and Benjamin Stephenson had been encouraging the Illinois and Wabash Kickapoos to meet in council and discuss the surrender of their lands in the Northwest. Finally, during the spring of 1819, word reached these officials that the Kickapoos were ready to consider the exchange of their Illinois and Wabash lands for a home in the West.

Benjamin Parke negotiated with the Wabash Kickapoos, while August Chouteau and Benjamin Stephenson dealt with the Kickapoos of the Illinois. After months of lengthy councils, during which tons of government provisions were used to feed the tribe and special gifts of horses and weapons were handed out to chiefs and headmen, the commissioners won their treaties. These agreements, the Treaty of Edwardsville, signed on July 30, 1819, with the Illinois Kickapoos, and the Treaty of Fort Harrison, completed August 30, 1819, with the Wabash Kickapoos, provided for the exchange of tribal lands in Indiana and Illinois for a new domain on the Osage River in Missouri. The Wabash Kickapoos received three thousand dollars worth of goods—blankets, weapons, hatchets, and trinkets—and were promised two thousand dollars in silver an-

---

[4] Harris to Tiffin, Vincennes, March 12, 1816, National Archives, Record Group 107, Secretary of War, Letters Received.

A Kickapoo family, about 1884. From a photograph by W. S. Prettyman.

BABESHIKIT, a Kickapoo warrior, 1894. From a photograph by Hillers(?).

nually for ten years; the Illinois Kickapoos received a similar issue of goods and a pledge of two thousand dollars a year in silver for fifteen years. In addition to supplying boats and conductors to carry out the removal, the United States was obligated to assure the Kickapoos peaceful occupation of their new home in Missouri and to restrain all whites from hunting or settling nearby.[5]

Throughout the removal arrangement, the neighboring Potawatomis and white traders, reluctant to see the powerful Kickapoos depart, used every ruse to upset the councils. Once the Kickapoos had agreed to move west, the traders and Potawatomis spread reports that the officials supervising the removal were really government spies assigned to lead the Kickapoos across the Mississippi and to deliver them up to the Americans at St. Louis for execution. In spite of these intrigues, however, most of the Kickapoos assented to Chief Pawatomo's policy of removal and began preparations for the westward journey soon after the treaties were signed.[6]

There was much relief and rejoicing in the settlements of the Northwest when, in the autumn of 1819, Paschal Cerré, officer-in-charge of the removal, began gathering the Kickapoos for the migration to the tribe's new home. Secretary of War John C. Calhoun, also relieved that the lengthy deliberations were finally and successfully ended, observed that at long last the Kickapoos were removing to the country west of the Mississippi, "where a more extended scope is afforded for the indulgence of their barbaric propensities and habits."[7]

Paschal Cerré, having collected nearly two thousand Kickapoos

[5] Prince to Secretary of War, Vincennes, April 15, 1819, *American State Papers, Indian Affairs,* II, 197; "Treaty of Fort Harrison, August 30, 1819," *American State Papers, Indian Affairs,* II, 196; Chouteau and Stephenson to Secretary of War, Edwardsville, June 7, 1819, *American State Papers, Indian Affairs,* II, 197; and "Treaty of Edwardsville, July 30, 1819," *American State Papers, Indian Affairs,* II, 196–97.

[6] Stephenson to Secretary of War, August, 1819, August Chouteau Papers, Missouri Historical Society.

[7] Calhoun to Parke, Washington, September 8, 1819, *American State Papers, Indian Affairs,* II, 200.

during September for the journey to the Osage River, was perplexed when the tribe suddenly divided into small parties and began an independent migration. The only band which remained with Cerré was that led by Blue Eyes, a village chief. The source of difficulty, Cerré soon found, was that Potawatomi warriors had been circulating the rumor through the camps that Cerré intended to deliver the Kickapoos to the Americans at St. Louis for slaughter. Overtaking several of the bands, Cerré sought unsuccessfully to persuade them to join the main party. Finally departing with sixty families composing Blue Eyes' band, Cerré found them "very shy and pretty hard to deal with." He later reported to August Chouteau that the Indians dreaded to pass through the American settlements, that they traveled very slowly and "with the greatest repugnance," and that they threatened at every navigable stream to stop for the winter. Nearing the Osage River, Cerré's charges absolutely refused to continue to their new home, and Blue Eyes announced that his people would wait for spring.[8]

Eventually the main body of the Kickapoos arrived in southwestern Missouri. Combining readily with Serena's western band, the Kickapoos, now with greater strength, brought new turbulence to the southwestern frontier of the United States. Besides waging an active war on the Osages, their historic enemy, the Kickapoos ranged far to the south, settling in small bands in the Indian Territory, Texas, and northern Mexico, and creating new trouble spots for the United States.

The removal of the Kickapoos from Illinois and Indiana to the Osage River was part of a broad national policy to evacuate a number of tribes to the area beyond the trans-Mississippi settlements. The plan included not only the Kickapoos, Miamis, Potawatomis, and other tribes of the Old Northwest, but the tribes of the Old Southwest as well, including the Cherokees, Creeks, Choctaws, Chickasaws, and Seminoles. While it was the idea of the government removal officials to transfer each tribe *in toto*, seldom was this accomplished, for small remnants both north and south of the

---

[8] Cerré to Chouteau, St. Louis, December 6, 1819, National Archives, Record Group 107, Secretary of War, Letters Received.

Ohio River defied removal attempts by force, by passive resistance, and by hiding from removal officials.

This was true also in the case of the Kickapoos, for while nearly 2,000 tribesmen migrated during 1819, there remained in Illinois two renegade bands, each numbering about 250 warriors, who repudiated the treaties of 1819 and refused to consider the subject of removal. It was not until around 1835 that the United States was able to induce the last of these recalcitrants to join the Kickapoos in the West.

One band, under Chief Mecina, was particularly irritated by the Treaty of Edwardsville, and would not accept the fact that the homeland of the Kickapoos had been surrendered to the United States. Mecina, when advised by William Clark and other Indian officials to join the western Kickapoos, regularly cited the old Indian doctrine of Tecumseh. With fanatic vigor he denied that his tribe or any other could unilaterally sign away tribal lands and the resting place of "the bones of their ancestors."[9]

Like their chief, the warriors who followed Mecina were diehard fanatics, choleric and troublesome, and for over a decade they defied the United States to evict them from their village near the head of Peoria Lake. Mecina's band subsisted on the corn and vegetables raised by the women and by local hunting. Each autumn the entire village moved to the Mississippi, moving west up the Missouri to hunt buffalo and to trade with neighboring tribes.[10]

The return of Mecina's band each spring was the signal for the women and children to prepare the fields for planting and for the braves to begin depredations. Wise enough to refrain from taking scalps, Mecina's warriors stayed near the edges of American settlements on the Sangamon and Illinois, sometimes ranging as far east as the upper Wabash, and terrorized settlers, looting isolated farmhouses, stealing horses, and shooting cattle and hogs.[11]

---

[9] Graham to Commissioner of Indian Affairs, St. Louis, January, 1825, National Archives, Office of Indian Affairs, Letters Received, Microcopy 234, Roll 747.

[10] Forsyth to Clark, Fort Armstrong, September 8, 1822, Indian Papers, Missouri Historical Society.

[11] Tipton to Cass, Fort Wayne, October 31, 1823, in Nellie A. Robertson and

The plunder gathered by these raiders, especially horses, was disposed of quickly, for the Kickapoos found an ever receptive market in the camps of the Potawatomis and renegade whites. These rapid transactions, while keeping Mecina's warriors well supplied with weapons, ammunition, and whisky, also had the advantage of clouding title of ownership, by implicating the receivers of the stolen property, thereby reducing Kickapoo blame.

The regularity of the brigandage by Mecina's band angered the citizens of Illinois, and soon settlers' associations began to petition the War Department and Indian Office to remove the cause of their trouble. Since William Clark, superintendent of Indian affairs at St. Louis, had regional jurisdiction over the Kickapoos, he received most of the complaints. One of these, prepared in 1824 by a settlers' association in Fulton County, Illinois, describes the threat to life and property posed by the Kickapoos:

> We the inhabitants of the county of Fulton in the military district for the state of Illinois respectfully petition that the inhabitants of this county have for a long time been so oppressed by the various tribes of Indians living on the military lands and its vicinity . . . that we think it incumbent upon us both for the safety of ourselves and families and protection and welfare of our property to petition the general government through you as a public agent for a removal of said Indians from our vicinity, particularly from the military lands. In many instances and various ways has our property been stolen and destroyed by said Indians consisting chiefly of the Potawatomie and Kickapoo. . . . We have no conception how the general government could grant to individuals lands by way of general warranted deeds, and yet leave these Individuals to the mercy of the savages if they presume to venture forth onto their lands at any distance from the settlement the Indians still being residing on those lands in many places which has been granted to individuals. We would respectfully suggest the propriety of having those Indians removed . . . upon their own lands. The depositions of several persons of respectability have been taken to prove the several depredations of said Indians. It has been a great hindrance to the settling of this part of the state. The Indians being so numerous

Dorothy Riker (eds.), *The John Tipton Papers,* I, 323–24; and "Incidents of Frontier Life," Illinois Historical Society *Journal,* XXXII (December, 1939), 529.

in our vicinity that people from a distance coming to view their lands give up all idea of bringing on their families so long as the Indians continue to reside in our neighborhood and amongst us.[12]

Clark also received complaints from state politicians. Acting Governor of Illinois A. F. Hubbard admonished Clark in 1825 that "during the last week a written communication has been received by me purporting to be signed by forty citizens of the North Fork of the Sangamon in this state. They prefer a complaint against a band of Kickapoo Indians who they say are infesting their neighborhood, killing their hogs before their eyes, and in defiance of the settlers, declaring the land is theirs and that the whites are intruders upon it; and that they will fight before they will leave it. That in two moons more the great man above will rain down Kickapoos enough to cover all that land. If I am not mistaken, the Kickapoos have stipulated to remove west of the Mississippi. They, I believe, are within your superintendency. It would be highly gratifying to our citizens that such steps should be taken" to quiet these disturbances.[13]

The removal of Mecina's Kickapoos and other bands from Illinois became an issue in state politics, and the Edwards and Hubbards, ever sensitive to those situations which threatened their control of Illinois, brought constant pressure on William Clark to carry out the terms of the Treaty of Edwardsville. Clark, popular with and trusted by the tribes of his jurisdiction, continued to follow the policy of peaceful suasion, regularly inviting Kickapoo delegations from Illinois to discuss removal. The years 1824 and 1825 were especially troublesome, as Mecina's Kickapoos increased their activities against the settlements. Clark sent an aide, Richard Graham, to visit the Kickapoos during January of 1825, in order to ascertain why this band persisted in its refusal to move to Missouri. Graham found them in their hunting camps on the Mississippi and, after talking with the headmen, was convinced that "not many of

---

[12] "Petition to General William Clark, Fulton County, Illinois, April 6, 1824," National Archives, Office of Indian Affairs, Letters Received, Microcopy 234, Roll 747.

[13] Hubbard to Clark, Vandalia, October 27, 1825, *Illinois Historical Society Collections,* IV, 91–92.

these Indians will remove without coercion . . . their attachment to the homes of their fathers is great . . . some of them say they had nothing to do in selling their lands."[14]

The patience of the citizens of Illinois grew thin as Mecina's Kickapoos continued to occupy the choice lands on the Sangamon. In 1828 pressure on the political leaders of the state led Ninian Edwards to virtually demand that William Clark take positive steps to remove this obstacle to the development of western Illinois: "You have done all that can be accomplished without actual coercion. Observing . . . repeated exertions have been made for the past several years to induce those Indians to remove from the seat of the lands of Illinois . . . I trust you must see the necessity of substituting force for persuasion."[15]

While Clark and other officials continued their efforts to move the Kickapoos from Illinois, a new threat to the American settlements in western Illinois and Wisconsin was emerging. By virtue of a series of treaties signed between 1804 and 1825, the Sac and Fox Indians had surrendered their lands in northwestern Illinois and Wisconsin. Under the leadership of Chief Keokuk, most of the members of these tribes had abandoned the old tribal center on Rock River and had moved to the West. A renegade band led by Black Hawk repudiated the cession treaties and refused to vacate. A series of councils held by Black Hawk on Rock River during 1829 attracted Mecina's Kickapoo warriors and, swayed by the eloquence of the Sac chieftain, most of them decided to move their families to Rock River and join Black Hawk's resistance movement.

Chief Mecina instructed his warriors to remain aloof from the Rock River intrigue, and in the dispute that followed, he joined the other Kickapoo band in Illinois—that led by Kennekuk. The leadership of Mecina's band fell to a younger war chief, Panoahah, who forthwith led nearly one hundred Kickapoo warriors along

---

[14] Graham to Commissioner of Indian Affairs, St. Louis, January, 1825, National Archives, Office of Indian Affairs, Letters Received, Microcopy 234, Roll 747.

[15] Edwards to Clark, Belleville, May 29, 1828, in Ninian W. Edwards, *The Edwards Papers*, 339–40.

with their wives and children from the Sangamon to the Rock River camps of Black Hawk.

The "nest of villainy" formed by Black Hawk on Rock River alarmed the frontier settlements, and in response to repeated appeals for military aid, Governor Reynolds of Illinois dispatched a sizable militia force to Black Hawk's village in the summer of 1831. After the Indian community was dispersed, white settlers rushed in to claim the lands vacated by Black Hawk's followers. Most of Black Hawk's Sac, Fox, Kickapoo, and Winnebago warriors crossed to the west bank of the Mississippi. About sixty Kickapoos remained in Illinois, moving to the headwaters of the Kaskaskia River where they rampaged through the settlements, killing stock and burning barns and homesteads.[16]

From his camp on the west bank of the Mississippi, Black Hawk plotted the reconquest of his homeland. After collecting large quantities of arms and ammunition, Black Hawk sent his son Whirling Thunder, with a party of Sac and Kickapoo warriors, south to circulate war belts among the Osages, Cherokees, and Southern Kickapoos. Visiting the Kickapoo camps on Red River and in Texas, Whirling Thunder's party recruited several warriors who hastened north to join Black Hawk's army on the Mississippi.[17]

During the early spring of 1832, word came to William Clark at St. Louis concerning the build-up of hostile forces near the mouth of the Iowa River. Clark alerted military and civilian officers in Illinois to this menace and warned that "those fellows must be punished severely, otherwise others will be encouraged to pursue the same course."[18]

On April 3, 1832, Black Hawk, with two thousand men, women, and children, crossed the Mississippi to Rock River with the stated purpose of recovering tribal lands appropriated by white settlers.

[16] Clark to Secretary of War, St. Louis, August 12, 1831, Clark Papers, Kansas Historical Society.

[17] Clark to Secretary of War, St. Louis, June 29, 1831, Clark Papers, Kansas Historical Society.

[18] Clark to Atkinson, St. Louis, April 16, 1832, Clark Papers, Missouri Historical Society.

Illinois militia units operating with a United States force from Jefferson Barracks forced Black Hawk's Indian army to turn north up Rock River into Wisconsin. Finally overtaken at Bad Axe on August 3, 1832, the Sac chieftain made a stand and was defeated by overwhelming odds. Black Hawk lost a total of 150 warriors and was himself taken prisoner by the United States. Most of the survivors fled west of the Mississippi. The Kickapoo supporters of the Sac chief, the remnants of Mecina's band now under the leadership of Panoahah, joined the Missouri Kickapoos, who were preparing to move from the Osage River to a new home near Fort Leavenworth. Thus Illinois was freed of a portion of the menace to its settlements, but there yet remained one band of Kickapoos in Illinois—a curious association led by Kennekuk, the Kickapoo Prophet.

Soon after the War of 1812, a pacifist faction had developed within the Kickapoo tribe. Opposed to the continuation of the historic Kickapoo tradition of status based on scalps and violence, this group sought to follow a policy of peace with the Long Knives, substituting the art of agriculture for the art of war and demonstrating a friendly willingness to learn the white man's ways. Leadership for this movement was provided by a Kickapoo brave named Kennekuk, a mystic who claimed supernatural powers, including a direct access to the Great Spirit. Ostracized by the tribe for his pacifist teachings and his congenial attitude toward the Americans, Kennekuk went into exile, establishing a religious center on the Vermillion where he collected about 250 followers from the Illinois and Wabash Kickapoos.

By 1819, Kennekuk had refined his teaching to a system of religion which he imparted to his followers through preaching, fasting, and meditation. Kennekuk's doctrines included a sacred chart which set forth the path through fire and water and which the "virtuous must pursue to reach the happy hunting grounds." His followers were "exhorted to remain where they were, and if they lived worthily, abandoning their native superstitions, avoiding quarrels among themselves and infractions of the white man's law, and resisting the seduction" of whisky, "they would at last inherit a land of plenty, clear of enemies." The badge of his followers was a wooden prayer stick engraved with mystic symbols and manipulated much like a rosary.[19]

The peaceful disposition of Kennekuk's followers won the interest of local settlers, and the fact that the Prophet defied the removal requirements of the treaties of 1819 by passive resistance enabled his band to enjoy the indulgence of William Clark and other government officials. Endowed with abundant native ability, Kennekuk was also exceedingly skilled in the art of delay. Several times each year Clark sent talks to the Prophet, reminding him of the obligations of the treaties of 1819 and encouraging him to move his people west of the Mississippi. Each time the Prophet supplied an obsequious reply, promising Clark that it was his wish to comply with the demand of the Great Father in Washington that they leave Illinois, but because the corn "was yet in the milk," or because of illness in his band, or, more often than not, because the Great Spirit had advised that this was not the time to move, the Prophet remained in Illinois.

At least once each year, Kennekuk paid an extended visit to Clark at his St. Louis headquarters. Clark kept a diary in which he recorded the important events connected with his office, describing each occurrence in cryptic language. Noting the arrival and departure of visiting Indian delegations, Clark also listed such events as the berthing of steamboats on the river and the weather reports. A laconic entry for February 10, 1827, reads, "Wind high. Kickapoo Prophet speaks."[20]

By 1832, Clark himself was able to use Kennekuk's methods, and in a letter to the Prophet on the subject of removal, Clark warned that "shortly you will be treated as enemies," and added, "I hope the Great Spirit will open your ears."[21] Finally, in 1833,

---

[19] Frederick W. Hodge (ed.), *Handbook of American Indians North of Mexico,* Bureau of American Ethnology *Bulletin No. 30,* I, 650.

[20] Clark Diary, Entry for February 10, 1827, Clark Papers, Kansas Historical Society.

[21] Clark to Kennekuk, St. Louis, August 31, 1832, Clark Papers, Kansas Historical Society.

the Prophet agreed to join the tribe in the West and began preparations for the move.[22]

Late that autumn Kennekuk led his followers to the West. It was not until the spring of 1834, however, that the entire band crossed the Mississippi, for one party of 116 members of the Prophet's followers, under the leadership of Wabanim, was stopped near Danville in December, 1833, by a disease called "milk sickness" which struck down their horses. Clark learned of their distress and sent provisions to last them through the winter, and in early March Wabanim's party resumed the westward journey.[23]

By spring of 1834, nearly fifteen years after the treaties of Edwardsville and Fort Harrison, the last of the Kickapoos had reluctantly departed from the old Algonquian range. Most of the tribes from the Old Northwest and the Old Southwest, once they settled in the West, were tamed by missionaries and government annuities. Their spirits were broken, and they were seldom—if ever—heard from.

This way of life was not for the Kickapoos. If they had been dangerous while in the East, their savagery expanded in the vastness of the trans-Mississippi region, and as they turned south to the Plains, the Kickapoos became a menace to the entire Southwest. They were dreaded by the settlements, feared and respected by the Plains' tribes, and their exploits were recorded from the Missouri River in the North to the very gates of Monterrey in the South.

[22] Clark to Kennekuk, St. Louis, January 16, 1833, Clark Papers, Kansas Historical Society.

[23] Hubbard to Clark, Danville, December 9, 1833, National Archives, Office of Indian Affairs, Letters Received, Microcopy 234, Roll 750.

8

Banditti on the Niangua

THE GOVERNMENT'S REMOVAL OF THE KICKAPOOS to the Osage River country, under the auspices of the treaties of Edwardsville and Fort Harrison, simply made official a movement which had been under way for nearly a century. From the times of the earliest French colonizers, the Kickapoos had ranged over the trans-Mississippi West, hunting and gathering furs for trade with the French and Spanish settlements. During the Spanish period, in 1763, a band of Kickapoos under Chief Serena settled permanently on the Missouri west of St. Louis.

Throughout the Spanish regime the Illinois and Wabash Kickapoos traveled west on the Missouri and south to the Arkansas and Red rivers each year on their winter hunts. The rhythm of these seasonal migrations was regular, and the tribe returned each spring to its eastern homeland for planting and for new mischief against the Anglo-American settlements. After 1770 several hundred Kickapoo warriors became more or less permanently attached to the Spanish as mercernaries. In return for Spanish arms, ammunition, rations, and scalp bounties, these warriors waged war on the Chickasaws, a Gulf tribe which had paralyzed communications between St. Louis and New Orleans by raiding Spanish commercial convoys on the Mississippi.

After driving the Chickasaws back to their towns in terror and forcing them to terms with the Spanish, the Kickapoos were turned on the Osages. This tribe had refused to accept the Spanish as their

Father, had closed all Spanish contact with the Southwest, and had even threatened the settlements on the Mississippi. Around 1790 the Spanish declared open season on the Osages. The Kickapoos, with Sac, Fox, Shawnee, and Delaware assistance, drove the Osages south into the Grand, Neosho, and Verdigris country.

Kickapoo bands settled on the lands taken from the Osages before the Spanish regime at St. Louis ended, forming a defensive buffer for the river settlements and protecting communications with the Southwest. By 1803, when the United States acquired the Missouri country through the Louisiana Purchase, a string of small, detached Kickapoo villages, running up the Missouri for well over a hundred miles and southward along the Osage and other tributary streams, had been established.

The year after the acquisition of Louisiana by the United States, the famous Lewis and Clark Expedition began preparations for the exploration of this vast new territory. As the expedition moved west across Missouri, its members came upon these Kickapoo villages and also met Kickapoo war and hunting parties. One Kickapoo hunting party accompanied the expedition for six days, supplying fresh meat for the explorers. On one hunt the warriors brought in four deer and received as a reward for their efforts two quarts of whiskey.[1]

On Chaurette Creek, nearly seventy miles above St. Louis, the expedition came upon a settlement of five French families. These Frenchmen lived by trading with a detached band of Kickapoos, and settlers living along the creeks and rivers west of St. Louis had built a series of forts to protect themselves from these Kickapoo warriors, "the most feared in this section."[2] Meriwether Lewis explained to William Clark that he had been detained at his camp in mid-February, 1804, by a visit from the principal chief of the Kickapoos, whom he had been "anxious to see for some time past for several reasons."[3]

[1] James K. Hosmer, *History of the Expedition of Captains Lewis and Clark,* I, 5.

[2] Francis A. Sampson, "Books of Early Travels in Missouri," *Missouri Historical Review,* IX (January, 1915), 97.

[3] Lewis to Clark, Camp at River DuBois, February 18, 1804, Voorhis Collection, Missouri Historical Society.

At about the time of the Louisiana Purchase, the Osages surged up Spring River, a tributary of the Grand, toward their old homeland in a new effort to drive out the Kickapoo intruders. With assistance from their allies, scattered bands of Sacs and Foxes, the Missouri Kickapoos welcomed this renewal of combat, and another war developed. The United States government, alarmed that this affair might involve additional tribes and paralyze the development of the newly acquired territory, instructed General James Wilkinson, governor of Louisiana Territory, to call an Indian peace congress and to attempt to resolve the differences between the Kickapoos and Osages. After many months of negotiations and promises of presents and provisions, a grand council convened at St. Louis in October, 1805. Delegations of Kickapoo, Osage, Sac, and Fox chiefs, headmen, and warriors were in attendance as well as representatives from the Pawnee, Missouri, Otoe, Delaware, Miami, Potawatomi, and Iowa tribes. Most of these were spectators, since the "talks" of Wilkinson were directed at the belligerents—the Osages on one side of the fire and the Kickapoos with their Sac and Fox allies on the other.

General Wilkinson's message was eloquent but irritating, as the Kickapoo rejoinder indicates. Admonishing the Kickapoos, Osages, Sacs, and Foxes to think only in terms of peace, Wilkinson charged the assemblage:

> Children, open your ears, listen to our words and let them sink deep into your heart. Your Father, the President of the United States loves his red children, he is desirous that you may hunt in safety, that you may live in tranquillity, that your trade may be increased and your happiness be advanced. This great and good Father, to whom you must look for everything, has heard bad talk from your nations, which fills his heart with grief. He has been told that some of his red children, who reside on the great rivers and their waters, do not live together like men and brothers, but like mad dogs they tear each other's flesh and spill the blood of the innocent and the helpless, not excepting your old men, your women and children. Children, your great Father, the head man of your white brethren who are more numerous than the hairs on your heads, has listened to these talks with sorrow. He la-

93

ments your madness and your folly and is determined to open your eyes to your own interests, and incline the ears of his red children to brotherly love.

Children of the Kickapoo, Sac, and Osage nations, we speak to you; hear what we say and remember what you hear. You call yourselves good and wise men, and you walk upright in the image of the Great Spirit, who found you; yet while the buffalo, the deer, and the bear who range your forests live together in peace, you are at war, killing each other. Did the Great Spirit place you on this earth to destroy each other, or that the strong should trample the weak under their feet? No. Men of the Kickapoo, Sac, and Osage nations, he placed you here and gave you the faculties and powers of human beings, to be employed for your glory and for your mutual comfort, peace, and happiness.

Why do you make war and spill each other's blood; why pursue each other, as the numerous wolf does the timid and defenseless deer? It is not for food or for land, because you have more of both than is sufficient for all your people, and by your wars, you will drive your traders away from you and this will make your clothing more scarce and more dear. . . . Look at your red brethren who live towards the rising sun. The Wyandots, Delawares, Shawnees, Miamis, Iowas, Chippewas, and others. You will find them living together like brothers pursuing their game without fear, planting their corn in peace and taking care of their wives, their children and their old men. . . . We have received you as brothers, and we hold you by the hands as friends. We entreat you to follow the example of your red brethren in the east, and to live in peace with each other. . . . If you will listen to the voice of your Father and will follow his advice, he will look on you as good children and will increase the number of his traders among you, to supply your wants and increase your comforts, but if you turn a deaf ear to his talks and go on quarrelling and acting like strange dogs in a camp, he will abandon you to your fate, he will turn his back upon you, he will prevent his traders from going among you, he will shut the doors of commerce and will leave you without clothing, powder, lead, or guns, if you continue your wars. . . .

Red men, Children listen to us for we are your friends. What do we ask of you—is it land? No. We have enough of it. Is it your skins and furs? No. We are able to buy them. Is it the assistance of your warriors? No. Our warriors are as numerous as the stars in the Heavens. What is it then? That red men may spare the lives of red men, that you may wipe away the tears of your wives and children. That you may live in peace with each other; cease to shed the blood of man and spill that of beast only. Then you may lay down to sleep without fear, you may hunt in safety and trade with security.[4]

Throughout Wilkinson's impassioned appeal for peace, his painted, plumed, and skin bedecked listeners sat at impassive attention. As the Governor closed his opening address, Pawatomo, a leading chief of the Kickapoos, rose to answer:

My Father, I pray you listen to me. . . . What you have told us . . . I received with pleasure. I see that you spoke from the heart. When you offered us the calumet . . . it was the manner in which our fathers conducted their councils. Why did we come among you? It was to listen to you. One thing, however, I did not like. You called us your little children, and at the same time, spoke to us with a degree of anger, instead of that mild way, always used by a father when speaking to his children. The Master of the World, when he placed us on this earth, took care to provide us with all the necessaries of life. He gave us stones to make our arms. The earth and clay to form our pots, wood for our bows and arrows to enable us to hunt our game. The French were our first Fathers. From them did we derive the supply to our wants. After them we had the British who supplied us in the same way. The Spaniards came after and aided with like manner. You came, my Father, you took us under your protection and recommended to us hunting, where at the same time you were depriving us of the means by taking our lands and suffering establishments to be made on the same, and on the very spot where we before were accustomed to hunt our game. Never did the French, Spaniards, or British suffer such an invasion of our rights. Never did they call on us to go to such distance to see our Fathers, as you, now do, to see our Grand Father, the President of the United States.

We did not come to this council fire to beg anything of you, we want nothing but our own. We came to see you and listen to your talks. . . . Excuse, my Father, the boldness of my talk, should it appear so to you, it is in our nature to speak as we feel. You threatened us to

[4] "Speeches of James Wilkinson and Others at Grand Council Fire, St. Louis, October 14, 1805," National Archives, Adjutant General's Office, Record Group 94.

withdraw your traders from among us; we do not want them; the Great Spirit has provided for us plentifully. He gave us the earth for a Mother, from whence we derive our subsistence; the wild animals for our game and the maintenance of our wives and children; we skin them and trade with them; hence do we derive our clothing and that of our wives and children. We do not then, look to you for those articles which we now procure by hunting; the only thing we ask is that we may not be deprived of it, by being dispossessed of our lands, and by that of our game.[5]

Before the council closed a truce was pledged by the belligerents, and all agreed to return to St. Louis before the next winter's hunt for more talk on the treaty of peace urged by Wilkinson. True to their pledge the Kickapoos and Osages arrived in St. Louis the first week in October, 1806, and signed an agreement providing that all hostilities should cease and that "friendly intercourse" should prevail "through all succeeding generations." A curious provision of this treaty, evidently aimed at substituting public administration of tribal law for the old *lex talionis* of the tribes, stated: "Lest the firm peace which is now so happily established should be disturbed by the misconduct of individuals, it is agreed by the contracting parties that for injuries done by individuals, no private revenge or retaliation shall take place, but instead thereof, complaint shall be made by the party injured, to the other and if no satisfactory remedy shall be obtained within a reasonable time, application shall be made to one of the superintendents of Indian Affairs, who shall interpose his influence and authority to effect a reconciliation."[6] Subsequent relations between the Kickapoos and Osages proved the historic law of vengeance to be too deeply ingrained in tribal mores, and this noble experiment was disregarded for the time being.

The United States government took the initiative in freeing the Kickapoos from the sanctions of the late treaty, for during 1807 the Osages went on a destructive rampage against the white settlements in Missouri, killing and maiming settlers, stealing horses and

[5] *Ibid.*

[6] "Kickapoo-Osage Treaty, St. Louis, October 8, 1806," National Archives, Record Group 107, Secretary of War, Letters Received.

cattle, and burning homes. The Kickapoos, the historic nemesis of the Osages, were called in. Meriwether Lewis made public in the spring of 1808 the steps he had taken to free the frontier of the Osage threat: "I have counciled with the Kickapoo, declared the Osage nation no longer under the protection of the United States, and have set the Kickapoo at liberty to adjust their several differences with the Osage and to drive them out of the country."[7]

The Kickapoo-Osage wars continued spasmodically until the outbreak of the War of 1812 when an increase in the Kickapoo warrior population of Missouri made continued hostilities too dangerous for the Osages. The division between the Illinois and Indiana Kickapoos over the question of joining Tecumseh and the Prophet caused a few Kickapoo bands to move to Missouri between 1808 and 1811. The defeat of the Prophet at Tippecanoe in 1811 set off another Kickapoo exodus to Missouri, as did the general conditions of the War of 1812. One band of sixty-three families came into Missouri as late as 1814. The general course of migration for these bands after crossing at Kaskaskia was to move southwest to the White River. Some settled on the Osage River, others on the Pomme de Terre.[8]

During the War of 1812, after the Kickapoo-Osage controversy had quieted, many of the Missouri Kickapoos were engaged in gathering skins for the American Fur Company. Agents for this firm lived in the field with the Kickapoos, establishing crude depots for trade goods in the Kickapoo villages and ofter accompanying hunting parties to the Arkansas and the Red.

More than fifty Kickapoo warriors, however, remained in Missouri and lived off the settlers. Led by a daring young war chief named Black Buffalo, and referred to as "banditti," these raiders ranged south from St. Charles, looting homes and stealing clothing, household goods, and horses.[9] Travelers in Missouri Territory were

[7] Meriwether Lewis to Harrison, St. Louis, May 26, 1808, published in Vincennes, Indiana, *Western Sun, June* 5, 1808.

[8] "Re Paschal Pensineau, Topeka, 1883," Fur Trade Papers, Missouri Historical Society.

[9] "Relief to Citizens . . . for Indian Depredations," *loc. cit.*

in constant danger of ambush by Black Buffalo's band, and their victims were shot down at the slightest provocation.[10]

The most valuable plunder for the Kickapoo raiders was horses. The first of the Woodland Algonquian tribes to be mounted, throughout their later tribal history the Kickapoos were known to be superb horsemen, top authorities on quality of horseflesh, and inveterate horse traders and thieves. A Kickapoo raid might spare human life, homes, and valuables, but Black Buffalo's warriors rarely passed up an opportunity to empty the settlers' corrals and pastures of livestock. Missouri pioneer citizens regularly filed complaints with the Indian Superintendency at St. Louis concerning Kickapoo depredations on their livestock. Once the Kickapoos were accused of taking a whitefaced, three-year-old sorrel mare from Adam Purcell of Upper Louisiana Territory. The reasoning of the officials in ascribing the theft to the Kickapoos was that "the Kickapoo know good horseflesh" and that the mare "is a remarkable runner."[11]

For the period 1811 through 1814, the Missouri Kickapoos plundered thirty-three thousand dollars worth of property, and the people of the territory, indignant at the insolence and audacity of these raiders, began asking Congress for relief from the devastation and desolation of their settlements. Petitions from the territory charged that Kickapoo raids were driving settlers from their homes and—worse still—were leaving the victims afoot to flee the country, for generally the Kickapoos swept the country clean of horses.[12]

The treaties of 1819, by sending the Indiana and Illinois Kickapoos to join the Missouri faction, strengthened the tribe considerably and added to the turbulence of the southwestern frontier. Their arrival in force caused the line of white settlement in Missouri to waver, for settlers understandably feared the warriors of this tribe, and the Kickapoos claimed that the encroaching white

[10] Sibley to Clark, St. Louis, March 17, 1814, Sibley Papers, Missouri Historical Society.

[11] Dearborn to Harrison, Washington, July 2, 1804, National Archives, Secretary of War, Letters Sent Relating to Indian Affairs, Microcopy 12, Roll 2.

[12] *Memorial of the State of Missouri in Relation to Indian Depredations.*

settlements annoyed them. To discourage and intimidate the settlers, the Kickapoos increased their depredations after 1819.

Officials at St. Louis, in the face of mounting settlers' complaints,
found it difficult to know what tribe to blame, for when the Kickapoos committed depredations, they often left Osage signs, cleverly
shifting the blame for many acts of violence. Soon after Missouri at-
tained statehood, leading citizens began demanding that the Kickapoos be removed beyond the limits of the state, and one citizen
warned the Secretary of War that "Missouri's sons are bold," and
that if the government would not "remove the intruders, the arms
of our frontier inhabitants will."[13]

Confronted with numerous complaints and claims for depredations committed by the Kickapoos and unable to hold the warriors
accountable for their acts through the tribal chiefs, William Clark
developed the policy of drawing on the Kickapoo annuity to pay
the claims. By the treaties of 1819, the Wabash and Illinois Kickapoo bands each had been granted annuities amounting to two
thousand dollars a year. Clark used this as a peace bond to bribe
their good behavior, but for many years, so active were the warriors
and so voluminous the complaints and claims against them, the
Kickapoos could expect no annuity at all at payment time, it having
been committed to pay depredations claims.[14] One raid carried out
in 1825 near Farmington, Missouri, netted considerable plunder
and a number of horses. Two horses taken on this *coup* cut heavily
into the Kickapoo annuity fund, for Clark allowed the owner $310,
an exorbitant value for two horses at the time.[15] By 1830 Kickapoo activity had been diverted to the West and South, so that their
arresting influence on the development of Missouri was gradually
reduced, although isolated bands of Kickapoos were stealing horses
and looting farmsteads in Missouri as late as 1832.[16]

[13] Green to Calhoun, St. Charles, December 9, 1821, Indian Papers, Missouri Historical Society.

[14] Graham to Secretary of War, St. Louis, June 1, 1821, National Archives, Record Group 107, Secretary of War, Letters Received.

[15] Clark to Vance, St. Louis, March 26, 1825, Clark Papers, Missouri Historical
Society.

[16] "Relief to Citizens . . . for Indian Depredations," *loc. cit.*, 5–9.

The Missouri chapter of Kickapoo history was not only one of continued brigandage on the settlements, but was also a period of intermittent warfare with the Osages. To the Osages, historic occupants of the Middle Border country of the trans-Mississippi West, the Kickapoos were intruders. After the Indiana and Illinois bands removed to the Osage River country, an estimated two thousand Kickapoos were in southwest Missouri. This large population placed a heavy drain on the fur and game resources of the region.[17]

As early as 1820 the Osages were complaining to Clark that the Kickapoos, authorized to settle in southwest Missouri by the treaties of 1819, were deliberately constructing their villages beyond the treaty line and dangerously close to those of the Osages in order to provoke an excuse for waging war. The secretary of war, on learning of this Kickapoo insolence, directed Clark to attempt to induce the Kickapoos to fix their villages at a greater distance from the Osages, for it was understandably "impossible for such near neighbors to live in peace."[18]

The Kickapoos further incensed the Osages by poaching on their hunting grounds on the Arkansas and Red rivers. Frequent brushes occurred when Osage parties came upon Kickapoo hunting camps in acknowledged Osage range. These skirmishes on the Arkansas and the Red produced repercussions in the Osage communities on the Verdigris and the Grand and the Kickapoo villages on the Osage, and full-scale war broke out several times between 1821 and 1826.

Pressed by the Kickapoos from the northeast, the Osages were also pushed by the Cherokees and Creeks, who were receiving lands west of Arkansas on the Grand and Canadian rivers. The Cherokee and Creek settlements flanked the Osages on the south and left them with only a corridor up the Neosho to the Plains.[19]

The tormented Osages became more surly and vindictive than

[17] McKinney to Secretary of War, Washington, March 25, 1828, National Archives, Office of Indian Affairs, Letters Sent, Microcopy 21, Roll 4.

[18] Secretary of War to Clark, Washington, July 20, 1820, in Carter (ed.), *op. cit.*, XI, 628.

[19] Chouteau to Clark, Osage Agency, April 6, 1831, Clark Papers, Kansas Historical Society.

ever. In March of 1826 a Kickapoo hunting party slew five Osages on Red River, claiming this avenged a Delaware and eleven Cherokees killed by the Osages the preceding year.[20] In council the Osage war chiefs demanded one hundred Kickapoo scalps to avenge this massacre, and heavily armed war parties moved on the Kickapoo and Delaware towns in southwest Missouri.

One Osage party intruded as far north as the Robideau Fork on the Gasconade River, where they surprised a Delaware hunting camp of three men, three women, two girls, and a one-year-old child. Only four Delawares escaped the attack that followed; the others were "killing and horribly mangled and the child was thrown into the fire." A Kickapoo scout discovered "the trail of this party where it crossed the Osage River near the mouth of the Neanger."[21]

These Osage invasions drew the Kickapoos and Delawares into battle readiness, and war seemed inevitable. Settlers on the borders of these nations fled to St. Louis and Booneville for safety. Agent Richard Graham, charged with keeping the peace on the southwestern frontier, worked hard to reconcile the Kickapoos, Delawares, and Osages, but apparently had no success. In desperation he recommended to William Clark that the belligerents "should be left alone to settle their own differences, and it is my advice that this course should be adopted on the present occasion. You are well aware that all attempts of the Government to force a peace between hostile tribes, and where hatred to each other has been deep rooted and amongst whom revenge is ranked among the first virtues, resulted in merely smothering for a time these hostile feelings. By permitting them to wage war, a more speedy and lasting termination will be put to their hostilities and a more permanent peace and friendship effected by it, besides I am certain that in the end it will be more humane."

It would also better serve the interests of the United States, Graham pointed out in his recommendation, if the Osage-Kickapoo

[20] Campbell to Graham, Delaware Village, March 16, 1826, Graham Papers, Missouri Historical Society.

[21] Graham to Clark, Delaware Village, May 29, 1826, National Archives, Office of Indian Affairs, Letters Received, Microcopy 234, Roll 747.

war were permitted to continue. If the Kickapoos could drive out or exterminate the Osages, the frontier might be relatively quiet, for the Osages "not only commit depredations on the surrounding tribes, but scarcely a caravan passes between Santa Fe and Missouri that does not feel the effects of their thieving and hostile disposition, as is witnessed by the larger demands made upon the government by individuals for losses sustained by the Osages."[22]

Still believing in the efficacy of councils and negotiations, William Clark did not subscribe to this view. Disregarding Graham's plan, Clark wrote to the Office of Indian Affairs recommending that "the government order a meeting in council . . . of chiefs, considerate men, and warriors of the several tribes of Osages, Kickapoos . . . for the purpose of explaining and settling all differences amongst them; which when settled, articles of agreement in the form of a treaty be entered into between them, binding themselves to conform to the treaty; and to refer all their disputes to the Superintendent of Indian Affairs or agents, and obliging themselves to comply with the decision of the government in all matters of controversy. To effect this compromise and meeting, a movement of troops may be necessary. I am inclined to believe that we shall not succeed in preventing entirely, depredations and disagreements of a hostile nature between these tribes, while they are scattered at every direction through the country. At this time a considerable portion of . . . Kickapoos . . . are scattered from the Lakes to Texas. For the purpose of preventing this evil in a great measure, as well as to commence the work of civilization, I must beg leave to suggest that authority be given . . . to exchange the lands which have been assigned to the . . . Kickapoo . . . within this state, for lands to be apportioned and laid off to them, outside of the state boundary, on or near the Kansas River, with authority to employ subagents and other suitable persons to collect the scattering families and bands, and move them on those lands; and when collected on the lands assigned them, the necessary assistance to be afforded them by the Government, in the erection of comfortable log houses,

[22] Graham to Clark, Delaware Village, April 29, 1826, National Archives, Office of Indian Affairs, Letters Received, Microcopy 234, Roll 747.

good fences to enclose their fields, breaking up their grounds and preparing it for cultivation, some provisions, stock and useful articles for agricultural purposes."[23]

Secretary of War James Barbour replied to Clark on July 14, 1826, noting "that new and aggravated differences have arisen amongst the Kickapoo and Osage." Curiously, he added, that "the Department has no authority . . . to interfere in the settlement of these differences, while the effects of them are confined to the Indians, in any other way than by mediation." Barbour directed Clark to call the proposed council "for the settlement of the existing differences among these tribes, and establishing such regulations as may be necessary to guard against them in the future." The Secretary of War remarked that "these tribes, by their restless, and predatory conduct, have occasioned the Government, at different times, considerable trouble and expense." Because of this Clark was directed to deliver to the belligerents in council a "strong and spirited representation . . . of the ingratitude and infidelity which they have manifested towards the Government, by disregarding its kind and often repeated admonitions, and their own promises to it of forbearance towards each other." Concerning the removal of the Kickapoos from Missouri, the Secretary of War agreed that this was most desirable, and suggested that when the council gathered, the chiefs and headmen should be sounded on the prospect of surrendering their Missouri lands.

On September 25, 1826, Kickapoo, Osage, and Delaware chiefs and headmen arrived in St. Louis for Clark's peace council. Clark stayed away from the council for several days, urging the delegates to effect a permanent peace without the interference of the government. After six days of warm debate and recriminations, when the council seemed on the verge of resuming the late war, the persuasive Clark was forced to take his seat among them, quickly bringing a calm to the council. So eager was he for an end to the border strife that he made presents to the relatives of the dead from his own accounts, made "advances to settle and quiet the differences be-

[23] Clark to Commissioner of Indian Affairs, St. Louis, June 11, 1826, National Archives, Office of Indian Affairs, Letters Received, Microcopy 234, Roll 747.

tween them," and "with much difficulty obtained their entire appro-
bation to the treaty."[24]

The painfully composed Kickapoo-Osage treaty, signed by the
chiefs and headmen on October 7, 1826, provided for perpetual
peace and friendship between the Kickapoos and Osages. The
Kickapoos agreed to pay to the Osages one thousand dollars to
cover depredations and murders and promised to refrain from hunting on Osage lands, pledging to stay in their own territory. It was
agreed by both parties that "no private revenge shall be taken for
any property stolen or destroyed or murders thought to have been
committed by either of the contracting parties; but that complaint
shall be made, in future, by the aggrieved party, or by their agent,
to the offending party, or their agent, for redress; and the agent
of the offending party is hereby authorized to compel the offenders
to make full and fair compensation to the injured party."[25]

After the treaty council and before the Kickapoos departed for
their villages, Clark met with them to discuss the subject of exchanging their lands on the Osage River for a new domain west
on the Missouri River. Clark pointed out that such a move would
not only prevent future collisions with the Osages over hunting
grounds, but would protect the Kickapoos from the pressure of the
American settlements. Clark admonished the tribal leaders to abandon their savage life and turn to agriculture. He promised that
when the tribe agreed to move to the Missouri River, he would arrange for breaking the ground for them; help them build fences
to divide the land into parcels for each family; furnish the tribe
with seed, fruit trees, cattle, and chickens; and have permanent
houses erected for the families.[26]

Kishko, a leading Kickapoo chief and spokesman for the delegation, reluctantly promised William Clark that his people would
send an inspection party out the Missouri, look over the land, and

[24] Clark to Secretary of War, St. Louis, October 12, 1826, *American State Papers,
Indian Affairs*, II, 673.

[25] "Treaty of Peace . . . between the Osage . . . and the Kickapoo, October
7, 1826," *American State Papers, Indian Affairs*, II, 673.

[26] Clark to Secretary of War, St. Louis, October 12, 1826, *American State Papers,
Indian Affairs*, II, 673.

report to Clark the decision of the council. Clark was fairly certain he could persuade the Kickapoos to move, for the tribe regularly visited St. Louis to complain about the treaties of 1819 and about the lands assigned to the tribe in southwest Missouri.

As a matter of fact, none of the tribes under the St. Louis Superintendency caused William Clark as much trouble as the Kickapoos. Keeping the southwestern frontier in constant turmoil with their raids on the white settlements and their Osage wars, the Kickapoos were also most difficult to deal with officially. Their choleric attitude toward the United States evolved from a traditional esteem for their benevolent French, Spanish, and British Fathers and an implacable hatred for their American Father, whom they considered to be an intruder and whose people plundered the land.

This antipathy for the Long Knives manifested itself in various ways in the course of Kickapoo history—one was the tendency of Kickapoo bands to migrate beyond the jurisdiction of the United States into Spanish territory and Texas during the Republic Period. Many moved to Mexico as early as 1839, and a substantial portion of the tribe remains there to this day. The antagonism showed also in official relations with the United States. Clark and other government officials were perplexed by the fact that while other tribes gradually became more amenable to American purposes and policies, the Kickapoos persisted in their hostility, "were exceedingly arrogant, the most uncooperative of all the tribes," and were constantly complaining. A probable reason for Clark's determination to move the Kickapoos far to the west on the Missouri was that after a decade of Kickapoo complaints, his remarkable patience was growing thin. Once they were settled far away, he would be less accessible to them. On one occasion in 1832 he confided to his son that "sixty Kickapoos from the Osage River have just arrived to plague me."[27]

Soon after their arrival in Missouri, the Kickapoos showed signs of discontent with their new home, and various chiefs began calling on Clark to protest the quality of the land and various other mat-

[27] Clark to Clark, St. Louis, June 8, 1832, Clark Papers, Missouri Historical Society.

ters. They even complained about the annuities. Chief Kishko, on a visit to St. Louis, charged that Clark was making an unfair division of the annuities, giving to Pecan, a Kickapoo war chief, far more than he deserved. Kishko claimed that although Pecan "tells you that he is a friend of the government, and will not go to the Red River, he intends to go as soon as the grass is ankle high. His object is to get as much as he can before he goes."[28]

Various Kickapoo chiefs complained about the wording of the treaties of 1819 whereby the tribe had received title to lands on the Osage River. During 1820, Chief Pawatomo charged that the American commissioners had forged the treaties of 1819 and had substituted the word "sold" for "exchanged." Pawatomo argued that the Kickapoos had not sold their lands in Illinois but rather had exchanged them for the Osage River domain, and demanded that the text of the treaty be changed, "stating positively" that the Kickapoos had "exchanged and not sold their lands" in Illinois.[29]

During the same year Chief Wawpeehangaw, with 130 Kickapoo warriors, journeyed to St. Louis to make a similar protest. Officials in the St. Louis Indian office were distraught over this visit, for besides having to listen to torrents of abuse from the Kickapoo orators, they also had to feed this large delegation during the week-long council.

Apparently the American commissioners had promised the Kickapoos that they could select their lands in Missouri. When the tribe arrived on the Osage River during the winter of 1819, they found the government had already surveyed a site for their new range. Kickapoo reaction to this affront was bitter and prolonged. Chiefs and headmen refused to settle their people on the designated lands and build their villages on the Niangua, a tributary of the Osage, twenty-five miles east of the boundary of their assigned lands. In the presence of William Clark these tribal leaders charged that August Chouteau and Benjamin Stephenson, the American treaty commissioners, had cheated them of their lands in Illinois, for as

[28] Hogel to Campbell, St. Louis, n.d., Frost Collection, Missouri Historical Society.
[29] Chouteau to Secretary of War, St. Louis, July 30, 1820, Pierre Chouteau Collection, Missouri Historical Society.

Chief Kishko proclaimed, "Father, what you have said is not what Chouteau and Stephenson told us, he showed us a large mark for our lands. You have shown a small one. You have placed us in a small hole. Chouteau and Stephenson told us to come on this side of the Mississippi and wherever we make our fires, there we should have our lands. You tell us different. They did not tell us truth. . . . We understood from them we were to pick our lands."[30]

Kickapoo resentment over the land assignment of 1819 persisted through the years. And when the Kickapoo chiefs and headmen returned from an inspection of a proposed domain on the Missouri near Fort Leavenworth, Chief Kishko traveled to St. Louis and reported to William Clark that certain Kickapoo chiefs and headmen had "visited the lands on the Missouri and found them good," that the nation had met in council and "had a talk on this," and that they were ready to discuss "exchange of lands in Missouri. We want all the principal men of our nation present because when the chiefs made the bargain with . . . Mr. Chouteau, the nation was not pleased for the bargain was a bad one, for us. . . . Many troubles have been between the whites and us since that treaty, and none would have happened if that treaty had not taken place in the way it did."[31]

William Clark could not negotiate a removal treaty with the Kickapoos until Congress approved the general policy of extinguishing Indian title to land in Missouri. Approval came in 1831, and, as the pressure of settlement on the Kickapoo domain increased and a growing number of warriors turned to the cheap whisky sold by frontier whites, the Kickapoo chiefs and headmen began firm negotiations with Clark late in 1831.[32]

After extended and troubled councils, a final session was held at Castor Hill, Clark's home near St. Louis, on October 24, 1832.

[30] Graham to Clark, St. Louis, October 3, 1822, National Archives, Record Group 107, Secretary of War, Letters Received.

[31] Talk of Kishko to Clark, St. Louis, September 16, 1829, National Archives, Office of Indian Affairs, Letters Received, Microcopy 234, Roll 749.

[32] Clark to Cass, St. Louis, September 2, 1831, Office of Indian Affairs, Fort Leavenworth Agency, Letters Received, Microcopy 234, Roll 300; Cummins to Clark, Delaware Agency, May 12, 1831, Clark Papers, Kansas Historical Society.

By the Treaty of Castor Hill, the Kickapoos surrendered title to their Missouri domain in exchange for a home on the Missouri River near Fort Leavenworth.[33]

The Kickapoo tribe, whose peregrinations extended from the St. Lawrence River and the Great Lakes to Central Mexico within a century, already had moved west across half the continent like a savage stream, leaving a trail of death and despair in the American settlements. When the Kickapoos accepted a new home near Fort Leavenworth the direction of the current suddenly turned south toward the Rio Grande. Along the way bands of Kickapoos separated from the main tribal movement and became permanently fixed in given areas. One of these tribal homes was formed near Fort Leavenworth. While most of the Kickapoos soon abandoned this government-assigned domain and moved south, a portion of the tribe settled there permanently, abandoned their wild ways, substituted the plow for the rifle and the hoe for the scalping knife, and became tamed to the ways of the white man.

[33] Charles J. Kappler (ed.), *Indian Affairs: Laws and Treaties,* II, 365–67.

9

The Kickapoo Prophet

By 1832, the year in which the Treaty of Castor Hill was signed, the Kickapoo tribe, numbering about two thousand, had split into a number of bands scattered from Lake Michigan to the Rio Grande. One Kickapoo community of 350, followers of the Prophet Kennekuk, remained in eastern Illinois. A large Kickapoo village of four hundred, under Chief Kishko, was located on the Osage River in Missouri. To the south in the Indian Territory roamed several Kickapoo bands, with a total population of about nine hundred, under the leadership of various war chiefs, including Pecan and Black Buffalo. Finally, a band of three hundred, headed by Chief Mosqua, had settled in the Mexican province of Texas on the Sabine River.

The Treaty of Castor Hill, whereby the Kickapoos exchanged their Osage River range for a new domain beyond the white settlements located on the Missouri River near Fort Leavenworth, was signed by the representatives of only two bands—Kishko's Missouri Kickapoos and Kennekuk's Illinois Kickapoos. The treaty finally rid Illinois of the Kickapoos, for by this agreement Kennekuk brought his people to the Missouri River in 1833. The state of Missouri, too, was at last cleared of the Kickapoos, since Kishko led the Osage River Kickapoos west to the new tribal home.

This move had another important result in that for a portion of the tribe—the followers of Kennekuk—wandering ceased and a permanent home was established. The descendants of this band still live on the lands assigned by the Treaty of Castor Hill in present Brown County, Kansas. For Kishko's band, however, moving west at this time was simply an interlude between migrations, and soon small parties were departing for the south, so that by 1865 only Kennekuk's people remained. Thereafter, the so-called Northern Kickapoos, having been rather thoroughly civilized, were seldom heard from except in the administrative reports of the Indian agent who annually recited for the commissioner of Indian affairs the production of Kickapoo farms, the educational advancement of Kickapoo children, the high moral condition of this segment of the tribe, its remarkable temperance in contrast to other tribes in the area, and the general Kickapoo progress along "the white man's road."

For the Northern Kickapoos the period 1832–65 is sufficiently disordered to be exciting and interesting. This disorder was caused by the presence, until 1865, of a number of nonconformist Kickapoos who exerted a troublesome influence. Although reduced in number through the years by a constant shearing off of small bands who joined the Southern Kickapoos, a hard core of recalcitrants remained in the north until virtually the close of the Civil War. This period, 1832–65, saw the development of the tribal schism which had started years earlier—a conflict between the warmakers and the peace-makers. The latter group, led by Kennekuk, wished to settle down and make at least a moderate adjustment to the way of life directed by United States Indian policy.

A mile south of the location selected by Kennekuk as a village site for his followers, Kishko directed his four hundred partisans to build a separate community. These two Kickapoo villages remained autonomous, and the inhabitants of Kennekuk's town generally shunned Kishko's followers, who were considered evil influences. The latter lived by hunting and trading, held Kennekuk's people in contempt because of their settled agricultural existence, denounced their friendly attitude toward the United States, and called the warriors of Kennekuk's band "squaws," the epitome of Indian derision. Each time a disagreeable situation, real or imaginary, developed in tribal affairs, various members of the protesting band would form a migration party and join the Southern Kickapoos, in this way gradually reducing the number and strength of the dissident party and, it should be added, reducing the frustration of the Indian agent assigned to the Kickapoo tribe in Kansas.

The Kickapoos had hardly settled on their new Missouri River domain when Kishko's band began to show signs of discontent. The chief complaint was that the land was inferior in quality and extent, and, as Kishko said, "not equal to his expectations."[1] The claim that the new Kickapoo domain on the Missouri River was considerably smaller than the Osage River range in Missouri is substantiated by a survey made in 1835 which shows that the Kickapoos surrendered 2,048,000 acres in Missouri and received 768,-000 acres in Kansas.[2]

The United States Indian Office, proud of the progress made by Kennekuk's band and gratified by the Prophet's co-operation was equally distressed by the arrogance of Kishko's followers. Upon learning of the mounting dissatisfaction, Elbert Herring, commissioner of Indian affairs, directed William Clark to have local agents convene the Kickapoos in council to quiet these disturbances, adding fatuously: "The discontent which they manifest in consequece of the alleged inferiority or unsuitableness of the land allotted for their Western residence must be removed. They ought not to imagine that they are ill-used and injured by the removal and that they have been constrained to accept of an inferior exchange. It is essential to their comfort and happiness that they should believe the policy of the Government in removing them was benevolent and had in view the promotion of their welfare. Such a persuasion would tend to remove a state of feeling prejudicial to themselves and unjust to the Government. Under that assurance of protection, which has been given to them by the United States, they should be so dealt with, as to feel that they have a faithful guardian and

---

[1] Clark to Commissioner of Indian Affairs, St. Louis, July 7, 1833, Clark Papers, Kansas Historical Society.

[2] *Report of the Commissioner of Indian Affairs for 1836*, 424.

a kind of protector. Under such a belief our influence over them would be great and of the right character. They would remain at peace, cultivate the arts of social life and advance in civilization."[3]

While producing such an attitude as Herring envisaged among Kennekuk's followers was easily achieved, for Kishko's irreconcilables it was at best wishful thinking. Beginning in September, 1833, United States Commissioner E. A. Ellsworth conducted a series of councils with the Northern Kickapoos at Fort Leavenworth for the purpose of convincing the tribe that the United States government was "the friend, not a wrong doer," a "faithful guardian and kind protector" of the Kickapoos, and on persuading Kishko's band to accept gracefully the lands assigned by the Treaty of Castor Hill.

During the council of September 2, Muscahtewishah, a war chief of Kishko's band, explained in colorful and candid terms the turmoil within the tribe. "Our young men and chiefs do not agree as they did some time ago. Some wish one thing, some another. Some would go to the prairie, where there is game. Some would stay and raise cattle and corn. We are like fish in the water, we jump at whatever is thrown." After Muscahtewishah's explanation of the dilemma, Commissioner Ellsworth made an extended appeal to the followers of Kishko to join Kennekuk's band and become peaceful tillers of the soil, for, warned Ellsworth, "the President will not permit the tribe divided," and he expected Kishko's people to accept their lands willingly.[4]

Ellsworth's final council with the Northern Kickapoos was held on November 13, 1833. At this meeting the Commissioner was gratified when, after a stormy, invective-laden speech by Kishko, Kennekuk, the Prophet, rose to say to Ellsworth, "you have been on our land and seen it. We leave it to you to say." After Ellsworth

[3] Herring to Clark, Washington, June 3, 1833, National Archives, Office of Indian Affairs, Letters Sent, Microcopy 21, Roll 10.

[4] "Talk of Muscahtewishah at Ellsworth's Council, Fort Leavenworth, September 2, 1833," National Archives, Office of Indian Affairs, Western Superintendency, Letters Received, Microcopy 234, Roll 921.

affirmed that it was the best land available, the Prophet sweepingly proclaimed, "We are then willing to accept the land and say no more about it."[5]

Kishko waxed belligerent, then sulked, and a few weeks after the November council he led a dozen irritated warriors and their families south to join their fellow tribesmen in the Indian Territory. Kishko's place as leader of the nonconformists band was filled by Chief Pashishi, who continued the tradition of resistance to government policies.

Kennekuk's band, meanwhile, continued to advance. The Treaty of Castor Hill provided many benefits for the tribe on the condition that it settle down to agricultural life. Kennekuk's people were the only Kickapoos to take advantage of these opportunities, which included a blacksmith to repair tools and farm equipment used by the tribe, three thousand dollars worth of farming tools, four thousand dollars for livestock, thirty-seven hundred dollars for the erection of various buildings, including a granary and a sawmill. The treaty provided for a resident agent who, among other duties, was required to instruct the Kickapoos in planting and animal husbandry.[6] Kennekuk's followers readily took advantage of these treaty benefits and were soon busily engaged in developing farms. By 1835 the agent noted that a cultural revolution was taking place. Only a few years earlier the warriors had regarded the plow and the hoe as implements intended only for the squaws and children; now "the men as well as the women were laboring astonishingly."[7] So advanced were these Kickapoos by 1838 that their efforts even caught the notice of the hypercritical Baptist missionary, Isaac McCoy, who, although he denounced the Prophet as a charlatan and a religious fraud, admitted that Kennekuk had so influenced his band that they had "commenced

[5] "Talk of Ellsworth to Kickapoo Council, Fort Leavenworth, November 13, 1833," National Archives, Office of Indian Affairs, Western Superintendency, Letters Received, Microcopy 234, Roll 921.

[6] Herring to Clark, Washington, April 2, 1833, National Archives, Office of Indian Affairs, Letters Sent, Microcopy 21, Roll 10; Kappler (ed.), *op. cit.*, II, 365–67.

[7] *Report of the Commissioner of Indian Affairs for 1836*, 392.

a promising career of improvements" by abandoning the chase and becoming conscientious farmers.[8]

On their new farms Kennekuk's people produced corn, beans, peas, potatoes, cabbage, turnips, and melons in such abundance that they made annual sales of their surplus at Fort Leavenworth. Their hides and surplus livestock they sold to the local trader. The commissioner of Indian affairs, amazed at the progress of Kennekuk's people along the "white man's road," observed that the Prophet's band of Kickapoos "is making great improvements, and are approaching fast to a system of farming and government among themselves not far inferior to white citizens."[9] These Indian farmers made good use of their mill too, for, besides supplying the band's total needs in meal, they felled trees from the tribal reserve and produced lumber for flooring, doors, and furniture in the log cabins which were fast replacing the traditional wickiup.[10]

By 1845, Agent Richard Cummins could report that the Kickapoos of Kennekuk's band had "progressed faster in civilization than any tribe I have knowledge of, particularly in agriculture."[11] It was well that these "thriving and prosperous people," who were "more advanced than any other tribe" of the Fort Leavenworth area and who presented such a "pleasing contrast to the other tribes" of the region, had moved so far toward self-sufficiency, observed the commissioner of Indian affairs in 1853, since "their annuity ceases this year,"[12]

The Kickapoo annuity, guaranteed by the Treaty of Castor Hill, consisted of five thousand dollars in goods and cash to be paid annually to the tribe for nineteen years on a per capita basis.[13] The tribe invariably chose that the annuity be paid in cash. Each year the Southern Kickapoos migrated to the Missouri River at

[8] Isaac McCoy, *Annual Register of Indian Affairs within the Indian Territory,* 67.

[9] *Report of the Commissioner of Indian Affairs for 1838,* 506.

[10] Clifton Wharton, "Expedition of Major Clifton Wharton in 1844," Kansas Historical Society *Collections,* XVI, 274.

[11] *Report of the Commissioner of Indian Affairs for 1845,* 540–41.

[12] *Report of the Commissioner of Indian Affairs for 1853,* 247.

[13] Kappler (ed.), *op. cit.,* II, 365–67.

payment time to receive their share of the annuity.[14] Their arrival was dreaded and their departure was always a relief. While the Southern Kickapoos lingered at the Leavenworth agency awaiting the annuity payment, they visited with relatives, swapped horses, and gambled, with blankets and guns for stakes.

Renegade traders, ready with casks of double-distilled whisky produced by Missouri border stills, lurked in the timber on the edge of the Kickapoo camps. Cutting their merchandise substantially with river water, they too awaited the annuity payment. A week of riotous drinking, brawling, and general disorder followed the payment, then the Southern Kickapoos departed for the Indian Territory, leaving behind them wrecked cabins and wickiups, and driving ahead of them horses stolen from the neighboring Peorias, Delawares, and Potawatomis.[15]

Generally the spree that followed the payment satisfied Pashishi's warriors for a time, but if any annuity money was left after departure of the Southern Kickapoos, the agency could expect a continuation of the drunken frolic. An example of this occurred following the payment of the 1836 annuity. After Pashishi's camp was little but shambles, his whisky-sated warriors rode wild through Kennekuk's village, wrecking homes, tearing down fences, and molesting women. Kennekuk, whose followers were abstainers, complained to the agent and to the military commandant at Fort Leavenworth, appealing for a restoration of peace. Captain Matthew Duncan rode with forty-five mounted troops to Pashishi's camp, "found the Indians in a deplorably drunk condition," and confiscated fifty gallons of whisky.[16]

This particular celebration grew out of a council held during the visit of the Southern Kickapoos. The festive occasion began when news reached the camps, just before payment time, that a

---

[14] *Report of the Commissioner of Indian Affairs for 1848*, 446.

[15] McCoy to Commissioner of Indian Affairs, Washington, May 14, 1838, Foreman Transcripts, Oklahoma Historical Society.

[16] Duncan to Dodge, Fort Leavenworth, May 25, 1835, National Archives, Office of Indian Affairs, Western Superintendency, Letters Received, Microcopy 234, Roll 300.

United States Army unit had been massacred by Seminole warriors in Florida. The United States government had been removing the various Southeastern tribes to the Indian Territory, but the Seminoles refused to honor the removal treaties, retreated to the Swamplands of Florida, and carried on a long and bloody war of resistance against the United States. Word of the massacre was happily received in Pashishi's village, and set off an extended celebration of dancing and general exultation.

When Kennekuk went to the post commandant and asked for armed assistance in quieting Pashishi's warriors, he also told of the recent celebration of the Florida massacre and warned the commandant to be careful, since the Southern Kickapoos and Pashishi's warriors had staged an extended war dance. Thus, when Pashishi and his head men were called to task after Captain Duncan's seizure of the whisky, they had to stand accountable not only for the damage done to Kennekuk's village, but, more seriously for the dances, which the officers at Fort Leavenworth regarded as treason.

At a council called by Agent Cummins and Captain Duncan during June, 1836, Pashishi was required to answer the charge read by Captain Duncan that the dances and celebration lately held were in approval of the Florida massacre and that the Kickapoo warriors had "exulted on account of the Seminole victory." He was asked to admit or deny that the celebrants had "declared that the time was near at hand when the white people would all be subdued, and red men restored again to their country." Duncan, speaking for the army, admonished that behavior of this sort, by "a nation of Indians against a Government which had done, and was still doing so much for its happiness was ungrateful and improper. . . . You have heard the charges against you. What have you got to say to them? Are these things true?"

Pashishi's answer was a tirade against his "red-headed Father at St. Louis," William Clark, who had induced him to leave the Osage River country and move up the Missouri River. The chief declared that since their arrival at Fort Leavenworth, his people had known nothing but trouble, and that Clark had deceived him. "If my red-headed Father had told me about the bad wind that is always blowing about the land at my village, he could not have persuaded me to move. . . . He said that my Father at the Garrison had very big eyes, and that he would watch my enemies and defend me against them. But instead of this, you my Father are watching me to see if I do anything wrong, for when the bad wind from my village blows to the ears of my father at the Garrison he writes it down and sends it off to his General. There has been a great deal of fuss about our dance. We do not deny that we have a dance. It is the right of our people to dance." Both Duncan and Cummins were dissatisfied with Pashishi's explanation, and pressed him for a direct answer to the charges. The chief continued to evade the question by presenting an extensive description of the intent of Kickapoo ceremonials, and when he finally offered a mild assurance that no insult to the United States was intended by the dances, the council closed.[17]

Pashishi's people, resenting the interference of the military in their domestic affairs, sulked for the remainder of the year, and early in 1837, over two hundred members of the band left for Red River, ostensibly to hunt, and did not return.[18] Thereafter, since only about one hundred nonconformist Kickapoos remained in the north, Kennekuk came to dominate affairs at the Leavenworth agency for this portion of the tribe, and he was recognized by the agent and the Bureau of Indian Affairs as the official spokesman for the tribe.

Now unchallenged as leader of the Northern Kickapoos, Kennekuk began missionary work among the neighboring tribes, preaching his unique doctrine of salvation for the Indian at meetings much like the frontier revivals conducted by the Methodists and Baptists. Kennekuk was most successful among the Potawatomis, winning over one hundred converts, who, at his invitation, moved

[17] "Proceedings of Kickapoo Council, Fort Leavenworth, June 13, 1836," National Archives, Office of Indian Affairs, Fort Leavenworth Agency, Letters Received, Microcopy 234, Roll 751.

[18] Pilcher to Cummins, Fort Leavenworth, October 5, 1839, National Archives, Office of Indian Affairs, Fort Leavenworth Agency, Letters Received, Microcopy 234, Roll 752.

onto the Kickapoo Reservation. By 1844 the Potawatomi followers of the Prophet had intermarried with the Kickapoos, and Kennekuk began a movement to permit them to unite officially with the Kickapoos to form one nation. Since annuity rights were involved, Kennekuk submitted an appeal to the commissioner of Indian affairs seeking authorization for the proposed union. On being advised that there were no government objections to the plan, Kennekuk held a series of tribal councils to confirm his unification program.[19]

Finally, in 1851, articles of agreement were signed providing that the Kickapoo and Potawatomi followers of Kennekuk "should constitute one nation, having equal rights" and sharing jointly in soil, resources, and money.[20] Thereafter, the annual tribal census for the Northern Kickapoos was complicated by the Potawatomis being counted as Kickapoos.[21] The adoption of the Potawatomi band by Kennekuk's faction widened the breach between the Northern and Southern Kickapoos, for the latter held the Potawatomis in low regard and resented the newcomers' usurping what they regarded as their share of Kickapoo annuities, land allotments, and benefits from the eventual sale of most of their Kansas reserve.

The land deals of the 1850's between the United States government and the Northern Kickapoos are important to tribal history in that they usher in a long and sordid chronicle of sharp deals and swindles, involving not only the Kickapoo property in Kansas but, eventually, the tribe's assigned lands in the Indian Territory, and implicating United States senators, Indian agents, railroad officials, and bankers. The creation of Kansas Territory in 1854 brought new trouble to the Fort Leavenworth agency. The tribes of this jurisdiction, especially the Kickapoos, occupied the choicest lands in the

19 Cummins to Clark, Fort Leavenworth, March 25, 1844, Clark Papers, Kansas Historical Society; Commissioner of Indian Affairs to Thomas, Washington, April 20, 1844, National Archives, Office of Indian Affairs, Letters Sent, Microcopy 21, Roll 35.

20 "Articles of Agreement, Kickapoo Agency, May 9, 1851," National Archives, Office of Indian Affairs, Fort Leavenworth Agency, Letters Received, Microcopy 234, Roll 271.

21 *Report of the Commissioner of Indian Affairs for 1859*, 144–45.

territory, and settlers' associations, coveting the sparsely settled Indian reserves, pressured the government to reduce tribal holdings and open the surplus land to white settlement.

Throughout the summer of 1853 white settlers, anticipating the opening, squatted on Kickapoo lands, fencing fields and pastures, erecting log cabins, and refusing the demands of the Kickapoo chiefs and headmen that they vacate the reservation. So numerous and troublesome had these trespassers become by September that the Kickapoos appealed to the commandant at Fort Leavenworth for aid in evicting the intruders.[22]

Through the work of United States commissioners sent to the West to negotiate with the tribes of the new territory, a truce between the squatters and the Kickapoos was signed, and councils were held to discuss liquidation of Indian title to the lands desired by the settlers. Late in 1853 the Northern Kickapoos authorized a delegation to travel to Washington for negotiations with the government on the diminution of the tribal reserve. Chief Kennekuk the Prophet had died in 1853. His son John Kennekuk, or Pakah-kah, who had succeeded to the leadership of the tribe, led the Kickapoo delegation, consisting of Kapioma, Nohawat, Peshagon, and Kewisahtuk, in the Washington councils with George W. Manypenny, United States commissioner.

As finally approved on May 18, 1854, the Kickapoo Treaty provided for the cession to the United States of 618,000 acres of the tribal land granted by the Treaty of Castor Hill. The tribe retained 150,000 acres on the Grasshopper River. In return the Kickapoos were to receive three hundred thousand dollars, one-third of which was to be invested in securities to produce income for the Kickapoo educational fund. The remainder, to be paid out in varying sums over a period of twenty years, was to be used for the erection of public buildings and houses, and for the purchase of livestock, tools, implements, seed, and other benefits for tribal members. The Northern Kickapoo Treaty of 1854 also authorized a railroad right-of-way across the Kickapoo reserve and permitted

---

[22] McClelland to Secretary of War, Washington, September 7, 1853, Indian Papers, Missouri Historical Society.

the President to order, at his discretion, the survey of Kickapoo lands and to assign each family an allotment in fee, the amount to be determined by the President.[23]

The last two provisions produced much evil for the Northern Kickapoos. A human wolf pack—speculators, bankers, railroad promoters, and United States senators—sensing easy prey, moved in for the kill. Even the United States Indian agents assigned to the Kickapoo tribe by the Bureau of Indian Affairs—although morally obligated by oath of office to protect the Indians and promote their welfare—were involved in personal ventures of questionable character. Using their influence over the tribal council to good advantage, they conspired with powerful outside interests to divest the Kickapoos of their lands and their treaty money. Partisan politics were apparent in Kickapoo affairs, too, for the Indian agents often acted as servants of party convenience rather than in the tribal and public interest. One letter, probably left inadvertently in the files of the Bureau of Indian Affairs, reveals the operation of the spoils system among the Indian nations. Abram Bennett, a Kickapoo agent in 1864, complained to W. P. Dole, commissioner of Indian affairs, that while "I am taxed $150 by the [Republican] party to bear the expenses of the last political campaign in my own state [Kansas]," yet "I give very freely as the result has saved much trouble and perhaps the Government itself."[24]

Unfortunately for the Kickapoos, the diminished reserve established by the Treaty of 1854 was strategically situated on the eastern terminus of the major highways of the West. Traffic from three overland trails—the northern branch of the Santa Fe, the California, and the Oregon trails—crossed the Kickapoo domain. In addition, a stagecoach and pony express trail from St. Joseph, an overland freighting and stagecoach road from Atchison, and a mili-

[23] Manypenny to Cummins, Washington, December 1, 1854, National Archives, Office of Indian Affairs, Letters Sent, Microcopy 21, Roll 50; Kappler (ed.), *op. cit.*, II, 634–36.

[24] Bennett to Dole, Kickapoo Agency, December 17, 1864, National Archives, Office of Indian Affairs, Kickapoo Agency, Letters Received, Microcopy 234, Roll 372.

tary road from Fort Leavenworth to Laramie crossed the lands of the Kickapoos.

California gold seekers, Mormons, and Pikes Peak adventurers all lingered on the Kickapoo reserve, fattening their livestock on the lush tribal pastures, cutting timber for firewood and wagon repairs, and often departing for the West with Kickapoo horses and cattle in their livestock herds. Worse yet, animals from the wagon trains frequently broke through the rail-fenced fields and destroyed Kickapoo corn and vegetable patches. The steady stream of migrants irritated the Kickapoos, who were attempting to make a fresh start on their new lands, and the livestock thefts, timber depredations, and desolated grain fields impoverished the tribe and increased its antagonism toward the whites. Thus there developed a new determination among the nonconformist Kickapoos to abandon Kansas Territory and join the Southern Kickapoos in the Indian Territoy. Even the pacifist followers of Kennekuk became aroused at the constant misuse of their lands and began to threaten the agent with plans to move south.

The steadily increasing volume of traffic across the Kickapoo reserve attracted local businessmen who enriched themselves by supplying weapons, tools, and staples to the wagon trains at speculative prices. One of the most active of these merchants was William P. Badger. While doing a substantial business each year with the overland trail travelers, Badger also reaped handsome profits as trader for the Kickapoos. At the same time he held a franchise for operating the Grasshopper River ferry on the Kickapoo reserve— a service all overland trail traffic was forced to use. Badger was also a perennial candidate for agent to the Kickapoos, and he redoubled his efforts after the treaty of 1854, which opened the way for allotments in severalty to tribal members. Badger's interest here was insuring that all lands not required to satisfy Indian homestead needs would be thrown open to white settlement. This became obvious in February, 1858, when the Kansas territorial legislature revealed that Badger was an active intermediary for a company seeking to purchase surplus Kickapoo lands for two hundred thousand dollars. In return for his influence, Badger reportedly was "to be remembered in the townsites he expected to locate therein."[25]

When the commissioner of Indian affairs learned of Badger's plan, he directed that, since the Northern Kickapoos seemed opposed to the sale of their lands to Badger or any other person, Badger and his associates were to be prohibited from entering the Kickapoo reserve or holding councils with the Kickapoos. The commissioner warned that unless Badger abandoned the Kickapoo land scheme, legal procedures would be instituted against him under provisions of the Indian Intercourse Act of 1834, which dealt heavy penalties to intruders on Indian lands.[26]

William P. Badger had friends in high places, however, and within five months after the legislative investigation—in spite of its damning revelations—he had been appointed agent for the Northern Kickapoos.[27] Badger wasted no time in exploiting the strategic advantage his new office afforded. While he turned over to relatives the mercantile monopoly he held among the Kickapoos, he openly retained the operation of his Grasshopper River ferry. For years travelers had complained that Badger's rates were too high, and in 1858, a Weston, Missouri, contractor, Oliver Diefendorf, sought a franchise to build a competing toll bridge across the Grasshopper. On learning of this project, Agent Badger objected, and in his protest asked that he be permitted to extend his holdings to include a toll road across the Indian reserve to be built from personal capital and Kickapoo tribal funds. That this would be a lucrative enterprise is shown by the volume of traffic on the main highway across the Kickapoo reserve, which was rated as the heaviest traveled road in Kansas Territory. Since the "gold excitement" there had been an average of fifty wagons a day, and "this

[25] Baldwin to Commissioner of Indian Affairs, St. Joseph, February 1, 1858, National Archives, Office of Indian Affairs, Kickapoo Agency, Letters Received, Microcopy 234, Roll 371.

[26] Commissioner of Indian Affairs to Secretary of the Interior, Washington, February 17, 1858, National Archives, Central Superintendency, Miscellaneous Coreespondence.

[27] Commissioner of Indian Affairs to Controller, Washington, August 89, 1858, National Archives, Office of Indian Affairs, Letters Sent, Microcopy 21, Roll 59.

did not include handcarts, wheelbarrows, horsemen," and pedestrians.[28]

While Badger's road scheme was too ambitious even for the callous Bureau of Indian Affairs, his ferry and trading franchises were maintained, and in spite of considerable pressure from competing interests, the Kickapoo agent continued his management of the agency store and the Grasshopper ferry. Most of his time as Kickapoo agent, however, was spent in conditioning the Northern Kickapoos to accept allotments in severalty.

Railroad expansion into the West was soon to reach its high point, and one of the most popular proposed routes traversed the new Kickapoo reserve. Farms, towns, and new businesses were expected to flourish when the railroad was completed. The railroad land deals initiated by Agent Badger in 1859 had a far-reaching impact on the Northern Kickapoos. Badger's allotment proposals split the tribe into two camps at a time when the old rifts were finally healing and irritated many of the Northern Kickapoos, causing more of them to join the Southern bands. The land problem involved the tribe in a dispute with the United States government which was not settled until 1865.

[28] Diefendorf to Commissioner of Indian Affairs, Western, Missouri, April 9, 1859, National Archives, Office of Indian Affairs, Kickapoo Agency, Letters Received, Microcopy 234, Roll 371.

10

The Kansas Land Sharks

THE ACTIVITIES of frontier railroad promoters, bankers, and businessmen in divesting the Kickapoos of their tribal lands in Kansas during the 1860's comprise a sordid chronicle of man's inhumanity to man. Their avarice was surpassed only by that of the "Shawnee Wolves," who plundered the Mexican Kickapoo domain in Oklahoma Territory around 1900. Ironically enough, officials of the Bureau of Indian Affairs legalized this frontier brigandage by instituting a program humanely calculated, so they claimed, to afford the Kickapoos a singular opportunity to advance in economic competence and the social graces of an Anglo-American civilization. This program was foisted upon the tribe by a "fixed" referendum, the substituting of government lackeys for unco-operative hereditary chiefs, and the active interference of at least one United States senator. Historical tribal land tenure concepts were replaced by a system of fee simple ownership through allotment in severalty assignment.

Using the Kickapoo Treaty of 1854, particularly the clause permitting the survey and allotment of tribal lands, as a guide, William P. Badger set out to acquire his new charges' consent to the dissolution of their reservation and the establishment of individual homesteads. Since the Northern Kickapoos numbered only 350, less than one-sixth of the 150,000 acres assigned to the tribe by the Treaty of 1854 would be required to satisfy allotment requirements, and a substantial residue would remain. This residue was the prize Badger and the interests he represented sought. With the eastern terminus of the projected trans-western railroad expected to cross the Kickapoo reservation, the tribe's surplus land promised, with a minimum risk, to undergo a phenomenal value increment through the townsites and farms expected to develop nearby, as well as through the revenue from commercial traffic on the new railroad.

Historically the Kickapoos had held their lands in common, with title vested in the tribe rather than in individuals. Fee simple ownership was a mysterious contrivance of the white men, and the proposal that each tribal member accept an individual allotment was heresy to orthodox Kickapoos, for tribal religion held that the Great Spirit had ordained their system of common ownership.

Pressed by railroad and townsite speculators, Badger prematurely reported to the commissioner of Indian affairs that the Kickapoos were ready to council on accepting allotments in severalty and surrendering their surplus lands to the government. Acting on Badger's assurances of Kickapoo readiness, Charles E. Mix, commissioner of Indian affairs, directed that inasmuch as the Kickapoos were "very desirous to have the allotment clause" carried out, and "as in the opinion of the Department a division of the lands in severalty will have a tendency to contribute to the advancement of the interests and general prosperity of the tribe," Agent Badger was to continue his councils with the Kickapoo chiefs on the subject of allotments. Commissioner Mix set three rules for Badger to follow: the tribe was to agree to bear the cost of surveying and allotting their lands; each family head was to receive eighty acres; and the remaining lands were to be reserved for the Southern Kickapoos, since it was the intention of the Bureau of Indian Affairs to "concentrate" these Kickapoos "within the reserve in Kansas."[1]

Commissioner Mix's plan for inducing the Southern Kickapoos to settle on the Kansas reserve was, at the least, unrealistic. It was highly unlikely that these marauders, who ranged from the Indian Territory into Northern Mexico, would be willing to abandon their

[1] Mix to Robinson, Washington, August 19, 1858, National Archives, Office of Indian Affairs, Letters Sent, Microcopy 21, Roll 59.

125

free, roving life for a sedentary existence on a postage-stamp allotment in Kansas. At any rate this proposal threatened to drastically
reduce the surplus lands anticipated by the railroad crowd. The
danger was easily turned aside, however, for as finally drafted, the
Kickapoo Allotment Treaty allowed each Southern Kickapoo only
forty acres on the Kansas reserve, and this paltry headright had
to be validated by continued residence within one year after ratification of the treaty.

While a few bands of Southern Kickapoos journeyed occasionally
to the Kansas reserve between 1861 and 1864, they did so not to
claim any land rights but to escape the confusion of the Civil War
on the border. After a brief stay these visitors from the south departed for the Indian Territory. One small party, leaving the Kansas reserve in 1864, served as guides for more than one hundred
Northern Kickapoos, under Nokowhat, a village chief, who were
incensed at the undue pressure and callous tactics the railroad
crowd used in order to induce the Northern Kickapoos to agree
to an allotment treaty.

Soon after Badger's appointment Nokowhat had been irritated
by the new agent's neglect of tribal interests and the undue attention he gave to the subject of allotments in the frequent councils
he called. Then, when Badger began visiting each Indian home, not
in order to look after the interests of his charges or to instruct
them in the arts of cleanliness, health, and husbandry—as one
would expect of an official of the Bureau of Indian Affairs—but
rather to sound the householders on accepting allotments and to
intimidate them into support of his proposal before the Kickapoo
Council, Nokowhat became openly hostile. Courageously speaking
out against Badger for neglecting his official duties and for squan-
dering his time on a matter the Kickapoos were clearly unprepared
and unwilling to accept, Nokowhat became the rallying point for
nearly a third of the Kickapoo population on the Kansas reserve.

Agent Badger, faced with growing opposition as the malcontents
flocked to Nokowhat's leadership, became increasingly impatient
and repeatedly recommended to the commissioner of Indian affairs

that allotments be made without further consultation with the tribe.[2] Before Badger's intrigue could be brought to a successful conclusion, however, he was removed from office, not for official misconduct, but because of party patronage.

The new Republican Party, having won its first national election in 1860, swept the Democratic appointees of retiring President Buchanan from the various government offices. By June, 1861, the Republican patronage managers reached the agencies of the Bureau of Indian Affairs, and assigned a new corps of agents to serve the Indian tribes. One of these Republican appointees was Charles B. Keith, who took his oath of office at the Northern Kickapoo Agency on June 1, 1861, as the replacement for Badger.

The Northern Kickapoos, expecting a respite from Badger's incessant scheming, were sorely disappointed by the choice of his successor. Agent Keith was well known to the tribe, for as Badger's brother-in-law, he had shared an interest in the mercantile monopoly Badger held on the Kickapoo reserve. And as subsequent events proved, Keith, also a minion of the railroad promoters, was as determined to thrust an allotment treaty upon the Kickapoos as his relative had been, the chief difference being that Keith was considerably more direct and effective than Badger had been.

Keith's efforts were aided greatly by national political developments and by influence from the United States Senate. The commissioner of Indian affairs was forced by political pressure to authorize the calling of a treaty council with the Kickapoos in 1862. In the year of Keith's appointment as Kickapoo agent, Kansas Territory was admitted to the Union. One of the United States senators selected to represent Kansas in the Congress was Samuel C. Pomeroy. Active in Kansas territorial politics, Pomeroy also had extensive business interests in the new country and was one of the leading figures in the organization of the Atchison and Pike's Peak Railroad. This corporation, formed in 1859 with Senator

[2] Badger to Commissioner of Indian Affairs, Washington, February 8, 1860, National Archives, Office of Indian Affairs, Kickapoo Agency, Letters Received, Microcopy 234, Roll 371; *Report of the Commissioner of Indian Affairs for 1859,* 146.

Pomeroy as its President, sought a right of way across the Kickapoo reserve and hoped to gain title to the surplus Kickapoo lands when the tribe accepted allotments.

Throughout the troubled period 1862–66, which saw treaty negotiations, Kickapoo renunciation of the treaty, and recriminations and investigations concerning the treaty, Senator Pomeroy was remarkably active in looking after and protecting the interests of the Atchison and Pike's Peak Railroad. His abundant correspondence on this subject is interesting for several reasons, not the least of which is the stationery he used. For routine matters concerning the corporation and its Kickapoo land interests, Senator Pomeroy used Atchison and Pike's Peak Railroad letterhead stationery and signed his letters as president of the enterprise. When, however, the force and influence of his official political office were required, Pomeroy used United States Senate stationery and signed these letters over the title "United States Senator."

The earliest evidence of Senator Pomeroy's interest in the Kickapoo Allotment Treaty appeared in a letter from the secretary of the interior to the commissioner of Indian affairs, dated February 20, 1862. Describing Pomeroy's visit to his office, the secretary of the interior reported that the Senator had stated that the Kickapoos were "anxious to make a treaty." By this same communication the commissioner of Indian affairs was directed to call the Kickapoos in council and submit "the treaty," if the commissioner judged it "expedient" to do so.[3]

Apparently an allotment agreement had already been drafted, and all that was required of the Kickapoos was ratification. Agent Keith made little mention of the Kickapoo treaty referendum in his annual report for 1862, noting only that the treaty was "generally satisfactory to the Indians."[4]

This agreement, submitted on June 28, 1862, by Charles B. Keith to the commissioner of Indian affairs with the agent's affir-

[3] Secretary of the Interior to Commissioner of Indian Affairs, Washington, February 20, 1862, National Archives, Office of Indian Affairs, Kickapoo Agency, Letters Received, Microcopy 234, Roll 371.

[4] *Report of the Commissioner of Indian Affairs for 1863*, 245–47.

mation that it had been properly approved, provided for the survey of the Northern Kickapoo reserve and subsequent assignment of an allotment in severalty to each person whose name appeared on the Northern Kickapoo roll. Chiefs were to receive 320 acres each; heads of families, 160 acres; and all others, 40 acres each. Those Northern Kickapoos who preferred to continue in community ownership could combine their allotments in a small reserve and live there until a new home could be found for them in the Indian Territory. Their combined allotments would then be sold, and the proceeds would pay for the new reservation established for them by the Bureau of Indian Affairs. The Southern Kickapoos were required to return to the reserve within one year in order to be eligible for their allotments, these to consist of forty acres each. Those Kickapoos accepting allotments were to receive patents of title, and under certain conditions the landowner could sell or otherwise dispose of his land. Upon certification of competency, each allottee ceased to be a member of the Kickapoo tribe and became a citizen of the United States. All land remaining after allotment—slightly over 125,000 acres—was to be sold to the Atchison and Pike's Peak Railroad for $1.25 an acre.[5]

Agent Keith had been so secretive in handling the allotment negotiations that it was not until the Kickapoo Allotment Treaty had been ratified by the United States Senate and signed by President Lincoln, in May of 1863, that the general public and most of the Northern Kickapoos were aware of what had been done. Most of the Kickapoos apparently thought the treaty was still in the discussion stage.

A volcano of protest erupted in northeastern Kansas upon publication of the Kickapoo Allotment Treaty. The naive Kickapoos, unschooled in the legal artifices of the white men, were championed by the attorney general of Kansas, W. W. Guthrie, in an extended campaign to negate the allotment treaty.

The indignation of the Kickapoos was based primarily on religious grounds; allotment in severalty was sacrilegious in that private ownership broke the law of the Great Spirit that the tribe

[5] Kappler (ed.), *op. cit.,* II, 835.

must hold its lands in common. Guthrie's indignation and energetic campaign to destroy the treaty was, so he claimed, based upon his duty to protect the Kickapoos from injustice and exploitation. Lurking in the background of the investigations that followed and producing evidence intended to discredit the Kickapoo Allotment Treaty, was a rival crowd of railroad promoters. This group, consisting mainly of businessmen from St. Joseph, Missouri, had formed the Hannibal and St. Joseph Railroad Corporation. Since this company planned to construct a competing line to the West, they resented the advantages given the Atchison and Pike's Peak Railroad Company by Keith's treaty.

Guthrie's investigation of the Kickapoo Allotment Treaty opened with a grand jury hearing, held in Topeka, during the spring of 1863, at which various Kickapoo leaders voiced their objections to the treaty and lodged charges of fraud against Agent Keith. Convinced there was sufficient evidence to challenge the treaty officials, Guthrie began an active campaign to call the attention of the commissioner of Indian affairs, the secretary of the interior, the president of the Senate, and the speaker of the House to the alleged fraud perpetrated upon the Northern Kickapoos by Agent Keith and the Atchison and Pike's Peak Railroad.

Even President Lincoln received a letter from Guthrie in which the Kansan charged that the treaty was "a fraud from its inception" and petitioned the President to dismiss Keith and to revoke the Treaty. Guthrie also gathered depositions from citizens who lived on the border of the Kickapoo reserve and who claimed to have intimate knowledge of Keith's machinations in gaining the treaty. These statements included descriptions of the nepotism of Keith and Badger; their operation of the reserve store and the exorbitant prices charged the Kickapoos; Keith's deposing of hereditary chiefs and elevation of "worthless" but co-operative Indians to tribal leadership; threats to withhold annuities and to call in troops if the treaty was not signed; and the use of outside influence to intimidate the tribe.

One affidavit produced by Guthrie involved M. W. Terrill, a trader who reportedly "had influence over the Kickapoo." This document charged that Terrill was persuaded by Keith and Badger to use his influence on tribal leaders to get them to sign the "railroad treaty." In return for his services, the Atchison and Pike's Peak Railroad Company pledged him "a 160 acre tract of land when the treaty was signed and the title was cleared."[6]

President Lincoln received a number of letters from local citizens claiming that "the treaty sickened even the settlers" living around the Kickapoo reserve. These letters charged that the treaty was a fraud; that among the people listed in the treaty draft as "chiefs and headmen" were a ten-year-old boy, a woman, and the tribal interpreter; that no council had been held to ratify the treaty as had been claimed; and that the whole matter was a "private family affair" involving Keith, Badger, their cousin, and a nephew.[7] Various Kansas citizens, interested, so they claimed, in gaining justice for the Kickapoos, raised three hundred dollars to pay the expenses of W. W. Guthrie for a proposed trip to Washington, D.C., where he planned to protest the allotment treaty in person before the President and Congress.[8]

In the face of this opposition the treaty was suspended, and an embarrassed Bureau of Indian Affairs began the task of determining the truth of the charges.[9] Immediately after the Senate approved the Kickapoo Allotment Treaty in May, 1863, Commissioner of Indian Affairs Charles A. Mix had hastily negotiated a contract for the survey of the Kickapoo reserve in preparation for allotment. Now, confronted by the threat of an investigation, he directed Edward Wolcott, a special agent from his office already in the field and ready to set the allotment program in motion, to

6 Deposition of W. W. Letson, Granada, Kansas, June 18, 1863, National Archives, Office of Indian Affairs, Kickapoo Agency, Letters Received, Microcopy 234, Roll 371.

7 "Citizens of Brown County, Kansas, to the President of the United States, June, 1863," National Archives, Office of Indian Affairs, Kickapoo Agency, Letters Received, Microcopy 234, Roll 371.

8 Horton to Pomeroy, Atchison, June 20, 1863, National Archives, Office of Indian Affairs, Kickapoo Agency, Letters Received, Microcopy 234, Roll 371.

9 Secretary of the Interior to President of the Senate, Washington, April 4, 1864, National Archives, Office of Indian Affairs, Kickapoo Agency, Letters Received, Microcopy 234, Roll 372.

discharge the survey crew, since the Commissioner deemed it "advisable to suspend survey ... operations ... until further notice."[10]

With the stigma of collusion attached to the administration of Commissioner Mix, a new commissioner of Indian affairs, William P. Dole, was appointed in late July, 1863. Dole considered the charges against the Kickapoo Allotment Treaty sufficiently grave to warrant a personal investigation. Traveling to Kansas in August, 1863, he conducted a series of hearings and collected a substantial file of evidence concerning the Kickapoo Allotment Treaty, with special emphasis upon the methods used by Agent Keith to gain approval of the agreement.[11]

Commissioner Dole established his headquarters at the Kickapoo Agency, and during the late summer and early autumn of 1863, he listened to the testimony of a number of witnesses concerning the embattled Kickapoo Allotment Treaty. W. W. Guthrie collected local businessmen, settlers, and Kickapoo tribal leaders —including Chiefs Nokowhat, Pashagon, Keoquark, and Miscopot—to offer testimony against Agent Keith and his treaty. Keith and former agents William P. Badger and Royal Baldwin appeared to defend the treaty.

Guthrie supplied the lengthiest testimony, repeating earlier charges and attempting, as he claimed, to expose "the villainous conspiracy" hatched by Keith and the Atchison and Pike's Peak Railroad. According to Guthrie, Keith had attempted to force the Kickapoos to sign the allotment agreement by threatening to bring in United States troops if the council failed to sign the proposed allotment treaty. Guthrie also stated that Agent Keith had threatened to withhold the tribe's annuity if the Kickapoos remained unco-operative; that he did hold up the annuity for three months in an attempt to bring the Kickapoos to terms; that failing in this coercion attempt, he had, "contrary to law and custom" of the Kickapoos, deposed Nokowhat, Pashagon, Keoquark, and Mis-

10 Commissioner of Indian Affairs to Wolcott, Washington, July 2, 1863, National Archives, Office of Indian Affairs, Letters Sent, Microcopy 21, Roll 71.

11 Commissioner of Indian Affairs to Wolcott, Washington, August 3, 1863, National Archives, Office of Indian Affairs, Letters Sent, Microcopy 21, Roll 71.

copot as chiefs of the Northern Kickapoos because of their sustained opposition to the treaty; and that the agreement as approved by the United States Senate had the signature of only one recognized Kickapoo chief, John Kennekuk, the son of the departed Kickapoo Prophet.

The other persons represented by Agent Keith as Kickapoo chiefs on the official treaty draft, asserted Guthrie, were Whirling Thunder, a "worthless, drunken Indian"; Parthee, who was not a chief; Stephen Pensineau, a boy of twelve and the son of the tribal interpreter, who had been adopted by John Kennekuk in 1862, receiving the name of Kennekuk and thus making his claim as chief-apparent somewhat legitimate; and the boy's mother, Mahmahsehecowah. Guthrie claimed to have discovered that since the legitimate chiefs, John Kennekuk excepted, had refused to call a treaty council or to sign the treaty, no council had ever been held, although Keith had certified otherwise. Rather, Guthrie said, the names on the treaty had been obtained one by one at Keith's home.

Commissioner Dole was again reminded that the Indians were not told the treaty had been sent to Washington until it was proclaimed. Guthrie closed his tirade with the statement that Keith had bribed M. W. Terrill and others to use their influence on the Kickapoos; and that Keith and Badger, who kept the only store permitted on the Kickapoo reserve, sold goods to the Kickapoos at exorbitant prices, retaining the tribal annuities to satisfy the credit extended the Indians. Chiefs Keoquark and Pashagon appeared next before Commissioner Dole and testified concerning the general neglect of their interests by Agent Keith. They offered as an example a request they had made to Keith during 1862 that he stop white men from stealing timber from the Kickapoo reserve. Keith had promised to act promptly but actually had done nothing, according to the chiefs, although there were twenty-five or thirty teams at a time on the Kickapoo reserve busily hauling away wagonloads of logs. On one occasion the chiefs discovered two acres of logs ready to be hauled away, but when they notified Keith, "he complained of a sore throat, and never came near," his illness reportedly lasting for four months. This infirmity, it was noted,

133

did not seem to interfere with his efforts to gain approval of the allotment treaty.

Agent Keith answered that he had diligently protected the interests of the Kickapoos, and that the treaty had been negotiated under the most honorable conditions. To discredit the testimony of Guthrie, Keith charged that instead of being the champion of Kickapoo justice, the Attorney General was in reality working with the rival Hannibal and St. Joseph Railroad Company. Keith charged Guthrie with hypocrisy in that he concealed his real motives under the claim of protecting the interests of a betrayed benighted people.

Keith was sustained by the testimony of William P. Badger, who, although he admitted that he had worked actively for the adoption of the treaty after his discharge as Kickapoo agent, swore that he knew "the signers of the treaty to be blooded chiefs, so recognized," and that "Guthrie was the agent of the Hannibal and St. Joseph Railroad Company, certain whiskey traders, and timber stealers." Royal C. Baldwin, also a former agent, admitted that he, too, had joined Badger and Keith in using his influence to win Kickapoo approval of the treaty. When, however, Commissioner Dole asked Baldwin under oath if he had been promised a 160-acre tract of Kickapoo land by the president of the Atchison and Pike's Peak Railroad in return for his work among the Kickapoos, Baldwin refused to answer.[12]

Returning to Washington during the winter of 1863, Commissioner Dole prepared a report of his findings for the secretary of the interior. Copies of Dole's report and a file of evidence concerning the Kickapoo Allotment Treaty were submitted to President Lincoln and the president of the Senate on April 4, 1864.[13]

[12] "Notes of Evidence Relative to the Kickapoo Treaty of 1863, November, 1863," National Archives, Office of Indian Affairs, Kickapoo Agency, Letters Received, Microcopy 234, Roll 372.

[13] Secretary of the Interior to the President of the Senate, Washington, April 4, 1864, National Archives, Office of Indian Affairs, Kickapoo Agency, Letters Received, Microcopy 234, Roll 372; Secretary of the Senate to the Secretary of the Interior, Washington, April 10, 1864, National Archives, Office of Indian Affairs, Kickapoo Agency, Letters Received, Microcopy 234, Roll 372.

Apparently through the active influence of Senator Pomeroy, and because of the allegation that W. W. Guthrie was a front for the Hannibal and St. Joseph Railroad Company, the suspension was lifted, and the Kickapoo Allotment Treaty was permitted to stand as negotiated by Keith. Preparations were then begun late in 1864 to divide the land among the Kickapoos and to transfer title of the surplus lands to the Atchison and Pike's Peak Railroad. Kickapoo allotments were approved by the Secretary of the Interior on February 21, 1865, and on the same date negotiations were completed with Senator Pomeroy, president of the Atchison and Pike's Peak Railroad, for purchase of the residue of nearly 125,000 acres at $1.25 an acre, as provided in the treaty of 1862.[14] By June of the same year, the Atchison and Pike's Peak Railroad had nearly completed its line across the old Kickapoo reserve, and before the summer was over, the railroad was selling the Kickapoo lands to settlers.[15]

Chief John Kennekuk, as ingratiating as his father the Prophet had been, presumably settled the treaty controversy in a letter to President Lincoln in which he reported the Kickapoos "have done as our Great Father wished us to do and fulfilled the words of our treaty. There is good feeling among us; we are all satisfied, and we are very glad."[16]

Kennekuk was more optimistic than the facts warranted. Because of religious compunctions—and probably also because of plain stubbornness—the allotment program met with passionate resistance. As late as 1869, only 93 Kickapoos had accepted allotments in severalty, while 172 continued to hold their lands in common.[17]

---

[14] Commissioner of Indian Affairs to Pomeroy, Washington, June 29, 1865, National Archives, Office of Indian Affairs, Letters Sent, Microcopy 21, Roll 77.

[15] Van Valkenberg to Pomeroy, Washington, August 19, 1865, National Archives, Office of Indian Affairs, Letters Sent, Microcopy 21, Roll 78.

[16] Kennekuk to President of the United States, Kickapoo Agency, January 11, 1865, National Archives, Office of Indian Affairs, Kickapoo Agency, Letters Received, Microcopy 234, Roll 372.

[17] *Report of the Commissioner of Indian Affairs for 1869,* 365.

The greed of the Kansas land sharks could not be satisfied. Since the allotment treaty provided for additional land to be available under certain conditions (i.e., those Indians eligible for allotments had to claim them within one year; those refusing allotments had to accept a new home in the Indian Territory, the lands reserved for them in Kansas to be sold to settlers), no effort was spared to bring these treaty terms into play. Edward Wolcott, a special agent assigned to supervise the Kickapoo allotments, had been in Kansas since the spring of 1863. He became well acquainted with Charles B. Keith and William P. Badger, and his correspondence with the commissioner of Indian affairs reveals an abiding interest in termination of land rights of absentee Kickapoos.

Over 150 Northern Kickapoos had departed from the Kansas reservation in protest of allotments and Wolcott asked the commissioner during December, 1864, about the availability for sale to whites of the lands not claimed. Commissioner Dole replied that although "absentees were to lose their rights . . . after one year had elapsed since the ratification of that treaty, thus making their rights terminate" on May 28, 1864, since the treaty had been delayed before the United States Senate because of the charges of fraud, "it was deemed just and equitable to consider the absentees to have preserved their rights to a period one year subsequent to the full operation of the treaty"—about July 1, 1865. Commissioner Dole added that lands should be set aside for the absentees, and if they did not return to occupy them within the specified limit, these lands could be sold to settlers "for the benefit of those who are upon the Reservation."[18]

The absentees Wolcott referred to consisted of two bands—one led by Nokowhat, the other by Keoquark. The determination of the government to enforce the allotment treaty and to sustain Charles B. Keith as Kickapoo Agent so infuriated Nokowhat that he gathered about one hundred followers and departed southward during August of 1864.[19]

[18] Commissioner of Indian Affairs to Wolcott, Washington, December 27, 1864, National Archives, Office of Indian Affairs, Letters Sent, Microcopy 21, Roll 76.
[19] *Report of the Commissioner of Indian Affairs for 1864,* 373.

At almost the same time, Keoquark led another band of fifty Kickapoos to western Kansas to protest the allotment program.

Confederate agents had been active among the Plains tribes for several years, provoking them to attack the settlements on the western edge of Kansas and to cut east-west communications. Actually, Keoquark's people had moved to southwest Kansas to hunt buffalo and to show their anger over the treaty. Several attempts were made to link Keoquark's absentee Kickapoos with frontier massacres actually committed by other Plains tribes. These Kickapoos were also charged with being in the pay of Confederate agents. The two charges were part of a calculated campaign to discredit the absentee Kickapoos and to inflame officials in Washington against the tribe, thus hastening the forfeiture of the Kansas lands held by absentees. Special Agent Wolcott was one of those writing letters to the commissioner of Indian affairs. He condemned the absentee Kickapoos as renegades and charged them with "carrying on murderous raids in western Kansas" and with being "paid by Confederate agents to do this."[20]

Probably more through design than coincidence, Charles B. Keith wrote a letter almost identical to Wolcott's which carried the same date. Keith claimed that the absentee Kickapoos were "carrying on murderous raids in western and southern Kansas" as a part of "an Indian conspiracy to drive through all of Kansas" and to terrorize the settlements of the new state. Depositions attesting to the truth of these charges were signed by William P. Badger, Stephen Pensineau, and Whirling Thunder.[21]

As it turned out, Nokowhat's band eventually settled temporarily in Mexico, and the old chief returned in 1867 with only a fragment of his followers to find that their rights, as provided by the Kickapoo Allotment Treaty, had been forfeited. Keoquark's band returned in 1865 before the termination date, settled briefly

[20] Wolcott to Commissioner of Indian Affairs, Muscotah, Kansas, August 20, 1864, National Archives, Office of Indian Affairs, Kickapoo Agency, Letters Received, Microcopy 234, Roll 372.

[21] Keith to Commissioner of Indian Affairs, Kickapoo Agency, August 20, 1864, National Archives, Office of Indian Affairs, Kickapoo Agency, Letters Received, Microcopy 234, Roll 372.

on the common reserve, and joined the Southern Kickapoos in the Indian Territory during 1874 after these border raiders had been persuaded to return from Mexico to the United States.

Along with forfeiture through non-residence and exchange of Kansas common reserve lands for new homes in the Indian Territory, there was yet another method by which the Northern Kickapoos could be separated from their land. The Kickapoo Allotment Treaty permitted those Indians who accepted allotments to sell their lands under certain conditions. Within a year after the allotment assignments had been made, several Kickapoos were giving in to white pressure and selling their lands. It is ironic that Whirling Thunder, one of the "paper chiefs" created by Charles B. Keith for Kickapoo Allotment Treaty of 1862, conveyed his allotment in fee to Senator Samuel C. Pomeroy in December, 1865.[22]

The Atchison and Pike's Peak Railroad, having acquired practically all of the Kickapoo lands assigned by the Kickapoo Treaty of 1854, continued to receive special favors from the United States government at the tribe's expense. An instance was the agreement worked out whereby the company could delay until 1871 payment on the surplus lands made available by the Kickapoo Allotment Treaty of 1862.[23]

The power and influence of United States Senator Samuel C. Pomeroy, president of the Atchison and Pike's Peak Railroad Company, continued to be felt in Kickapoo affairs. An interesting example of the manner in which officials of the Bureau of Indian Affairs jumped to serve the Senator is found in the Kickapoo timber depredations correspondence of 1865. The Kickapoo surplus lands consigned to the Atchison and Pike's Peak Railroad Company were set aside as a reserve pending completion of the purchase agreement. Because of financing difficulties the deal was not brought to a close until August 16, 1865. Heavy timber stands on the railroad reserve attracted lumber poachers. The Kickapoos had regularly

[22] Secretary of the Interior to the Commissioner of Indian Affairs, Washington, December 12, 1865, National Archives, Office of Indian Affairs, Kickapoo Agency, Letters Received, Microcopy 234, Roll 372.

[23] *Report of the Commissioner of Indian Affairs for 1869*, 365.

complained to their various agents about lumber depredations, but little if anything had ever been done to protect their interests in this regard.

The Atchison and Pike's Peak Railroad Company planned to use the timber for roadbed ties, bridge timbers, and trusses as the line extended across the Kickapoo country. Word reached Senator Pomeroy in late January, 1865, that renegade lumbermen were making a shambles of the reserve forests. The Senator, on January 30, reported the lumber thefts to the commissioner of Indian affairs and charged that Ab Bennett, the agent who had replaced Charles B. Keith at the Kickapoo Agency, "does not make the least objection." Pomeroy's note is interesting in that he *directed* the commissioner to send Agent Bennett a "pointed letter" concerning the depredations and to order him to "attend to it at once."[24]

Pomeroy apparently considered the matter quite grave, for instead of using Atchison and Pike's Peak Railroad Company stationery and signing himself as "President" of the company, he used official Senate stationery and signed his note over the title "United States Senator." An interesting sequel to Pomeroy's demand is the alacrity with which Commissioner Dole attended to the matter. On the same day of Pomeroy's letter, January 30, 1865, the Commissioner answered the Senator with assurances that the matter was being attended to. Also on the same day, Commissioner Dole sent a strong directive to Agent Bennett, reminding him that "it is the special duty of the Agent in charge to zealously guard and protect all the rights, and interests of the Indians under their care. . . . It is as much your duty to protect from trespassers the lands which under the late treaty are to be sold to the Railroad Company, until such time as such sale shall be fully consummated."[25]

The Kickapoo Allotment Treaty and the courageous stand taken

---

[24] Pomeroy to Commissioner of Indian Affairs, Washington, January 30, 1865, National Archives, Office of Indian Affairs, Kickapoo Agency, Letters Received, Microcopy 234, Roll 372.

[25] Commissioner of Indian Affairs to Bennett, Washington, January 30, 1865, National Archives, Office of Indian Affairs, Letters Sent, Microcopy 21, Roll 76.

by most of the tribe to thwart its consummation marked the end of an era for the Northern Kickapoos. Those Kickapoos who for cultural and personal reasons could not accept the fundamental changes produced by the treaty joined the Southern Kickapoos. Those who accepted allotments soon were shorn of their historic tribal pride, haughtiness, and sense of superiority. These allotted citizens—not of the Kickapoo tribe, but of the state of Kansas and the United States—became mere statistical quantities in routine agency reports after 1865. It remained for the Southern Kickapoos to preserve the tribal traditions, religion, lore, and reputation for invincibility among the Indian nations, as well as the historic hatred for the white man and his culture. This the Southern Kickapoos did with a passion and a vengeance, maintaining their resistance to the "taming process" into the middle of the twentieth century.

11

Lords of the Middle Border

ON THE GREAT PLAINS—from Canada south to the plateau and mountain country of west Texas and northern Mexico—ranged the wild Kiowas, Comanches, Cheyennes, and Arapahoes. These warlike tribesmen comprised a formidable barrier to free east-west movement for other Indian tribes as well as for expeditions from the Spanish, Mexican, and Anglo-American settlements. Between this savage region in the West and the settlements in Missouri, Arkansas, Louisiana, and east Texas, there existed for many years a corridor about one hundred miles wide and extending from the Missouri River southward into the upper reaches of Coahuila, Mexico—a middle border which came to be occupied by emigrant tribes from various locations in the United States.

For centuries the middle and northern portion of this corridor had been the hunting range of the Osages. The Kickapoo-Osage wars, lasting from 1790 to 1827, had driven the Osages from their home in Missouri, and new Osage settlements had been made on the lower Neosho River, a major stream of the corridor. As early as 1800, several Kickapoo bands had flanked the Osage settlements on the Neosho and then had moved southward to the Red River.

Through the years the Kickapoo population in this middle border region increased, and the tribe came to be the dominant power in the corridor. Regularly challenging the Osages and forcing this tribe to turn more and more to the West for a hunting range, the

141

Kickapoos also established an interesting *modus operandi* with the Kiowas and Comanches, serving as middlemen between these tribes and the American posts at Fort Gibson and Fort Smith for the return of white captives and the payment of ransom. The Kickapoos were also remarkably successful traders with these and other tribes on the southwestern frontier.

Various portions of the middle border range were reduced from time to time, and each reduction was resisted by the Kickapoos. Encroaching Texas settlements irritated the Kickapoos and involved the tribe in a long and bloody war with the Texans which did not end until 1880. A substantial area was carved out of this corridor by the United States government as a new home for the Five Civilized Tribes. Designated as the Indian Territory, the region from Arkansas west to the one-hundredth meridian and south from the thirty-seventh parallel north latitude to the Red River was assigned to the Cherokee, Choctaws, Chickasaws, Creeks, and Seminoles. The Kickapoos resented this intrusion and for several years intimidated the Chickasaws, threatening to exterminate them if they dared settle on the lands assigned by United States removal officers and causing the Chickasaws to cower in the safety of Choctaw settlements near Fort Towson. The Creeks wisely invited the Kickapoo bands to settle in the western part of their new domain to protect the nation from incursions by the Plains' tribes.

The inclination of about one-fourth of the Kickapoo tribe to accept a settled life on the Missouri River reservation assigned by the Treaty of Castor Hill stimulated the development of a schism in the nation which did not become absolute until around 1865. Each year various bands of Southern Kickapoos migrated to the Fort Leavenworth Agency to receive annuities guaranteed by the Castor Hill Treaty. Marriages and family ties between the Northern and Southern Kickapoos caused considerable visiting back and forth among relatives. Northern Kickapoo bands spent their annual hunt in the Indian Territory with their Southern brethren. Bands of Northern Kickapoos, irritated by United States Indian policy, abandoned the settled life of the Missouri River reservation and joined the Southern Kickapoos. One of the largest of these migrations occurred in 1864 when Chief Nokowhat led about one hundred followers south in protest over the Kickapoo Allotment Treaty. These contacts diminished through the years, however, and after Nokowhat's departure in 1864, virtually ceased.

The growing tribal split produced some interesting results. Official relations with the United States government were possible only for the Northern Kickapoos. An Indian agency with a full-time resident agent had been established near Fort Leavenworth in 1832 for this faction of the tribe. Regarded by the United States government as the official spokesmen for the entire nation, the Northern Kickapoos were regularly consulted by government commissioners on treaties and agreements concerning land cessions, annuities, and tribal schools. The Southern Kickapoos, ranging widely over the middle border region, were not encumbered with an Indian agent and had no relations with the United States except for occasional skirmishes with the military. Frequent references to the Southern Kickapoos appear in the agency reports of the Cherokee, Choctaw, Chickasaw, Creek, and Seminole agents, and these generally cast an unfavorable light on the tribe.

The Southern Kickapoos, numbering about fifteen hundred at peak strength and seldom comprising an integrated Indian community, were by 1860 scattered in bands of from fifty to three hundred on the Canadian and Washita rivers in the Indian Territory, on the Sabine and the Brazos in Texas, and on the Remolino in Northern Mexico. In 1804, soon after the retreat of the Spanish and French from Louisiana, Spanish officers on the Texas frontier began inviting Kickapoo bands and remnants of other tribes to migrate to their jurisdiction.

Since the southwestern boundary of the United States on the Red River was not affirmed until 1819 by the Adams-Onis Treaty, Spanish officials planned a frontier defense for Texas which included settling emigrant tribes from the United States in a line north of the Red River on the Washita and Blue, and south of the Red at various strategic points. Not only were these tribes intended to serve as a buffer against United States territorial expansion, but warriors from the Kickapoo, Shawnee, Delaware, and Cherokee tribes were also expected to protect the Spanish settlements in Texas from raids by the Kiowas and Comanches.

Colonel Don Antonio Cordero was governor of Texas at this time and was largely responsible for persuading the Kickapoos and other tribes to join in the defense of Spanish interests on the southwestern frontier. Cordero sent numerous talks to the Kickapoos and other tribes who ranged the middle border, "explaining the many advantages arising from" Spanish patronage. The Governor pointed out examples of the heartless actions of the Anglo-Americans in forcing the Indian nations to abandon their old homes and migrate. Cordero also established a policy of distributing presents and barrels of *aguardiente* (brandy) each year in an effort to woo Indians from north of Red River into the Spanish periphery.[1]

By 1805, Cordero's efforts were bearing fruit, for bands of Kickapoos and remnants of other tribes were moving into Spanish territory. One Kickapoo band, at the Governor's encouragement, settled on the lower Washita.[2] Spanish frontier defenses tightened under the active attention of Governor Cordero. His desire to thwart the Anglo-American advance in the Southwest strongly appealed to the Kickapoos and various other tribes of the middle border who held historic grudges against the United States. Cordero, in summarizing the condition of Spanish defenses in 1806, explained how he had exploited this antipathy. "In my various contacts with the Indian Tribes . . . of the North who are coming into this area, I have done my utmost to show the difference between our gentle government and that of those ambitious people the Americans who wish to appropriate all the land by forcibly driving out of it those persons who have peacefully been possessing it, as they have done with so many Indian tribes."[3]

Not long after Governor Cordero's elaborate Indian defense system had been established, there began a gradual decline of Spanish

[1] "Cordero to the Friendly Tribes of Louisiana, San Antonio de Bexar, June 20, 1804," San Antonio de Bexar Archives, University of Texas Library.

[2] Cordero to Commandant General, San Antonio de Bexar, September 25, 1805, San Antonio de Bexar Archives, University of Texas Library.

[3] Cordero to Commandant General, San Antonio de Bexar, May 4, 1806, San Antonio de Bexar Archives, University of Texas Library.

Courtesy Bureau of American Ethnology

GAGAN-I-CHIKA, a Kickapoo living with the Sauks.
Photographed at the Omaha Exposition, 1898.

A Kickapoo prayer stick, made of maplewood with characters on one side.

power in the northern provinces, and the Kickapoos and other Spanish mercenaries, accustomed to looking to San Antonio for direction and annual presents, were abandoned to shift for themselves. Even with the waning of Spanish rule, however, the Southern Kickapoos continued in their role as lords of the middle border, a position they held until the outbreak of the American Civil War, although they were forced by Anglo-American pressure and the challenge of other tribes to exert every faculty of the warrior craft to survive and to sustain their unique status.

A number of Kickapoo bands remained in Texas, having by 1815 established substantial villages on the Sabine and Angelina rivers, and were involved in the Cherokee settlements established by Chief Bowles two years later. Several thousand Cherokees had migrated to Arkansas between 1795 and 1817. Many of them, displeased with tribal politics and government Indian policies, began separating from the western faction of the Cherokee Nation between 1815 and 1817, and scattered much like the Kickapoos in widely dispersed bands over the middle border. Frequently these Kickapoo and Cherokee bands confederated, roaming and hunting together, and mutually sharing adventures.

One notorious Kickapoo-Cherokee combination, under Chief Tahchee, established a village on the Red River directly across from the mouth of the Kiamichi. From this base of operations, Tahchee's warriors preyed regularly on white traders and trappers stationed on the Mountain Fork, the Boggy, and the Blue. Horseherds as far north as Fort Gibson suffered from their depredations. One foray by Tahchee's raiders touched off a vendetta with the Osages. Near Chouteau's Post on the Verdigris they found an Osage camp. Taking a warrior's scalp, the Kickapoo-Cherokee band departed with a number of horses.

The Osages' patient wait for revenge was rewarded when they discovered an undefended Kickapoo camp on Red River in 1827. The Osage party took seven scalps and captured a woman and child. Tahchee's warriors bided their time, stalked the Osages, and during the next hunting season caught an Osage band on a fork of the Arkansas, killed one, fatally wounded another, and took the group's horses.[4] For several months thereafter Tahchee's Kickapoo and Cherokee warriors lurked on the edge of the Osage villages on the Verdigris and Neosho, bringing such terror that the missionaries were forced to close the schools and missions in the Osage country.[5]

Tahchee's warriors also terrorized the white settlements which were fingering up the Red from Arkansas and Louisiana. Herds of hogs belonging to the settlers roamed the timber on the riverbank feeding on mast. Claiming that animals roaming the forests belonged to all, Tahchee's foragers hunted the swine much as they would deer and buffalo. Settlers along the Red protested the destruction of their livestock, banded together for protection, and retaliated by ambushing isolated Indian families and running off Indian horseherds. Mutual insults and injuries provoked Tahchee's warriors to threaten a war of extermination on the encroaching whites, causing the settlers to retreat to safety in the frontier towns of Arkansas and Louisiana.[6]

The erection of Fort Towson on Gates Creek near Red River in 1824 brought some protection for the pioneer communities on the Red River, and most of the settlers returned to their abandoned farmsteads. Since the troops at Towson were a constant deterrent to violence, the Kickapoo and Cherokee renegades satisfied themselves with nuisance raids which left a train of burned haystacks, barns, and cabins, stampeded livestock, and stolen horses. Finally, in response to repeated appeals, during the spring of 1828 an army of Arkansas militia under the command of Major Theodore Pierson moved into the Kickapoo-Cherokee village, drove the Indians to cover, and completely desolated Tahchee's community.[7]

Most of the survivors of Pierson's raid fled southward and settled in the confederated Indian communities established by Chief

[4] Grant Foreman, *Indians and Pioneers*, 205–208.

[5] Morris L. Wardell, "Protestant Missions Among the Osages, 1820–1838," *Chronicles of Oklahoma*, Vol. II (September, 1924), 294–95.

[6] Jamison to Secretary of War, Red River Agency, Natchitoches, May 20, 1818, National Archives, Record Group 107, Secretary of War, Letters Received.

[7] Porter to Izard, n.p., June 11, 1828, National Archives, Office of Indian Affairs, Letters Sent, Microcopy 21, Roll 5.

Bowles. This Cherokee leader had left Arkansas in protest against the Cherokee Removal Treaty of 1817 and had immigrated to East Texas, where he established a chain of villages on the Trinity, Neches, Angelina, and upper Sabine rivers for his followers. Along with eight hundred Kickapoos, bands of Shawnees and Delawares were also permitted to settle in this Texas Indian community. A loose intertribal confederation was established, and Chief Bowles was regarded as the nominal leader of the immigrant Indian association.[8]

After the successful war for independence in 1821, Mexico succeeded to sovereignty over Texas. The new revolutionary government permitted the immigrant Indians to remain in the region selected by Chief Bowles, and in return for fealty to the Mexican government, the Indians were promised title to the lands they occupied.

Encouraged by the friendly attitude of the new rulers of Texas, the confederated Indians flourished. Substantial farms were developed with broad fields of corn, pumpkins, melons, beans, and squash. Large herds of horses and cattle prospered on the lush, open pastures. Abundant buffalo, deer, wild turkey, and fur-bearing animals made the home selected by Chief Bowles for his people as attractive for the huntsman as for the farmer. José Sánchez, a representative of the Mexican government, traveled through this Indian Eden in 1828, and was impressed by the opulence of the villages. One of Sánchez's most striking experiences during his journey was a chance meeting with two Kickapoo warriors, whom he described as mounted on excellent horses, each carrying a freshly killed deer, and of an appearance "more fierce than that of any other Indians, revealing in their manners a certain pride which is their characteristic."[9] For the first time in many years, the Kickapoos and other vagabonds of the middle border were satisfied to settle and live in peace.

[8] Juan N. Almonte, "Statistical Report on Texas—1835," *Southwestern Historical Quarterly,* Vol. XXVIII (January, 1925), 222.

[9] José M. Sanchez, "A Trip to Texas in 1828," *Southwestern Historical Quarterly,* Vol. XXIX (April, 1926), 280.

The tranquil bliss of this Indian utopia was shattered by the nemesis of the Kickapoos and every other Indian tribe—that "great land animal, the American people." The same generous Mexican government that had sponsored Chief Bowles's confederated Indian community began soon after independence from Spain to develop a lavish land grant system which quickly attracted a horde of Anglo-American settlers. The immigrants soon grew restive under Mexican rule, and separatist tendencies developed, culminating in the ill-fated Fredonian Revolution of 1826. Emissaries from the American settlements visited the Indian tribes of Bowles's confederacy seeking their assistance in this abortive bid for independence. The Kickapoos, because of their reputation for bravery and fighting prowess, were especially courted by the Fredonian conspirators. But this tribe, "one of the strongest and most warlike of the associated tribes, cherished sentiments of deadly hostility toward the whole white population," remained aloof, and refused to join the revolt.[10]

The collapse of the Fredonian insurrection was only an interlude in the Anglo-American drive for independence from Mexico. By 1835, internal difficulties had weakened the Mexican government, and the Anglo-American population in Texas had increased to the point that another attempt was made by the Texans to throw off Mexican rule. Bowles's Indian confederacy was again approached by the Texans as insurrection developed among the American settlements. Sam Houston, a leader in this independence movement, was appointed by the Texan Revolutionary Convention to head a delegation to negotiate with the chiefs of the tribes of Bowles's confederacy.

Houston was instructed to offer these tribes a grant of land from the Texas Republic. The area proposed, situated in the general area of present Cherokee and Smith counties, Texas, would have substantially reduced the range used by these tribes for hunting purposes and would have left them with a limited reservation for

[10] Ernest W. Winkler, "The Cherokee Indians in Texas," *Texas State Historical Association Quarterly,* Vol. VII (October, 1903), 145.

farming and pasture.[11] In return for title to this grant from the Texas Republic, the chiefs of the confederated tribes were expected to pledge "a firm and lasting peace forever" with Texas, thus assuring their neutrality while the Texan armies were in the field against the Mexican forces. All Indians of the confederated tribes were to move to the assigned reservation by November, 1836, surrendering to the Texas Republic all other lands they had been using for hunting and other purposes and permitting the peaceful entry, settlement, and use of these lands by Texans.

The proposed treaty met with considerable opposition among the chiefs of Bowles's Confederacy, and it was nearly rejected by the Indian delegates on several occasions. Largely through the influence of Houston, who was well known among these tribal leaders and who was esteemed and trusted by most of them, the agreement was finally approved by the chiefs of Bowles's confederacy in February, 1836.[12]

Houston's treaty, which neutralized the immigrant tribes so that Texan armies could devote full attention to the Mexican army of Santa Anna, was especially unpopular with the Kickapoos. These lords of the middle border remembered too well the constant reduction of tribal hunting grounds by American treaty commissioners in Indiana, Illinois, and Missouri, and to them the Houston treaty seemed a painful repetition.

Ironically, this treaty, which forced the immigrant tribes to abandon the use of so much territory, was unsatisfactory to the first Texas Congress when Houston's agreement with the confederated tribes came up for ratification. Several senators challenged the right of the immigrant tribes to a single acre of Texas land, claiming that these tribes had migrated from the north, abandoning reservations already assigned to them by the United States. Other senators charged that these tribes had negated any right to Texas lands or even the right to remain in Texas, because, through

[11] Grant Foreman, *Last Trek of the Indians,* 160–61.

[12] "Treaty between Texas and the Cherokee Indians," February 23, 1836," in Dorman H. Winfrey (ed.), *Texas Indian Papers, 1825–1845,* I, 14.

recent alleged depredations on the Texas settlers, they had become "savage and ruthless enemies" of the new republic.[13]

In the light of these charges ratification of the treaty was held in abeyance by the Texas Senate for well over a year. Finally during December, 1837, in spite of President Houston's support for the territorial rights of the confederated tribes, the Texas Senate rejected his Indian treaty.[14] The action by the Texas government left a dark cloud of uncertainty over the land rights of Bowles's confederacy. The situation was further confused by the rapid movement of the Texans to the range of the associated tribes.

During 1837 mutual depredations threatened to bring all out war. The encroaching whites sought to further discredit the tenure rights of the Indians by charging that they were in league with various Mexican agents sent to Texas to foment a counterrevolution among the Mexican settlements. President Houston, continuing his defense of the land rights of the confederated tribes, ordered a survey of the boundaries of the proposed reservation in the hope that this might at least temporarily deter the frenzied rush of settlers to the Indians' lands and thus quiet the threat of war.

In the midst of this confusion, Houston was succeeded by Mirabeau B. Lamar as president of the Texas Republic late in 1838. As hostile to the Kickapoos and other tribes of East Texas as Houston had been friendly, President Lamar left no doubt as to his intentions when he declared in his inaugural message that "the sword should mark the boundaries of the Republic" during his administration. Charging that the immigrant tribes were guilty of conspiring with Mexican agents and asserting that they posed a threat to the internal security of Texas, he declared that it was his intention to force these tribes to return to the United States.[15]

The new President's avowed hostility to the confederated tribes and his declared intention of expelling them from Texas encouraged

13 R. Earl McClendon, "The First Treaty of the Republic of Texas," *Southwestern Historical Quarterly,* Vol. LII (July, 1948), 46–45.

14 James Mooney, *Myths of the Cherokee, Nineteenth Annual Report* of the Bureau of American Ethnology, Part I, 144.

15 *Ibid.,* 145.

white settlers to push even farther into the Indian country. The accelerated settlement forced the Kickapoos and others to defend their hunting grounds, fields, and villages. Depredations were returned in kind, and less than a month after Lamar's inauguration, a series of needless Indian wars had been precipitated in central and east Texas which continued until the outbreak of the American Civil War.

12

Affair at Kickapoo Town

THE CHAIN OF EVENTS which led to the expulsion of the Kickapoos and other tribes of Chief Bowles's confederated Indian community from East Texas in 1839 had been set in motion four years
earlier. The Southern Kickapoos, numbering about fifteen hundred
at the time of Texas independence with about half this number
living in Texas, were more sensitive to the Anglo-American usur-
pation of their hunting than were the other confederated tribes.
Long accustomed to settling tribal problems by violence, the Kickapoos were the first to break the peace which Chief Bowles had
been able to maintain among his associated tribes since 1817.

The first recorded Kickapoo foray in Texas occurred in 1835 on
the western edge of the confederated tribes' hunting grounds near
present Belton, Texas. Joseph Taylor, a prominent Texas pioneer,
had migrated to Little River, built a cabin for his family, and
begun a frontier farm in the heart of a choice Kickapoo hunting
area. Eleven Kickapoo warriors on a hunt discovered Taylor's
place and, irritated by this unexpected trespassing upon their range,
killed the livestock in the corrals and besieged the family. Repeatedly driven from the cabin by Taylor's stout defense, the party
was suddenly surprised by a force of local militia. Retreating to
safety, the Kickapoo raiders left two of their fallen comrades in
Taylor's dooryard. The militiamen decapitated the slain warriors
and stuck their heads on long poles to dry in the sun—a grim warning to all the other Indians who were in this area.[1]

This ghoulish insult provoked the Kickapoos, and the Taylor raid inaugurated a long war of vengeance on the Texans. During 1836 the Kickapoos gradually expanded their depredations on the Texas settlements, although generally confining themselves to stealing horses.[2] A year later, however, Kickapoo depredations had become so numerous and destructive of life and property that the more daring settlers who had been edging into present Cherokee County, Texas, fled to Nacogdoches for safety. Three families delayed in joining the exodus were massacred by the Kickapoos. Chief Bowles denied Cherokee participation in these raids, and fearing reprisals from the Texans, he declared the Kickapoos to be renegades and no longer recognized members of his Indian community. Bowles's rejection made the Kickapoos more surly and dangerous than ever, and when Mexican agents began recruiting an army for a counterrevolution among the Mexican and Indian communities of East Texas, the Kickapoos listened readily to their overtures.[3]

The Mexican government, anxious to humble the young but proud Texas Republic and to restore it to the national dominion, began a vigorous campaign to create discord and foment insurrection intended eventually to generate a successful reconquest of Texas. Mexican communities and Bowles's Indian confederacy, especially the Kickapoos, were cultivated as potential allies for a Mexican army of invasion.[4] At this time the most prominent chiefs among the Southern Kickapoos were Pacana, formerly a terror on the Middle Border but now aging and conservative, and the young, impulsive Wapanahkah, son of the famous Kickapoo raider Black Buffalo and known to the Mexicans as Captain Benito.

Benito had been an active leader in the attacks on the Texas settlements during 1836 and 1837, and was the Indian chief most

---

[1] James DeShields, *Border Wars of Texas*, 136.

[2] Rex W. Strickland, "History of Fannin County, Texas, 1836–1843," *Southwestern Historical Quarterly*, Vol. XXXIII (April, 1930), 287.

[3] Armstrong to Herring, Choctaw Agency, May 6, 1836, Cass Manuscripts, Division of Manuscripts, University of Oklahoma Library.

[4] Irion to Hunt, Houston, September 20, 1837, in George P. Garrison (ed.), *Diplomatic Correspondence of the Republic of Texas, Annual Report* of the American Historical Association for 1907 and 1908, I, 259.

sought after by the Mexican agents. A veritable army of envoys from Mexico, headed by Vicente Cordova, Juan Flores, and Pedro Miracle, lurked in the Indians camps and Mexican villages of Texas. These agents were instructed by the Mexican government to organize the Indians and the Texas Mexicans into small raiding parties and to incite these bands to harass the Texans in every way possible, including burning homes and businesses, stealing horses, cutting communications, ruining commerce, and punishing all Indians and Mexicans friendly to Texans. The Kickapoos and other Mexican partisans were admonished to "spare the defenseless of all ages and sexes." In return for their support, the Indians were promised by Cordova, Flores, and Miracle that the country they had settled and to which they had become so attached would be forever theirs.[5] The Kickapoos and other tribesmen were reminded that "they need expect nothing from those greedy adventurers," the Texans.[6]

Having gained assurances of Kickapoo support from Pacana and Benito, Vicente Cordova, leading agent in the Nacogdoches area, gathered a force of two hundred Mexicans from the villages near this important East Texas town and established a rebel post on the Angelina River. During September, 1838, Cordova received sufficient arms and ammunition from Mexico to supply his followers, and in early autumn small bands of his guerrillas roamed the countryside terrorizing the Anglo-American settlements.

Benito's Kickapoos were also active, stalking survey camps established in their hunting grounds. Texas land locators, anxious to obtain the choice tracts, had hired a number of survey crews to venture beyond the settlements and lay out sites for farms and towns. The Kickapoos well knew the significance of the transit and compass—"the thing that steals the land"—and regarded it as an instrument of evil much like the plow, "which buries the buffalo."

On September 8, 1838, a band of three hundred Kickapoo warriors, squaws, and children on Richland Creek in Navarro County,

[5] Jones to Texian Delegation, Washington, November 26, 1838, Foreman Transcripts, Oklahoma Historical Society.

[6] J. W. Wilbarger, *Indian Depredations in Texas,* 152.

killing and processing buffalo for winter stores, discovered a survey party of twenty-three members at work. A night ambush took the survey camp by surprise, and dawn revealed the work of Benito's warriors. Sixteen Texans had been slain, and only seven escaped, five of them critically wounded.[7] Anglo-American settlers who followed on the heels of the survey parties changed the name of the massacre site from Richland Creek to Battle Creek.

After the Battle Creek massacre Benito's people returned to their village at Kickapoo Town, a polyglot village in northeastern Anderson County containing, along with the host Kickapoos, several Caddo, Delaware, Shawnee, and renegade Cherokee families. To the south, Vicente Cordova's Mexican guerrilla army, after a series of attacks on the Anglo-American settlements, was accosted by a Texas militia force of six hundred men under General Thomas J. Rusk. Wheeling northwest to escape a trap set by Rusk's army, Cordova hurried to Kickapoo Town to join Benito's Kickapoo warriors. The combined Mexican-Indian force surprised the tiny frontier community of Killough, and the butchery carried out there caused new terror in the Anglo-American settlements. The settlers demanded that all Indians be driven from East Texas.

The Killough massacre brought General Rusk's army on the double to Kickapoo Town. Unable to risk an all out attack on Benito's warriors before this time, the Texas forces were driven to this dangerous undertaking by public revulsion and indignation over the Killough episode. Reaching Kickapoo Town on October 15, 1838, General Rusk sent his army into Benito's lair at dawn the following day.[8]

Driven from their village by Rusk's assault, the Indian and Mexican forces separated, and the Mexicans were not heard from again. The Kickapoos, however, fought a savage defensive battle to cover the evacuation of their women and children, then counterattacked several times in an unsuccessful attempt to retake their village and recover their stores of food, skins, and ammunition. Brisk fighting continued for three days, and according to a Texan

---

[7] DeShields, *op. cit.*, 247.

[8] John H. Brown, *Indian Wars and Pioneers of Texas*, 56.

who survived the battle of Kickapoo Town, the Kickapoos took cover in the ravines about their captured town and "fought like fury. . . . These Indians were brave warriors and experts with the rifle, and were not inferior to the Texans in bushwhack warfare."[9]

Their warriors' supply of ammunition nearly exhausted, Pacana and Benito disagreed on continuing hostilities. General Rusk had offered a truce, and the aging Pacana was in favor of ending the battle and meeting the Texans in council. Benito insisted on fighting to the end. The chiefs compromised, deciding that Benito would withdraw his partisans in order not to hazard Pacana's negotiations with General Rusk. When finally affirmed, Rusk's agreement with Pacana included a surrender by the old chief, a pledge of peace with Texas, and assurances that he would gather his warriors, women, and children and remove from Texas to the Indian Territory. Pacana received credentials from General Rusk declaring the friendly intent of his band and providing a safe conduct through the Texas settlements to the Red River.[10]

General Rusk's victory at Kickapoo Town quickly brought the question of the right of the confederated tribes to occupy lands in East Texas to a head. Pedro Miracle, a prominent Mexican agent, was slain on Red River by Texas troops during 1838.[11] Among the effects found on his body, according to the Texas government, was his personal journal which revealed that he had held councils with the Kickapoos and that this tribe had agreed to join the Mexican government in waging war on the Texans.[12]

In the same year the Texas government announced that Juan Flores, another leading Mexican agent, had been taken and that a captured mail pouch yielded correspondence and documents which implicated the Mexican government in the Indian-Mexican outrages. One letter, reportedly signed by Valentine Canalizo, an

[9] "J. H. Greenwood, Early Texas Pioneer," *Frontier Times,* Vol. II, No. 4 (January, 1925), 20–23.

[10] Kingsbury to Commissioner of Indian Affairs, Boggy Depot, May 13, 1839, Foreman Transcripts, Oklahoma Historical Society.

[11] Irion to Jones, Houston, November 29, 1838, in Garrison (ed.), *op. cit.,* I, 350.

[12] Jones to Forsyth, Texan Legation, Washington, December 31, 1838, 32 Cong., 2 sess., *Sen. Exec. Doc. No. 14,* 11.

official of the Mexican government, and containing a "talk" addressed to Captain Benito and other Kickapoo leaders, encouraged the confederated tribes to wage a relentless war on the Texans.[13]

These revelations, the Cordova-inspired insurrection among the Mexican communities of Texas, and especially the Kickapoo massacres at Battle Creek and Killough provided President Lamar with the means to overcome former President Houston's contentions concerning Indian rights in East Texas. Suspecting that even Bowles's Cherokees were about to defect to the Mexicans, Lamar sent Vice-President David Burnett and Secretary of War Albert Sidney Johnston to the confederated tribes to discuss removal to the Indian Territory.[14] The delegation was authorized to negotiate with Chief Bowles for the purchase by the Texas government of all Indian improvements. Bowles was also informed that the government would furnish aid in transporting the confederated Indians and their families out of Texas. Bowles's council postponed a final decision, and the delay caused considerable irritation and anxiety. The Texas government considered the Indian menace to be more dangerous than the threat of a Mexican invasion, and warned the settlements they could expect "more danger from [the tribes] than the Mexicans."[15]

At Mustang Prairie—while the negotiations were in progress—Benito's Kickapoo raiders slaughtered several white families in revenge for Rusk's destruction of Kickapoo Town.[16] In early July the Texas government charged the entire confederated Indian community with actively conspiring with Mexican envoys, and a Texas army under General Kelsey H. Douglas marched on the main Cherokee villages on the Angelina River on July 15, 1839. After a stout defense of their homes and fields, Bowles's people fled in

[13] William L. Mann, "James O. Rice—Hero of the Battle of San Gabriels," *Southwestern Historical Quarterly,* Vol. LV (January, 1952), 40.

[14] Lamar to Burnet, Johnston, et al., Houston, June 27, 1839, in Winfrey (ed.), *op. cit.,* I, 67; Burnet to Dunlap, Houston, May 30, 1830, Garrison (ed.), *op. cit.,* I, 396.

[15] Irion to Jones, Houston, August 7, 1838, Garrison (ed.), *op. cit.,* I, 343.

[16] Roberts to Johnston, Fannin County, May 28, 1839, Winfrey (ed.), *op. cit.,* I, 59.

panic when the venerable Cherokee chief was slain. The villages of the confederated tribes were burned by the invaders, and most of the Cherokee, Caddo, Shawnee, Delaware, and Kickapoo families fled north to the Red River and into the Indian Territory.[17]

One band of eighty Kickapoos and a few Delaware, Shawnee, and Cherokee warriors traveled southeast between San Antonio and the Gulf shore, heading for Matamoras. Upon arriving there, the warriors reported to the leading Mexican officials and were issued guns, ammunition, clothing, and rations. The Kickapoo-led band was then inducted into the Mexican army for service against the Republic of Texas. For many years the Mexican army of the northern frontier contained Kickapoo units generally serving—with pay—as scouts. Various revolutionary governments extended recognition to these Kickapoos, confirming land grants made to the tribe by earlier administrations. As the Kickapoo population in northern Mexico increased through successive migrations of the Northern band, the Mexican government integrated the tribe into a northern defensive buffer against raids by the wide-ranging Kiowas and Comanches.[18]

The initial Kickapoo migration to Mexico in 1839 to escape the retribution of the armies of the Republic of Texas is significant in the history of the tribe, for it marks the beginning of the so-called Mexican Kickapoos. This band was augmented by various Kickapoo migrations into Mexico during the 1850's and 1860's, and there is a direct link between the Kickapoo pioneers in Coahuila and the substantial portion of the tribe resident in Northern Mexico in the middle of the twentieth century.

Soon after being mustered into Mexican service in 1839, the Kickapoos were moved by border officials up the Rio Grande near Morelos. There a village was established which served as a base of operations for Kickapoo raiders, enabling them to strike laterally at the settlements and communications on the San Antonio periphery. From their sanctuary south of the Rio Grande, the Mexi-

[17] Mooney, *Myths of the Cherokee*, 145.

[18] "Relations of the United States with Mexico," 45 Cong., 1 sess., *House Report No. 701*, 222–23.

can Kickapoos became the scourge of the Southwest, and their terrorizing raids on Texas ranches, farms, settlements, and communications extended into the 1880's.

The first recorded Kickapoo raid into Texas from south of the Rio Grande occurred in February, 1840. A party of six Texans, accompanied by two Mexican servants, was ambushed on the San Antonio road by Kickapoo marauders. The Texans were slain, their bodies stripped and mutilated, and their personal effects looted. The two Mexican servants were taken as prisoners to Mexico.[19]

The Mexican Kickapoos were also used by the Mexican government in espionage activities. After the destruction of Chief Bowles's confederated Indian community by Texas armies in 1839, most of the Indians of East Texas fled north to the Indian Territory, carrying with them a strong resentment toward the Texas government. Mexican agents accompanied by small parties of Kickapoo warriors slipped by the western edge of the Texas settlements and crossed the Red River into the Indian Territory. There both the Mexicans and the Kickapoos intrigued in the camps of the Indians recently driven from Texas, urging them to return to Texas and to kill, plunder, and burn among the northern settlements of their former oppressors.[20]

Those Indians most receptive to the plans of the Mexican emissaries were the Kickapoos who had fled north during 1838 and 1839. Pacana, with a safe conduct pass from General Rusk, had moved along the Red River with four hundred warriors, women and children to the lower Washita and had established a village on Wild Horse Creek. Benito's followers—those who had not gone to Mexico—had come to the Indian Territory during the great Indian exodus of 1839. Angry with Pacana for abandoning the fight at Kickapoo Town and for capitulating to the Texans, Benito settled his 350 followers on the Blue, a tributary of the Red which drained the lower middle Indian Territory.

Smaller bands of Kickapoos straggled in, settling either with

<hr>

19 Report of the United States Consul at Matamoras to Secretary of State, Matamoras, March 3, 1840, Foreman Transcripts, Oklahoma Historical Society.
20 *Ibid.*

Pacana on the Washita or with Benito on the Blue, until by 1841 the combined population of the two bands was near twelve hundred. The return of the Kickapoos to the Indian Territory produced new turbulence on the middle border, and in their restive drive for supremacy among the tribes of the region, the Kickapoos created numerous problems for the Western Superintendency (the United States' administrative center for Indian affairs in this sector) and for the agents of the Five Civilized Tribes.

William Armstrong, head of the Western Superintendency, lamented the return of the Southern Kickapoos to the Indian Territory, for as he pointed out, this branch of the tribe was attached to no agency and had no connection with the United States government, but because of its sagacity and ferocity, the tribe "exercised a peculiar influence over border affairs." So overpowering was the Kickapoo threat to the peace of the middle border that the United States found it necessary to build two military posts, Fort Washita and Fort Arbuckle, within the Kickapoo range in the Indian Territory in an attempt to curtail the warriors' forays into the Chickasaw towns on the east and the Texas settlements on the south.

Pacana's band had scarcely begun the construction of a new village on Wild Horse Creek when his followers began displaying their warrior craft. In the first week of May, 1839, at a rendezvous less than twenty miles from Boggy Depot, a trade center in the western Choctaw Nation, Kickapoo stalkers killed a white trapper. Choctaw light-horsemen found the unfortunate man in the midst of a wrecked and plundered camp, scalped and his body mutilated with a tomahawk. Within a week the Kickapoos killed another trapper on the Blue River. Also during May, a Kickapoo war party returning from a raid on the north Texas settlements was seen driving a sizable herd of horses through the upper Choctaw Nation toward the settlements in Arkansas, where a ready market awaited their plunder. Before the month was out, the Kickapoos had driven a band of Osage horse thieves from the southern Indian Territory, taking two scalps.

The middle border was in turmoil again, and the relative peace which the tribal leaders and agents for the Five Civilized Tribes had worked so hard to establish in the Indian Territory evaporated with the return of the Southern Kickapoos. White traders and trappers on the Washita, Blue, and Boggy had fled to the safety of the Choctaw settlements and dared not venture out. The Chickasaws, who had recently been granted a home in the western portion of the Choctaw Nation, were afraid to settle in their new domain, for the Southern Kickapoos claimed it as their range and challenged the Chickasaws to drive them out.[21]

During 1840 the Chickasaws, eager to get settled in their Indian Territory home, cautiously began to move beyond Boggy Depot and to establish towns, plantations, farms, and ranches. Kickapoo raiders struck violently at these settlements, terrorizing the Chickasaws with threats of the tomahawk and scalping knife, looting and burning their cabins, killing their hogs and cattle, and stealing their horses. William Armstrong regularly sent "talks" to the Southern Kickapoo chiefs, reminding them that their people had no right to remain in the Indian Territory, that they must remove to the Northern Kickapoo domain on the Missouri River, and that if the tribe would co-operate with his request, the United States government would pay for their removal and support them en route.

Chiefs Pacana and Benito ignored Armstrong's entreaties. At this time the Choctaws and Chickasaws were united under a single tribal constitution and shared a common government. As the Kickapoos became increasingly insolent toward the Chickasaws and more brazen in their raids, the Choctaw-Chickasaw Council began to adopt resolutions of protest and to issue threats that unless the Kickapoos removed voluntarily, the Council would organize a special Indian militia and drive the intruders out with force of arms. The Kickapoo answer to these threats was that if a Choctaw-Chickasaw army were formed to drive them out, they would immediately drive eastward into the Choctaw settlements, where they

21 Kingsbury to Commissioner of Indian Affairs, Boggy Depot, May 8, 1839, Foreman Transcripts, Oklahoma Historical Society; Armstrong to Commissioner of Indian Affairs, Choctaw Agency, May 16, 1839, Foreman Transcripts, Oklahoma Historical Society.

would massacre the inhabitants and burn and destroy all property of the Choctaws.

The Kickapoo chiefs sent word to the Choctaw-Chickasaw Council that they would welcome an opportunity to wage such a war of annihilation, and promised that their warriors "could and would whip the Choctaws." A. M. Upshaw, Chickasaw agent, was genuinely concerned for the safety of the tribe, and he resented the Kickapoo interference with the orderly settlement and development of the home assigned the Chickasaw Nation by the United States. In an appeal to General Matthew Arbuckle, military commander of the Indian Territory with headquarters at Fort Gibson, Agent Upshaw reported that five hundred Kickapoo warriors roamed the Chickasaw Nation and that the principal reason they found that area so attractive was its strategic proximity to Texas. The Kickapoos considered themselves at war with the Republic of Texas, Upshaw advised Arbuckle, and regularly crossed the Red River to kill and plunder among the settlements of north Texas. Returning to the sanctuary of the Choctaw Nation, he continued, they killed the cattle and hogs and stole the horses of the Choctaws and Chickasaws. This, he warned, could set off an Indian war which would involve the entire West, and if "ever dragoons were wanted in any of the Indian countries West they are wanted in this Nation at this time."[22]

Apparently cowed by Kickapoo threats of monstrous retaliation, the Choctaw-Chickasaw Council never organized the promised militia force. Instead, the Chickasaws fled to the safety of the Choctaw settlements and sent tribal delegations to Agent Upshaw, Superintendent Armstrong, and General Arbuckle protesting the Kickapoo depredations on their property and the continued trespass on their treaty lands, and soliciting military assistance in removing these oppressors.[23] It is surprising that the small Kickapoo

[22] Upshaw to Arbuckle, Chickasaw Agency, February 5, 1841, National Archives, Office of Indian Affairs, Western Superintendency, Letters Received, Microcopy 234, Roll 923.

[23] Chickasaw Delegation to Upshaw, Blue Water, Choctaw Nation, n.d., National Archives, Office of Indian Affairs, Western Superintendency, Letters Received, Microcopy 234, Roll 923.

nation of—at the most—twelve hundred members could hold at bay for several years two great nations, the Choctaws and Chickasaws, whose combined population around 1840, estimated most conservatively, would amount to at least twenty thousand.

Finally, in response to repeated requests for United States military aid, during April, 1841, General Arbuckle sent two companies of dragoons from Fort Gibson under Captain B. D. Moore to the Chickasaw country. Upon his arrival in the Kickapoo villages, Captain Moore found that a greater show of strength would be necessary in order to intimidate the warriors of Pacana and Benito, and in response to his request for re-enforcements, an additional dragoon company arrived in May. William Armstrong, reporting on Moore's councils with the Southern Kickapoos, observed they were stormy and that for several days the Kickapoo chiefs refused to even consider Moore's proposal that they evacuate the Chickasaw Nation. Moore was remarkably patient in his negotiations with the tribal council, and finally elicited a promise that the Kickapoos would voluntarily abandon the Chickasaw Nation in thirty days. Armstrong, wondering where the Kickapoos might go, reported that there were rumors they would settle in the Cross Timbers and that the Creeks were considering adopting the Southern Kickapoos and inviting them to settle in their country. Wherever they went, Armstrong warned, they must be watched carefully, for they were dangerous, and he added that the Kickapoos possessed great influence over the Comanches and Kiowas. He closed his report of Captain Moore's councils on a note of doubt, recommending that a military post be established on the Washita to keep the Kickapoos west and to protect the Choctaws and Chickasaws from depredations by "these haughty people."[24]

True to their pledge to Captain Moore, the Kickapoo chiefs evacuated their villages in the lower Chickasaw Nation and moved at the invitation of the Creeks to a location high on the Canadian. As a reward for keeping their agreement, and to repay the tribe

[24] Armstrong to Commissioner of Indian Affairs, Choctaw Agency, May 26, 1841, National Archives, Office of Indian Affairs, Western Superintendency, Letters Received, Microcopy 234, Roll 923.

for the loss of their corn fields on the Washita and Blue, Captain Moore offered the Southern Kickapoos subsistence at government expense for one year. The Kickapoos proudly refused. This action alarmed Superintendent Armstrong, who interpreted their rejection of United States assistance as a sign of arrogance and a new threat to the peace of the middle border. Armstrong reminded the commissioner of Indian affairs of the danger posed by such a population of irreconcilables on the southwestern frontier, pointing out that the Kickapoos "are formidable not only in point of numbers, but are the best warriors." He warned further that the Kickapoos were a nucleus around which the disaffected of all tribes could gather.[25]

Superintendent Armstrong's doubts of Kickapoo intentions were corroborated, for as soon as Captain Moore's dragoons departed, bands of Kickapoo raiders returned to their old haunts on the lower Washita, stealing horses and Negro slaves from the Chickasaw settlers. When reports of the renewed Kickapoo forays into the Chickasaw Nation reached Fort Gibson, plans were made to follow Superintendent Armstrong's earlier proposal that a military post be constructed on the middle border. During April, 1842, General Zachary Taylor led an expedition to the lower Washita and directed the construction of a military post which he named Fort Washita.[26] The new post was strategically situated about twelve miles east of the so-called "small Cross Timbers," astride a well-worn highway running from the Canadian across the Red and into northern Texas.[27]

Under the patronage of the United States Army garrison at Fort Washita, the Chickasaws moved to their treaty lands with confidence, and before 1842 ended, even tribal leaders—"among them some of the largest planters" in the nation—were venturing into

[25] Armstrong to Commissioner of Indian Affairs, Choctaw Agency, September 23, 1841, National Archives, Office of Indian Affairs, Western Superintendency, Letters Received, Microcopy 234, Roll 923.

[26] William B. Morrison, *Military Posts and Camps in Oklahoma*, 81.

[27] Grant Foreman, *The Five Civilized Tribes*, 105.

the rich valleys of the Washita, the Boggy, and the Blue.[28] Thus, although Fort Washita served as a buffer between the Kickapoos and other tribes of the middle border, it did not stop their raids into Texas and into the Indian nations to the east; if anything, Fort Washita forced the Kickapoos to be more cautious and to diversify their tactics.

[28] *Report of the Commissioner of Indian Affairs for 1842,* 460.

13

The Pawnee Hunters

THE YEAR 1842 was a critical one for the young Republic of Texas. Mexico still hoped to destroy the surprising military vigor of the new nation and to extend Mexican domination to the Red River. After several abortive attempts at reconquest, military men and politicians in Mexico planned to launch a major offensive north of the Rio Grande during 1842. The line of Texas settlements directly across the Red River from Indian Territory had prospered and expanded substantially in the six years following independence. The master invasion plan for the reconquest of Texas envisaged a massive intertribal army driving through these north Texas settlements in co-operation with a national army invading from south of the Rio Grande.

The Indian Territory literally swarmed with Mexican agents during the early spring of 1842, each carrying talks to the various chiefs reminding them of the many old scores yet unsettled with the Texans, of the rich plunder the warriors could expect from the towns, farms, and ranches on the south side of the Red, and of the vast territorial prizes awaiting each participating tribe on the day of victory.[1] While these envoys hoped to enlist warrior bands from all the tribes of the Indian Territory, past events had proved that the Southern Kickapoos were the most adamant of all

[1] Smith to Jones, Fannin County, April 22, 1842, in Winfrey (ed.), *op. cit.*, I, 125.

166

tribesmen in their hatred for Texans, the most active in seeking vengeance, and therefore the most vulnerable to Mexican overtures. The Kickapoos felt they had suffered a monstrous injustice when the Texas government ordered their expulsion in 1839, and they resented "being forced to leave Texas when they were in occupation . . . of lands before the Texans took possession."[2]

These lords of the middle border smarted under their more recent exile from the choice range in the lower Chickasaw Nation. Heavily armed dragoon patrols operating out of Fort Washita had restricted their movement to the south during the early part of 1842, and for the first time since their expulsion from Texas, the warriors were inactive.

Crossing into the Indian Territory, the Mexican agents assigned to the Southern Kickapoos learned that after being forced out of the lower Chickasaw Nation, the tribe had settled to the north in two separate locations. One band of five hundred Kickapoos under Chiefs Papequah and Benito had established a series of villages on Wild Horse Creek, a tributary of the middle Washita. Arriving in the Wild Horse Creek villages during late March, 1842, the envoys from south of the Rio Grande began their enlistment campaign. Reminding the warriors of the desolation of their villages in east Texas by General Rusk and General Douglas, reminding them that vengeance had yet to be taken, and promising that when the Texans had been humbled in military defeat, the Southern Kickapoos and other tribes could return to Texas and live unmolested on the Angelina and the Sabine, the agents received a pledge of support. During the first week in April, Papequah's raiders began slipping past the dragoon patrols on the Red into Texas. When the invasion was discovered, fast-riding couriers spread the alarm through the settlements and frightened Texans fled across the river to safety at Fort Towson. The north country abandoned to them, the Kickapoos cut a path of destruction from the mouth

---

2 Armstrong to Commissioner of Indian Affairs, Choctaw Agency, April 2, 1842, National Archives, Office of Indian Affairs, Western Superintendency, Letters Received, Microcopy 234, Roll 923.

of the Washita east to the Kiamichi, plundering and burning farms and ranches, killing cattle, and collecting their most valuable loot —horses.[3]

The middle border was galvanized to action by these forays. William Armstrong, head of the Western Superintendency with headquarters at Doaksville in the Choctaw Nation, considered the situation so potentially dangerous that he placed an embargo on the sale of powder, lead, and weapons among the tribes of his jurisdiction and threatened all traders who violated his order with confiscation of goods and expulsion from the territory. As an added precaution, he appealed to General Zachary Taylor at Fort Gibson for stronger military protection. General Taylor responded by sending two extra companies of dragoons to Red River. These re-enforcements were stationed at strategic crossings to intercept Kickapoo war parties.[4]

Before the Mexican agents, who had instigated the activity from Wild Horse Creek, could reach the upper villages of the Southern Kickapoos on the Canadian in the western Creek Nation, their plot was discovered. United States officials, learning of the activities of these operatives among Papequah's Kickapoos, took steps to counteract their influence among the tribes of Indian Territory.

At about the time that Papequah and Benito settled their band on Wild Horse Creek, Chiefs Pecan and Mothakuck, at the invitation of the Creeks, led nearly a thousand Kickapoos north to the Canadian and established villages on the western frontier of the Creek Nation. During April, 1842, messengers reached the Canadian with talks from William Armstrong inviting the chiefs and headmen to an intertribal council to be held at the Creek Agency. A Kickapoo delegation headed by Pecan and Mothakuck joined representatives from the Seminole, Choctaw, Chickasaw, Osage, and host Creek tribes in mid-April, 1842. After the Creeks, famous

[3] Armstrong to Commissioner of Indian Affairs, Choctaw Agency, April 12, 1842, National Archives, Office of Indian Affairs, Western Superintendency, Letters Received, Microcopy 234, Roll 923.

[4] Armstrong to Commissioner of Indian Affairs, Choctaw Agency, April 9, 1842, National Archives, Office of Indian Affairs, Western Superintendency, Letters Received, Microcopy 234, Roll 923.

as peacemakers on the middle border, had entertained the visiting delegations with feasts, intertribal ball games, horse races, and orations by their chiefs, Superintendent Armstrong delivered a lengthy speech on the new threat to peace in the Indian Territory. Reporting on the activities of the Mexican agents, Armstrong warned the tribal leaders to shun the "Texas-Mexican affair."[5]

Agreeably surprised that the Southern Kickapoos were represented, Armstrong went to special pains to praise their chiefs and headmen for showing an interest in the councils of peace. After the adjournment of the council, Armstrong arranged for the Kickapoo delegation to receive an invitation to visit Fort Gibson, where added attempts were made to impress the tribe favorably and to persuade the leaders not to interfere in the contest between Texas and Mexico. Before the Kickapoos departed for their villages on the Canadian, the officers at Fort Gibson lavished tobacco and other presents upon each delegate.[6]

The Southern Kickapoo councils at Fort Gibson extended into the summer of 1842, and when the chiefs and headmen finally departed for their villages on the Canadian, it was late July. Having spent the spring and early part of the summer in councils, the tribal leaders were to spend another week or two in yet another council. A delegation from south of the Red River had arrived on the Canadian weeks before the Kickapoo leaders returned from Fort Gibson and anxiously awaited their arrival. This delegation consisted of commissioners representing the Republic of Texas.[7]

The Texas government had concluded the expulsion of the Southern Kickapoos in 1839 had really solved no problems, but had created a host of new ones—specifically the sustained Kickapoo depredations in north Texas. The various commercial interests and

[5] Armstrong to Commissioner of Indian Affairs, Choctaw Agency, May 24, 1842, National Archives, Office of Indian Affairs, Western Superintendency, Letters Received, Microcopy 234, Roll 923.

[6] Armstrong to Commissioner of Indian Affairs, Choctaw Agency, August 4, 1832, National Archives, Office of Indian Affairs, Western Superintendency, Letters Received, Microcopy 234, Roll 923.

[7] Terrell to Van Zandt, Houston, August 19, 1842, in Garrison (ed.), *op. cit.,* I, 596.

emigrant associations in Texas charged that the threat of continued Kickapoo retribution and the tribe's intrigue with Mexican agents were delaying the settlement and economic development of the northern frontier of the new republic.

It was in an attempt to overcome this very real obstacle to peace and security in north Texas that the commissioners ventured to the Canadian villages of the Southern Kickapoos during the summer of 1842. Coolly received, the commissioners were nonetheless permitted to speak before the tribal council. Their mission was to invite the Kickapoos to return to Texas. The tribal assembly was reminded that the Kickapoos had hunted on the Clear Fork of the Brazos while they were affiliated with Chief Bowles's confederated Indian community in east Texas. The Brazos country, where game still abounded, was far enough beyond the Texas settlements (assured the commissioners) to insure a long, undisturbed occupancy for the tribe. In return for a pledge of peace from the tribe, the commissioners reported that the Texas government was ready to reserve the Clear Fork region as a permanent home for the Southern Kickapoos. The tribal council considered the proposal, and after some deliberation about a third of the Canadian band, led by Mothakuck, decided to accept the invitation.[8]

Small parties of Mothakuck's band began departing before autumn, and by the spring of 1843 his three hundred followers had located on the Clear Fork, where they once again lived comfortably on "the choicest delicacies of the wilds. Honey, Bear, Venison, Turkey, [and] Buffalow."[9] With the departure of Mothakuck's people, the Southern Kickapoos were divided into three bands. There were three hundred with Mothakuck on the Brazos; Papequah's band of five hundred on Wild Horse Creek; and about the same number were with Pecan on the Canadian. Through the years these three bands visited back and forth, often hunting together and joining for the celebration of religious rites and festivals. They

[8] Armstrong to Commissioner of Indian Affairs, Choctaw Agency, September 13, 1842, National Archives, Office of Indian Affairs, Western Superintendency, Letters Received, Microcopy 234, Roll 923.

[9] Elijah Hicks, "Journal," *Chronicles of Oklahoma*, Vol. XIII (March, 1935), 77.

remained in close contact with one another until the outbreak of the American Civil War, when the tribe collected on Wild Horse Creek for the race to southern Kansas—the prelude to their migration to Mexico.

During the time these bands lived apart, each developed an interesting specialty. Mothakuck's people concentrated on hunting and became famous throughout the middle border for their heavy traffic in furs and hides. Randolph B. Marcy, a United States army officer who traveled through the range of the Southern Kickapoos during the 1840's and 1850's as a government explorer, was impressed by the prowess of the three bands of Southern Kickapoos, and noted that Mothakuck's warriors were "well armed with good rifles, in the use of which they are very expert, and there are no better hunters or warriors upon the border. They hunt altogether on horseback, and after a party of them has passed through a section of country, it is seldom that any game is left in their trace." Marcy characterized them as "intelligent, active, and brave," and unafraid of meeting in battle the wild Kiowas and Comanches— upon whose hunting range they regularly trespassed—"provided the odds are not more than six to one against them."[10]

Concerning their fierce pride, Marcy observed that when some Kickapoo hunters came into his camp one evening, "we could not but remark the striking contrast between them and the Wichitas. They [the Kickapoo] were fine looking, well-dressed young men, with open, frank and intelligent countenances, and seem to scorn the idea of begging; while the others . . . are incessantly begging every article they can see."[11]

At least twice each year Kickapoo families from the Brazos villages traveled to Edwards' Trading House on the Canadian, where they exchanged their furs for the latest weapons, a new store of ammunition, blankets, and trade goods.[12] So well acquainted did Mothakuck's warriors become with central and western Texas that

---

[10] Randolph B. Marcy, *Thirty Years of Army Life on the Border,* 93–96.

[11] Grant Foreman (ed.), *Adventure on Red River,* 131.

[12] Douglas Cooper, "A Journal Kept by Douglas Cooper" (ed. by Grant Foreman), *Chronicles of Oklahoma,* Vol. V (December, 1927), 383n.

they were much in demand as guides and scouts for Anglo-American expeditions into the Southwest. They received one of their most notable assignments in 1846 when Pierce Butler, former governor of South Carolina and Cherokee Agent at Fort Gibson, recruited scouts and guides from Mothakuck's warriors to lead his party into Texas for the purpose of finding and negotiating a treaty with the Comanches. The report of this expedition attests not only to the competence of the guides, but also to the hunting ability of Mothakuck's band, for Butler's party, during the trek across Texas, came upon three hundred Kickapoo hunters—men, women, and children. Butler reported that the Indians' horses were heavily laden with peltries after a successful hunt and that his party purchased buckskins, moccasins, bear meat, and venison from them.[13]

While Papequah's Kickapoo community on Wild Horse Creek supported itself in part by hunting and by raising patches of corn, pumpkins, and beans, its chief economic specialization was trading. The members of this band became famous on the middle border as merchants dealing in a wide range of goods, including a lively traffic in humans. Trading only on a limited basis with the tribes east of the Cross Timbers because of the competition of white merchants there, they concentrated on the Comanches. These fierce tribesmen were feared both by the frontier whites and the tribes of the Indian Territory. The Comanches shunned the settlements and trading houses generally, and few white traders dared work among them. Dr. R. Glisan, an army surgeon who accompanied the Marcy Expedition of 1851, noted the daring of the Kickapoo traders who ventured to the Comanche country and rated the Kickapoos "more than a match for many times their number of wild Indians," for "better marksmen or braver men than these Indians are not to be found anywhere."[14]

William Armstrong noted the commercial activities of the Kickapoo band on Wild Horse Creek, and although he resented the fact that the Southern Kickapoos were independent of any Indian

[13] Grant Foreman, "The Texas Comanche Treaty of 1846," *Southwestern Historical Quarterly*, Vol. LI (April, 1948), 320.

[14] R. Glisan, *Journal of Army Life*, 106–107.

agency affiliation, he admitted that their role on the middle border had some advantages even for the United States, since the Kickapoo traders comprised the only channel of communication between the eastern settlements and the Comanches. He added that the Kickapoo merchants exercised a "peculiar influence on border affairs," that "they showed great shrewdness and intelligence in dealing with the whites," and that "their character for superior courage and sagacity being so well established . . . the wild tribes seldom venture to attack them."[15]

The Kickapoos, almost alone among the tribes of Indian Territory in holding no fear of the Comanches, made annual visits to Comanche camps for trading, horse racing, and hunting. Each summer after the corn had been laid by, bands of Kickapoos from Wild Horse Creek collected at the trading houses on the middle border. The three establishments which attracted most of their business were Coffee's two stations on Red River and Edwards' House on the Canadian at the mouth of Little River. Of these, Edwards' was the favorite for the merchants from Wild Horse Creek. A cosmopolitan center in the western Creek Nation, Edwards' House had been condemned by the commissioner of Indian affairs as "admirably situated for carrying on all sorts of nefarious transactions. . . . those having it under their management . . . not at all backward or slow to avail themselves of the results."[16]

From the trading houses enterprising Kickapoo merchants collected a stock of goods—tobacco, paint, knives, calico, utensils, wampum, and beads—which were "of utmost importance" to the Comanches and "which, if necessary, they will make great sacrifices to procure." Traveling in small parties with caravans of pack animals burdened with trade goods, the Kickapoos journeyed beyond the Cross Timbers and moved about at will visiting the camps of the Comanches. The most popular commodities of exchange were the horses and mules the Comanche raiders had taken from the

[15] Armstrong to Commissioner of Indian Affairs, Choctaw Agency, September 30, 1845, National Archives, Office of Indian Affairs, Western Superintendency, Letters Received, Microcopy 234, Roll 923.

[16] *Report of the Commissioner of Indian Affairs for 1849,* 194.

Texan and Mexican settlements.[17] These animals, collected in herds, could be readily and quickly driven east of the Cross Timbers. By dealing largely in horses and mules, the Kickapoo traders were not encumbered with bulky plunder on the return trip, and there was always a ready market at Coffee's or Edwards'.[18]

Horse buyers from the Missouri and Arkansas settlements gathered each year at these trading houses to buy the horse and mule herds brought in by Kickapoo traders. Through the years this traffic increased because of demands for more animals from the eastern settlements, and the pressure exerted by Kickapoo traders on the Comanches to supply the animals had the effect of extending Comanche depredations on Texas and Mexican settlements.[19]

The Kickapoos, always well armed themselves, frequently carried in their trade goods a stock of firearms which they distributed among the various Comanche bands. Whisky was also a very popular item vended by Kickapoo traders among the Indian nations east of the Cross Timbers rather than the Comanches. Raw frontier whisky produced in north Texas distilleries was purchased by the Kickapoo traders at thirty cents a gallon and hauled in five-gallon kegs slung on pack horses in rawhide netting into the Indian Territory, where it fetched two dollars a gallon. The Choctaw and Chickasaw camps beyond Boggy Depot provided a ready market for this "Red River Head-knock," and the National Council regularly complained of this traffic, finally discouraging it somewhat by detailing squads of lighthorse police along the Red River with instructions to intercept the Kickapoo whisky caravans and confiscate and destroy the contraband.[20]

One of the most bizarre aspects of Middle Border trade involved a regular traffic in humans. Kickapoo parties from Wild Horse

[17] Eldredge to Houston, Washington, December 8, 1843, Winfrey (ed.), *op. cit.*, I, 266.

[18] Marcy to Cooper, Washington, January 15, 1855, Miscellaneous Documents Relating to Marcy Expedition, Division of Manuscripts, University of Oklahoma Library.

[19] Foreman (ed.), *Adventure on Red River,* 173.

[20] *Report of the Commissioner of Indian Affairs for 1853,* 402; Foreman, *The Five Civilized Tribes,* 129.

Creek frequently plundered plantations in north Texas and on the Boggy and Blue rivers in the Choctaw-Chickasaw Nation, carrying off Negro slaves who were then sold to planters in the Creek Nation.[21] A single raid into the Chickasaw Nation carried out in 1844 by Papequah's warriors created "great excitement and alarm" and netted scalps from a man and a woman, two Negro boy captives, and a herd of horses.[22] In their dealings with the Comanches, Kickapoo traders sometimes acquired Negro slaves whom the Comanches had collected along with their booty in horses and mules. Every year the Comanches also swapped a number of Mexican children to the merchants from Wild Horse Creek. These captives the Kickapoos sold, as they did the Negroes, to the Creek planters.[23] As slaves and half-adopted children these Mexican captives were eventually absorbed into the Creek Nation.[24]

The most desirable captives in the middle border trade, however, were those children taken by the Comanches from the Anglo-American settlements in Texas and from the wagon trains bound for the Far West. A regular chain of negotiations was developed to provide for the ransoming of these white captives. Each year, inquiries came to the officers at Fort Gibson from anxious relatives. Kickapoo traders were called in, a description of the captives was provided, and a reward was agreed upon. The Kickapoos, as middlemen in this chain, inquired at the Comanche camps on their next trade trip concerning the captive. When the prisoner was located, the Kickapoos bartered him away from his captors and on their return trip, after disposing of the horse and mule herds at Edwards' on Little River, continued to Fort Gibson, where they delivered the captive and collected the reward.

A white boy and girl taken from their Texas home by the Comanches when they were quite young were sought for years by anxious relatives. Kickapoo traders were requested to search for the pair in the Comanche country, and late in 1842 they delivered

[21] *Report of the Commissioner of Indian Affairs for 1841*, 340.

[22] "The Chickasaw Massacre, March 26, 1844," Draper Manuscript Collection, Kentucky Papers, Wisconsin Historical Society.

[23] *Report of the Commissioner of Indian Affairs for 1851*, 386.

[24] Angie Debo, *The Road to Disappearance*, 129.

the boy to Fort Gibson, stating that the boy's sister had been located and could be ransomed with further negotiations. For this service the Kickapoo middlemen received four hundred dollars.[25]

During the same year, General Zachary Taylor paid $240 for another white boy whom Kickapoo traders had delivered from the Comanche camps.[26] Because of "the peculiar influence" the Kickapoo traders from Wild Horse Creek exercised on Middle Border affairs, they became the most important link of communications between the Anglo-American settlements and the wild Plains tribes, and they were regularly called upon by General Zachary Taylor and other leading United States officials for special assignments, particularly the return of white captives.[27]

The third band of Southern Kickapoos, headed by Chief Pecan and consisting of about seven hundred men, women, and children, lived on the Canadian River in the western Creek Nation. While these people supported themselves on hunting and agriculture, and replenished their horseherds through trading and raids into Texas, their special function between 1842 and 1860 was to supply protection for the Creek Nation.[28]

The Creeks were prominent peacemakers on the middle border, and because of their pacifism, they were regularly imposed upon by marauding bands of Indians from the north and west. Far-ranging Pawnee war parties from the Platte struck terror each year into the Creek settlements, stealing horses and carrying away Creek women and children. The nearby Osages seldom missed an opportunity to raid the Creek settlements, and there was the constant threat of Kiowa and Comanche incursions from west of the Cross Timbers.

[25] Mason to Bliss, Fort Gibson, August 24, 1842, National Archives, Fort Gibson Letterbook for 1842, Adjutant General's Office.

[26] Spencer to Secretary of State, Washington, October 5, 1842, 32 Cong., 2 sess., *Sen. Exec. Doc. No. 14,* 88.

[27] Armstrong to Commissioner of Indian Affairs, Choctaw Agency, May 24, 1842, National Archives, Office of Indian Affairs, Western Superintendency, Letters Received, Microcopy 234, Roll 923.

[28] *Report of the Commissioner of Indian Affairs for 1846,* 276.

A'H-TEE-WAT-O-MEE, a Kickapoo woman, with wampum and silver
brooches in profusion on her neck. From a painting by George Catlin.

KIWAKOUK, or Stunned by Lightning, a chief of the Kansas Kickapoos
and a delegate to Washington in June, 1898.
From a photograph by De Lancey Gill.

Soon after the Southern Kickapoos had been ejected from the lower Chickasaw Nation by United States dragoons in 1841, the Creek National Council extended an invitation to the Kickapoos to settle on the western frontier of their nation. In return for a permanent home the Kickapoos were to serve the Creeks as mercenaries, ready to defend them from invasions by Pawnee, Osage, Kiowa, and Comanche war parties. "Allowed no other privilege than a home" and with nothing "expected in return except protection," the warriors of Pecan's band patrolled the northern and western borders of the Creek Nation in search of marauders, while their "women and children made corn on the Canadian."[29]

Before Pecan's Southern Kickapoo band settled on the Canadian, life and property in the Creek Nation had been in constant jeopardy, and after repeated appeals from the Creek National Council and various officials of the Bureau of Indian Affairs, the United States government had seriously considered establishing a military post on the Creek frontier to curb the forays by the wild tribes. Pecan's Kickapoo warriors brought almost immediate peace to the Creek Nation, and William Armstrong, who had for years recommended the erection of a military post in the Creek Nation, could report in 1845 that no military garrison was needed in the Creek Country, for "ample protection was afforded by the Kickapoo at no expense to the government. . . . These stragglers," he noted, while not connected with any agency and relying mainly on the chase for subsistence, were "in courage and sagacity as hunters and warriors . . . unsurpassed, and perhaps unequalled by any other Indians."[30]

During the late summer of 1845, bands of Pawnees ranging south on horse-stealing expeditions into the Creek Nation tried repeatedly to crack the Kickapoo defenses. Each time the marauders were driven back with heavy losses. Armstrong repeated his earlier assurance to the commissioner of Indian affairs that there was no

[29] *Ibid.,* 279.
[30] Armstrong to Commissioner of Indian Affairs, Choctaw Agency, June 8, 1845, Foreman Transcripts, Oklahoma Historical Society.

need to station United States troops in the Creek country, since the "Kickapoo, who live on the Canadian," adequately "protect the Creeks."[31]

The consequences of a Pawnee raid during the summer of 1845 illustrates the savagery of Kickapoo warfare. A Kickapoo hunting party was surprised on Little River by a Pawnee band. The Pawnees killed the Kickapoo in charge of the horses and made off with the herd. A pursuit was quickly begun, and after a close chase the Kickapoo party came upon the Pawnees. The Kickapoo warriors made a sweeping attack, killing one of the intruders, wounding several others, and recovering their horses. "As a token of their vow" to exact additional vengeance, the Kickapoo warriors consumed the flesh from the elbow to the wrist of one arm of the slain Pawnee. "The arm thus mutilated was . . . brought to the Creek Agency."[32]

The three bands of Southern Kickapoos thus engaged—Mothakuck's people largely as hunters, Papequah's as traders, and Pecan's as defenders of the Creeks—the lords of the middle border continued in their specialties until the beginning of the Civil War. The rhythm of their activities was interrupted only occasionally—once by Wildcat's colonizing scheme in Mexico, another time by the renewal of Kickapoo warfare with the Texans.

[31] Armstrong to Commissioner of Indian Affairs, Choctaw Agency, September 30, 1845, National Archives, Office of Indian Affairs, Western Superintendency, Letters Received, Microcopy 234, Roll 923.

[32] Grant Foreman, *Advancing the Frontier*, 231.

14

Texas' Greatest Enemy

IN THE DECADE preceding the outbreak of the American Civil War, the Southern Kickapoos were as active, restless, and dangerous as ever. The year 1861 marked the end of their occupation of the middle border until 1873, when various bands were returned from Mexico to the Indian Territory as captives and were forced to accept a small reservation in the Sac and Fox country. At least three significant movements in the tribal history of the Southern Kickapoos occurred during this pre–Civil War period. One was their participation in Wildcat's scheme of pan-Indian unity, which involved a migration to Northern Mexico and a quick return to the Indian Territory. Another was a general renewal of Southern Kickapoo warfare with Texas. The third was the shifting of fragments from the three Southern Kickapoo bands—until 1850 somewhat permanently domiciled on the Canadian, Wild Horse Creek, and the upper Brazos—to the Leased District, a special reserve carved out of the southwestern Indian Territory as a home for the Kiowa, Comanche, Wichita, and Caddo tribes.

Wildcat (Coacoochee), a warrior from one of the leading families of the Seminole Nation, had led resistance to attempts of the United States government to remove the Seminoles from Florida to the Indian Territory. Wildcat finally capitulated to the United States Army in Florida on the assurance that his people would receive adequate land and other special considerations when they removed to their new home in the West. Arriving in the Indian

179

Territory, Wildcat, who had anticipated an independent existence for his people, was disillusioned by the plan of the United States government to attach the Seminoles to the Creeks. His disappointment was heightened by his failure to become the leader of the Seminole Nation.

Exceedingly ambitious and an indefatigable organizer, Wildcat turned his abundant energy and talent to other pursuits and soon developed a grand plan of confederation for the Southwestern tribes, in which the members would be fused by unity against Anglo-American expansion and by intertribal trade.[1] Between 1846 and 1850, Wildcat traveled widely over the Southwest in search of a territory beyond the jurisdiction and interference of the United States where he could move his followers. After a series of talks with the Mexican government, Wildcat decided to establish the center for his proposed Indian community south of the Rio Grande in Coahuila. Wildcat then visited the Kickapoos, Comanches, Kiowas, Caddoes, and Wichitas, persuading these tribes to join his proposed intertribal community. With a single exception, the tribes rejected his invitation.[2]

The Southern Kickapoos alone showed considerable interest. Wildcat's emphasis on the injustices to Indians committed by the Anglo-Americans, the evils of contact with these intruders, and the necessity for a unified Indian resistance to their eternal impositions had a familiar ring to the Kickapoos. The teachings of Tecumseh and the Prophet, Elskwatawa, which lingered in the traditions of the Southern Kickapoos, were much like the Seminole leader's theories, so that Wildcat's words were welcomed by the Kickapoos. The long-standing determination of the Southern Kickapoos to live apart from their brothers on the Missouri River, who had become rather thoroughly tamed by the Anglo-American civilization, was a measure of their implacable hatred of the "white man's road."

This hatred, and the Southern Kickapoos' remarkable penchant

---

[1] Kenneth W. Porter, "The Seminole in Mexico, 1850–1861," *Hispanic American Historical Review*, Vol. XXXI (February, 1952), 3.

[2] Edwin C. McReynolds, *The Seminoles*, 263.

for leading or at least becoming involved with daring, trouble-some, and dangerous schemes, explain best of all why this indomit-able tribe—of all tribes solicited by Wildcat—chose to participate in his plan to establish an Indian colony south of the Rio Grande. By early 1850, Wildcat was ready to launch his enterprise, and in that year 250 Seminole and Kickapoo warriors (the Kickapoo contingent led by Papequah, the valiant warrior-chieftain from Wild Horse Creek) and the entire party headed by Wildcat mi-grated to the Rio Grande and settled temporarily at Piedras Negras in Northern Mexico.[3]

Mexican officials in Coahuila, faced with regular and devastating forays by Kiowa, Comanche, and Apache raiders into the northern Mexican settlements, welcomed Wildcat and his Seminole and Kickapoo followers. They permitted the Indians to settle on the border of Mexican settlements in Northern Coahuila, granted lands to both the Seminole and Kickapoo tribesmen, and promised to furnish these newcomers livestock and farming tools. In return the military colonies, composed of Seminole and Kickapoo warriors and their families, were to disperse in villages along the Rio Grande frontier and to defend against the Kiowa, Comanche, and Apache raids.[4]

With his project well under way, Wildcat returned to the Indian Territory during the late spring of 1850 for the purpose of recruit-ing additional mercenaries for the Mexican government's fron-tier defense system. Again only the Kickapoos, of the tribes Wild-cat contacted, responded to his proposal. Visiting the Southern Kickapoo camps on the Canadian and on Wild Horse Creek, Wild-cat made an earnest appeal for recruits to accompany him to Mexi-co. Chief Pecan, head of the Canadian River Kickapoos, was op-posed to warriors' leaving his band for Mexico since his people were obligated to remain and defend the Creeks from Osage, Paw-nee, and Comanche attacks.[5]

---

[3] Walter Prescott Webb, *The Texas Rangers,* 133.

[4] Porter, "The Seminole in Mexico, 1850–1861," *loc. cit.,* 1–7.

[5] March to Jones, Washington, November 25, 1851, Foreman Transcripts, Okla-homa Historical Society.

On Wild Horse Creek, Chief Pacanah, aging Kickapoo leader and nominal head of this band while Chief Papequah was in Mexico, also warned his warriors against departing for the Rio Grande with Wildcat. Through the influence of Pecan and Pacanah, all of the older warriors and most of the women and children remained in their villages in the Indian Territory. Wildcat persevered, however, and finally persuaded two hundred young warriors from the two Kickapoo bands to accompany him by promising them all the booty taken from the Comanches and Apaches and assuring them that the Mexican government would pay them well for their services.[6]

Along with the contingent of warriors from Wild Horse Creek and the Canadian, Wildcat also won over a small party from the Brazos Kickapoos, and by May, 1850, his recruits were en route for the Coahuila frontier.[7] Wildcat's Seminole-Kickapoo warriors patrolled the northern Mexican border during late 1850 and 1851, and so formidable was their defense that none of the wild tribes ventured a single raid. Late in the summer and in early autumn of 1851, however, Comanche and Apache bands flanked Wildcat's military colonies on the west and crashed into the Mexican settlements. The alarm was sounded, and the Seminole-Kickapoo defenders soon rallied and drove the enemy north of the Rio Grande.

Relentlessly tracking the marauders across the wastelands of West Texas, the Seminole-Kickapoo army time and again cornered Comanche and Apache bands, took scalps, and recovered a substantial amount of plunder as well as several hundred horses and mules. On returning to their villages in northern Coahuila, the victorious warriors found that Chiefs Pecan and Pacanah had traveled all the way from the Southern Kickapoo camps in the Indian Territory to attempt to persuade their young warriors to return to their people on the Canadian River and Wild Horse Creek. After several days of pleading, the chiefs won out, and the entire Kick-

6 Page to Adjutant General, Fort Smith, November 18, 1854, 33 Cong., 2 sess., *House Exec. Doc. No. 15*, 9–15.

7 Duval to Commissioner of Indian Affairs, Seminole Sub-Agency, May 30, 1850, Foreman Transcripts, Oklahoma Historical Society.

apoo faction of Wildcat's army departed for the Indian Territory, leaving the Seminole leader with only forty Seminoles and about eighty Negroes. The Kickapoos took with them the entire assortment of plunder, horses, and mules retrieved from the Comanches.[8]

The two hundred Kickapoo warriors returning from Mexico, considered by the officers at Fort Washita and Fort Arbuckle to be as "good as can be found," were permitted to settle again on Wild Horse Creek and the Canadian, and to "plant corn as long as they behaved themselves."[9] Resentful of the increasing military surveillance of the valley of the Washita, their great highway into Texas, parties of Kickapoos from both the Canadian and Wild Horse Creek bands began to drift westward. Joining Mothakuck's recently arrived Kickapoo band on Big Beaver Creek, they brought trouble to the string of Anglo-American settlements fingering up the river valleys in a westward flow across Texas.

From the earliest days of the Republic, Texans had resented the barrier comprised by the various tribes to the expansion of their settlements. Just as in the frontier areas of the United States, when Indian tribes happened to be in the path of westward-moving settlements, the human barrier was generally disposed of by frontier militia either through wholesale extermination or through a forced removal, so was the case in Texas. Like the United States, Texas sometimes resorted to farcical treaties to legalize its Indian land extortions. Very early in the history of the Republic, Texas armies and county militia units, called rangers, took to the field to clear Indian communities from the line of settlement.

By 1839 the immigrant Indians of Chiefs Bowles's confederacy had been driven from the Sabine and the Angelina into the Indian Territory. The Texans turned then to the Wacos, Tawakonis, Ionies, Anadarkos, and scattered bands of Caddoes and Wichitas, pushing them west and north with a merciless and relentless pressure. An interesting apologia for the Texans' treatment of these

[8] Page to Adjutant General, Fort Smith, November 18, 1854, 33 Cong., 2 sess., *House Exec. Doc. No. 15,* 14.

[9] Henshaw to Holmes, Fort Arbuckle, July 9, 1852, and Henshaw to Page, Fort Smith, July 18, 1852, Miscellaneous Documents Relating to Marcy Expedition, Division of Manuscripts, University of Oklahoma Library.

Indians is furnished by J. W. Wilbarger, who admitted that while "the 'old Texans' have not infrequently been censured by some of the maudlin, sentimental writers . . . for having treated poor Lo [the Indian] in a few isolated cases in a barbarous manner," yet, "such writers probably never saw a wild Indian in their lives— never had their fathers, mothers, brothers or sisters butchered by them in cold blood; never had their little sons and daughters carried away by them into captivity, to be brought up as savages, and taught to believe that robbery was meritorious, and cold-blooded murder a praiseworthy act, and certainly they never themselves had their own limbs beaten, bruised, burnt and tortured with fiendish ingenuity by 'ye gentle savages,' nor their scalps ruthlessly torn from their bleeding heads, for if the latter experience had been theirs, and they had survived the pleasant operation (as some have done in Texas) we are inclined to think the exposure of their naked skulls to the influences of wind and weather might have so softened them to permit the entrance of a little common sense."[10]

In 1845 the Republic of Texas was annexed by the United States, and Indian affairs south of the Red River, formerly attended to in a very limited way by the Texas Indian Bureau, were taken over by the United States. One of the first United States agents appointed to look after the Texas tribes was Robert S. Neighbors, who inherited a mountain of Indian problems in the change-over. Most of the problems involved the Southern Kickapoos, either directly or indirectly.

One situation that required Neighbors' immediate attention involved the Comanches, who each year rampaged through the the western edge of the Texas settlements from the Red to the Rio Grande, killing, looting, and burning. Neighbors soon discovered that the Southern Kickapoos were indirectly involved in these raids, for the leading motive in the seasonal Comanche forays was to acquire plunder as a trading medium with the Kickapoo merchants from Wild Horse Creek who held a monopoly in furnishing the Comanches with weapons, tobacco, fabrics, and other items.

10 Wilbarger, *op. cit.*, 6.

Neighbors, with an associate agent, Jesse Stem, attempted to limit the Kickapoo traders' influence on the Comanches by holding periodic councils with the Comanches, distributing gifts, and establishing government-licensed trading houses where the Comanches could obtain more cheaply the goods and trinkets they went to such lengths to acquire from the Kickapoo merchants. Neighbors and other United States Indian officials throughout the Southwest, noting the high toll in human life and property taken each year by the Comanches in their attempt to gather sufficient plunder for the wily Kickapoo traders, agreed that the Kickapoos were "as void of principle as any Indians can be."[11]

Learning that their commerce with the Comanches was threatened by the proposed government councils and trading houses, Kickapoo traders visited the Comanche camps each time a council with the United States agents was planned. They warned the impressionable Comanches that the United States agents were really enemies of the Comanches, and, once in a council, would "spread smallpox among them, give them poison, or cut their throats when they were asleep." As a result of this rumor campaign, government attempts to convene the Comanches in council were seldom successful, and the Kickapoo commerce with the Comanches continued to flourish.[12]

Jesse Stem, agent in charge of the Clear Fork Valley Agency, labored for years to overcome the influence of Kickapoo traders among the Comanches. Repeatedly Kickapoo traders warned Stem to desist from his efforts to curtail their Comanche commerce. In early 1854, Stem resigned his commission as Indian agent and established a farm near Fort Belknap. In the spring of 1854, Stem and a friend were ambushed by a Kickapoo war party less than ten miles from the fort. After mutilating their victims and taking their scalps, the Kickapoos looted Stem's wagon and drove off his mule team. This bloody incident stirred terror through the settlements around Fort Belknap, and an indignant group of citi-

[11] *Report of the Commissioner of Indian Affairs for 1847,* 885.
[12] Rupert N. Richardson, *The Comanche Barrier to South Plains Settlement,* 140–41.

zens posted a five-hundred-dollar reward for the capture, dead or alive, of the Kickapoo assassins.[13] While the Kickapoo killers were finally located on Wild Horse Creek and justice was done, the efforts of Neighbors and Stem to curtail the Kickapoo trade among the wild Plains' tribes were of no avail, and their commerce continued unabated until 1861.[14]

Another problem facing Agent Neighbors was the westward extension of the Texas settlements. This movement exerted a painful pressure on the Wacos and other small tribes, and each year Neighbors received insistent demands that these tribes be removed from the path of settlement. Finally a small reservation, situated fifteen miles below Fort Belknap, was established for these tribes, and nearly fifteen hundred Wacos, Tawakonis, Ionies, Anadarkos, Kichais, and scattered bands of Wichitas and Caddoes were collected. The Kickapoos on the Brazos disdained any invitation to join these co-operative Indians, and made life miserable for them by plundering isolated camps on the reserve, stealing corn, killing Indian cattle, and running off horses. The misery of these unfortunates was heightened during 1858, for the line of white settlements was approaching the reserve and the settlers were demanding that the Indians either remove north of the Red River or face extermination.[15]

The troubles of the reserve Indians were compounded by Kickapoo raiders along the forward line of Texas settlements. The marauders left signs which implicated the reserve Indians. Their plight was finally brought to the attention of the commissioner of Indian affairs, who authorized their immediate removal to the Indian Territory.[16] Agent Neighbors lost no time in gathering the fifteen hundred Wacos, Tawaconis, Ionies, Anadarkos, Kichais, Wichitas, and Caddoes, and escorted by two infantry companies and two

13 "Broadside Notice of Reward for Indian Murderers, Fort Belknap, March 23, 1854," Robert S. Neighbors Papers, University of Texas Library.

14 Marcy to Cooper, Washington, January 15, 1855, Miscellaneous Documents Relating to Marcy Expedition, Division of Manuscripts, University of Oklahoma Library.

15 *Report of the Commissioner of Indian Affairs for 1859*, 5.

16 Commissioner of Indian Affairs to Neighbors, Washington, July 19, 1858, Robert S. Neighbors Papers, University of Texas Library.

cavalry companies of United States troops, he crossed the Red on August 9, 1859, and delivered his charges to S. A. Blaine, head of the Wichita Agency.[17] Ironically, Neighbors had scarcely returned to Texas after this mission when he was slain by a settler in an altercation over Indian policy.

Before his untimely death, Neighbors had been faced each year with a growing list of Texas depredations committed by the Kickapoos. He had appealed repeatedly to the commissioner of Indian affairs for some means of checking these costly forays. The annuity had been used to good advantage as a peace bond with some tribes to control their activities, and Neighbors had suggested using the five-thousand-dollar Kickapoo annuity provided by the Treaty of Castor Hill to recompense the Texans who suffered losses at the hands of Kickapoo raiders.

Since most of the annuity went to the Northern Kickapoos, and since this branch of the tribe was becoming more co-operative with the United States, the commissioner advised Neighbors that "it would be great injustice to the orderly and well disposed part of the tribe to take their means to pay for the outrages committed by the unworthy." The commissioner, in a move that was more hopeful than realistic, directed Neighbors to inform the Southern Kickapoos "that measures will be taken and orders given to prevent a repetition of these lawless acts."[18]

The delay in carrying out this stern threat had tragic results for the Texas settlements. Kickapoo depredations south of the Red River between 1847 and 1852 consisted largely of nuisance raids and seldom involved the taking of human life. The raiders generally restricted themselves to horse-stealing and cattle-killing, intending to intimidate settlers and to slow down the steady westward movement of Texas settlements, which had begun to intrude into their hunting grounds on the forks of the Brazos and upper Colorado.

Several other Kickapoo grievances against the whites were build-

[17] Neighbors to Blaine, Camp on Red River Crossing, August 9, 1859, Robert S. Neighbors Papers, University of Texas Library.

[18] Medill to Neighbors, Austin, April 7, 1848, National Archives, Office of Indian Affairs, Letters Sent, Microcopy 21, Roll 40.

ing up by 1852. The efforts of Agents Stem and Neighbors to destroy their Comanche trade irritated the Kickapoos, especially the trading band from Wild Horse Creek. A stiffening frontier defense manned by Texas ranger companies and United States troops, plus the extension of military posts both in Texas and the Indian Territory, further restricted their range.

This combination of factors—the intrusion of the Texas settlements into their hunting range, government meddling in their Comanche trade, and an increased surveillance and control of their freedom of movement by ranger patrols and United States troops—evoked a deadly hostility among the Southern Kickapoos and drove these lords of the middle border to an all out war on Texas. So devastating and ruinous had their forays become by 1858 that Agent Neighbors charged "that it can be conclusively shown by evidence . . . that they have committed more depredations than any other Indians . . . in Texas."[19]

The buildup of fighting power which enabled the Kickapoos to launch this war of vengeance began in 1851, when Mothakuck's Southern Kickapoo band, located for years on the upper waters of the Brazos, retreated northward before the intruding line of Texas settlements, finally crossing the Red and settling on Big Beaver Creek. Most of the two hundred young warriors from Wildcat's military colony in Coahuila, who returned to the Indian Territory in 1852, stayed for a while with their people on Wild Horse Creek and the Canadian, then moved westward to Mothakuck's village.

The new Kickapoo location was included in a reservation created in 1855 by the United States government. The area, known as the Leased District and extending from the ninety-eighth to the one-hundredth meridian, had been leased from the Choctaws and Chickasaws to provide a permanent home for the Kiowas, Comanches, and other wild tribes of the Southwest. It was hoped by officials in the Bureau of Indian Affairs that once settled on this new reserve and free from white intrusion, the wild tribes would aban-

[19] Neighbors to Gibson, San Antonio, January 21, 1858, Robert S. Neighbors Papers, University of Texas Library.

don their predatory ways and become adjusted to a sedentary life. Kiowa and Comanche bands did settle in the Leased District, but instead of turning to peaceful pursuits, their warriors joined parties of Kickapoo marauders from Mothakuck's village, situated on the eastern edge of the district, and using this new domain as a sanctuary, depredated throughout the southwestern settlements. Dr. R. Glisan, an army surgeon from Fort Arbuckle, visited Mothakuck's Kickapoo warriors and was impressed by the fact that "they can use both bow and rifle equally well, and are as brave as Spartans," adding that they were "more than a match for many times their number of wild Indians."[20]

Kickapoo raiders, ranging from the Leased District south to the Red and into the Texas settlements, at times operated in league with Kiowa and Comanche parties, and by 1857 Indian officials were reporting that all depredations in Texas could be traced to the Kickapoos who were linked with various Kiowa and Comanche bands. A noticeable change in Kickapoo depredation patterns emerged during this period of intensified warfare on the Texas settlements, for their forays not only extended over a much wider range, but there was a substantial increase in the amount of plunder they gathered from each raid.

Whereas Kickapoo raids during the 1840's had been of brief duration and limited range, and had seldom netted over fifty horses, their raids during the 1850's were prodigiously successful. This is illustrated by a foray which occurred during the autumn of 1857. A small party of Kickapoos from Big Beaver Creek slipped into the ranching communities on the headwaters of the Leon, killed two Texans, and returned to their lair in the Leased District with well over four hundred horses.[21] In the same season as the Leon River raid, another Kickapoo war party struck the forward settlements on the Brazos and Colorado rivers. The toll from this frenzied series of attacks included seven Texans killed, six

[20] R. Glisan, *op. cit.*, 93.
[21] Neighbors to Commissioner of Indian Affairs, Brazos Agency, December 18, 1857, Robert S. Neighbors Papers, University of Texas Library.

hundred horses stolen, and an estimated sixty thousand dollars worth of property destroyed.[22]

The year 1858 marked the summit of Kickapoo successes in Texas. Jack County and the surrounding area were fairly swept clean of horses; cattle were maliciously destroyed; homesteads were looted and burned; and settlers fled in panic in all directions to safety. Wide-ranging Kickapoo raiders accompanied by Kiowa and Comanche parties cut a swath of destruction along the El Paso mail route. Isolated settlements west of the Pecos were sacked, and near Fort Davis in far western Texas, Kickapoo warriors attacked two California immigrant trains, killed four guards, wounded a fifth, and ran off a sizable horseherd and two hundred head of cattle.[23]

A curious role was played by a Kickapoo party on a raid near Jack County in early 1858. Abner Mullins, a Texas rancher, had lost a horseherd of four hundred animals in a Kiowa-Comanche raid. A United States Army patrol headed by Major Earl Van Dorn, in hot pursuit of the brigands, met this Kickapoo party and enlisted the warriors to serve as guides. In doing so, according to Agent Neighbors, Van Dorn had placed himself "in the hands of the greatest enemy Texas ever had—the Kickapoo." These "guides led them through all sorts of bad places and abandoned them on Red River." Van Dorn continued the search north to the Canadian and finally gave up the chase.[24]

Aroused and apprehensive over these increasingly daring and destructive Kickapoo forays, the Texas Legislature in 1858 authorized an increase in ranger companies for duty on the northwestern frontier. Colonel John S. Ford, a prominent Indian fighter, was directed to muster a force of 190 rangers, proceed to Red River,

[22] Neighbors to Commissioner of Indian Affairs, San Antonio, January 17, 1858, Robert S. Neighbors Papers, University of Texas Library.

[23] Neighbors to Commissioner of Indian Affairs, San Antonio, September 10, 1858, Robert S. Neighbors Papers, University of Texas Library.

[24] Neighbors to Gibson, San Antonio, January 21, 1858, Robert S. Neighbors Papers, University of Texas Library.

and "pursue and chastize the Indians" wherever they were found.[25]

The better part of Ford's frontier army was in the field by the early spring of 1858, scattered in patrols guarding the crossings on the Red River from the Indian Territory into Texas. Kickapoo war parties filtered through Ford's defensive cordon, swept through Jack County, and returned to their villages on Big Beaver Creek with their plunder and stolen horseherds before the alarm could be sounded. Colonel Ford, convinced that this whirlwind raid was a Kickapoo enterprise, sent Caddo and Anadarko scouts across the Red to reconnoiter the Big Beaver Creek villages. They returned with the news that, according to the squaws, all the warriors were absent, "buffalo hunting." The scouts also learned from Jonas Masifield, a white trader, that Kickapoo warriors had recently returned to their villages with great herds of Texas horses, which they had driven on to the east. Ford advised the governor that from this reconnaissance all evidence pointed to the Kickapoos "as prime movers in murders and depredations recently committed in Jack and contiguous counties," and assured him that "there can be no doubt of the existence of an alliance between the renegade Kickapoo . . . and Comanche in making war on Texas."[26]

Ford's Indian scouts also searched for Comanche signs, and in May, 1858, they discovered a sizable camp, identified as Iron Jacket's band, on the upper Washita. Ford's entire ranger force swiftly crossed the Red, and catching the Comanches unawares, won a smashing victory. The rangers killed the inveterate plunderer, Iron Jacket, dispersed his band, and took seventy-six scalps and ten prisoners.[27]

The ranger's daring example shook the United States Army on the southwestern frontier from its defensive inertia. During September, 1858, four companies of United States cavalry and one of

[25] Neighbors to Commissioner of Indian Affairs, Austin, February 3, 1858, Robert S. Neighbors Papers, University of Texas Library.

[26] Ford to Runnels, Brazos Agency, July 5, 1858, Robert S. Neighbors Papers, University of Texas Library.

[27] Bernard to Neighbors, Waco, May 26, 1858, Robert S. Neighbors Papers, University of Texas Library.

infantry, under the command of Major Earl Van Dorn, moved out of Fort Belknap and headed for the Leased District. On Otter Creek in the lower district, the troops established a base which they named Camp Radziminski. From here, army patrols headed by Tonkawa and Anadarko trailers searched the Leased District for hostiles. On October 1, 1858, near Rush Springs, Van Dorn's forces caught a Comanche band of five hundred returning from Texas. Striking hard and fast, Van Dorn's troopers killed fifty-six Comanches, burned all the lodges, captured three hundred horses, and scattered the survivors afoot without blankets, shelter, weapons, or horses.[28]

Life in the Leased District was becoming increasingly dangerous for the Kickapoos, Comanches, and other resident tribes. While the Kickapoos had so far escaped the heavy retribution which the Texas rangers and United States Army brought to the Comanche camps, there was every possibility that their villages on Big Beaver Creek would be next. United States Army patrols from Camp Radziminski swarmed over the district, watching the Kickapoos closely. In October, 1859, the defensive net in the district was tightened by the construction of Fort Cobb at the mouth of Cobb Creek on the Washita. Thoroughly intimidated, the Kickapoos on Big Beaver Creek quietly packed their camp gear during the late winter of 1859–60 and slipped back into the Kickapoo villages on the Canadian River and Wild Horse Creek, where they languished for nearly a year. With the outbreak of the Civil War in 1861, however, United States troops were evacuated from the posts of the Indian Territory and Texas, and danger returned to the middle border, for the Southern Kickapoos were again in their element.

[28] Walter Prescott Webb, *op. cit.,* 155–60; Morrison, *op. cit.,* 105.

15

The Battle of Dove Creek

THE OUTBREAK of the American Civil War in 1861 had a far-reaching impact on the Indian tribes of the middle border. Federal troops stationed at Fort Cobb, Fort Washita, and other southwestern military posts were ordered to the eastern United States to defend against a threatened Confederate invasion. General Earl Van Dorn, Confederate commander in Texas, immediately rushed the First Texas Mounted Riflemen across the Red. Colonel H. E. McCulloch, leader of this crack regiment, seized the abandoned military stores and equipment at Cobb, Washita, and Arbuckle in the name of the Confederate States of America, and manned these posts with companies of wide-ranging troopers, largely for the purpose of checking forays by Kickapoo, Comanche, and Kiowa raiders into the frontier settlements of Texas.[1]

While most of their military energy was focused in the East, Confederate planners were not unmindful of the potential of the West, and they soon developed plans for bringing the trans-Mississippi region under the control of the Confederacy. The Indian Territory, with its abundant lead and salt reserves, great herds of cattle and horses, and the acknowledged fighting prowess of the Indian nations, figured prominently in Confederate designs for the West. During the spring of 1861, General Albert Pike of Arkansas, well

---

[1] Van Dorn to McCulloch, San Antonio, May 25, 1861, *War of Rebellion: A Compilation of the Official Records of the Union and Confederate Armies,* Series I, Vol 1, 576 (hereafter cited as *War of Rebellion Records*).

known among the tribes of the middle border, was appointed special commissioner by the new government at Richmond and was assigned the duty of integrating the tribes of the Indian Territory into the Confederacy.

Because of their numbers and their remarkable cultural advancement, the Five Civilized Tribes—Cherokees, Chickasaws, Choctaws, Creeks, and Seminoles—were expected to play an active military and economic role in the affairs of the Confederacy. The Kickapoos, Comanches, Kiowas, and other tribes west of the Five Civilized Tribes were also sought by the Confederacy, but for different reasons. Since Texas, a Confederate state, had long been exposed to devastating raids by these tribes, Pike's primary mission to these fierce people was to gain assurances of neutrality, so that Texas would be freed from maintaining an extended frontier defense and could turn its attention to the Union armies.[2]

Beyond this, being well aware of the courage and remarkable fighting ability of the Kickapoos, General Pike hoped that he would be able to recruit a battalion of Kickapoo warriors for service in the Confederate Army. This was revealed in a letter of instructions from Pike to Matthew Leeper, agent in charge of the Wichita Agency, which was situated near Fort Cobb.

General Pike wrote that while he continued his negotiations with the Five Civilized Tribes, Leeper was to prepare for his coming to the Washita country by visiting the tribes of the Leased District. Leeper was instructed to travel eastward to the Kickapoo villages on the Canadian and Wild Horse Creek and to inform the chiefs and warriors of Pike's hope of recruiting a battalion of mounted troops for the Confederacy. Leeper was directed to impress upon the Kickapoos and other tribes of the region that Texas was now a member of the Confederacy, and therefore no longer an enemy, and he was especially to "assure the Kickapoo, that if they have any cause of complaint against any of the people of Texas, it will be inquired into, and reparations made, and that they must in no case commit any act of hostility against Texas." Leeper was au-

[2] Hemphill to Walker, Montgomery, March 20, 1861, *War of Rebellion Records,* Series I, Vol. 1, 618.

thorized to promise the Kickapoos that if they would form a battalion, the warriors would "be paid like other mounted men, receiving 40 cents a day for use and risk of their horse, in addition to their pay, rations, and clothing."[3]

During the summer of 1861, General Pike won treaties of alliance and assurances of military assistance from the Choctaw, Chickasaw, Creek, and Seminole nations, and a promise of later negotiation from the Cherokees. Turning next to the Kickapoos and the other tribes of the western sector of the middle border, Pike sent Seminole couriers to their villages, informing them that he was preparing to travel to their country and would meet them in council at Fort Cobb in early August.

General Pike's Seminole messengers found the Southern Kickapoos in their villages. In the decade preceding the Civil War, tribal leadership had changed. The elder Pecan, venerable chief of the Canadian River Kickapoos, had died around 1860, and a younger relative with the same name was regarded as the leading spokesman for this band. Papequah, chief of the Wild Horse Kickapoos, remained young and daring enough to command the respect and loyalty of his warriors. Mothakuck, leader of the Brazos Kickapoos, had been eclipsed by a tried and proven warrior named Machemanet. This band, after a long residence on the Brazos, had lived briefly in the Leased District, but in 1860, because of the stiffening army defense, had moved east of the ninety-eighth meridian, some of the warriors and their families settling with Papequah's people on Wild Horse Creek, others moving north and joining Pecan's people on the Canadian.

Chiefs Pecan, Papequah, and Machemanet, already alerted to General Pike's mission by an earlier visit from Matthew Leeper, called their warriors in council to discuss the tidings carried by Pike's Seminole scouts, and they agreed to accept General Pike's invitation. Around August 1 the Kickapoo delegation arrived at Fort Cobb and joined representatives from the Caddo, Reserve Comanche, Wichita, Tonkawa, Waco, Ionie, Kichai, and Anadarko

---

[3] Pike to Leeper, Fort Smith, May 26, 1861, Hume Papers, Division of Manuscripts, University of Oklahoma Library.

tribes. At Agent Leeper's insistence the visiting delegations moved their camp sites eight miles east to the Wichita Agency, where he could more readily supply them until General Pike arrived. On August 8, 1861, Pike and his Seminole bodyguard arrived at Wichita Agency, and the long-awaited council got underway.[4]

Before the Confederate commissioner presented his treaty terms to the assembled delegations, he astutely wove a "talk" of Confederate concern for the Indian nations, reminded his listeners of Union ambitions to take their hunting grounds, and assured them of Confederate protection from their oppressors in Washington. Next General Pike purchased nearly two thousand dollars' worth of presents at Shirley's Trading House, near Wichita Agency, and distributed them among the visiting chiefs and headmen.[5]

The Indian delegates, pleased with the hats, saddles, trousers, kettles, guns, ammunition, coffee, and tobacco which General Pike lavished upon them, were called back into council to hear his treaty terms. Each item of the proposed agreement was explained to the chiefs and headmen through interpreters. By its terms the signatory tribes would place themselves under the laws and protection of the Confederate States of America "in peace and war forever," and the Confederate States of America promised "during all time" to protect the signatory tribes. All hostilities with Texas were to cease, and all enmities toward Texans were to end—to be "forgotten and forgiven." The new patron of the tribes agreed to furnish its wards agricultural implements, tools, livestock, seed, and rations of flour, "sugar and coffee, salt, soap, and vinegar," until the tribes could become self-sustaining, and each warrrior was promised a rifle and ammunition.[6]

By August 12 the terms of Pike's proposed treaty were clearly understood by all the Indian delegates, and the chiefs of the Wichitas, Caddoes, Reserve Comanches, Anadarkos, Tonkawas,

[4] Shirley's Post Ledger, Hume Papers, Division of Manuscripts, University of Oklahoma Library.

[5] *Ibid.*

[6] "Articles of Agreement, Wichita Agency, August 12, 1861," *War of Rebellion Records,* Series IV, Vol. 1, 542.

Ionies, Kichais, and Wacos stepped forward "to touch the pen." The Kickapoo delegation alone held back, chiefly because of the stipulation requiring the tribe to abandon its historic antipathy toward the Texans. In spite of Pike's entreaties and warnings of Confederate reprisals, Pecan, Papequah, and Machemanet remained adamant, and on the evening of August 12 the Kickapoos, sullen from the pressure applied to them, left Wichita Agency for their villages.[7]

Clearly confused by the war between sections of the United States, and unwilling to suddenly become allies of a people—the Texans—for whom they had maintained an unremitting hostility for nearly half a century, the Southern Kickapoos were divided on what steps to take. Fearing reprisals for their refusal to sign Pike's treaty, the Kickapoo villages on Wild Horse Creek and the Canadian were beehives of activity during the autumn of 1861. The Wild Horse Creek band departed for the north in September and traveled all the way to southern Kansas, finally settling on the Walnut River. The Canadian Kickapoos, consisting of about six hundred, divided. Most of the band followed Chief Pecan to southern Kansas, where a temporary village was established on the upper Neosho. Some of Pecan's people, about fifty warriors and their families, had heard of a neutral band of Creeks and Seminoles under Chief Opothleyaholo gathering on the Deep Fork.[8]

This small Kickapoo band joined Opothleyaholo, and soon the Creek chieftain and his followers were forced by successive Confederate Indian attacks to flee north from the Indian Territory. Having driven off the Confederate forces on three occasions, Opothleyaholo's motley Indian army suffered a crushing defeat at Chustenalah on December 26, 1861, and the Creek, Seminole, and Kickapoo survivors fled northward across the deep snow to a sanctuary in southern Kansas. Settling first on the Verdigris, the South-

[7] Whipple to Commissioner of Indian Affairs, Kickapoo Agency, August 30, 1865, National Archives, Office of Indian Affairs, Kickapoo Agency, Letters Received, Microcopy 234, Roll 372.

[8] "Re Paschal Pensineau, Topeka, Kansas, 1883," Fur Trade Papers, Missouri Historical Society.

ern Kickapoo survivors migrated to the Northern Kickapoo villages near Fort Leavenworth.[9]

The year 1862 was an active period for the Southern Kickapoos. The famous Indian Brigade was being recruited from among the refugee Indians in Kansas for the purpose of undertaking the reconquest of Indian Territory. Feeling was especially strong among the neutral Creek and Seminole survivors who had suffered severe losses at the hands of the Confederate Indians. Union recruiters were able even to enlist fifty-four Southern Kickapoo warriors from the camps on Walnut River and from among those Kickapoo survivors who had settled at the Northern Kickapoo Agency at Fort Leavenworth for service in the Indian Brigade. Unable to comprehend the issues involved, the Southern Kickapoo enlistees signed up, simply declaring they would "join any side but that on which the Texans fight."[10]

The Southern Kickapoos, temporarily located on the Walnut and upper Neosho, supported themselves in various ways during their stay in Southern Kansas. They depended in part on buffalo hunting and some trading. Most of their supplies, however, came from plunder which they gathered up in lightning raids into the Indian Territory. Since the Five Civilized Tribes had officially declared for the Confederacy, Union officials in Kansas had pronounced open season on the lives and property of Confederate Indians, and the refugee tribes in Kansas were encouraged to raid, burn, plunder, cut communications and supply lines, and in general terrorize the disloyal nations. The Southern Kickapoos, operating from their villages on the Walnut and Neosho rivers, were the most active of the refugee Indians in in this undertaking, not because of any degree of loyalty to the Union, but for the adventure and coup-counting opportunities this license allowed.[11]

Ranging between the Grand and the Arkansas rivers and south to the Canadian, Kickapoo raiders brought in great stores of plunder and huge herds of cattle and horses, which they delivered for

[9] *Report of the Commissioner of Indian Affairs for 1862*, 115.
[10] Ibid., 116.
[11] Ibid., 164

sale at Fort Scott, Kansas. Union army contractors, dependent upon the cattle to provision armies in the field, welcomed the arrival of Kickapoo raiding parties and their loot from the Indian Territory. A single Kickapoo raid during the summer of 1862 into the Creek Nation netted over one thousand head of cattle and horses.[12]

One of the most daring and spectacular sorties of the Civil War in the West was inspired and led by the Kickapoos, and occurred in the autumn of 1862. The chiefs and headmen of the Southern Kickapoos still smoldered with resentment at the tactics used by General Albert Pike to induce them to sign his Confederate treaty the year before at Wichita Agency. They recalled the insolent behavior of the Wichitas, Caddoes, and Tonkawas toward them when they refused "to touch the pen" as the other Indian delegations had done. The Tonkawa abuse was especially irritating, because Tonkawa scouts had zealously watched their movements during 1859 and 1860 and reported them to Earl Van Dorn, army commander for the Leased District.

Thirsting for vengeance and adventure, about one hundred Southern Kickapoo warriors, together with a band of Shawnees and Delawares, rode all the way from their Walnut and Neosho river villages to the Washita and slipped up the river to the Wichita Agency. The garrison of Texas militia at nearby Fort Cobb had been withdrawn earlier in the year, and the post and agency were protected by a force of about two hundred Confederate Tonkawa Indians. Arriving at Wichita Agency on the afternoon of October 23, 1862, Papequah's Kickapoo warriors remained in hiding under a cut bank until late evening, then took their positions and struck the agency buildings. The raiders killed three white traders, left Confederate Indian Agent Matthew Leeper for dead, looted the agency stores, and burned the structure to the ground.

The Tonkawa defenders fled at the first sign of the enemy, but their fresh trail was picked up by the relentless avengers, and by noon the next day, Kickapoo scouts had found the Tonkawas downriver, cowering in a blackjack thicket. The main force was called in, and Papequah's warriors sated their vengeance by taking well

[12] Annie H. Abel, *The American Indian as Slaveholder and Secessionist,* III, 77.

over one hundred Tonkawa scalps. That afternoon, laden with plunder from the Wichita Agency and driving a large horseherd before them, the victorious Kickapoos turned north toward their camps on the Walnut and Neosho. Papequah delivered to Union officers a bundle of papers taken from Leeper's files which he had carefully wrapped in a Confederate flag.[13]

Soon after Papequah's return, dissatisfaction developed in the Southern Kickapoo camps. While many of the warriors seemed satisfied for the time being to live in southern Kansas and prey on Confederate Indian property in the Indian Territory, a growing faction was becoming irritated by the constant pressure put on them by Union army recruiters to sign up for organized service in the Indian Brigade. Also, there was constant trouble with neighboring Indian tribes. Along with nearly five thousand refugee Indians scattered in camps across southern Kansas, there were the Osages—historic enemy of the Southern Kickapoos. The Osages were constantly protesting to United States officials, charging the Kickapoos with stealing their horses and maliciously trampling their cornfields. Machemanet became the leader of the discontented Kickapoos, who numbered about six hundred, and they decided late in the autumn of 1862 to leave Kansas and go beyond the Indian Territory to the unsettled portions of west Texas or northern Mexico, where they would be free from the bothersome Osage protests and the constant solicitation of the Union agents.[14]

Traveling west in Kansas, then turning south beyond the one-hundredth meridian and taking every precaution to escape detection by Texas Confederate patrols, Machemanet's followers traveled without incident until they arrived, during late December, 1862, on the Little Concho River, Tom Green County, in far southwest Texas. While camped on the river, Machemanet's band was sighted by a mounted Confederate battalion. The Texas troops noted the Indians' large horseherd and struck at it. The warriors,

[13] "Battle at Wichita Agency, October 23, 1862," Hume Papers, Division of Manuscripts, University of Oklahoma Library.

[14] "Relations of the United States with Mexico," 45 Cong., 1 sess., *House Report No. 701*, 222–23.

warned of the danger, rallied quickly and recovered the horseherd, then drove back repeated charges sent against them. After sixteen Texans had been shot from their saddles, the battalion retreated for re-enforcement, and the lull enabled the Kickapoos to gather and load their camp gear and hasten toward Mexico. Fording the Rio Grande at the north end of the Sierra del Carmin Range, Machemanet's band followed the mountains down into Coahuila and settled near Nacimiento, where Mexican officials, remembering the earlier service to the Republic furnished by Kickapoo defenders, welcomed them. Northern Mexico had become a veritable scalp alley for savage Comanche and Apache bands, and no Mexican community in Coahuila was safe from their terrorizing and destructive raids. The Mexican government made a grant of land to Machemanet's followers in return for a pledge from the Kickapoos to drive out the Comanche and Apache raiders and protect the northern frontiers of Mexico.[15]

Twice before, Southern Kickapoo bands had migrated to Mexico, one group arriving in 1838 and another in 1850—the latter as a part of the famous Wildcat enterprise. The Kickapoo followers of Wildcat had remained in northern Mexico for only about a year before returning to the Indian Territory. The first Kickapoo immigrants to Mexico, numbering about eighty, had fled south of the Rio Grande in 1838 to escape avenging Texas armies. This group had settled near Morelos and had provided good service to the northern Mexican armies as scouts and couriers. Their reputation for bravery and endurance was well established, and the Kickapoo mercenaries were highly esteemed by the Mexican government.[16]

Machemanet's band joined the Morelos Kickapoos, and the combined tribal community became the nucleus for additional Kickapoo migrations, so that by 1865 all the Southern Kickapoos had removed to Mexico. Thereafter the Southern Kickapoos were known as the Mexican Kickapoos, an identification which is still applicable in the twentieth century. Machemanet's people, impressed by the

---

[15] "Affairs of the Mexican Kickapoo," 60 Cong., 1 sess., *Sen. Exec. Doc. 215,* III, 1886.
[16] *Report of the Commissioner of Indian Affairs for 1868,* 87.

laissez faire Indian policy of the Mexican government, and grateful for the sympathetic reception they received, longed to have the Southern Kickapoos on the Walnut and Neosho join them in Mexico. Machemanet began sending small delegations of Kickapoo subchiefs and headmen to the Kansas camps of the Southern Kickapoos, inviting and encouraging them to immigrate south of the Rio Grande.[17]

The Southern Kickapoos were becoming more and more receptive to making a move. The Indian Territory had been swept fairly clean of plunder by the Kickapoo raids and by locally based "free companies." Union armies had conquered all the Indian Territory south to the Canadian, and Kickapoo forays into the Cherokee and Creek nations were no longer legitimate. Their disputes with the meddlesome Osages increased daily, and United States Indian officials constantly admonished the Southern Kickapoos to abandon their wild, ruthless habits, accept a permanent reservation, and become tame, co-operative Indians like their brothers, the Northern Kickapoos.

Pecan and Papequah held numerous councils during 1863 to discuss the invitation of the Mexican government brought to them by couriers from Machemanet's band in Coahuila, and to determine the future course of the Southern Kickapoos. During the summer of 1864, over one hundred Northern Kickapoos from the Fort Leavenworth Agency arrived in the camps on the Walnut and Neosho. The newcomers were led by Chief Nokowhat, and his separation from the Northern Kickapoos was in protest to the Kickapoo Allotment Treaty and the tactics used by Agent Charles B. Keith to gain the agreement from the tribe. The arrival of Nokowhat's band spurred the Southern Kickapoos to action.

Welcoming their northern brethren, they decided to accept the invitation of the Mexican government and join Machemanet's band in Coahuila. Abandoning their camps in southern Kansas in September, 1864, about seven hundred Kickapoos, led by Papequah, Pecan, and Nokowhat and guided by a party of scouts from Mache-

[17] Commissioner of Indian Affairs to Secretary of the Interior, Washington, July 14, 1868, 40 Cong., 2 sess., *House Exec. Doc. No. 340*, 2.

manet's band, traveled due west. Moving slowly, hunting buffalo, and processing the meat and hides for winter's use, the emigrants turned south through the Texas Panhandle during the autumn of 1864.[18]

Since they were traveling with their women, children, and old people, the warriors hoped that they could escape discovery by the Texans and have a peaceful journey to the new country across the Rio Grande. Therefore the tribe followed a carefully selected course far to the west of the Texas settlements, and each day's route was studied beforehand by wide-ranging scouts.

By New Year's Day, 1865, the Kickapoo caravan had reached the South Concho River. Only a few days' journey from the Rio Grande and safety, and having traveled to this point without incident, Pecan, Papequah, and Nokowhat decided to camp for several days to allow the ponies a much needed rest, Dark clouds indicated that a storm was on the way, and the chiefs wisely selected a camp site on a flat divided by Dove Creek, a Concho River tributary, with a high bluff to the windward side. The lodges were quickly erected, the squaws and children gathered a supply of wood, and before the end of New Year's day, the weary travelers settled warmly in their lodges to sit out the extended snowstorm which moved in during the night.

So angry were the winds and so bitter cold the snow that the chiefs believed it unnecessary to post scouts, so that every member of the party was under cover except for three young warriors assigned to watch the horseherd pastured in a draw below the camp. Later events proved that the failure to keep scouts in the field was a disastrous error in judgment on the part of the chiefs, for had the regular detail patrolled the camp area, the Kickapoos would have known that danger was close at hand.

A few days earlier, a troop of twenty Texas Confederate scouts, commanded by Captain N. W. Gillentine of the Second Military

[18] George A. Root (ed.), "No-ko-aht's Talk—A Kickapoo Chief's Account of a Tribal Journey from Kansas to Mexico and Return in the Sixties," *Kansas Historical Quarterly*, Vol. I (February, 1932), 155 (hereinafter cited as Root, "No-ko-aht's Talk").

District, had crossed the trail of the Coahuila-bound Kickapoos in the course of a routine patrol. The trail, about one hundred yards wide, indicated a large body of Indians moving slowly in a south-westerly direction. Following the trail for some distance, Gillentine's scouts discovered an abandoned camp site with outlines of lodges and the customary camp debris. On the edge of the camp site, the Texans found a freshly made grave. Over the protests of some, the grave was opened, ostensibly so that the scouts could learn the identity of the tribe they were following. The work yielded the body of a young squaw, neatly dressed in buckskin garments and adorned with many colorful trinkets. These were divided among Gillentine's men as souvenirs and were proudly displayed, although the more cautious warned that this plunder might prove "to be bad medicine" for them. The men did not suffer the consequences of their ghoulish act until the battle, a few days later, with the Kickapoo Indians they had been trailing. According to one of the scouts, "every possessor of a trinket met death in the fight."[19]

Captain Gillentine sent couriers with news of his discovery to state militia units throughout the Second Military District and to the Confederate regulars at Fort Chadbourne. Captain S. S. Totten of the Second Military District gathered a militia force and rushed to the Concho Country where he met Captain Henry Fossett from Fort Chadbourne, their combined forces totaling about four hundred men.[20] Gillentine's scouts led the Confederate army along the broad trail to the approaches of the Kickapoo camp on Dove Creek. Reconnoitering the Indian position on the morning of January 8, 1865, Gillentine reported that the Kickapoo camp was strung along the creek for nearly a quarter of a mile, and that his scouts had flanked the lodges and located the horseherd in the draw. Fossett and Totten held a hasty council in a clump of timber scarcely a mile and a half from the camp. The plan was for the forces to divide—Captain Totten to drive through the north end of the camp

[19] James K. Greer, *A Texas Ranger and Frontiersman*, 184–86.

[20] William C. Pool, "The Battle of Dove Creek," *Southwestern Historical Quarterly*, Vol. LIII (April, 1950), 376–77.

[21] Floyd J. Holmes, *Indian Fights on the Texas Frontier*, 41–47.

while Captain Fossett struck from the south, dividing his command between the lodges and the horseherd.[21]

The Texans formed a thin assault line, about one mile in length, and a "pell-mell charge was made for three miles." Most of the Texans dismounted toward the end of their run because of the rough ground on the east edge of Dove Creek and waded through hip-deep water into the Kickapoo camp on the west bank. The surprise of the attack stunned the warriors momentarily, but recovering quickly, they scooped up their weapons and retreated to the brush-choked ravines back of their camp. Their modern, long-range rifles took a deadly toll among the troopers; in a matter of minutes their withering fire had cut down thirty of Totten's men, including four officers. After a half-hour of close fighting, the Confederate line broke, and many of the Texans ran to their horses in panic. The Kickapoos counterattacked on foot and pulled several soldiers "from their saddles and slew them with demoniac fury." Fossett's line wavered after capturing the horseherd, and a Kickapoo force flanked his troops, recaptured the horses, and killed several of his confused troopers.[22]

A "scattering fire was exchanged until dark," when the Texans retreated to safety on the ridges to the east of the Indian camp. There the officers counted their casualties and discovered that the Kickapoo sharpshooters had slain twenty-six Texans, critically wounded sixty others, and shot down sixty-five of their mounts.[23] During the late evening of January 8, the Texans made a painful retreat with nothing to subsist on but horse meat. Just after dark the snow began falling again, and by morning it had built up to a foot in depth, increasing the misery of the survivors, both Texan and Indian.

With the retreat of the Confederate army, Pecan, Papequah, and Nokowhat counted their dead and found that fifteen warriors had fallen in battle.[24] Unaware that they had won a decisive victory and expecting another attack at dawn from the Texans, the

[22] "Battle of Dove Creek," *Frontier Times,* Vol. I (July, 1924), 17–20.
[23] Holmes, *op. cit.,* 41–47.
[24] Root, "No-ko-aht's Talk," *loc. cit.,* 157.

chiefs directed the families to pack hastily only their necessities, abandoning great quantities of plunder, buffalo robes, and dried meat, and before midnight of January 8, 1865, the Kickapoos rushed off into the bitter night's cold for the Rio Grande. The Battle of Dove Creek was the most disastrous defeat ever suffered by the Texans in their long history of Indian wars, and their shame was such that an official investigation was held to inquire into the conduct of Captains Fossett and Totten. General J. D. McAdoo was appointed special investigating officer and after a month of probing, he reported that the Kickapoos had been doing their utmost to avoid contact with the Texans, that there had been no depredations committed by them on this trip, that their destination was Mexico, and that "they were not in the pay of Union agents in Kansas, assigned the duty of desolating the Texas frontier, as had been charged by Fossett and Totten." McAdoo reported that he could discover nothing to indicate that at this time the tribe was anything but friendly, and he charged that Fossett and Totten, "without any council of war, without any distribution of orders, without any formation of line of battle, without any preparation, without any inspection of camp, without any communication with the Indians, or inquiry as to what tribe or party they belonged to, without any knowledge of their strength or position," had given the command, "Forward," at which a "pell mell charge was made for three miles." General McAdoo found that one of Fossett's officers had suggested that the Texans "try to communicate with them and see if they were friendly," and Fossett had answered that "he recognized no friendly Indian on the Texas frontier." The General's report continued: "An Indian went out from the encampment with two children to Captain Fossett . . . unarmed, with hands raised, and told Captain Fossett that they were friendly Indians, and that if he would see their principal chief all would be satisfactory. Fossett told the Indian that he recognized no friendly Indians in Texas. The Indian then told him he was his prisoner. Fossett's reply was 'we take no prisoners here.' Thereupon he ordered him shot which was done. He also, it is said, ordered the children shot, but the men opposed and they were taken as prisoners and they subsequently made their escape in the retreat."[25]

The survivors of the Dove Creek fiasco reported that their chance of success seemed certain, just as it had in earlier battles with the Comanches and Apaches, who, when pushed, always turned and ran. The Kickapoos, however, stood fast and counterattacked, so that for the Texans "the fight began to look like something else than a picnic." Finally the flight became "a rout and a disgraceful one too," and the Texans ended up "hungry, tired, and licked." Trooper Scrutchfield's laconic diary entry for January 8, 1865, best describes the battle—"made the attack. Got whipped."[26]

No matter what Kickapoo intentions toward Texans had been before the Battle of Dove Creek, they became deadly certain after January 8, 1865. After their chilling flight to the Rio Grande, the Southern Kickapoos rested in Machemanet's Nacimiento village, nursed their ailing back to health, and plotted savage schemes of vengeance for the Texans. Considering the attack at Dove Creek to be a declaration of war by the Texans, the Kickapoos were able to rationalize their merciless campaign along the Rio Grande until the 1880's.

[25] McAdoo to Burke, Gatesville, February 21, 1865, *War of Rebellion Records,* Series I, Vol. 48, Pt. 1, 26–29.

[26] "The Dove Creek Battle," *Frontier Times,* Vol. V (November, 1927), 60–61; Greer, *op. cit.,* 192–96.

16

Raiders from Remolino

PAPEQUAH'S EMBATTLED FOLLOWERS finally reached Machemanet's village in upper Coahuila in mid-January, 1865. Impoverished and hungry, they burned with wrath over the surprise attack at Dove Creek, and were eager for vengeance on the Texans. Their arrival sparked festivities, rejoicing, and a warm welcome from the tribal brothers who had preceded them to Mexico three years earlier. The newcomers found that the Mexicans had been sincere in their invitations to the Southern Kickapoos. Vicente Gurza, former *Jefe Politico* of Coahuila, true to the terms of his pledge to the tribe, had set aside a permanent reservation for them near Nacimiento, about 120 miles from Piedras Negras, and near the location of Machemanet's band. The chief purpose of the Mexican officials in attracting the Kickapoos to Coahuila was to establish a fighting force able to turn back the Comanche and Apache marauders whose raids had made a shambles of Mexican settlements on the northern frontier. Machemanet's warriors, in the short time of their residence of Coahuila, had done this well, and an appreciative Mexican government, in addition to the Nacimiento land grant, had bestowed upon the tribe seed, implements, and oxen.[1]

Machemanet's people, numbering about six hundred, had readily adapted to their new environment, and sustained themselves by agriculture, hunting, weaving mats and baskets, and dressing deerskins. Other sources of support, although irregular, were the plun-

[1] Deposition of Manuel Ban, 43 Conp., 1 sess., *House Exec. Doc. No. 257*, 20.

208

der they captured from marauding Comanche and Apache bands and the scalp bounties paid by the Mexican government. The arrival of Papequah's band increased the Mexican Kickapoo population to about thirteen hundred, and although this number was reduced by about one hundred when Nokowhat and his Northern Kickapoos returned to the Fort Leavenworth Agency in 1867, the slim resources of the appointed reserves, even with the hunting in the near-by mountains, scarcely furnished the tribe subsistence. After 1865 there was a substantial decline in Comanche and Apache raids into Coahuila, which reduced the amount of plunder the Kickapoos could expect to confiscate.[2]

The new situation was the result of a revision in United States Indian policy in the Southwest after the Civil War. A serious obstacle to the development of the West in the post-bellum period was the constant threat poised by savage Comanche, Kiowa, and Apache bands. Notoriously active during the Civil War, these raiders comprised a deadly barrier to westward expansion after 1865. The Indian policy adopted by the victorious Union government was to reoccupy the existing military posts in the Indian country, construct new ones at strategic locations, garrison each with specially trained cavalry units, and force the wild tribes to accept fixed reservations in the Indian Territory.

This policy had a very direct effect upon the Mexican Kickapoos, for the punitive expeditions led by Ranald Mackenzie and other western commanders drastically reduced the depredation range of the Comanches, Kiowas, and Apaches and gradually caused these tribes to accept reservation homes near Fort Sill in the Indian Territory. Before long, therefore, the *raison d'être* for Kickapoo residence south of the Rio Grande was eliminated. While Comanche, Kiowa, and Apache raids in Northern Mexico continued sporadically for a number of years, their frequency and severity were drastically reduced, not because of Kickapoo strength south of the Rio Grande, but because of the network of United States defenses.

The Mexican Kickapoos were not slow in developing a new

2 Statement of William Schuchardt, Washington, January 14, 1878, 45 Cong., 2 sess., *House Report No.* 701, 35–36.

modus vivendi with the officials and citizens of Coahuila. The new operation emerged from their recent suffering at the hands of the Texans, which had intensified their hatred for the people north of the Rio Grande. The entire Mexican Kickapoo community held deep animosity toward the Texans for historic reasons, and because they had twice been set upon by Texas armies during their attempts to reach asylum in Mexico.

Beginning in the spring of 1865, the Mexican Kickapoos, claiming that Texas had declared war on the tribe by the attack at Dove Creek, launched a twenty-year offensive against Texas which is unmatched for calculated viciousness, vindictiveness, and destruction of life and property. Before Kickapoo vengeance was finally satisfied, marauding bands raiding from the sanctuary in Coahuila across the international boundary had destroyed millions of dollars' worth of property, massacred hundreds of Texas citizens, carried countless children into captivity, and completely desolated entire counties on the Texas side of the Rio Grande. The war also embroiled the United States in a dispute with Mexico which saw Mexican soil invaded countless times by United States armed forces in hot pursuit of Kickapoo marauders, and provoked a diplomatic tiff which involved an embarrassed United States Congress, the secretary of state, and the President.

The Mexican Kickapoos carried on this murderous attack with a dedicated vengeance, cool precision, and remarkable success. The pattern of warfare was consistently destructive, and proved highly lucrative for the Kickapoos, not only in satisfying their desire for scalps and gore, but also in providing their new means of support. Soon discovering the economic possibilities of their warfare north of the Rio Grande, Kickapoo warriors came to rely less and less on agriculture and hunting, and more and more upon Texas plunder for the principal support of their families.

The Kickapoo war on Texas was carried out by squads of about thirty, never over fifty, well-mounted, fast-riding warriors. They were armed with hatchets, knives, and the latest models in repeating rifles, supplied by Mexican merchants, in the use of which they were rated as "capital marksmen." Bows, arrows, and lances were used to good effect too, especially on occasions where silence was desired. These projectiles were fitted with razor sharp metal points produced in Mexican blacksmith shops at Santa Rosa and Morelos. Certain Kickapoos who excelled in exploits north of the Rio Grande came to be regarded as *coup* chiefs, and warriors vied to ride with the more famous ones.[3]

Machemanet, Papequah, and Pecan represented the tribe in its relations with Mexican government officials, conducted the tribal councils, and looked after the Kickapoo festivals and religious observances. But the power of the petty war chiefs increased through the years, for their status was based not on heredity, but on daring and success in the field. Among the more prominent *coup* chiefs during the tribal war on Texas were Cheeno, who later became a principal chief, Mosquito, John Taylor, and Caballo Blanco. Taylor was the most vicious and notorious of the war leaders, and was best known and feared in the Mexican towns for his boasting of the men, women, and children he had slain in Texas and for the long female tresses he wore braided into his knife belt.[4]

The range of the Kickapoo war on Texas extended on the south from Laredo east to the far edge of Duval County and west on a crescent which curved just below San Antonio, running through Bandera and Edwards counties, and dropping southward again to the Rio Grande in Terrell County above Piedras Negras. The Texans in this battle zone, when comparing the Kickapoos, Comanches, and Apaches, considered the Kickapoo raiders "the worst of the lot," by far the most vicious, calculating, and enterprising for savagery.

Soon becoming well acquainted with the trails and fords that laced the Rio Grande country, Kickapoo war parties generally used the cover of the dark of the moon to slip into Texas, each foray lasting from three to four days.[5] A favorite target for Kickapoo raiders was Atacosa County, just below San Antonio. Between 1865 and 1873 the Kickapoos swept this area clean of horses and

---

[3] Deposition of James O. Luby, 45 Cong., 2 sess., *House Report No. 701*, 217–20.

[4] Deposition of Albert Turpe, 43 Cong., 1 sess., *House Exec. Doc. No. 257*, 22.

[5] Deposition of James O. Luby, 43 Cong., 1 sess., *House Exec. Doc. No. 257*, 15.

cattle and so thoroughly terrorized the ranchers with their barbarities that the survivors fled to San Antonio for safety.

On a single raid into Atascosa County in 1868, Kickapoo raiders killed two Negroes, took a boy captive, and drove off one hundred horses from French's Ranch; then they struck the community of Pleasanton where they killed one white man and took three hundred head of horses. Returning two months later, they scalped four men on Sandy Creek and made off with 250 horses. Concentrating again on Atascosa County, Kickapoo marauders came back in three weeks, scalped a Mexican sheepherder, and drove off fifty horses. When a party of ranchers caught up with the Indians and sought to recover their livestock, they were overwhelmed by a fierce Kickapoo charge in which every man in the ranchers' posse was wounded, one of them fatally. Back again the following year, Kickapoo raiders made away with a number of women and children, some of whom they were reported to have murdered, others they held as captives. The last Kickapoo raid in Atascosa County occurred during February, 1873. The warriors killed two men near the Sanchez Ranch, took a large herd of horses, and captured two boys. A survivor of the Kickapoo wars in this embattled county recalled that their murderous raids made life and property "very insecure," and that the dire uncertainty of existence was "worse than playing monte."[6]

Duval County was also a popular area for the Mexican Kickapoos. One raid near San Diego in 1866 illustrates a characteristic feature of Kickapoo depredation patterns during the war on Texas —malicious destruction. Cattle, horses, and captives they could deliver to Mexican merchants for a profit, but sheep could not be driven great distances at a high rate of speed and so were of no value as plunder. Yet the Kickapoo war parties seldom ignored an opportunity to devastate sheep ranches by scalping the herders and running the flocks to death. Adolph Labbe, a leading citizen in Duval County, stocked his ranch near San Diego in 1866 with five thousand head of sheep. In the same year a Kickapoo war party cut through the region. At Labbe's ranch the marauders killed four

[6] Deposition of Joseph A. Durand, 45 Cong., 2 sess., *House Report No. 701*, 220–21.

herders and scattered the five thousand sheep over the countryside, where they were lost or perished. Labbe's ranching enterprise was completely wiped out by this foray.[7]

Another characteristic of the Kickapoo depredations in Texas was wantonness such as that shown in a raid near Fort McKavett in Schleicher County during 1866. The local ranch houses were ransacked and all valuables were loaded on pack horses. That which couldn't be carried off was destroyed. Chickens and sheep were killed; pillows and mattresses were slashed open, the feathers thrown into the wind. One man was slain, stripped of his clothing, and his back was mutilated with arrows. One little girl was dangerously wounded with a vicious lance thrust. Completing their "saturnalia of blood and destruction," the Kickapoo marauders gathered up a thousand head of cattle and drove them across the Rio Grande.[8]

Kickapoo strategy in fighting off or eluding Texas or United States troops while on these forays was inventive and effective. There is no record of an entire Mexican Kickapoo war party ever being completely annihilated by Texans or United States Army defenders. Even when they were forced to make a stand, Kickapoo casualties were generally few, seldom over one or two on any given foray. Mexican Kickapoo population declined between 1865 and 1870 from about twelve hundred to nine hundred, not because of battle casualties but because of a smallpox epidemic which struck the Nacimiento community in 1869. Because of Kickapoo fighting prowess, mobility, and tactical skill, Texans generally paid dearly for venturing a stand against the raiders from Coahuila.[9]

The so-called "Fight on the Frio" is a good example of Kickapoo tactical skill. During 1865, while the Martin Settlement in Frio County was celebrating the Fourth of July with a dance, Kickapoo raiders struck the horse corral. The settlers interrupted their festivities, named an experienced Indian fighter, Levi English, as

[7] Deposition of Adolph Labbe, 43 Cong., 1 sess., *House Exec. Doc. No. 257,* 16.

[8] "Great Indian Raid near Fort McKavett in 1866," *Frontier Times,* Vol. IV (June, 1927), 51–43.

[9] Schuchardt to Secretary of State, Piedras Negras, July 1, 1869, National Archives, Office of Indian Affairs, Kickapoo Affairs, Letters Received, Microcopy 234, Roll 373.

leader, and the twelve-man posse took up the chase. Following a fresh trail, the English group soon sighted the Kickapoo raiders traveling slowly westward in the evening sun. English counted eighteen Indians on horseback and, considering this a fair match, led the Texans on a reckless charge toward the Indians. Too late the pursuers discovered the decoy, for when the Texans rode into rifle range, the Indians—mounted double—paused momentarily. The warriors riding behind slipped into the tall grass and formed a firing line facing the Texans, while the mounted Indians divided, rode furiously to each side, and flanked the Texans. When the ranchers' posse finally retreated, nine had been wounded, three fatally.[10]

The cattle, horses, plunder, and captives swept up from south Texas by Kickapoo war parties found a ready market in Coahuila. Santa Rosa, Musquiz, and other North Mexican towns—until the Kickapoo war on Texas scarcely more than poverty-stricken, sprawling adobe villages—were transformed overnight into bustling commercial towns, their new opulence a result of the Kickapoo spoils of war. This commerce produced some interesting economic and political relationships among the local political chiefs, the merchants, and Kickapoo raiders.

Strife-ridden Mexico had little control over Coahuila and the other northern states during the time of the Kickapoo wars on Texas, and local war lords in Coahuila, fairly true to the pattern of particularism arising throughout Mexico, were commonly characterized as "more or less temporary and utterly unscrupulous."[11] These political chiefs, whenever the occasion demanded, gave official sanction to the depredations of the Kickapoos by supplying *coup* chiefs with passports and title to stolen livestock, and they were linked with a group of merchants chiefly from Santa Rosa. With Mexican customs officers at Piedras Negras and Nuevo Laredo they formed a ring to receive and dispose of the Kickapoo

---

[10] John S. Ford, "Fight on the Frio," Texas State Historical *Quarterly,* Vol. I (October, 1897), 118–20.

[11] Statement of General E. O. Ord, Washington, December 7, 1877, 45 Cong., 2 sess., *House Report No. 701,* 1–2.

booty. Herds of horses and cattle driven across the Rio Grande by Kickapoo marauders were collected in a spacious and protected canyon near their villages at Nacimiento. Local buyers from Santa Rosa visited this rendezvous regularly and purchased the stock, generally dealing through Jesus Galan, who represented the Mexican Kickapoos as their business agent. The buyers then obtained forged transfer documents from their compatriots in the Customs Office. These papers made their transactions legal in Mexican courts, and with them they were able to drive the stolen cattle and horses to Saltillo without fear of confiscation.[12] Color of title was increased by the fact that Santa Rosa and other towns permitted all cattle and horses brought in by the Kickapoos to be marked with the brand of the local municipal corporation. This made the livestock "good and transferrable property," and all purchasers could buy with complete safety.[13]

This phase of the ring's operation involved the local alcaldes, who also came in for their share of the spoils of the Kickapoo wars. In one instance an alcalde, because he was considered an honorable man, was assigned the duty of holding the proceeds from the sale of a consignment of stolen Texas cattle until the money could be divided among the ring members. On the appointed day the alcalde discovered to his dismay that the money entrusted to him was missing, having apparently been extorted from his account by the fiscal or some other officer.[14]

Other official parasites who lived off the Kickapoo plunder were the local war lords, who, in return for the "protection" they furnished the towns, exacted a toll of from ten to thirty per cent of the proceeds from the traffic in Texas booty. In addition these military commanders frequently appropriated entire herds of Texas cattle and horses for use by their troops. Between 1868 and 1873, Kickapoo war parties supplied the Mexican army in Coahuila with Texas beef and kept the ragged troops of Colonel Juan Flores

[12] Schuchardt to Hunter, Piedras Niegras, July 15, 1872, 45 Cong., 2 sess., *House Report No. 701*, 213–14.

[13] Schuchardt to Secretary of State, Piedras Negras, December 26, 1872, 45 Cong., 2 sess., *House Report No. 701*, 215.

[14] Deposition of Edward N. Gray, 45 Cong., 2 sess., *House Report No. 701*, 219–20.

mounted on horses and mules stolen from north of the Rio Grande. Texas stockmen frequently crossed into Coahuila and attempted to recover their livestock, but only on rare occasions were they successful, for local authorities at Santa Rosa usually refused to surrender stolen property on the grounds that it was "spoils of war" legitimately obtained by the Kickapoos in their war on Texas. Several Texans reported seeing in the cattle markets of Santa Rosa on various occasions herds of cattle and horses bearing the brands of Richard King, Tom Beldon, John Robb, W. W. Wright, T. H. Clark, and William Hale.[15]

During 1870, a Kickapoo war party ran off more than forty horses near Fort Clark. Two ranchers watched the raiders cross the Rio Grande twenty-one miles above Eagle Pass, followed them to their camp near Santa Rosa, and while the warriors slept, slipped the horseherd away. Near Santa Rosa the ranchers were arrested by a patrol of Captain Antonio Guerra's company of Flores' army on suspicion of stealing horses. When the Kickapoos came to Santa Rosa to reclaim the horses, the Texans brought suit against the Indians in the local courts. The Kickapoos were represented in the recovery suit by Jesus Galan. His argument before the court was that inasmuch as the Kickapoos were at war with the Texans, they had a perfect right to steal north of the Rio Grande. Captain Guerra, a power in local politics, interposed his influence because he was related to one of the protesting ranchers, and this alone influenced the court to award seventeen of the horses to the Texans. It was a hollow victory, however, for the horses had been so exhausted by the long drive into Coahuila that most of them died before the ranchers reached Texas.[16]

Most important of the businessmen who dealt with the Kickapoos during the Texas war was Jesus Galan, who had established a trading house near the villages at Nacimiento. The stolen cattle and the horseherds were often delivered to Galan and payment was made, each Kickapoo warrior receiving his share of the proceeds.

---

[15] Depositions of Albert Turpe and Edward N. Gray, 45 Cong., 2 sess., *House Report No. 701*, 219–20.

[16] Deposition of Manuel Ban, 43 Cong., 1 sess., *House Exec. Doc. No. 257*, 20.

Between raids, the fighting men received goods on credit at Galan's store. There they could buy jerked beef, grain, trinkets, sugar and coffee, tobacco, guns, ammunition, and whisky. After each raid the warriors settled their accounts with Galan's firm. Cattle worth fifteen to twenty dollars a head in Texas were purchased from the Kickapoo war parties by Galan for three dollars. He later sold the cattle to buyers from Santa Rosa and Saltillo for five dollars a head. While the going price for mules was the same as for cattle, the price for horses varied, depending on the type of animal, condition, and age. Kickapoo warriors knew good horseflesh and generally culled the horseherds they brought in, keeping the top animals for their personal string and selling Galan the remaining animals. Kickapoo raiders had become so efficient and audacious by 1877 that they were actually taking "commercial orders" from interested parties in Mexico for particular types and numbers of animals, such as "a pair of large black mules." The regular rate for the recovery of a white captive brought to Nacimiento by Kickapoo war parties was $250. Relatives from Texas usually got prompt results when they contacted the local political chief, who then went through Jesus Galan to the captors. Each party to the negotiation received a share of the ransom. A tragic twist was given to one recovery attempt involving a boy and an adult female. When the ransom for both was posted, only the boy was delivered, and it was explained that the woman could not be ransomed since she had been taken as a concubine by a chief's son.[17]

Soon after the outbreak of the Kickapoo war on Texas, distressed citizens began to seek relief. Those who dared to defend their families and property generally paid dearly for their courage, for the speed, firepower, reckless daring, and savage ferocity of Mexican Kickapoo marauders was devastating. The tragic result of the "Fight on the Frio" bears this out. Some settlers, after a Kickapoo raid, formed expeditions with neighbors and pursued the plunder-laden raiding parties to the Rio Grande. The Kickapoos, after crossing the international boundary into Mexico, where the south bank was a sure refuge and barrier, frequently waited for their pur-

---

[17] Deposition of John R. Burleson, 43 Cong., 1 sess., *House Exec. Doc. No. 257*, 10.

THE KICKAPOOS

suers, and when the Texans reached the north bank, the Indians hurled insults and mocked them.[18]

Texans also sought to recover the property stolen by Kickapoo war parties and transferred quickly to local buyers in Mexican courts. Again they were disappointed. One rancher, after repeated failures to recover his cattle and horses from the corrals at Santa Rosa, reported that "it is evident to anyone who tries to receive stolen property from these Indians that they are protected by the Mexican authorities and the citizens of Santa Rosa, as well as the merchants there, who . . . conduct an illicit trade with the Indians, encouraging them to raid into Texas."[19] This information was corroborated by an official United States agent sent to Santa Rosa to to investigate the Mexican Kickapoos. His report revealed that while many Mexican officials and businessmen were involved in the savage war the Kickapoos were waging on the Texans, Jesus Galan was the prime mover, the leader "of the Mexican ring who for years have used the Kickapoo to rob, plunder, and murder in Texas for pecuniary profit of said ring."[20]

While attempting to defend their homes and families against the Coahuila Kickapoos and to recover their property from the markets of Santa Rosa, Texas ranchers along the Rio Grande also sought to enlist help from the state and national governments in freeing the country "of this terrible scourge—the Kickapoo." County conventions and grand juries in the battle zone prepared many petitions each year for the Texas Legislature and United States Congress setting forth in the most solicitous terms the terrors the ranchers faced daily and urgent appeals for aid.

During the earlier years of the Kickapoo war, Texas was still in the hands of a fumbling reconstruction government, and the Legislature responded only hesitatingly to the ranchers' appeals. One hopeful measure was adopted in 1870 when the Texas Legisla-

[18] Schuchardt to Gautier, Piedras Negras, May 6, 1871, 45 Cong., 1 sess., *House Report No. 701*, 203–204.

[19] Deposition of John P. Fries, 43 Cong., 1 sess., *House Exec. Doc. No. 257*, 11.

[20] Williams to Commissioner of Indian Affairs, San Antonio, March 27, 1874, National Archives, Office of Indian Affairs, Kickapoo Agency, Letters Received, Microcopy 234, Roll 374.

ture authorized the formation of twenty companies of Texas Rangers to protect the Texas frontier from Indian depredations. Poor financing, however, nullified the force of this measure; only about half of the companies were ever formed, and these were disbanded in 1871. The counties in the Kickapoo depredation range had become so impoverished by 1873 that the Texas Legislature suspended the payment of ad valorem and poll taxes in the desolated zone. There were indications that many of the south Texas counties might even be completely abandoned until the Kickapoo threat had passed.

South Texas grand juries and conventions also sent petitions to the United States Congress and to various government officials, including the President, the secretaries of war and the interior, and the commissioner of Indian affairs, soliciting their active and early assistance. One of the most melancholy of these Texas petitions came from Uvalde County, where in the autumn of 1868 a grand jury gathered to prepare a report on the harsh conditions in the county and an appeal for relief. The Uvalde grand jury's findings revealed that local Kickapoo depredations over a three-year period had taken the lives of at least sixty-two persons, whose bodies had been fiendishly mangled by the marauders. Many citizens had been wounded; several thousand dollars worth of property had been looted and stolen; and recovery of livestock and other property was next to impossible. "So rapid are their movements that they can't be overtaken, and the nearness of Mexico offers them a safe and sure retreat. There they publicly sell our horses, mules, and cattle. Our lives are in continual danger and our property in daily hazard."[21]

Throughout 1870 and 1871 Congress received a steady stream of letters, petitions, and appeals concerning the Kickapoo war on the Rio Grande, the problem local governments faced in dealing with the raiders, and the need for early United States intervention. The South Texas Wool Growers' Association complained to Con-

[21] "Grand Jury Petition, Uvalde County, Texas, Fall Term, 1868," National Archives, Office of Indian Affairs, Kickapoo Agency, Letters Received, Microcopy 234, Roll 373.

gress that Kickapoo raiders "scatter our sheep far and wide, leaving them for weeks a prey to wild beasts, because their shepherds have been driven off or killed. They destroy our sheep-camps. They plunder our houses. They drive off our horses. Yet these all might be endured until eventually overcome, were it not for more fearful horrors which attend them. They kill, and then horribly mutilate, all whom they encounter—old and young, men and women, and prattling children, and smiling babes. Our houses are filled with sorrow, and our hearts with gloom; our hopes, so fondly cherished, are blasted forever; and life's anticipations are shrouded in the darkest night."[22]

Texas Indian fighters, confident and competent in handling the Comanches, Kiowas, and Apaches, admitted they were now fighting a foe without equal in cunning, bravery, and tactical skill. The whirlwind assaults of the Kickapoo marauders vexed Ranger veterans, for they made the tried and proven methods of Indian fighting obsolete. The Texans learned that "the tough, wiry Kickapoo . . . by changing horses . . . will get over an incredible quantity of ground in a short time and drive a large herd of horses before them shooting down those that give out. When overtaken they will fight to the death with the fury of ancient crusaders; but they are seldom overtaken for the reason that they always get a good start before the settlers in the thinly populated frontier counties can get together."[23]

The desperate situation along the Rio Grande finally received the full attention of the United States government. But before peace was restored on the Rio Grande, the Mexican Kickapoos had by their war of vengeance on Texas involved the United States Congress in a long series of investigations of conditions along the Rio Grande; the United States Army in a war of retribution on the Mexican Kickapoos which saw the invasion of Mexican territory on at least twelve different occasions; the commissioner of Indian

[22] Alexander Sweet and Armory J. Knox, *On a Mexican Mustang Through Texas*, 532.

[23] *Ibid.*, 509–10.

affairs in a long and frustrating campaign to persuade the Mexican Kickapoos to remove peacefully to the Indian Territory; and the State Department in a bitter controversy with Mexico over national responsibility and sanctity of national territory.

17

The Miles Mission

IN RESPONSE to the increasing numbers of petitions, letters, and memorials from distressed Texans along the Rio Grande, the national government finally began around 1871 to give serious attention to the Kickapoo war. Various Congressmen had been offering resolutions and bills of relief on behalf of the south Texas ranchers for several years, but it was not until 1871 that Congress took a real interest in the Kickapoo-Texas feud. In February, 1872, Congress adopted Joint Resolution Number 101, a measure authorizing an investigation into the Kickapoo war on Texas and directing that three commissioners be appointed to carry out the inquiry.[1]

Under authority of the resolution, Thomas P. Robb, Richard H. Savage, and Thomas O. Osborn were appointed commissioners to Texas. Arriving on the Rio Grande during the summer of 1872, the commissioners held sessions at Laredo, Eagle Pass, Fort Clark, Uvalde, and San Antonio, their inquiry lasting into May, 1873. Hundreds of witnesses appeared before the investigators to tell of their sufferings and losses at the hands of Kickapoo plunderers, and well over one thousand depositions were taken, all of which furnished "the most thorough proofs . . . as to the cattle stealing raids with the full record of the deeds of . . . the Kickapoo."[2]

Among the tribes of the Southwest, the United States commis-

1 *Congressional Globe,* 42 Cong., 2 sess., 1115.
2 "Report of the United States Commission to Texas," 43 Cong., 1 sess., *House Exec. Doc. No. 257,* 1–3.

sioners found, the Mexican Kickapoos were "especially distinguished for a bitter animosity to the inhabitants of Texas, and for unceasing activity in their bold raids." Their incursions had "two main objects," according to the investigators—stealing "horses and the kidnapping of children. Murder is an invariable accompaniment, for these Indians have shown a disposition to fight bitterly with the settlers, and the gloomy record of their deeds is found in the many depositions taken upon the subject." The commissioners observed that Texas offered "in its vast desert plains and in its unexplored hill regions . . . abundant facilities for the concealment of the Indian marauders" to meet, barter captives and plunder, and conjure up new trouble for the Texans. The commissioners noted that "the extended frontier, open and only dotted here and there with military posts," gave the "Indians a decided advantage," and that raiding parties could "retire in almost any direction and find some means of escape."

The commissioners found their investigation interrupted from time to time when witnesses "appearing before the Commission to record their losses by Indian raids" were suddenly "called away by the news of fresh attacks upon their residences and property." Robb, Savage, and Osborn personally traversed much of the territory exposed to the raids of the Kickapoos and found that the desolated zone began in the vicinity of San Diego and stretched "in a semi-circle as far as San Antonio, the settlements such as San Diego, Laredo, Fort Ewell, Eagle Pass, Fort Clark, Uvalde, and their vicinities . . . continually harassed by the bold and desperate raids of these invaders."

In their final report the commissioners charged that the Kickapoos, settled near Santa Rosa in Coahuila, were "under the protection of the Mexican Authorities," and that the Indians carried "on a trade with a circle of degraded merchants who are their accomplices, these receiving at a nominal sum, cattle and horses stolen from Texas for their goods and munitions, and that the Kickapoos were "answerable for murders and deaths without number." In studying Kickapoo depredation patterns, the commissioners observed that the Indians "cross the Rio Grande at almost any point between San Diego and Fort Clark, whirl around the settlements, kill shepherds, travelers, and others, attack ranchers and drive away to Mexico herds of horses, leaving a trail of broken down animals, dead bodies, and pillaged ranches behind them." The commissioners noted that there were "spies and emissaries aiding the nefarious traders who inform, through them, the Indians of any suitable opportunity for a descent. With regret the commissioners report that at the town of Laredo the feeling was so strong in connection with the debasing circle of Mexican local influence, illicit trade, and hostility to Americans, that, although the drum had been beaten on one occasion to rally the inhabitants of that town . . . to repel an attack of the Kickapoo," and although "bodies of men murdered by them often had been brought in the town, but few resident witnesses could be found who could state what tribes of Indians depredated upon them."[3]

The commissioners, after months of hearing testimony, estimated that the Kickapoo desolation of south Texas ranches had been so complete that in 1872 there remained only one-tenth of the livestock population tallied in 1865. Cumulative loss estimates supplied by witnesses revealed that between 1865 and 1872, five hundred thousand head of cattle and fourteen thousand horses had been stolen in Texas by Kickapoo marauders and Mexican outlaws. Roger Q. Mills, a Texas political leader commenting on the reports of the United States Commission to Texas, praised the investigation for setting forth "in a plain unvarnished tale of horror" the grievances of Texas citizens against the Mexican Kickapoos. Besides heavy property losses, Mills added, "men have been murdered in cold blood in almost every conceivable way. They have been shot, stabbed, burned alive, and strangled, and their bodies have been indecently mutilated. Women have been captured, their persons violated; children have been stolen and sold as slaves. . . . [Mexicans] have made large profits by shipping and selling our stolen beef to the Spanish army in Cuba. Their mounted troops in government service ride our stolen horses and the local authorities super-

[3] "Depredations by Indians," 45 Cong., 2 sess., *House Report No. 701*, 217–18.

intend and regulate the stealing and share in its profits. . . . When the adventurers return with their stock, the *Alcalde* charges them so much per head for the privilege of passing through his jurisdiction, and upon payment of the fee he gives them a paper that invests them with the title to the property which was not even asserted before."[4]

In mid-1873 the commissioners closed their investigations with the observation that the Kickapoo war on Texas could be speedily concluded by the removal of these Indians to a reservation in the United States, and by "the performance of plain duty by Mexican authorities, and the equitable adjustment" of the claims for damages lodged by the Texans. The published report of the United States Commission to Texas was widely read in Washington by members of Congress and officers in other branches of the government, and its startling revelations were of primary importance in bringing about concerted attempts to remove the Mexican Kickapoos to the Indian Territory.[5]

When Congress turned its attention to the Kickapoo war on the Rio Grande, the Bureau of Indian Affairs also began to take notice of the Kickapoo-Texas vendetta. During 1869 the commissioner of Indian affairs had called attention to the necessity for prompt action to end the Mexican-based Kickapoo raids, warning that serious difficulties might arise with Mexico "should the citizens of Texas, suffering beyond further endurance at the hands of these marauders, undertake to redress their grievances by invading the territory of the Republic in pursuit of the offenders." The commissioner declared that although the Kickapoos, by their long residence in Mexico and by their savage war on a state of the Union, had forfeited any right to United States protection or benefits from the government—including the reservation in Kansas they had long since abandoned—yet, in view of the suffering and destruction their raids had produced, he recommended steps "be taken as early

4 Roger Q. Mills, *Speeches of Roger Q. Mills of Texas,* 4–5.

5 "Report of the United States Commission to Texas," 43 Cong., 1 sess., *House Exec. Doc. No. 257,* 27–32.

as practicable" to return them to the United States to a reservation somewhere in the Indian Territory.[6]

In the following year the commissioner of Indian affairs, beset by increasing appeals from south Texas ranchers, again called attention to the need for an immediate removal of the Kickapoos from Mexico to the United States, and he recommended to the secretary of the interior that in view of the warlike disposition of the Mexican Kickapoos, the most suitable home in the Indian Territory for them would be a reservation in the old Leased District situated west of the Chickasaw country near Fort Sill.[7] No firm decision on a home for the Mexican Kickapoos was made, however, and in later United States councils in Coahuila, the inability of American commissioners to offer a specific home in the Indian Territory and their evasive answers to the questions of the Mexican Kickapoo chiefs and headmen were responsible in part for the failure of the United States Commission to effect a removal.

No official contact had yet been made with the Mexican Kickapoos on the proposed move to the Indian Territory, but rumors abounded throughout 1869 and 1870 that the chiefs were ready to terminate their wars on Texas and return peacefully to the United States. These rumors produced optimism in the Bureau of Indian Affairs on the chances of an early and successful removal and stirred hope in the hearts of the Texans.

William Schuchardt, close to the Mexican Kickapoos in his post as United States consul at Piedras Negras, declared that these rumors were "utterly false" and warned that no stock should be placed in them. His assertion was based on the belief that "so long as the Kickapoo have the protection of the Mexican Government and cross into Texas to loot, rob, plunder, and as long as these acts are countenanced by citizens of Mexico, and as long as the Kickapoo can find a ready market for their booty they will never willingly quit."[8]

[6] *Report of the Commissioner of Indian Affairs for 1869*, 8.

[7] *Report of the Commissioner of Indian Affairs for 1870*, 7.

[8] Schuchardt to Secretary of State, Piedras Negras, July 1, 1869, National Archives, Office of Indian Affairs, Kickapoo Agency, Letters Received, Microcopy 234, Roll 373.

The operation of the Bureau of Indian Affairs, as a result of President Grant's so-called "Indian Peace Policy," was at this time in the hands of leaders of various religious denominations. Representatives from the Society of Friends dominated the official positions in the Bureau of Indian Affairs, and their philosophy of executive action was not based upon the cynical realism espoused by most professional politicians, but upon hope, trust, and abiding faith in good intentions. This attitude explains in part the optimism prevalent in the Indian service around 1870 concerning the willingness of the Mexican Kickapoos to abandon their war on Texas and to remove peacefully to the Indian Territory. In spite of Schuchardt's warning, therefore, the commissioner of Indian affairs made preparations during 1870 to establish contact with the Mexican Kickapoos, and by the spring of 1871 all was in readiness.

Quaker Indian Agent Jonathan B. Miles, assigned the mission of establishing contact with the Mexican Kickapoos and inviting them to return to the United States, departed with Nokowhat, Parthe, and Keoquark, Northern Kickapoo chiefs, and John Anderson, interpreter, from Muscotah, Kansas, on April 11, 1871.[9] Nearly six weeks later Miles' party arrived at Fort Duncan, Texas, on the Rio Grande. After a brief rest Miles and the Kickapoo chiefs, in company with Colonel Z. R. Bliss, post commander, and William Schuchardt, United States consul at Piedras Negras, crossed the Rio Grande and set out for the Mexican Kickapoo villages at Nacimiento. Miles later learned that before his departure, two Mexican spies had ridden south from Piedras Negras to Santa Rosa to warn Mexican officials and Kickapoo plunder merchants of the mission of the American party. Forewarned, the local authorities and businessmen were ready for Miles when he arrived in Santa Rosa.[10]

Near Morelos on the Santa Rosa road, Miles came upon a temporary Kickapoo camp consisting of the warriors and families of a war

[9] Miles to Hoag, Muscotah, Kansas, March 13, 1871, National Archives, Office of Indian Affairs, Kickapoo Agency, Letters Received, Microcopy 234, Roll 373.

[10] Miles to Hoag, Muscotah, Kansas, July 13, 1871, National Archives, Office of Indian Affairs, Kickapoo Agency, Letters Received, Microcopy 234, Roll 373.

band headed by Cheeno. The American party was kindly received by Cheeno, and his people seemed particularly pleased to receive a visit from representatives of their people from the north. Cheeno and his warriors supplied an escort to Santa Rosa, where Miles was greeted by a large delegation of Kickapoos who had traveled in from their villages at Nacimiento. Again the Commission was welcomed, and Miles noted that the Mexican Kickapoos seemed "perfectly delighted to meet our delegation, and receive intelligence from the north, and to give us information relative to themselves."[11]

From this band Miles learned that most of the Mexican Kickapoo warriors were away from their Nacimiento villages "hunting." Messengers were sent out to locate them and to deliver tidings of the arrival of the American Commission and of the proposed council to be held at Nacimiento. While waiting for the Kickapoos to gather, Miles visited among those present and told them of the friendly purpose of his mission and of the many advantages the tribe would derive from accepting "the kind offer made by their great White Father in Washington." Miles noted that quite a number of them, particularly the squaws, expressed a positive determination to return to the United States.[12]

Commissioner Miles soon discovered a plot conceived by local government officials and merchants at Santa Rosa to discredit the American Commission and to persuade the Kickapoos to remain in Coahuila. In talking with the Indians, Miles found that they firmly believed, because the Mexicans had told them, that "the Civil War still rages" and that Miles' purpose in coming to Coahuila was to set a trap for the Kickapoos by luring them over into Texas, where, warned the Mexicans, "the terrible slaughter of 1865 [Dove Creek] by rebel Texans" would be repeated. Miles found that the Mexican Kickapoos still hated the Texans and that the Indians placed implicit faith in the false warnings given them by the Mexicans.[13]

[11] *Report of the Commissioner of Indian Affairs for 1871,* 192–96.

[12] Miles to Hoag, Muscotah, Kansas, July 13, 1871, National Archives, Office of Indian Affairs, Kickapoo Agency, Letters Received, Microcopy 234, Roll 373.

[13] Miles to Hoag, Santa Rosa, June 7, 1871, National Archives, Office of Indian Affairs, Kickapoo Agency, Letters Received, Microcopy 234, Roll 373.

Promises of presents, annuities, rations, and land if they would return to the United States seemed to be of little interest to the Mexican Kickapoos, and Miles soon discovered the reason. Shortly after the Kickapoos arrived in Coahuila during the American Civil War, the Mexican government had promised the Indians an award of ten thousand dollars for their border defense service against the wild Indians, the money to be used by the tribe to continue the agricultural development of the Nacimiento farms established by earlier grants-in-aid. This money had been delivered to the governor of Coahuila, who had "held it in trust" for the benefit of the tribe. Soon after news of Miles' mission reached the governor's office at Saltillo, a Mexican Indian supply commissioner suddenly appeared in Santa Rosa with five thousand dollars, which he expended in the local stores for trinkets, saddles, grain, and meat, and began distributing presents among the Kickapoo families gathered at Santa Rosa ostensibly to council with Miles on the subject of their removal to the United States. Commissioner Miles, who could bestow only promises upon the Kickapoos, observed that "it seemed strange . . . that it should so happen that this commissioner should be in Santa Rosa issuing supplies just as we were there, and it is equally miraculous that the Governor of Coahuila should discover these $10,000 lying in the treasury vaults just at the time when he must have known that our government . . . was taking steps to effect the removal of the Kickapoo from Mexican soil." Commissioner Miles concluded even before the council convened that his chances of success were very slight, since the "people of Santa Rosa . . . were decidedly opposed to the removal of the Kickapoo, giving for their reason . . . that the city of Santa Rosa and the whole community would be invaded at once by Mescalero Apaches, Lipans, and other marauding bands of Indians; that the Kickapoo were their only defense; and not only this, but . . . the Kickapoo trade was a matter of no mean importance to them."[14]

As the days passed, Kickapoo bands straggled in, and by June 15, the date set for the council, most of the Indians had reached Santa Rosa. Each arriving band received its quota of presents and

[14] *Report of the Commissioner of Indian Affairs for 1871*, 192–96.

rations from the Mexican Indian supply commissioner, along with whispered warnings of the "American plot" from local officials and merchants.[15] The chiefs and headmen were resolutely courteous to the American party, but they evidenced a growing coolness to the proposal that they return to the United States. Miles, sensing the diminishing chance for a successful mission, confided to officials in the Bureau of Indian Affairs that "we have fearful odds to work against. Therefore, don't expect too much from us. P. S. 105° in the shade makes us Northerners pant."[16]

Commissioner Miles planned to hold his council in the American camp, "under a tree." The Mexican authorities graciously offered the Santa Rosa courthouse as a meeting place. When Miles just as graciously rejected the alcalde's invitation, the mayor directed that unless the council was held in the courthouse, there would be no council. Given no choice, the American party gathered in the courtroom at Santa Rosa on June 15, 1871. The council was presided over by the alcalde and his deputies. Commissioner Miles was permitted to extend an invitation to the Mexican Kickapoos from the United States government, asking that the tribe return to the United States where a suitable home in the Indian Territory would be provided for them. The chiefs and headmen asked many questions about their proposed home, most of which Miles could answer only in general terms. Throughout the opening session the alcalde and his deputies raised questions, interrupted Miles and the chiefs, and generally succeeded in creating dissatisfaction by "misinterpretations, and evil misrepresentations, which were accepted as truth" by the impressionable Kickapoos. Little of value having been accomplished on the first day, the council was recessed until the following morning.[17]

During the night Wapakah, a band chief favorable to removal,

[15] Bliss to Adjutant General of Department of Texas, Fort Duncan, June 15, 1871, National Archives, Office of Indian Affairs, Kickapoo Agency, Letters Received, Microcopy 234, Roll 373.

[16] Miles to Hoag, Santa Rosa, June 7, 1871, National Archives, Office Indian Affairs, Kickapoo Agency, Letters Received, Microcopy 234, Roll 373.

[17] Miles to Hoag, Muscotah, Kansas, July 13, 1871, National Archives, Office of Indian Affairs, Kickapoo Agency, Letters Received, Microcopy 234, Roll 373.

came to Miles' quarters and expressed regret that the American proposal was "lost." He advised Miles to abandon his mission, for those favorable to returning to the United States were at that very moment being won over by Mexican presents and promises. Miles discovered that the presents distributed by the Mexicans during the night had included a large quantity of liquor, and by the time for the council on the following day, most of the warriors were drunk. Only a few of the chiefs were sober enough to attend the second session, and this meeting was quite brief. The chiefs thanked the American commissioners for their visit and for the invitation they carried from "the great White Father in Washington," but for various reasons they declined to accept. Smarting under their defeat at the hands of the Mexican officials and traders, the American commissioners prepared to return to the United States, disheartened at their failure but compassionate enough to note that a number of squaws and many children "had come from their camps, already packed on their ponies for the trip north, and quite disappointed" that the chiefs had decided to remain in Mexico.[18]

In summarizing the causes of the failure of his mission to the Mexican Kickapoos, Miles noted that his group had no official status, and that the alcalde of Santa Rosa had properly raised this question on many occasions. "We were intruders in a foreign country without documents to show our lawful authority for crossing the Rio Grand," the Quaker agent pointed out to officials in the Bureau of Indian Affairs, and he recommended that on the next removal attempt the State Department should be called upon to prepare the way. With documents from the secretary of state, the commissioner of Indian affairs, and the secretary of the interior endorsed by the Mexican minister, concluded Miles, the authorities at Santa Rosa would assuredly "be more cooperative."[19]

After receiving Jonathan Miles' recommendations, the secretary of the interior informed Secretary of State Hamilton Fish of the difficulties "interposed by Mexican officials" in the negotiations for

---

[18] *Report of the Commissioner of Indian Affairs for 1871,* 192–93.

[19] Miles to Hoag, Santa Rosa, June 7, 1871, National Archives, Office of Indian Affairs, Kickapoo Agency, Letters Received, Microcopy 234, Roll 373.

the removal of the Kickapoos from Mexico, and requested the active assistance of the State Department in subsequent attempts. The State Department, while willing to co-operate fully in the Kickapoo removal project, was in close touch with political conditions in the Mexican capital. And because of the revolution threatening the Juárez regime, Secretary of State Hamilton Fish, skeptical of the efficacy of an appeal to the Mexican government, reflected this doubt in his note of instructions to Thomas Nelson, United States minister to Mexico: "It is presumed that any remonstrances which may be addressed to the Mexican Government . . . would have little or no effect. You may, however, say unofficially that it may become our duty at least to weigh the expediency of pursuing the hostile Indians into Mexico, without the consent of that government, if it shall not adopt measures towards checking the robberies referred to."[20]

The War Department, gradually building up the strength of military posts on the southwestern frontier during the early 1870's, was hopeful of the success of Miles' mission, since a peaceful Kickapoo removal would free much-needed troops for other assignments. The failure of the American commissioners to induce the tribe to return to the Indian Territory made the need for an extended defense in south Texas all the more evident. Chief of Staff William Tecumseh Sherman, sensitive to the international boundary, which frustrated his cavalry in their operations against the Kickapoos on the Rio Grande, asked during August, 1871, that the State Department apply to the Mexican government for permission for United States troops to cross the Rio Grande when in "hot pursuit" of Kickapoo war parties. This request the Mexican government promptly rejected.[21]

Minister Thomas Nelson continued to seek the assistance of the Mexican government in removing the Kickapoos, and repeatedly he suggested the alternative of permitting United States troops to

[20] Fish to Nelson, Washington, June 26, 1871, 45 Cong., 2 sess., *House Report No. 701*, 204.

[21] Davis to Nelson, Washington, August 7, 1871, 45 Cong., 2 sess., *House Report No. 701*, 204–205.

enter Mexico when in pursuit of the hostiles. Governmental turmoil during the early 1870's had caused a number of shifts in the Mexican cabinet which made Nelson's task of communicating the American protests and proposals concerning the Mexican Kickapoos more than trying. Stability was restored in part during the summer of 1871 when Ignacio Mariscal became minister of foreign affairs. In a belated reply to Minister Nelson's many notes on the subject of the Kickapoo war on Texas, Mariscal claimed that he had not been informed of improper interference in the Miles mission by local authorities at Santa Rosa, but he promised to prevent, if possible, any similar intervention on the part of government officials in the future. He assured Nelson that the Mexican government would present no obstacle to the enactment of a "humane and peaceful policy" toward the Mexican Kickapoos. Mariscal promised Nelson that he would confer with President Juárez on the most feasible method of aiding the United States in removing the Kickapoos, and expressed the opinion that since the Mexican presidential election was over, "there would be no great difficulty in procuring the sanction of Congress to an act authorizing the passage" of American troops across the Mexican boundary in chastizing Kickapoo war parties. Interestingly, Mariscal added that while the Mexican government lacked the power "without the authority of Congress, to permit the entrance of foreign troops" into Mexico, yet, "if it should become an imperious necessity" for United States troops "to pursue savage and hostile Indians . . . into Mexico," Mariscal assured Nelson "unofficially, that the Mexican government, in his opinion, would not seriously complain."[22]

A grim mockery of these efforts to stop the Kickapoo war on Texas was that tribal raids north of the Rio Grande increased after the failure of the Miles mission. Texas demands for relief increased in proportion to the fury of the new assaults from Coahuila. Texas newspapers, becoming increasingly strident in their demands that the "Kickapoo scourge" be destroyed, were bitterly critical of the Mexican government for its innocous Indian policy and for har-

[22] Nelson to Fish, Mexico City, August 30, 1871, 45 Cong., 2 sess., *House Report No. 701*, 205–206.

boring and protecting "the enemies of Texas." The venerable Benito Juárez, revolutionary leader and president of the Republic after the Maximilian era, died in July, 1872. In spite of efforts by Porfirio Díaz to succeed to the Mexican presidency, Sebastián Lerdo de Tejada was installed as Juárez' successor. The ambitious Díaz led revolutionary activity in various Mexican states and was constantly on the watch for an excuse to overthrow the anxious and wavering Lerdo regime. Officials of the new administration were therefore irritatingly evasive in dealing with the demands from the American State Department that United States troops be permitted to enter Mexico in pursuit of the Kickapoos. The Lerdo administration was also resentful of the bitter criticism it received from Texas newspapers for its alleged failure to act decisively to stop the Coahuila-based Kickapoo war. In an attempt to quiet the rising tide of criticism and to rationalize its position, the Mexican government during 1872 organized the Rio Grande Commission and sent it north to investigate the many charges made against the Kickapoos and the local government officials and businessmen. After months of investigations along the Rio Grande, the Mexican Commission reported that the American charges of official complicity with Indian raids on Texas were "preposterous and utterly false." The Kickapoos in Coahuila were exonerated of any blame for the alleged war on Texas. The Mexican Commission charged all depredations in Texas to the Comanches and other tribes of the north, as well as to Texas desperadoes and cattle rustlers who attacked Texas communities disguised as Kickapoo Indians.[23]

The findings of the Mexican Rio Grande Commission increased the skepticism among officials in the American government concerning the intentions and ability of the Mexican government to deal with the Kickapoo problem. Secretary of State Hamilton Fish, observing that as late as January, 1873, the Kickapoo war on Texas still raged, reflected this doubt in a note to Minister Nelson: "The Federal Government of that republic appears to be so apathetic on this subject, or so powerless to prevent such raids, that sooner or

[23] *Report of the Committee of Investigation, Sent in 1873 by the Government to the Frontier of Texas.*

234

later this governmnent will have no other alternative than to endeavor to secure quiet on the frontier by seeking the marauders and punishing them in their haunts, wherever these may be. Of course we would prefer that this should be with the consent, if not with the cooperation, of Mexico. It is certain, however, that if the grievance shall be persisted in, the remedy adverted to will not remain untried. It is not, however, expected, that for the present at least, you will make a formal representation . . . to this effect."[24]

Minister Nelson was, however, soon requested to obtain clearance and credentials for a new American commissioner assigned to attempt the peaceful removal of the Kickapoos from Coahuila to the Indian Territory. While these preparations were being made by the Bureau of Indian Affairs, another branch of the United States government—the War Department—thoroughly unco-ordinated but equally as desperate, was planning its own solution for the Kickapoo problem. To the army planners the "imperious necessity" mentioned by Ignacio Mariscal existed, and the task of defeating the Kickapoos in their Mexican lair was assigned to the daring and resourceful Colonel Ranald Mackenzie.

[24] Fish to Nelson, Washington, January 16, 1873, 45 Cong., 2 sess., *House Report No. 701,* 214.

18

The Mackenzie Raid

THE YEAR 1873 was one of drastic change for the Kickapoos. These Indians had resisted for several hundred years the attempts of the French, the British, the Spaniards, and the Americans to subjugate them. The United States, sometimes using subtle and peaceful methods, but more often resorting to overt martial activity, had overwhelmed most of the tribes of North America. These tribes, drastically reduced in population and unable to maintain the tribal traditions, had succumbed to reservation life by 1870. The Kickapoos (Kennekuk's band excepted) continued to defy the United States, and opposed with savage vehemence the nation's Indian policy, which offered a choice between reservation life and annihilation.

Having successfully resisted American control for almost a century, the Southern Kickapoos were suddenly turned out of their Nacimiento home by an invading (and trespassing) American force. The return to the United States marked the end of their historic, savagely won freedom and the beginning of the reservation life they had scorned for so many years. The circumstances which brought about this revolution in Kickapoo tribal history were produced in Washington, where two divergent programs for handling the "Indian Problem" were in operation—the "Force Policy" of the War Department and the "Peace Policy" of the Bureau of Indian Affairs. Ironically enough, emissaries of both factions reached the Mexican Kickapoos at virtually the same time.

During the early spring of 1873, Thomas Nelson, United States minister to Mexico, advised Mexican Minister of Foreign Affairs Lafragua that the American government, through the Bureau of Indian Affairs, planned to send a second mission to the Mexican Kickapoos to promote the peaceful removal of the Texas marauders to the United States. Since special agents would be appointed to carry out this assignment during the month of May, Nelson asked that the Mexican government "take such measures as will not merely prevent the recurrence of that interference of the local authorities of Coahuila" which frustrated the efforts of Miles' mission in 1871, "but will throw the moral and material weight" of the Mexican government behind the project.[1]

Upon receiving assurance from Lafragua of unlimited co-operation, the Bureau of Indian Affairs made final plans for the mission to Coahuila.[2] Henry M. Atkinson of Brownsville, Nebraska, and F. G. Williams of San Antonio, Texas, were named special commissioners to negotiate for the removal of the Kickapoos to the Indian Territory. The commissioners were to establish contact with the commandant at Fort Duncan, and if they were successful in persuading the Kickapoos to return to the Indian Territory, the post commandant was to provide a military escort across Texas. Atkinson and Williams were to deliver all transit Kickapoos to Warren's Station in the Leased District, where a special agent would be waiting to take charge. The sum of ten thousand dollars was deposited for use by the commissioners in gathering and subsisting the Indians in Mexico preparatory to conducting them across the Rio Grande, and an additional two thousand dollars was provided for presents to be distributed "among the most influential . . . Indians."[3] The American commissioners carried credentials from the Mexican minister in Washington authorizing their mission and calling on the governor of Coahuila to give them every assistance.

[1] Nelson to Lafragua, Mexico City, April 22, 1873, 45 Cong., 2 sess., *House Report No. 701*, 215–16.

[2] *Ibid.*, 216–16.

[3] Commissioner of Indian Affairs to Atkinson, Washington, March 31, 1873, National Archives, Indian Office Letterbook No. 112.

The Bureau of Indian Affairs carefully planned this second removal attempt, and every effort was made to avoid the mistakes evident in the Miles mission of 1871.

While these elaborate preparations were being made to arrange for the peaceful removal of the Mexican Kickapoos to the United States, preparations of a different sort were being made by the United States Army. Colonel Ranald S. Mackenzie, fresh from his dazzling victories in the north over the Comanches, had been ordered to the Rio Grande during the early spring of 1873 with his famous Fourth Cavalry to smash the seemingly invincible Kickapoos. Establishing his command headquarters at Fort Clark just above Eagle Pass, Mackenzie set up a special training camp near Bracketville, where his hardy troopers of the Fourth were bivouacked.

During April, 1873, General Philip Henry Sheridan, commander of the Department of Missouri, and Secretary of War William Belknap arrived at Fort Clark for a secret three-day council with Colonel Mackenzie. According to Captain R. G. Carter, Mackenzie's adjutant, the sessions were largely devoted to outlining strategy for the Kickapoo campaign. The climax of the council occurred when Sheridan pointed out that Mackenzie had been ordered to the Rio Grande to relieve General Wesley Merritt and the Ninth Cavalry and to bring the Kickapoo war on Texas to a close. Sheridan was reported to have directed Mackenzie "to *control* and *hold down* the situation, and to *do it in your own way*. I want you to be bold, enterprising, and . . . when you begin, to let it be a campaign of *annihilation, obliteration* and *complete destruction*. . . . I think you understand what I want done, and the way in which you should employ your force." Mackenzie, according to Carter, then inquired upon what authority he was to act, and Sheridan replied "Damn the *orders!* Damn the *authority!* You are to go ahead on your own plan of action, and your authority and backing shall be General Grant and myself. With us behind you in whatever you do to clean up this situation, you can rest assured of the fullest support."[4]

[4] R. G. Carter, *On the Border with Mackenzie,* 422–23.

After the departure of Sheridan and Belknap, Mackenzie's Bracketville camp became a beehive of preparation for one of the most daring exploits in the annals of southwestern Indian warfare. The campaign was astutely planned and was carried out with a machine-like precision which delighted the military tacticians; it was an operation which turned the tide of the Kickapoo war on Texas and resulted in the return of most of the Mexican Kickapoos to the Indian Territory.

Cavalry mounts were pampered to allow them to build up flesh and recuperate from the arduous Comanche campaigns. Pack mules received the same attention. Saddles and pack gear were inspected and repaired where necessary. The troopers drilled daily and were "subjected to the most rigid discipline," including daily carbine practice. Simulated field operations were carried out with "company, platoon, and every movement in column and in line, mounted and dismounted . . . thoroughly worked out, especially rapid fighting on foot and to the right and left."[5] Carter "was especially directed to see in as quiet a way as possible that all sabres in the command were ground to a *razor edge*. This stunt was a very great 'puzzler' " to all the men and they complained of "such a fool proposition . . . for we had never, thus far, *carried such encumbrances as sabres on an ordinary Indian campaign.*"[6]

While the men of the Fourth Cavalry speculated on the mission for which they were making such extreme preparations, only Colonel Mackenzie and Captain Carter knew the true purpose of the intensive training, and each kept his secret until the regiment was well into Coahuila. That this was to be no "ordinary Indian campaign" was evidenced by the long hours Colonel Mackenzie devoted to map study, and briefing by his scouts, and by the watchful eye he kept on the Fourth Cavalry as the unit sharpened its tactical skill, endurance, and discipline.

Near the Kickapoo villages at Nacimiento was a Negro community with its population made up of the descendants of former Creek and Seminole slaves, locally called Muscogees, who were the

5 *Ibid.*, 425.
6 *Ibid.*, 427.

residue of the Wildcat colony of the 1850's.[7] The Kickapoos held these Negroes in contempt, and there was bad blood between the two communities. Therefore, when Colonel Mackenzie established contact with the Negro leaders for the purpose of recruiting spies to watch the Kickapoo villages, the Muscogees welcomed the opportunity to inform on their insolent Indian neighbors. Additional information for the regiment's future mission came to Colonel Mackenzie from his three scouts. Ike Cox, the post guide at Fort Duncan, teamed with Green Van and Art McLain, local ranchers who had suffered heavy losses from repeated Kickapoo depredations and who were well acquainted with the country north and south of the Rio Grande. The three worked for weeks scouting the country south of the Rio Grande for Mackenzie, and preparing rough sketch maps of trails and river fords, as well as the location, layout, and strength of the Kickapoo villages. These sketches and notes Mackenzie and Carter studied carefully, so that the Fourth could travel steadily at night "with nothing but stars for points of direction."

On the night of May 16, 1873, the Fourth Cavalry settled to a weary sleep after a long, tiring day of drill, inspections, and simulated attack patterns. A few minutes before midnight Ike Cox rode into Fort Duncan. Arousing Colonel Mackenzie, Cox reported that Muscogee spies had relayed to his post the news that during the day the entire Kickapoo warrior force had left the Nacimiento villages, riding west.[8] By two o'clock in the morning a courier from Fort Duncan had reached the Bracketville bivouac to rouse the men with orders to pack and saddle up immediately. By the light of "crackling campfires" the Fourth Cavalry packed, stood inspection, and by early dawn had moved out to rendezvous with Colonel Mackenzie on the Rio Grande. Waiting for the cover of night to ford the river, the entire column of six companies, amounting to nearly four hundred men, crossed on a ford near El Moral at eight o'clock on the evening of May 17.[9]

[7] Ritzenthaler and Peterson, *The Mexican Kickapoo Indians,* 19.

[8] Mackenzie to Adjutant General, Fort Clark, May 23, 1873, National Archives, Office of Indian Affairs, Kickapoo Agency, Letters Received, Microcopy 234, Roll 374.

240

A Kickapoo war club, about 33½ inches in length.

NIGANITHAT, or He Who Flies First,
a member of the Kickapoo delegation to Washington, April, 1895.
From a painting by Dinwiddie.

Avoiding the better-known trails in order to escape detection, scouts Cox, Van, and McLain led the Fourth along faint game runs, cattle paths, and mule trails which wound through dense cane-brakes and chaparral, up and down rocky mountain ravines, and over brief desert flats. The objective, known only to Mackenzie and Carter, was to strike the Kickapoo villages at dawn. Mackenzie's scouts had checked the distance on their crude maps and had found that the best possible route required a brisk seventy-mile ride in the time allotted.[10] The cavalry set a faster pace than the heavily laden mule train could match, and on several occasions during the early part of the night's ride, the horsemen had to pause to allow the pack train to catch up. Both Mackenzie and Carter knew that speed would give them the advantage of surprise in a dawn assault, and after a number of frustrating halts, Carter proposed that the packs be cut from the mules and abandoned. Mackenzie agreed and directed Carter to notify the troop commanders that the column would halt for "just five minutes to cut the packs loose," adding that the men were to fill their pockets with hard biscuits from the abandoned packs.

This accomplished, the column moved forward at a steady pace. Carter recalled that "sleep almost overpowered us, and yet, on, on we went. Conversation had long ago begun to lag. Nothing was heard save the ceaseless pounding of the horses and the jingle of the steel equipment."[11] At false dawn the Fourth Cavalry had reached a crucial landmark on their mission—the Remolino, a stream that flowed past the Kickapoo villages on its upper fork. The troopers dismounted and quenched their thirst and that of their mounts in the cool pools. Saddles were checked, girths were tightened, the column was given a rapid inspection, and all was ready for the charge. As the troopers moved slowly up the stream bed in the full light of early dawn, using the high banks for cover, the scouts suddenly paused to confer with Mackenzie, and in seconds runners were moving along the column with instructions to

[9] Carter, *op. cit.*, 429.
[10] Philip H. Sheridan, *Records of Engagements with Hostile Indians*, 35.
[11] Carter, *op. cit.*, 436.

"form platoons" and "prepare to charge." Moving out of the stream bed, the Fourth Cavalry struck formation for the assault on the Kickapoo villages, visible a mile away. Front to rear the orders— "Gallop! March! *Charge!*"—rang out.

And then there burst forth such a cheering and yelling from our gallant little column as that Kickapoo village never heard before. It was caught up from troop to troop and struck such dismay in the Indians' hearts that they were seen flying in every direction. The distance was nearly a mile over fairly open but rough ground. Our reserve ammunition was neither carried on the pack mules, with a possible loss by stampede, nor in the saddle pockets on the horses, as was done by Custer in the Battle of Little Big Horn, and captured by the Indians when the dismounted men became separated from their mounts, but on the persons of the troopers *safely stowed in the pockets of their blouses.* Although it was an uncomfortable burden, Mackenzie, as a successful Indian fighter never took any doubtful chances in action with such a slippery enemy who always took advantage of any culpable errors. Our formation for the charge was in columns of platoons. The order was for the leading platoon to deliver its fire by volley, then wheel to the right, turning back and up the length of the villages again; each succeeding platoon to do the same from the front to rear of the column, and then reloading and falling in rear, still continue following down the length of the three villages. The leading platoons of 'I' Troop were to pursue the fleeing Indians out to open ground, and through and beyond the lodges. . . . I had witnessed the battle of Upperville, Va., during the Civil War . . . between the Cavalry Corps of the two armies under Generals Alfred Pleasanton and J. E. B. Stuart, on June 22, 1863. . . . I saw many charges . . . during that day, but I never saw such a magnificent charge as that made by those six troops of the Fourth U. S. Cavalry on the morning of May 18, 1873, at Rey Molina, Mexico.[12]

The Kickapoo villages, undefended—the warriors having departed the day before—were caught completely by surprise. The Indian population, women, children, and old men, was panic-stricken, but even they fought like demons when the terror of the surprise assault passed. Rushing to the thickets and brush-choked

[12] *Ibid.,* 440–41.

ravines on the edge of the villages with whatever weapons they could lay their hands on, the Indians defended themselves as best they could from the probing sallies of "I" Troop.[13] After the first charge a detail of troops prepared long grass tapers, ignited them, and ran through the streets firing the lodges. In a matter of minutes the Kickapoo villages were a shambles, "the fierce crackling of the flames mingling strangely with loud reports of carbines, sharp crack of rifles, cheers and yells. The destruction was complete."[14]

Methodically the troopers hunted out the hiding Indians, killed those who resisted, and took prisoner the more placid ones. Captain Carter, in charge of the prisoner detail, recalled that in a thicket on the creek bank he "witnessed one of those most singular and pitiable spectacles incident to Indian warfare. A small but faithful cur dog was at the entrance of what appeared to be a cave far under the bank of the stream, savagely meancing our advance. Near him . . . seemed to be more bodies. It was necessary to kill the dog before we could proceed further. The men reaching in, then drew forth two small children, respectively two and four years of age, badly shot through their bodies. One was dead, the other nearly so. Opening the bush still further for more revelations, way in the rear we saw the form of a young squaw, apparently unhurt, but badly frightened. Her black, glittering eyes were fastened upon the group of blue-coated soldiers with a fascinating stare, not unlike that of a snake, expressing half fear, half hatred and defiance. We made signs for her to come out, but, as she refused, she was quietly, and without harm, dragged forth. We thought this was all, but almost covered up under the immense flags, we found a third child, a girl of about twelve, badly wounded."[15]

Mackenzie's secret mission had been accomplished, and "ruin and desolation now marked the spot—a cyclone could not have made more havoc or a cleaner sweep" where scarcely an hour before had stood the prosperous villages of the Mexican Kickapoos.

[13] Mackenzie to Adjutant General, Fort Clark, May 23, 1873, National Archives, Office of Indian Affairs, Kickapoo Agency, Letters Received, Microcopy 234, Roll 374.

[14] Carter, *op. cit.*, 442.

[15] *Ibid.*, 443.

Fearing an early return of the warriors, the Fourth Cavalry gathered up forty women and children, mounted them on ponies captured from the many horseherds that grazed near the villages, and beat a hasty retreat to the Rio Grande. The officers urged greater speed from the column, but just as the mule train had slowed the pace the day before, the Kickapoo prisoners reduced the pace of the Fourth Cavalry on the return trip.[16]

The captives were mounted two or three on a horse, and toward morning of May 19, the column stopped a number of times to pick up children who had fallen asleep and rolled off the horses onto the trail. Finally the order was sent down to secure the captives, and each prisoner was tied to his horse, some bound two and three together. The anxious column finally reached the Rio Grande and safety at dawn on May 19, 1873. As they prepared to ford the river, Captain Carter noted that while the cavalrymen had suffered almost beyond endurance from the expedition, the prisoners probably had suffered even more, for their condition "was pitiful in the extreme. They had been riding, lashed on the captured ponies, doubled up and by threes. The children, half naked and streaked with dust and sweat, deprived, by being bound, even of the privilege of lying down upon their ponies' necks, were fast asleep, their black heads and swarthy skins presenting a striking contrast to the blue-coated troopers who surrounded them."[17]

Mackenzie feared an attempt by massed Kickapoo war parties to recover the Indian women and children, and to reduce the hazard, he rushed the captives to military headquarters at San Antonio under strong military escort.[18] After a brief rest in the stockade at San Antonio, where they were permitted to recuperate from the ordeal of their journey, the captives were sent to Fort Gibson in the Indian Territory as "prisoners of war," and despite efforts

[16] Mackenzie to Adjutant General, Fort Clark, May 23, 1873, National Archives, Office of Indian Affairs, Kickapoo Agency, Letters Received, Microcopy 234, Roll 374.

[17] Carter, *op. cit.*, 451–54.

[18] Mackenzie to Adjutant General, Fort Clark, May 23, 1873, National Archives, Office of Indian Affairs, Kickapoo Agency, Letters Received, Microcopy 234, Roll 374.

of the Bureau of Indian Affairs to obtain custody, the War Department refused to surrender them.[19]

In his official report on the Kickapoo raid, Mackenzie described the "sharp skirmish" the Fourth Cavalry experienced in accomplishing their mission, and the Colonel heaped praise on his troopers for their "bravery." It is surprising that the gallant Mackenzie, who struck the Kickapoo villages only after his scouts reported that the Kickapoo warriors had departed, would dignify his official report of the raid with the claim of a "sharp skirmish" and cite the "bravery" of the troopers, especially when their only antagonists were women, children, and a few old men able to inflict only three slight wounds on the ranks of the Fourth Cavalry.[20]

On May 18, 1873, the very day the Fourth Cavalry smashed the Kickapoo villages at Nacimiento—an overt expression of the United States "Force Policy"—a United States Commission from the Bureau of Indian Affairs, seeking to apply the "Peace Policy," had arrived in Saltillo, capital city of Coahuila, and was waiting for an audience with Governor Cepeda. The American commissioners, Henry M. Atkinson and F. G. Williams, presented their credentials and were cordially received by Governor Cepeda, who promised to render every assistance in removing the Kickapoos and issued a call to all citizens of Coahuila to co-operate.[21]

From Saltillo, Atkinson and Williams journeyed north to Santa Rosa to begin negotiations with the Kickapoo chiefs for removal to the Indian Territory. When they arrived in Santa Rosa, the American commissioners found the townspeople in a high state of excitement and alarm. News had just come in of Colonel Mackenzie's raid on the Kickapoo villages. The citizens, fearful of an attack by the United States Army, were suspicious of Atkinson and

[19] Upshaw to Adjutant General, Fort Gibson, July 24, 1873, National Archives, Fort Gibson Letterbook for 1873, Adjutant General's Office.

[20] Mackenzie to Adjutant General, Fort Clark, May 23, 1873, National Archives, Office of Indian Affairs, Kickapoo Agency, Letters Aeceived, Microcopy 234, Roll 374.

[21] Atkinson to Commissioner of Indian Affairs, Saltillo, May 19, 1873, National Archives, Office of Indian Affairs, Kickapoo Agency, Letters Received, Microcopy 234, Roll 374.

Williams, believing them to be American agents sent to spy on them. The commissioners were in the town for several days before the townspeople would even talk with them. After repeated inquiry, Atkinson and Williams finally learned that Indian messengers had reached the warriors and that they had returned to the ruins of their villages. Collecting the women, children, and old people who were still in hiding, the Kickapoos had divided into small bands, and fearing another attack by the Americans, had scattered over Coahuila and Chihuahua. After several unsuccessful attempts, the American commissioners finally were able to establish contact with a small Kickapoo band headed by Chequamkako.

The chief, understandably shy and suspicious, came in when he was offered gifts and food for his people. Mackenzie's troopers had burned the tribe's store of provisions, and the Indians were in dire straits. But when the rations were issued, resentful citizens from Santa Rosa warned the hungry Kickapoos not to eat the American food because it was poisoned. Only after Atkinson and Williams ate of the issued rations would the suspicious Indians accept the food gifts. After the band had been fed for several days, Chequamkako gradually warmed to the American commissioners, especially when Atkinson promised him fifteen hundred dollars for his assistance in bringing in the scattered bands and using his influence to promote the removal of the tribe to the United States. Thereafter Chequamkako became the firm ally of Atkinson and worked hard to make the removal attempt a success.[22]

Chequamkako's band numbered only about sixty, but the Kickapoo population in the American camp gradually increased to about three hundred as hungry bands came in, largely through the influence of Chequamkako, to draw rations from the American commissioners. On June 1, Atkinson held his first council with the Mexican Kickapoos and presented the invitation of the United States government that the tribe accept a new home in the Indian Territory. The American commissioners were helped considerably by Alfredo

[22] Atkinson to Commissioner of Indian Affairs, Washington, July 9, 1874, National Archives, Office of Indian Affairs, Kickapoo Agency, Letters Received, Microcopy 234, Roll 374.

Montero, Governor Cepeda's personal deputy, who had been sent to Santa Rosa to assist in promoting the removal. Montero arrived shortly before the council, and he warned that any Mexican citizen who interfered in any way with the removal negotiations would be arrested. The American commissioners had the highest praise for Montero, noting that he worked honestly and faithfully for the removal of the Kickapoos and that the United States could not "attach any blame to him or his government should we fail in our mission." Montero also addressed the council and strongly urged the Kickapoo chiefs to lead their people to the new home in the Indian Territory. In spite of Montero's warning, local businessmen, whose trade would suffer if the Kickapoos returned to the United States, circulated among the Indian camps at night, warning the warriors that if they dared cross the Rio Grande, they would be killed as soon as they entered Texas. The Kickapoo chiefs responded to Atkinson's proposal with a reminder that the tribe had been attacked by Texans when they had crossed the state some years earlier, and that recently innocent women and children had been killed and many taken prisoner by the United States troops. The chiefs closed their presentation with a unanimous statement that until the captives were returned, "they would not talk about returning to the United States." In his report on this initial council with the Mexican Kickapoos, Atkinson confided to the commissioner of Indian affairs that he did not "believe the Indians would go through Texas, if they go at all," adding that he could not "tell yet what effect the raid by Mackenzie will have but at present it appears to be the chief obstacle in the way of our success."[23]

Most of the Kickapoos who had gathered at Santa Rosa to attend Atkinson's council were in some way or another related to Mackenzie's captives, and the safe return of the prisoners seemed to be their major concern. After several days of fruitless negotiation, Atkinson concluded that the only way he could persuade the Mexican Kickapoos to remain in Santa Rosa and confer on the removal

[23] Atkinson to Commissioner of Indian Affairs, Santa Rosa, June 1, 1873, National Archives, Office of Indian Affairs, Kickapoo Agency, Letters Received, Microcopy 234, Roll 374.

proposal was to first consider the subject of the captives and their return. There was still much mourning in the Kickapoo camps for the women and children slain in Mackenzie's surprise attack, and grief and anxiety for the captives, strongly evident among the squaws, was noticeable among the warriors, too. Convinced that the American mission to the Mexican Kickapoos—that of persuading the tribe to abandon Coahuila and return with the commissioners to the United States—was deadlocked until the status of the captives was determined, Atkinson proposed to the assembled chiefs that he journey to San Antonio for the purpose of negotiating with the United States Army for the return of the women and children. The Kickapoo chiefs agreed and selected Chequamkako to accompany Atkinson, promising the American commissioners that they would keep their people in Santa Rosa until the commissioners returned, and pledging that if the captives were returned to them in Santa Rosa in good condition, the tribal council would consider very favorably the invitation to return to the United States. Atkinson, accompanied by Chequamkako and Alfredo Montero, hastened to San Antonio to negotiate for the return of the Kickapoo captives.

Atkinson's conference with General Augur, commandant of the Department of Texas, was disappointing, and the American mission to the Mexican Kickapoos seemed doomed to certain failure. Not only did the army refuse to turn over the captives to Atkinson, but the War Department had ordered the captives transferred to Fort Gibson in the Indian Territory and refused to transfer the Kickapoo "prisoners of war" to the custody of the Bureau of Indian Affairs until the Kickapoos in Mexico had arrived in the Indian Territory.[24]

Dreading to return to Santa Rosa with these gloomy tidings, Atkinson squarely faced the task of finding some other means of persuading the Mexican Kickapoos to return to the United States. Recalling the strong affection of the Kickapoo warriors for their

[24] Atkinson to Commissioner of Indian Affairs, San Antonio, June 15, 1873, National Archives, Office of Indian Affairs, Kickapoo Agency, Letters Received, Microcopy 234, Roll 374.

women and children, he reasoned that the Army's custody of the captives could be turned to advantage by the American commissioners, for the captives, if properly exploited, could be the "bait" to lure the entire tribe to the Indian Territory. The chiefs' threat that unless the captives were returned to Santa Rosa soon, the bands would scatter again and forever abandon negotiations with the United States on removal to the Indian Territory appeared to Atkinson to be a bluff.

Atkinson became more convinced of the wisdom of this approach when he recalled that the major reason the bands collected to council with him in the first place was not the rations and gifts—although these influenced the Indians somewhat—but the fact that the American commission was the tribe's only link with the wives and children held as "prisoners of war" by the United States Army. Atkinson therefore decided to make it completely clear to the Mexican Kickapoos that while the captives would be returned, the restoration would be on United States terms, not Kickapoo terms; in other words the only way the women and children could rejoin their grieving husbands, fathers, mothers, and other relatives was for the Mexican Kickapoos to return to the Indian Territory, where the reunion would take place. Atkinson planned to place his emphasis not on whether or not they would return, but on how soon the journey could take place and the preparations which must be made. Atkinson also recalled that his substantial gift to Chief Chequamkako had helped greatly in winning the support and active assistance of this tribal leader, reasoning that if a leading chief were susceptible to material persuasion, lesser chiefs and warriors must have their price also. The ten-thousand-dollar appropriation to pay for gathering and subsisting the Mexican Kickapoos preparatory to removal was nearly gone, and the two-thousand-dollar allocation for presents for "the most influential Indians" had long since been spent, fifteen hundred dollars going to Chequamkako.

Nearly out of ration money and faced with a Congress slow to appropriate the additional fifteen thousand dollars he had requested, the resourceful Atkinson called on a fellow townsman and close friend of Commissioner Williams, C. W. Brackenridge, president of the Bank of San Antonio. Brackenridge, like other leading businessmen of south Texas, was anxious to see the Kickapoos removed to the Indian Territory and agreed to advance Atkinson the fifteen thousand dollars interest free, to be repaid from the expected congressional appropriation. The United States controller telegraphed approval for this transaction, and the chances of a removal seemed brighter. Atkinson, through the good offices of Brackenridge, next established credit at a number of San Antonio stores for future purchases.[25]

Commissioner Atkinson returned to Santa Rosa, convened the Kickapoo council, bluntly presented the only way in which the captives could be restored to their families, and then began to discuss the many presents he planned to buy for those who agreed to follow him to the United States. He asked the chiefs and headmen to plan carefully with him on the needs of the tribe for the long journey. Having already promised Chequamkako fifteen hundred dollars, Atkinson had private talks with Chiefs Thahpequah and Wahpesee and promised each of them one thousand dollars in cash and five hundred dollars in presents for their support. For each of the lesser chiefs he pledged one hundred dollars in cash.[26]

Overwhelmed by Atkinson's promises and longing to be reunited with their people at Fort Gibson, the three hundred Mexican Kickapoos at Santa Rosa began to prepare for their migration to the Indian Territory. Made destitute by the destruction of their tools, weapons, utensils, food stores, clothing, and blankets in the Mackenzie raid, the Mexican Kickapoos had to be completely supplied for the trip to the Indian Territory. During early August heavy shipments of goods began arriving at Santa Rosa, supplied by San Antonio merchants on the credit extended to commissioners Atkinson and Williams. On August 26, 1873, just before the Mexican

<hr />

[25] Atkinson to Commissioner of Indian Affairs, San Antonio, September 13, 1873, National Archives, Office of Indian Affairs, Kickapoo Agency, Letters Received, Microcopy 234, Roll 374.

[26] Atkinson to Commissioner of Indian Affairs, Washington, July 9, 1874, National Archives, Office of Indian Affairs, Kickapoo Agency, Letters Received, Microcopy 234, Roll 374.

Kickapoos departed for the Indian Territory, well over eight thousand dollars worth of rations, weapons, riding gear, and utensils were issued to them. The supply included an arsenal of weapons, more than were necessary for mere hunting, and this can possibly be explained by the warriors' determination to have the means to defend themselves against possible attacks by the Texans and the United States Army. The inventory list shows that Atkinson issued to the Kickapoos 53 Colt revolvers; 20 Kentucky rifles; 50 Enfield rifles; 4 Spencer carbines; 1 pistol, holster, and belt; 13 Winchester carbines; 300 gun tubes; 100 pounds of powder; 300 pounds of lead; 50 pounds of buckshot; 200 boxes of percussion caps; 5,000 Winchester cartridges; 4,000 Enfield cartridges; 600 Spencer cartridges; 160 hatchets; 301 butcher knives; 104 Texas saddles; 100 pairs of spurs; 150 riding bridles; 180 saddle girths; 34 pairs of stirrup straps; 4 fancy saddles for chiefs; 50 yards of German silver plate; 150 brass kettles; 5 dozen covered canteens; 600 tin cups; 3 dozen coffeepots; 6 dozen frying pans; 3 Mexican ropes; 21 pounds of soap; 1 fancy blanket; 12 yards of calico; and 1 pound of sassafras.

Atkinson purchased twelve thousand dollars worth of provisions for the trip, including 22 sacks of coffee; 1,000 pounds of salt; 157 beeves; 8,000 pounds of sugar; 251 sacks of flour; 1,150 bushels of corn; 15,000 pounds of bacon; 36 boxes of tobacco (800 pounds); 4 bales of leaf tobacco (400 pounds); 4 barrels of molasses; 6 barrels of crackers; and 8 boxes of assorted candy (400 pounds). To provide transportation, the American commissioners paid another twelve thousand dollars for horses and mules, which included one hundred "average" horses, one hundred "average" mules, and "three horses extra fine for the chiefs, and three jack asses extra fine" also for the chiefs.[27]

Armed, provisioned, and mounted, 317 Mexican Kickapoos broke camp for the last time at Santa Rosa on the morning of

[27] "Special Issue to Mexican Kickapoo Inventory List, Remolino, August 26, 1873," National Archives, Office of Indian Affairs, Kickapoo Agency, Letters Received, Microcopy 234, Roll 374.

August 28, 1873, and headed northwest.[28] While their ultimate destination was the Indian Territory, the tribe remembered well the difficulties of earlier attempts to cross Texas. Escorted by United States commissioners Atkinson and Williams, the long column of Indians followed an itinerary that would place them far to the west of the settled areas beyond the Rio Grande. This circuitous route, checked each day by scouts, made their journey to the Indian Territory longer by well over a month, but safer. Moving first in a northwesterly direction, the Kickapoos forded the Rio Grande west of the mouth of the Pecos, then struck due north, and on December 1, 1873, the advance party, consisting of Chief Wahpesee and six warriors, reached Fort Sill to report that the trip had been safe and their people were fifty miles southwest.[29]

The main Kickapoo force arrived at Fort Sill on December 20. After a council with Atkinson at the Kiowa-Comanche Agency, Wahpesee and Thahpequah led the 317 Kickapoos to the upper Washita. There they erected winter lodges, welcomed the captives, and awaited the spring, when tribal leaders would decide upon a permanent home in the Indian Territory.

[28] Upshaw to Commissioner of Indian Affairs, Fort Gibson, November 4, 1873, National Archives, Fort Gibson Letterbook for 1873, Adjutant General's Office.

[29] Atkinson to Commissioner of Indian Affairs, Fort Sill, December 2, 1873, National Archives, Office of Indian Affairs, Kickapoo Agency, Letters Received, Microcopy 234, Roll 374.

19

A New Home

THE SOUTHERN KICKAPOOS were among the last of the Indian tribes of North America to accept a reservation in the Indian Territory. Commissioner Henry Atkinson probably could not have induced the 317 warriors, women, and children to accompany him across the Rio Grande and into the Indian Territory had it not been for the Mackenzie raid. Most of the Kickapoos who returned with Atkinson were related in some way to the captives, who were being held as "prisoners of war" at Fort Gibson by the United States Army, and it was the attraction of kinship more than anything else that finally caused about half of the Southern Kickapoos to abandon their exciting life in Coahuila and join their loved ones on a reservation in the United States.

The reservation era for the Southern Kickapoos extended from 1874 to 1895. During the stormy twenty-one-year period the United States government sought to transform these proud, insolent people from resourceful, arrogant raiders into co-operative, complacent wards. Probably no other tribe in the history of American Indian policy caused as much difficulty for Indian agents as the Kickapoos, for they persistently resisted civilizing attempts and remained unequivocally unchanged at the end of the reservation period. The Quaker Agents, supporters of the "Peace Policy," were full of patience, good will, and trust, and were excited at the prospect of turning the former "Lords of the middle border" into civilized, educated, peaceful Christian Indians. Their optimism was reflected by Quaker leader Enoch Hoag, head of the Central Superintendency, in a letter of January 20, 1874, to the commissioner of Indian affairs: "The Mexican Kickapoo, late depredators and raiders for a long period on the border of Mexico are now ready to settle down after the example of the Kansas Kickapoo who are self-supporting. The Mexican Kickapoo should have homes opened for all heads of families, grounds plowed, fenced, and cultivated, and a supply of necessary implements at an early day, and their children provided with schools, looking to early self-support."[1]

The first problem facing Bureau of Indian Affairs officials, when they learned that about half of the Mexican Kickapoos were en route to the United States, was to select a suitable reservation for the tribe. With characteristic efficiency the Quaker agents looked over the available areas. Their first thought was to locate the immigrants in Kansas with the Northern Kickapoos. This reservation, assigned the entire tribe by the Treaty of Castor Hill in 1832, had been drastically reduced by railroad land thefts and allotments to certain Northern Kickapoos so that only a small fragment of the original cession remained. Also, anxious alarm flared in north Kansas when news arrived that there was a possibility that these "wild Indians" would be located so near heavily settled white communities. It was therefore decided to select a reservation for the Mexican Kickapoos in the Indian Territory. Andrew Williams was appointed special agent and directed to select a suitable reservation, erect agency buildings, and be ready to receive the immigrants when they arrived in the Indian Territory.[2]

Special Agent Williams traveled over the Indian Territory and finally settled on a site just west of the Osage and Kaw reservations and due south of the Kansas line. The area was bounded on the east by the Arkansas River, on the south by the Salt Fork River,

[1] Hoag to Commissioner of Indian Affairs, Lawrence, January 20, 1874, National Archives, Office of Indian Affairs, Kickapoo Agency, Letters Received, Microcopy 234, Roll 373.

[2] Commissioner of Indian Affairs to Miles, Washington, September 26, 1873, National Archives, Central Superintendency, Kickapoo File No. 73.

and west by range one of the Indian Meridian. On Bitter Creek, Williams supervised the erection of two double log-houses for agency buildings.[3]

By November 5, 1873, the agency buildings had been completed, and Williams had received a shipment of rations and blankets. Also on that day the Kickapoo captives from Fort Gibson were delivered to him. Williams supervised the settlement of his new charges, most of whom erected the traditional bark lodges for shelter against the coming winter's cold, and eagerly awaited the December arrival of their husbands, fathers, and relatives from Mexico.[4]

The 317 Mexican Kickapoos had hardly arrived in the Indian Territory when they provided Indian bureau officials with an example of the difficulties the United States government would have in trying to adapt the tribe to the routine of reservation life. In spite of the extensive preparations made by Superintendent Hoag, Agent Williams, and others to receive the immigrants at the Bitter Creek Agency, the Kickapoos refused, with a calculated belligerence, to accept the assigned reservation. During the December council held at the Kiowa-Comanche Agency near Fort Sill in the southwestern Indian Territory, the tribal leaders reminded Atkinson that in agreeing to accompany him to the Indian Territory, one of the conditions they had set was the right of the Kickapoo chiefs and headmen to select for their people a new home in the Indian Territory. The chiefs expressed disappointment and concern over finding a reservation already selected for them, not only because the selection of the site by United States officials violated Atkinson's agreement with the tribe, but—worse still—because the new home proposed by the Bureau of Indian Affairs was situated next to their old enemies the Osages, and "they would be constantly liable to get into trouble" in settling old scores. The chiefs also

---

[3] Williams to Hoag, Lawrence, January 15, 1874, National Archives, Office of Indian Affairs, Kickapoo Agency, Letters Received, Microcopy 234, Roll 374.

[4] Upshaw to Commanding General, Department of Texas, Fort Gibson, November 5, 1873, National Archives, Fort Gibson Letterbook for 1873, Adjutant General's Office.

declared that they "wanted to be free from molestation by the 'thieving Kaws,' " who were settled near the Bitter Creek Agency. Chief Thahpequah made it clear to Atkinson that his people would not accept the reservation selected for them, and that the tribe would winter on the Washita and select a new home in the Indian Territory in the spring. He reminded Atkinson that the Southern Kickapoos had kept their promise to return to the United States, and that they expected the United States to honor the promises made by commissioners Atkinson and Williams, which included pledges to restore all captives immediately upon arrival and to issue blankets and provisions to carry the Kickapoos through the winter. Since at least four hundred Kickapoos had remained in Mexico, and because the treatment received by this band would largely determine the success of future removal attempts, Atkinson provided for the return of the captives as promised, permitted the Kickapoos to winter on the upper Washita, and arranged for them to receive blankets and winter provisions from the Cheyenne Agency and the Wichita Agency.[5]

At the first sign of spring Chief Thahpequah led a delegation of twenty lesser chiefs and headmen from the Washita camps on a wide search over the Indian Territory for a new home. Their explorations revealed that great changes had taken place in the Indian Territory during their stay in Mexico. The domain of the Five Civilized Tribes, who had held title to most of the Indian Territory before 1861, had been drastically reduced after the Civil War, and the surplus lands appropriated by the federal government for settling immigrant tribes from various sections of the United States. As a consequence, few unassigned areas remained for the Kickapoos to choose from.

After examining vacant sections of the Chicksaw Nation and the Cherokee Outlet, Thahpequah's party continued east to the old Kickapoo range on the Canadian, where for years their villages had extended to the North Fork as a frontier defense for the hos-

[5] Atkinson to Commissioner of Indian Affairs, Brownsville, Nebraska, December 26, 1873, National Archives, Office of Indian Affairs, Kickapoo Agency, Letters Received, Microcopy 234, Roll 374.

pitable Creek Nation. Changes had taken place there too, they learned, for their old village site had been assigned to the Shawnees. Most of the land north and east was the home of the Sac and Fox tribes. There was an unassigned area just west of the Sac and Fox domain, bounded on the north by the Deep Fork, on the south by the North Canadian, and extending westward to the Indian Meridian.

Since the tribe strongly preferred this portion of the Indian Territory, and the Sacs and Foxes and Shawnees spoke a language similar to their own, Thahpequah's party decided this would be the new home for their people. Returning to the Washita camps, Thahpequah announced the selection, and by early April, the entire band had moved to the Deep Fork country. Only a few days after their arrival, the women were clearing patches and planting corn and vegetables. Superintendent Enoch Hoag, anxious to have the tribe settled and satisfied, journeyed from Lawrence, Kansas, to visit the tribe upon learning of their decision to settle west of the Sac and Fox. In a council with the Kickapoo chiefs and headmen held at the Sac and Fox Agency on May 10, 1874, Hoag agreed to the selection and placed the tribe under the jurisdiction of the Sac and Fox Agency.[6]

The Kickapoos turned to establishing new homes, and before the summer was out, they had "the most elegant and substantially built little village of bark houses in the Indian Territory." These traditional structures, common shelter for the Kickapoos for centuries, were approximately sixteen feet long, twelve feet wide, and ten feet high, oval-framed with poles, secured with bark strips and rawhide, and covered with bark mats. Their early days in the Indian Territory were happy ones—especially for the women since their warriors were not exposed to the fearful risks of raids on Texas—and families had been reunited by the restoration of the captives. Tribal health was good; the small patches of corn, squash, beans, and pumpkins furnished a bountiful harvest; and the war-

[6] Hoag to Commissioner of Indian Affairs, Lawrence, May 15, 1874, National Archives, Office of Indian Affairs, Kickapoo Agency, Letters Received, Microcopy 234, Roll 374.

257

riors found good hunting. At first the Sac and Fox agent, well acquainted with the deadly reputation of the Kickapoo warriors, had restricted the tribe to their reservation, but when he became convinced of their peaceful intention, he issued passes which permitted bands of about twenty each to spend several weeks at a time hunting in the western Chickasaw Nation and on the upper waters of the Washita.

During their first year in the Indian Territory, the Kickapoos supported themselves so well that they required no aid from the government, managing to sustain themselves by their hunting, the corn and vegetables the women raised, and the income from the skins they dressed and sold to local traders. Indian officials watched the Mexican Kickapoos carefully, noted their industriousness, and praised them for "doing incredibly well considering their restless disposition," observing that "in spite of the fact that the Mexican Kickapoo bring a bad reputation, we may be able to promote their advancement. We can't expect too much of them too early," for "after spending twelve years roving from place to place in quest of plunder, as they have, it is a rather sudden change to settle down to quiet farm work, and they have not done as much as they might. And yet they have done as well as anyone acquainted with their former life could expect, and, everything considered, there are hopeful signs of their becoming settled and peaceful Indians. They are not lazy, as their flying marauding trips have educated them to be sharp and stirring, and, once thoroughly interested in farming, they will excel most other tribes."[7]

But trouble was brewing for the Mexican Kickapoos. The laissez faire policy of the government changed gradually to one of direct intervention, as officials became anxious to push the tribe from hunting, trapping, and subsistence farming to a sedentary life based completely on agriculture—the warriors becoming farmers, the women, homemakers, in the traditional pattern of the American rural family. Indian officials became distressed at the carefree Kickapoo attitude toward life, and they resented the "time wasted"

[7] *Report of the Commissioner of Indian Affairs for 1874*, 213; *Report of the Commissioner of Indian Affairs for 1875*, 65.

by the warriors and their families in native religious observances, tribal festivals, dances, and games. The Kickapoos were inveterate gamblers, and Indian agents were concerned over their influence on other tribes. The Sacs, Foxes, and Shawnees, before the Kickapoos became their neighbors, had made remarkable progress in agriculture, were developing habits of thrift and industry, and had enrolled their children in the agency schools. The effect of the Mexican Kickapoos upon these tribes was almost immediate. Sac, Fox, and Shawnee families joined the Kickapoos in religious rites, became disdainful of the missionaries laboring among them, rejected Christian teachings, and neglected their fields and livestock herds to participate in the Kickapoo dances, festivals, and games. The Indian agents charged that during the early summer when the Kickapoo, Sac, Fox, and Shawnee warriors were expected to be in the fields working their crops, they left the chores to the women and children while they visited the tribes of the territory, racing horses on wagers, gambling, and "exchanging or 'smoking' ponies, a practice demoralizing, expensive, and useless, as it inclines to stimulate their nomadic disposition and foster their indifference in regard to the value of property and goods, which are ostensibly gifts, but in reality doubly paid for."[8]

There was a growing resentment, too, among the Chickasaws, Kiowas, Comanches, Wichitas, and Cheyennes concerning the Kickapoo hunting expeditions, for when the Kickapoos received passes from the Sac and Fox Agent to hunt on their lands, Kickapoo huntsmen, as in days of old, swept the country almost clean of game and fur-bearing animals. Consequently there were increasing demands from the various agencies that no more hunting passes be issued to the Kickapoos. Various tribes also charged that while on these hunting expeditions, Kickapoo warriors stole horses, although the Kickapoos hotly denied this.[9]

Indian officials were reluctant to move too swiftly, however, in attempting to tame the Mexican Kickapoos, for four hundred tribes-

[8] *Report of the Commissioner of Indian Affairs for 1877*, 106.
[9] Smith to Hoag, Washington, November 14, 1874, Kickapoo Affairs, Sac-Fox Agency File, Oklahoma Historical Society.

men still remained in Coahuila, and the commissioner of Indian affairs hoped to move them to the Indian Territory. The commissioner feared that if the resident Kickapoos were forced into the reservation routine too quickly, the chances of obtaining a complete evacuation of the Kickapoos from Mexico would be prejudiced, either by unfavorable reports reaching the Mexican branch from their tribesmen in the Indian Territory, or by a wholesale return of the Deep Fork band to Mexico. It was decided, however, that in view of their damaging influence on the neighboring tribes, some cautious step toward civilizing the Kickapoos had to be taken—and soon.

It had long before been discovered that one of the most effective weapons against Indian culture was education, and Indian officials decided that a school for Kickapoo children would do more to overthrow the "old ways" than any other plan the Government could contrive. The school would be an innovation that would not prejudice the Deep Fork band against remaining in the Indian Territory, nor discourage the Coahuila band from joining their people in the United States. In making this decision the Bureau of Indian Affairs sadly miscalculated Kickapoo attitudes, for while the warriors would have resisted to some degree allotments in severalty, adoption of "citizen dress," or just about any alternative policy the government could have devised as a first step in the taming process, the prospect of being required to enroll their children in a white man's school was too dreadful to even consider. Indian officials, puzzled at first by the tribal council's violent rejection of their proposal that a government school be established on the Deep Fork Reservation, finally found the reason—not in tribal stubbornness, although this was a factor in all Kickapoo dealings with the government during the reservation period, but in honest religious convictions. Investigators discovered that rigid Kickapoo habits, superstitions, and notions, including their aversion to education, were derived from a fanatical attachment to the Great Spirit, that Kickapoo religion was "traditional and antagonistic to civilization," and that a tribal member who patronized the white man's schools or followed the customs of the whites was "stigmatized as a traitor to their Great Spirit." Officials also learned that the Kickapoos believed "that had the Great Spirit intended them to become white men, he would so have created them. They regard it as a transgression against the supreme law, and a sin against the Great Spirit to make white men of their children by giving them an education."[10]

Suspicious of the Kickapoos from the beginning, John H. Pickering, Sac and Fox agent, was none too pleased by Superintendent Hoag's action in assigning the new arrivals on the Deep Fork to his jurisdiction. Pickering did not share the optimism of his superiors in the Bureau of Indian Affairs concerning the prospects for a quick tribal adjustment to reservation life. In the field and regularly in contact with the tribe, he soon discovered that the Mexican Kickapoos understood "enough about civilization to know how to repel its advances." Concerning the prospects for their eventual acculturation, Pickering noted that one of their favorite chiefs, Saganah, a youth of twenty-three, had been elevated to the headship of one of the bands in the Deep Fork community for having killed and scalped fifty-seven Texans![11]

The Sac and Fox Agent also doubted the wisdom of the Bureau of Indian Affairs in working so hard to persuade the four hundred Kickapoos still in Mexico to return to the United States, for their coming, Pickering believed, would multiply many times over the difficulties he already faced in attempting "to lead the resident Kickapoo along the white man's road." Despite Agent Pickering's urging that the Kickapoos already in the Indian Territory were trouble enough, the United States government continued its efforts to persuade the Kickapoos in Mexico to join their brothers on the Deep Fork. Because of his success in bringing in nearly half of the Mexican Kickapoos in 1873, Henry Atkinson was prevailed upon to head another removal mission to Mexico. The commissioner of Indian affairs appointed William M. Edgar to assist Atkinson, and

[10] *Report of the Commissioner of Indian Affairs for 1874,* 230–31; *Report of Commissioner of Indian Affairs for 1875,* 263.

[11] Pickering to Commissioner of Indian Affairs, Sac and Fox Agency, June 2, 1874, National Archives, Central Superintendency, Kickapoo File No. 98.

the reliable Chequamkako accompanied the American commissioners and labored diligently throughout 1875 to persuade the Mexican
Kickapoos to return to the United States, spurred by the promise
of five hundred dollars bounty for each band he helped deliver to
the Indian Territory.[12]

During December, 1874, the American commissioners departed
from the United States and traveled to Saltillo, capital of Coahuila,
for the purpose of presenting their credentials and receiving authority to negotiate with the Mexican Kickapoos. Atkinson was
surprised to learn that Governor Cepeda had been overthrown
earlier in the year by a revolutionary coup caused, it was rumored,
by his co-operation with the Kickapoo removal the preceding year.
At Atkinson's request, Governor Carillo, Cepeda's successor, telegraphed Mexico City for instructions. When the central government, prodded by the American minister, directed Carillo to co-
operate with the United States commission in attempting to remove the Kickapoos, he appointed Jesus del Moral as commissioner
to represent the Mexican government and called upon local officials throughout Coahuila to assist in the removal venture.

Properly accredited, the joint Kickapoo Removal Commission
traveled to Santa Rosa, where the commissioners learned that the
tribe, still fearful of another Mackenzie-type raid, was scattered
in small bands over northern Coahuila, west across Chihuahua,
and south into Durango, some of them six hundred miles distant.
Atkinson discovered that these bands looked to Cheeno as principal
chief, and it was common knowledge that the old raider was un-
yielding in his determination to remain in Mexico. After weeks of
searching over Coahuila, Atkinson managed to attract about 120
Kickapoos to the commission headquarters near Santa Rosa. The
largest band in this group was headed by Mosquito, the chief
spokesman for the assembled Indians in the absence of Cheeno,
who was hunting in Durango and, according to reports from messengers sent out by Atkinson, would not return until February.

While the rations and presents the American commissioners

[12] Hoag to Pickering, Lawrence, May 28, 1875, Kickapoo Affairs, Sac-Fox Agency
File, Oklahoma Historical Society.

offered them had some influence, the strongest attraction for Mosquito's followers was the news Chequamkako brought them of their people in the Indian Territory. Throughout the winter the American commissioners fed Mosquito's Kickapoos, issued them blankets, and told of the pleasant life of their fellow tribesmen in the Indian Territory. In spite of these urgings and the influence of Chequamkako, however, Mosquito and his councilors refused to negotiate with Atkinson until Cheeno and the other band chiefs returned in February.[13]

Spring, 1875, came and there was no sign of Cheeno and the band chiefs. Atkinson's patience grew thin, for not only was he disappointed by the failure of the other Kickapoos to join him for councils at Santa Rosa, but he was also faced with a renewed campaign of intrigue by local Mexican officials and businessmen. While Mosquito had several times during the winter showed a strong inclination to lead his people to the Indian Territory, his enthusiasm was overcome by gifts and promises from Santa Rosa citizens. From his earlier experience Atkinson had expected this conspiracy to develop, and he went to great lengths to counter each attempt to dissuade the Indians, but he found the Mexican officials and businessmen "more determined than ever before to prevent the removal of the remaining Kickapoos as they claim with some truth that it would leave them subject to constant depredations" from the Apaches who had recently come from New Mexico and Arizona territories to settle in northern Mexico, where they were raiding indiscriminately north and south of the Rio Grande.[14]

In an effort to negate the influence of businessmen and officials at Santa Rosa, and anxious to contact Cheeno and other band leaders, Atkinson moved his headquarters to Zaragoza, in the Mexi-

---

[13] Atkinson to Commissioner of Indian Affairs, Santa Rosa, December 26, 1874, National Archives, Office of Indian Affairs, Kickapoo Agency, Letters Received, Microcopy 234, Roll 374.

[14] Atkinson to Commissioner of Indian Affairs, Santa Rosa, December 26, 1874, National Archives, Office of Indian Affairs, Kickapoo Agency, Letters Received, Microcopy 234, Roll 374; Atkinson to Commissioner of Indian Affairs, San Antonio, March 22, 1875, National Archives, Office of Indian Affairs, Kickapoo Agency, Letters Received, Microcopy 234, Roll 374.

can state of Durango. Mosquito's people followed the removal commission to the new rendezvous, and messengers were again sent out inviting Cheeno and other band chiefs to come in, receive presents from their "Father in Washington," and council with Atkinson. Within two weeks all the chiefs, including Cheeno, had arrived, and discussions on the proposed removal were begun. Only Mosquito and his followers were in favor of returning to the United States. The other band chiefs stood solidly with Cheeno in the decision to remain in Mexico. José Galindo, a daring raider chieftain and a leading councilor to the formidable Cheeno, showed his disdain for the United States and its offer of a home for his band by averring that as long as he was welcome in Coahuila and Durango, he would remain there and should the people of these states tire of him, then he would try every one of the remaining states of Mexico and if none would accept him, only "then he would return to the United States." Besides having to cope with the stubbornness of Cheeno and Galindo, Atkinson found his negotiations imperiled by "the most persistent opposition from the Mexicans, and the arbitrary course of their officials" was a "serious source of trouble." General Fueno and Colonel Aguillar, commanding troops on the Durango frontier, raised "serious objections to the removal of the Kickapoo," but assured the American commissioners of full co-operation in removing the Apache bands, saying on several occasions that Atkinson and Edgar could "take the others but they want the Kickapoo to stay." Atkinson discovered that even Commissioner Moral was secretly working against the Kickapoo removal, and he confided to the commissioner of Indian affairs that Governor Carillo "had instructed him to work against us for he feared a revolution by the Mexican people" if his government co-operated in making the removal a success.[15]

Commissioner Atkinson, before he reached Zaragoza, had assumed that only the citizens of Santa Rosa were opposed to the

[15] Atkinson to Commissioner of Indian Affairs, Zaragoza, March 22, 1875, National Archives, Office of Indian Affairs, Kickapoo Agency, Letters Received, Microcopy 234, Roll 374.

Kickapoos leaving Mexico, and it came as a surprise to him that even the people in Zaragoza, six hundred miles southwest of Santa Rosa, also were dependent upon the Kickapoo warriors for defense against the recently arrived Apache bands. One incident typical of many that worked against Atkinson's attempts to win over the Kickapoos at his Zaragoza rendezvous illustrates the lengths to which the Mexican officials were willing to go in order to discredit the American commissioners. Atkinson issued daily rations to the Kickapoos from the first day of contact with them during December, 1874, until his departure for the United States in April, 1875.

Some of his early stores had come in from San Antonio, but the distance of Zaragoza from American sources of supply and his diminishing ration funds forced Atkinson to replenish his supplies from local merchants. As they had in his earlier removal attempt, Mexicans warned the Kickapoos that the American flour, bacon, and coffee were poisoned. The first consignment of flour Atkinson purchased in Zaragoza made most of the Kickapoos deathly ill, seemingly affirming the Mexican charges, and the Kickapoos—except for their weakened condition—would have flown from Atkinson's rendezvous. Only after Atkinson proved to the satisfaction of the chiefs that the flour he had purchased in Zaragoza had come from a warehouse owned by the alcalde of Zaragoza, one of the most active opponents to removal, was "the opposite effect of that planned" achieved.[16]

In spite of Atkinson's remarkable patience and the persuasion of Chequamkako, only Mosquito's band of 115 Kickapoos would agree to return to the United States. Working fast before the opponents of removal could dissuade Mosquito from his determination, the American commissioners outfitted each family, issued provisions for the journey, and on April 15, 1875, the second wave of Kickapoo immigrants was bound for the Indian Terri-

[16] Atkinson to Commissioner of Indian Affairs, Zaragoza, March 27, 1875, National Archives, Office of Indian Affairs, Kickapoo Agency, Letters Received, Microcopy 234, Roll 374.

tory. Following the same route taken by the first party and led by Chequamkako, the travelers were in high hopes of arriving on the Deep Fork reservation by June.[17]

Commissioner Atkinson, through his many months of energetic negotiation, came to know the Mexican Kickapoo character exceedingly well, and in spite of the trials he had endured and his disappointment, he continued to hold for these wild, erratic people a deep regard. For years to come those Kickapoos who had followed him to the Indian Territory looked to him for advice and help in many problems that came to them as government wards. While most Indians during this reservation period wrote to the President of the United States or the commissioner of Indian affairs when confronted with problems, the Kickapoos at the Deep Fork reserve, through their agent, wrote to Atkinson, confiding their problems and conveying their trust and love for him. Henry Atkinson, with all the burdens of his office as commissioner of pensions, always took the time to look after the interests of, and intercede for, his former charges. An interesting example of Atkinson's personal concern for Kickapoo welfare is found in his letter to Superintendent Enoch Hoag alerting him that Mosquito's band would soon arrive in the Indian Territory and reminding him that "all will need rations and blankets and I trust they will be well fed. . . . I have been duly installed as Commissioner of Pensions and have my hands full of business. . . . Treat my Kickapoos honestly and fairly."[18]

Commissioner Edgar remained in Mexico and continued attempts to negotiate with the Kickapoos, but his efforts were for the most part in vain. Soon after the departure of Mosquito's band for the Indian Territory, Galindo and other chiefs scattered with their partisans over Coahuila and Durango to hunt. Edgar followed the Kickapoos to their hunting camps, and although he was courteously received and the chiefs "said they would study the subject

17 Atkinson to Commissioner of Indian Affairs, Washington, April 30, 1875, National Archives, Office of Indian Affairs, Kickapoo Agency, Letters Received, Microcopy 234, Roll 374.

18 Atkinson to Hoag, Washington, May 26, 1875, Kickapoo Affairs, Sac-Fox Agency File, Oklahoma Historical Society.

of removal," it was evident they were tired of Edgar and the American councils.[19]

Learning of a tribal festival to be held at the old Kickapoo village site at Nacimiento in October, when all the bands would be together again, Edgar decided to stay over and make one last effort at removal. After a week of talks Edgar could persuade only Mahquatauthena, a subchief of the Cheeno band, and thirty followers to accompany him to the United States, the chief attraction being their many close relatives in the Mosquito band already settled in the Indian Territory. After the October council Edgar despaired of persuading any additional bands to remove, for, besides the strong attachment the remaining Kickapoos seemed to hold for their free life in Mexico, the Mexican influence was too great to overcome. Edgar informed the commissioner of Indian affairs that throughout his October council, citizens and officials from Santa Rosa came out to Nacimiento and interfered in various ways. They not only lavished presents, bribes, and promises upon the Kickapoos, but the leaders "took up a collection among the citizens to buy supplies to induce them to stay." Edgar recommended to the commissioner of Indian affairs, just before he departed for the Indian Territory with Mahquatauthena's small band, that the United States abandon its efforts to attempt further removals. He suggested as an alternative that the State Department propose that the Mexican government remove the Kickapoos away from the Rio Grande border to a reservation in the interior of Mexico so distant from Texas that no further depredations would be possible.[20]

Commissioner Edgar's relocation proposal, favorably received by the Bureau of Indian Affairs, was transmitted through State Department channels to the Mexican government. On February 29, 1876, Juan de Arias, Mexican minister of Foreign affairs, informed the United States government that the Mexican government had

[19] Edgar to Commissioner of Indian Affairs, San Antonio, September 5, 1875, National Archives, Office of Indian Affairs, Kickapoo Agency, Letters Received, Microcopy 234, Roll 374.

[20] Edgar to Commissioner of Indian Affairs, San Antonio, October 27, 1875, National Archives, Office of Indian Affairs, Kickapoo Agency, Letters Received, Microcopy 234, Roll 374.

decided to comply with the recommendation, and that the Kickapoos resident in Mexico would be assigned a reservation near Mapimi in Durango, nearly eight hundred miles from the Rio Grande, and sufficiently distant to discourage depredations in Texas.[21]

This was a declaration of intent only, and the plan was never carried out by the Mexican government, for by 1876, Kickapoo war parties based in camps across Northern Coahuila and Chihuahua were again raiding into Texas, generally preying on isolated ranches west of Fort Clark. The Santa Rosa merchants, while not as brazen as before, continued to encourage the Kickapoos in their forays and to traffic in the cattle and horses the marauders brought in. A noticeable difference was the higher prices paid for the Kickapoo loot, for merchants at Zaragoza had become active in the plunder traffic and were competing with the Santa Rosa ring for stolen goods.[22]

Since well over half the tribe was now on the Deep Fork reservation in the Indian Territory, there were fewer Kickapoo warriors in Mexico to muster for raiding parties, but the band chiefs, notably José Galindo, were just as daring as before; the Kickapoo forays were as savage as in the days preceding removal; and the diminished ranks of raiders still brought in a surprising amount of plunder. During the autumn of 1876, Galindo's partisans audaciously raided to the very picket lines of Fort Clark, collected one hundred horses and three hundred head of cattle, and delivered the animals to dealers at Zaragoza. The following spring Galindo's Kickapoos made a lightning attack on Hondo and New Fountain which netted over two hundred head of horses. The renewal of Kickapoo raids in Texas took its usual high toll in human life. American army investigators found that Kickapoo depredations in southwestern Texas during the winter and spring of 1877 had taken the lives of seventeen ranchers. General Philip Sheridan's reports on this renewed Kickapoo activity north of the Rio Grande reveal the

[21] Arias to Foster, Mexico City, February 29, 1876, 45 Cong., 2 sess., *House Report No. 701,* 234.

[22] "Texas Frontier Troubles," 45 Cong., 2 sess., *House Report No. 701,* 41–45.

brutality of their forays—during April, 1878, Kickapoo raiders killed four Texans, including a Mexican shepherd and his wife who were shot, tied together, and thrown across a panicked horse. In the same month, a Kickapoo war party shot one Texan near Escondido, Texas, and at Coyotes Gordos, the Indians killed a sheepherder and threw him into the camp fire with the result that his lower extremities were consumed. On a single raid on April 17, 1878, the Kickapoos killed six ranchers.[23]

In addition to their sorties north of the Rio Grande, the Kickapoos were defending the north Mexican settlements against immigrant Indians. Apache bands in northern Coahuila and Durango had been troublesome during 1877, not only competing with the Kickapoos in terrorizing Texas, but also murdering and robbing Mexican citizens near Santa Rosa. During July, 1877, the Apaches ran off an entire horseherd from a Kickapoo band camped near Nacimiento. Thirty Kickapoo warriors followed them on foot, discovered their camp, and surprised the Apaches with a dawn attack which killed all the women and seventeen warriors, including the notorious band chiefs Colorado, Tejano, and Enrique. The victorious Kickapoos returned to Santa Rosa with seventeen scalps and 125 horses they had captured from the Apaches.[24]

The Kickapoo attacks on southwestern Texas ranches which began early in 1876 represent the last bloody activities of these fierce, martial people. By 1877 United States troops were deployed in a long line of defense on the Rio Grande. Whenever American scouts ranging widely over northern Mexico, brought in reports of a Kickapoo location, cavalry expeditions were sent across the river, with or without approval of Mexican officials, to destroy the Indian camps and disperse the Indians. Each time a cavalry unit struck, women and children were slain. Texas Rangers units were becoming more active, too, and Kickapoo war parties found it difficult to locate a ford on the river which was not blocked by heavily armed patrols. In 1879, General Sheridan reported the Kickapoos

---

[23] Sheridan, *Records of Engagements*, 76–78.
[24] Schuchardt to Secretary of State, Piedras Negras, August 7, 1877, 45 Cong., 1 sess., *House Exec. Doc. No. 13,* 208.

"less active" than before—although there were still some killings—because raiding in Texas had become extremely hazardous. By 1880 the Mexican Kickapoos had completely abandoned their war on Texas, given up plundering as a means of support, and returned to peaceful pursuits—the warriors hunting and the women tending patches of corn, beans, and pumpkins.

20

The Cold War on the Deep Fork

As LONG AS there was a possibility that the entire Southern Kickapoo community in Mexico could be induced to return to the United States, the Bureau of Indian Affairs had sought to avoid irritating Thahpequah's Kickapoo band by moving too fast in leading them "along the white man's road." But with the safe arrival of Mosquito's 115 followers on the Deep Fork in late July, 1875, and with the assurance of Atkinson and Edgar of the futility of attempting to persuade the remaining 350 Kickapoos in Mexico to return to the United States, the government turned in earnest to de-barbarizing the resident Kickapoos and transforming them into co-operative, law-abiding, self-sustaining citizens of the Indian Territory.

The system used in civilizing other tribes was generally followed in dealing with the Kickapoos. The tribe was placed under the administrative jurisdiction of the Sac and Fox agent. Since the agent's headquarters was nearly thirty-five miles east of the Deep Fork reserve, a station was established near the main Kickapoo village. The buildings, all of log construction, included a warehouse, blacksmith shop, schoolhouse, and dwellings for station employees. A station superintendent, appointed during March, 1875, with duties similar to that of a sub-agent, was assigned to oversee Kickapoo activities, report regularly to the Sac and Fox agent on tribal progress, and issue rations, blankets, and other supplies to be furnished to the tribe by the government until the Indian families became

271

self-supporting. The superintendent's staff also included a station farmer who was to instruct Kickapoo families in farming methods, equipment use, and livestock care.[1]

The Deep Fork Indian community also had the services of the Sac and Fox agency physician, who attempted from time to time to make calls on Kickapoo families. Only rarely, however, was he cordially received, since the Indians generally preferred to treat their illnesses "in the old way." Even less popular with the tribe than using health facilities was the proposal advanced periodically by John Pickering, Sac and Fox agent, that the Kickapoos take advantage of the government educational opportunities by permitting their children to be counted, so that he could employ a teaching staff and put the empty schoolhouse to use. The tribal council persistently refused to allow the enrollment of Kickapoo children in the proposed government school, and even threatened to burn the building if the government forced the educational question. By 1876 the building erected to educate the youth of the tribe had been converted to a storehouse for hay, grain, and harness.

The Kickapoo tribal council did agree during 1875 to accept farming equipment and livestock from the government, and by 1880 the Sac and Fox agent had managed to furnish each Kickapoo family with a plow, a harness, a mule or ox team, and a number of mowers and hayrakes for common use. The tribe received also seed herds of dairy and beef cattle, hogs, chickens, and other domestic animals as the government stepped up its program to make the tribe less reliant upon hunting and government rations to enable each family to support its members in a comfortable fashion.[2]

Another feature of the government's Indian program was persuading each tribe to abandon common ownership of land and accept allotments in severalty. It was supposed that such a step would break down one of the bulwarks of tribal unity, destroy a basic custom, and shift the focus from the tribe to the land-owning

[1] Clum to Pickering, Washington, March 9, 1875, Kickapoo Affairs, Sac-Fox Agency File, Oklahoma Historical Society.
[2] Nicholson to Woodward, Lawrence, April 26, 1877, Kickapoo Affairs, Sac-Fox Agency File, Oklahoma Historical Society.

WAH-PE-CAT-QUA, head chief of the Mexican Kickapoos
from 1901 to 1908.

Village scenes in the Kickapoo country, Mexico.

family—a unit more amenable to government purposes and interests and in effect a bureaucratic application of the "divide and conquer" principle. This proposition, which the Kickapoos greeted much the same way as they had the plan for a government school, was brought before the council by Agent Pickering on several occasions and each time received the same reception—a cold rebuff. But Pickering persisted, pointing out to officials in the Bureau of Indian Affairs that since the Southern Kickapoos in "disposition, history, and character" were in "such direct antagonism to civilization and its advances," bold administrative action was necessary in order to shock the tribe into a full realization of the new role its members must take up if they were to survive.

After a year of frustration, disappointment, and failure in attempting to induce the Kickapoos to accept allotments in severalty, educate their children, and adopt other features of the government's acculturation program, Pickering confided to Enoch Hoag, head of the Central Superintendency, that since the Mexican Kickapoos were "very bold, conniving, and superstitious" and would "probably object pretty strongly to anything" tending to "do away with their regular tribal customs," and since the tribe was expecting to receive additional rations for the coming year as well as livestock and implements, the government would "never have a more propitious time to settle them on allotments than now. It should be made a condition in giving them the implements that they have a piece of land which they may select allotted to them. I believe it will be a good policy for the government to give them an additional incentive to accept allotments—that of furnishing a certain amount of lumber, nails, *etc.* to each one who will erect a house on his land. We had better press this question now when they are entirely dependent than to give them a certain amount of territory in common, as they will then say it is their own and claim the right to do as they please about allotments. . . . This matter should be determined at once, as they should take their allotments before putting in spring crops."[3]

[3] Pickering to Hoag, January 2, 1875, National Archives, Central Superintendency, Kickapoo File No. 98.

The Bureau of Indian Affairs authorized John Pickering to proceed with his plan to force allotments upon the Kickapoos by withholding promised farming implements, livestock, and rations until the tribal council capitulated. The Kickapoo chiefs and headmen, when faced with Pickering's ultimatum, cleverly countered by threatening to return to Mexico if the agent brought up the subject of private land ownership again or if he made it a condition of the tribe's receiving the promised farming implements, livestock, and rations. Rather than permit such a dangerous threat to develop, Pickering abandoned the allotment proposal and began to issue the promised items.[4]

The officials of the Bureau of Indian Affairs probably knew less about the character of the Southern Kickapoos than that of any tribe under its jurisdiction. From the time of American independence, this segment of the tribe had successfully evaded the administrative control of the United States, and the first and only reservation the Southern Kickapoos had ever acknowledged was the one they occupied after their return from Mexico in 1874. The pattern of reservation life which worked so well with most of the captive tribes of the United States—including the Osages, Senecas, Potawatomis, and even the cultural cousins of the Kickapoos, the Sacs, Foxes, and Shawnees—was a completely new experience for the Southern Kickapoos and was anathema to them.

Indian officials were puzzled by their studied belligerence and lack of co-operation, and they came to regard the Kickapoos as ingrates because the tribe did not appreciate the material support and educational opportunities the government stood ready to extend to them. After a number of unsuccessful attempts to fit the Kickapoos into the reservation mold, Agent Pickering, who considered the Southern Kickapoos to be the most dangerous, haughty, suspicious, and crafty people in the Indian Territory, the most difficult to manage, and the single tribe "tenaciously continuing to be Indians," returned to a "hands off" policy, waiting for a more opportune time to convert the tribe to government purposes.

4 *Report of the Commissioner of Indian Affairs for 1876,* 68.

Sensing the victory they had won over the Sac and Fox agent, the Kickapoos brazenly ignored agency edicts regarding disposal of government property, relations with other tribes, hunting privileges, gambling, and possession of whisky. When, during early 1876, word came to Agent Pickering that these "perennial troublemakers" were busily developing farms and making rails for fences, he was surprised and doubtful, and decided to make a personal inspection. Upon arrival he found the Deep Fork reserve a beehive of industry, but not a single Kickapoo warrior was at work. It seems "some Mexicans had found their way to this tribe and were doing most of the work" along with some Negro and Creek laborers who had been hired to clear timber from the cornfields and split rails.[5] Curious about how the Kickapoos paid their help, Pickering discovered that these resourceful Indians had accumulated some cash from the sale of skins taken during the winter hunt, and, as he learned later, from the sale of some government issue blankets.

For excitement the Kickapoos roamed the Indian Territory on hunting expeditions, and their heavy annual harvests of dried meat, hides, and skins corroborated Pickering's belief that they were "the most successful hunters of any of the tribes in this part of the country." Other popular pastimes were stealing cattle from Texas herds being driven across the Indian Territory to the Kansas cow towns and running off oxen belonging to government survey parties which swarmed over the Indian Territory during the late 1870's.[6]

The Kickapoos found a ready market for this stolen livestock on the western edge of their reservation in the so-called Unassigned Lands, where a community of renegade whites, reportedly numbering over one hundred "lawless characters," had established an outlaw camp called "Ragtown." "Well-armed with Spencer and Winchester rifles, besides Colt revolvers," these desperadoes were "a terror to the law-abiding people of the surrounding country."

---

[5] Pickering to Commissioner of Indian Affairs, February 1, 1876, National Archives, Central Superintendency, Kickapoo File No. 98.

[6] Pickering to Commissioner of Indian Affairs, June 1, 1875, National Archives, Central Superintendency, Kickapoo File No. 98.

Kickapoo families frequented this community, for it was one of the few places where they could exchange their stolen booty and government issue blankets and rations for whisky, ammunition for hunting, and other necessities.[7] Through the years several hundred head of high-bred dairy and beef cattle issued to the Kickapoos by the Sac and Fox agent to build up herds for the tribe were driven into the Unassigned Lands, where they were swapped for whisky and shells.[8]

The reservation era made little if any impact on tribal culture, for even as late as 1887, after thirteen years under United States patronage, the Kickapoos were reported to be living in bark lodges, wearing blankets, and the only Indians under the jurisdiction of the Sac and Fox Agency who refused to send their children to school.[9] The traditional religious observances and feasts continued, as did tribal games—including lacrosse—which furnished entertainment and tested the skills of both warriors and squaws. The Kickapoo villages on the Deep Fork became popular gathering places for neighboring tribes, and to the disappointment of the various agents, Sac, Fox, Shawnee, Potawatomi, Iowa, and even some Creek, Seminole, and Wichita families joined the Kickapoos in celebrating various feasts, participating in tribal games, especially the famous races where the entire family estate often was wagered on a certain pony. The Kickapoos were reputed to be among the top judges of good horseflesh, and each autumn they went west to run their best animals against the highly touted Comanche ponies.

An interesting aspect of Kickapoo reservation life was the "cold war" the tribe carried on with the United States government. With all the freedom of action the Kickapoos had been able to extort from the Sac and Fox agent by their threat to return to Mexico, the tribe was clearly dissatisfied with reservation life, and their disillusionment and disappointment found expression in a calcu-

[7] *Report of the Commissioner of Indian Affairs for 1879*, 80.

[8] Marble to Shorb, Washington, November 2, 1880, Kickapoo Affairs, Sac-Fox Agency File, Oklahoma Historical Society.

[9] *Report of the Commissioner of Indian Affairs for 1887*, 95.

lated campaign of constant criticism, fault-finding, and open defiance of agency rules. The brunt of their offensive was received by the officer they held responsible for their misery—imagined or otherwise—the Sac and Fox agent. The Southern Kickapoos, under other circumstances a friendly and hospitable people, were insolent and haughty toward John Pickering and his successors, most of whom were well-intentioned, honorable men who went out of their way to please and pamper the irreconcilables from Mexico. The station superintendent and the reserve farmer were frequently charged with being incompetent and immoral, and life was made so generally miserable for them that there was a heavy turnover of personnel at Kickapoo Station; seldom did a superintendent or farmer last longer than a year before he resigned or begged for a transfer. The agency physician was criticized for failing to make calls on the Kickapoo reserve, yet when he did venture to the Deep Fork, he more often than not was informed that tribal health was good and his services were not needed. Every month or so the Kickapoos sent crude letters to the commissioner of Indian affairs, written by the one literate Indian in the entire tribe, Johnson Warsano, complaining of the poor work of the station blacksmith and the sorry quality of their rations, especially the wormy flour and the short supply of tobacco and sugar in certain issues. More often than not these letters included a denunciation of the agent, and a charge that he failed to visit the Kickapoo villages and look after their interests. Yet when the commissioner directed the Sac and Fox agent "to visit the Kickapoo more frequently so that the tribe would not feel neglected or uncared for," and when more frequent visits were made, the Kickapoos accused the agent of spying on them and interfering in tribal affairs. No trip to Deep Fork was complete without a denunciation of the agent, the United States, the rations, and the proposals of allotments in severalty and a school for Kickapoo children.[10] The venerable despot Chief Thahpequah, usually the tribal spokesman, was characterized by Pickering as

[10] Upshaw to Neal, Washington, August 20, 1886, Kickapoo Affairs, Sac-Fox Agency File, Oklahoma Historical Society.

the epitome of Kickapoo arrogance and recalcitrance, for "he seems to be dissatisfied with everything done for his tribe, and says he does not find things here as he expected or as promised him."[11]

The continued Kickapoo dependence on government rations was a paradox, for the tribe occupied one of the most attractive reservations in the Indian Territory, a well-watered, timbered tract of over two hundred thousand acres laced with rolling prairie and bottom land on the North Canadian and Deep Fork. And the Southern Kickapoos were "not lazy," according to the Sac and Fox agent, "as their flying, marauding trips have educated them to be sharp and sturdy," and he characterized them as "energetic, aggressive, and up and stirring early in the morning, resourceful, and very sharp traders." That the tribe could be self-reliant was proved during their first year in the Indian Territory, when, left much to themselves, the Kickapoos had supported themselves in comfortable fashion on the corn, beans, squash, and pumpkins raised in the patches which the families had carved out of the Deep Fork wilderness, and by trading and hunting, without a single cent of expense to the government. Only when the Bureau of Indian Affairs began to attempt to integrate the Mexican Kickapoos into the traditional reservation pattern, which included pressure to abandon their old tribal ways and strong encouragement to take up "the white man's road," did a noticeable change occur in tribal attitudes.

When the Sac and Fox agent began attempts to force the Kickapoos to enroll their children in the government school, to accept allotments, and to abandon hunting for farming, the reaction set in. Rations were issued by Sac and Fox Agent John Pickering, beginning in 1876, as an inducement to the Kickapoos to abandon their hunting trips over the Indian Territory, settle permanently in their villages, and rely on government issues of food, clothing, and blankets until the families became self-sufficient through farming and stock raising. These rations, consisting of meat, flour, soap,

[11] Pickering to Commissioner of Indian Affairs, Sac and Fox Agency, February 1, 1876, National Archives, Central Superintendency, Kickapoo File No. 98.

sugar, coffee, tobacco, and salt, were distributed to the Indian families each quarter by the superintendent at Kickapoo Station.

Intended by the Bureau of Indian Affairs as a stopgap measure to sustain the tribe until the Kickapoos could become self-supporting under a government commercial farming program, the quarterly ration came to be regarded as a right, and for the remainder of the reservation era, nearly twenty years, the tribe received the rations. The quarterly ration became a symbol of victory for the Kickapoos over the United States Government, a form of tribute exacted by the tribe. The Kickapoos, the only Indians of the six tribes attached to the Sac and Fox Agency to draw rations, zealously guarded this assumed right and considered themselves severely imposed upon if the rations were late or of inferior quality.[12]

The original purpose of the quarterly issue of Government rations was clearly to furnish only temporary sustenance for the Kickapoos, to relieve the warriors of the necessity of wandering over the Indian Territory on hunting expeditions, and to enable them to devote their time to developing farms and livestock herds, thus elevating their families above the subsistence level. The Kickapoos were determined to retain their historic economic patterns and, in effect, to remain only at the subsistence level. As late as 1886, over ten years after their return from Mexico, the tribe had only 175 acres in cultivation—less than half an acre per person; in 1887 the total was 250 acres, and even in 1890, only about 300 acres. During the same period the United States government had spent well over one hundred thousand dollars on farm machinery, tools, harnesses (largely accepted as "curiosities" and allowed to rust and rot into uselessness), and mules, oxen, and dairy and beef cattle, most of which were traded or slaughtered by the tribe. The Kickapoos placed an economic value on rations for, since the tribe could take care of itself, the ration was an added source of wealth which each family could and did trade for other goods or money. Whenever the government threatened to stop the ration issue, withhold it temporarily, or change the method of issue, the resourceful Kick-

12 *Report of the Commissioner of Indian Affairs for 1886*, 144.

apoos found ways to check the government. In 1883, Sac and Fox Agent Levi Woodward decided to abolish the issue station on the Kickapoo reservation and require the Kickapoos to travel thirty-five miles to the Sac and Fox Agency to draw their rations. This change was an evident inconvenience to the tribe and "caused a great deal of dissatisfaction among them." Woodward soon received word that the Kickapoos had threatened to leave the Deep Fork and that twenty-seven families already were as far west as the Antelope Hills, and he decided to re-establish the issue station on the Kickapoo reservation.[13] Woodward was verbally chastized for his interference by that articulate old rebel Thahpequah, who reminded the Sac and Fox agent that "this country rightfully belongs to them [the Kickapoo] and that the white man was placed here to work for them, and should give them one-half of all that he makes."[14]

Over the years various agents had suspected that the Kickapoos were drawing more rations than the tribal population justified, but they had been unable to learn the exact number of Kickapoos on the Deep Fork reserve. When approached, the Kickapoos steadfastly refused to be counted for rations or for any other purposes, for they feared that a census was a part of some diabolical government plot to force them to accept allotments or enroll their children in school. When the new Sac and Fox agent, Moses Neal, determined to force the tribe to terms in 1886 by threatening to withhold rations until they were counted, the Kickapoos refused to submit, began packing for a "visit to Mexico," and won out again, for no census was taken.[15]

If the reservation era was an exasperating and disappointing period for those Bureau of Indian Affairs officials assigned the seemingly impossible task of civilizing the Mexican Kickapoos, it was a time of anxiety and confusion for the tribe. Problems of control by the Sac and Fox agent and of adjustment for the tribe were

---

[13] *Report of the Commissioner of Indian Affairs for 1883,* 85–86.

[14] *Ibid.,* 85–86.

[15] Upshaw to Neal, Washington, June 14, 1886, Kickapoo Affairs, Sac-Fox Agency File, Oklahoma Historical Society.

intensified in 1889 when the Unassigned Lands, situated in the very heart of the Indian Territory and flanking the Kickapoo reservation on the west, were opened to settlement. Overnight Oklahoma Territory metamorphosed from a frontier wilderness to a settlers' haven complete with homesteads and a number of bustling towns, including Guthrie, the territorial capital, Stillwater, Norman, and Oklahoma City. The settlers in eastern Oklahoma Territory helped themselves to timber on the Kickapoo reserve, cut hay and pastured their stock on the Kickapoo meadows, and hunted at will over the Kickapoo land.[16]

These encroachments added to the problems facing Lee Patrick, Sac and Fox agent, for the Kickapoos became increasingly belligerent and intractable as the trespasses became more numerous. When the tribe protested, the agent found that he was powerless, since his agency Indian police force was too small to patrol the Kickapoo reservation and eject all intruders. Reports were sent to the commissioner of Indian affairs describing the situation and requesting that he arrange through the War Department for troops to come in from Fort Reno and expel the trespassers, but no action was ever taken against the intruding settlers from Oklahoma Territory. Military action was taken against the Kickapoos, however, when the warriors determined to take matters into their own hands. Alarm spread through the settlements of Oklahoma Territory when it was learned "the Kickapoo were going on the warpath." The citizens demanded protection, and a company of United States cavalry rushed to the Deep Fork, intercepted the warrriors, and confiscated their rifles and ammunition. The laxity of the government in protecting their reservation against settlers and the army's apparent willingness to defend the settlers but not the Kickapoos made the tribe more surly and unco-operative than ever.[17]

The opening of Oklahoma Territory proved unfortunate in many ways for the Kickapoos, for the new territory attracted not only the

---

[16] Wahpahoqua to Thomas, Kickapoo Village, March 11, 1895, Kickapoo Affairs, Sac-Fox Agency File, Oklahoma Historical Society.

[17] Snyder to Morgan, Idelah, Indian Territory, December 19, 1890, Kickapoo Affairs, Sac-Fox Agency File, Oklahoma Historical Society.

trespassing settlers, but gamblers, whisky peddlers, and practically every breed and stripe of huckster. These parasites soon discovered that the resourceful Kickapoos generally had cash, from the sale of skins and government rations, or ponies to trade, and they began to make regular visits to the Deep Fork reserve, lurking about the Kickapoo villages and pandering to their impressionable customers. During the spring of 1894, soon after the Kickapoos had been forced by the government to sell most of their reserve to the United States so that the land could be opened as new settlement area, the tribe received about $5,000 of the total purchase price of $64,650 in per capita payments of approximately $15.00 cash. Thus a family of four to six persons would suddenly have a substantial amount of cash. When the news of the Kickapoo payment got out, saloon-keepers, sewing machine salesmen, gamblers, and other "desperate characters" from Oklahoma City, Guthrie, and other towns of the Territory rushed to the Indian villages on the Deep Fork and the North Canadian, set up their camps, and prepared for the harvest. Agent Edward L. Thomas became alarmed over this sudden influx, and in answer to his request to the commissioner of Indian affairs for instructions, he was directed to banish "all saloon-keepers, gamblers, and evil persons of whatever character" from the Kickapoo domain before payment was made.[18]

Agent Thomas' precautions only delayed the theft of the Kickapoo payment, for less than a week after disbursal, most of it had gone to pay the saloon-keepers and gamblers in nearby Choctaw City and Oklahoma City for the generous credit they had extended to the tribe. The growing addiction of the Kickapoos to whisky was another symptom of their boredom with reservation life and of their individual disappointments and disillusionment, and was in disturbing contrast to their life in Mexico before 1874, when they had been characterized as "sternly temperate." Soon after arriving in the Indian Territory, some of the warriors had taken to drink, but they generally limited their frolics to periodic sprees or to celebrations of a particular event. Whisky peddlers became ac-

[18] Commissioner of Indian Affairs to Thomas, Washington, May 1, 1894, Kickapoo Affairs, Sac-Fox Agency File, Oklahoma Historical Society.

tive on the Deep Fork reserve soon after the arrival of Thahpequah's people, and the warriors could always trade for a supply of strong drink at the renegade "Ragtown." The disturbing increase in the consumption of whisky by the tribe, however, came after the opening of Oklahoma Territory and involved a greater proportion of the tribe. Even the women drank, and all were apparently attempting to insulate themselves from the confusing times by consuming heavy quantities of rotgut whisky.

Missionaries estimated that as many as twenty-five per cent of the tribe had become drunkards by 1893, four years after the opening of Oklahoma Territory, and that probably seventy-five per cent of the warriors drank at least occasionally. The former lords of the middle border, rated by many observers as the bravest and proudest warriors in North America, came to be regarded as the heaviest drinkers in the Indian Territory. This sordid reputation, probably exaggerated, involved a malicious twisting of the facts which implicated even the temperate members of the tribe. This was revealed by a report on conditions on the Kickapoo Reservation prepared by the Indian Rights Association in 1893. The report by this organization, entitled "How Deputy Marshals Make Their Fees," described the naïve Kickapoo's introduction to the white man's system of justice in Oklahoma Territory.

An army of United States deputy marshals had been required during the 1870's and 1880's to impose law on the Indian Territory. By 1895 most of the famous outlaw bands had been destroyed or dispersed, but the horde of marshals continued in their appointment under a minor patronage system, although most of them were pushed to find a *raison d'être* for continued employment. The findings of the Indian Rights Association show that some of the more resourceful marshals found steady employment, collecting regular and substantial fees, by enforcing the "bone dry laws" on the Kickapoo reserve. The venality of these law enforcement officers came to light in 1893 when Indian Rights Association investigators learned that two of the most temperate and respected members of the Kickapoo tribe, Parthee and Papashekit, were going to jail in Oklahoma City "for a few days." Elizabeth Test, the resident Quaker missionary disclosed that they had been arrested on a charge of bringing whisky to the Deep Fork reserve, and she assured the Indian Rights Association representatives that Parthee and Papeshekit were "good men" and that she was "confident that they were innocent." Further investigation showed that a conspiracy existed between certain deputy marshals and dishonest lawyers in Oklahoma City. Their formula for implicating the unlettered Kickapoos included "planting" whisky on the reservation. A deputy marshal with a blank warrant then filled in some Indian's name:

> He is arrested; employs an attorney if he has money or ponies; a bond is given for his appearance if someone will sign it. When the trial comes off, under advice, he pleads guilty and is sentenced to a few days' confinement in jail. This secures to the deputy his fees and mileage ... when he takes him to jail. A friend of the Indians, a Mr. Sweeney, who lives on the line of the reservation ... was on such bonds to the extent of at least $50,000. He had no hesitation about signing them, as he knew that nothing would come of it, and he thus lessened the time of the Indians' imprisonment. He said nothing was needed to convince anyone of the trumped up and fraudulent character of these charges, made for the sake of the fees, than to consult the records of the court; that the U. S. Treasury was robbed of thousands of dollars ... and the Indians were subjected to endless annoyance. My advice to the Indians was that, in the first place, they should never go to town except on business, and when there regard any and every man an enemy who offered them drink; that they seize any man, Indian or white, found on the reservation with whiskey ... that when arrested they should not employ a lawyer; that they should not take their own pony or saddle when they went to court, or anything that could be levied upon; that they should not plead guilty, but require the Marshal to make out his case, and when sent to jail, to eat all they could, thus reducing the profits to a minimum, and making the expense to the government as large as possible, so that when there was no profit to Marshals or shysters in these arrests, they would probably cease.[19]

These measures did much to reduce the number of fraudulent arrests and kangaroo court convictions of innocent Indians in

[19] *Twelfth Annual Report* of the Indian Rights Association, 46–48.

Oklahoma Territory. Also, the redoubtable Elizabeth Test began accompanying the accused warriors to court and confronting the judicial officers and lawyers with sharp questions. By 1895, after the exposure of the Oklahoma judiciary through the publication of the Indians Rights Association report, "the whisky ring" on Deep Fork reserve was broken up.

The problems of reservation routines caused the Mexican Kickapoos to react in various ways; most of them withdrew and maintained an unremitting hostility to the government's projects; many sought to escape the new order through strong drink; and a few, by 1890, began to sense the futility of resistance and capitulated to civilization. Early in the spring of 1878, a band of forty Kickapoos under Chief Keoquark left the Northern Kickapoo reserve in Kansas and migrated to the Indian Territory to join the Mexican Kickapoos on the Deep Fork. Having been exposed to civilization for a longer time than the Mexican Kickapoos, the newcomers were more amenable to adopting the "white man's way," and they became the nucleus around which a gradually increasing number of Mexican Kickapoos gathered.[20]

By 1881, the agent could detect a slight breakthrough, a growing sentiment "among the young men of the tribe to break away from the leadership of chiefs, separate, and build houses and fields for themselves, and give up 'the common for all' way of living."[21] This slowly growing group became the basis for a faction in the tribe, quite evident by 1890, which was called the "Progressive Kickapoo." The recalcitrants, those conservatives who refused to submit to the government, were called the "Kicking Kickapoo."

Corrosive forces which had been at work since 1873 on tribal customs, religion, and the despotic control of the chiefs and headmen over tribal affairs were beginning to have their effect by 1895. One of these was the active intervention of the Bureau of Indian Affairs in tribal politics. Tribesmen were encouraged by the agent to make decisions and settle problems on an individual basis rather

---

[20] *Report of the Commissioner of Indian Affairs for 1878,* 69.

[21] Kickapoo Superintendent's Report, Kickapoo Station, July 3, 1881, Kickapoo Affairs, Sac-Fox Agency File, Oklahoma Historical Society.

than through the tribal council. When Thahpequah died in 1884, his cousin, Johnson Warsano, was regarded as his successor. The commissioner of Indian affairs, upon learning of this choice, directed the Sac and Fox agent to inform the tribe that since it was the policy of his office "to discourage as far as possible the election or appointment of 'chiefs' among the Indians at the various agencies," and since "the Indians did not require an officer of this kind, and should manage their own affairs without subjecting themselves in any manner to the whims or control of a Head Chief," his "advice to them would be not to appoint or elect one."[22] While the Kickapoos ignored the commissioner and the tribe's historic custom continued in force well past the turn of the century, the unity of earlier times, which had been a mainspring of tribal power, gradually disintegrated as the "Progressive" element increased in numbers and influence to the point that they dared defy the will of the chiefs and headmen.

The most decisive blow to the old Kickapoo ways came through education. In 1875, soon after the arrival of the Southern Kickapoos from Mexico, the government had erected a school on the Deep Fork reserve, and for several years Bureau of Indian Affairs officials attempted unsuccessfully to persuade the tribe to enroll Kickapoo children. Finally the school supplies purchased for the Kickapoo children were distributed to the nearby Sac, Fox, Shawnee, and Potawatomi schools, and the Kickapoo schoolhouse was converted into a government storeroom. During 1882 the school proposal was brought up again when the Society of Friends proposed to the Bureau of Indian Affairs that the Quakers organize a school and mission among the Kickapoos and attempt to persuade the tribe to accept a missionary and teacher.[23] The government approved the request, and Quaker John Clinton and his wife came to the Kickapoos in 1883. From their first day on the Deep Fork, the

[22] Commissioner of Indian Affairs to Taylor, Washington, November 18, 1884, Kickapoo Affairs, Sac-Fox Agency, Oklahoma Historical Society.
[23] Price to Townsend, Washington, March 17, 1882, Kickapoo Affairs, Sac-Fox Agency File, Oklahoma Historical Society.

Clintons were insulted, threatened, and intimidated. While the "Progressive" element favored their proposed school, this group had little influence, and the "Kickers" remained adamant, voicing the fear "should they send their children to school, that the Great Spirit would abandon them, and then the world would come to an end."[24] Faced with constant hostility from the conservative element, who declared that "if they took up the white man's learning and religion the Great Spirit would kill them" and who pledged "to kill any missionary who attempted to convert them," the Clintons abandoned their work among the Kickapoos after nearly a year of disappointment and failure.[25]

The Society of Friends, not easily discouraged, noted that education was popular among the other tribes of the Sac and Fox Agency, for each year Sac, Fox, Shawnee, and Potawatomi families sent from seventy to one hundred of their children to Chilocco and other Indian boarding schools after the students had received a solid primary education at their respective reservation schools. Only the Kickapoos refused to educate their children, and the Quakers, possibly the only religious denomination in the United States with the stamina and patience to persist in the face of such opposition, determined to win the tribe to the cause of civilization and Christianity. After the Clintons' departure, the Quakers sent another missionary, Elizabeth Test, to the Kickapoos in 1885, and after five years of heartbreak and disappointment which would have defeated most people, this indomitable little woman finally cracked the wall of Kickapoo reserve, overwhelmed their bitter hostility and resistance with love and good works, and managed to establish a loyal following, particularly among the women of the tribe.

Miss Test's first contact with the tribe did not seem to promise a successful future with them. When she first arrived in 1885, she found most of the Kickapoos belligerent; her school was boycotted —not a single pupil enrolled for over a year—and she was treated

24 *Report of the Commissioner of Indian Affairs for 1886,* 144.
25 Rayner W. Kelsey, *Friends and the Indians,* 214.

as an enemy seeking to overthrow the Great Spirit. Her health broken, she left the Deep Fork reserve to rest and work with the more agreeable Iowa tribe, located just north of the Kickapoos.

By 1890 the "Progressive" element had grown to nearly one-third of the tribal population of four hundred. The group felt strong enough to assert itself, and so, over the protests of the "Kicking Kickapoo," they invited the Society of Friends to return to Deep Fork. Elizabeth Test, her health improved, purchased a tent and re-established her school among the Kickapoos with an enrollment of nine pupils. Surprisingly the school prospered, and Miss Test, using one thousand dollars of her own money, supervised the construction of a permanent frame schoolhouse near present McLoud.[26]

Near the Kickapoo schoolhouse Charles W. Kirk and his wife established a small Quaker church in 1891, and they co-ordinated their missionary work with Miss Test's educational labors. Miss Test's school was more readily accepted by the tribe than Reverend Kirk's church, for the teacher also spent considerable time in the Kickapoo homes, instructing the women in home care, cooking, and sewing; nursing the sick; "endeavoring to gain their confidence, and give them, in the school room, in their camps, and on their farms, such instruction and assistance as they need."[27]

Her work brought praise from the Bureau of Indian Affairs and in 1892 she accepted an appointment as Kickapoo Field Matron, on government salary, continuing also as teacher, representing the Society of Friends.[28] Her first report as Field Matron reveals her personal devotion and dedication to her work, as well as an insight into Kickapoo family life:

> To the present day I have visited nearly all the homes and many of them a number of times, making in all thirty-five families visited and 180 visits made. Counting children and all who come to our mission home, we have had over 800 visits from them, and as I have mingled

[26] *Ibid.*

[27] *Twelfth Annual Report* of the Indians Rights Association, 43.

[28] Commissioner of Indian Affairs to Test, Washington, April 20, 1882, Kickapoo Affairs, Sac-Fox Agency File, Oklahoma Historical Society.

with them day by day I find it a very needy field, calling loudly for sympathy and help. The difficulties in the way are great. The women are so ignorant and satisfied with their ignorance that it will require a long continued, patient, earnest effort aided by wisdom and power from above, to lead them in the desired way. Yet their case is not hopeless, for they are very friendly and apt enough to learn anything that does not conflict too much with their superstitious ideas. They have no houses, only those the women make of poles covered with bark for summer and flag matting for winter; no windows, one mat for a door; no chairs, bed, or table; but an elevated platform on three sides of the room serves the purpose for all. They have no stoves; instead, a fire on the earth floor with an open space in the roof for the escape of smoke. Their cooking utensils consist of iron ovens, brass kettles, and a coffee pot. They have some dishes, but few of the families have sufficient for all, and several will sit very contentedly around a wooden bowl and eat their soup in their respective turns from one wooden ladle. They wash their clothing at a creek, without washboard or tub and often without soap. The women carry all the water, cut the wood, build the houses, and aid in planting and tending the crops, besides their house work and sewing. When they can afford it they have coffee and flour, but their food is mostly corn, which they pound into meal or hominy, beans, and pumpkin, which they raise on their small fields. They are also able still to procure some wild game. They are very fond of lightbread, and their interest in making it is increasing. At first I had to watch when they would have flour; take yeast and show them how to use it; but of late several have come to ask for yeast. If they had a more convenient way of baking it they would enjoy it more, and some expres a wish for cooking stoves. Many of them have been bringing their sewing to our mission that we may aid by stitching on the machine. This makes a good opportunity to give them some instruction and suggestions about cutting and fitting, a great deal is done in this line for them. I have also had very profitable and pleasant times with the small girls, and when I visit a village or even where there are only one or two wickiups, I take with me pieces for patchwork, needles, and thread. As the little ones gather around me each one is supplied and taught, and when the classwork closes each receives as her own what she has pieced. They are very much delighted with this kind of work and try to do just as they are shown.

289

Their hearts are open wide for teaching and aiding in caring for their sick. Some bring in their suffering ones, others send for me to come and see them. I have had more than one hundred applications for medicine, which I have furnished. What has been done in this direction has won their confidence more than anything else and created a bond of sympathy and friendship between us, which makes them more willing to trust to my guidance in other matters. Having our home right among them gives many opportunities for teaching them which we could not have in any other way. When they visit us we try to make whatever work we are engaged in an object lesson to them. Surrounded as they are by temptations to drink, we find great need of temperance work. More than thirty of their men and boys have promised to drink no more and are wearing the little knot of blue ribbon. We have Bible reading and prayer with all of them who will come to meet with us, and we are pleased to note that their interest seems to be rather on the increase.[29]

This propitious beginning unfortunately lost much of its momentum a few years later, when the government forced allotment in severalty on the Kickapoos and opened their surplus lands to settlement. From 1895 to 1915, the Southern Kickapoos, kept in a constant state of confusion and anxiety by unscrupulous Indian agents, land pirates, and dishonest attorneys, were unable to appreciate and take advantage of the humanity and aid so lavishly afforded by Elizabeth Test and the Society of Friends.

[29] *Report of the Commissioner of Indian Affairs for 1892*, 406–407.

21

The Great Kickapoo Swindle

THE INDIAN TERRITORY, which had been closed to settlers except under certain restricted conditions since its establishment in
the early nineteenth century, by 1880 represented the homestead-
er's last frontier. Most of the arable land in the trans-Mississippi
West had been claimed and developed to some degree, and various
sources exerted great pressures on the United States government
to extinguish tribal title to the sparsely settled Indian Territory
and open it to settlement. Professional "Boomer" leaders C. C.
Carpenter, David L. Payne, and William L. Couch, organized
Oklahoma colonies in southern Kansas and led determined homeseekers into the territory during the late 1870's and 1880's. Although these colonies were promptly expelled by the United States
troops, the "Boomer raids" attracted national attention through
wide coverage in the press.

Despite the organized and articulate opposition of the Indian
nations, notably the Five Civilized Tribes, the United States government gave in to political and economic pressure, and in 1889
began the partition of Indian Territory by authorizing the opening of the Unassigned Lands to settlement. This rectangle of land
situated in the heart of the Indian Territory was surveyed and
staked into 160-acre farmsteads and townsites; prospective settlers
were permitted to line up on the four sides of the Unassigned Lands;
and at noon, April 22, 1889, the first race for homesteads began.
Within a few hours, some sixty thousand people had staked claims

to farm and town locations in the Unassigned Lands, and overnight Oklahoma Territory was born.

The first land run only whetted the appetite of homeseekers over the United States for more land in the Indian Territory. Oklahoma Territory grew and Indian Territory shrank as sustained pressure on the government forced the opening of new areas to settlement. The opening of the Unassigned Lands was a small problem because the area belonged to no Indian nation. The Creeks and Seminoles held a so-called "residual interest" which was easily disposed of, and the territory was immediately made available, since it was unoccupied except for a few scattered ranches.

Subsequent openings presented a much greater problem, for the remainder of the Indian Territory belonged to various tribes and was populated to some degree. Indian title had to be extinguished and the land needs of the tribes concerned taken care of by allotments in severalty; then the remaining land, declared surplus, could be opened to settlement. In a rapid series of negotiations, the Iowa, Sac and Fox, Potawatomi, and Shawnee lands were allotted and the residue opened in 1891; the Cheyenne and Arapaho reservation in 1892; and the fabulous Cherokee Outlet in 1893.

The Kickapoo reservation, containing some of the richest bottom land, timber, and meadows in the Southwest, had attracted the attention of homeseekers since the first run, and the government had attempted to gain an agreement from the Kickapoo council at the same time the other tribes of the Sac and Fox Agency agreed to allotment in severalty and the opening of their surplus lands to settlement. The Kickapoos refused under any circumstances to accept allotments in severalty, and after three unsuccessful negotiations an exasperated government commission literally stole the Deep Fork reserve with a forged agreement. This official swindle set in motion a series of annuity frauds, land thefts, and expensive lawsuits which troubled the tribe until 1915.

The United States government had attempted from the very beginning of the Kickapoo reservation era to convince the tribe to accept allotments in severalty, believing that by replacing tribal common ownership with fee title, it would destroy a source of the

292

Kickapoo power of resistance. Since the tribe regarded common ownership of land as an ordinance of the Great Spirit, even discussion of the subject was considered a sacrilege.

In June, 1889, soon after the opening of the Unassigned Lands, the government ordered a three-man commission headed by Lucius Fairchild, of Wisconsin, to the Indian Territory to negotiate with the resident tribes for extinguishment of title under the terms of the General Allotment Act of 1887. Popularly known as the Cherokee Commission and sometimes called the Jerome Commission for David H. Jerome, ex-governor of Michigan, who succeeded Fairchild as chairman soon after its organization, the Commission visited various tribes, including the Kickapoos, during late 1889, describing its purpose and encouraging the Indians to be ready to negotiate on allotments in severalty when the Commission returned.[1]

After a successful swing through the Indian Territory, the Cherokee Commission returned to the Deep Fork reserve in late June, 1890, the members apparently expecting a quick and successful negotiation. It soon became clear to the Commission, however, that the Kickapoos were not as docile as their neighbors and that the chiefs and headmen stood together, unalterably opposed to accepting allotments. Although the tribe had split over the question of adopting some of the government reservation policies, allotment in severalty was too revolutionary even for the "Progressives," and the factions closed ranks to face the Cherokee Commission as a unified tribe. Upon the arrival of the Cherokee Commission, the Kickapoos withdrew and for several days refused to council, hoping that their tormentors would go away. This failing, "Kicker" Chief Wapeneshawa and "Progressive" Ockquanocasey, with their headmen, grudgingly received the Cherokee Commission and heard the members out as they explained the government's proposal. When the Kickapoo delegation rejected the offer, claiming that such action "would offend the Great Spirit," the Commission denounced the Kickapoos as "the most ignorant and degraded In-

[1] Berlin B. Chapman, "The Cherokee Commission at Kickapoo Village," *Chronicles of Oklahoma,* Vol. XVII (March, 1939), 62.

dians" they had met, admitting at the same time that they were "possessed of an animal cunning, and obstinacy in a rare degree."[2]

The Cherokee Commission returned to the Kickapoo country a third time in June, 1890, brimming with impatience and determined to force an agreement one way or another. The chiefs and headmen were reminded by Chairman Jerome that the Deep Fork reserve had for years been occupied by the Kickapoos only by the sufferance of a charitable government; that President Arthur's executive proclamation of 1883, setting the boundaries of the Deep Fork reserve, had granted the Kickapoos the "right of occupancy" only, thereby making them tenants subject to the will of the United States government as sole proprietor; and that any benefit the tribe received from their negotiations with the Cherokee Commission was strictly gratuitous, for the Kickapoos had no right or title to the property. Apparently the Commission's technical and verbose argument, intended to impress the unlettered Kickapoos, was understood by the council, for when Wapeneshawa rose to reject the government's offer, he presented in simple terms a painfully direct argument, explaining that "the reservation was no larger than sufficient for their needs; that to become definitely located would be to destroy their visiting, feasts, and dances; that if they did not own the reservation, it would not be right to dispose of what did not belong to them, and if it was theirs they did not wish to sell."[3]

Thwarted again, a chagrined Cherokee Commission retreated to Oklahoma City. In a few days there arrived on the Deep Fork reserve one John T. Hill, who claimed to be an intermarried citizen of the Creek Nation. With his brother Joe, he had ranched in the Indian Territory for a number of years, even grazing his herds at times on the Kickapoo reserve. John Hill was best known to the Kickapoos as a former United States deputy marshal who had been active in making arrests for possession of whisky among the Indians, and because he had represented the law in the past, the Kickapoos feared him. John Hill assured the anxious Indians that his

[2] *Ibid.,* 64.
[3] *Report of the Commissioner of Indian Affairs for 1891,* 364.

purpose in being on the Kickapoo reservation was not to make arrests, but to help the tribe.[4]

Investigations by a Senate committee and the Indian Rights Association reconstructed subsequent developments in the following manner. Through the tribal interpreter, Joe Whipple, Hill explained that he knew the Cherokee Commission members well, that he could reason with them and possibly enable the tribe to escape allotment in severalty. Further, he had just learned that there was some money in Washington for the tribe, and there was a good chance that he could get it for them. Hill's promise of assistance was welcomed by the chiefs and headmen, and seven leading Kickapoos agreed to accompany him to Oklahoma City to continue the council. This council ended when the Indian delegation signed a paper, interpreted by Whipple, investing Hill, two Indians to be selected by the tribe, and Whipple with power of attorney to journey to Washington and negotiate on behalf of the tribe for all money due them and for preservation of the tribal right of common ownership of the Deep Fork reserve.[5] The Kickapoo delegation returned to the reservation, and Hill's proposal was ratified by the tribal council when it was made clear the trip would be made at government expense. Chief Ockquanocasey and Keeshocum, a leading headman, were selected to represent the tribe with Hill and Whipple before the secretary of the interior and the commissioner of Indian affairs.[6]

On the train en route to Washington, the Kickapoo members of Hill's party were surprised to see the three Cherokee Commission members in the same car with them. They thought it more than mere coincidence that when they reached Secretary of the Interior Noble's office, these same commissioners were already there talking with the Secretary. The Indians became anxious, and to put them at ease, Noble had them taken to a small private room where

---

[4] *Indian Advocate,* January, 1894.

[5] "Affairs of the Mexican Kickapoo Indians," 60 Cong., 1 sess., *Sen. Doc. No. 215,* III, 1887.

[6] *Twelfth Annual Report* of the Indian Rights Association, 39–40.

Hill showed them a paper. Whipple explained this document to them, and when the Indians insisted they were confused and did not understand it, they were "taken on a boat down to where there was 'Big Water'." The following day the Indians were returned to the little room just off Secretary Noble's office and told to sign the paper they had seen the previous day. Ockquanocasey obliged but Keeshocum refused, insisting that the paper still was not clear to him. Whipple and Hill, plainly irritated, conducted the Indian to the hotel and attempted to intimidate the adamant Keeshocum, finally threatening that he "would be taken down to the 'Big Water' and thrown in." Fearful that "he would never get back home" unless he signed, Keeshocum finally capitulated. Keeshocum's "ride home . . . was sad and solitary, and immediately on his arrival he denounced the others as having betrayed, in some way" which was not entirely clear to him, the trust the Kickapoo council had placed in them.[7]

Keeshocum's charges caused some anxiety among the Kickapoos, but it was not until 1893, two years after the Washington trip, that they realized how badly they had been treated. The first intimation of what had actually taken place came during August, 1893, when Special Agent Moses Neal appeared on the Deep Fork reserve with a commission from the commissioner of Indian affairs directing him to supervise the assignment to each enrolled member of the Kickapoo tribe an allotment of eighty acres, and to disburse in per capita shares a portion of the money the Kickapoos were to receive from the sale of their surplus lands, as provided in the act of Congress approved on March 30, 1893.[8]

The tribe was first stunned, then infuriated, when it became clear to them that they had been duped. Stirred to action, the Kickapoos unanimously refused to be enrolled, to receive allotments, or to accept the per capita payments, and they raised a fund among the warriors to pay the expenses of a representative to Washington to protest before the Congress and the "Great White Father." Sus-

7 *Ibid.*, 39–40.

8 Commissioner of Indian Affairs to Neal, Washington, August 30, 1893, Kickapoo Affairs, Sac-Fox Agency File, Oklahoma Historical Society.

picious of Joe Whipple, the council selected a trusted headman, Papashekit, who spoke a little English, as tribal delegate. Turned away, insulted or ignored by the various government bureaus and Congressional committees, Papashekit finally made his way to the headquarters of the Indian Rights Association, an agency which looked after the interests of the American Indian, where he was courteously received. Association officials, plainly skeptical of Papashekit's account of John T. Hill's treatment of the Kickapoos, agreed that Papashekit either "was repeating with exactness what really occurred, or that as a liar, he was an accomplished artist," and decided to send an investigator into the field to examine Papashekit's charges. The Indian Rights Association investigator, after spending several weeks in Washington examining government documents and interviewing persons connected with the Hill affair of 1891, traveled to the Deep Fork reserve during the fall and early winter of 1893 and continued the inquiry. The published report stated that John T. Hill and Joe Whipple had been the tools of the Cherokee Commission, and that these three officials had called in Hill and Whipple after the Commission had been thwarted three times in negotiating with the Kickapoos for allotments in severalty. The report also charged that "the Cherokee Commission, . . . inspired and supported by Secretary Noble, who seemed to have had the ambition to open as many acres as possible of Indian land to settlement, put back the cause of Indian civilization . . . more than fifty years" by the Kickapoo negotiations.[9]

The Association's investigation revealed that Hill's promise of government money for the Kickapoos was a ruse, for the only government money the Kickapoos could expect would be funds received by the tribe in payment for their surplus lands once they had accepted allotments. The power of attorney, granted Hill and Whipple by the tribe, to negotiate to preserve common ownership of the Deep Fork reserve and to exact from the government a guarantee that allotment in severalty would not take place was used for the opposite purposes. The Kickapoo allotment agree-

[9] *Twelfth Annual Report of the Indian Rights Association,* 44.

ment, certified by the Bureau of Indian Affairs and the Department of the Interior to be properly negotiated and unanimously approved by the Kickapoos was, according to the Indian Rights Association, "a palpable forgery." The document submitted by the secretary of the interior to Congress for approval contained the signatures (printed names followed by marks) of what was claimed to be the total adult male population in the Kickapoo tribe.[10]

These signatures were discredited by subsequent investigations, which produced, among other evidence, a protest signed by nineteen Kickapoos. The names of the adult male members of the tribe could not have been available because the Kickapoos had steadfastly refused to be enrolled for any purpose whatever. Knowing that there were fifty adult males, Joe Whipple undoubtedly had supplied a clerk in Secretary Noble's office with fifty names, relying on his memory and fabricating names when that failed. The list contained the names of several Kickapoos dead and in their graves before 1891. According to Okemah and other Kickapoos who signed the affidavit of protest, they

> . . . were in 1891 and for many years prior thereto residents of the Kickapoo Reservation in Oklahoma; that they were present at a council of said Kickapoo tribe called by the Commission known as the Gerome Commission, held near the village of Wellston, in the month of June, 1891. That at the said council speeches were made both by the members of the Commission and by the headmen of the Kickapoo tribe; that finally a vote was taken as to whether or not the said Kickapoo tribe should consent to the allotment of their lands and the making of the treaty there presented by the said Gerome Commission; that upon said vote one adult Indian and his two minor sons only voted for the acceptance of said treaty and that all the remainder of the said Kickapoo tribe then present voted against the making of said treaty; that no paper was at that time presented for the signature of the members of the said tribe, and that no person signed any treaty or agreement of any kind; that some time during the month of August thereafter, one John T. Hill came to said reservation and took with him to the city of Washington two members of the said Kickapoo

10 *United States Statutes at Large,* XXVII, 557.

tribe, namely Ocquanocasey, Kishocamme, and one Joseph Whipple, a white man in no manner connected with the said tribe; that the said two Kickapoo Indians so taken to Washington, D.C., were instructed by the Kickapoo tribe at a council of said tribe to protest against any attempt to allot their said lands or to in any manner interfere with the title thereof as then held by them; that upon the return of the said two Indians from the city of Washington the said Kickapoo tribe was informed by them that they had so protested and that no treaty whatever had been made or accepted by them. Notwithstanding said statement, shortly thereafter came Government surveyors and the United States Indian agent saying that they were authorized to survey and allot said reservation under a treaty made by said John T. Hill, Ocquanocasey, and Kishocamme; that thereupon all of said Kickapoo tribe, with the exception of ten heads of families left the better part of said reservation and removed themselves to the most inaccessible part thereof, and that they in no manner participated in the said allotment, but protested constantly against the same, and refused to accept the payment of money provided by the terms of said treaty to be paid to each member of the Kickapoo tribe; that today, for the first time, there is now shown to them a copy of the said treaty so alleged to have been made . . . that they have had read to them the signatures attached thereto; that they find signed thereto the name Pameethout; that they are of the opinion that the said Pameethout refers to the only Pamethot who has ever been in Oklahoma Territory upon their reservation; that there has never been but one Pamethot on said reservation and that he is a Kansas Kickapoo enrolled in Kansas prior to said treaty and allotted there subsequent to the date of said treaty and is not a member of the Mexican band of Kickapoo in Oklahoma; that the said name of Pameethout appears twice in the signatures and attached to said treaty; that the name N-dee-thow, attached to said treaty, is not a Kickapoo name and no such person was ever connected with said tribe; that the name Takekakthoe, thereto attached, is not a Kickapoo name, and that no such person was ever connected with the said tribe or lived upon said reservation; that the name Meereajquaw, attached to said treaty, is not a Kickapoo name nor did any such person ever reside upon said reservation, nor was he a member of said tribe; that the name Theoroughnaugh is not a Kickapoo name and no such person ever resided upon said reservation, nor was he a member of said tribe; that the name Theocann is not a Kickapoo name and no such person ever resided upon said reservation, nor was he a member of said tribe; that the name Payahnough is not a Kickapoo name and that no such person ever resided upon said reservation, nor was he a member of said tribe; that the name Chaughcotow is not a Kickapoo name and that no such person ever resided upon said reservation, nor was he a member of said tribe; that the name Maysooppatteesaut is not a Kickapoo name and that no such person ever resided upon said reservation, nor was he a member of said tribe; that the name Westsacttosauth is not a Kickapoo name and that no such person ever resided upon said reservation, nor was he a member of said tribe; that the name Chestkeeaugh is not a Kickapoo name and that no such person ever resided upon said reservation, nor was he a member of the tribe; that the name Kamkeneynay, subscribed to said treaty, is not a Kickapoo name, and that no such person ever resided upon said reservation, nor was he a member of said tribe; that the name Mass-Mc-carmic is the name of a Pawnee Indian married to a Kickapoo woman who was at that time resident upon said reservation, but was not a member of said tribe, nor had he ever been recognized by said tribe as such; that the name Sopuckawaw is undoubtedly intended for the Kickapoo named Sopuckemah, who died more than five years prior to the date of the attempted making of said treaty by said Gerome Commission; that the name Paughthesislught is not a Kickapoo name and that no such person ever lived upon said reservation, nor was he ever a member of said tribe; that the name Mackaureyer is not a Kickapoo name and that no such person ever resided upon said reservation, nor was he ever a member of said tribe; that the name Aughpautthousepyeare is not a Kickapoo name and that no such person ever resided upon said reservation, nor was he ever a member of said tribe; that the name Patthesathe is not a Kickapoo name and that no such person ever resided upon said reservation, nor was he at any time a member of said tribe; that the name Emnestatte is not a Kickapoo name and that no such person ever resided upon said reservation, nor was he ever a member of said tribe; that the name Nectootauquawpaw is supposed to be the name of the Kickapoo named Nickotocapee, who was a Kickapoo Indian, said reservation, and member of said tribe, but who died some six years prior to the date of the attempted making of the said agreement by said Gerome Commission; that they and none of their people ever authorized the said Ocquanocasey, Keesocomme, and John T. Hill, or either of them to represent the said tribe, or to attach the signature of the tribe or any of its members, to any treaty or agreement whatsoever, but that on the contrary, they protested at all times against the making of said agreement and the execution thereof.[11]

According to the Indian Rights Association report, Joe Whipple was a mixed-blood Cherokee who, in return for his services to the Kickapoos as their interpreter, had been adopted as a citizen of the tribe. Interviews with people in the Kickapoo country who knew Whipple corroborated the charge that he was dishonest, and that he was "a man whose word no one would accept as true unless it was for his interest to speak the truth."[12] Elizabeth Test, a perceptive judge of character, remarked that while Whipple was the only member of the tribe who "speaks sufficient English to transact business understandably . . . he is almost white, and cannot be depended upon to interpret truthfully."[13]

The report of the Senate committee investigating Kickapoo affairs included a deposition furnished by Benjamin F. Beveridge, a Washington, D.C., hotel operator, which implicated John T. Hill and revealed another facet of Whipple's character—cupidity. Beveridge swore that

> . . . about the 1st of September, 1891, a delegation arrived at the Baltimore and Ohio depot, from Oklahoma Territory, consisting of two Kickapoo Indians and two white men, one of whom, I was told, was an adopted Kickapoo Indian. His name was Joe Whipple. I remember distinctly the arrival of said party because I sent a carriage to meet them, which the white man, John T. Hill, who seemed to be in control of the party, refused to take. He engaged another carriage and drove with his party, direct to the Indian Office. The Commissioner of Indian Affairs detailed a messenger who brought the party on foot to my house. The two white men seemed to guard and to prevent any person from talking to the two full-blood Indians who were with them. Joe Whipple, the adopted Indian of the party, told me that he and Hill had brought the Indians to Washington to try to get them to

[11] "Affairs of the Mexican Kickapoo Indians," *loc. cit.*, III, 1899.
[12] *Twelfth Annual Report* of the Indians Rights Association, 45.
[13] *Report of the Commissioner of Indian Affairs for 1894*, 258.

make a treaty; that he spoke the Kickapoo language, and would do the interpreting. About the 10th of September this man Whipple became very much dissatisfied. He said that Hill was to be paid $5,000 for fooling the Indians into a treaty, and that Hill had agreed to pay him $500 and give him a good time in Washington for helping to fool the Indians; that he had misinterpreted to them and was afraid that he would be killed when he went back to the Oklahoma country for lying to them because they did not understand they were making any treaty; that he thought Hill was acting in bad faith with him, and he said if Hill did not pay him he would go back to the Secretary of the Interior and give the whole thing away. During the winter of 1895 a delegation of Kickapoo Indians also stayed at my house. They were very persistent in declaring to me that they had not made any treaty, and said they never would take their allotments.[14]

John T. Hill received $5,172 from a grateful United States government for his Kickapoo success, characterized by the Indian Rights Association as a "palpable fraud." This amount, to be deducted from the total of $64,650 which the Kickapoos would receive for the nearly two hundred thousand acres of their reserve declared surplus, was written into the statute "for services rendered said Kickapoo Indians and . . . recommended by the Secretary of the Interior."[15]

The House Committee on Indian Affairs, after a study of the Kickapoo Agreement Bill, submitted it to Congress with a recommendation that it be approved, adding to its report a commendation for John T. Hill:

> The Government acquires by this agreement 206,000 acres of valuable land with the payment of the nominal sum of $64,650. The land immediately south of it acquired from the Potawatomie Indians was opened to homestead entry at the price of $1.50 per acre, and therefore it was thought advisable to charge the settlers the same price for the land. The bill makes ample provisions for the protection of the honest settler. Fifty-five thousand dollars . . . appropriated is to remain in the Treasury of the United States at five percent interest. Four thousand four hundred and seventy-eight dollars is to be paid to

[14] "Affairs of the Mexican Kickapoo Indians," *loc. cit.*, III, 1895–96.
[15] *United States Statutes at Large*, XXVII, 577.

the Indians per capita, and five thousand one hundred and seventy-two dollars is to be paid to John T. Hill. The Kickapoo Indians are very self reliant, but wild and uncivilized tribe of Indians. They are great traders, intrepid gamblers, and farm in a small way, and are self-supporting. They have had but little to do with the white people and are averse to associating with them. The Cherokee Commission made four efforts to make an agreement with them in regard to allotting their lands and selling the surplus. They did not succeed. The Indians finally called into their council John T. Hill, and after nearly two years of residence and labor with them, suffering many privations, he finally succeeded in bringing about the written agreement, and brought the Indians with the commission to Washington to consult with the Secretary of the Interior. The Indians in council entered into an agreement with John T. Hill to look after their interest and said agreement lies here approved by the Secretary of the Interior. It was utterly impossible for the commission to make an agreement with the said Indians, and had it not been for the knowledge that Mr. Hill had of their customs and habits, and the long acquaintance he had with the Indians, and their confidence in him, no agreement could have been made.[16]

This report not only ignored the methods used to secure the Kickapoo allotment agreement, but it also failed to point out the obvious injustices it contained: that while the Potawatomis and other neighboring tribes received $1.50 an acre for their surplus lands, the Kickapoos received only about thirty cents an acre; and that while few tribes in the Indian Territory had to submit to allotments of less than 160 acres (several of them receiving twice or more this amount), the Kickapoos were to receive eighty acres each. The injustice was compounded by the fact that the Deep Fork reserve contained enough land for the tribe to receive the customary 160-acre allotment with a substantial surplus to satisfy the land-hungry settlers.[17]

Disregarding the Kickapoos' claim that they had not agreed to allot their lands and ignoring the charges that Hill's allotment

16 "Kickapoo Indians in Oklahoma," 52 Cong., 1 sess., *House Report No. 1662*, 1–2.

17 *Indian Advocate*, January, 1894.

agreement was fraudulent, Congress accepted the report of the Committee on Indian Affairs and approved the Kickapoo Allotment Act on March 30, 1893. The Department of the Interior lost little time in preparing the Deep Fork reserve for the settlers who were "perched like vultures" around the Kickapoo country waiting for the slightest excuse to appropriate its rich lands. Before the Kickapoo reservation could be opened to homesteaders, however, a government survey had to be made and a statutory allotment of eighty acres assigned to each member of the tribe. In spite of the efforts of the Department of the Interior to meet these obligations as quickly as possible, most of the Kickapoos utterly refused to co-operate with the enrollment officers, and their calculated resistance, itself a monument to tribal endurance and tenacity, held up settlement in the Kickapoo country for well over two years.

22

Boomers on the Deep Fork

GOVERNMENT SURVEYORS and enrollment officers arrived on the Deep Fork reserve during the summer of 1893. The "Kicking Kickapoo," comprising nearly two-thirds of the tribe, were sullen and unco-operative, sulked in their lodges, and refused to be enrolled or to give the names of their children. The "Progressive" Kickapoos, on the other hand, were somewhat more agreeable, for after much coaxing, including the promise of a special ration of tobacco, sugar, and fresh beeves for a celebration, they reluctantly enrolled themselves and their children. Special Agent Moses Neal persuaded "Progressive" Chief Wahnahkethahah, successor to the deposed Ockquanocasey, to provide the names of as many of the "Kicking Kickapoo" as he could recall, so that by early 1894 a tribal roll containing 283 names had been compiled. The government surveyors having completed their work, Neal and his staff escorted the "Progressive Kickapoo" about the Deep Fork reserve, assigning eighty-acre allotments as the Indians made their selections. Neal attempted to communicate with the "Kicking Kickapoos" without success and finally made arbitrary homestead selections for them.

The next step was to persuade the Kickapoos who had accepted allotments to abandon their communal village life, move to their new homesteads, and begin improvements. Again the "Kickers" frustrated the government plan for opening the Kickapoo surplus lands to settlement. About twenty members of "Kicker" Chief

305

Wahpahhoko's band were converted by Neal's promise of a special ration and cash per capita payments from the sale of tribal surplus lands. By September, 1894, 123 Kickapoos had been persuaded to move to their homesteads, while, according to Neal, there remained with "Kicker" Chief Wahpahhoko 160 followers who refused to abandon their communal life, accept cash payments, or even recognize that an allotment agreement had ever been made with the United States.[1]

Special Agent Neal's allotment roll left uncounted nearly fifty men, women, and children, members of a band hunting on the upper Washita when the final draft of Neal's allotment roll was drawn. A tribal census contained in the report of the commissioner of Indian affairs for 1892 noted that the Deep Fork reserve contained 325 Kickapoos entitled to receive allotments. Yet Neal's allotment roll, approved by the Bureau of Indian Affairs less than two years later, showed 283 names. When the hunting band returned and some of its members demanded allotments and per capita payments, they were refused. The secretary of the interior, pressed by homeseeker groups, railroads, and powerful interests in Congress to hold the amount of land assigned to the tribe to a bare minimum so that a maximum number of 160-acre homesteads would be available, ruled that since the allotment schedules already had been approved by the commissioner of Indian affairs and the remaining land on the Deep Fork reserve had been declared surplus, no additional allotments could be made. In 1898 the landless Kickapoos, angered by an administrative cupidity which denied them even a cash settlement, departed for Mexico to join their kinsmen on the Nacimiento, the vanguard of a greater Kickapoo migration to take place in a few years.[2]

The Kickapoo country contained approximately 206,000 acres of land described by "Boomer" enthusiasts as "the choicest part of the Indian Territory. Its wonderful richness gives assurance of

[1] Secretary of the Interior to the Speaker of the House, Washington, January 18, 1895, 53 Cong., 3 sess., *House Exec. Doc. No. 222*, 1–2.

[2] Commissioner of Indian Affairs to Patrick, Washington, September 1, 1898, Kickapoo Affairs, Sac-Fox Agency File, Oklahoma Historical Society.

prosperity to those who may be so fortunate as to secure claims in it. The reservation is simply a magnificent park. In the Kickapoo country is a succession of rich bottom lands with soil as black and rich as Illinois prairie loam. The central and eastern portions of the country are high prairie lands, interspersed with timber. Among the woods are beautiful circular glades in which the tall, sweet blue stem grasses wave in the wind. In these glades bunches of Indian ponies and cattle have browsed until they fairly roll in fat. Along the eastern border, where it adjoins the Sac and Fox country, the land is practically without timber, but is excellent farming land. In the northern part of the country is a region of blackjack oak, which never grows luxuriantly unless it has plenty of sand. The country is . . . rich in timber, and particular mention is made of the pecan, wild plum, hickory, elm, red-oak, post-oak, burr-oak, white-oak, and walnut. It is also well watered. The south central part is described as rich in springs. . . . In one place it is said, there are a number of springs within 100 feet of each other giving forth enough water to supply a city of 50,000 people."[3]

When allotment assignments had been completed, it was found that the government had made remarkably economical use of the 206,000 acres comprising this "Savage Eden," since only about 18,000 acres had been needed to provide each enrolled Kickapoo with an 80-acre allotment. The remaining 188,000 acres the government declared surplus. This would be the amount of land available to settlers when the Kickapoo country was opened. Not all of it would be subject to homestead entry however, for the new Territory of Oklahoma, guaranteed two sections from each township for the support of its public schools, had not received the promised amount in the earlier land openings, either through improper filings or because Indian allotments were made on areas customarily reserved for school purposes. Oklahoma Territory anticipated a deficiency of about 87,000 acres by 1894, and the secretary of the interior proposed to settle this claim by awarding approximately this amount of land to Oklahoma Territory from the Kickapoo surplus lands. Homeseekers could settle on this land—most of it situ-

[3] Guthrie, Oklahoma, *Daily Oklahoma State Capitol,* March 27, 1895.

ated in the northern portion of the old Kickapoo reservation—but only on a lease basis, and their lessor would be the government of the Territory of Oklahoma.

In 1894 Chief Wahpahhoko, irritated by the pressure exerted on the "Kickers" to settle on their allotments and frightened by the preparations being made to open the Kickapoo country to settlement, led the "Kickers" to the indemnity school lands, where a new village was established and the old communal life was continued. This trespass on Oklahoma Territory property alarmed Governor William C. Renfrow, who was making arrangements to lease the school lands in 160-acre tracts as soon as the Kickapoo country was opened. He demanded on several occasions that the Indians be evicted, but even after the opening, which occurred in May, 1895, Wahpahhoko's people remained.[4]

In 1896, when the land had already been leased and settlers had begun demanding possession, Sac and Fox Agent Edward L. Thomas recommended that the government call in a company of cavalry from Fort Reno to force the "Kickers" to vacate the school lands and move to their allotments, most of which were located in the North Canadian valley. Before this drastic step was taken the commissioner of Indian affairs appointed Martin J. Bentley as special agent to attempt to persuade these Kickapoos to move to their allotments. To everyone's surprise, the new agent had the "Kickers" settled on their homesteads and, according to Bentley, actually making some improvements by early 1897.[5]

The Kickapoo land run was the last of those colorful and exciting races for homesteads used by the government to settle the surplus lands of the Indian nations. After the Kickapoo run of 1895, because of the violence, "Soonerism," and the many disputed claims that attended this race, quieter methods such as lotteries and auctions were adopted by the United States General Land Office. The Kickapoo run was probably the most highly anticipated of them all, not only because of the valuable land awaiting the successful set-

[4] Commissioner of Indian Affairs to Thomas, Washington, January 22, 1896, Kickapoo Affairs, Sac-Fox Agency File, Oklahoma Historical Society.

[5] "Affairs of the Mexican Kickapoo," loc. cit., III, 1888.

tler, but also because the delay in opening caused by tribal resistance attracted much attention across the United States through press coverage and produced an avalanche of letters and petitions to the Congress from eager homeseekers, causing a congressional inquiry into the reasons for the delay.

Charles Curtis, later vice-president of the United States and at the time a Republican representative from Kansas serving on the House Committee on Indian Affairs, had for years promoted the dissolution of the Indian nations, allotment in severalty, and the opening of surplus Indian lands to homeseekers. Because he was regarded nationally as the settler's friend, his office received the lion's share of homeseekers' petitions.[6] With characteristic directness Curtis sponsored a resolution during January, 1895, inquiring of the Department of the Interior why there had been a delay in opening the Kickapoo reservation.[7] Secretary of the Interior Hoke Smith furnished Curtis with a complete account of the frustrating attempts of his office to carry out the will of Congress as expressed in the Kickapoo Allotment Act of 1893—to open promptly the surplus lands on the Deep Fork reserve to the homeseekers. Secretary Smith explained that the principal problem was the refusal of most of the Kickapoos to accept and settle on their allotments or to receive the cash payments for the sale of their surplus lands. Smith explained that these intractables were "encamped on unallotted lands, having deserted their homes and the enclosed fields that were allotted them (selected for them by the officers of the Department)" and that with few exceptions these Indians were "bitterly opposed to education, civilization, or in any manner changing their mode of living or becoming as they express it, 'like white men.' " Smith added that Wahpahhoko's band contended that "they never made the agreement of 1891; that they were mis-

[6] Oklahoma City *Daily Oklahoman*, May 17, 1895. That Congressman Curtis, himself of Indian blood, was remarkably active in making as much land as possible available for the homeseekers is further shown by his attempts to open the Potawatomie and Kickapoo lands in Kansas to settlement, and by his promotion of legislation for right-of-way across the Indian Territory for various railroads, see *Congressional Record*, 53 Cong., 3 sess., XXVII, Pt. II, 1199.

[7] *Congressional Record*, 53 Cong., 3 sess., XXVII, Pt. I, 728.

represented in the negotiations; and that they have religious scruples against taking allotments."[8]

Curtis and other interested congressmen were assured that the Department of the Interior would use all dispatch in bringing the Indians under control in order to satisfy the demands of the home-seekers for an early opening, and the official word went out that the presidential proclamation authorizing settlement in the Kickapoo country would come before the end of spring, 1895. By March prospective settlers began to gather on the fringes of the Kickapoo country, setting up crude camps and awaiting the promised proclamation.

As in earlier land runs the geographical background of the candidates for homesteads was varied, for there were homeseekers from Texas, Arkansas, Missouri, New York, Massachusetts, and Michigan. One colony of 412 was expected by rail from Lexington and Louisville, Kentucky, and the leader described his people as "men of means" and requested local agents in Oklahoma City to have all preparations made, including horses, since the Kentuckians "would all want to buy cheap ponies to run on."[9] Every train into the Territory during May overflowed with homeseekers, wagons, teams, and farm equipment; hotels and boarding houses in Oklahoma City and Shawnee were "full to the brim ... reaping a harvest for a few days" as they catered to those prospective settlers who disdained the camps on the rim of the Kickapoo country.[10]

Oklahoma City, Shawnee, and Choctaw City, all near the Kickapoo line and principal centers for outfitting, "were full of gamblers, thugs, and thieves. Games were run wide open and many of the prospective settlers were robbed. At Shawnee ... an infuriated mob threatened to hang the 'Butterfly Kid' and 'Kechi' two noted characters, and had the rope around their necks when stopped by Sheriff Deford and his deputies. They had robbed several of the settlers by means of a shell game. There were thirty-six saloons in

[8] Secretary of the Interior to the Speaker of the House, Washington, January 18, 1895, 53 Cong., 3 sess., *House Exec. Doc. No. 222, 1–2.*

[9] Oklahoma City *Daily Oklahoman,* May 21, 1895.

[10] *Ibid.*

Shawnee, each of which had a gambling attachment. The three-card monte and shell game men plied their trade on barrels and boxes in front of the saloons unmolested by the officers."[11]

If the homeseekers managed to escape the clutches of the gamblers, con men, and desperadoes who swarmed through the towns and camps, they still ran the risk of being cheated by less obvious forms of graft. For every previous land run involving Indian allotments, "Boomer" leaders had printed and distributed free of charge, months before the opening, neat little guidebooks containing maps showing the area to be opened, the sections reserved for Indian allotments (which were closed to entry), and the location and legal description of each homestead open for entry with detailed instructions on how to select and file. Because of the uncertainty of Kickapoo allotments, the official allotment map for the Deep Fork reserve was not prepared by the Bureau of Indian Affairs until February, 1895, and for some reason its contents were not made public, as had been the custom. Some enterprising officer or clerk in the Bureau traced a copy from the original and sent it out to confederates in Oklahoma City who printed several hundred copies and sold them to eager homeseekers for fifty dollars each. This bonanza met a sudden death when public-spirited newspapers in Oklahoma City and Guthrie purchased a copy of the plat, published it, and thereby cut the cost from fifty dollars to a few cents—the price of a daily newspaper.[12]

All persons intending to make the run for a homestead in the Kickapoo country were required to register their intent at the General Land Office booth in Oklahoma City. Since the booth was to be opened only a few days before the run, it was important to register early and be back at the starting position on the Kickapoo line, ready for the signal. Town loafers, bums, and others, with no intention of participating in the run, formed a line at the registration booth several days ahead of time and then offered their places to homeseekers for prices ranging, according to position, from five dollars to over one hundred dollars. Number one position sold four

[11] Guthrie, Oklahoma, *Daily Oklahoma State Capitol,* May 24, 1895.
[12] Guthrie, Oklahoma, *Daily Oklahoma State Capitol,* March 27, 1895.

days before the run for $110, and its former owner received in addition wages of $5 a day to hold it, "the purchaser being a lady."[13]

Correspondents from a number of leading newspapers spent several weeks in the Kickapoo country sending in news and feature stories on the Kickapoo run. Permitted by United States officials to travel over the Deep Fork reserve several days before the opening, the reporters were dismayed by the abundance of "Sooners" settled on choice locations and were agreed that the settler waiting on the line for the signal stood slight chance of finding a claim not already taken. W. C. Richardson, Kansas City *Star* correspondent, reported to his paper that the Kickapoo Country "was full of Sooners, enough to take the claims several times over," and the *Daily Oklahoman* representative noted that the "ravines and brush along the river contains hundreds of Sooners who are only awaiting the blast of the trumpet to hop out, and onto the claims, and if they don't hear the blast they'll do the hopping act anyway. Deputy United States marshals are in the country arresting all they can find; but a 'five' will go a long way with them, make them blind, deaf, and dumb, if necessary."[14]

The Guthrie *Daily Leader* correspondent discovered the "Sooners" had conjured "a new scheme . . . to deceive settlers." It seems that "Sooners" had "gone upon the land and planted fraudulent stakes, purporting to tell that the particular section is an allotment or school section, to cause honest homeseekers to go past it for open land further on. Then the planter of the stakes will follow leisurely, pull them up and use them to cook his coffee with Thursday night on the site of a carefully chosen and unlawfully gotten claim."[15]

President Grover Cleveland issued the Kickapoo opening proclamation on May 18, 1895, authorizing the race for homesteads to take place five days later, May 23, at high noon. As the starting shots were fired on the east, south, and west sides of the Kickapoo

13 Oklahoma City *Daily Oklahoman,* May 21, 1895.
14 Oklahoma City *Daily Oklahoman,* May 22, 1895.
15 Guthrie, Oklahoma, *Daily Leader,* May 22, 1895.

country, a noisy mob of ten thousand surged into the Deep Fork reserve "on horses, mules, bicycles, wagons, buggies, and vehicles" of every description and soon "disappeared in a whirl of dust and confusion. Hundreds of women started and exhibited the same amount of enthusiasm as the men."[16]

The *Daily Oklahoman* correspondent wrote that ". . . the run was a magnificent sight. . . . Some of the best horses in the West, ridden by some of the best horsemen, took part and it was a sight calculated to stir the blood of the coldest mortal in existence. In many localities the country is heavily wooded, and as the horses wound in and out among the trees, going at their highest speed, first one ahead and then another, it was a race which will not soon be forgotten by those who witnessed it."[17] The Guthrie *Daily Leader* representative described the change of the Kickapoo country in his account:

> At dawn a wilderness, at midday a seething, rushing, rioting mob, at eve a settled community; such is, in brief, the history of one day's wonderful transition in the land of the Kickapoo. The sun rose on the Kickapoo Reservation; it set at night on settled parts of Lincoln, Oklahoma, and Pottawatomie counties. Wednesday night the stars shone over a stretch of silent prairie which has known nothing but the monotonous whirr of the cricket and the warble of the thrush and the tread of the ghost dance and thump of cowskin drum; last night they glinted above a community of men contending in courts; levying, collecting and paying taxes; and setting in motion all the machinery that the civilized man needs for progress, a progress which in improving what nature has given him, departs as far as possible from nature's models and designs. Amid all this rush and change the Indian looks on in bewilderment and wonder, saying nothing, doing nothing. . . . There was something singularly pathetic in this farewell scene of the Kickapoo tribe."[18]

The Kansas City *Star* was not as charitable and seemed to take particular delight in the fact that this land rush would, according

---

[16] Guthrie, Oklahoma, *Daily Oklahoma State Capital,* May 23, 1895.

[17] Oklahoma City *Daily Oklahoman,* May 24, 1895.

[18] Guthrie, Oklahoma, *Daily Leader,* May 24, 1895.

to the *Star's* editor, "wipe out the name Kickapoo," so that eventually it would be "dropped from history and from the memory of men." The editor continued with the pompous assertion that the Kickapoo "encounters the fate he invites. In over two hundred years of intercourse with white people the Kickapoo never learned any good; never became of any value or use to humanity or the world; never invented anything. Savages in the seventeenth century they remained savages in the nineteenth. Hence all efforts in their behalf were defeated by themselves. Unfit to occupy the soil they were removed as cumberers of the ground. Such is the alternative offered the races of man. The tree that bears no good fruit of civilization, peace and progress, is cut down."[19]

Actually this was not a "farewell scene" for the Kickapoos, for in a few years these Indians were again very much in the public eye. With their eternal penchant for becoming involved in the dramatic and sensational, the Kickapoos between 1900 and 1915 were probably the best known of the Indian tribes in the United States. The Kickapoo land scandals, a monument to evil genius and deceit; the Bentley scheme, implicating leading United States officials; and a Senate investigation which allegedly "covered up quite as much as it revealed" furnished choice copy for newspapers in the United States for fifteen years.[20] And if the tribe bore "no good fruit of civilization," it was in large measure because of the sordid education they received from the many instructors in villainy who gathered about their domain to betray Kickapoo trust and exploit their innocence.

The chain of events which shortly restored the Kickapoos to public notice began quietly and innocently enough in 1896 with the appointment of Martin J. Bentley as special Indian agent for the "Kicking Kickapoos." This band, led by Wahpahhoko, had refused to accept allotments and, in order to maintain their old communal life, had squatted on Oklahoma Territory indemnity school lands situated in the northern portion of the old tribal reserve. The

[19] Kansas City *Star,* May 22, 1895.
[20] Joseph B. Thoburn and Muriel H. Wright, *Oklahoma—A History of the State and Its People,* II, 558.

government of Oklahoma Territory, pushed by farmers who had leased these lands and were demanding possession, was putting inordinate pressure on the Bureau of Indian Affairs to evict the trespassing Kickapoos, and in fact had threatened to use the territorial militia to drive the Indians from the school lands. The commissioner of Indian affairs, desperate for a solution, was surprised to receive a petition from the "Kicker" band in 1896 requesting that Martin J. Bentley be appointed agent to look after their interests, his services to be of no expense to the government since the tribe would pay his annual salary. While this request was highly irregular, matters had reached a crisis, and the commissioner appointed Bentley as special agent for the "Kicking Kickapoo" band.[21]

Martin J. Bentley—an attorney by profession, an adventurer by disposition—had spent most of his early years in Kansas, where he engaged in land speculation and railroad promotional schemes. Endowed with a keen imagination, forceful personality, and remarkable foresight, Bentley was aggressive, striking in personal appearance, and highly articulate, with a notable ability to overcome his opposition. Bentley belonged to that legal wolf pack which ranged restlessly up and down the American frontier during the 1890's seeking wealth and power. Many had ended their quests in the Indian nations, plundering tribal treasuries and Indian estates, and appropriating rich coal, lead, zinc, and oil royalties under the guise of promoting justice for the unlettered tribesmen of the Indian Territory.

Even before the Kickapoo opening, lawyers from various towns in Oklahoma Territory and as far away as Topeka and Kansas City, denouncing the "great injustice" which had been perpetrated upon the Kickapoos by the Allotment Agreement of 1893 whereby the tribe received only thirty cents an acre for surplus lands while neighboring tribes had been paid $1.50 an acre, swarmed to the Deep Fork. One law firm offered to manufacture a case for the Kickapoos to recover the difference for a fee of twenty-five per cent of any award received; another agreed to attempt recovery

[21] *Report of the Commissioner of Indian Affairs of 1900,* 336–37.

for fifteen per cent of the take. Since most of the tribe refused to recognize that an allotment agreement had ever been negotiated, and approved, the Kickapoos could not accept these proposals and most of the lawyers left. Bentley remained, took up his residence among the Kickapoos, and began to take a deep interest in their affairs.[22]

Bentley ingratiated himself by defending the Kickapoos without charge on whisky-possession counts, and interceding on their behalf when designing white men attempted to have themselves appointed guardians of Indian minors in order to control their allotments. An indication of the tribe's growing trust in their new protector was that in guardianship cases, Bentley was the choice of the Kickapoo council. By 1900 he controlled the property of practically every minor in the tribe. Bentley's popularity with the "Kickers" increased when he gained hunting privileges for small parties in the western Chickasaw Nation. And only six months after his appointment as special agent for the Kickapoos—to the wonderment of the officials in the Bureau of Indian Affairs—he had the "Kicking Kickapoos" settled on their allotments, where, according to the annual reports Bentley submitted to the commissioner of Indian affairs, his charges "were making remarkable progress." His statement for 1899, more enthusiastic than any previous reports, claimed that he had produced a transformation among the "Kicking Kickapoos" and reminded the commissioner that "by purely persuasive means," he had "succeeded in moving them to their allotted lands in the North Canadian valley. At that time but two of them spoke any English, and that very imperfectly. None could read or write, or had ever attended school. . . . Today fifty of them can speak English enough for ordinary business intercourse; twenty can read and write . . . conditions are most satisfactory, and the Kickapoo are making extensive improvements on

[22] "Proceedings of the Kickapoo Indian Tribe, Kickapoo Village, Oklahoma Territory, May 11, 1895"; Commissioner of Indian Affairs to Thomas, Washington, July 24, 1895; Commissioner of Indian Affairs to Thomas, Washington, October 2, 1895; and Commissioner of Indian Affairs to Thomas, Washington, February 24, 1897, Sac-Fox Agency File, Oklahoma Historical Society.

their lands, fencing, plowing, clearing, planting, putting up hay. . . . the habit of labor is well and thoroughly established among the Mexican Kickapoo."[23]

The "Progressive" Kickapoo band, those Indians who had accepted allotments and other government programs, had continued under the jurisdiction of the Sac and Fox agent after the Kickapoo run. Bentley had regularly suggested to the commissioner of Indian affairs that the "Progressive" Kickapoos also be assigned to his administration, pointing out that it was inefficient and at times awkward to have the tribe divided between two agents. So impressed was the commissioner of Indian affairs by the reported progress Bentley had made with the "Kicking Kickapoos" that in 1899 he directed the Sac and Fox agent to turn over to Bentley's "exclusive jurisdiction and control" the "Progressive" Kickapoos, thus uniting the tribe administratively.[24]

A year after the union took place, Bentley claimed that "the Mexican Kickapoo Indians . . . who were considered the meanest, least civilized, and most worthless of all the Indians of Oklahoma Territory, when I was appointed their agent, are today the most progressive. From worthless, poverty-stricken idlers, they have become successful tillers of the soil. . . . The Kickapoo are now living in contentment and upon their own allotments."[25]

In spite of this reported progress, Bentley was suddenly relieved of his duties as special agent for the Kickapoos late in 1901. He was replaced by a veteran of the Indian service, Frank Thackery, who came to the Kickapoos with a long term of service as head of the Wichita Agency at Anadarko. Former Agent Bentley, with characteristic aplomb, accepted his dismissal "with deep regret," adding for the benefit of the commissioner that he left his assignment with the assurance that the Kickapoos were in a "prosperous and satisfactory condition," it having "taken six years of the best energy of my life to bring about and make possible this system of

[23] *Report of the Commissioner of Indian Affairs for 1899*, 291–93.

[24] Commissioner of Indian Affairs to Patrick, Washington, April 15, 1899, Kickapoo Affairs, Sac-Fox Agency File, Oklahoma Historical Society.

[25] *Report of the Commissioner of Indian Affairs for 1900*, 336–37.

progress, and in its accomplishment it has not been a matter of compensation. My appointment as agent was made upon the petition of these Indians, and my services have been paid from their funds at their request. Thus I have been not only their agent, but the agent of the Government, and now that the Department seems to have wisely chosen a new general policy in the management of these Indians by placing them under the jurisdiction" of Frank Thackery, Bentley continued, "I retire from the service with the absolute confidence of the Indians and with the most kindly feeling toward the Department and my superiors. . . . During my administration I have discouraged sale of lands by the Indians under my charge, even to the extent of having to go to court to defeat the efforts of speculators who had themselves appointed guardians of Indian children for the single purpose of acquiring their lands and the proceeds."[26] But Bentley's dismissal as special agent for the Kickapoos did not end his association with the tribe.

[26] *Report of the Commissioner of Indian Affairs for 1901*, 338–40.

23

The Bentley-Thackery War

MOST OF THE MEXICAN KICKAPOOS were shocked, grieved, and angered by Martin J. Bentley's summary dismissal as their agent. The tribe had come to trust and to respect him, and he was the most popular agent ever assigned the tribe. The Kickapoos recalled that Bentley had defended them without cost in the white man's courts, had looked after the affairs of Kickapoo minors as guardian, and had gained hunting permits for the warriors. They appreciated the fact that Bentley had not required them to work their lands but, after they had moved onto their allotments, had arranged to lease the pasture and crop land to neighboring white farmers, thus freeing the Kickapoos to observe their festivals, hold their dances, and visit other tribes. He permitted them to race their horses and did not meddle in family affairs by requiring Kickapoo children to attend school. The tribe also remembered Bentley's promise that if they moved to their allotments and were discreet, he would see to it that in the very near future they would have a new home where the tribe could once again live in a communal village, hold their lands in common, worship their tribal gods without the interference of missionaries, and live by hunting, all as the Great Spirit had ordained.

What the Kickapoos did not know at the time of his dismissal, and upon learning later, most refused to believe, was that Bentley had, according to investigators, ingratiated himself and used his official position to build up a system of influence over the tribe which would ultimately give him control of all Kickapoo allotments in Oklahoma Territory and all the funds which he extracted from Congress in the name of humanity and justice for the Kickapoos.[1] The commissioner of Indian affairs began to doubt Bentley's good intentions in 1900, when he was advised by the State Department that a Martin J. Bentley of Shawnee, Oklahoma Territory, had been in correspondence with the Mexican government concerning a grant of land for an Indian tribe resident in Oklahoma Territory; that Bentley had made a number of personal visits to Mexico on behalf of this request; and that he had sent delegations of Kickapoos to Mexico with letters of introduction to President Díaz "relative to moving from the United States to Mexico."[2]

Bentley's critics were found outside the government too; these included the farmers and ranchers who had negotiated leases with Bentley for the use of Kickapoo allotments. By 1900, Bentley had reportedly become so despotic in handling Kickapoo lease matters and, it was alleged, so "callously open in favoring his friends," that certain leaseholders formed an association and carried on a campaign to have Bentley removed as Kickapoo agent. This association wrote letters of protest to Bentley's immediate superior, the Sac and Fox agent, the secretary of the interior, and the commissioner of Indian affairs. One of these letters corroborated the Mexican relocation scheme and charged that "Bentley lies and defrauds us in every conceivable way and furthermore we can never find him in his office. He is either gone on some railroad deal or else on a trip to Mexico trying to locate the Kickapoo . . . down there. We want to deal with an agent whose word will be considered worth at least something and not one who is totally and wholly undesirable."[3]

Bentley was warned by the commissioner of Indian affairs in

---

[1] "Memorandum of Inspector Dickson's Investigation, December 1, 1905," Kickapoo Affairs, Sac-Fox Agency File, Oklahoma Historical Society.

[2] Bentley to Clayton, Shawnee, July 28, 1900, National Archives, Office of Indian Affairs, Bentley Case Papers.

[3] "Lessees of Kickapoo Lands to Patrick, Dale, Oklahoma Territory, June 17, 1901," Kickapoo Affairs, Sac-Fox Agency File, Oklahoma Historical Society.

March, 1900, that the government was aware of his "unwarranted and unofficial action" in the Mexican land grant attempts, and directed him to return to his duties as special agent for the Kickapoos and abandon these "adventures," or face dismissal from the service. Bentley ignored the warning and continued his attempts to obtain a land grant in Mexico for the purpose of relocating the Kickapoos. When the secretary of the interior learned, through the Department of State, of Bentley's insubordination, he wrote the commissioner of Indian affairs that "in the matter of the correspondence had by Mr. Bentley with the Ambassador of Mexico, it may be proper to state that . . . you personally called his attention to his unwarranted and unofficial action in this affair, directing him not only to discontinue his efforts in the matter of these land grants, but to return at once to his official duties and thereafter to devote his time to the legitimate work of his office. From the correspondence herewith returned, it is apparent that Mr. Bentley has ignored your instructions . . . and is guilty of insubordination and has violated in the most flagrant manner the rules of official etiquette and regulations of the Department. I find no extenuating circumstances which would in any aspect tend to justify his conduct, which so far as I can learn, stands without parallel. I am of the opinion that his case demands summary action, and I have therefore to recommend that he be dismissed from the service to take effect upon the appointment and qualification of his successor."[4]

Frank A. Thackery, formerly of the Wichita Agency at Anadarko, replaced Bentley as special agent for the Kickapoos on October 1, 1901, and for a solid fifteen years, from the first day of his assignment, Thackery carried on a running battle with Bentley for control of the Kickapoos and their property. Bentley opened a law office in Shawnee soon after his dismissal and established a peculiar and apparently lucrative liaison with the Kickapoos. Thackery found that most of the Indians were openly hostile and resentful toward him, were indifferent to his suggestions for im-

[4] Secretary of the Interior to the Commissioner of Indian Affairs, Washington, August 29, 1900, National Archives, Office of Indian Affairs, Bentley Case Papers.

proving their status by working their allotments and enrolling their children in the government school, and spent their time in Shawnee loafing in and around Bentley's office.[5]

After several months of patient but futile attempts to make headway with his new charges, Agent Thackery concluded that the primary cause of his frustration was the mysterious hold Bentley seemed to have over the Kickapoos. Curious and desperate, Thackery finally discovered that Bentley's control derived from his popularity; the Kickapoos liked Bentley because he had encouraged their native feasts, rituals, games, dances, and religion rather than attempting to obliterate all traces of indigenous culture, as was the policy of the Bureau of Indian Affairs at this time. The Kickapoos appreciated Bentley for the many favors he had done the tribe, such as representing the members in the white man's courts and managing tribal finances. They were grateful for the zealous protection Bentley had provided from all other white men—Bureau of Indian Affairs officials, missionaries, and private citizens alike—and in this connection Thackery charged that Bentley had successfully conditioned the Kickapoos to trust no white man but Bentley and to rely on his advice only. Bentley's most powerful attraction, Thackery learned on the streets of Shawnee, was that he had promised the Kickapoos that in the near future he, like a modern Moses, would lead the tribe to a promised land where they could once again hold their lands in common and "live in the old way," free of interference by scheming white men and the United States government.[6]

Checking Bentley's reports to the commissioner of Indian affairs on the progress he claimed he had made in leading the Kickapoos along the "white man's road," Agent Thackery reported examples of deliberate misrepresentation. Instead of the Kickapoos settling

[5] Thackery to Commissioner of Indian Affairs, Shawnee, December 19, 1901. "Affairs of the Kickapoo Indians," *loc. cit.*, II, 1713. By Bentley's own testimony it was revealed "the M. K. and T. and Southern Pacific, and Mexican International Companies for a time paid the rent" for the M. J. Bentley and Co. office in Shawnee. Bentley added that he "solicited business for the three companies."

[6] Thackery to the Commissioner of Indian Affairs, Shawnee, April 6, 1902, Kickapoo Affairs, Sac-Fox Agency File, Oklahoma Historical Society.

on their allotments, opening fields, building fences, and developing habits of thrift and industry, as Bentley had claimed, Thackery charged that most of the Kickapoo allotments had been leased to white farmers and ranchers during the Bentley regime and that the Kickapoos had lived a life of ease, indulging themselves in Indian pleasures while sustained by rations Bentley purchased for them from funds appropriated for the specific purpose of purchasing farming equipment and maintaining a school for the tribe. Where Bentley boasted that fifty Kickapoos were able to speak and understand English well enough for ordinary business purposes and twenty were competent in reading and writing English, Thackery found the "Kicker" faction of the tribe totally illiterate and discovered that both factions required the services of a paid interpreter. Thackery reported that a strong reason for Bentley's popularity with the tribe was his promise "to fix it" so that the Kickapoo children would not have to attend school. Bentley constantly reminded them that if they co-operated with the new agent, they could expect forced school attendance for their children. When Thackery revealed these alleged discrepancies to the commissioner of Indian affairs, an inspector was dispatched to the Kickapoo agency. After attempting to check the financial records for the Bentley period, the investigator gave up in dismay over "the very loose fashion" in which he claimed Bentley had kept his accounts.[7]

According to investigators from the Bureau of Indian Affairs, when Bentley learned that Thackery was looking beneath the surface of his administration as Kickapoo agent, he responded with a clever campaign of diversion to divert attention from himself to the opposition, a strategy he used skillfully and effectively many times in his long struggle with Thackery for control of Kickapoo property and tribal funds.[8] In this instance, well-turned letters signed by Kickapoo leaders in Oklahoma Territory began to arrive in the offices of the commissioner of Indian affairs, the secretary

[7] Secretary of the Interior to the Commissioner of Indian Affairs, Washington, January 30, 1902, National Archives, Office of Indian Affairs, Bentley Case Papers.

[8] "Memorandum of Inspector Dickson's Investigation, December 1, 1905," Kickapoo Affairs, Sac-Fox Agency File, Oklahoma Historical Society.

of the interior, and certain congressmen and senators belittling Thackery's handling of Kickapoo affairs, and complaining of his neglect of official duties, his incompetence, and his vicious personal habits.[9]

Bentley was also engaged in railroad promotion, land speculations, and other assorted enterprises. When the Chickasaw Nation was allotted soon after 1900, Bentley traveled among the booming towns of Fitzhugh, Ada, and Roff as an agent for the Chickasaw Development Company, speculating in coal, oil, and grazing and cotton lands.[10] The question of the source of Bentley's capital for these investments was raised, and Kickapoo Agent Frank Thackery, trying to build a case against Bentley with the hope of breaking his hold on the tribe, reported that Bentley received fifteen hundred dollars annual salary, along with various allowances and unlimited travel passes from several major railroads interested in townsite and coal lands in the Chickasaw Nation. By far the major resource for Bentley's "financial adventures," according to Thackery, was the Kickapoos. As tribal attorney Bentley was paid an annual salary. Since he was also tribal trustee, all money coming to the Kickapoos for lease fees and per capital shares of the proceeds from surplus land passed through his hands, and Thackery charged that he had induced the Indians to invest much of this in what he referred to as "the tribal pool," promising the tribe that this money would eventually enable him to relocate them in Mexico. Thackery alleged that aside from holding power of attorney for practically every member of the tribe, a prerogative he exercised "whenever possible" in transacting their business, Bentley was legal guardian for all Kickapoo minors and had absolute control of their lands and other property.[11]

Thackery claimed that Bentley planned to gain title to the lands

9 Wahpechequa to Commissioner of Indian Affairs, Shawnee, January 13, 1902, National Archives, Office of Indian Affairs, Bentley Case Papers.

10 Bentley to Clark, Roff, Indian Territory, November 6, 1904; Chickasaw Development Company to Bentley, Ada, Indian Territory, May 19, 1904, Kickapoo Affairs, Sac-Fox Agency File, Oklahoma Historical Society.

11 Thackery to Commissioner of Indian Affairs, Shawnee, April 20, 1904, Kickapoo Affairs, Sac-Fox Agency File, Oklahoma Historical Society.

of the Kickapoos. Moses Neal, allotting agent from the Bureau of Indian Affairs, had selected the best land on the old Deep Fork reserve for the Kickapoos when he made their homestead assignments in 1894. Many of the allotments he had selected for the tribe were situated in the rich bottom of the North Canadian, while seven Kickapoo allotments were located on the edge of the fast-growing town of Shawnee. It was conservatively estimated that these seven eighty-acre allotments alone were worth at least three hundred thousand dollars for real estate development purposes. Under the terms of the Kickapoo Allotment Act of 1893, the Indians were to receive patents of ownership, but title to each Indian homestead was to be held in trust by the government for twenty-five years unless these restrictions were removed by an act of Congress. Thus, while the landowner could use or lease his land, he could not dispose of it during the restricted period. The single exception was inherited land. The control and use of the lands of Indian minors was directed by a court-appointed guardian.

Agent Thackery charged Bentley with manipulating the heirship clause of the Kickapoo Allotment Act. By 1904 many of the older Indians who had accepted allotments had died, and under the terms of the act their survivors could sell the inherited land. It was the practice at several Indian agencies to dispose of the land at public auction, thus obtaining a fair, competitive price for the heirs. Frank Thackery attempted to persuade Kickapoo heirs to follow this practice, but they would do nothing without first seeking Bentley's advice. Agent Thackery claimed that when a landowner died, Bentley rushed the heirs away to visit relatives in Mexico, and thereby was able to control the signing of the deed and the price paid, receiving his customary commission as well as custody of the purchase money, since much of the heirship money went into the "tribal pool." Bentley spent very little money on this sort of transaction, Thackery reported, since "those Indians going to Mexico are given passes on the railroads." Thackery noted that Bentley's alleged heirship machinations also worked a hardship on "any ordinary farmer or other person who cannot afford to go to Mexico to get his deed signed and no doubt

325

will object to paying some rascal from one to two to three hundred dollars to get his deed signed by the proper Indians."[12]

Agent Thackery charged that the Invalid Allotment Rule was another source of profit for Martin Bentley. The General Land Office had established the rule, honored by the courts, that if an Indian died before the government issued patent of ownership for his allotment, the allotment passed to the public domain rather than to the heir and was opened for entry by any settler who could prove prior death of the owner. The tribe's reluctance to record information concerning births, deaths, and other vital statistics made the Kickapoos easy targets for this activity. While there were at least six instances of attempts to apply the Invalid Allotment Rule, the most dramatic case involved Wapanakeskaha, who died soon after the tribe had been allotted. Former agent Lee Patrick persuaded Wapanakeskaha's heirs to sell the allotment to him for $1,804, and although Kickapoo Agent Thackery protested that "the land would bring a considerably larger amount" than Patrick had paid for it, the transaction stood until a local farmer, Jackson Davis, brought proceedings to have the allotment vacated so that he could make a homestead entry, claiming that Wapanakeskaha had died before the allotment patent was issued. Davis substantiated his claim with several sworn affidavits signed by certain Indians who claimed to have knowledge of the date of Wapanakeskaha's death. Thackery produced affidavits to the contrary, and the heirs were allowed to keep the purchase money while title passed to Patrick. What few of those people involved knew, according to Thackery, was that Jackson Davis had engaged Martin Bentley to provide affidavits which would have, if accepted, transferred Wapanakeskaha's allotment to the public domain, and that Davis had deposited one thousand dollars in the Oklahoma National Bank to be paid to Bentley when he could prove that Wapanakeskaha had died before the patent was issued.[13]

[12] Dickson to Commissioner of Indian Affairs, Shawnee, April 14, 1905; Thackery to Commissioner of Indian Affairs, Shawnee, December 6, 1908; Thackery to Commissioner of Indian Affairs, Shawnee, April 30, 1903, Kickapoo Affairs, Sac-Fox Agency File, Oklahoma Historical Society.

Thackery pointed out to the commissioner of Indian affairs that these were small activities, however, compared to Bentley's scheme for appropriating title to all Kickapoo lands, "a conspiracy so bold and callous that it defied the most extravagant imagination." Thackery charged that Bentley gave his closest attention to this project. Leading men in Congress were persuaded that the Kickapoos were unhappy on their allotments, that these Indians were unremitting in their determination to resist the attempts of the Bureau of Indian Affairs "to lead them along the white man's road," that money spent in attempting to achieve this was money wasted, and that the Kickapoos longed to join their fellow tribesmen in Mexico. Proposals were introduced in Congress to remove all restrictions on the sale of Kickapoo allotments "in order that the tribe could dispose of their property in the United States and return to Mexico and make a fresh start." It was further recommended that all money and interest yet due them from the sale of their surplus lands be paid at once, and that a sum of $215,000 be appropriated to settle the "injustices" of the Hill Agreement, which had forced the Kickapoos to accept thirty cents an acre for their surplus lands rather than the customary $1.50[14] Taking frequent trips to Washington to promote these measures, Bentley also chaperoned a number of Kickapoo delegations to the congressional committees for added emphasis. As early as 1903, Thackery reported, Bentley had begun shipping railroad cars of government issue farming equipment, saddles, mules, horses, and entire Kickapoo families to Mexico through Eagle Pass.[15]

Bentley's preparations so excited the Kickapoos that Agent Frank Thackery's efforts to establish rapport with the Indians and to work with them to improve their lot were futile. Discouraged, Thackery shared his problem with the commissioner of Indian affairs, charging that Bentley had made "all sorts of representations

[13] Thackery to Commissioner of Indian Affairs, Shawnee, December 8, 1904, Kickapoo Affairs, Sac-Fox File, Oklahoma Historical Society.

[14] *Congressional Record,* 59 Cong., 1 sess., 5788–90.

[15] Thackery to Commissioner of Indian Affairs, Shawnee, January 9, 1903, Kickapoo Affairs, Sac-Fox Agency File, Oklahoma Historical Society.

... to these Indians ... to prejudice them against me such as that I was a school man and had been sent here to force the children in school, and the only way they could keep the children from going to school would be to remove them out of the country to Mexico. . . . In September, a large number of these Indians, more especially the Indian children, were shipped to Mexico." Thackery added that he and Elizabeth Test, the Quaker missionary, had "seen several receipts issued to certain of the Kickapoo by Martin J. Bentley wherein he acknowledged the receipt of large sums from the Indians who had been paid money derived from the sale of heirship land," which Bentley had placed in the "tribal pool" to pay the colonizing expenses. Thackery added "there is no question but that the majority of the Kickapoo have turned a large part of their money received from the sale of heirship land over to Mr. Bentley."[16]

Agent Thackery was personally responsible for all government property issued to the Kickapoos, and when he found that Bentley was shipping large quantities of farming equipment and livestock to Mexico, he began stopping the cars to recover the government property. But even in the exercise of what was clearly an official responsibility, Thackery was placed in a bad light by Bentley, who wrote Senator Matthew S. Quay excusing the attempted appropriation of government property as an "honest mistake" by innocent Indians, particularly Pakotah, who had supervised the loading of the railroad cars for this particular shipment. Pakotah, confided Bentley to Quay, was resentful of the "miserable treatment" he had received at the hands of Agent Thackery, and he was leaving his allotment for a new home in Mexico "because he was being persecuted and felt that his life was in danger here."[17]

While efforts to remove restrictions from the selling of allotments and to award the Kickapoos a money settlement were unsuccessful during the legislative years of 1903 and 1904, early in 1905 a Kickapoo land bill was reported favorably. Bentley was in

---

[16] Thackery to Commissioner of Indian Affairs, Shawnee, November 4, 1903, Kickapoo Affairs, Sac-Fox Agency File, Oklahoma Historical Society.

[17] Bentley to Quay, Shawnee, January 1, 1903, National Archives, Office of Indian Affairs, Bentley Case Papers.

Washington during January, 1905, and when victory seemed near, he confided to Joseph Clark, his secretary in Shawnee, that "the prospect is good for getting what I came for, or part of it, and I expect to come west for a few days in the Indian Territory. Have a copy of the Kickapoo Allotment Roll made."[18]

As matters developed, a compromise was necessary and only a part of the Kickapoo proposal was approved at this time. This was a satisfactory beginning, however, for restrictions were abolished on the seven choice allotments bordering the Shawnee city limits. By the Indian Omnibus Act of March 3, 1905, the secretary of the interior was directed to issue patents in fee to Okemah, Thithequa, Wahkethehah, Noten, Thapathethea, Shuckequah, and Neconopit, and all limitations to the sale of their allotments were lifted.[19]

Even before the act was signed, according to affidavits furnished Thackery by tribal members mentioned in this legislation, Bentley transported the seven Kickapoos mentioned to Mexico, settled them temporarily with Mexican Kickapoo relatives at Nacimiento, and secured warranty deeds from each. By April 1, 1905, less than a month after passage of the act, Bentley was back in Shawnee arranging for transfer of the allotments to Shawnee real estate interests. The top price Bentley was offered by the Shawnee Townsite Company was $43,970; another offer amounted to $39,000; and the lowest offer for an eighty-acre tract was $28,300. This represented a phenomenal return on investment since, Thackery claimed, Bentley had received the warranty deeds from the Kickapoos for considerations ranging from $300 to $1,500 in Mexican money. All went well until Thapathethea, a Kickapoo woman and one of the landowners listed in the act, arrived in Shawnee from Mexico during the late spring of 1905, found surveyors platting her allotment, and was informed that her land had been purchased from Bentley by the Shawnee Townsite Company. Thapathethea went to Agent Thackery and denied that she had sold

[18] Bentley to Clark, Washington, January 29, 1905, Kickapoo Affairs, Sac-Fox Agency File, Oklahoma Historical Society.

[19] Kappler (ed.), *op. cit.,* III, 140.

her land; she claimed that Bentley had told her to "touch the pen, a symbol of signing the paper," in order to authorize him to lease her land, and that Bentley had paid her $300 in Mexican silver as "advance lease money."[20]

With Thapathethea's affidavit—affirming that she had been assured by Bentley that she had signed a lease and not a deed to her allotment—as evidence, Agent Thackery requested the commissioner of Indian affairs, in view of what he felt to be a "palpable fraud" perpetrated by Bentley on the seven Kickapoo allottees, that the patents in fee to the seven allotments be withheld and that the Bureau of Indian Affairs undertake a thorough investigation of Bentley's activities as tribal attorney and trustee for the Kickapoos. Inspector Charles H. Dickson was promptly assigned to look into Bentley's management of Kickapoo affairs. His investigation, the first of several formal inquiries, reported evidence of deceit, abuse of Kickapoo trust, and outright fraud, and his report was so conclusive that it attracted the interest of the Department of Justice. Curiously, the Congress completely disregarded the evidence these investigations produced. Henry Teller regularly defended Bentley and his management of Kickapoo affairs before the United States Senate, and during 1906 and 1908, Congress passed into law all of the Kickapoo proposals, including one which authorized payment of over twenty-six thousand dollars to Bentley for his services to the Kickapoos.[21]

[20] Thackery to Commissioner of Indian Affairs, Shawnee, April 6, 1905, National Archives, Office of Indian Affairs, Bentley Case Papers; "Affidavit of Thapathethea made at Kickapoo Camp, Shawnee, August 2, 1905," Kickapoo Affairs, Sac-Fox Agency File, Oklahoma Historical Society.

[21] For a speech by Senator Teller defending Bentley and promoting the second Removal of Restrictions Act, see *Congressional Record,* 59 Cong., 1 sess., 5788–91.

24

The Shawnee Wolves

WHEN INSPECTOR CHARLES DICKSON arrived in Shawnee, Oklahoma Territory, during April, 1905, Agent Frank Thackery briefed him on the latest Kickapoo developments, including the news that Bentley had sponsored the migration to Mexico of more than two hundred Kickapoo landowners. According to Thackery, only about one hundred Kickapoos remained on their allotments, and these comprised the last of the "Progressives." With Thackery's help Dickson finally persuaded the leaders of this band to council with him, and after some hesitancy they began to furnish evidence against Bentley, ranging from such minor complaints as "rents for land under Bentley were very low" to heated denunciations of "Bentley's big steal." Keotuck, a headman, offered: "You know what these Indians here think. . . . White people coax the Indians and tell them what they have to do. White people told Indians that Government law is to take the children away. . . . Bentley tells them that the Government will force their children to school and make the Indians pay taxes. . . . He is always trying to frighten them." Muchaninni, another headman, recalled that "when Bentley was agent he urged all the Indians to sell their land." Muchaninni added that the Kickapoos were "very much troubled by Bentley, who keeps the Indians stirred up all the time. These Indians are like children, and they do not know what to do. The Government ought to protect the Indians, because they cannot protect themselves . . . and white people take advantage of them. Bentley has given the Indians a good deal of trouble. Some way should be found to stop this and let the Indians have rest."[1]

From interviews with Agent Thackery, Dickson learned that a "considerable number of the businessmen of Shawnee" were interested in Bentley's plan to obtain removal of restrictions and gain control of the Kickapoo allotments. Thackery charged that this enterprise was "backed by a notorious set of grafters and rascals who are smart enough to deceive these poor Indians into their way of thinking by misrepresenting matters to them . . . and leading them to believe that they are going to a place where they can forever have their happy hunting ground and live as old time Indians in the full sense of the term."[2]

Following this lead, Dickson reported that he had discovered that even as Kickapoo agent, Bentley had had secret agreements with businessmen and farmers in and around Shawnee to deliver deeds to certain pieces of heirship land for a fee. A notable instance of Bentley's collusion, Dickson claimed, involved his contract with a group of Shawnee bankers organized as the Pottawatomie County Fair and Driving Association. The association was interested in obtaining an allotment near Shawnee as a site for the fairgrounds, and in 1903 the bankers engaged Bentley to acquire it for them. The owner of the allotment died and the heirs were co-operative. Bentley received ten shares of stock in the association, worth approximately twenty-five hundred dollars, for these services.[3]

The decorous Elizabeth Test informed Dickson that "Bentley was doing everything in his power to induce the Indians to remove to Mexico and that as the Indians told her, he was telling them that there would be soldiers sent here; that if they did not go away there would be war, the Indians would be killed, that all the Indians who remained here would have their children taken away and sent to distant schools . . . that he was going to get lands for these In-

[1] "Proceedings of Council at Muchaninni's Camp, Shawnee, April 15, 1905," National Archives, Interior Department File No. 6, Kickapoo Affairs.

[2] Thackery to Dickson, Shawnee, July 30, 1905, National Archives, Kickapoo Affairs, Interior Department File No. 6.

[3] *Bentley* v. *Benson*, Amended Petition in District Court, Potawatomie County, Oklahoma Territory, 1906, Sac-Fox Agency File, Oklahoma Historical Society.

dians in Mexico, where they would be entirely free to hunt and
their children would not have to go to school; that he commenced
to work upon the minds of the Indians by sending small parties
down to Mexico to see their relatives."[4]

From Shawnee, Dickson traveled to Saltillo, Mexico, where he
held interviews with Governor Miguel Cárdenas, of Coahuila, for
the purpose of learning the attitude of the Mexican government
toward the two hundred Kickapoos who had recently followed
Bentley to Mexico. Cárdenas declared that the Kickapoos resident
in Mexico near Nacimiento were regarded as citizens of the Republic and were respected by all for their independence, thrift,
and industry, but that the members of Bentley's colony were regarded as shiftless drunkards and were unwelcome in Mexico. Governor Cárdenas informed Dickson that since his government had
refused to permit the recent emigrants to settle on the Kickapoo
reservation at Nacimiento, Bentley was attempting to find land for
them elsewhere, and that he had rented a pasture near Musquiz
as a temporary camp. Cárdenas closed the interview with the charge
that Bentley's Kickapoos were "vicious in their habits, drunken,
and troublesome," and that Coahuila "would most gladly get rid
of them as they were no benefit, but on the contrary a detriment."[5]

Before returning to the United States, Inspector Dickson visited
the Oklahoma Kickapoo camp near Musquiz. His report to the
commissioner of Indian affairs of this visit—a chronicle of degeneracy—afforded tragic contrast to the glowing reports of Kickapoo
pride, honor, fearlessness, and independence made by Marcy, Glisan, and others scarcely a half century before. Dickson found the
descendants of the lords of the middle border debauched and nearly
destitute:

> In all my experience I have never seen any Indians so low in the
> scale in both mental and moral conditions, so dissipated through

---

[4] Statement of Elizabeth Test, Shawnee, September 9, 1905, National Archives,
Kickapoo Affairs, Interior Department File No. 6.

[5] "Memorandum of interviews with Governor Miguel Cardenas, Saltillo, Coahuila, July 17, 1905," National Archives, Kickapoo Affairs, Interior Department
File No. 6.

strong drink, and all its attendant evils, so entirely lacking in all the elements which make for manhood and civilization as are these . . . Kickapoo Indians. Degradation and misery are plainly manifest and there is apparent helplessness and hopelessness among them all. While a few of the leading Indians made professions of being satisfied with their present condition, I am satisfied from information that the large majority are discontented and unhappy. Promises made to them have been unfilled, and they begin to realize that the roseate pictures painted for them will not be realized. The children particularly, or many of them, looked as if they were sickly and did not have regular and nourishing food. Some of them appeared to be scurvy. When we first visited the Indian camp there seemed to be real destitution, but in a few days some Indian hunters returned to camp with dried venison in good quantity, when this condition was temporarily relieved. But the great trouble with these Indians (freely admitted by Mr. Bentley) is the plentiful use of ardent spirits, (almost pure alcohol) which can be bought anywhere at any saloon, without restriction, for about 15 to 20 cents per quart in Mexican money. . . . That Mr. Bentley has had, and has now, an undue influence over these Indians in Mexico, was plainly manifest to me (as I observed carefully his actions toward them) in all his dealing with them, and on the other hand there was an apparent dread or fear of him on the part of these Indians. On several occasions the fear of Bentley on the part of the Indians was plainly in evidence. In fact some three or four of them told me that they would like to talk with me, but they were afraid of Bentley. They really did not dare to be seen at our quarters in Musquiz. The Mexican officials . . . remarked that Mr. Bentley seemed to have the mastery over these Indians, and held them completely in his power. Through this undue influence . . . and with the assistance of others, Mr. Bentley has been able to impose and perpetrate upon these Indians one of the most glaring and flagrant instances of misrepresentation, deceit, and fraud.[6]

Dickson's report on his investigation of Kickapoo affairs shocked the Bureau of Indian Affairs and the Department of the Interior. Since a bill was already before the Congress to lift all restrictions

[6] "Memorandum of Inspector Dickson's Investigation, December 1, 1905," Kickapoo Affairs, Sac and Fox File, Oklahoma Historical Society.

on the sale of Kickapoo allotments, the commissioner of Indian affairs furnished a copy of Dickson's report on Bentley's activities to the secretary of the interior and recommended that he request Congress to reconsider the first Removal of Restrictions Act, which had opened seven choice Kickapoo allotments to sale and that the new owners be required to vacate the seven allotments so they could be restored to the Indians. The commissioner warned that the proposals to lift restrictions on the selling of all Kickapoo allotments, presently before the Congress, would, if approved, produce gravest consequences.[7]

Obviously it was essential to the success of Bentley's plan that the Oklahoma Kickapoos be as far removed from Shawnee as possible when Congress passed the second Removal of Restrictions Act, in order to avoid interference from outside interests. Governor Cárdenas' order had frightened some of the Kickapoos, and several of them were talking about returning to their allotments in Oklahoma. Bentley shared his concern with his associate, Walter Field: "Hell is to pay and I do not know what to do. The Oklahoma Kickapoo are ordered off the reservation and Roman [Galan] says they are camped in his pasture. I do not want them to come straggling back to Shawnee and think it is best to rent a place to put them and hold them there."[8]

Renting a campsite near Musquiz and leaving his secretary, Joseph Clark, to watch over the Kickapoos, Bentley traveled extensively across West Texas looking over possible sites for the Kickapoos' "Promised Land." Ranging widely north of the Rio Grande during late May and early June, 1905, without success, Bentley stopped at Spofford, Texas, on June 14 to bring Field up to date on his progress. Bentley's intent is clear in the note to Field: "I am fully determined to buy land on this side of the river. Our means

---

[7] Commissioner of Indian Affairs to Secretary of the Interior, Washington, December 14, 1905, Kickapoo Affairs, Sac-Fox Agency File, Oklahoma Historical Society.

[8] Bentley to Field, Eufaula, Indian Territory, May 14, 1905, Kickapoo Affairs, Sac-Fox Agency File, Oklahoma Historical Society.

is too limited to tackle Mexico and life is too short. We will buy us a team and outfit here within 100 miles of Eagle Pass, and the Indians will be suited, they will have to be in fact."[9]

Soon after Dickson's visit to Musquiz, Governor Cárdenas, his attention apparently diverted to other matters, relaxed his pressure on the Oklahoma Kickapoos. Bentley, taking this as permission for the Oklahoma Kickapoos to remain in Mexico, abandoned his attempt to purchase land for his Indian followers and prepared to travel to Washington, where several matters required his attention. On his way north Bentley stopped in Shawnee to write to Field on October 19, 1905, that he was to "meet Congressman Curtis at Kansas City to get him to help us out."[10]

Congress, paying little attention to the Dickson report, passed the Kickapoo Removal of Restrictions Act in early June, 1906. Senator Henry Teller made a vigorous defense of Bentley and the removal of restrictions measure just before passage.[11] The act lifted restrictions on the sale of all Kickapoo allotments held by nonresident adult members of the tribe, and directed that the Kickapoos be paid in per capita shares all the money plus interest due them by the Hill Agreement of 1891.[12]

In late May, 1906, when passage of the bill was assured, Bentley hastened to Mexico. Ominous tidings had come to him from friends in Shawnee; several Oklahoma capitalists, closely watching the status of the second Kickapoo Removal of Restrictions Act, had formed a combination, pooled their resources, and planned to go to Mexico and purchase the entire block of Kickapoo allotments as soon as the act went into effect. The "nonresident Kickapoo" clause of the Second Removal of Restrictions Act was, according to Thackeray, a stratagem to force the Kickapoos to leave the country in order to dispose of their allotments and to eliminate all com-

[9] Bentley to Field, Spofford, Texas, June 14, 1905, Kickapoo Affairs, Sac-Fox Agency File, Oklahoma Historical Society.

[10] Bentley to Field, Shawnee, October 19, 1905, Kickapoo Affairs, Sac-Fox Agency File, Oklahoma Historical Society.

[11] *Congressional Record,* 59 Cong., 1 sess., 5788–91.

[12] Kappler (ed.), *op. cit.,* III, 230.

Kickapoo Indians migrating to Mexico. From a print
furnished by Martin J. Bentley, agent for the Kickapoos, February, 1907.

JOHN MINE, a Kickapoo, and Martin J. Bentley, agent for the tribe, 1906.
From a photograph by De Lancey Gill.

petition for deeds once transfer of title was lawful. Thackery reported that Bentley was earnestly alarmed and desperate when he discovered that the Shawnee group was preparing to travel to Mexico and tamper with his Kickapoos. Thackery suggested that his desperation probably accounted in part for the extreme methods he adopted in acquiring deeds, for he had always controlled these Indians by non-violent measures; faced with the threat of interference, Bentley added brutality to deceit.[13]

Henry Murdock, a semiliterate Kickapoo, later made a deposition relating the events which followed. In late May, 1906, a few weeks before the second Kickapoo Removal of Restrictions Act went into effect, Bentley and Walter Field called a council of the Oklahoma Kickapoos at their camp near Musquiz. Bentley directed Murdock to interpret the news of the passage of the bill and to transmit Bentley's warning that the Indians "must not sell their Oklahoma lands, but they must allow him . . . to trade or swap their Oklahoma lands for other lands in Mexico." Bentley reminded the tribe that they had come to Mexico "to hold their lands in common so that they could live like the Indians lived hundreds of years ago"; that "they would have no taxes to pay in Mexico and would not have to work or do anything else but hunt"; and—most important of all—that "their children would not have to go to school." Murdock threw the council into turmoil by adding, on his own initiative, a plea to his fellow tribesmen not to sign any papers for Bentley until they were sure that they fully understood the contents of the deeds Bentley and Field had prepared. Murdock pointed out that other buyers would probably soon arrive in Mexico for their lands, and that if they were determined to sell their allotments in Oklahoma, they should wait for the highest price. Murdock's words infuriated Bentley; a Mexican policeman was called in, and Murdock was arrested and jailed at Musquiz. Bentley and Field promised him his freedom if he would co-operate, but when Murdock refused, he was forced to work on the city streets as a public prisoner. When Murdock finally agreed not to interfere with the coun-

13 Thackery to Commissioner of Indian Affairs, Shawnee, August 18, 1907, Kickapoo Affairs, Sac-Fox Agency File, Oklahoma Historical Society.

cils and promised to leave Mexico, he was released—after paying a twenty-five dollar fine. Murdock reported to government investigators that at least fifty Oklahoma Kickapoos in Mexico were anxious to return to their allotments, but "if they attempt to do so, they are immediately arrested for debts purported to be owed by them to . . . Roman Galan who has been working in conjunction with . . . Bentley for the past several years."[14]

Murdock's advice to the Kickapoo council caused some members of the tribe to oppose Bentley and Field, who were working feverishly to obtain deeds to the Oklahoma Kickapoo allotments before the land buyers from Shawnee arrived. According to statements subsequently made by other Kickapoos, threats of arrest brought many of the recalcitrants to terms, while actual imprisonment in the Musquiz jail induced others to sign. Mack Johnson stated under oath that when he refused to acknowledge the deed to his allotment which Bentley and Field had prepared, a Mexican policeman and one of Roman Galan's servants pinned his arms while another Galan employee pistol-whipped him. Johnson added that during his punishment, since his "wife and female relations were there, excited and crying . . . I signed the paper Bentley wanted me to sign. They did not read the paper to me and I did not know what it was, but suppose it was relating to my land."[15]

Bentley's fear of outside interference was justified, for after the first of June, 1906, and before he had finished taking deeds, Musquiz fairly swarmed with land buyers from Oklahoma Territory. The newcomers, numbering about fifteen, were for the most part from the towns around the Kickapoo country—some from Harrah, Dale, and McLoud, but most of them from Shawnee, which soon gave rise to a name used by the Indians for these tormentors, "Shawnee Wolves." A Senate investigating committee which probed

[14] Deposition of Henry Murdock made for Maverick County, Texas, June 9, 1906, Kickapoo Affairs, Sac-Fox Agency File, Oklahoma Historical Society.

[15] Statement of Mack Johnson, Musquiz, June 22, 1906; Statement of Ahetenjetuck, June 11, 1906; Statement of Homer Anderson, Musquiz, June 11, 1906; Statement of Paphshe, Musquiz, June 5, 1906; Statement of Tepeathepea, Musquiz, June 26, 1906; Statement of Wahthechonahah, Musquiz, June 21, 1906, National Archives, Kickapoo Affairs, Interior Department File No. 6.

Kickapoo affairs the following year was able to identify three different factions among the land buyers. The most active group included Charles J. Benson, who furnished the capital for this combine, W. L. Chapman, and Al Brown; Willard Johnston, C. M. Cade, and Russell Johnson comprised another faction with capital supplied by Johnston and Cade; and the third faction, John Garrett and James Jacobs, was supported by Garrett's money. Three other interested persons, dealing directly with the Oklahoma Kickapoos and at various times associated with all three factions, were L. C. Grimes, R. C. Conine, and Tony Alexander. It was reported that this trio terrorized the Oklahoma Kickapoos.[16]

When Bentley learned of the arrival of the Shawnee crowd, he took strict security measures to keep the newcomers from molesting his Indians. According to government investigators in Mexico for the United States Department of Justice, Alberto Guajardo, the *jefe político* at Musquiz was paid by Bentley not only to certify Bentley's deeds for Kickapoo allotments as each was taken and to allow Bentley to use his jail, but also to protect Bentley from outside interference.[17]

According to the Senate committee which investigated this struggle for power, Musquiz, a typically serene North Mexican town, was transformed during the late spring and early summer of 1906 as the Shawnee crowd waged a vigorous campaign to break Bentley's hold on the Oklahoma Kickapoos and to open the Indian camp to their agents. It appeared there was an unwritten agreement among the three factions that the common enemy was Bentley; to destroy him was the important consideration, and when this had been accomplished, there would be plenty of land for all. Instead of fighting among themselves, they concentrated on defeating Bentley. The leaders of the three factions remained in their Musquiz hotel rooms and left Bentley to Grimes, Conine, and Alexander.[18] Investigators from the Department of Justice reported it was ap-

---

[16] "Affairs of the Mexican Kickapoo Indians," *loc. cit.*, I, 3–14.

[17] Report of George Outcelt, Musquiz, Coahuila, May 29, 1906, Kickapoo Affairs, Sac-Fox Agency File, Oklahoma Historical Society.

[18] "Affairs of the Mexican Kickapoo Indians," *loc. cit.*, I, 3–7.

parent to Grimes, Conine, and Alexander that "he who controls Guajardo controls Bentley and the Oklahoma Kickapoo," and since the Oklahoma combine offered more for his services than had Bentley, Guajardo's attitude toward Bentley suddenly changed.[19]

Bentley found himself in jail; his staff was ejected from the Kickapoo camp by Guajardo's police; Grimes, Conine, and Alexander were installed in power; and, according to the Senate report, the Oklahoma Kickapoos were terrorized until most of the eligible allottees—and some who were not eligible—had deeded their Oklahoma property to the "Shawnee Wolves." Groups of Kickapoos were herded to Eagle Pass under close guard, held incommunicado in a wagon yard, and taken out a few at a time to sign deeds before Texas notaries and courts of record. Those Indians who protested or resisted were arrested, placed in chains, and put to work on the streets of Musquiz; many of the recalcitrants, the report continued, were bullied or pistol-whipped. Those Kickapoos who, in spite of all manner of threats, physical violence, and coercion, would not "touch the pen" were abandoned as hopeless, and the Shawnee agents forged their marks on allotment deeds.[20]

Other obvious cases of forgery, according to the Senate report, included signed deeds to allotments. In one case the allottee had been dead five years when the alleged signature was made; in several other instances it was proved that the Indians involved were in Oklahoma at the time the signatures were received; and at least three Kickapoos living on choice allotments on the Canadian in Oklahoma, who had no intention of becoming nonresident under the terms of the second Kickapoo Removal of Restrictions Act, were taken to Musquiz by henchmen of the Shawnee crowd and forced to sign deeds. Senate investigators noted that although the Shawnee combine had acquired deeds to most of the nonresident Kickapoo allotments in Oklahoma by early autumn, there remained in Oklahoma fine pieces of property belonging to Kickapoo minors.

[19] Report of George Outcelt, Tecumseh, Oklahoma, December 6, 1906, Kickapoo Affairs, Sac-Fox Agency File, Oklahoma Historical Society.

[20] "Affairs of the Mexican Kickapoo Indians," *loc. cit.*, I, 47.

The allotment of each Indian minor was controlled by a court-appointed guardian until the child achieved majority. Several of the minors who owned allotments had accompanied their parents to Mexico, and among them were boys and girls ranging in age from fifteen to eighteen. The Senate report stated that Grimes, Conine, and Alexander gathered up at least six of these young Kickapoos, took them to Eagle Pass, swore before a Texas notary they were of marriageable age, and had them married by civil ceremony, thus releasing them from guardian control. Deeds were taken immediately for their allotments. Later investigation showed that in every case these "matchmakers" had selected young people who had no marital interest in each other, and that after satisfying the Shawnee crowd by signing deeds, they lived not a single day together as man and wife.[21]

Department of Justice and Senate investigators looking into the activities of the "Shawnee Wolves" among the Kickapoos charged that Conine and Alexander went even further. The money that Oklahoma capitalists Benson, Cade, and Garrett put up to pay for the Kickapoo allotments was deposited in various Eagle Pass banks. As the Indians signed deeds to their allotments, each received a check for the amount listed in the transfer document. Eighty-acre allotments, appraised at five thousand dollars and sold almost immediately to other parties for ten thousand dollars, went for fifteen hundred dollars. The checks were then deposited in the same Eagle Pass banks by Conine, Grimes, and Alexander. The Senate committee reported that soon after the money had been deposited, Indians accompanied by Conine or one of his colleagues would confront the cashier with cash drafts and draw a portion or all of the money in their accounts. Later the real Kickapoo depositors would appear and find that their accounts had been cleaned out by imposters. Senate investigators charged further that Conine and Alexander used the same Indians, men and women, to impersonate various Kickapoo depositors, identifying them for the cashiers as genuine depositors. Since, as the bank employees

[21] *Ibid.*, I, 4–5.

claimed, "all the Kickapoo looked alike to them," the checks were honored, and, the report noted, Conine generally paid his Indian confederates fifty dollars for each impersonation.[22]

After obtaining deeds to the most desirable Kickapoo allotments, the Shawnee crowd relaxed its guard over the Oklahoma Kickapoos, and the bewildered, frightened Indians fled their Musquiz camp in small groups to hide in the mountains. Bentley finally secured his release from Guajardo's jail and, with characteristic resourcefulness, turned to the task of salvaging what he could from the wreckage caused by the Oklahoma combination. By mid–1907, Bentley had regained his favored position with most of the Oklahoma Kickapoos and had avenged himself on the Shawnee crowd, for their Mexican adventures were brought to the attention of the United States government. In the investigation which followed, Bentley served as Kickapoo tribal attorney, assisted in the embarrassing inquiry and litigation which ruined most of the principals, and managed to gain for himself the esteem of the Congress for protecting the interests of a benighted people. Bentley thus turned disorder to order and apparent defeat to sweet victory.

Gathering together as many of the scattered Oklahoma Kickapoos as possible and persuading them that he alone could protect them from the "Shawnee Wolves," Bentley announced that he still intended to "swap" their Oklahoma allotments for lands in Mexico where they could live communally as of old. Bentley then led them far into Northern Sonora twenty miles south of the Arizona line near Douglas, where he settled them on an abandoned ranch and, through Walter Field, arranged for ultimate purchase of the land. Leaving one of his agents, John W. Gostin, in Sonora to look after the Kickapoos, Bentley, as Kickapoo attorney, turned to exposing the Mexican activities of the Oklahoma combination. He also improved his position with the Oklahoma Kickapoos by establishing a trust agreement for the tribe. The trust arrangement designated Bentley, his wife Ida Bentley, and W. W. Ives, an Indiana real estate broker and former Bentley business associate, as trustees, and authorized him legally to receive the deeds to Oklahoma Kick-

[22] *Ibid.*, I, 5, 488.

apoo allotments, hold them in trust, and sell the allotments. From the proceeds, after deducting "reasonable expenses and compensation," Bentley was to purchase land in Mexico for the tribe.[23]

With his own house in better order, Bentley went at the Oklahoma combination with a vengeance. By authority of a resolution introduced by Henry Teller and approved by the Senate, an investigation of the Mexican adventure was begun in February, 1907.[24] Chairman Clapp of the Senate Committee on Indian Affairs appointed a subcommittee, which included Senators Curtis and Teller, and this body occupied itself for the remainder of 1907 with extended hearings in Washington, D.C.; Shawnee, Oklahoma; Eagle Pass, Texas; and Douglas, Arizona. Several hundred witnesses testified, and thousands of documents were introduced as evidence. Along with several leading Kickapoos, all the principals of the Oklahoma combination were called to appear before the Senate subcommittee, and Curtis and Teller were merciless in their questioning of Benson, Grimes, Conine, Cade, and Chapman. Bentley was in a unique and strategic position, for as Kickapoo tribal attorney, he examined each witness. He settled personal scores with the Oklahoma combination members by subjecting them to tortuous interrogation.[25]

From the Indian witnesses Bentley elicited answers which reflected credit upon himself. Bentley presented hundreds of affidavits, letters, and other items which further incriminated the "Shawnee Wolves." His own management of Kickapoo affairs was brought up by United States attorneys representing the Bureau of Indian Affairs before the subcommittee, and as a witness Bentley answered their questions with poise and calculated evasion. Senators Curtis and Teller were sympathetic in their examination of Bentley. The printed testimony clearly shows that Bentley was in command of the hearings throughout, interrupting witnesses, offering asides, correcting testimony, and constantly submitting exhibits in evidence.

[23] *Ibid.,* I, 609.
[24] *Congressional Record,* 59 Cong., 2 sess., 1197, 2743.
[25] "Affairs of the Mexican Kickapoo Indians," *loc. cit.,* I, 568.

The Senate subcommittee's report, submitted after the close of hearings in December, 1907, consisted of a stinging denunciation of the Oklahoma combination and a charge that "the conduct of the men, who were on the ground representing the Chapman-Grimes-Conine people in their efforts to secure the valuable lands owned by the Mexican Kickapoo Indians in Oklahoma" was "criminal and brutal in the extreme." The subcommittee's report revealed also that "outrages were shamelessly perpetrated by them, and their conduct has never been equalled in the history of any dealings to secure lands from American Indians. The names of the Indians were wilfully and deliberately forged to the deeds claimed to have been taken in Mexico. . . . The treatment of these Indians by the Chapman, Grimes, and Conine people, whom they took to Eagle Pass, was outrageous, and the treatment of the Indian women by these same people at Musquiz was such as to condemn them in the eyes of all decent people. . . . The evidence taken before your committee is conclusive that these Chapman, Grimes, and Conine people deliberately bought Mexican officials to assist them in their nefarious and criminal practices. There is evidence to the effect that L. C. Grimes told one of the witnesses that they had paid Alberto Guajardo, a Mexican official, $75 Mexican money for each deed executed."

Martin Bentley was completely vindicated by the report. The senators found that "many of the deeds taken by Mr. Bentley under the act of June 21, 1906, were taken simply for the purpose of protecting the Indians against what has been denominated as the Chapman-Grimes-Conine people . . . and whatever errors he committed were errors of judgment due in many cases to his zeal in protecting the Indians' interest, and there is no evidence whatever that he has diverted the said funds or any part thereof from their proper use." The published report of the investigation noted that Bentley had been somewhat indiscreet in handling tribal funds, but it added "that Mr. Bentley in his desire to properly serve the Indians in this regard, went further than he should have gone while acting as an agent, yet he and the Indians testified that this was done to secure what was known as a fight or expense

344

fund for the Indians and that he, Bentley, was not to derive any benefit therefrom. While your committee is satisfied that in this regard Mr. Bentley made a mistake for which he should be criticized, yet, the evidence warrants the committee in the conclusion that he did it in his zeal to do something beneficial to the Indians."

Concerning charges brought by the Bureau of Indian Affairs that Bentley had used coercion and deceit in acquiring deeds to Kickapoo allotments, the Senate subcommittee noted: "There has not been shown any evidence of force, or treachery or other culpable conduct on the part of Mr. Bentley or any of those associated with him, but on the contrary, it is shown that he has been ever watchful and zealous in the interests of these Kickapoo people."

Referring to the deeds taken for Oklahoma Kickapoo allotments, the report continued: "We find that the persons whom we have designated as belonging to the Chapman, Grimes, and Conine people, and all those claiming under them, secured their said pretended title by acts of violence, corruption, and fraud, intimidation, and debauchery, and some by committing the crime of forgery, and that they have no valid titles, but the deeds they hold are such a cloud upon the title that it is the duty of the Government to at once bring action to set the same aside." In order to accomplish this, the subcommittee recommended that a special attorney, "not heretofore connected with the investigation of Kickapoo affairs in Mexico, be employed by the Department of Justice, to have sole charge of the . . . cases, with authority to select his own assistants, and take such steps as may be necessary for the protection of the Mexican Kickapoo Indians, and promptly recover for them the lands from the parties claiming to hold title under the . . . act, except the parties Martin Bentley, Ida Bentley, and W. W. Ives holding lands in trust for said Kickapoo Indians."[26]

The vindication of Bentley by Senator Teller's subcommittee clearly gave him a monopoly over Kickapoo allotments, since, according to the report, only those deeds taken under the auspices of his trust agreement were to escape recovery suits by the United States. But the Oklahoma Kickapoos still had a tenacious cham-

26 *Ibid.*, I, 3–14.

pion in Agent Frank Thackery, who, despite private threats, official censure, and senatorial condemnation, stood by his claim that Martin Bentley was as dangerous for the Kickapoos as were the "Shawnee Wolves."

25

Justice for the Kickapoos

The Senate investigation of Oklahoma Kickapoo land frauds by no means closed inquiry into the affairs of Martin Bentley. In fact, officials in the Bureau of Indian Affairs and the Department of Justice redoubled their efforts to remove the Kickapoos from his control. The Bureau of Indian Affairs and Department of Justice investigators were puzzled by the ease with which Bentley could achieve approval by Congress of special Kickapoo legislation.

The most persistent and successful of the government investigators was Kickapoo Agent Frank Thackery. Because of Bentley's promises, about two hundred Kickapoos had left their allotments near Shawnee for Mexico during 1905 and 1906, and Thackery, with only about one hundred Kickapoos, members of the "Progressive" faction, to watch over, spent most of his time collecting evidence concerning Kickapoo affairs. The Bureau of Indian Affairs, anxious to follow up Inspector Charles H. Dickson's report on Bentley's mismanagement of Kickapoo interests, had detailed Thackery to work in liaison with Department of Justice investigators on the matter. Thackery was in Mexico taking depositions against Bentley when the Oklahoma combination arrived, and Bentley diverted attention from himself by accusing Thackery of being in league with the Chapman-Grimes-Conine crowd. Bentley's counterattack discredited Thackery in the eyes of Senator Teller's subcommittee. But it is to Thackery's credit that when he discovered the intent of the Oklahoma combination, he worked just as hard to destroy its hold over the Kickapoos as he had in the case of Bentley. Thackery furnished evidence against both the Oklahoma combination and Bentley before Senator Teller's subcommittee.

Because of Thackery's determination to continue his investigation after the Teller committee had destroyed the Oklahoma combination and vindicated Bentley, the commissioner of Indian affairs and the secretary of the interior began receiving protests from Teller concerning Thackery's interference. Senator Teller wrote Secretary of the Interior James R. Garfield during 1908 that in his estimation Thackery was unfit to handle Kickapoo affairs and that the commissioner of Indian affairs should "immediately withdraw from him supervision over any connection with the affairs of these Indians."[1]

Thackery apparently was not intimidated by the Senator's pressure, for he answered that justice had yet to be done the Kickapoos and claimed that he had been put in a bad light by a manipulation of the incriminating evidence he had submitted to Senator Teller's committee. Thackery contended that much of the evidence he had submitted to the committee on Bentley had been suppressed, particularly the sheaves of correspondence and copies of telegrams sent by Bentley in Mexico to various senators and lobbyists in Washington, of which only a few were entered and those "doctored" in the text of the published report.[2] Thackery charged that testimony had also been deliberately changed in order to show Bentley to the public more favorably than Thackery's investigations warranted. He concluded: "It is singular that these omissions, changes or mistakes all tend to weaken that part in the affairs which I have stood for and, on the other hand, to strengthen the Bentley-Field side of the controversy."[3]

While it was clearly not Thackery's duty to investigate United States senators, certain names appeared with increasing regularity

[1] Teller to Secretary of the Interior, Washington, March 4, 1906, Kickapoo Affairs, Sac-Fox Agency File, Oklahoma Historical Society.

[2] "Affairs of the Mexican Kickapoo Indians," loc. cit., II, 1560. 1154-67.

[3] Thackery to Secretary of the Interior, Shawnee, April 11, 1908, Kickapoo Affairs, Sac-Fox Agency File, Oklahoma Historical Society.

as his investigation of Bentley's relations with the Kickapoos continued. In the course of collecting correspondence related to the Kickapoo land frauds, Thackery had come upon letters affirming Senator Teller's active intervention on Bentley's behalf while Bentley was taking deeds in Mexico during 1906. The services of a United States consul were required to affirm the deeds. The commissioner of Indian affairs, seeking to protect the Indians and prevent Bentley from gaining control of their allotments, had requested the secretary of state to instruct United States consuls in Mexico not to co-operate with Bentley. Bentley protested to Teller concerning this order, and Teller, by letter to Robert Bacon, acting secretary of state, had promptly instructed the State Department to disregard the commissioner's request and to co-operate with Bentley:

> I was instrumental in securing the adoption of this portion of the bill, and I know the intention of Congress was that Mr. M. H. Bentley, the attorney for the . . . Indians should manage their affairs for them, as he had been doing for some time, with the entire approval of these Indians now in Mexico. The committee having this matter in charge know that the Commissioner of Indian Affairs was not friendly to Mr. Bentley, but did not suppose he would pursue the course he has since the passage of the act. . . . I understand that the consul at Diaz, Mexico was instructed by your Department to refuse to accept acknowledgments for Mr. Bentley. In this connection I desire to say that if this order is not withdrawn, the Department will be put in the position of attempting to nullify an act of Congress, which position I am sure your department will not care to be placed. . . . I hope that the above order will be withdrawn and that the consul at Diaz will be instructed to use all proper means to assist Mr. Bentley in carrying out the wishes of Congress.[4]

The active interference of Teller and Charles Curtis on Martin Bentley's behalf seemed to increase as Thackery continued his investigation. While attempting to gather evidence sufficient to warrant prosecution of Bentley on conspiracy and fraud charges,

---

[4] Teller to Bacon, Denver, July 13, 1906, Kickapoo Affairs, Sac-Fox Agency File, Oklahoma Historical Society.

Thackery was also obligated as Kickapoo agent to remove the Kickapoos from Bentley's influence and restore the tribe to the control of his agency and the Bureau of Indian Affairs. But during December, 1907, when Thackery sought through United States Attorney John Embry at Guthrie, Oklahoma, to have Bentley discharged as guardian for a number of Kickapoo minors, Teller wrote Embry that "Bentley as trustee for the Oklahoma Kickapoo should not be interfered with in looking after their interests" and that Embry should cancel Thackery's leases and sustain Bentley's leases. Teller's letter to Embry closed with an endorsement by Senator Curtis, "We trust that you will see that action is taken looking to the discontinuance of such practice" as discharging Bentley in favor of Thackery, and Curtis added "I gladly join Senator Teller in the above."[5]

John Embry's appointment as United States attorney semed to be in jeopardy during 1908, and Senator Curtis wrote to Embry assuring him that he would do what he could to assist in pushing Embry's appointment, but the Senator made it clear that Embry's cause would be helped if he would more diligently dismiss Kickapoo guardianship and lease cases brought by Thackery against Bentley. The Senator closed with the hope that Embry could see his "way clear to order dismissal of the cases. . . . If you will write me fully in regard to the matter, it will give me pleasure to do all I can to assist you. I have not had a talk with Senator Teller but will see him at the first opportunity."[6]

Thackery confided to Marke Goode, a Shawnee attorney, that he had it on good authority there was "no doubt as to the connection of Senator Curtis with Bentley's move," but Thackery expressed the "hope that it will not turn out so, for Curtis has always been a friend of mine, and I have always regarded him as a friend of the Indians. Clark says that when the restrictions were removed from the seven allotments, that Bentley did most of his business

[5] Teller to Embry, Washington, December 18, 1906, Kickapoo Affairs, Sac-Fox Agency File, Oklahoma Historical Society.

[6] Curtis to Embry, Washington, January 24, 1908, Kickapoo Affairs, Sac-Fox Agency File, Oklahoma Historical Society.

with Sam Powell, that between Powell and Dr. Linn at Washington, D.C., Curtis was reached. Clark says that he understands Curtis to be under great obligation to Linn in Kansas politics." Thackery thought "there was no doubt but that Powell was down here some months ago insisting upon the payment of some obligation by Bentley."[7]

The "obligation by Bentley" was explained to Thackery when, in the course of his investigation, he came upon copies of several telegrams between Bentley and Sam Powell, a Washington attorney. These messages, all concerned with the passage of the Kickapoo Removal of Restrictions Act of 1906, kept Bentley posted on developments. One wire sent from Powell in Washington to Bentley in Mexico on June 21, 1906, read, "Indian Bill signed. No change. Attend to matter of checks by wire."[8]

The activities of Bentley, Curtis, Teller, and other leading figures were revealing in an investigation which followed the passage by Congress on April 30, 1908, of a $215,000 appropriation to be paid the Oklahoma Kickapoos for settling all differences caused by treaties and agreements with the United States. While until this time Thackery had been concerned primarily with Kickapoo land dealings, he now had to face the problem of investigating the distribution of the money to the Indians. One of the depositions concerning this matter came from Lee Patrick, a former Sac and Fox agent who had become a Chandler, Oklahoma, banker. During his interrogation, which occurred on April 10, 1909, Patrick not only told how the appropriation was managed and how it was to be used, but also gave testimony on the background of the Kickapoo Removal of Restrictions Act of 1906. Patrick said that he had met with Bentley and Field during late 1905 to discuss the wording and cost of the desired legislation; Patrick recalled that Bentley and Field "claimed they needed about fifteen hundred dollars" as a beginning. In response to the question, "Did Mr. Bentley say . . .

---

[7] Thackery to Goode, Shawnee, July 16, 1907, Kickapoo Affairs, Sac-Fox Agency File, Oklahoma Historical Society.

[8] Powell to Bentley, Washington, June 12, 1906, Kickapoo Affairs, Sac-Fox Agency File, Oklahoma Historical Society.

that of course Senator Teller would have to have ten percent of the profits from the deal," Patrick could not remember that a specific amount was mentioned, but that they had "argreed that Teller would have to be taken care of." Patrick added that no formal agreement was reached during this meeting concerning the division of the Kickapoo allotments and that Bentley and Field had continued without him when the bill was finally approved. Patrick said that Bentley and Field met with him again during 1907 to discuss the formation of a corporation for handling Kickapoo allotment sales and any money appropriated for the tribe by Congress. Patrick remembered Bentley's proposed $215,000 settlement was the chief topic of conversation during this meeting, particularly the methods to be used in promoting its adoption. Patrick's subsequent answers were as follows:

Question: [Was] any suggestion made as to how much it would cost to secure the appropriation of that amount or as to how such appropriation should be handled when secured?

Answer: I don't think there was any amount suggested for legislation at that time. It was talked that when the appropriation was secured that it would be handled by Mr. Bentley and Mr. Field and that a good portion of it would be deposited in our bank at Stroud and Chandler and that we should furnish the money to purchase Mexican land and pay for the same out of this fund.

Question: What security had you that the legislation would be enacted or that you would get your money out of an appropriation not yet made?

Answer: Nothing whatever except that they seemed to have been successful in getting such matters through.

Question: Were you a part of the firm that met Bentley and Field aboard the Senatorial special car on the way from Shawnee to St. Louis after the meeting closed at Shawnee?

Answer: I accidentally got onto the train with them at Chandler to go to Stroud.

Question: Was the appropriation of two hundred and fifteen thousand discussed on that trip?

Answer: Only casually.

352

Pеhкотаh, a chief of the Mexican Kickapoos, 1907.
From a photograph by De Lancey Gill.

O-ke-ma (Окем아), head man of the Mexican Kickapoos,
Coahuila, Mexico, 1908. From a photograph by De Lancey Gill.

Question: Didn't you enter into an agreement to assist Bentley to get off as much of those Indians as possible to Mexico?

Answer: Yes, but that was by correspondence.

Question: Didn't you receive some telegrams concerning the matter?

Answer: Yes, I received telegrams from both Field and Bentley.

Question: Now, do you remember substantially the contents of those telegrams?

Answer: They were concerning the removal of the Kickapoos to Mexico and the number that he wanted taken.

Question: How many Indians did they want sent to Mexico?

Answer: I think they said they needed thirty some odd.

Question: About what was the date of this telegram?

Answer: Just a short time prior to the passage of the Act.

Question: What was the other telegram if you now remember?

Answer: I think it called for nine more.

Question: Now at this time, Mr. Patrick did you have any working agreement with Bentley? . . . and state . . . as full as you can with special view of showing why you expected to get these Indians to go to Mexico.

Answer: We were to establish a trust company . . . and the expense incurred in removing Indians was to be paid for by the trust company. The stock was to be issued to the several parties interested.

Question: Who were the interested parties or supposed to be?

Answer: Field, Bentley, . . . some of Field's Washington friends and myself.

Question: How much did Curtis have?

Answer: Ten thousand I think it was.

Question: How much did Senator Teller get?

Answer: I think it was the same.

Question: Now, Mr. Patrick, I want to ask you if you did not enter into an agreement with Bentley and Field, to get those Indians off down there, enough of them at least to give Bentley a majority, and was the consideration to be procured in the manner just outlined through a trust company plus some other profits as the firm might make in handling land of other Indians than the Kickapoo who might desire to go to Mexico and sell their allotments?

Answer: Yes.

Question: Did you . . . not call on Mr. Thackery about April 12, or 13 to talk to him about the situation?

Answer: Yes sir.

Question: If at that time were you not in receipt of a telegram from Bentley . . . reading substantially as follows, the first addressed to you, dated Washington, April 12, Thackery wanting trouble; getting Indians to protest; council his office tomorrow; call him off. Signed M. J. Bentley. The second dated the same at Washington, . . . Senator says call Thackery off immediately, signed M. J. Bentley?

Answer: Yes sir.

Question: Was anything during any of these discussions ever said or discussed by you gentlemen as to taking these Indians down to Mexico, robbing them of their property and pocketing the proceeds?

Answer: Yes sir, it was discussed.

Question: Was that the object of your conversation?

Answer: The object of it was to get hold of as much of the land as we could and make a profit out of it along with other people who might be in the same business.[9]

The *Congressional Record* showed that in the course of debate on the $215,000 appropriation Chairman Clapp of the Senate Committee on Indian Affairs had identified this measure "as a matter in which the Senior Senator from Colorado [Mr. Teller] is very much interested."[10] Apparently Thackery's investigation of Bentley's Kickapoo conspiracy, which had implicated Teller and Curtis, was becoming more than embarrassing for the Senators by 1909.[11]

As Thackery continued his search for evidence, it became more and more apparent that the Senate was deeply involved, and pressure from that source to abandon the inquiry of Kickapoo affairs diminished, enabling Thackery to make some progress. His first victory over Bentley in his fight to restore the Kickapoos to his agency and the Bureau of Indian Affairs came in 1908.

In that year Congress passed the $215,000 appropriation. The very language of the statute was loose, allowing for easy manipulation of the entire appropriation. The act directed that the lump

[9] Deposition of Lee Patrick, April 10, 1909, Kickapoo Affairs, Sac-Fox Agency File, Oklahoma Historical Society.

[10] *Congressional Record,* 59 Cong., 2 sess., 2274.

[11] Spencer to Thackery, Kansas City, April 7, 1909, Kickapoo Affairs, Sac-Fox Agency File, Oklahoma Historical Society.

sum of $215,000 be "paid by the Secretary of the Treasury as authorized and directed by a majority of the members of said Mexican Kickapoo tribe in council assembled. Such council shall be composed of a majority of those surviving members of said tribe, male and female, heretofore allotted in Oklahoma. The authorization . . . and the proceedings of said council shall be attested by a clerk of the United States District Court of the Territory of Arizona. Said sum shall be immediately available."[12]

Thus, the Kickapoo council, rather than the Congress, as was customary, was to determine the method of distributing the $215,-000. And the council which would determine the method of disbursal, was to be held, not at Shawnee, where the Kickapoo Agent could easily supervise the proceedings, but in Arizona, near Bentley's Kickapoo colony in Sonora, and this a mandate since the United States district court clerk of Arizona was specifically designated as the attesting officer. Clearly it was to Bentley's advantage to remove the council as far from Thackery's control as possible and to use the Kickapoos in Sonora as a core of support.

Bentley, as Kickapoo tribal attorney, called the council to convene at Douglas, Arizona Territory, May 16, 1908. When Thackery became aware of the possibilities of this plan, he worked hard to assure a majority of anti-Bentley Kickapoos. Since many of the Indians at Shawnee had no funds to pay their train fare to Douglas, Thackery raised money from private sources to buy tickets and food for the trip.[13]

It was found there were 157 original Kickapoo allottees living— each entitled to a vote in the council—and Thackery and Bentley kept score on one another as the council date approached. An affidavit signed by Samuel Bosley, a Kickapoo, charged that when it appeared that Thackery had mustered a majority and therefore would control the council Bentley rushed to Shawnee and attempted to bribe allottees with promises of one hundred dollars for each vote cast for his plan. According to Bosley, Bentley attempted to

12 Kappler (ed.), *op. cit.*, III, 337.
13 "Kickapoo Council Proceedings, McLoud, Oklahoma, May 11, 1908," Kickapoo Affairs, Sac-Fox Agency File, Oklahoma Historical Society.

force those who refused to remain in Shawnee, while at least two Kickapoo allottees he "shanghaied" to Sonora just before the Douglas council to receive instructions on voting.[14]

The council convened as planned, and it was found that of the 157 Kickapoos eligible to vote, Thackery had 82 while Bentley could muster only 75. After a heated opening, a compromise was worked out whereby Bentley would not control the total appropriation—a victory for Thackery because his following would receive some benefit from the $215,000. The council agreed to divide the money between the two bands. Bentley's following insisted that he receive an award of twelve and one-half per cent of the $215,000, or $26,875, for his services as tribal attorney in getting the legislation adopted. Upon their return to Shawnee, each of Thackery's Kickapoos received $1,200, the per capita share of the $215,000. Bentley's partisans authorized Bentley to use their share, nearly ninety thousand dollars, in developing the Kickapoo colony in Sonora.[15]

Thackery turned next to the task of recovering Kickapoo allotments. This was a most complex undertaking, since both Bentley and the Shawnee crowd had taken deeds to Kickapoo allotments, and certain Kickapoo allottees had signed as many as three deeds for a single allotment. The situation was further complicated by the fact that both Bentley and the Shawnee factions had resold the allotments to outside parties, thus adding color to title. And if the Kickapoo land question were not sufficiently confused already, the confusion was compounded by the fact that a number of innocent farmer-purchasers had negotiated mortgages on the Kickapoo allotments.[16]

Despite these obstacles the commissioner of Indian affairs appeared determined to see justice done the Kickapoos. Encouraged

14 Deposition of Samuel Bosley, Potawatomie Country Court, Shawnee, May 23, 1908, Kickapoo Affairs, Sac-Fox Agency File, Oklahoma Historical Society.

15 Secretary of the Interior to Chairman, Committee on Indian Affairs, House of Representatives, Washington, August 12, 1911, Kickapoo Affairs, Sac-Fox Agency File, Oklahoma Historical Society.

by Agent Thackery's report of the methods used by Bentley to obtain his deeds to Kickapoo allotments, and armed with the strong recommendations of Senator Teller's investigating committee concerning the legal action the government should take to regain the deeds to Kickapoo allotments obtained by the Shawnee combination, the commissioner requested the United States Department of Justice to file suits on behalf of the government for the purpose of recovering all Kickapoo allotments taken under the act of 1906.[17]

This series of recovery suits, involving approximately one hundred choice Kickapoo allotments, began a legal circus which cluttered federal and state dockets from Oklahoma to Texas and Mexico and included counter suits; civil and criminal proceedings; charges of libel, bribery, fraud, and forgery; and heated extradition hearings. While the central purpose of the legal proceedings was the government's attempt to recover title to the one hundred allotments in order to restore them to Indian owners, public interest was attracted by the sordid side issues. The public soon forgot Wahpahoko's Oklahoma Kickapoos, cast adrift in small bands to wander aimlessly over northern Mexico, suffering every privation and hopefully awaiting word from Frank Thackery that he had won back their land allotments—that they had a home to return to. John Embry, United States district attorney for the western District of Oklahoma, joined forces with Frank Thackery and, apparently undismayed by the legal maze, tenaciously worked for restoration of the one hundred allotments to the dispossessed Indians. Thackery's heavy file of evidence on Kickapoo land thefts was exposed in its entirety, and the proof left no doubt about the guilt of Bentley on the one hand and the Shawnee crowd on the other.[18] Between late 1907, when the government suits were first filed, and 1911, when

[16] Buntin to Brosius, Shawnee, August 3, 1914, Kickapoo Affairs, Sac-Fox Agency File, Oklahoma Historical Society.

[17] Commissioner of Indian Affairs to Thackery, Washington, June 12, 1907, Kickapoo Affairs, Sac-Fox Agency File, Oklahoma Historical Society.

[18] Embry to White, Guthrie, March 29, 1909, Kickapoo Affairs, Sac-Fox Agency File, Oklahoma Historical Society.

they finally were given a full hearing, Embry built his case for the Kickapoos.[19]

On January 19, 1911, United States District Judge John H. Cotteral sustained the government's position and directed that the Kickapoos receive their land free of all encumbrances. This meant that the defendants not only lost all the money they had invested in the Kickapoo land conspiracy but also had to go to the additional expense of clearing the titles they had encumbered with quick sales to innocent purchasers, and of liquidating all mortgages then in effect on Kickapoo allotments.[20]

Appeals by the defendants held up final settlement until 1914, when the United States Circuit Court of Appeals sustained the Government's case. Embry could write the United States attorney general on August 13, 1914, that the Kickapoo cases had been "finally disposed of, and the troublesome litigation concerning the same concluded."[21] While the United States government bore most of the expenses for the long battle with Bentley and the Shawnee crowd, each Indian who benefited from the restoration decision was assessed a token charge of $165 "to settle up this old trouble," to be paid from money received by the Indians from leases on their lands and various other income.[22]

Thackery and Embry were warmly congratulated by the commissioner of Indian affairs, the secretary of the interior, and the attorney general for finally winning justice for the embattled Kickapoos, and promotions were promised for both.[23] Private groups concerned with the welfare of the American Indian, having carefully watched the Kickapoo land cases and offered what support they could—particularly the Indian Rights Association and the'

[19] Grimes to Thackery, Harrah, January 30, 1911, Kickapoo Affairs, Sac-Fox Agency File, Oklahoma Historical Society.

[20] Attorney General to the Secretary of the Interior, Washington, April 10, 1911, Kickapoo Affairs, Sac-Fox Agency File, Oklahoma Historical Society.

[21] Embry to Attorney General, Guthrie, August 13, 1914, Kickapoo Affairs, Sac-Fox Agency File, Oklahoma Historical Society.

[22] Green to Matapene, Shawnee, April 8, 1916, National Archives (Fort Worth), Kickapoo File, Shawnee Agency.

[23] Commissioner of Indian Affairs to Thackery, Washington, February 1, 1911, Kickapoo Affairs, Sac-Fox Agency File, Oklahoma Historical Society.

Society of Friends—heaped accolades and citations on Thackery and Embry.[24]

Now that the Oklahoma Kickapoos had homes to which they could return, Thackery and other officers in the Indian service worked to bring them back, but this was not an easy task. Although a few families from Wahpahoko's band had returned to their allotments on the Canadian by 1916, most of the Kickapoos in Mexico continued to wander, spending a season now and then at Nacimiento with their Mexican Kickapoo kinsmen, returning to the old Bentley colony near Sonora for brief stays, and infrequently venturing visits to their allotments in Oklahoma.[25]

In the early years following restoration of allotments Wahpahoko's "Kicking Kickapoo" rarely remained for any extended period on their Canadian homesteads. These Indians carried deep scars and bad memories. The historic Kickapoo law of vengeance, in former times a positive means of gaining satisfaction and the only way these people knew how to handle their problems even in the early twentieth century, was forbidden by the white man's law to which they were now subject. Unlettered in the white man's way yet subject to his rules, they had suffered time and again because of laws, lawyers, and the courts. Until Frank Thackery and John Embry championed their cause and by these same laws and courts won back their allotments, the Kickapoos had never seen this legal machinery used for any purpose other than evil. Thackery and other officials in the Indian Service continued their attempt to assure the wary Indians that neither the "Shawnee Wolves" nor Bentley could ever harm them again, but the Kickapoos remained doubtful, and with some good reason, for their years of privation had been caused by the strange disappearance of their share of the Douglas money. Bentley had still had the support of the "Kicker" faction when the $215,000 settlement money was paid to the Oklahoma Kickapoos in 1908 by the United States government. Ex-

24 Brosius to Thackery, Washington, January 24, 1911, Kickapoo Affairs, Sac-Fox Agency File, Oklahoma Historical Society.

25 Makeseah to Guard, Shawnee, November 1, 1927, National Archives (Fort Worth), Kickapoo File, Shawnee Agency.

ploiting their loyalty to him, Bentley gained for himself not only the attorney's fee of $26,875, but also complete control of the nearly $90,000 awarded to the "Kicker" faction as its share of the settlement. Bentley assured his Kickapoos the money would be used to improve their common reservation in Sonora. Government investigators later found this "promised land," where the "Kicking Kickapoo" could at long last hold their lands in common, consisted principally of rocky desert country hardly sufficient to sustain a herd of mountain goats.[26]

The ninety thousand dollars disappeared; only token improvements were made; and in subsequent recovery suits, Bentley reportedly claimed that he had invested this money with the Oklahoma City firm of Miller and Mitschner, which in a few short months was bankrupt.[27] Without money, Wahpahoko's band remained destitute for years, sustaining themselves in an uncertain way by hunting in Mexico, some trading, and the lease money they received each year from the farmers leasing their allotments. Their fellow tribesmen in Mexico at Nacimiento and their "Progressive" kinsmen in Oklahoma also helped to support them. The "Progressive" Kickapoos were generally prosperous, most of them having accepted the per capita payments Thackery had wrested from Bentley when the $215,000 settlement was paid, for under Thackery's supervision and with his encouragement, they had used this money to improve their allotments. The impact of Bentley's mismanagement of their ninety thousand dollars was not fully realized by the "Kickers" until they visited the "Progressives" in Oklahoma during 1910, fleeing a famine which threatened their drouth-ridden, impoverished reservation at Bacerac, and saw with their own eyes the prosperity of their "Progressive" brethren. When Wahpahoko's headmen called at Bentley's comfortable headquarters in Shawnee they learned he was in Washington looking after "Kickapoo busi-

26 Buntin to Commissioner of Indian Affairs, Shawnee, March 12, 1914, Kickapoo Affairs, Sac-Fox Agency File, Oklahoma Historical Society.

27 Deposition of Ahkiskuck, Shawnee, February 2, 1910, Kickapoo Affairs, Sac-Fox Agency File, Oklahoma Historical Society.

ness." The "Kicker" faction undertook recovery proceedings and soon learned of the dissipation of their trust fund.[28]

Although this was an expensive lesson, the Kickapoos learned well, and if the "Kickers" failed to prosper materially for many years, their education produced considerable spiritual and moral improvement. They remained vagabonds for many years, but their restlessness gradually sated itself, and by the late 1920's many of them had taken up residence on their allotments on the Canadian.

In attempting to reconstruct the Kickapoo character, the chiefs and headmen worked long and hard to overcome the immoral habits various white men had evoked among the warriors. In due time the grandsons of the lords of the middle border came to share the pride and spirit of their elders, and they directed the tribe along a course that was conciliatory with the white man only when survival itself became a clear and immediate question; in general they held to the old ways. The Kickapoos had always led among the other tribes, and the old Kickapoo ego now seemed to reassert itself. The result of their proud independence is that a pure Indian culture, or as pure as can exist among the tribes of the United States today, resides among the Kickapoos.

[28]. *Ibid.*

Bibliography

I. MANUSCRIPTS

National Archives (Washington, D.C.)
  Interior Department File No. 6, Kickapoo Affairs
  Office of Indian Affairs
    Bentley Case Papers
    Central Superintendency, Miscellaneous Correspondence
    Central Superintendency, Kickapoo Files No. 98 and 73
    Letters Received (Fort Leavenworth Agency, Kickapoo Agency, and Western Superintendency) (Microcopy 234).
    Letters Sent (Microcopy 21)
    Michigan Superintendency
  Old Army Files
    Adjutant General's Office, Record Group 94
    Secretary of War, Letters Received
    Secretary of War, Letters Sent Relating to Indian Affairs (Microcopy 12)
    Fort Gibson Letterbooks, 1838–80
National Archives, Regional Branch, Fort Worth, Texas
  Office of Indian Affairs
    Shawnee Agency Files
National Archives, Regional Branch, Kansas City, Missouri
  Office of Indian Affairs
    Kansas Kickapoo Agency Files
Bureau of American Ethnology (Washington, D.C.)
  Mooney Field Notes
  Jones Field Notes

Great Lakes Indian Archives Project (Bloomington, Indiana)
  Kickapoo Files (1600–1957)
  Mascoutin Files (1600–1800)
Indiana Historical Society (Indianapolis, Indiana)
  Harrison Miscellaneous Collections
Kansas Historical Society (Topeka, Kansas)
  Clark Papers
  Diary of St. Mary's Mission
Library of Congress (Washington, D.C.)
  Marcy Papers
  Sherman Papers
  Sheridan Papers
Missouri Historical Society (St. Louis, Missouri)
  Auguste Chouteau Papers
  Pierre Chouteau Papers
  Chouteau-Moffitt Collection
  Chouteau-Papin Collection
  Clark Papers
  Forsyth Papers
  Frost Collection
  Fur Trade Papers
  Graham Papers
  Indian Papers
  Sibley Papers
  Voorhis Collection
Oklahoma Historical Society (Oklahoma City, Oklahoma)
  Foreman Transcripts
  Sac-Fox Agency File
Presbyterian Historical Society (Philadelphia, Pennsylvania)
  Kickapoo Missionary Papers
University of Oklahoma Library (Norman, Oklahoma)
  Cass Manuscripts
  Hume Papers
  Marriott Papers
  Miscellaneous Documents Relating to the Marcy Expeditions
University of Texas Library (Austin, Texas)
  Robert S. Neighbors Papers
  San Antonio de Bexar Archives
Wisconsin Historical Society (Madison, Wisconsin)

Draper Manuscript Collection
  Clark Papers
  Croghan Papers
  Harrison Papers
  Kentucky Papers
  Preston and Virginia Papers
  Tecumseh Papers
  Houck Transcript of Spanish Papers in the *Archivo General de Indias,* Sevilla

II. GOVERNMENT DOCUMENTS AND PUBLICATIONS

American State Papers, Indian Affairs. 2 vols. Washington, 1834.
Annual Reports of the Commissioner of Indian Affairs, 1829–1906.
Benton, Thomas H. *In the Senate of the United States.* Washington, 1824.
Carter, Clarence E. (ed.). *Territorial Papers of the United States.* Vols. I–XV. Washington, 1934–51.
Congressional Record, 1890–1915.
Correspondence on the Subject of the Emigration of Indians. 2 vols. Washington, 1835.
Donaldson, Thomas. *The George Catlin Indian Gallery in the National Museum.* Smithsonian Institution *Annual Report,* Pt. 2, 1885. Washington, 1886.
Ewers, John C. *George Catlin, Painter of the Indians of the West.* Smithsonian Institution *Annual Report,* 1955. Washington, 1956.
Gannett, Henry. *Gazeteer of Texas.* U.S. Geological Survey *Bulletin No. 224.* Washington, 1904.
Hodge, Frederick W. (ed.). *Handbook of American Indians North of Mexico.* Bureau of American Ethnology *Bulletin No. 30.* 2 vols. Washington, 1907, 1910.
Jenks, Albert E. *The Wild Rice Gatherers of the Upper Lakes. Nineteenth Annual Report* of the Bureau of American Ethnology, Pt. 2. Washington, 1900.
Jones, William. *Ethnography of the Fox Indians.* Bureau of American Ethnology *Bulletin No. 125.* Washington, 1939.
Journal of the Congress of the Confederate States of America, 1861–1865. Washington, 1904.
Kappler, Charles J. (ed.). *Indian Affairs: Laws and Treaties* (Laws). 3 vols. Washington, 1913.

————. *Indian Affairs: Laws and Treaties* (Treaties). 3 vols. Washington, 1904.

Memorial of the State of Missouri in Relation to Indian Depredations. Washington, 1826.

Michelson, Truman. *Algonquian Indian Tribes of Oklahoma and Iowa. Explorations and Field Work* of the Smithsonian Institution, 1928. Washington, 1929.

————. *Notes on Fox Mortuary Customs and Beliefs. Fortieth Annual Report* of the Bureau of American Ethnology. Washington, 1925.

Mooney, James. *The Ghost Dance Religion and the Sioux Outbreak of 1890. Fourteenth Annual Report* of the Bureau of American Ethnology, Pt. 2. Washington, 1896.

————. *Myths of the Cherokee. Nineteenth Annual Report* of the Bureau of American Ethnology, Pt. 1. Washington, 1900.

Report on Indians Taxed and Indians not Taxed. Eleventh U.S. Census, Washington, 1894.

Sheridan, Philip H. *Records of Engagements with Hostile Indians.* Washington, 1882.

Swanton, John R. *The Indian Tribes of North America.* Bureau of American Ethnology *Bulletin No. 145*. Washington, 1952.

United States Congress, House of Representatives: 22 Cong., 1 sess., *House Exec. Doc. No. 38;* 29 Cong., 2 sess., *House Exec. Doc. No. 76;* 33 Cong., 1 sess., *House Exec. Doc. No. 129;* 33 Cong., 2 sess., *House Exec. Doc. No. 15;* 40 Cong., 2 sess., *House Exec. Doc. No. 340;* 42 Cong., 3 sess., *House Exec. Doc. No. 63;* 42 Cong., 3 sess., *House Report No. 98;* 43 Cong., 1 sess., *House Exec. Doc. No. 39;* 45 Cong., 1 sess., *House Exec. Doc. No. 13;* 45 Cong., 2 sess., *House Report No. 701;* 45 Cong., 3 sess., *House Report No. 188;* 48 Cong., 1 sess., *House Exec. Doc. No. 16;* 48 Cong., 1 sess., *House Report No. 765;* 49 Cong., 1 sess., *House Report No. 642;* 52 Cong., 1 sess., *House Report No. 1662;* 53 Cong., 3 sess., *House Exec. Doc. No. 222;* 53 Cong., 3 sess., *House Report No. 1624.*

United States Congress, Senate: 23 Cong., 1 sess., *Sen. Doc. No. 512;* 29 Cong., 1 sess., *Sen. Exec. Doc. No. 1;* 30 Cong., 1 sess., *Sen. Report No. 171;* 32 Cong., 2 sess., *Sen. Doc. No. 14;* 32 Cong., 2 sess., *Sen. Exec. Doc. No. 54;* 36 Cong., 2 sess., *Sen. Exec. Doc. No. 1;* 45 Cong., 2 sess., *Sen. Misc. Doc. No. 23;* 47 Cong., 1 sess., *Sen. Report No. 233;* 48 Cong., 1 sess., *Sen. Exec. Doc. No. 18;* 60 Cong., 1 sess., *Sen. Doc. No. 215,* 3 vols.

United States Statutes at Large, XXVII.

War of Rebellion: A Compilation of the Official Records of the Union and Confederate Armies. Washington, 1896.

Yarrow, H. C. *A Further Contribution to the Study of the Mortuary Customs of the North American Indians. First Annual Report* of the Bureau of American Ethnology. Washington, 1881.

III. SPECIAL SOURCES

Annals of the propagation of the faith, a periodical collection of letters from the bishops and missionaries engaged in the missions of the old and new world, and of . . . documents relating to those missions, and the Institution of the Propagation of the Faith. 65 vols. Baltimore, 1868–1902.

Billet, Viola. "Indian Diplomacy in the Northwest Territory. 1783–1795." Unpublished M.A. thesis, Northwestern University, Evanston, Illinois, 1937.

Caldwell, Norman W. "The French in the West, 1740–1750." Unpublished Ph.D. dissertation, University of Illinois, Urbana, Illinois, 1936.

Dockstader, Frederick J. *The American Indian in Graduate Studies.* Heye Foundation, Museum of the American Indian. New York, 1957.

Dunham, Douglas. "The French Element in the American Fur Trade, 1760–1816." Unpublished Ph.D. dissertation, University of Michigan, Ann Arbor, Michigan, 1950.

Illinois Historical Society *Collections.*

Indian Rights Association *Annual Reports.* Washington, 1885–1932.

Kinietz, William V. "The Ethnology of the Illinois Indians." Unpublished M.A. thesis, University of Chicago, Chicago, Illinois, 1933.

Mexican Government. *Report of the Committee of Investigation, Sent in 1873 by the Government to the Frontier of Texas.* New York, 1875.

Michigan Pioneer and Historical Collections, vols. I–XL.

Murdock, George P. *Ethnographic Bibliography of North America.* New Haven, 1953.

Nasatir, Abraham P. "Indian Trade and Diplomacy in the Spanish Illinois, 1763–1792." Unpublished Ph.D. dissertation, University of California, Berkeley, California, 1926.

Nunn, William C. "Texas During the Administration of E. J. Davis." (Unpublished Ph.D. dissertation, University of Texas, Austin, Texas, 1938).

Pennsylvania *Archives.* 1st Series. Philadelphia, 1853.

Pennsylvania *Colonial Records.* Harrisburg, 1852.

Saeger, Armin L. "Extent of Participation of the Kickapoo Indians in Oklahoma in Community Activities." Unpublished School of Social Work paper, University of Oklahoma, 1957.

Silverberg, James. "The Cultural Position of the Kickapoo." Unpublished M.A. thesis, University of Wisconsin, Madison, Wisconsin, 1949.

Wisconsin Historical Society *Collections,* vols. 1–17.

Woodstock Letters, Woodstock College, Montreal, 1882, XI.

Wilson, Clyde W. "The Kickapoo Indians: An Ethno-History." Unpublished M.A. thesis, University of Texas, Austin, Texas, 1953.

IV. NEWSPAPERS

Army and Navy Chronicle, 1836–38.

Army and Navy Journal, 1873.

Cherokee Advocate, Tahlequah, Cherokee Nation, 1844–52.

Daily Leader, Guthrie, Oklahoma, 1892–98.

Daily Oklahoman, Oklahoma City, 1891–1916.

Daily Oklahoma State Capital, Guthrie, 1890–96.

Indian Advocate, 1889–1906.

Kansas City *Star,* 1894–96.

Missouri Republican, St. Louis, 1831–33.

Niles' Weekly Register, 1812–20.

Western Sun, Vincennes, Indiana.

V. ARTICLES

Abel, Annie H. "Indian Reservations in Kansas." *Kansas Historical Collections,* VIII (1903–1904), 72–109.

Almonte, Juan N. "Statistical Report on Texas—1835," *Southwestern Historical Quarterly,* Vol. XXVIII (January, 1925), 177–222.

Angle, Paul M. "Nathaniel Pope, 1784–1850," Illinois State Historical Society *Transactions,* 1936, 111–81.

Barry, Louise. "William Clark's Diary, May, 1826–February 1831," *Kansas Historical Quarterly,* Vol. XVI (February, May, August, and November, 1948), 1–39, 136–74, 274–305, 384–410.

"Battle Creek Fight in Navarro County," *Frontier Times,* Vol. IV (February, 1927), 57–60.

"Battle of Dove Creek," *Frontier Times,* Vol. I (July, 1924), 17–20.

Berryman, Jerome C. "A Circuit Rider's Frontier Experiences," *Kansas Historical Collections,* XVI, (1923–25), 177–226.

THE KICKAPOOS

Biggs, William. "Letter Written by William Biggs," Illinois State Historical Society *Journal*, Vol. VI (April, 1913), 129–33.

Blasingham, Emily J. "The Illinois Indians, A Study in Depopulation," *Ethnohistory*, Vol. III (Summer, 1956), 193–217.

Brainerd, Ezra. "Jeremiah Hubbard, Hoosier Schoolmaster and Friends Missionary among the Indians," *Chronicles of Oklahoma*, Vol. XXIX (Spring, 1951), 23–31.

Brennan, George A. "De Linctot, Guardian of the Frontier," Illinois State Historical Society *Journal*, Vol. X (October, 1917), 323–67.

Brown, Stuart. "Old Kaskaskia Days and Ways," Illinois State Historical Society *Transactions*, 1905, 128–44.

Buntin, Martha. "The Mexican Kickapoo," *Chronicles of Oklahoma*, Vol. XI (March, 1933), 691–708.

Caldwell, Norman W. "Fort Massac: The American Frontier Post, 1778–1805," Illinois State Historical Society *Journal*, Vol. XLIII (Winter, 1950), 265–81.

———. "Shawneetown: A Chapter in the Indian History of Illinois," Illinois State Historical Society *Journal*, Vol. XXXII (1939), 193–205.

———. "The Chickasaw Threat to French Control of the Mississippi in the 1740's," *Chronicles of Oklahoma*, Vol. XVI (December, 1938), 465–92.

Carr, Lucien. "The Mascoutins," American Antiquarian Society *Proceedings*, XIII (1900).

Chapman, Berlin B. "The Cherokee Commission at Kickapoo Village," *Chronicles of Oklahoma*, Vol. XVII (March, 1939), 62–74.

Cooper, Douglas. "A Journal Kept by Douglas Cooper," ed. by Grant Foreman, *Chronicles of Oklahoma*, Vol. V (December, 1927), 381–90.

Craig, Oscar J. "Ouiatanon—A Study in Indian History," Indiana Historical Society *Publications*, II (1893), 318–48.

Croll, D. D. "Thomas Beard, The Pioneer and Founder of Beardstown, Illinois," Illinois State Historical Society *Journal*, Vol. X (July, 1917), 207–36.

Custer, Milo. "Kannekuk, the Kickapoo Prophet," Illinois State Historical Society *Journal*, Vol. XI (April, 1918), 48–56.

———. "Masheena," Illinois State Historical Society *Transactions*, 1911, 115–21.

Daniell, Forrest. "Texas Pioneer Surveyors and Indians," *Southwestern Historical Quarterly*, Vol. LX (April, 1957), 501–506.

Douglas, Walter B. "Jean Gabriel Cerré, Illinois State Historical Society *Transactions,* 1903, 275–88.

"Dove Creek Battle," *Frontier Times,* Vol. V (November, 1927), 60–61.

Dunn, Jacob P. "Documents Relating to the French Settlements on the Wabash," Indiana Historical Society *Publications,* II (1894), 407–42.

———. "The Mission to the Ouabache," Indiana Historical Society *Publications,* III (1902), 255–330.

Ernst, Ferdinand. "Travels in Illinois in 1819," Illinois State Historical Society *Transactions,* 1903, 150–65.

Ford, John S. "Fight on the Frio," Texas State Historical Association *Quarterly* Vol. I (October, 1897), 118–20.

Foreman, Grant. "The Texas Comanche Treaty of 1846," *Southwestern Historical Quarterly,* Vol. LI (April, 1948), 313–32.

French, Maude C. "The Last Years of Kaskaskia," Illinois State Historical Society *Journal,* Vol. XXXVII (September, 1944), 228–41.

Gallatin, Albert. "A Synopsis of the Indian Tribes," American Antiquarian Society *Transactions and Collections,* II (1836).

Garraghan, Gilbert J. "The Kickapoo Mission," St. Louis *Catholic Historical Review,* Vol. IV (1922), 25–50.

Goggin, John M. "The Mexican Kickapoo Indians," *Southwestern Journal of Anthropology,* Vol. VII (1951).

Graveley, Ernestine. "Fifty Years Ago in Shawnee and Pottawatomie County," *Chronicles of Oklahoma,* Vol. XXX (Winter, 1953), 381–91.

"Great Indian Raid near Fort McKavett in 1866," *Frontier Times,* Vol. IV (June, 1927), 41–43.

Hall, Claude V. "Early Days in Red River County," East Texas State Teachers' College *Bulletin,* Vol. XIV (June, 1931), 49–79.

Hauberg, John H. "The Black Hawk War, 1831–1832," Illinois State Historical Society *Transactions,* 1932.

Henderson, Harry M. "The Surveyors' Fight," *Southwestern Historical Quarterly,* Vol. LVI (July, 1952), 25–35.

Henderson, James C. "Reminiscences of a Range Rider," *Chronicles of Oklahoma,* Vol. III (December, 1925), 254–88.

Hicks, Elijah. "Journal of Elijah Hicks," *Chronicles of Oklahoma,* Vol. XIII (March, 1935), 68–99.

Hoecken, Father Christian. "Letter of Father Hoecken," *U. S. Catholic Magazine,* 1847.

Howe, R. D. "The Opening of the Kickapoo Country," *Sturm's Oklahoma Magazine,* Vol. VI (June, 1908), 52–56.

Hume, C. Ross. "Historic Sites Around Anadarko," *Chronicles of Oklahoma,* Vol. XVI (December, 1938), 410–24.

"Incidents of Frontier Life," Illinois State Historical Society *Journal,* Vol. XXXII (December, 1939), 529.

"J. H. Greenwood—Early Texas Pioneer," *Frontier Times,* Vol. II, No. 4 (January, 1925), 20–23.

Johnson, William. "Letters from the Indian Missions in Kansas," *Kansas Historical Collections,* XVI (1923–25), 227.

Jones, William. "The Algonkin Manitou," *Journal of American Folklore,* Vol. XVIII (July, 1905), 183–90.

"Kickapoo Indian Raid," *Frontier Times,* Vol. II (August, 1925), 25–26.

Koch, Lena C. "The Federal Indian Policy in Texas, 1845–1860," *Southwestern Historical Quarterly,* Vol. XXVIII (January, 1925), 223–34.

Linton, Ralph. "The Indian History of Illinois," Illinois State Historical Society *Transactions,* 1916, 51–57.

Lutz, J. J. "Methodist Missions Among the Indian Tribes in Kansas," *Kansas Historical Collections,* IX (1905–1906), 160–235.

McClendon, R. Earl. "The First Treaty of the Republic of Texas," *Southwestern Historical Quarterly,* Vol. LII (July, 1948), 32–48.

McVicker, George G. "Indians in Illinois in 1812," Illinois State Historical Society *Journal,* Vol. XXIV (July, 1931), 342–43.

Mann, William L. "James O. Rice—Hero of the Battle of San Gabriels," *Southwestern Historical Quarterly* Vol. LV (January, 1952), 30–42.

Mead, James R. "The Little Arkansas," *Kansas Historical Collections,* X (1907–1908), 7–14.

——. "The Wichita Indians in Kansas," *Kansas Historical Collections,* VIII (1903–1904), 171–177.

Michelson, Truman. "Once More Mascoutens," *American Anthropologist,* n.s., Vol. XXXVII (January-March, 1935), 163–64.

——. "The Identification of the Mascoutens," *American Anthropologist, n.s.,* Vol. XXXVI (April-June, 1934), 226–33.

——. "The Punishment of Impudent Children Among the Kickapoo," *American Anthropologist,* Vol. XXV (April-June, 1923), 281–83.

Mooney, James. "Kickapoo Indians," *Catholic Encyclopedia,* VIII, 635–36.

Moulder, Klaris. "McLoud, 1895–1949," *Chronicles of Oklahoma,* Vol. XXVIII (Spring, 1950), 89–94.

"Narrative of the Capture of William Biggs by the Kickapoo Indians in 1788," Illinois State Historical Society *Transactions,* 1902, 202–15.

Nasatir, A. P. "The Anglo-Spanish Frontier in the Illinois Country During the American Revolution," Illinois State Historical Society *Journal*, Vol. XXI (October, 1928), 291–358.

Peterson, Frederick A. "The Kickapoo Indians of Northern Mexico," *Mexican Life*, Vol. XXX (February, 1956), 50–54.

Peterson, Frederick A., and Robert E. Ritzenthaler, "The Kickapoos Are Still Kicking," *Natural History*, Vol. LXIV (April, 1955), 200–204.

"Pigeon Roost Massacre," Indiana Historical Society *Publications*, II (1890), 128–34.

Pool, William C. "The Battle of Wove Creek," *Southwestern Historical Quarterly*, Vol. LIII (April, 1950), 367–85.

Pope, Richard K. "The Withdrawal of the Kickapoo," *The American Indian*, Vol. VIII (Winter, 1958–59), 17–27.

Porter, Kenneth W. "Seminoles in Mexico, 1850–1861," *Chronicles of Oklahoma*, Vol. XXIX (Summer, 1951), 153–68.

———. "The Seminole in Mexico, 1850–1861," *Hispanic American Historical Review*, Vol. XXXI (February, 1952), 1–36.

———. "The Seminole Negro-Indian Scouts," *Southwestern Historical Quarterly*, Vol. LV (January, 1952), 358–77.

Ragland, Hobert D. "Missions of the Society of Friends Among the Indian Tribes of the Sac and Fox Agency," *Chronicles of Oklahoma*, Vol. XXXIII (Summer, 1955), 169–82.

Root, Frank A. "Kickapoo-Pottawatomie Grand Indian Jubilee," *Kansas Historical Quarterly*, Vol. V (February, 1936), 15–21.

Root, George A., ed. "No-ko-aht's Talk—A Kickapoo Chief's Account of a Tribal Journey from Kansas to Mexico and Return in the Sixties," *Kansas Historical Quarterly*, Vol. I (February, 1932), 153–59.

Sampson, Francis A. "Books of Early Travels in Missouri," *Missouri Historical Review*, Vol. IX (January, 1915), 94–101.

Sanchez, José M. "A Trip to Texas in 1828," *Southwestern Historical Quarterly*, Vol. XXIX (April, 1926), 249–88.

Shepard, Edward M. "Early Springfield," *Missouri Historical Review*, Vol. XXIV (July, 1930), 50–65.

Silverberg, James. "The Kickapoo Indians," *The Wisconsin Archaeologist*, Vol. XXXVIII, No. 3.

Stevens, Frank E. "Illinois in the War of 1812–1814," Illinois State Historical Society *Transactions*, 1904, 62–197.

Steward, John F. "Destruction of the Fox Indians in 1730," Illinois State Historical Society *Transactions*, 1902, 148–54.

Strickland, Rex W. "Establishment of Old Miller County, Arkansas Territory," *Chronicles of Oklahoma,* Vol. XVIII (June, 1940), 154–70.

———. "History of Fannin County, Texas, 1836–1843," *Southwestern Historical Quarterly,* Vol. XXXIII (April, 1930), 262.

Tilton, Clint C. "Gurdon Saltonstall Hubbard and Some of His Friends," Illinois State Historical Society *Transactions,* 1933, 83–178.

———. "The Genesis of Old Vermilion," Illinois State Historical Society *Journal,* Vol. II (April, 1927), 63–97.

Volwiler, Albert T. "The Imperial Indian Department and the Occupation of the Great West," Illinois State Historical Society *Transactions,* 1925, 100–107.

Wallace, Edward S. "General Ranald S. Mackenzie," *Southwestern Historical Quarterly,* Vol. LVI, (January, 1953), 378–96.

Wardell, Morris L. "Protestant Missions Among the Osages, 1820–1838," *Chronicles of Oklahoma,* Vol. II (September, 1924), 285–97.

Webster, Homer J. "William Henry Harrison's Administration of Indiana Territory," Indiana Historical Society *Publications,* IV (1907), 266–71.

Wharton, Clifton. "Expedition of Major Clifton Wharton in 1844," *Kansas Historical Collections,* XVI (1923–25), 272–315.

Wilson, Glen O. "Old Red River Station," *Southwestern Historical Quarterly,* Vol. LXI (January, 1958), 350–58.

Winfrey, Dorman H. "Chief Bowles of the Texas Cherokee," *Chronicles of Oklahoma,* Vol. XXXII (Spring, 1954), 29–41.

———. "Mirabeau B. Lamar and Texas Nationalism," *Southwestern Historical Quarterly,* Vol. LIX (October, 1955), 184–205.

Winkler, Ernest W. "The Cherokee Indians in Texas," Texas State Historical Association *Quarterly,* Vol. VII (October, 1903), 95–165.

VI. BOOKS

Abel, Annie H. *The American Indian as Slaveholder and Secessionist.* 3 vols. Cleveland, 1915.

Adams, Richard C. *A Brief Sketch of the Sabine Land Cession in Texas.* Washington, 1901.

Albach, James R. *Annals of the West.* Pittsburgh, 1857.

Alford, Thomas Wildcat. *Civilization.* Norman, 1936.

Alvord, Clarence W., ed. *Kaskaskia Records, 1778–1790, Virginia Series,* II. *Collections of the Illinois State Historical Library,* V. Springfield, 1909.

———. *The Illinois Country, 1763–1818.* Chicago, 1922.

———, and Clarence E. Carter, eds. *The New Regime, 1765–1767, British Series*, II. *Collections of the Illinois State Historical Library*, XI. Springfield, 1916.

———, and ———, eds. *Trade and Politics, 1767–1769, British Series*, III. *Collections of the Illinois State Historical Library*, XVI, Springfield, 1921.

Atwater, Caleb. *Indians of the Northwest*. Columbus, 1850.

Bakeless, John. *Road to Glory*. Philadelphia, 1957.

Barce, Elmore and Robert A. Swan. *History of Benton County, Indiana*. Fowler, Indiana, 1930.

Barclay, Wade C. *Early American Methodism, 1769–1844*. New York, 1950.

Barnhart, John D. *Henry Hamilton and George Rogers Clark in the American Revolution*. Crawfordsville, Indiana, 1951.

Battey, Thomas C. *The Life and Adventures of a Quaker Among the Indians*. Boston, 1903.

Beach, W. W., ed. *The Indian Miscellany*. Albany, 1877.

Beckwith, Hiram W., ed. *Collections of the Illinois State Historical Library*, I. Springfield, 1903.

———. *The Illinois and Indiana Indians. Fergus Historical Series No. 27*. Chicago, 1884.

Benton, E. J. *The Wabash Trade Route in the Development of the Old Northwest*. Johns Hopkins University *Studies in Historical and Political Science, No. 21*. Baltimore, 1903.

Biggs, William. *Narrative of the Captivity of William Biggs Among the Kickapoo Indians in Illinois in 1788*. New York, 1922.

Blair, Emma H., ed. *The Indian Tribes of the Upper Mississippi Valley and Region of the Great Lakes*. 2 vols. Cleveland, 1911.

Bledsoe, S. T. *Indian Land Laws*. Kansas City, Missouri, 1909.

Boaz, Franz. *Race, Language, and Culture*. New York, 1940.

Boggess, Arthur C. *The Settlement of Illinois 1778–1830*. Chicago, 1908.

Bower, Reuben E. *The Unreached Indian*. Kansas City, Missouri, 1920.

Brice, Wallace A. *History of Fort Wayne*. Fort Wayne, 1868.

Brinton, Daniel G. *American Hero Myths*. Philadelphia, 1882.

Brown, Henry. *The History of Illinois*. New York, 1844.

Brown, John H. *Indian Wars and Pioneers of Texas*. Austin, n.d.

Brownell, Charles D. *The Indian Races of North and South America*. N.p., 1857.

Buck, Solon J. *Illinois in 1818*. Chicago, 1918.

Buley, R. Carlyle. *The Old Northwest*. 2 vols. Bloomington, 1951.

Carter, R. G. *On the Border with Mackenzie*. Washington, 1935.

Carver, Jonathan. *Three Years Travels Through the Interior Parts of North America*. Philadelphia, 1784.

Cass, Lewis. *Consideration on the Present State of Indians*. N.p., n.d.

Catlin, George. *Catlin's Notes of Eight Years' Travels and Residence in Europe with his North American Indian Collection*. London, 1848.

———. *North American Indians . . . Written during Eight Years' Travel Amongst the Wildest Tribes of Indians in North America, 1832–1839*. 2 vols. Edinburgh, 1926.

Charlevoix, Pierre F. *Histoire et description generale de la Nouvelle France*. 6 vols. Paris, 1744.

Chittenden, Hiram Martin and Alfred Talbot Richardson, *Life, Letters and Travels of Father Pierre—Jean De Smet, S.J., 1801–1873*. 4 vols. New York, 1905.

Clark, W. P. *The Indian Sign Language*. Philadelphia, 1885.

Cleaves, Freeman. *Old Tippecanoe—William Henry Harrison and His Time*. New York, 1939.

Cockrum, William M. *Pioneer History of Indiana*. Oakland City, Indiana, 1907.

Collot, Victor. *A Journey in North America . . . 1796*. Firenze, 1924.

Croghan, George. *A Selection of George Croghan's Letters and Journals Relating to Tours in the Western Country, November 16, 1750—November, 1765*. In Thwaites' *Early Western Travels (q.v.)*, I, 45–173.

Debo, Angie. *The Road to Disappearance*. Norman, 1941.

Densmore, Frances. *The American Indians and Their Music*. New York, 1926.

DeShields, James. *Border Wars of Texas*. Tioga, Texas, 1912.

Dillon, John B. *A History of Indiana*. Indianapolis, 1859.

Drake, Samuel G. *Indian Biography*. Boston, 1832.

———. *Life of Tecumseh*. Cincinnati, 1841.

———. *The Aboriginal Races of North America*. New York, 1880.

Dunn, J. P. *Indiana*. Boston, 1891.

Edwards, Ninian W. *History of Illinois*. Springfield, 1870.

———. *The Edwards Papers*. Chicago, 1884.

Eggan, Fred, ed. *Social Anthropology of North American Tribes*. Chicago, 1937.

Eggleston, Edward. *Tecumseh and the Shawnee Prophet*. New York, 1878.

Elkins, John M. *Indian Fighting on the Texas Frontier.* Amarillo, 1929.

Esarey, Logan. *A History of Indiana from Its Exploration to 1850.* 2 vols. Indianapolis, 1915.

———, ed. *Messages and Letters of William Henry Harrison.* 2 vols. Indianapolis, 1922.

Fabila, Alfonso. *La Tribu Kickapoo de Coahuila. Biblioteca Enciclopedica Popular No. 50.* Mexico, 1945.

Finley, James B. *Life Among the Indians.* Cincinnati, n.d.

Flagg, Edmund. *The Far West.* In R. G. Thwaites' *Early Western Travels (q.v.),* XXVII.

Foreman, Grant. *Advancing the Frontier.* Norman, 1933.

———, ed. *Adventure on Red River.* Norman, 1937.

———. *Indians and Pioneers.* New Haven, 1930.

———. *Last Trek of the Indians.* Chicago, 1946.

———. *Marcy and the Gold Seekers.* Norman, 1939.

———. *Pioneer Days in the Early Southwest.* Cleveland, 1926.

———. *The Five Civilized Tribes.* Norman, 1934.

Frost, John. *Indian Battles, Captives, and Adventures.* New York, 1857.

Garraghan, Gilbert J. *Catholic Beginnings in Kansas City, Missouri.* Chicago, 1920.

———. *The Jesuits of the Middle United States.* 3 vols. New York, 1938.

Garrison, George P. ed. *Diplomatic Correspondence of the Republic of Texas.* 3 vols. *Annual Report* of the American Historical Association, 1907 and 1908. Washington, 1911.

Glisan, R. *Journal of Army Life.* San Francisco, 1874.

Gillett, James B. *Six Years with the Texas Rangers, 1875–1881.* New Haven, 1925.

Goebel, Dorothy B. *William Henry Harrison—A Political Biography.* Indianapolis, 1926.

Graves, William W. and others. *A History of the Kickapoo Mission and Parish.* St. Paul, Kansas, 1938.

Greene, Evarts B. and Clarence W. Alvord, eds. *The Governors' Letter Books, 1818–1834, Executive Series,* I. *Collections of the Illinois State Historical Library,* IV. Springfield, 1909.

Greene, Max. *The Kansas Region.* New York, 1856.

Green, James K. *A Texas Ranger and Frontiersman.* Dallas, 1932.

Hagan, William T. *The Sac and Fox Indians.* Norman, 1958.

Haley, J. Evetts. *Fort Concho and the Texas Frontier.* San Angelo, Texas, 1952.

Hennepin, Louis. *A New Discovery of a Vast Country in America*. With introduction, notes, and index by R. G. Thwaites. 2 vols. Chicago, 1903.

Hitchcock, Ethan Allen. *A Traveler in Indian Territory—the Journal of Ethan Allen Hitchcock*. Ed. by Grant Foreman. Cedar Rapids, 1930.

Hoad, Louise. *Kickapoo Indian Trails*. Caldwell, Idaho, 1946.

Holmes, Floyd J. *Indian Fights on the Texas Frontier*. Fort Worth, 1927.

Hosmer, James K., ed. *History of the Expedition of Captains Lewis and Clark*. 2 vols. Chicago, 1903.

Houck, Louis. *A History of Missouri*. 3 vols. Chicago, 1908.

———, ed. *The Spanish Regime in Missouri*. 2 vols. Chicago, 1909.

Humphreville, J. Lee. *Twenty Years Among Our Hostile Indians*. New York, 1899.

Hunter, J. Marvin, ed. *The Trail Drivers of Texas*. Nashville, 1925.

Hunter, John D. *Memoirs of Captivity*. London, 1823.

Irving, John Treat. *Indian Sketches*. Ed. by John F. McDermott. Norman, 1955.

Irving, Washington. *The Western Journals of Washington Irving*. Ed. by John F. McDermott. Norman, 1944.

James, James A., ed. *George Rogers Clark Papers, 1771–1781., Virginia Series*. III. *Collections of the Illinois State Historical Library*, VIII. Springfield, 1912.

Johonnot, Jackson T. *The Remarkable Adventure of Jackson T. Johonnot ... Containing an Account of His Captivity, Sufferings, and Escape from the Kickapoo Indians*. Greenfield, Massachusetts, 1816.

Jones, William. ed. *Kickapoo Tales. Publications* of the American Ethnological Society, *No. 9*. New York, 1915.

Kellogg, Louise P. *The British Regime in Wisconsin and the Northwest*, Madison, 1935.

Kelsey, Rayner W. *Friends and the Indians*. Philadelphia, 1917.

Kennedy, J. H. *Jesuit and Savage in New France*. New Haven, 1950.

Kingston, W. H. G. *Adventures Among the Indians*. Chicago, 1889.

Kinietz, W. Vernon. *The Indians of the Western Great Lakes, 1615–1760*. Ann Arbor, 1940.

Kinnaird, Lawrence, ed. *Spain in the Mississippi Valley, 1765–1794*. 3 vols. *Annual Report* of the American Historical Association for 1945. Washington, 1949.

Lahontan, Louis Armande de Lom d'Arce. *New Voyages to North-America*. Ed. by R. G. Thwaites. 2 vols. Chicago, 1905.

Lang, John D. and Samuel Taylor. *Report of a Visit to Some of the Tribes of Indians Located West of the Mississippi River.* New York, 1843.

Leupp, Francis E. *The Indian and His Problem.* New York, 1910.

Lewis, Meriwether. *Original Journal of the Lewis and Clark Expedition, 1804–1806 . . . .* Ed. by R. G. Thwaites. 8 vols. New York, 1904–1905.

Lindley, Harlow, ed. *Indiana as Seen by Early Travelers. Indiana Historical Collections,* III. Indianapolis, 1916.

Linton, Ralph. *Use of Tobacco among North American Indians. Anthropology Leaflet No. 15,* Field Museum of Natural History. Chicago, 1924.

Lucas, Jannette M. *Indian Harvest—Wild Food Plants of America.* Philadelphia, 1945.

Lyons, Emory J. *Isaac McCoy: His Plan of and Work for Indian Colonization.* Fort Hays Kansas State College *Studies, No. 9.* Fort Hays, Kansas, 1945.

McCoy, Isaac. *Annual Register of Indian Affairs within the Indian Territory.* Washington, 1838.

———. *History of Baptist Indian Missions.* Washington, 1840.

McKenney, Thomas L. and James Hall, *The Indian Tribes of North America.* 3 vols. Edinburgh, 1934.

McNamara, William. *The Catholic Church on the Northern Indiana Frontier, 1789–1844.* Washington, 1931.

McReynolds, Edwin C. *The Seminoles.* Norman, 1957.

Mallery, Garrick. *Sign Language among North American Indians.* Washington, 1881.

Marcy, Randolph B. *Thirty Years of Army Life on the Border.* New York, 1866.

Matson, N. *French and Indians of Illinois River.* Princeton, Illinois,1874.

———. *Memories of Shaubena.* Chicago, 1878.

Melish, John. *Travels Through the United States of America, 1806–1811.* Belfast, 1818.

Mills, Roger Q. *Speeches of Roger Q. Mills of Texas.* Washington, 1878.

Mohr, Walter H. *Federal Indian Relations, 1774–1788.* Philadelphia, 1922.

Moore, J. H. *The Political Condition of the Indians and the Resources of the Indian Territory.* St. Louis, 1874.

Morris, Captain Thomas. *Morris Journals.* In R. G. Thwaites *Early Western Travels (q.v.),* I.

Morris, William B. *Military Posts and Camps in Oklahoma*. Oklahoma City, 1936.

Morse, Jedidiah. *A Report to the Secretary of War of the United States on Indian Affairs*. New Haven, 1822.

Murphy, Edmund R. *Hnery de Tonty—Fur Trader of the Mississippi*. Baltimore, 1941.

Murray, Charles A. *Travels in North America*. 2 vols. London, 1839.

Nasatir, A. P. ed. *Before Lewis and Clark*. 2 vols. St. Louis, 1952.

O'Callaghan, E. B., ed. *Documents Relative to the Colonial History of the State of New York*. 15 vols. Albany, 1855–87.

Oskisson, John M. *Tecumseh and His Times*. New York, 1938.

Owen, Mary A. *Folklore of the Musquakie Indians of North America*. London, 1902.

Parker, W. B. *Notes Taken During the Expedition . . . Through Unexplored Texas*. Philadelphia, 1856.

Parkman, Francis. *A Half Century of Conflict*. Boston, 1893.

———. *The Conspiracy of Pontiac*. 3 vols. Boston, 1898.

———. *Count Frontenac and New France Under Louis XIV*. Boston, 1902.

———. *The Oregon Trail*. Boston, 1902.

Pease, Theodore C., ed. *Illinois on the Eve of the Seven Years War, 1747–1755, French Series*, III. Collections of the Illinois State Historical Library, XXIX. Springfield, 1934.

———, ed. *The French Foundations, 1680–1692, French Series*, I. Collections of the Illinois State Historical Library, XXIII. Springfield, 1934.

Pike, James. *Scout and Ranger*. Princeton, 1932.

Quaife, Milo M. *Chicago and the Old Northwest, 1673–1835*. Chicago, 1913.

———, ed. *The Western Country in the Seventeenth Century—the Memoirs of Lamothe Cadillac and Pierre Liette*. Chicago, 1947.

Raymond, Dora N. *Captain Lee Hall of Texas*. Norman, 1940.

Richardson, Rupert N. *The Comanche Barrier to South Plains Settlement*. Glendale, 1933.

Ridings, Sam P. *The Chisholm Trail*. Guthrie, Oklahoma, 1936.

Rister, Carl Coke. *Fort Griffin on the Texas Frontier*. Norman, 1956.

Ritzenthaler, Robert E. and Frederick A. Peterson. *The Mexican Kickapoo Indians*. Milwaukee Public Museum *Publications in Anthropology*, No. 2. Milwaukee, 1956.

Robertson, Nellie A. and Riker, Dorothy, eds. *The John Tipton Papers.* 3 vols. Indianapolis, 1942.

Roe, Frank G. *The Indian and the Horse.* Norman, 1955.

Rowland, Dunbar and A. G. Sanders. *Mississippi Provincial Archives, 1729–1740.* 3 vols. Jackson, 1927.

Santleben, August. *A Texas Pioneer.* New York, 1910.

Schoolcraft, Henry R. *Information Respecting the History, Condition, and Prospects of the Indian Tribes of the United States.* 6 vols. Philadelphia, 1851–57.

———. *Personal Memoirs of a Residence of Thirty Years with the Indian Tribes.* Philadelphia, 1851.

———. *The American Indians.* Rochester, 1851.

———. *The Indian in His Wigwam.* New York, 1848.

Scott, L. *Narrative of the Captivity of Mrs. Mary Smith.* Providence, 1815.

Seymour, Flora W. *Indian Agents of the Old Frontier.* New York, 1941.

———. *The Indians Today.* Chicago, 1926.

Shea, John G. *Early Voyages Up and Down the Mississippi.* Albany, 1861.

———. *History of the Catholic Missions Among the Indian Tribes of the United States, 1529–1854.* New York, 1881.

Smith, James. *An Account of the Remarkable Occurrences in the Life and Travels of Colonel James Smith.* Cincinnati, 1907.

Smith, William H. *The History of the State of Indiana.* 2 vols. Indianapolis, 1903.

———. ed. *The St. Clair Papers.* 2 vols. Cincinnati, 1882.

Snider, Brainerd C. *Story of the Kickapoos.* Lincoln, Illinois, 1951.

Stevens, Frank E. *The Black Hawk War.* Chicago, 1903.

Stone, Will Hale. *Twenty-four Years a Cowboy and Ranchman.* Headrick, Oklahoma Territory, 1905.

Sullivan, James, ed. *The Papers of Sir William Johnson.* 12 Vols. Albany, 1921–57.

Sweet, Alexander E. and J. Armoy Knox. *On a Mexican Mustang Through Texas.* London, 1905.

Tatum, Lawrie. *Our Red Brothers.* Philadelphia, 1899.

Thatcher, B. B. *Indian Biography.* New York, 1839.

Thoburn, Joseph B. and Muriel H. Wright. *Oklahoma—A History of the State and Its People.* 4 vols. New York, 1929.

Thornbrough, Gayle, ed. *Outpost on the Wabash, 1787–1791: Letters* of *Brigadier General Josiah Harmar and Major John Hamtramck*. Indianapolis, 1957.

Thwaites, Reuben G. *Early Western Travels, 1748–1846* . . . . 32 vols. Cleveland, 1904–1907.

———. *How George Rogers Clark Won the Northwest*. Chicago, 1915.

———. (ed.) *The Jesuit Relations and Allied Documents*. 73 vols. Cleveland, 1896–1901.

———., and Louise P. Kellogg. *Frontier Defense on the Upper Ohio, 1778–1783*. Madison, 1912.

———., and ———. *The Revolution on the Upper Ohio, 1775–1777*. Madison, 1908.

Trumbull, Henry. *History of the Indian Wars*. Boston, 1846.

Turner, G. *Traits of Indian Character*. 2 vols. Philadelphia, 1836.

Turner, Katharine C. *Red Men Calling on the Great White Father*. Norman, 1951.

Verrill, A. Hyatt. *The American Indian*. New York, 1927.

Volwiler, Albert T. *George Croghan and the Westward Movement, 1741–1782*. Cleveland, 1926.

Weatherwax, Paul. *Indian Corn in Old America*. New York, 1954.

Webb, George W. *Chronological List of Engagements Between the Regular Army of the United States and Various Indian Tribes . . . 1790–1893*. St. Joseph, 1939.

Webb, Walter Prescott. *The Texas Rangers*. Cambridge, 1935.

Wilbarger, J. W. *Indian Depredations in Texas*. Austin, 1935.

Wilder, D. W. *The Annals of Kansas, 1541–1885*. Topeka, 1886.

Williams, Harry. *Texas Trails—Legends of the Great Southwest*. San Antonio, 1932.

Williams, Samuel C. *Adair's History of the American Indians*. Johnson County, Tennessee, 1930.

Winfrey, Dorman H., ed. *Texas Indian Papers, 1825–1845*. 2 vols. Austin, 1959–60.

Winslow, Charles S., ed. *Indians of the Chicago Region*. Chicago, 1946.

Winsor, Justin. *Cartier to Frontenac*. Boston, 1894.

Wood, Charles S. *On the Frontier with St. Clair*. Boston, 1902.

Wright, Muriel H. *A Guide to the Indian Tribes of Oklahoma*. Norman, 1951.

Wyeth, Walter N. *Isaac McCoy—Early Indian Missions*. Philadelphia, 1895.

Yoakum, H. *History of Texas*. 2 vols. New York, 1856.

Index

381

of which *The Kickapoos*: Lords of the Middle Border is the seventieth volume, was inaugurated in 1932 by the University of Oklahoma Press, and has as its purpose the reconstruction of American Indian civilization by presenting aboriginal, historical, and contemporary Indian life. The following list is complete as of the date of publication of this volume:

1. Alfred Barnaby Thomas. *Forgotten Frontiers:* A Study of the Spanish Indian Policy of Don Juan Bautista de Anza, Governor of New Mexico, 1777–1787. Out of print.
2. Grant Foreman. *Indian Removal:* The Emigration of the Five Civilized Tribes of Indians.
3. John Joseph Mathews. *Wah'Kon-Tah*: The Osage and the White Man's Road. Out of print.
4. Grant Foreman. *Advancing the Frontier, 1830–1860.* Out of print.
5. John Homer Seger. *Early Days among the Cheyenne and Arapahoe Indians.* Edited by Stanley Vestal.
6. Angie Debo. *The Rise and Fall of the Choctaw Republic.*
7. Stanley Vestal (ed.). *New Sources of Indian History, 1850–1891.* Out of print.
8. Grant Foreman. *The Five Civilized Tribes.* Out of print.
9. Alfred Barnaby Thomas. *After Coronado:* Spanish Exploration Northeast of New Mexico, 1696–1727. Out of print.
10. Frank G. Speck. *Naskapi:* The Savage Hunters of the Labrador Peninsula. Out of print.
11. Elaine Goodale Eastman. *Pratt:* The Red Man's Moses. Out of print.
12. Althea Bass. *Cherokee Messenger:* A Life of Samuel Austin Worcester. Out of print.
13. Thomas Wildcat Alford. *Civilization.* As told to Florence Drake. Out of print.
14. Grant Foreman. *Indians and Pioneers:* The Story of the American Southwest before 1830. Out of print.

15. George E. Hyde. *Red Cloud's Folk:* A History of the Oglala Sioux Indians.
16. Grant Foreman. *Sequoyah.*
17. Morris L. Wardell. *A Political History of the Cherokee Nation, 1838–1907.* Out of print.
18. John Walton Caughey. *McGillivray of the Creeks.*
19. Edward Everett Dale and Gaston Litton. *Cherokee Cavaliers:* Forty Years of Cherokee History as Told in the Correspondence of the Ridge-Watie-Boudinot Family. Out of print.
20. Ralph Henry Gabriel. *Elias Boudinot, Cherokee, and His America.*
21. Karl N. Llewellyn and E. Adamson Hoebel. *The Cheyenne Way:* Conflicts and Case Law in Primitive Jurisprudence.
22. Angie Debo. *The Road to Disappearance.* Out of print.
23. Oliver La Farge and others. *The Changing Indian.* Out of print.
24. Carolyn Thomas Foreman. *Indians Abroad.* Out of print.
25. John Adair. *The Navajo and Pueblo Silversmiths.*
26. Alice Marriott. *The Ten Grandmothers.*
27. Alice Marriott. *María:* The Potter of San Ildefonso.
28. Edward Everett Dale. *The Indians of the Southwest:* A Century of Development under the United States. Out of print.
29. Adrián Recinos. *Popol Vuh:* The Sacred Book of the Ancient Quiché Maya. English version by Delia Goetz and Sylvanus G. Morley from the translation of Adrián Recinos.
30. Walter Collins O'Kane. *Sun in the Sky.*
31. Stanley A. Stubbs. *Bird's-Eye View of the Pueblos.*
32. Katharine C. Turner. *Red Men Calling on the Great White Father.*
33. Muriel H. Wright. *A Guide to the Indian Tribes of Oklahoma.*
34. Ernest Wallace and E. Adamson Hoebel. *The Comanches:* Lords of the South Plains.
35. Walter Collins O'Kane. *The Hopis:* Portrait of a Desert People. Out of print.
36. Joseph Epes Brown. *The Sacred Pipe:* Black Elk's Account of the Seven Rites of the Oglala Sioux.
37. Adrián Recinos and Delia Goetz. *The Annals of the Cakchi-*

quels. Translated from the Cakchiquel Maya, with *Title of the Lords of Totonicapán,* translated from the Quiché text into Spanish by Dionisio José Chonay, English version by Delia Goetz.

38. R. S. Cotterill. *The Southern Indians:* The Story of the Civilized Tribes before Removal.
39. J. Eric S. Thompson. *The Rise and Fall of Maya Civilization.*
40. Robert Emmitt. *The Last War Trail:* The Utes and the Settlement of Colorado.
41. Frank Gilbert Roe. *The Indian and the Horse.*
42. Francis Haines. *The Nez Percés:* Tribesmen of the Columbia Plateau. Out of print.
43. Ruth M. Underhill. *The Navajos.*
44. George Bird Grinnell. *The Fighting Cheyennes.*
45. George E. Hyde. *A Sioux Chronicle.*
46. Stanley Vestal. *Sitting Bull:* Champion of the Sioux, A Biography.
47. Edwin C. McReynolds. *The Seminoles.*
48. William T. Hagan. *The Sac and Fox Indians.*
49. John C. Ewers. *The Blackfeet:* Raiders on the Northwestern Plains.
50. Alfonso Caso. *The Aztecs:* People of the Sun. Translated by Lowell Dunham.
51. C. L. Sonnichsen. *The Mescalero Apaches.*
52. Keith A. Murray. *The Modocs and Their War.*
53. Victor W. von Hagen (ed.). *The Incas of Pedro de Cieza de León.* Translated by Harriet de Onis.
54. George E. Hyde. *Indians of the High Plains:* From the Prehistoric Period to the Coming of Europeans.
55. *George Catlin. Episodes from "Life among the Indians" and "Last Rambles."* Edited by Marvin C. Ross.
56. J. Eric S. Thompson. *Maya Hieroglyphic Writing:* An Introduction.
57. George E. Hyde. *Spotted Tail's Folk:* A History of the Brulé Sioux.
58. James Larpenteur Long. *The Assiniboines:* From the Accounts

of the Old Ones Told to First Boy (James Larpenteur Long).
Edited and with an introduction by Michael Stephen Kennedy.

59. Edwin Thompson Denig. *Five Indian Tribes of the Upper Missouri*. Edited and with an introduction by John C. Ewers.
60. John Joseph Mathews. *The Osages:* Children of the Middle Waters.
61. Mary Elizabeth Young. *Redskins, Ruffleshirts, and Rednecks:* Indian Allotments in Alabama and Mississippi, 1830–1860.
62. J. Eric S. Thompson. *A Catalog of Maya Hieroglyphs.*
63. Mildred P. Mayhall. *The Kiowas.*
64. George E. Hyde. *Indians of the Woodlands:* From Prehistoric Times to 1725.
65. Grace Steele Woodward. *The Cherokees.*
66. Donald J. Berthrong. *The Southern Cheyennes.*
67. Miguel León-Portilla. *Aztec Thought and Culture:* A Study of the Ancient Nahuatl Mind.
68. T. D. Allen. *Navahos Have Five Fingers.*
69. Burr Cartwright Brundage. *Empire of the Inca.*
70. A. M. Gibson. *The Kickapoos:* Lords of the Middle Border.

Certainly more stories will be told about this era. To the best of our abilities, we tried to tell what we know & what we can remember. It's likely that people & events have been left out, but that will be someone else's story. The different perspectives & voices here reflect the collaborative, adventurous spirit that defined the early punk-rock scene in Los Angeles. We couldn't have & didn't want to do it alone.

—John Doe
Richmond, Calif.

Contents

Foreword

by Billie Joe Armstrong

Green Day finally made it to Los Angeles for a gig in 1990. We were roughly ten years too late for a scene that spawned some of the best bands ever. We played the god-awful Coconut Teaszer on Sunset Boulevard. We were all under twenty-one, so we weren't allowed inside the club.

We waited our turn outside, sandwiched in between a strange lineup of bands that were trying to get signed to a major label.

The stage wrangler hauled us in, and we played our twenty-minute set on borrowed gear. It was a good set, and people were genuinely into it. But before we got a chance to bask in the glory, we were asked to leave.

And that was my first impression of Los Angeles.

I sat outside on the curb kinda sad. I wondered if maybe Exene and John would walk by and bum a smoke off me. Or just maybe Leonard and Stan Lee possibly caught our set.

Or by some weird chance Jane Wiedlin would invite me to a party at the Canterbury . . . NOPE.

None of these things happened.

But what DID happen is that their music made its way to the painfully small town I came from in Northern California. And it made me want to slam dance my way out of it.

Finding like-minded weirdos at the Gilman Street scene in Berkeley who also had dreams of "almost" hanging out with Darby Crash and the Light Bulb Kids in the *Decline of Western Civilization.*

However, "almost" isn't good enough. You have to take whatever spirit is left and make it your own. History only happens for a second, and you have to do everything you can in that moment.

Thank god for Alice Bag. Good lord! And Pat Smear, for that matter. The thing that makes these people brilliant is the fact that the music and ideas they created are still relevant today. Songs like "Los Angeles," "We Got the Neutron Bomb," and "Lexicon Devil" don't have expiration dates. And that's at a time when the entire decade of the eighties WAS a giant expiration date.

These are the kids before the kids. And then there are the kids after that. And so on.

I'm not much of a kid anymore, but I still got all these songs stuck in my head.

So even if the Coconut Teaszer wasn't exactly the Masque, I still had all that graffiti in my brain.

Imagination can take you a long way.

Roughly,
Billie Joe Armstrong

Preface
Post-Apocalyptic Clowns

by Tom DeSavia

I wasn't there, but it was about to change my life.

Living in the suburbs outside of Los Angeles, punk rock was simply the scary legend that came from the big, dirty metropolis. Punk itself was kind of a pop-culture mythology proven to exist only by the desolate outsider occasionally spotted wandering our streets, causing the community to collectively clutch their pearls and pray they were just passing through. In our minds these punks shared space only with the homeless and war vets, except they scared us more because it was obviously a rebellious choice they had made to live this way. Punk was dangerous, a gateway drug to a dark, violent world. This wasn't teenage rebellion—this was alarming, ugly, and threatening.

The first time I became aware of punk rock was as a lad in 1976. There was TV coverage of the Sex Pistols in America—the only footage I recall was showing the audience spitting on this hideous band of post-apocalyptic clowns. The only reason I even recall it was because of the distaste it drew from my parents, and I couldn't have agreed with them more. It was disgusting, obviously immoral, and seemingly

devoid of all melody. Also, they seemed angry. As did the crowd. It was shocking on all levels; the newscasters reporting enthusiastically agreed.

I was young enough to be intimidated by the images that came over the local news channel that day but just becoming old enough to begin to sort of learn what rebellion meant. Those images stuck with me strong . . . and I always associated them with my folks being so offended by this. Perhaps that was why I needed to find out more. More images started to creep in, mostly in the pages of the rock magazines I began to devour religiously: *Circus*, *Creem*, even *Rolling Stone*.

I wasn't even ten years old, but I was just starting to realize the world was a real fucked-up place. Saigon fell in 1975, ending the Vietnam War. Hippies were turning into cultists and murderers. This Nixon guy seemed to have fucked up a lot of shit. Basically it seemed folks were prepping for the arrival of four horsemen. In only a few short years the hippies became unflinching heartless businessmen, greed was good, and Reagan would introduce Jesus Christ into the Republican Party. Combine with that pop radio so smooth that flute solos were replacing guitars, and you had a larger sect of the American mainstream ready to accept punk rock in their hearts, just as our compatriots on the other side of the pond had been doing for a few years.

Looking back on that time, I suppose the hippies and the punks had more in common than they would have chosen to believe, especially back then: political rebellion, the rise of counterculture activism, economic uncertainty, and needing art that spoke to these and other issues in an unflinching way.

As the 1970s were starting to come to a close, suddenly the radio really began to sound different: songs by bands

like The Clash, The Pretenders, Blondie, and Devo were creeping into our bedrooms, some even going on to become pop hits. I remember hearing DJs on rock stations make fun of punk as they were obviously forced to play some of the bigger tunes due to listener demand. Devo's "Whip It" and the Vapors' "Turning Japanese" were straight-up pop-radio smashes, so was Blondie's disco-ish/new-wave hybrid "Heart of Glass," which soon led me backward to discover the band's less radio-friendly tunes, like the alarming "Rip Her to Shreds." Nick Lowe's power-pop masterpiece "Cruel to Be Kind" single-handedly enabled me to unearth the whole Stiff Records culture. I had discovered a treasure map with so many roads to follow, and I was equally overwhelmed, enthralled, and confused.

This Reagan guy had arrived in office and was suddenly the target of and inspiration for a whole wave of US punk anarchy. Politically charged bands and songs began to creep into our consciousness, with not-so-subtle Reagan Youth, the UK's Crass and The Subhumans, and, of course, the West Coast's own Dead Kennedys and Avengers, who took fierce and unapologetic aim at both political figures and policies with such brutal imagery (both lyrical and visual) that they would make more melodic activists like The Clash and the Sex Pistols blush.

At the same time, '70s arena rock was making its evolution into what would become labeled, accurately, "corporate rock." And lines in the sand were officially drawn. You picked a team: you liked Journey or you liked Black Flag. Never both. Not ever. The punk kids and the heavy-metal kids did not play nicely, though as a result of this postmodern Montague/Capulet war, I never saw Motörhead, arguably a great punk band, as clad in leather as they may have been. I'm not sad I never saw Journey. Fuck them.

It was around that time that friends led me to a Sunday night show on KROQ by the most nontraditional DJ I had ever heard, Rodney Bingenheimer. At first I found both his unconventional voice and on-air awkwardness annoying, but after a while his fan-boy exuberance became not only endearing but vital. And then there was the music: I was hearing hefty doses of bands called The Ramones and The Runaways and that band from the news a couple of years back, the Sex Pistols. There was bad and good—some were novelty records, some were plain ol' weird, and some seemed brilliant. I listened intensely with the headphones on . . . it was my secret. The folks would be worried if they knew what I was listening to, I knew that. I liked that.

That year I made bona fide punk-rock friends. They were my age, but they had all these records by bands with names like The Flesh Eaters, Christian Death, the Circle Jerks, and Agent Orange. The records were harsher than what I was used to, and the accompanying art was often shocking. They didn't get along with their parents that well, so while trying to listen to these records in darkened bedrooms after school, the tunes were regularly drowned out by the sounds of mothers and fathers and kids screaming at each other. This was the uncomfortable compromise that came with hearing new music then—and it became normal in its own weird way. These were the misfits, I guess, and they had the best and most interesting record collections. These were the kids who told their folks to fuck off and the parents just walked away. What kind of world was this?

Another constant in the suburbs was the local paper, the *Los Angeles Times*. Every Sunday featured a pullout section called *Calendar*, which provided a fantasy into a world of clubs that I could only dream of—I wondered what these places looked like inside. In it were also reviews filled with

words I didn't understand, so I usually just liked to stare at the album covers that accompanied them and fantasize about having them in my collection. It was about that time when there was a lot of press about this band called X. I had heard Rodney play them before, and once I got past jarring harmonies unlike anything I had ever heard, I decided I really liked them. I saved up my money and bought their album *Wild Gift* at the local Music Plus after I had heard "We're Desperate" and "The Once Over Twice" at a friend's house. I didn't really understand what they were singing about, but I got lost in the words anyway. And I couldn't stop listening. I played it every day.

In 1981 or 1982 I discovered this record store in the San Fernando Valley called Blue Meanie. It was a great import and alternative record shop specializing in punk, metal, and new wave. I would save up all my money to spend there, and when I went, I would literally stay for hours . . . getting dropped off to go through every record in the store. I spent so much time at the store that I soon befriended two of the clerks there, two mods who were about my age named Lance and Jeff. It was a great, unique store where I learned of The Damned, The Jam, and even classic soul. It was also the store where those clerks led me into the living world of punk rock.

I already knew some of the counterculture stuff that I liked: the aforementioned Stiff Records canon and a lot of the British new wave and punk that I was really starting to dig. Soon enough I was hanging out with Lance and Jeff outside of the store and listening to records at their homes, but this time we had cigarettes and beer and weed. Holy shit. This was teenage rebellion, and I was really starting to get that it had a soundtrack. The words were starting to make more sense. I was a kid from a slightly lower-middle-class

family living in an apartment in an affluent suburb—I wasn't exactly desperate, but now I longed to be.

It was then, during my fifteenth year, when my new mod pals took me to my first punk-rock show. When we walked into the club we walked into a nightmare: everyone there looked like they belonged—I stood out. I didn't have the right haircut or clothes. Everyone looked pissed off or drunk or both. I was way out of my element and wasn't happy about it. And I was scared. Full-on I'm-gonna-crap-my-pants scared. I was going to be killed here, or at least have the shit beat out of me. I still remember the argyle sweater I was wearing and how it looked among the ripped T-shirts and mohawks. I found a spot in the very back of the club and pushed myself so hard into that wall that I felt I could have gone through it—and it would have been a welcome escape from this unspeakable land of Oz that I wandered into. All the records I had listened to and all the photos I had stared at, and I still wasn't prepared for this world. Not even a little bit.

We were there to see X. I had been so excited to finally see this band I loved, but I had envisioned something different. I envisioned seats and appropriately timed applause, and probably a clean snack bar. Also we had arrived to the show in a "borrowed" car and ingested a good amount of cheap beer and San Fernando Valley weed, making the evening all the more surreal. I quietly prayed to myself that if I made it out alive, I would not put myself in this situation again—in the same way a kid bargains with God to get them through a night of alcohol poisoning: survive and you'll never touch the sauce again.

But at some point during that gig—once the sensory overload of the environment slightly subsided—the music began to come into focus and enveloped me whole. I knew

everything would be different after that, whether I liked it or not. I had lost my virginity, innocence gone. Good riddance.

Through the thunderous white noise of the crowd the music began to come into focus. Everything else vanished and I sat there transfixed. Like anyone who has ever seen X perform, I was completely captivated by Exene and John. She was gripping the mic with both hands, leaning in almost menacingly and defiantly toward the adrenaline-filled crowd, the two of them soundtracking the scene unfolding before me perfectly with high-decibel poetry and a brash dual lead vocal like I'd never heard:

> *I play too hard when I ought to go to sleep*
> *They pick on me 'cause I really got the beat*
> *Some people give me the creeps*

Song after song, I was getting dragged in deeper. Not everything was sounding like the albums—songs were faster, louder, and Exene's vocals would often trail off into undecipherable guttural growls. John Doe and DJ Bonebrake played like no rhythm section I'd seen before or since, and of course, Billy Zoom, poised—almost motionless among the chaos—eerily grinning like I'd seen in dozens of photos.

Still, all these years later, if I close my eyes, I can recall every bit of the sensory overload of that night: the smell of stale cigarettes and sweat, the way my face flushed with panic and humiliation at the stares I knew I was getting, and the eventual exhilaration at the feeling that I had discovered a new world that was mine, that was dangerous and challenging, that would give me a new identity. It wasn't exactly acceptance—I didn't need acceptance—it was more a feeling that challenged everything I thought I knew. I had gone through the mirror. I liked it.

Now I felt indoctrinated into a world where The Flesh Eaters' Chris D. scared the shit out of me way more than an Ozzy Osbourne ever could. It was wonderful. We had known of the legend of the clubs that had already closed; the Masque, Hong Kong Café, and the Starwood were the stuff of punk-rock legend to us. We would endlessly fantasize out loud about how we wished we had been able to experience them. But venues still remained for us: in the form of the Whisky a Go Go, the Cathay de Grande, the Anti-Club, the 818's own Country Club, bigger settings like the Santa Monica Civic, downtown LA's Olympic Auditorium, and a host of other fly-by-night—and I'm guessing hardly legal—rooms that would host bands like The Gun Club, Meat Puppets, The Cramps, The Vandals, Social Distortion, The Plugz, 45 Grave, Agent Orange, T.S.O.L., the Circle Jerks, Wasted Youth, D.I., Fear, Tex and the Horseheads, and literally countless others.

I wasn't there for the birth, but I was there for the evolution. When members of X, The Blasters, and The Red Devils formed The Knitters and made it okay for us to like real country music. When bands like Lone Justice, The Beat Farmers, Long Ryders, Rank and File, Green on Red, and Blood on the Saddle challenged our thoughts on "modern rock" and brought influences from both punk and the world of roots music. When The Plugz and Los Lobos opened our eyes to a Chicano artistic subculture that we, as suburban white kids, were painfully unaware existed. The treasure map was expanding, and so was our knowledge of the world that came before punk: the worlds of Eddie Cochran, Merle Haggard, Muddy Waters, Ritchie Valens, Gram Parsons, the Sir Douglas Quintet, Carl Perkins, Johnny Cash, Chuck Berry, Motown, Stax and Chess Records, and so many more.

That's how punk rock changed my life. I know that's how punk rock changed a lot of folks I know, and an army of those I'll never meet. It's an education and lifestyle we always keep with us. And those early bands, completely unbeknownst to them, became our teachers, role models, and influencers.

In 1996 I went to work as an A&R man at Elektra Records, once the home of my favorite punk-rock band. I was hired by the legendary Seymour Stein, arguably one of the most important architects of bringing punk rock to the mainstream. During my interview process I pitched the idea of an X anthology—the company bit. I slowly reached out to the band, one by one, and we assembled what would become *Beyond and Back: The X Anthology*, a two-disc career retrospective tracing back to the band's roots. It was amazing fun to put together . . . and even resulted in a Tower Records autograph-signing appearance that would reunite the four original band members together for the first time in over ten years, spurring the second wave of the band's existence.

During the process of assembling the compilation, somewhere between going through a million old shitty cassette tapes, John Doe became my pal. As I began to chat with John I would very surreptitiously dig for stories from the scene, soon discovering that a lot of what I thought I knew from those early days of LA punk was wrong. There had been no real documentation from that time, save for some salvaged fanzines, films like Penelope Spheeris's groundbreaking *The Decline of Western Civilization* and *Urgh: A Music War*, some brilliant writing by the likes of Chris Morris in the sort-of-underground *LA Reader*, and the mainstream press reviews in the *Los Angeles Times*. And, of course, W. T. Morgan's X documentary, *The Unheard Music*.

To unapologetically generalize history: the New York punk-rock scene was born from the city's art scene and community, while London's influence came from both reggae and the UK invasion of the New York punk scene. Both landscapes produced stars, widely documented and deservedly securing their place and stories forever in history. At the same time it was evident that there was very little being said about the LA scene; it was becoming a footnote—if not overlooked entirely—in articles and documentaries chronicling the rise of punk rock. With very little documentation of that era easily accessible, it seemed it was also falling to revisionist history. LA punk was born from rock 'n' roll, from country and blues and Latin music, the true next step—and one of the last steps—in the evolution of rock 'n' roll music. Although legends were born from this scene, there were very few stars and really no celebrities.

This is an attempt to tell the story. When John and I first spoke of writing this book, I told him I thought it was important for the true story of LA punk rock to be told. He replied that everyone in the scene probably had their own truth to tell. He would be interested in *that* story, regardless of whether it matched his own memory. So here it is— the many true stories from a mostly undocumented era in cultural history. This book is about that time. The time before the major label deals and the mainstream press. This is about the birth of the true second coming of rock 'n' roll—a story most haven't heard, told from the voices of those who were there.

CHAPTER 1

Something's Happening Here

by John Doe

It could've been 10 p.m. in July in a painted, plywood hallway upstairs at the Whisky a Go Go. There was a corner w/ red & black linoleum squares on the floor. This corner was at one end of another short hall & staircase that led down to the stage. I stood there breathing short breaths waiting for the rest of X to join me before we'd walk down those stairs. I imagined Jim Morrison & Ray Manzarek or Otis Redding or Arthur Lee or Marvin Gaye & Tammi Terrell standing on the very same spot, waiting for the rest of the world to catch up to them. It wasn't the first time I'd been here & this had become a kind of ritual. But it was the first time in 1978 that the show was sold out & the Whisky added another. This was a place where you knew that something was definitely happening, that you were definitely headed somewhere. I would look down at my shoes and those red & black squares and think that we were part of something, like others had been part of something else. Where the people in their audience had known something

that other people did not & were about to see something the rest of the world might see soon.

When we walked down those stairs, I knew it would go from zero to a hundred in a blink, cymbals would crash & DJ Bonebrake would hit his drums so hard that he'd probably knock something over or snap a hi-hat pedal in two. I might pull the cord out of my guitar & stop the giant, rumbling bass. And we would forget about the asshole soundman who said we were too loud. After all the nights of rehearsals & learning songs, bad equipment at the Masque & other DIY shows, this would be louder than hell & there would be sounds hurtling past & swirling around us all & somewhere amidst that mayhem, there would be a moment when everything would slow down & I would see things slo-mo. I'd catch someone's face distorted by a shoulder or the palm of another's hand. Or Exene's hair would rise into a fan as she flipped it into or out of her face. I would glimpse her dark red lips making wonderful sounds that I knew were the only sound that could be made at that moment. She would tell the truth to all these people who knew she would tell the truth. There would be flashing lights & sharp, piercing guitar notes & monstrous chords & Billy would look like he was straddling a wide creek w/ a smile that was genuine & scary & somewhat practiced because a fan of his rockabilly band had said he looked like he wasn't having fun while he played. I knew Exene & I would bounce around the stage unhinged, but Billy would stay still, play so fast & true & smile & wink at girls. There would be people's faces upturned to the lights & we would recognize over half of those faces & they knew where & about who the songs had been written. There would be sweat and DJ would have no shirt on. He would shine w/ the power of his driving hands & arms & legs & his eyes would roll back in his head & his chin would

tilt upward and sometimes steam would rise from his back. And we knew then that we were unstoppable & that we had power. And that something was definitely happening here.

There had been so many other nights when the roles were reversed and Exene & I were in the audience seeing something—a band?—that was not fully formed but breaking something to pieces, getting to the bottom of some core. When The Screamers stretched heavy, black plastic across the entire front of the stage to obscure all that lay behind, only to slit it open w/ a knife & begin their jagged, distorted performance, it didn't matter what the sounds were, whether they were good or smart or accomplished. It didn't matter if they were pretty or polished. They had an edge & were cool & probably dangerous. You could just tell. And it was happening now, right now, in front of your face & no one had seen this before. Tomata du Plenty could've been wearing a straightjacket, could've escaped from the asylum, no one knew, but our imagination allowed anything to be possible— the wilder the better. It throbbed & pulsed & was part music, part theater & all live experience. No one cared whether they could buy a record later. No one cared to have a souvenir T-shirt. The band, any band, dropped complete onto this stage, right now & we may never see them again after this night was over. Rik L Rik from F-Word or John Denney from The Weirdos both seemed to move like they were dodging imaginary bullets, swerving & bending, choking the mic stand as their eyes bugged out of their heads. They had practiced & were prepared to meet whatever was thrown, sometimes literally, at them, but there was nothing calculated in what they did. The bands pounded & roared & droned & fell down & broke shit & got too high to play right, but it was all happening right there in front of our eyes.

DECEMBER

X

(2 shows)

SAT **TH FIRST**
at the HONG KOng
SAT WITH The
GEARS

WEND.
19Th aT The
WHISKY

THE
CROWD

FEAR &

9TH - cuckoo's NEST in
Costa mesa

21,22 GEARY ST. SAN
FRANCISCO
WITH MUTANTS

GOGOS

28 **29**
week end
**HONK
KONG**

& ||||| BLACK FLAG

FRI. **14** hope st. hall

Tba

1329
S. HOPE
WITH: **GERMS**

CHAPTER 2

A Seamless Race

by Exene Cervenka

1976 was the bicentennial of the United States of America. Two hundred years of red, white, and blue. Fireworks and celebration. Meanwhile the carnage of a generation of young people drafted or volunteered into the Vietnam War had just ended. The hippies had won, or so it seemed. But Jim, Jimi, and Janis were among the dead, victims of nascent rock stardom, drugs, or maybe something much more sinister. FM radio, reeling from the blow of losing the most important voices of that generation, made the conscious choice to hold on tight to the memories and the music. Classic Rock was born. And mixed into that were The Eagles, Linda Ronstadt, Fleetwood Mac, Frampton, Steely Dan, David Bowie—and disco.

Everything was quieting down. Los Angeles nestled its soft rockers on fluffy pillows of white cocaine, upon which their dreams of fame came true.

Walking up the hills of West Hollywood side streets to get to Sunset and Crescent Heights, I would see real limousines

probably headed to the Record Plant, where reels of tape were spun into multimillion-selling LPs. Limos full of pretty groupies and skinny rock stars, dressed in velvet and wrapped in scarves. Snorting blow. Drinking expensive champagne. But I never wanted to be them. Not the groupie nor the rock star. I thought they were excessive, alien, obsolete, funny.

It felt like The Doors were light years behind us. I loved them; my first realization that music was life-changing, soul-stirring, and cosmic came when I was 12. I had just heard the long version of "Light My Fire" on the car radio. But only 7 years later, after their mystical Whisky a Go Go days—I was only 20 then—some of the younger kids (teens) in the LA scene didn't have as much knowledge about hippies and the '60s music and culture. These kids grew up with KISS and what their brothers might have played, usually going back to metal, but not rockabilly, blues, or Little Richard. But we all learned from each other. Bits and pieces of Brit pop, glam, country, old music, new music, old cars, East LA sugar skulls and lowriders, Hells Angels with their choppers lined up on the Sunset Strip—it was a sexy, scary thrill to walk the gauntlet of all those biker eyes.

We thought we were doing something new and revolutionary, but really we were handed the torch, and it was a seamless race from jazz, to poetry, to be-ins, to love-ins, to beatniks, to hippies, to protesters, to punk. Not a lot of time passed, considering that 200 years of history—it was maybe 25 years' time.

But in so many ways we punks were different. We were angry—or pretended to be—to ward off the jocks and mockers. We were flip and funny, bratty and aloof, scared and brave. We were the kind of fearless that comes from not knowing how dangerous what we were doing really was.

San Francisco had a commie, loving side. New York had the dark side, the no-wave scene. I thought The Ramones were just as dark as James Chance with their pale skin, skinny leathers, and a kind of *West Side Story* Jets legacy. Los Angeles had the wild, reckless humor, drugs, and beer yet close-knit community side covered. We were fun. We wanted the world to revolve around us. I had picked the right city to land in when I made my escape from Tallahassee, Florida.

I thought punk was gonna end the corporate takeover of America's rock 'n' roll, our real music, and we would never have to give in to the dumbing-down, mass-minded crap of the now-ruined radio.

The sunny afternoons on Sunset Boulevard—walking past Schwab's drugstore, where you could sit at the counter, order a Coke, and sip the lie that said that Veronica Lake (maybe it was Lana Turner) was discovered right here—would turn into nights traipsing up Hollywood Boulevard to the Masque basement, where we would make our descent into the pitch black of a new light. When X played there, or at a rented hall, or even the Whisky or Starwood, I loved the blur between band and crowd, taking my turn jumping around in the mix of friends and weirdos then back to the band.

I loved floating on a small sea of people who knew we weren't rock stars or even fans; we were all the same freedom-loving rebels, doing our job as young people do—changing and destroying, creating and rebuilding culture.

We were in a vortex, a vacuum, an underground scene so secret and so beautiful, it was hard to believe it was happening. I could wear my same Florida thrift-store dresses and antique jewelry and vintage shoes with ripped-up stockings or black straight-leg jeans that I would take in by hand

'cause all I could find in stores were flares and bell bottoms. We didn't go to malls or grocery stores or school. We didn't have to.

Rent was cheap, 3 or 4 hundred bucks split 2 or 3 or 4 ways. We made all our own fliers and took them to Charlie Chan's on Hollywood Blvd to get them printed, 2 cents each. Wheat paste and a paintbrush—those were all the ads we needed.

But I also felt so sophisticated some nights, drinking martinis at the Whisky a Go Go, watching Blondie or The Damned or playing the same stage Johnny Rivers and The Doors had played, sitting in the same red booths.

We had it made. We were called up to serve our country or we volunteered for battle. Even in the early days of our scene there were casualties. Darby Crash, who died in 1980, was a deep and sensitive young man and the first martyr. His death hit us all very hard, and losing him injected the scene with the new drug of sadness, and forced us to grow up. The rest of us had to go on. We were playing the best music and doing the most creative performance art. We were a living spectacle that terrified and confused the traffic on Sunset and Vine, that broke the TV, replaced the radio, infiltrated the record companies, became the big stories the media was forced to tell, and maybe gave the government a bit of a scare.

But the best thing we had going for us was originality. Nothing quite like LA punk had ever existed or would ever again. We won.

CHAPTER 3

... a hundred lives are shoved inside

by John Doe

When Exene & I lived in West Hollywood, from 1979 to 1982, there wasn't a moment's rest. It seemed every day & every night someone was knocking on the door of our tiny duplex w/ a couple quarts of Eastside beer, a Bukowski-endorsed local brew. There were only 4 rooms, including the bathroom, which had aluminum foil for wallpaper. 1118 N. Genesee Ave was half a block north of Santa Monica Blvd, the Spike (a popular leather bar) & the strip, where most of the gay hustlers worked, even one of our friends who went by the name Tony the Hustler. I believe the rent was $250 & the place was just south of the heart of the beast.

Exene had an eye for decoration, loved anything— especially bark cloth—from the 1930s & '40s. Our place had as many pieces of that as she could bring from Flor- ida & what we found at junk stores. We loaded our mantel- piece w/ as much scary voodoo-type stuff as we could find,

hoping it would discourage people from breaking in. Of course, there was nothing to steal except maybe a couple guitars, a rhinestone tiara, or some engineer boots. Billy Zoom slept on the couch for 3 months or more. Our biker roadie, Chuck, fell asleep smoking in a chair, set fire to it & the prized leather jacket he was wearing. I remember waking at 3 a.m. to smoke, Chuck & Billy yelling & someone, maybe me, hoisting the smoldering chair out the door, over the wall of the four-step, tiny balcony/landing that led to our front door & onto the curb. We drenched it with the garden hose & crawled back to bed. We were roused again an hour later by a fire truck clanging up to our duplex & hosing down that beautiful, tenacious & now sad 1940s chair. After playing two shows at the Whisky a Go Go, we were filmed in that living room, high on speed, drinking & tattooing each other for *The Decline of Western Civilization.* I believe we had an impromptu wake there for Exene's sister Muriel. In the middle of the night I gave teenage runaway Gary Ryan a black eye for screaming that I had slept w/ his wannabe girlfriend Lorna Doom of The Germs. Only now I can admit that I had. And in that Hollywood duplex we wrote or lived all of the songs for *Wild Gift* & *Under the Big Black Sun.*

CHAPTER 4

The Canterbury Tales

by Jane Wiedlin

Living at the Canterbury
Fighting off the roaches
Like being in a dormitory
Till rental due approaches
Don't know where we'll get the cash
Spent it all on drink
I don't know, but sometimes
It's better not to think
And sometimes I don't like to think
Living at the Canterbury
My friends think I'm a fool
Living at the Canterbury
*I guess it's pretty cool**

---

*"Living at the Canterbury," performed by The Go-Go's, written by Jane Wiedlin.

It was 1976, and I'd just started college at Los Angeles Trade Tech, a cheap-ass school in downtown LA where kids from "the ghetto" went to learn a trade.

I wanted to be a fashion designer and desperately wanted to go to a chic, trendy school like Parsons, Otis, or FIDM. In typical style, my midwestern parents informed me that art school was a damn waste of their good money and if I truly wanted to be a fashion designer, all I really needed to learn was the trade and the tech. I was already plenty creative, so off to Trade Tech I went. I became, after growing up in the very white, very middle-class San Fernando Valley, *a minority*. Even though I wanted to be somewhere fancy and artsy, I loved college. After the loathed high school, it was a relief to finally be taking classes, learning things I was actually interested in, like pattern making, sketching, and sewing. In high school I'd had good friends, a small tight-knit group of kids called the Hollywooders because of our obsession with "glitter rock." We lived for David Bowie, Roxy Music, T-Rex, and Sparks. The rest of the school (other than the stoners and the geeks, whom we got along with just fine) despised us and called us fags and trash. The jocks and the surfers were particularly antagonistic toward us. Later, in a life-imitates-art moment, hostilities temporarily ceased after Bernie the surfer Romeo fucked Nancy the glam Juliet. If memory serves, the cease-fire was short-lived.

We glitter rockers had our own hangout on a set of steps dubbed the Hollywood Stairs, which was our tiny kingdom (queendom?) at Taft High School. We all rechristened ourselves with "cool" glam names. I was Tiffany Teardrop, and some of my friends were Limor Lovestar, Nicki Northwind, Chelsie Vixen, and Benni Electra. We wore satin and sequins and ridiculous platform shoes. The high point of high school

was when Joan Jett (who was already a locally famous up-and-comer) enrolled in our school for a semester. For thrills, on weekends our gang would sneak out and take the bus to Sunset Boulevard to go to Rodney Bingenheimer's English Disco. All the English rock stars visited Rodney (a strange little man who later became a DJ on KROQ) when they were in town, and young girls were served up to them like fresh meat on platters. I never did fuck a rock star, but we met lots of wannabes like Zolar X, Silverhead, and a then-unknown Iggy Pop.

Once, a well-known promoter dragged me into the walk-in cooler in the back of the joint and started rubbing up against me. I remember him complaining about my belt buckle being in the way. In the way of what? I was numb, confused, scared, but just stood there, paralyzed. I was young and inexperienced, but after I went back out to the dance floor and saw the mess on my satin hot pants, I figured it out. Oh, precious youth.

I'd been struggling with severe depression since puberty had hit me like a freight train at the tender age of eleven. In the early seventies a lot of young people (and probably a lot of adults too) were convinced that at any moment nuclear bombs were going to blow the world to smithereens. My conviction that this was true, combined with raging hormones and a brain that was naturally colored blue, made me sweet and sensitive and a huge mess. I was completely convinced that life was utterly pointless. Just before my sixteenth birthday, crushed by the rejection of Ron, a boy at school with an *actual David Bowie hairdo*, I took three bottles of phenobarbital in an attempt to end it all. My suicide note was a love letter to David Bowie. One of my many brothers discovered me unconscious and I was rushed to a hospital.

I was in a coma for days, and it was feared that I was going to be blind and have kidney damage, but I (obviously)
survived. My poor, besieged parents wanted to put me in a
loony bin, but the psychiatrist next door (who later turned
out to be a wife beater) told them to just get me a good
shrink. This was before the days of antidepressants (praise
Dog for them!). The two things I remember about my sessions, both solo and group, are, one, the shrink kept trying
to get me to admit that I masturbated, and, two, one of the
boys in my group therapy was suicidal because his cock was
crooked. I never did admit that I masturbated, but I reckon
that doctor helped me get through high school alive. Once
I escaped high school and moved out of my long-suffering
family's home, I was still depressed as hell, but I was at
least finally living the life I wanted. As an aside, it is so wild
that I found life so pointless as a teenager, when just a few
short years later I would be part of a band that was number
one in the charts. You just never know what the future will
bring. Painful, yes. Pointless, no.

In late 1976, a few months into college, I was reading the
fashion newspaper *Women's Wear Daily* when I came upon
an article on *punk-rock fashion*! At this time I was still pretty
immersed in the whole glitter-rock thing (which, like punk
rock, was equal parts look, music, and attitude). Music was
everything to me, though I never dreamed I could actually *be* in a band. I was going to be a famous rock 'n' roll
clothing designer. Anyway, that day, looking at the photos
of these *wild*-looking kids on Kings Road in London, I was
instantly smitten. Suddenly everything changed for me. I
started reading everything I could about punk rock. I started
making my own punk-rock clothes and dressing in them,
much to the chagrin of my teachers, to whom I'd previously

been a pet. I still had my 4.0 grade point average, but now everyone labeled me a nut job. One weekend I visited a store on the Sunset Strip called Granny Takes a Trip. GTAT had been a glitter-rock clothes store for years, but they had started to lean in favor of the new punk-rock style. The Brit running the place liked my stuff (even though he had a lot of good ideas on how to improve my designs, which I ignored) and ordered a bunch of it. I was ecstatic. While I was there another girl came into the shop to hawk *her* wares, and we got to talking. Her name was Pleasant (I thought it was a fake name but I was wrong), and she was also a former glitter-rock fan. In fact, she had recently met some other kids who were also transitioning from glitter to punk. Kids she'd hung out with while stealing room-service food in the hallways of the Continental Riot (Hyatt) House Hotel. Food that had been eaten by the members of the band Queen! Some of those kids ended up becoming The Germs. Pleasant informed me that punk rock was not just in London; it was in *Hollywood* too! Well, you coulda knocked me over with a feather. I was so excited! She gave me a flyer to a new club called the Masque. I wanted to be part of something glorious and revolutionary and, most of all, infuriating to grownups. With the death of glam came the birth of punk, and I was *all in*. Pleasant and I became great pals and had an on-again, off-again fling going. We'd get wasted at parties and slip off to a quiet corner to mess around. It was all good fun, and as David Bowie had taught me, "Bi is best." (I actually *said* this to my parents as a teenager! Oh, my poor mom and dad. What they went through with me!) The boys, and then the men, came and went in both our lives, but Pleasant and I are still dear friends nearly 40 years later.

The Masque was in the basement of the Pussycat, a porno theater. You entered through the back alley, down a long set of stairs. It was dark, filthy, and smelly. I thought I'd died and gone to heaven. The first show I saw was The Alley Cats and The Controllers. There were about 40 kids there, and I knew right away I'd found my home. I made some friends, including Chloe, a tiny woman who was a wannabe hairdresser and gave me some really revolting hairstyles! Five different colors, four different lengths, all short, of course. Wouldn't want to be mistaken for a *hippie*, who I quickly learned were "our" arch enemies. My hair was so wild that when I got a waitressing job at Norm's Coffee Shop on La Cienega, I would have to wear a wig to work. Norm's was an old-school Googie-type building, a restaurant frequented by the ancient Jews who lived in the Fairfax district. We served food like liver and onions, and I was frequently rewarded for my hard work with a quarter for a tip. "Here ya go, dearie!" Even then, 25 cents did *not* make a tip, but most of the patrons were really nice. My bravest act back then was to spit in the food of customers who were mean to me. I've always hated bullies. Chloe the fake hairdresser lived with the incredible band The Screamers, who, along with The Weirdos, were arguably the kings of the Hollywood punk scene. The Screamers lived in an old run-down house everyone called the Wilton Hilton. The guys in the band were handsome, sophisticated, and a bit older. They approached music from the art-school angle and were unbelievable live. So intense. So scary. So great. I hung around but was always nervous and shy. These guys were beyond me—and everyone else—in every way, and they knew it. They wrote songs about people like Eva Braun and Twiggy. They were twisted and fabulous. Everyone thought they'd be the breakout stars of our scene, but that is another story.

As I got more and more into the Hollywood punk movement, it got harder and harder to live at home in the Valley.
My mom would burst into tears when I'd come home with
yet another ridiculous/fabulous hairdo. She even asked me
whether I was mentally ill, which was kind of a compliment
at the time. After my first suicide attempt at fifteen, my entire family, including, of course, my parents, *never spoke of it.*
Ever. So in retrospect I can see why she was worried about
me when I went punk.

Finally, after what felt like an eternity, I moved out of the
Valley and into the Canterbury, a 1920s apartment building at the corner of Cherokee and Yucca, just one block
from the Masque. The year was 1977. The Canterbury had
previously catered to the influx of starlets in Hollywood's
glamour days, and though it was run down, it was still a fantastic building. It still had the original built-in vanities, huge
walk-in closets, and a beautiful-if-decrepit fountain courtyard. I couldn't afford the $185-a-month rent on my own,
so I met a girl also looking for an apartment. Debbie Dub
was just returning to California after living in London for
a few years. Poor Debbie! I was a selfish, spoiled teenager
and immediately took the one bedroom and *all* the closets,
leaving her nothing but the Murphy bed in the living room.
I ripped up all the old carpeting and painted everything, including the floorboards, bright white. I was really into surrealism at the time, so nothing nonwhite was allowed into
"my" space. I turned one of the huge closets into a sewing
room and hauled my enormous industrial antique sewing
machine in there, where I continued to make punky clothes.
The manager of The Weirdos, my favorite band, actually approached me about designing their stage wear (they always
looked like hot/crazy men in their mismatched thrift-store
finery), but alas, it didn't end up happening. Still, I saw

The Weirdos (and The Screamers and every other band that formed) dozens of times. I don't think I slept for years; between school, jobs, and shows, there *was* no time to sleep, and that was fine with me. During the day, after a brief few hours of sleep the night before, I took crystal meth to stay awake at my job. I worked in a sweatshop factory downtown, where I wrote my punk-rock poetry (later to become lyrics) onto the patterns I was making for mass-produced cheap men's sportswear.

Pulling up the old carpets left a huge gap around the baseboards in my trashy-chic starlet apartment. That, in turn, created a superhighway for every cockroach in Hollywood to come visit us. It didn't help that, though I wanted to live in a perfect surreal setting, I was also a teenager. Naturally I was lazy about taking out the garbage. The stockpiled bags of trash in the kitchen created a truly horrendous roach and rat problem that I had no idea how to deal with. So I ignored it. I lived on Top Ramen, Kraft Mac & Cheese, and trail mix in those years, and my "grocery store" was the corner liquor store. I'd save coins to eat, and when I didn't have enough money, I'd steal food. My apartment had a fire escape outside the kitchen window that I used like a balcony. I liked to sit out on my "balcony," swigging beer, smoking cigarettes, and watching the hookers ply their wares. It was just the sort of life I pictured when I became a punk rocker. The biggest treat for me and the rest of the gang was saving up our pennies to eat at Johnny's Steakhouse on Hollywood Boulevard, just east of Cherokee Avenue, where the Canterbury was. For $1.99 you could get a real steak dinner with all the fixings. Never mind that the windowsills were covered with flies, dead and alive. It was *steak*!

I fell in love with Terry very early into my new life. He was deathly white, with huge brown eyes and a shock of dark spiky hair (once he got the right haircut of course). He liked Kerouac and Bukowski. He claimed he was just a fan and didn't play an instrument. Later it turned out he was actually a fine drummer, and he joined The Bags and then The Gun Club. I invited Terry to move into my Canterbury apartment rent-free, without first asking or consulting Deb Dub, of course. Jesus, I was a dick then! Terry didn't pay rent and didn't have a job. At first I didn't care—it was punk to be unemployed! Later it became an issue, as I made almost nothing and was now working for two. When I meekly asked him to get a job to help pay rent, he dutifully went out and got one. He'd disappear "to work" every day, nine to five. I was so happy to have a working man for a boyfriend. Terry would come home to my all-white-but-filthy flat at night, tie me up, and (consensually) abuse me. "Oh Bondage, Up Yours!" It was my first real-life experience with BDSM after having obsessively read *Story of O* and *9½ Weeks* over and over as a teenager. I was a total closet perv, too ashamed to talk about it or admit it. Luckily the punk scene was loaded with BDSM imagery (check out Vivienne Westwood's early T-shirts!), and Terry really "got" me. I understand now why. Back then so many punk rockers—especially me—were enamored with legendary fifties pinup star Bettie Page. Bettie Page was the undeclared gorgeous queen of my "tribe": half devil-girl, half angel. Of course I adored her. Still do. Bettie was the perfect physical embodiment of a divided soul. Sadly, my punky-pervy honeymoon with Terry proved to be short-lived. I learned from friends that instead of working, Terry was actually spending his days wandering Hollywood Boulevard, hanging out in

the many used-book stores and crappy coffee shops, reading and caffeinating. Looking back on this almost 40 years later, I think this was clever and funny and, of course, *very punk rock*. At the time, though, I was heartbroken. Sayonara, Terry.

Punks quickly took over the entire Canterbury, and it really *was* like a dormitory. Doors were left open and unlocked. Girls and boys would be running through the hallways at all hours of the night and day, borrowing guitars, food, booze. A typical night out involved walking 400 feet to a show at the Masque, or possibly some other seedy temporary club location. The audience consisted of the same 100 kids—the scene had grown a lot in a year!—most of whom were in bands themselves. Most times it would just be a night of swapping, kids going from audience to stage then back again. It felt like Our Scene. It *was* our scene. There was an endless stream of boozing, barfing, dancing, and fucking. As I mentioned earlier, I grew up in a boring middle-class neighborhood, but I was no Pollyanna. I was working to be as good at being bad as I possibly could. Most of the punk kids I knew had been raised Catholic like me. There was just something about that religion that brought out the inner rebel in teenagers. If you grew up in that cult, you had an understood, unspoken frame of reference. We called it Catholic Damage. It made you want to be as bad as possible, all while still being a little bit scared of Hell way deep down inside.

Bands were forming and re-forming faster than you could keep track of. Everyone was welcome, girls included. It was even okay to be gay in the Hollywood punk scene. It was an inclusive scene, centered on art, creativity, and fun rebellion against grownups. By 1978 nearly everyone was in a band, except for a lone few girls. That was how The

Go-Go's formed. Belinda Carlisle lived across the courtyard from me with her best friend, Lorna Doom of The Germs. Belinda was beautiful and glamorous and always perfectly put together, even when she was wearing a trash bag for a dress. She kept her makeup in a cookie tin and made spare money on the foreign currency trading market. How the hell she knew how to do this, I still have no idea.

Eventually it became painfully obvious that you needed no prior knowledge to form a punk band and that we were the only kids left who hadn't done so. So Belinda, Margot Olavarria (an adorable girl with rainbow-colored hair just back from two years in London), and I decided *we* were going to be a band too. Hey, why not? We were perfectly capable of being just as incompetent as everyone else. No matter that we didn't know how to play our instruments— we were going for it! The manager of the Canterbury (who also happened to be some kind of shyster Pentecostal minister) started letting everyone use the basement of the building as a rehearsal room. Soon our little fledgling band was down there too, learning to play our instruments, cranking out fast, loud music, and having a blast. With Belinda living in one apartment and me in another, it only made sense that we'd use the basement, even though it was in no way a safe situation. It was spooky as fuck down there, and Hollywood was a dangerous town in those days. After rehearsing a bit, we would wheel our amps a block down the street to the Masque and play shows to an ever-growing "crowd" of enthusiastic friends/fans. It was so exciting! After a few short months Charlotte Caffey, a *real* musician, joined our group. Char actually knew how to *read music*. You may as well have told me she spoke ancient Aramaic, it was so exotic and so impressive. Charlotte and I later

became a songwriting team, and to this day I am still in awe of her genius.

After The Go-Go's formed, things really started heating up in Hollywood. Bands began to perform at real clubs, like the Whisky a Go Go on the Sunset Strip. This was about as prestigious as it got in those days, and I'll never forget the night that X was there, playing a two-set sold-out night in 1980. I was there, of course. *Everyone* was there. X was now the biggest, best band on the scene. In between the two sets Exene discovered that her sister Mirielle had been killed in a car crash on the way to the show. Exene was understandably inconsolable. Nobody knew what to do. Everyone was in shock. John Doe threw a chair through the big plate-glass window of the dressing room, unable to handle his feelings. I remember sitting on the floor in a corner of that dressing room. I wasn't really a friend; I was too in awe of them to be that. I was just another part of the tribe, and bands didn't really have private dressing rooms back then. I didn't know what to do. I was so uncomfortable being in the midst of this insane tragedy. I started cutting myself with a piece of glass from a broken beer bottle and playing with the blood to distract myself from the horror of it all. Later I read an article in the *Los Angeles Times* in which the journalist talked about that night, mentioning a little punk girl ritualistically cutting herself in a nihilistic way. It was like he was a scientist observing the behavior of some far-flung tribe from the deep jungles of the Amazon. It felt so strange that some total stranger had noticed me as I was doing something meaningless to me. That he'd assigned meaning to what I'd been doing. That I was part of the narrative. X played the second set anyway, and they were more brilliant than ever. I felt like the club was going to burst into flames, the intensity was so great.

Yup, the Canterbury was like a dormitory—a dormitory with heroin, rape, and plenty-loud punk-rock music. A schism, based on drug use, started forming pretty early on. We were *all* in agreement that *nobody* was allowed to smoke pot. Pot was for dirty hippies. The Great Punk Divide happened because some of us stuck to booze, pills, speed, and hallucinogens, while others moved on to shooting heroin and dilaudid, a synthetic opiate kids took when they couldn't score the real thing.

The idea of shooting drugs was really scary to me. I still had a few lines I was afraid to cross, needles being the primary one, though I do remember smoking angel dust one afternoon in the early days. I don't know why I did it or where I got it, but I got so high, I thought I was having a nervous breakdown. I wandered over to the Masque and climbed down the stairs to hide. The guy hired as caretaker there, a Scientologist named Larry, found me in a corner of the basement freaking out. Scientology was a new thing then, and they had their headquarters on Hollywood Boulevard. We used to try to mess with them, taking their tests and lying about everything. It was something to do, a way to pass the time. Anyway, after smoking the dust, I was crying, crumpled up on the filthy floor. Larry the Scientologist held my hand for hours until I came down from the high. Maybe he tried to recruit me; if so, I don't remember! Either way, it was a kind moment. It did not stop me from being a wild child, but I did stay away from angel dust thereafter.

I remember the excitement in the apartment building one day when it was discovered that the bag lady who we called Miss Conehead had died. Bag ladies were people who, back in the days when the government helped people, lived on SSI, money you could get if you were declared crazy. Miss

Conehead had lived in the Canterbury far longer than any of us and was a real character. She always wore a tall, pointy hat and a wimple, like a princess from the Middle Ages—hence her nickname. I thought she looked about a hundred years old, though for all I know she could have been in her fifties. I had a less-than-firm grasp on such things in those days, plus she *was* crazy. I often wonder if Miss Conehead had been in the building since its heyday, an aspiring starlet who just never caught a break. Anyway, Miss Conehead lay dead in her apartment for days—sad that—when finally the coroner came and took her body away. Her apartment just sat there, untouched, for weeks. Her family had obviously abandoned her long ago. When it became painfully clear that no one was coming to remove her possessions, I snuck in there and stole one of her dresses, a lovely white 1950s sundress that I still own to this day. I can't bear to part with it, and sometimes I think I'm the only person alive who still remembers her and still thinks about her . . . of course partially because I still feel guilty about stealing that dress. Catholic Damage.

Parties happened nearly nightly at the Canterbury. One night I was at a get-together with my good friend Alice Bag, a girl I'll call The Vampire, and Shannon, a newer member of the punk tribe who later started the Castration Squad. Alice lived in the Canterbury with her boyfriend, Nickey Beat, the hard-hitting but sweet drummer for The Weirdos. Alice was gorgeous and ferocious, and the lead singer of The Bags. The Vampire had crazy, jacked-up-looking teeth, pointy and menacing. She was volatile and frightening . . . truly frightening. She looked like goth before goth existed. The three girls had recently started a joke girl-gang they called The Pyranas.

That night someone offered me some pills that I, of course, immediately swallowed, no questions asked. We were all drinking cheapo wine, getting drunk as skunks. The Vampire started into this long tirade about how she was really and truly a *genuine* vampire and that she was the real reincarnation of Drusilla, sister of Caligula. (This next part is told by Alice, because I had blacked out from the pills and wine by then.) Everyone was laughing at her and dared The Vampire to prove her claims. The Vampire got pissed, grabbed my arm, and started sucking on it. I protested feebly, so then, of course, everyone started laughing at *me* and pounced on me, covering me with bites and hickeys. (Trust me, this was no big thing back then.) Later that night I made my way back to my apartment, still in my zombie blackout, where my boyfriend, Terry Bag, awaited me. Terry was so irate that I'd been "raped" by them (I hadn't—I'd been pranked punk-rock style, but still) that he spray painted "Pyranas Suck" all over the elevator of the building. He was furious, and I appreciated his gallantry, but I felt more embarrassed than anything by this event, and that was only because *I couldn't remember what actually happened.* The big problem then became that Terry was the drummer of The Bags, and The Bags was Alice's band! So eventually Terry's outrage at my "assault" morphed into him claiming he was just mad that *he hadn't been there to watch the action go down* (bow chicka wow wow). A classic Canterbury Tale.

There were parties for the "regular" kids (my word) and parties for the shooters. Of course, lots of the IV users had come from the same normal background as me, but at some point two paths emerged then diverged. It was sad to see that divide in a scene that was already pretty fucking small. I remember Rob. He came from Arizona and was the cutest,

sweetest boy ever, but he got caught up with the shooting crowd and ended up dead. This was a guy who started off looking like the president of the Chess Club and ended up looking like the Walking Dead. I remember Greg, gorgeous and sexy. I had a mad crush on him. We "dated" for a little while, but there was always a strange space between us. He was so secretive. It even turned out that he was seeing Charlotte while he was seeing me! Charlotte and I later wrote the song "He's So Strange" about him. Go's before Bro's.

I didn't know what Greg's secret was (heroin) until he ended up dead. Shannon, one of The Pyranas, died in the nineties of AIDS complications, caused by IV drug use. The Vampire was another one of the members of the "other crowd." She was a real tough broad and mean as hell when cornered. The Vampire had no problem picking a fight with *anyone*—bikers, cops, she didn't give a shit. She was fearless. When she got raped one night at the Canterbury, things took an awful turn toward the dark. If that tough-as-nails chick was vulnerable, *everyone* was.

There were a lot of turning points in the Hollywood punk scene. I always remember when I started feeling like the scene had grown a little *too* much. When guys from Orange County started showing up, ready for a bit of the old ultra-violence. When it went from being female friendly and gay friendly to more testosterone driven. When mock fighting became real fighting. And when people started dying from drugs. Meanwhile The Go-Go's got more and more (and more) popular. We started getting accused of being sellouts. We started playing places other than Southern California, until finally we weren't part of the Hollywood scene at all anymore. The scene continued on without us, and the history books erase The Go-Go's from the chronicles of

those days, because it is just too much work to try to imagine how we had ever been a part of it. But we *were* part of it. I feel incredibly lucky to have experienced what I did, to have been there at the beginning when everything was possible and everyone was welcome. I feel even more lucky to have survived it. It was the time of my life.

ANOTHER *slash* DiSASTER ?

CONCERT

WITH   PLUS

DILS X

AND
FROM SaN FRaNCiSCO

AVENGERS

FRiDAY ØCTOBER 21st

LaRCHMONT HALL

118 NORTh LARCHMONT

2 BLOCKS EAST oF VINE / 1 SOUTH OF BEVERLY

CaLL 469-5760
$3.00   FoR INFo   9 P.M.

CHAPTER 5

A Nonstop Crazy Party

by Pleasant Gehman

It took a moment to realize that the handsome silver-haired man handing me a lit joint was Tony Curtis. I'd arrived in Los Angeles—and turned sixteen—less than two weeks before, but somehow I had the social savvy to act as though it was completely normal to be getting high with a movie star. Taking a huge hit and choking out "Thank you!" as I handed the reefer back to him, I silently marveled at my good fortune.

Being in LA was surreal, something I'd dreamed about constantly since I'd discovered *Creem* magazine, *Rock Scene*, and *Andy Warhol's Interview* at the age of twelve. I was absolutely certain that once I got to the City of Angels, everything would pan out the way I'd always daydreamed it would. A rock 'n' roll–obsessed girl, I saw myself hanging out backstage at the Whisky and the Rainbow sipping champagne with rock stars, or riding in the backseat of a vintage convertible, cruising past pastel mansions and towering palm trees on my way to the beach. To manifest this opulent

fantasy lifestyle, I channeled the glamour of silent film star Clara Bow, dying my ass-length hair bright red with henna, piling on way too much black eye-makeup and muddy maroon lipstick.

I'd taken the 83 bus down to the Santa Monica Civic Auditorium for a concert. I felt extremely *foxy* in my stained crepe 1930s evening gown, a frayed antique velvet jacket, and the pair of mile-high silver glitter platforms that had cost me three weeks' worth of waitressing pay and tips . . . and now I was getting wasted with the leading man from *Some Like It Hot*! It was March 29, 1975, and along with the rest of the sold-out two-thousand-seat house, I was waiting breathlessly to see Queen.

As Mr. Curtis handed the joint back to me with a beatific smile, a pair of amazing-looking boys passing my seat suddenly diverted my attention. The taller one was slender and dark, with a long black satin cape billowing out behind him as he strode down the aisle. Barefoot and shirtless, he wore heavy Egyptian eyeliner, and his kinky hair splayed out from his head in a Sphinx-like wedge. The other one looked like a real-life David Bowie action figure, attired completely in white, his fluorescent red rat-tail mullet framing icy blue eyes and powdered pale cheeks with a perfectly rendered lightning bolt zigzagging across his baby face.

Sharing a reefer with a movie star was one thing, but what I was seeing was quite another. In that moment it seemed that all my fervent prayers were being answered. Never one to ignore an omen, I took fate into my own hands, borrowed a pen from Tony Curtis, and scrawled a note on a matchbook:

Aladdin Sane, You Cosmic Orgasm—Call Me!!!

To further drive the point across, I added stars, a moon, a Saturn, and a lightning bolt. With the precision of a crackerjack pitcher, I threw the matchbook across a few rows of seats just as the house lights were dimming, certain my life was about to change.

The next day they called me, constantly grabbing the receiver from each other for the hour or so we stayed on the phone. Our affinity was immediate. Because they lived by the beach and I lived in LA proper, we decided to take the bus to meet at the median point of Westwood. We became a trio on a regular basis, cutting school, day drinking while listening to records, vandalizing office buildings, and hanging out at Santa Monica's Lifeguard Station #26, known as the "juvenile delinquent" beach. We'd prowl Hollywood Boulevard, another haunt for high school students who were ditching class. At night we'd invade Sunset Strip to hear The Motels, Van Halen, The Quick, and the newly formed Runaways play the Whisky, where I'd gotten the coveted job as ticket taker in the box office. After the show we'd score Quaaludes for a dollar in the Rainbow parking lot.

Of course I had crushes on both guys and couldn't decide which one I liked better until the dark-haired one made a move and I officially became his First Girlfriend. Their names were Paul Beahm and Georg Ruthenberg—they hadn't yet switched to the monikers Darby Crash and Pat Smear.

Historians might argue that LA punk didn't get its "official" start until 1977. It was definitely a year of benchmarks, with the April 16 Weirdos/Zeros/Germs Orpheum show, followed the next day by the first visit of a UK punk band, The Damned, at the Starwood, *Slash* magazine's debut in May, and the opening of Brendan Mullen's club the Masque

in August. However, the scene had actually been bubbling under the surface since 1975. That year two key punk-precursor events occurred in quick succession: glam rock haven Rodney's English Disco closed, and Patti Smith's debut album, *Horses*, was released. Suddenly everyone on the scene chose sides, pledging allegiance to one of two distinct camps. Those who were interested in frivolously dancing the night away kept their Farrah hair and French bellbottom jeans, embracing disco. The others—like me—who were interested in a darker form of hedonism gravitated toward what was soon to coalesce as the original LA punk scene.

Along with Georg/Pat and Paul/Darby, almost everybody I knew was in high school. Most of us were seriously unsupervised latchkey kids, completely alienated by the bland seventies pop culture that society relentlessly shoved down our throats and into our ears. We actually *read books*, something that seemed like a truly archaic pastime and was frowned upon during The Disco Years. Horrified by the stupidity of *Charlie's Angels* and *The Six Million Dollar Man*, we infinitely preferred subversive "art house" fare: the racy foreign films, Manson Family documentaries, John Waters's *Pink Flamingos*, and *Reefer Madness* that showed as midnight movies at the Nuart or the Fox Venice.

We were disgusted with the syrupy garbage on the radio, the infinitely stupid, effervescent saccharine of The Carpenters or The Captain & Tennille. We chose the sonic mayhem of The Stooges, the salaciously macabre Alice Cooper, Kraftwerk's robotronic void, and the tawdry, homoerotic fabulosity of Lou Reed, David Bowie, and the succession of British bands influenced by them. There wasn't a snowball's chance in hell any of that would ever be broadcast on Top Forty radio, so we never expected to hear it on anything but

our cheap Sears Roebuck stereos or our painstakingly curated homemade cassettes.

Underfed intellectually and refusing to conform to
a dumbed-down vanilla sensibility, we were constantly
searching for like-minded souls, people who shared the
same arcane frame of reference. Soon a scene began to develop. In addition to disenfranchised kids from LA's vast array of suburbs, we began meeting people who were slightly
older than us. Aside from a love for unadulterated rock 'n'
roll, we all seemed to have a blend of the Beats' appreciation for literature and art combined with the louche, Harry
Crosby–informed *laissez faire* of Paris in the twenties or the
drug-addled debauchery of Andy Warhol's Factory or the
notorious Back Room at Max's Kansas City. Once night fell,
we were sincerely on the prowl and, as the New York Dolls
said, "Lookin' for a Kiss" . . . or more, if we could get it—
and usually, we could.

My crowd and I were streetwise teenagers, sophisticated
enough to be experimenting with drugs and sex but hid-
eously below the legal age of consent. Most of us hitchhiked
or took the bus to Hollywood Boulevard because many
weren't even old enough to have a driver's license, let alone
own a car. With Rodney's closed, we hung out in Westwood
at the Sugar Shack, a San Fernando Valley teen club where
you were carded to prove you were under 21.

Our favorite late-night gathering spots were the all-night
coffee shops—Arthur J's on Santa Monica Boulevard and the
two similar Hollywood Boulevard institutions, Danielle's
and the Gold Cup, later immortalized in Black Randy's
song "Trouble at the Cup." We fit in at these places, which
were full of street crazies, leather daddies, and 75-year-old
women with capped teeth who'd come to Hollywood in

the 1950s as aspiring starlets. Trannie hookers turned tricks in the ladies' room while rent boys straight out of John Rechy's *City of Night* worked the sidewalk. Mostly we hung out at these establishments after hitting the United Artists Theater in Westwood to see *The Rocky Horror Picture Show* for the millionth time. None of these dives served liquor, so they didn't card anyone. Whether you were male or female, you could be totally at home in your ripped fishnets, heavy *maquillage*, and Sally Bowles's fierce, divinely decadent attitude. Who was going to hassle you about your appearance—a stoned drag queen?

Because it was The Swingin' Seventies, our nascent sexuality was also one big fat gray area—and it's not like anyone was keeping tabs either! Our youthful, carnally adventurous spirit fit in with the prevalent freewheeling attitude of the time. Mixed with the handfuls of pills we took, washed down with the Mickey's Big Mouth and Olde English 800 tallboys we guzzled in back alleys, it made any sort of sexual classification totally irrelevant. My crowd's prurient interests, which had taken hold during glam rock and informed many factions of LA's early punk scene—included but weren't limited to fluid-gender identities and nonspecific sexual roles, uniform fetishes, multiple partners, and, especially, openly gay and bisexual experimentation.

The people I ran with were all fun and interesting. My schoolmate Randy Kaye introduced me to Dennis Crosby, delinquent grandson of Bing. Dennis was an absolute riot—openly gay and so casually out, everyone accepted him. He was like an outlaw rock 'n' roll version of Liberace. He'd wear my 1960s Peter Max mini-dress with a thick leather and rhinestone KISS belt, cowboy boots, and a Lone Ranger mask to school. Through Randy and Dennis I met their mutual

friend from Rodney's, Joan Jett, just as The Runways were being formed. We'd cut school nearly every day to watch the band rehearse at SIR Studios in Hollywood. Joan introduced me to their manager-producer Kim Fowley, and the guys who wrote the *Back Door Man* fanzine, Phast Phreddie and Don Waller. The Runaways actually played their first show in Torrance . . . in Phast Phreddie's living room!

Around the same time I'd met a kid whose thrift-store, pachuco-pimp clothes belied his amiable nature and vast musical knowledge, Brian Tristan. He became my roommate and changed his name to Kid Congo before joining The Gun Club and, later, The Cramps. Brian worked as a clerk at Greg Shaw's Bomp! Records. Though it was located in the vast wasteland of the San Fernando Valley, Bomp! might as well have been Mecca, and everyone made the pilgrimage, staying for hours because the English import 45s we all read about in Brit music papers *Sounds* and *NME* were always in stock. Anna Statman, who went on to be an A&R person at Slash Records, and Jeffrey Lee Pierce, who was the president of Blondie's fan club before forming The Gun Club, both practically lived there.

The double-trouble blond duo Belinda Carlisle and Terry Ryan (later known as Germs bassist Lorna Doom) made the long trek from Thousand Oaks to Hollywood almost nightly. Likewise, brother and sister Paul and Kira Roessler and their pal Michelle "Gerber" Bell had left the surfer life, abandoning Station #26 in favor of hanging out on Sunset Strip or at the Starwood. The gals from Backstage Pass—Johanna "Spock" Dean, Holly Vincent, Marina Del Rey, and Genny Body—looked like tough sixties B-movie stars and were ubiquitous scene makers: wherever you went, they were already there or walking in just behind

you. Photographer Theresa Kereakes, whose appearance was fairly "normal" (she was just starting at UCLA), began spending every night out at the clubs documenting the bands playing. Alice Armendariz and Patricia Rainone (later known as Alice and Pat Bag) were always on the scene. A few other gals constantly out on the town were Natasha, a petite redhead who'd been around at Rodney's, and sisters Jade and Zandra, who wound up documenting the LA scene in their fanzine, *Generation X*. Along with Exene, they all rocked a vampy 1920s look with a modern streetwise twist. I'd met Jane Wiedlin long before The Go-Go's existed. We were both at the Sunset Strip sister-store of the famed London rock 'n' roll boutique Granny Takes a Trip, trying to sell our original T-shirts. Mine were covered with dirty words stenciled on with spray paint; hers had two zippers down the front, which, when opened, would reveal the breasts. Jane swears I was the first punk she'd ever met, and she immediately began hanging out in Hollywood.

I can't remember the first time I encountered Hellin and Trudi, but it was probably while in line waiting to get into the Whisky. Manager Jim La Penna had a habit of letting teenagers in for free if we could prove we maintained a B average—he'd actually make us show him our report cards! Hellin, Trudi, and I formed a trio immediately, a mutual admiration society based on similar taste. Hailing from the beach community of Palos Verdes, they looked and acted anything but suburban. A slutty symphony in black and white, it was as though they'd come to life from the pages of a 1950s pulp men's magazine. Their dyed black hair was always snarled, and they wore torn vintage black slips, lacy bullet bras, and battered stiletto-heeled pumps. By accident or design, their vampire-white bare arms and legs were usually covered in an assortment of scratches and bruises.

One night while driving from the beach to LA, they got in an accident that totaled Hellin's mother's car. After that, they moved in with me so they could be closer to Hollywood. Though my mom detested the fact that our pillowcases were routinely stained bright pink or electric blue due to the Rit Fabric Dye we'd taken to using on our hair (Krazy Kolor hadn't hit the market yet), she was actually the one who named Helen "Hellin Killer," and the name stuck. We'd study the postage stamp–sized photos of Kings Road punks in the English rock rag *Sounds*, trying to absorb their ferocious attitude. Because there wasn't any punk gear available in America, Hellin, Trudi, and I made do wearing dog collars from the pet store and bought $4.00 studded leather cock rings from the Pleasure Chest to wear as wristbands. Soon Hellin chopped off her bed-head hair, styling it into a crew cut with two points in front, then shaved her eyebrows and pierced her cheek with a large safety pin, emulating Soo Catwoman of the Bromley Contingent, a group of Sex Pistols fans that included Siouxsie Sioux and Billy Idol. Around this time Belinda started showing up at gigs in Hefty trash bags that she'd fashioned into dresses.

Though our attitudes—and the way we expressed them in our DIY fashion—were shocking to "normal" people, we soon fell in with a crowd of slightly older hipsters who were in their twenties and thirties; their arty outrageousness was so professional, it made us look exactly like what we were: *kids.* Every night there'd always be a bunch of new cool people congregating in Hollywood. Many of them had been involved in various other fringy subcultures. They came from all over Southern California and beyond, including major cities like New York, San Francisco, Seattle, Chicago, and London as well as even obscure places like Oklahoma State University, where Dangerhouse Records founders K. K.

Barrett and Pat "Rand" Garrett had fled. John Doe hailed from Baltimore, Exene and Farrah Fawcett Minor had left Florida; the three eventually settled into a large single apartment in the alley behind Circus Books. Located across the street from the legendary rock club the Starwood, the apartment where X's song "Adult Books" was written, it soon became infamous for noisy after-hours parties. The constant influx into Hollywood was like a seasonal mass migration, happening as if by instinct. In those days you absolutely *could* judge someone on appearance alone, because nobody in mainstream society looked the way we did. God knows where they all came from or how we all found each other, but we were always excited to meet. There'd be an almost tribal moment of stunned recognition—you could practically see everyone thinking, *Holy shit, there's other people like me?*

One night early in March 1977 at the Whisky I was in the balcony with Joan, Hellin, and Randy, trying to act nonchalant as we sipped the illegal Long Island Ice Teas that waitress Marsha Perloff had slipped to us. She'd get us drunk every night by putting our cocktails on some hapless record exec's tab . . . not that they ever noticed. The Runaways' *Queens of Noise* had recently been released, and Joan had just returned from London. She'd left for the UK wearing her customary battered white platform boots, high-waisted French bellbottom jeans, and a baseball shirt, but she returned clad in straight-legged Levis, Converse sneakers, a black leather jacket, and a necklace made of safety pins. She regaled us with tales of what was going on with rock 'n' roll in the UK, and we were all fascinated to hear a firsthand account. We were grilling her about English punks as The Damned's "Neat Neat Neat" blared over the PA, when suddenly our minds were blown to bits as we first laid eyes on The Screamers.

As Tomata du Plenty and Tommy Gear walked through the front door, our mouths fell open in unison. They were *magnificent*; it was as though they were a pair of ambassadors who'd been sent from another planet to educate earthlings on punk cool. Both had black spiked hair and wore wraparound sunglasses and pegged black pants. Gear had on a 1950s black motorcycle jacket and a hardware-store chain around his neck fastened with an industrial padlock. Tomata was in a red sharkskin suit jacket with a huge wooden coat hanger shoved into the shoulders. As if hypnotized, we all walked onto the dance floor to talk to them. I immediately became obsessed with The Screamers, as did everyone else. Even though they hadn't played yet, their looks alone were so impressive that we all bowed down. Brian/Kid Congo soon became the president of their fan club.

I hung out daily at The Screamers' place, dubbed the Wilton Hilton. A dilapidated Craftsman duplex, it was two blocks away from Dangerhouse, the pad where Screamers K. K., David Braun, and their friend Rand McNally lived and founded LA's infamous underground record label of the same name. Tomata and Gear lived in the top half of the Wilton Hilton with Chloe, wide-eyed professional makeup artist whose crew cut changed colors every week. A stunning redhead named Fayette Hauser (who shared a matching crudely done Kewpie doll tattoo with Tomata) lived there too. She and Tomata had been a part of The Cockettes, San Francisco's celebrated, outrageously gender-bending cabaret drag troupe. According to Tomata, William Randolph Hearst had built the place in the 1930s as a love nest for Marion Davies before Paramount Studios bought it to house their starlets. Apparently at some point in the 1960s all or most of the GTOs had resided there; after they left, it was occupied by a Satanic cult. It seemed credible—the floors had

large circles burned into the wood that could've been used for rituals, and the downstairs family's dog constantly dug up cat skulls from the backyard. The hallways were painted matte black, and at the base of the steps there was a huge wall safe and a framed newspaper clipping from August 6, 1962, that declared in French *"Marilyn Est Mort!"*

Hanging out at the Wilton Hilton was like attending punk-rock finishing school. The Screamers taught me how to crash strangers' parties and make a French Exit, which meant you left by slipping out suddenly without saying good-bye to anyone. They showed me how to screen telephone calls, a necessary art in the days preceding answering machines. Gear demonstrated picking up the phone with your voice disguised, and when the caller asked if you were home, you'd say, "Let me see . . . " as you put your hand over the receiver, wait, then come back on the line and say, "No, I'm sorry—can I take a message?"

Everyone visited The Screamers; it was like paying homage to their greatness. I was so obsessed with them that I kept a CIA-like dossier on them in my journal, surreptitiously noting down pertinent facts such as their real names, the people they knew (Divine, John Waters, The Ramones, Blondie), and even what they *ate*. Hellin, Trudi, and I would sit quietly, amazed that they considered us friends and awed with the parade of cool people trickling into their house. Their entourage included Seattle cohorts Gorilla Rose and Suitcase, ex-Warhol star Mary Woronov, Black Randy, Hal Negro, and houseguests from San Francisco like The Nuns, Don Vinyl from The Offs, Chip and Tony Kinman of The Dils and The Avengers, plus their mutual manager, Peter Urban. The Screamers were constantly photographed, and the screaming spike-headed logo that artist Gary Panter created

for them became one of the most recognized punk-rock images ever.

The spring of 1977 turned out to be a huge turning point in the Hollywood scene; the punk-rock storm clouds that'd been gathering and building steadily turned into a killer tornado. Word spread quickly on the street that The Damned, the first UK punk band to visit America, were playing a two-night, four-show run at the Starwood. Anticipation ran high because since their first album had come out in February, The Damned had usurped The Clash as our favorite English band. For weeks you could walk into any apartment at the Canterbury at any hour of the day or night and hear "New Rose" or "Fan Club" playing. In fact, The Damned album was always blaring so loudly, you didn't even have to be *in* the building—the sound carried out the open windows and you could heard it all the way down on Hollywood Boulevard. Once Brian/Kid Congo spilled the beans that The Damned were making an in-store appearance at Bomp! on April 16, we all made giddy plans to be there.

Bomp! was a madhouse, so packed that the crowd spilled onto the sidewalk. Everyone was there, even Rodney and Kim Fowley. It was *an event*. It was also the first time many of us had seen each other in daylight. Randy Kaye and Brian were elbow nudging me as Angelyne sauntered in wearing a powder-blue marabou-trimmed satin corset, her white Barbie-doll hair piled in a high bouffant, with a face full of stage makeup, which, in the afternoon sun, looked like a scary doll-head mask. At the time, well before her billboards had gone up all over LA, Angelyne was in an excruciatingly bad bar band called Baby Blue, made up of shag-headed *poseurs* trying valiantly to ride on the coattails of the punk scene. As though a chorus of angels heralded their arrival,

The Damned appeared with the vampirical Dave Vanian, sending every punkette's heart aflutter. Hellin, Trudi, Mary Rat, and I were absolutely dumbstruck—and even more so years later when Pat Bag wound up marrying him!

Lots of us were drinking or had shown up already drunk, like Darby Crash (who was going under Bobby Pyn at the time) and Pat Smear. They were proudly wearing their new mustard-yellow band T-shirts, emblazoned in velvet iron-on letters GERMS. The shirts had been made at a store where they charged by the letter, and their first choice of band name, Sophistifuck and the Revlon Spam Queens, simply wasn't affordable. A band that none of us had ever seen before, The Weirdos, showed up, and their appearance was so extreme—a pastiche of 1960s vinyl raincoats, white patent leather belts, bits of trash, metal chains, and Japanese toys—that they momentarily diverted everyone's attention from The Damned. The Germs and I introduced ourselves and found out they were promoting their show that evening at the Orpheum Theater, with Peter Case's band The Nerves and a band from San Diego called The Zeros. Ready to stir up some trouble, I announced that The Germs were a band and that they should open the show—and they got invited onto the bill.

We were already tipsy before leaving Bomp! but because Chris Ashford was driving and was over the legal drinking age of twenty-one, we stopped at a liquor store to get a few bottles of Cold Duck before adjourning to my mom's house so The Germs could get ready for their debut show. Bobby/Darby had purchased ten or so packages of red licorice whips, so we spent the hours before the show tying them around his whole body, over his clothes, knotted bondage style, while popping Quaaludes washed down with the

cheap champagne. We got so wrecked that all I remember from the ride up to the Sunset Strip was being crammed into the backseat, giggling hysterically as the Cold Duck spilled all over Bobby's licorice whip–wrapped body, making him a sticky mess.

The Orpheum wasn't a regular rock venue, just a small black-box theater that Peter Case had somehow managed to rent for this gig, which I believe was the first—and last—rock show ever held there. Located just off the Sunset Strip, kitty-corner from Tower Records on the tiny dead-end Nellas Street, the entrance was in the back, and as our carful of crazies arrived, there was already a number of punks congregated in the alley drinking, including Belinda, who was dressed in a light blue disco jumpsuit and spike heels, with a giant flower in her hair. She hadn't yet started rockin' the look she had in The Go-Go's. The place was pretty crowded; lots of people who'd been at Bomp! earlier were there. When The Screamers showed up with The Damned in tow, sitting on top of the theater's seat backs, it proved the show was definitely *the place to be.*

The Germs set was a huge mess, and that's an *understatement.* Aside from the 'ludes and Cold Duck, they'd never really played before and only had minimal rehearsals, and it showed. Even setting up took them ages. Their show was actually pretty funny it was so bad, but a lot of people were horrified, especially when the peanut butter came out, setting a sloppy, condiment-oriented precedent for their future shows. It was meant as a tongue-in-cheek tribute to Iggy, but it created a gigantic, disgusting mess. The plug was pulled and The Germs were thrown out. The Zeros were on next and were amazing. They were so young and cute, like fetal versions of The Ramones, and really tight as a band. "Don't

Push Me Around" was so catchy, it became a new anthem for many, including me. The Weirdos were flat-out astonishing. Everyone went crazy. Their insane appearance was the perfect foil for their music, which was like a sonic wall of sludge, with John Denney lurching around the stage like an escaped mental patient. With his tongue lolling out of his mouth and eyes rolling as he growled out unintelligible lyrics, he was a rock 'n' roll version of a Pieter Bruegel demon.

The next evening The Damned played the Starwood. It was a pure revelation and also sort of legitimized the LA punk scene. Local power-pop faves The Quick opened for them, which might seem odd now but wasn't at the time, though it did explicitly illustrate the difference in what was actually punk and what would soon be called new wave. The Damned played at lightning speed with violent energy. Dave Vanian was fierce and scary-sexy onstage, Captain Sensible dropped trou, and Rat Scabies stood up behind his drum kit, spitting beer and flipping the audience off.

It was the first time I stayed out all night, blowing off my curfew and my ride home. In anticipation of a wild night, I'd taken my schoolbooks to the Starwood, parking them upstairs at the VIP bar while I watched the show. I went to Cantor's with The Damned afterward, engaging in a food fight before going to party at the infamous Tropicana Motel. The next morning, at Duke's Coffee Shop, Tom Waits took in my hungover appearance—whipped cream and maple syrup congealed in my hair and staining my homemade Damned shirt—and admonished me in his gravelly voice, "Pleasant, for God's sake, stay in school!"

I assured him I would and, looking like a hot drunk mess, was chauffeured down Santa Monica Boulevard to school in the back of Rodney Bingenheimer's vintage black Caddy,

the envy of Randy Kaye, Dennis Crosby, and Lisa Curland, who'd made the mistake of adhering to their curfews.

After that there was a summer-long string of benchmark events and uproarious gigs, all with a full attendance roster of those who'd eventually become celebrated as "LA's First Hundred Punks." The Germs had their first official gig at Kim Fowley's punk series at the Whisky, which resulted once again in a huge mess of food, this time because they'd requested their fans to bring condiments, and everyone obliged. They'd moved into a nearby apartment on Holloway Drive, Joan and Lisa had rented an apartment on San Vicente, across the street from both Licorice Pizza and the Whisky, and Brian/Kid Congo, Ann McLean, Dennis Crosby, and I moved into 909 Palm—all our pads were within walking distance of each other. Our 909 parties were epic and never-ending. At the end of the night, no matter where we were, there was always a standing invitation for *everyone* to come over, and they did.

Slash magazine held a coming-out bash at a ballroom at the Santa Monica Ramada Inn, because their offices were nearby. Hotel guests were staring at us in sheer terror. I was in disbelief that such a cool punk magazine had an "old" publisher—Steve Samiof—who also had a *beard*! Nevertheless, I knew a good thing when I saw it, hitting him up for a staff writing position, which he agreed to. My name appeared on the masthead in the next issue, and my first piece was the Germs interview I did, though to my chagrin, the story went uncredited. When *Slash* moved to a loft on Pico and Redondo in LA, they had many insane parties there, not the least of which was the May 1977 Screamers debut and a party for Devo in July, after which I slipped on a puddle of spilled Mickey's Big Mouth and fell over the Germs'

second-story balcony. Phast Phreddie and K. K. rushed me
to the hospital, where I got five stitches in my chin . . . and
stole a plastic "Patient Belongings" bag to use as a purse.

Soon two events occurred, spawning a party of mythical
proportions at my place: my mom left to work out of town
for a week, and Hellin and Trudi got a settlement for their
car accident. Because I'd let them stay at my house for so
long and they were now rollin' in dough, we went on a
shopping trip to the Pleasure Chest. We bought matching
black-leather spiked slave collars and more cock rings, a cat-
o'-nine-tails, various bullwhips, paddles, and an authentic
regulation canvas straightjacket with leather straps. Because
my mom was gone, in order to show off our kinky loot, we
decided to have a party. We got cases of beer, lots of vodka,
and avocados to make guacamole; we spent the afternoon
calling everyone to invite them. Among the first to show up
were Joan Jett and Lisa Curland, already many sheets to the
wind on Quaaludes and vodka. Our other guests all arrived
in various states of inebriation too. By the time Cherie the
Penguin, Tony the Hustler, John Doe and Exene, and everyone from Dangerhouse and the Wilton Hilton showed up
toting six-packs of Mickey's Big Mouth beer, we'd run out of
chips. I dared Tomata to try the guacamole with a dog bis-
cuit, and he did, declaring it "fabulous." Suddenly everyone
had to do it. The downstairs bathroom was commandeered
as a dungeon, with Joan, Lisa, Hellin, Trudi, Gear, and I taking turns bending anyone who was willing over the rim of
the bathtub and whipping them as hard as we could.

We started a game with the straightjacket and a stop-
watch, having a contest to see who could last the longest
amount of time; some people took dares to escape but
couldn't. When K. K. emerged from a really long bathroom

session with Trudi and Joan Jett, I convinced him to try it. He was drunk so he obliged, but none of us—even K. K.— realized he was claustrophobic! Once the buckles were in place, he flipped out and made a dash for the open front door, running down the street screaming and body slamming against the palm trees in an attempt to escape. Of course a neighbor called the cops and the party was busted immediately. The clean-up was challenging; there was blood on the bathroom walls, guacamole and crushed dog biscuits everywhere, and for months any time a piece of furniture was moved, a booze bottle or beer can rolled out.

When the Masque opened in August, it became our amazing secret clubhouse. The steep concrete stairway—which, in hindsight, I'm shocked no one ever tumbled down and died on—led to a warren of subterranean rooms, with the walls already covered in punk graffiti from the bands who practiced there. The stage was small and low, and the sound system sucked, but we were in heaven! It was also conveniently located within crawling distance of the Canterbury and the Hollywood Boulevard Jack in the Box, where you could buy pills. The vast public parking lots behind the Masque functioned as a free motel—the 'ludes-fueled make-out sessions that started in the Masque bathrooms would inevitably be consummated there. We'd select the nicest cars we could find, try the doors, which were mostly left unlocked, and climb in the backseat for some lovin', leaving the windows fogged up as we made a hasty exit to catch the next band. Sex in those extremely pre-AIDS days was louche and fun, and the hook-ups weren't always heterosexual. One night at Larchmont Hall, during an X show, Alice Bag and I got *very cozy* while guzzling Southern Comfort on the fainting couch in the ladies' room. Her boyfriend, Nickey Beat of

The Weirdos, burst in and a huge brawl ensued. My other constant make-out companions—all on a friend-with-benefits basis, with no strings attached—were Joan Jett and Lisa Curland (who were in a relationship at the time), Bobby/Darby, and Go-Go's Jane and Belinda. My affair with Jane, which had started at the Masque, spanned years, continuing into our respective relationships with Levi Dexter of The Rockats and his drummer, Dean Thomas, though neither of the guys ever knew about it!

1978 started off with a January 14 Sex Pistols gig at the Winterland Ballroom in San Francisco. Tickets were a whopping *three dollars*, and the migration from LA was massive. Brad Dunning, Randy Kaye, Brian/Kid, Nancy Nagler, and I all crammed into Theresa Kereakes's tiny Honda to make the pilgrimage. But a few others got a head start: Hellin, Trudi, and a bunch of other chicks from the Canterbury had gone to Texas to catch the shows there. It was rumored that Hellin lost her virginity to Sid and that Alice Bag and Pat Bag had followed suit with Paul Cook and Steve Jones. I reported on this salaciously in my fanzine, *Lobotomy* (which I started with Randy Kaye in 1978), though now I'm not entirely sure whether these rumors were actually true and who did what to whom! A few days after Winterland the Sex Pistols broke up and the Masque was shut down by the LA fire marshals. The huge Save the Masque benefit took place at the Elks Lodge, with The Dickies, Black Randy, The Avengers, Dils, Weirdos, X, Bags, Screamers, Randoms, and many others taking the stage.

Things rolled along, with events happening thick and fast. There were now so many local bands, plus New York and English bands touring, that there were multiple choices of things to do on any given night.

In 1979, with the release of *GI*, produced by Joan Jett, The Germs morphed from a seminovelty band into a serious force to be reckoned with. Their legions of slavish followers, fresh "Germs Burns" blistering their hands, were sort of annoying and cultish to me and quite a few of the other original punks. Also, beach punks and Cromagnon-esque jocks from Orange County had begun to infiltrate our scene, and many of us, especially the women, were put off by it because of the violence in the slam pits. Instead of the pogo-dancing fun we'd been accustomed to at the Masque, the idiots who just months before had been screaming at us from car windows and beating us up had suddenly decided that punk was "cool" and the original scene began to splinter.

Many of the punkettes made a swift turn to the neo-rockabilly movement, perpetrated by Levi & the Rockats, an English band managed by the legendary Leee Black Childers of Bowie's MainMan Productions. Brian/Kid and I had seen them at Max's Kansas City in New York, opening up for the Cramps, and they were astounding. When they moved to LA and took up residence at the Tropicana Motel, Jane Wiedlin and I were among the first punk chicks to convert, followed quickly by Belinda, Connie Clarksville, Rosemarie "Wyline" Patronette, Anna Statman, Ann McLean, and many more. Though we all still adored punk, rockabilly shows were a much safer bet for us physically, and the guys were more courtly in a 1950s throwback way. Guys were converting too, including Jeffrey Pierce, Billy Persons (of The Falcons), and Brian/Kid. I reported on this trend with my first article, "Rockabilly Redux," for the *LA Weekly*, and after that they gave me my own gossip column, the infamous "La De Da," which I wrote for years, first by myself and later in tandem with Craig Lee and other contributors.

By early 1980 Anna Statman and I discovered The Blasters just before their first album came out. Even though I still continued going to punk shows, writing for *Slash*, *LA Weekly*, and *New York Rocker*, and publishing *Lobotomy*, the punk scene had lost its initial lustre for me. The rampant violence at shows, constant police harassment, and the rise of heroin as the drug of choice within the scene had left me seriously disenchanted. The quick rise—and subsequent fall— of The Germs, the concert series for *The Decline of Western Civilization*, and, in December, the untimely death of Darby Crash sealed it for me. I not only lost a dear friend, someone I felt I'd already lost to heroin, but I was also sure that the scene I'd loved so much had ended for real. At the time I blithely moved on to other things—more writing, starting my own band, the all-female Screamin' Sirens, in 1983, and becoming the full-time booker for the seminal LA clubs Cathay de Grande and Raji's.

In retrospect—and not just because I was so young—the years between 1975 and 1980 really were beyond incredible. Los Angeles was a crazy nonstop party, and the punk scene was chock-full of interesting, wildly creative people. It was so much fun, most of us didn't even have time to stop and notice that history was being made.

CHAPTER 6

Murphy Beds

by John Doe

Behind Circus Books on Santa Monica Boulevard stood an unassuming, chalk-white, 1920s apartment bldg. Circus Books was a typical dirty bookstore from the '60s, when pornography was for perverts & homosexuals. We loved it for its lawlessness, people watching & service to a community right in the heart of the gay hustler district, West Hollywood.

At the end of the hall on the ground floor was Exene & Farrah Fawcett Minor's apartment. They were both lapsed Catholics from Florida, both of which usually lead to bad behavior. They had a talent for egging each other on to great heights of chaos. On any given night Farrah would throw a drink in someone's face and make it seem like it was the person's fault or, at least, they deserved it. Exene always had her back & occasionally instigated the fracas.

The studio apartment was unremarkable except for a few sturdy built-in cabinets that were part of any building from the 1920s or 1930s. Naturally there was a Murphy bed & a

fold-out couch where they slept. More punk rockers slept on & did who knows what on Murphy beds than you could count. It's a testament to the functionality & practicality of the invention. (Thank you, Mr. Wm. Murphy & your SF opera star paramour.) Exene & Farrah's front door opened directly into the main room. An attached bathroom and kitchen was somewhat divided by those built-ins. It was perfect for any aspiring starlet or punk-rock girls looking for an affordable lifestyle that left plenty of time for dreaming, writing, drawing, or generally fucking off.

The greatest benefit of the place was its location, directly across from the Starwood, the Whisky a Go Go's main above-ground competition for live music. When DIY shows at veteran halls weren't happening or the Masque was shut down, we saw countless punk-rock shows there. The Damned's debut w/ flour billowing up from the floor-tom as the first, rocketing song was counted off. Devo, as they left everyone speechless w/ their airtight, mid-west, rhythm section, catchy songs, uniforms & dance moves to boot. Cheap Trick, before they graduated to the Top Ten & arenas. The Germs' penultimate show, which everyone hoped wasn't the end but secretly knew it was.

The apartment on La Jolla was ground zero for the party before & after almost every show. To her friends, Farrah went by the name Fay, which, not surprisingly, was also a pseudonym. She was a hellion then & during that time earned a place in history by inspiring several songs. Owing to her Southern roots, she would transform their small space into the most inviting party atmosphere. I always thought of her as a character from Tennessee Williams or Truman Capote. Exene was an able cohort & stylist of the environs. Florida souvenir ashtrays & pillow covers were cleaned & placed just so. The Murphy bed folded up, the decks cleared & low light

from table lamps all set before everything went to hell or at least pretty damn haywire. The drink Fay invented she called the "fast gin fizz," Gordon's gin & Nehi strawberry soda. It tasted pretty horrible (Darby Crash once announced, "This tastes like GAASSS!"), but the sugar from the soda pop seemed to inject the gin straight into your veins, brain & heart of crazy. Anyone who went to any show at the Starwood in 1977 or '78 probably passed through this door. At the time word of mouth was king & news spread quickly when the gig or the party & the gin was on. Somewhere there's even a few rolls of film that Jenny Lens shot of a beautiful shit-show that was crowned by Cherie the Penguin swanning out of the bathroom with nothing on but strategically placed pieces of wet toilet paper—or was it shaving cream? K. K. Barrett, drummer for The Screamers & Fay's boyfriend at the time, was an artist who excelled at re-creating the reentry rubber stamp placed on people's wrists by the Starwood staff. One or two people would pay to get in & the rest of us would get in w/ fake hand-drawn stamps—genius!

This is how bonds & alliances were made & broken. This is how a bunch of outsiders, fuckups & loners turned into a bohemian, punk-rock community. People exchanged stories of where they came from, crazy shit they had done in their young lives, ideas of what was & wasn't cool or what was or wasn't punk rock. It was like going to the strangest, coolest graduate school of music, art & life, even though everyone was just fucking around & having a wild time. This place was the same as dozens of other apartments or houses where other friendships, partnerships & insanity took place. A short time after Fay & Exene moved out, a group of women—Trudi, Hellin Killer & Mary Rat—would move into another ground floor apt in the same building, which was aptly dubbed the Plunger Pit.

BOYCOTT

$6.50

SCREAMERS

TRACHODON

Profit.
That's The
Name Of
Our Tune.

$

CHAPTER 7

You Better Shut Up and Listen

by Chris Morris

I was a stranger in a strange land. Then I found other strangers, stranger even than me.

I arrived in Los Angeles on Good Friday of 1977. That January I had been ejected from my job as an all-night disc jockey at a freeform FM station in Madison, Wisconsin. I had hopped on a train for an already-plotted vacation in LA, where I stayed with an old high school buddy for a few days in Beverly Glen. In the dead of winter I had walked beneath a night-blooming jasmine tree in Westwood, and my destiny was sealed in the moment I inhaled its perfume.

After my return to Madtown I was morosely swilling a beer in my favorite saloon one night when the phone rang. "It's for you," Mitch the bartender said. My friend was on the other end of the line—he knew where to find me. He was well connected in the movie business. He told me that if I got on a plane at O'Hare in Chicago two days later, there was a job waiting for me on the Left Coast.

On my arrival I was hired on the spot by the three partners who ran Parallax Theatre Systems. The outfit, later
known as Landmark Theatre Corporation, operated a chain
of revival movie houses around the country, including the
Nuart in LA, the Rialto in Pasadena, and the Sherman in
Sherman Oaks. (They later acquired the Fox Venice.) I had
minored in film at college and could push two words together and, thus, was deemed suitable for the position. I
was charged with writing the film notes on the back of the
free theater calendars and coordinating publicity. I rented a
cheap, utilitarian apartment with a cottage-cheese ceiling in
Westwood Village. For the first few months I lived in the city;
a typical evening's entertainment involved buying a six-pack
at the liquor store below the company's offices on Santa
Monica Boulevard, walking a hundred yards to the Nuart,
and drinking the night away in the back row of the theater
as a double feature of classic films unspooled on the screen.

I hadn't lost my love of music, but I had grown alienated from the status quo during my days spinning records
in the Midwest. I'd wearied of the daily requests from frat
boys and sorority queens seeking their minimum daily requirement of Fleetwood Mac, The Eagles, and Boz Scaggs.
The stuff sent me around the bend with boredom. Moreover, the radio biz was driven by everyday corruption, and
I'd wearied of its sordid perquisites. I recall a time when a
hundred-count LP box arrived at the station from a label
with which we were doing no current promotions. Upon
opening it, we discovered that the generous regional promo
man had sent us hundreds of peyote buttons. This was the
way it worked.

But something else had been going on, and it had occasionally seeped onto the airwaves at the station. I was a fan

of Patti Smith's writing for *Creem* and was delighted when a copy of her Mer single "Hey Joe"/"Piss Factory" materialized in the studio. After Patti's debut album, *Horses*, was released in 1975, I had interviewed her for the station; she had thumbed desultorily through an issue of *Down Beat* while I grilled her but still graciously signed my copy of her book *Seventh Heaven*: "TO RADIO FREE MADISON TONGUE OF LOVE PATTI SMITH." Among the real or imagined crimes that had led to my dismissal was my decision, during a midafternoon substitute shift, to play The Ramones' debut album in its entirety at 2:30 p.m. as the day's featured LP. The studio telephone glowed white with listener outrage.

Those acts had already played LA by the time I landed, but I wasn't prepared to sally forth in search of the new music immediately. The size of the city was terrifying and daunting, and I didn't drive (and still don't), so I was slow to learn the lay of the land. However, in the summer of '77, a first fire got lit under my uncertain ass.

I was sitting at my IBM Selectric in the small space I shared with Parallax's art director when I heard a knock at the door. A swarthy young guy in a sports coat walked in with some newspapers under his arm. He introduced himself as Steve Samiof. He told me he was publishing a magazine devoted to new music in LA and asked whether my company would be interested in running some ads for its theaters in its pages. When advised that I had nothing to do with purchasing advertising for the company, Samiof shrugged and dropped the papers on my desk, told me to get in touch if there was any possibility of a buy, and walked out the door.

I took the three magazines Samiof had left—the first three issues of *Slash*—home with me. I studied them in amazement.

A scene of some unprecedented sort was developing in town. Like the one that had grown in New York, it was a small one, so infinitesimal as to be, at that point, almost undetectable, but it was populated by a fascinating-looking pack of musicians. I had no idea what they sounded like, but their contorted, painted visages and ripped-up togs were alluring, and their names—Tomata du Plenty, Exene, Alice Bag, Bobby Pyn—promised something strange, dangerous, and adventurous. The writing in the mag was raucous and hectoring; much of it was penned by a sardonic and obscene scribe who called himself Kickboy Face (who, I would later learn, was actually a French émigré named Claude Bessy). It appeared from the reviews and interviews in the mag that the local bands played at a subterranean Hollywood firetrap/dungeon called the Masque.

I was still too timid and unsure of my geographical footing to explore any gigs, but I did a little poking around. One afternoon I climbed into the Parallax van with our driver, Dave Cohlmeyer, a skinny metal dude with lank blond hair that spilled over his shoulders, to pick up some film cans from a Hollywood depot. On the way back I suggested that we stop by the Masque to scope out the center of the punk vortex. Parking the van on Cherokee, we cautiously walked down the alley behind the Pussycat porn theater. Finding an open door, we stared down the dark, narrow, graffiti-splattered staircase that led into the bowels of the Masque. We heard a stirring below, and a figure emerged at the foot of the stairs. Looking up at two hirsute intruders, the man glared at us with a bleary, poisonous eye and began to yell in a thick Scottish accent: "We're not open! Fuck off!" Dave and I beat a hasty retreat.

I had been 86ed by Brendan Mullen, the man who gave LA punk its first home.

I was still looking for my crew. I found it at Rhino Records. I occasionally walked past the tiny Westwood Boulevard store on my way home from the office. I started dropping in on a regular basis. The place specialized in the new music—they carried everything from New York and England, and local singles were beginning to trickle out—and its clerks were knowledgeable, funny, and loudly opinionated . . . my kind of people. The shop soon became my living room, to the dismay of some of its employees, who would sometimes honor me with a slot on the store's Worst Customers List, a Top Ten of muso infamy.

I can't recall whether I made my first trip to an LA punk gig with one of the Rhino habitués or a like-minded Parallax colleague—several of my coworkers were already cocking an ear to the local bands—but in January 1978 I found myself standing in front of the stage of the Whisky a Go Go, the grande dame of Sunset Strip clubs, for a show by The Screamers and X.

In an instant I was sold, and something like a new life began.

Had anyone ever seen anything like The Screamers? Today they exist more as a rumor or a legend than as a band, consigned to murky YouTube footage and bootlegged concert recordings and demos. They never issued an official recording during their brief lifetime. Back then they couldn't be compared to anything on the scene—or anything in the world, actually. Unlike the vast majority of the bands I would soon hear, they eschewed electric guitars; their sound was a wall of loud, demonically distorted keyboards, played by band mastermind Tommy Gear and David Braun (aka David Brown, cofounder of Dangerhouse Records), the latter soon supplanted by Paul Roessler. Drummer K. K. Barrett pushed the music with an incessant pulse inspired by

such krautrock skin men as Jaki Liebezeit of Can and Klaus Dinger of Neu!

The band's main attraction was vocalist Tomata du Plenty, who brought to the stage an ardent, ingratiating theatricality, no doubt bred by his time with San Francisco's Cockettes and Seattle's Ze Whiz Kidz. He skittered across the boards like a marionette with its strings tangled, waving his hands before his face, doing a bunny hop, prancing like an impatient child, declaiming such alternately twisted and yearning tunes as "Vertigo," "I Wanna Hurt," "A Better World," "Punish or Be Damned," and "Peer Pressure" in a choked yelp.

An invariable highlight of the group's sets came in the middle of the rocketing "122 Hours of Fear," when the convulsive song would suddenly slam to a stop and Tomata would topple to his knees. Milking the silence until the audience began to shriek, he would leap back up to the microphone and command, *You better shut up and listen!* And the music would roar anew.

The Screamers were a flabbergasting thing, and I would go on to see them every chance I got, waiting in vain for one of the small local labels that had begun to spring up to document their music. The band had its own ideas and ambitions, and by the end of 1978 they had virtually disappeared to hole up in an overheated makeshift studio at Melrose and Heliotrope in East Hollywood, where they hunkered down with Austrian film director Rene Daalder, plotting a prescient multimedia project that never came to fruition. Shows at the Whisky and the Roxy in 1979 were chaotic and disjointed, and the band was already atomizing. Daalder's dreadful dystopian musical *Population: 1*, starring Tomata with art direction by K. K. (who would later find

great success as a production designer for director Spike Jonze) would serve as a kind of epitaph for LA punk's most stellar unit.

You will hear a great deal about X straight from the horse's mouth elsewhere in these pages, so I will attempt to be brief. The band was as much of a revelation to me that night at the Whisky as The Screamers (whose lead singer's name was invoked on X's debut single "Adult Books"). It was love at first sight, really.

Their songs immediately bowled me over: their hurtling, imagistic lyrics betrayed John Doe and Exene's roots in poetry and fused influences like William S. Burroughs and Raymond Chandler in a grimy homebrew. Their performance was like a kinetic sculpture, as John bounded around the stage and Exene thrashed in its center as if the mic stand was the only thing holding her to the Earth. Drummer Don (later DJ) Bonebrake pushed every tune in your face. Their instrumental weapon was unlike any other: blond, pompadoured guitarist Billy Zoom, a rockabilly veteran, who stood, splay-legged, on the boards in a silver leather jacket and an insolent grin splitting his face as he slapped antique Chuck Berry and Cliff Gallup licks against the songs' amped grain. I would see the band literally dozens of times over the course of the next eight years, during which they established themselves as LA's most accomplished and important group.

By the time I witnessed that epochal Whisky show, the Masque era was essentially over; the club was shuttered under intense pressure from the LAPD and the Hollywood city fathers in January of '78, and it operated sporadically, essentially as a private venue, until late that year. Brendan briefly reanimated it at a bombed-out location at Santa Monica and Vine, but it too folded in early 1979 after an astonishing

show by The Cramps, The Dead Boys, and Pure Hell. (Brendan distinguished himself as a club booker at Club Lingerie and later as a Boswell of the LA punk scene before his sudden death in 2009.)

With the demise of the Masque, the MK1 punk bands scattered like roaches under a kitchen light, moving into whatever venues proved hospitable to the music. The Whisky and the Starwood on Santa Monica were safe havens until their respective closures in 1982 and 1981. Less upscale joints—well, some of them were toilets, really—picked up the slack: Blackie's on La Brea, Club 88 on Pico in West LA, the Hong Kong Café in Chinatown, Al's Bar downtown, The Vex in East LA, the Cathay de Grande in Hollywood. I wound up pursuing the music at most of these down-at-the-heels nightspots after I became the music critic for the *Los Angeles Reader*, a new alternative weekly, in October of 1978.

I got to know many of the OG punk musicians. You would run into some of them on the street. I encountered Randy Stodola and Dianne Chai, respectively the guitarist and bassist for The Alley Cats, as they handed out flyers for one of their shows in front of the Whisky one night. They were small, soft-spoken people, almost doll-like. With her ratted bouffant and brightly painted cupid's-bow mouth, Dianne reminded me of a mussed-up Ronnie Spector. Given their looks, it was surprising that, with drummer John McCarthy, they made some of the toughest, most nihilistic music on the scene. Song titles like "Nothing Means Nothing Anymore," "Too Much Junk," "Nightmare City," and "Escape from Planet Earth" pretty much encapsulate their worldview. They whacked their streetwise *weltschmerz* across with a snarling guitar vengeance.

The Alley Cats seemed to lose the thread after a brief and thoroughly unlikely association with MCA Records

and a reincarnation as The Zarkons, and then they disappeared into the cracks in the sidewalk. In the new millen-
nium Randy resurfaced with a new group playing under The
Alley Cats handle; at last report Dianne was married to the
band's former manager Marshall Berle (son of the early TV
icon Milton Berle) and working as a travel agent in Florida.

I only got to know The Plugz, one of the first acts on
Slash's in-house record label, after hearing the trio's debut
album *Electrify Me*, the first self-released LP by an LA punk
band. I loved their energy and charging original songs—
"Electrify Me," "A Gain A Loss," "Berserk Town"—and their
cranked-up cover of Ritchie Valens's "La Bamba." I subsequently saw several club gigs—at one of which, at the Hong
Kong Café, drummer Charlie (Chalo) Quintana, all of seventeen at the time, was given the heave-ho for being underage. After one show I approached the band's sardonic
singer-guitarist Tito Larriva and asked whether I could call
him to interview him for a *Reader* story about LA punk.
"Yeah, sure," he said. "My number's in the run-off groove of
the record." And so it was.

With members born in Mexico (Tito) and on the Texas-
Mexico border (Chalo), The Plugz were probably the most
prominent of several early LA punk bands featuring Latino
musicians—an appropriate contingent in a burg with the
largest Hispanic population outside Mexico City. The Zeros, a quartet of whey-faced transplants from Chula Vista
(including Javier Escovedo, brother of Alejandro Escovedo,
the guitarist for San Francisco's Nuns), made their bones at
the Masque and released a pair of ass-kicking 45s on Greg
Shaw's Bomp! label. The Bags, a first-gen Masque act, was
distinguished by the ferocious presence of its lead singer,
Alice Bag (née Armendariz), whose raw-voiced vocals put
across such early local anthems as "Survive" and "We Don't

Need the English." Acts like The Brat and Los Illegals would succeed them.

Tito Larriva was responsible for introducing LA punk-dom to a soon-to-be-prominent Chicano group who had never performed outside of East LA. After an act dropped off the support bill for a May 1980 concert by Public Image Ltd., led by former Sex Pistols front man John (Johnny Rotten) Lydon, Tito asked an East Side folk quartet whether they might be interested in subbing. The crowd greeted the group with a hail of refuse and spit. The next time they appeared in front of a punk audience, the members of Los Lobos came armed with electric guitars. To this day some of them suspect that Tito set them up.

One got used to rubbing elbows with the drunk, the drugged, and the deranged at LA punk shows—it was an outlaw music, after all, and a modicum of madness went with the terrain. But there were still certain bands to which I gave a wide berth. One of them was Black Randy and the Metro Squad. Because their front man was a founding partner in Dangerhouse Records, the group was well documented, on hilarious singles like "Trouble at the Cup" and the elegantly titled LP *Pass the Dust, I Think I'm Bowie*, largely a slab of fucked-up punk funk. But by all reports Black Randy was the loosest of cannons who lived out his skeevy lyrics; I was somewhat apprehensive about a guy who left go-cups of his own shit as booby traps on nightclub floors—I kept my distance.

Likewise, I kept The Germs at arm's length. Established as a local moving violation before the Masque even reared its head, their early shows were anything-goes trainwrecks that attracted a following notable for its destructive dementia; their homemade, Nazi-emulating armbands bearing the

band's blue circle logo were an effective stop sign for me. My closest encounter came after a show at Club 88. I had just missed their performance, and I entered the men's room to discover stalls festooned with wet toilet paper as well as shattered sinks and toilets lying in pools of brown water on the floor. (The fans couldn't destroy the urinals, which were metal troughs bolted into the walls.)

On occasion I would see lead singer Darby Crash wandering amid the crowd at the weekend record swap meets in the parking lot of the Capitol Records building on Vine Street. Clad in leather, sullen and acne encrusted, he wasn't a guy I wanted to chat up.

Only fifteen years after his suicide by overdose in December 1980 did I learn the facts about Darby while researching a story about his life and career. He was a glam-obsessed graduate of the West Side's Uni High, where he attended a frankly loco alternative studies program. With a head filled with Nietzsche, Hitler, Manson, L. Ron Hubbard, Werner Erhard, Bowie, and Iggy, he attacked the nascent LA punk scene like a baby-faced one-man demolition derby, too smart for his own good and bent on some kind of pestilent stardom.

The Germs' early singles "Forming" and "Lexicon Devil" (the latter of which was Slash Records' inaugural release) in no way prepared me or many other skeptical listeners for *G.I.*, the band's lone LP, released in 1979. Produced by Joan Jett of The Runaways, it bristled with slovenly, furious intelligence and grim, tumbling poetry. They followed it up with a few scathing tunes for the soundtrack of William Friedkin's much-maligned gay-themed noir *Cruising*. But by the time one of the Germs' outré performances was immortalized in Penelope Spheeris's 1981 documentary *The Decline of Western Civilization*, Darby had been sucked under

by the terminal whirlpool of his reckless and frankly miserable life. A biography and a low-budget Hollywood biopic would follow years later in the wake of Darby's canonization by some hardcore punk flag wavers. In the end it struck me as one sorry-ass legacy to leave behind.

A dozen years after Darby's self-designed exit, The Germs' guitarist, Darby's Uni classmate Pat Smear, would be recruited to play behind another similarly ill-fated, posthumously lionized musician, Nirvana's Kurt Cobain.

I initially found Chris D. of The Flesh Eaters as forbidding a figure as Darby. Glowering and beetle browed, he slouched through the local clubs like a bad dream made flesh. At one point he experienced some kind of eye trouble, and the eye patch he wore only accentuated his unnerving presence. He seemed to maintain a kind of force field around himself. Yet he managed to capture my imagination, for he crafted some of the most feral word-spew on the scene, on his band's rampaging tracks for the anthology *Tooth and Nail*, and The Flesh Eaters' album *No Questions Asked*, both of which he released on his own label, Upsetter Records.

My true Flesh Eaters epiphany came with *A Minute to Pray, A Second to Die*, an astonishing amalgam of fiery punk, swamp blues, and jazzy atonality cut in 1981 by an all-star lineup comprising members of X and The Blasters. The record was virtually all I listened to during a protracted siege of pneumonia that year, and it was a perfect soundtrack for my fever. I attended the handful of shows this dazzling unit performed, including one at Myron's Ballroom, where they blew The Fall back to Manchester, and I quickly learned that Chris was a soft-spoken, deeply thoughtful guy with a passion for movies of all stripes and the darkest veins of literature.

No one-shot, Chris followed *A Minute to Pray* with a pair of albums, *Forever Came Today* and *A Hard Road to Follow*, which featured paint-peeling work by lead guitarist Don Kirk. Ever the renaissance man, he backed up those early achievements with a decades-long succession of equally hair-raising Flesh Eaters releases plus a couple of fine poetry collections, stints as a film actor (in Alison Anders's punk drama *Border Radio*) and screenwriter-director (of the vampire film *I Pass for Human*), and a long run as a programmer for the American Cinematheque in Hollywood.

Sometime in late 1978 or early 1979 I had a fateful meeting with a then-neophyte musician who would ultimately make some big ripples and raise a few hackles. One afternoon in the reggae section at Rhino Records, I struck up a conversation with a fellow browser, a pudgy, moonfaced kid with bleached-blond hair who began to jabber excitedly about Lee Perry. Waves of chatter, punctuated by breathless explosions of nervous laughter, poured from him ceaselessly. It turned out that, like me, he was also a blues fan, so we ended up cruising down to the Santa Monica specialty store Muskadine Records to pick through the bins as the manager eyed us with suspicion. On his recommendation I bought a Bo Weavil Jackson LP that day.

The kid's name was Jeffrey Lee Pierce. A San Fernando Valley product, he was at that point president of the Blondie fan club, a sometime scribe for *Slash* (under the handle Ranking Jeffrey Lee), and a former member of some short-lived ad hoc punk bands, which had included as members such friends of mine as Phast Phreddie Patterson, editor of *Back Door Man* and later front man of his own band Thee Precisions, and Anna Statman, briefly a Parallax coworker and subsequently a Slash Records A&R rep.

Jeffrey was ubiquitous in the local clubs and harbored continuing ambitions for his own band. I dutifully attended the shambolic early-1980 debut of his group the Creeping Ritual at the Hong Kong Café; its lineup included my colleague Don Snowden, a music writer at the *Los Angeles Times*, and a skinny, frail-looking teen with a caterpillar mustache named Brian Tristan. Taught to play in open tuning by Jeffrey himself, Brian soon rechristened himself Kid Congo Powers and joined The Cramps as their guitarist.

Jeffrey finally drew together a stable lineup for his band, renamed The Gun Club at Keith Morris's suggestion, sometime in 1980. That quartet, which included guitarist Ward Dotson and the former rhythm section of The Bags, Rob Ritter and Terry Graham, stirred a forceful blues-soaked noise, which took some of its cues from The Cramps, behind Jeffrey's soul-baring lyrics and wavering vocals, all captured to perfection on the 1981 debut *Fire of Love* (produced by Chris D. and Tito Larriva).

Live, the act was an iffier proposition. Jeffrey liked—nay, *demanded*—attention, and he didn't particularly care what kind. On some nights the band would simply tear your face off; on others, Jeffrey would get loaded, bait the audience, and maybe curl up in Terry's bass drum for a while. He was an exasperating combination of addled genius, mammoth ego, and brittle insecurity. There were times when I wanted to wrap my fingers around his throat, but I never lost my affection for him.

A prophet bereft of honor in his hometown, Jeffrey still managed to record a dozen Gun Club albums and solo projects and found some adulation in Europe. The recognition probably hastened his demise, his body broken by a flood of poisons, at the age of thirty-seven, in 1996. Some

years later I interviewed Kid Congo at a garage-rock festival in Portland. Naturally Jeffrey's name came up, and in an instant we both found ourselves crying.

By 1981 to 1982 the original punk-rock scene in LA had atomized thoroughly. Some of the original fixtures of the scene—acts like The Skulls, The Eyes, and The Controllers—had vanished. Others, like that art project in motion The Weirdos, authors of such indelible singles as "Destroy All Music" and "We Got the Neutron Bomb," I would not encounter until much later.

The beach-punk posse had made its incursion within the city limits around the turn of the decade, leading to confrontations with the police that made 1979's St. Patrick's Day riot-squad assault on a punk show at MacArthur Park's Elks Lodge look like a family picnic. My favorite group among the new breed was The Minutemen, a smart, gale-force San Pedro trio who took their cues from the hypereconomical UCLA-spawned punk trio The Urinals. The Port-of-LA band shattered their songs into minute fragments of churning funk and darting, politically pointed punk. They liked Blue Öyster Cult and Creedence Clearwater Revival too. I adored them from my first listen to their debut 1981 long-player *The Punch Line*, and they only gained in skill and ambition as they relentlessly soldiered on.

The rest of the hardcore bands were more difficult to love, and I came to associate their scene with outbreaks of violence. For instance, in October 1980 I left a show at the Whisky early. Out on the sidewalk writer Richard Meltzer, who was also contributing to the *Reader* at the time, suggested we head over to Baces Hall to catch some of Black Flag's set. I climbed into Meltzer's car and we drove east. You could see the police helicopter hovering above the venue

from a mile away. By the time we pulled within a block of
the venue, chaos had poured out of the hall; uniformed
police were chasing punks down the middle of the street,
aiming nightsticks at their close-cropped heads. Like many
another Flag show of the era, this one had quickly devolved
into a full-scale riot.

Four months later, still curious, I decided to take my life
into my hands and attended a Black Flag show at the Stardust Ballroom, an antique big-band venue on Sunset Boulevard that occasionally played host to punk shows. I walked
into the place and was immediately confronted with the
spectacle of twenty or so skinheads kicking, beating, and
punching a long-haired concertgoer across the open floor.
Entering the men's room a few minutes later, I found the
guy crumpled and unattended in a corner on the floor, covered in blood. It would be some years before I attended
another Black Flag show.

Old-school punk types who declined to mingle with
maniac skinheads a decade their junior retreated to musical entertainment less likely to involve bloodletting and/or
arrest. It struck me as hardly coincidental that the arrival of
the hardcore bands in Hollywood coincided with the flour-
ishing of a contemporaneous roots-punk wave, populated
largely by LA punk elders.

The impulse was already there: The Gun Club and The
Flesh Eaters were steeped in swampy blues. Levi and the
Rockats, an émigré Brit unit fronted by Pleasant Gehman's
significant other Levi Dexter, had developed as a Masque-era
attraction. Brothers Chip and Tony Kinman of the left-tilting,
Clash-aping group The Dils founded the cowpunk outfit
Rank and File with Alejandro Escovedo. In 1980 the Downey-
born American music band The Blasters hit the scene like a

bomb; they would successfully sponsor such kindred acts as Los Lobos and hardcore honky-tonker Dwight Yoakam, who became a bona fide country star after breaking in on the postpunk circuit. Blood on the Saddle, Pleasant's own band The Screamin' Sirens, and Lone Justice rose in their wake.

I first encountered Lone Justice's rodeo-sweetheart vocalist Maria McKee sitting in at a Blue Monday show at the Cathay de Grande, where Top Jimmy and the Rhythm Pigs held their sodden weekly punk-blues revels under the basement's sagging ceiling tiles. Jimmy, our own Howlin' Wolf, friend and familiar of X, also did the pouring at the after-hours spot the Zero Zero on Cahuenga Boulevard, where the old punk crew would drink themselves to sunrise on the weekends.

Recognition for LA's punk pioneers would be late in coming, but even in the day a couple of the acts managed to make an impression on the national consciousness. Fear, which had been haranguing local audiences successfully with low humor, vile epithets, and in-your-face noise since 1977, brought full-on disorder to a 1981 *Saturday Night Live* telecast, thanks to the beneficence of their number-one fan, John Belushi. And The Go-Go's, the all-female quintet who had been a perennial punk opening act since their 1978 Masque bow, upped their commercial game, scored a hit on tour with Madness in the UK, signed to I.R.S. Records, and sold 2 million copies of their perky, radio-friendly 1981 debut album *Beauty and the Beat*.

Strange days had found us. Today some would call it history. Back then we called it fun.

CHAPTER 8

Acid, Meet Catholicism

by Tom DeSavia

We—the generation that came in later—were transfixed by punk logos: The Dead Kennedys' "DK" symbol was the easiest to draw, but the Black Flag logo was by far our favorite. I knew the Flag emblem before I knew the music, of that I am certain, and it was that logo that led me to my first hardcore show, a multiband bill at the Santa Monica Civic in 1983—Black Flag, The Misfits, The Vandals. I didn't really like going to hardcore shows initially—they felt *mean*, there were real fistfights with fans being carried out bloodied, and I always felt like a potential victim. And it was way harder to decipher lyrics at these gigs—way harder. But much like the punk shows that preceded it, the poison began to seep in, and I started to love the adrenaline rush I got from going to these more "dangerous" gigs. I didn't really own any hardcore records, so I bought a couple: the Flag's *Damaged* and Angry Samoans' *Back from Samoa*—both, honestly, because I thought they had cool album covers.

Those covers—and, really, almost all punk album covers—were half the fun of the experience. They felt forbidden. They *would* have been forbidden had they been discovered. In our elders' eyes these images, like the music, would lead to no good—so I kept them expertly hidden, tucked away between more acceptable discs, knowing that my parents—wonderful folks from a different generation—had no interest in hearing anything in my collection. If my sweet mother had discovered any of the Pettibon artwork that adorned some of them, it would have been curtains, both for the records and for me.

I would stare at the *Damaged* album cover endlessly. That image of Rollins—reflected in front of a just-punched cracked mirror, fist bloodied by the impact—had the intensity of a Scorsese film, violent and savage. And it didn't look staged.

"Cover Photo—Ed Colver" was one of the few credits, and it was noted prominently on the back of the LP. For whatever reason, his name stuck with me as much as any band member. His name started to pop up more and more as I went deeper, not only on Flag records but also on discs by Wasted Youth, T.S.O.L., The Adolescents, and the Circle Jerks. Whoever this dude was, he seemed to have the coolest job.

Flash forward to the very early nineties: while at dinner in Silverlake one night with my friend, the songwriter Dave Bassett, our conversation turned to drugs. I confessed that, unlike most of my pals, I had never tried acid, but wanted to. At that point Dave pulled out his wallet and revealed two tabs he had bought the night before outside of the Coconut Teaszer, a rock club we all used to frequent. Without

hesitation, I put the little piece of paper under my tongue as instructed and let it dissolve, being reassured that we'd have plenty of time to drive to my apartment before the effects of the drug took hold. A friend volunteered to serve as our designated tour guide, with our first stop being the old brewery lofts in downtown LA to visit another buddy. Loft living was taking hold in downtown—it was relatively cheap, and the buildings were filled with artists and musicians putting their own personal stamp on this creative living space. At some point, after the acid really started to kick in, it was suggested we pop in on our friend's next-door neighbor. So we crawled through his window, out on a fairly large segment of roof, and entered the window of the neighbor's loft. That was how I found myself in the home of . . . Ed Colver.

In this virginal drug haze I don't remember much about the night other than the bottom floor of Colver's loft being an art installation, with a weaving path that led through different pieces: I'll never forget passing "A Well-Hung Klansman"—a mannequin gussied up in KKK garb hanging from a noose overhead; another dummy swaddled from head to toe in an American flag, wrapped tightly with rope, dubbed "Bound for Glory"; a coffin atop a bunch of Campbell's soup cans; empty film canisters everywhere—with the body inside adorned with a Warhol mask and a *Sticky Fingers* album cover placed, appropriately, below the torso.

When I reached the end of this maze—and after being captivated by a suspended, spinning infinity cube for either five hours or five minutes—I focused on an upside-down cross at the very end of the path. Suddenly the implanted Catholic fear/guilt/paranoia of my upbringing came out all at once, and I remember literally crumbling into a fetal

position, unable to move. At some point someone or several people rescued me and I was ushered back through the maze of artifacts to safety. I never did acid again, but I will never forget getting lost in Colver's labyrinth. I still have panic attacks to this day as to what would have happened if I would have destroyed something. Or if Satan would have gotten me.

I barely remember meeting Ed Colver that night. I think he was tall.

Photo: Ed Colve

CHAPTER 9

Take My Picture ...

by Tom DeSavia

It was a photo of Exene: a black-and-white shot, her extra-wide open eyes peeking out from her bangs under a shock of jet-black hair, her arms in front, upright, crossed at the forearms to form the letter X, framing her face.

I think I saw the photo before I ever heard a note. And that photo said everything: it was supposed to shock, I suppose—it did—but mostly it was hypnotic. I remember staring at it, showing it to friends, eventually pinning it up on my wall. The photo was by Ed Colver. He, along with Frank Gargani, Jenny Lens, Gary Leonard, Melanie Nissen, Ann Summa, and a host of other emerging photographers, would become documentarians of the history of the Los Angeles punk-rock scene.

Each of these artists captured images so iconic, they almost instantly became as important as the music, not only defining the subculture but also differentiating it from sister scenes going on in New York and the UK. B&W was the preferred exposure for most—although some utilized the

vibrant, somewhat shocking contrasting colors present in fashion and hair dye—often with scenes of the West Coast's decaying glamour providing the backdrop. The marriage of music and photography was natural; for those too young to be in the center of the actual scene, these very images were what resonated with us as much as anything else did.

> I shot the first lineup of Black Flag in front of Frederick's of Hollywood on Hollywood Boulevard, and after two or three frames one of the members put his foot through the huge plate-glass window and it shattered, crashing down in thousands of pieces—but I got the shot—it ran in *No* magazine.
>
> —Frank Gargani

These photos showed us the desperate faces, at any moment capturing rage, defiance, apathy . . . sometimes all in one moment. The snapshots of the live shows often conveyed the tension of an authentic underground and its unearthly inhabitants. Occasionally the gritty reality of the performers resembled early-twentieth-century crime scene photography, a havoc-laden Weegee-like alternate universe where the "victims"—covered in chaotic tattoos and sometimes spit, thrown beer, and occasionally blood—were the center of attraction, violently gripping microphones and guitars in midperformance. They introduced images of mosh pits and stage diving that would serve as instructional blueprints for those who saw them. It was all part of the most mesmerizing visual cautionary tale since rock 'n' roll's first real evolution in the mid-1960s.

Exene standing on the toilet at the Masque—her pose, that grimy graffitied stall, those skinny jeans and orthopedic shoe-boots. So tough and cool.

—Ann Summa

Screamers on the Bus Bench perfectly encapsulates the cultural revolution. Young men with their spiky hair (so radical for its time), jeans with holes during a time most ironed on patches or threw them out, pointed boots, and other unique clothing versus a little old lady with her cat-eyeglasses, neck brace, and checkered dress says more about the visual and societal changes than any other photo from LA or any other city in 1977.

—Jenny Lens

1979, Hong Kong Café, The Germs—best live photos I ever shot. I got punched in the face by a rabid Germs fan and I struck back by tackling him; we ended up onstage in Don Bolles's drum kit and the show went on.

—Frank Gargani

There were the anticelebrity icons who were born: the Darbys and Exenes and Rollinses. But just as captivating were the crowds, the kids from the street, the scenesters expressing fashion, the reactions of proletariats interacting with the undesirables.

I took a picture of Carlos Guitarlos and Mayor (Tom) Bradley. I was covering a celebrity (singer Vikki Carr) getting her star on the Hollywood Walk of Fame, and I invited Carlos to come along. He hung out in the background while

I shot, and as the ceremony was ending, I asked Carlos if he wanted his picture with Mayor Tom Bradley, who was officiating the proceedings. I went to Mayor Bradley and I said, "Can I take a picture of you and my friend Carlos Guitarlos?" Being a politician, he of course said yes, and then did the most spectacular double-take when he saw Carlos. I knew I had captured something: the first black mayor meeting a punk rocker. This was such a native view, and that photo screamed, "This is Los Angeles, this is happening, this is taking place."

—Gary Leonard

Fashion and music seemingly evolved together, and the photos brought to life a punk-rock look that would eventually become a defining, widely adopted style, born from vintage thrift-store finds. A mix of garage-sale chic with nods to the Brandos and Bettie Pages that came before adorned the musicians and the fans alike. Just mentioning the word "punk" to any God-fearing citizen would conjure up a look, a style, a knot in the stomach. Punk was associated with one noise—and it was way worse than just loud, fast, and out of control. Mission accomplished.

Punk photography and my style of shooting were a match made in heaven. I have always shot very quickly, no fear of getting close, and I was very body language and personality oriented, with a bit of fashion thrown in. Fast, just like the music.

—Melanie Nissen

The visuals, the creativity, and the music drew me. The fashion was amazing, the music loud and crazy and pretty much like nothing I'd ever heard before. It felt like a revolution.

—Ann Summa

I used to turn the camera at an angle—it really was my signature during that time—I related most to Diane Arbus and Garry Winogrand. This was about documenting. As for his signature style for the first few years, Gary observed, "I got into this angular portrait thing. I grew out of it and no longer do it—it really is the one little affectation that seems to work at that time—not straight or vertical, but filling the frame to a different view.

—Gary Leonard

I merely wanted to capture the energy, fun and excitement, and, most of all, creativity of what I was feeling and seeing. I used my camera to support the musicians and the scene.

—Jenny Lens

At the shows I shot as fast as I could, with an on-camera flash powered with a battery pack, on a Nikon F. That way I could keep up with the music. I liked the live photos to be very high-key, hard-edge b&w.

—Frank Gargani

Everything was frenetic, so one had to be organized and at the same time keep one eye on your subject and the other to protect yourself and gear from the craziness around you. I had two cameras with different lenses on each so I wouldn't miss a shot.

—Ann Summa

I bought darkroom gear using a credit card. I taught myself
how to roll film, develop negatives, print proof sheets, and
make prints (all of which I hated! Hated! Hated!). I taught
myself to reach out to magazines and record companies to
get my photos into the world. I also moved from the Valley
to Hollywood to be near all the action.

—Jenny Lens

LA has historically been dubbed a cultural wasteland; the
rest of the country, generally even the world, have looked
down their collective noses at us at one time or another. Our
culture was too new, our architecture and literature boorish,
our artistic aesthetic subpar or even nonexistent. To the outside world we lived in a shallow paradise. We snacked on
fresh citrus fruit and listened to The Eagles whilst sipping
margaritas on chaise lounges by our pools in year-round
perfect weather. This, undoubtedly, was either not the reality for most punks or served as the main source of rebellion
for the ones who came from that existence.

I've always been on a mission to chronicle this city in a
very intuitive way. I wanted to put out a native point of
view. I get the romance of Los Angeles—that romantic ideal
that captured those who were from out of town. It was always about the place, about recognizing the history of the
city. It was a moment in LA history that hadn't occurred
before—and it wasn't confined like before to those early
days of the strip and along Sunset Boulevard; it really was
everywhere. What drew me to the scene was all the different
places that they had to be—in small clubs in Hollywood,
downtown, in Chinatown. . . . I mean that was amazing,
music in Chinatown?

—Gary Leonard

These were the days before the outskirts of Los Angeles were filled with high-priced lofts and the trendiest restaurants and clubs. Downtown LA was a scary place of homelessness and crime, of abandoned buildings and gutted shops. Just west was MacArthur Park, which, riddled with its infamous large population of heroin addicts, prostitutes, and (probably) dirty cops, was even worse. As such, these also became not only affordable neighborhoods for burgeoning artists to settle but also a haven for makeshift venues to pop up, many with the lifespan of a firefly. The raw loft spaces and the rest of the nearly abandoned real estate proved perfect locales for artistic types to gather and settle. Clubs such as Al's Bar, Madame Wong's, and the Elks Lodge coexisted alongside plenty of tried-and-true dirty dive bars, surrounded by bona fide skid rows to rival that of any doomed metropolis.

The moment I entered the Elks Lodge it felt like I walked into the first chapter of *On the Road*. Visually it was stunning. One of the first scenes I saw was a guy showing off his newly refinished bass and the girl who appeared to be with him. I got a photo of them, and they turned out to be John Doe and Exene. Those two nights changed my life and gave me a direction, a focus for my photography. This was more than a revolution for me; I'd call it an antirevolution.

—Frank Gargani

It was easy to recognize that there was a pure counterculture going on. In LA there was the mainstream and this counterculture. That was it.

—Gary Leonard

The punk demi-world brought together downtown art-damaged artists, South Bay head-banging skinheads, East LA muralists, Valley fans, and Hollywood runaways/squatters into one big mess. It wasn't organized enough to be called a revolution, but thanks to *Slash* and Kickboy Face (né journalist Claude Bessy) and Dangerhouse Records, at least it was documented.

—Ann Summa

The importance of the birth of *Slash* magazine in May 1977—not only to the LA movement but also to punk rock in general—is immeasurable and cannot be overstated. The large-format fanzine/tabloid, the brainchild of Steve Samiof and photographer Melanie Nissen as well as a handful of artists, musicians, and scenesters, not only brought the exploits of the LA scene to the world in its own underground way but also helped set forth a style both in imaging and text that would go on to instantly define punk rock for eternity. "Steve Samiof showed me an article in the *Los Angeles Times* about a new music scene that was underway in London," recalled Nissen. "Everything about it sounded intriguing and exciting—the music, visuals, fashion, and politics. We also heard that The Damned were coming to perform at the Starwood, and we went and checked it out. It was love at first listen.

We talked about doing a magazine, and The Damned were going to be the first group we worked with. I took the photo of Dave Vanian backstage that night for the first cover of *Slash*, Steve designed the logo, and we were ready to start. We then heard about The Screamers and that The Damned were going to be at their place, so we went over to their

house and took more photos. The Screamers were the first
LA punk band we met, so I did a photo session with them
too. We also met The Germs there. That was a great hangout party house, a great place to shoot photos. And so the
first issue of *Slash* started coming together.

—Melanie Nissen

I knew that punk was more than music. I merely wanted
to capture the energy, fun and excitement, and, most of all,
creativity of what I was feeling and seeing. I wanted the
groups to be successful.

—Jenny Lens

Success? Success seemed the furthest possibility. Radio was
not going to play this music, the mainstream press would
mostly cover their disdain for it, save for a handful of established critics, from Gonzo journalist Lester Bangs at *Creem*
to Kristine McKenna from the *Los Angeles Times.* More accessible than *Slash* was the *LA Reader,* the alternative weekly
where emerging columnist Chris Morris began covering the
scene and converting many an impressionable youth along
the way. But still, many in the community seemingly shared
Lens's sentiment: at the root they *wanted* it to be successful.
This could be the viable alternative the world needed. Rock
'n' roll reborn—but instead of inspiring a sexual revolution,
this was a counter-counterculture artistic, political, and cultural movement, full of poets, burgeoning activists, and sophisticated derelicts. This *could* be a revolution.

There was the art, arguably led by Ray Pettibon's show
flyers and album art. Pettibon's work defined the look of
SST Records, the label owned and operated by his brother,
Black Flag's Greg Ginn. His artwork, usually created with

simply black ink, was often antiestablishment and sometimes violent in its imagery. It defined an uprising, didn't
pretend to be gentle, and identified a segment of punk rock.
Pettibon's Black Flag logo remains one of the most recognizable rock 'n' roll emblems in existence.

Exene herself possessed a hand-lettering technique so
unique that it became synonymous with the scene and,
eventually, punk rock in general. Her work was emblazoned
not only on the printed lyrics in X's albums but also in
the songbooks they created in the early years and then later
adopted liberally by anyone anywhere wanting to present
something resembling a credible punk aesthetic.

It could be argued that nothing challenged the com-
placency of 1970s visual, mind-numbing glitz than the
rise of the punk-show flyer. All it took was some 8-by-11
paper, glue, a razor blade, and a stack of old magazines,
schoolbooks, some old porno mags as well as access to a
copy machine. These seemingly hastily put-together show
promos were showing up everywhere: record stores, skate
shops, bars, and, most of all, telephone poles, club walls,
boarded-up construction sites—basically anywhere that was
ripe for plastering. Angular and uncomfortable layouts challenged our senses, typography design delivered the shock
of a ransom note: dictators, celebrities new and old, 1950s
science-fiction imagery, sacrilegious Christian iconography,
Ronald Reagan's forehead emblazoned with the number of
the beast—these were all de rigueur.

The flyer culture held such significance that today these
Xeroxed concoctions have received the museum and coffee-
table respect given to fine and modern art. Deservedly so:
a case can be made for these handbills paving the way for
more conventional outsider art that took hold at the rise of

the twenty-first century, including Shepard Fairey, Banksy, and the like.

The revolution wasn't televised, but it was photographed. It was given immortality through the visual artists who were there, through an oftentimes unspoken shared vision with the musicians whose songs brought the scene together. Architects of not just a time but a movement. It turns out it *was* a cultural revolution all along, and although very few saw fame and riches from the birth of the Los Angeles punk-rock scene, they left behind an influential legacy more lasting than one assumes anyone could have imagined.

After the end of the Vietnam War, when the hippies decided to forget it and get high, I was extremely let down. After all, the sixties revolution was supposed to change the world, but where did that go? The punk movement was crazy and hectic and energetically full of life. I believe the statement punk made at that time was prophetic of where we are as a society today.

—Frank Gargani

VOLUME ONE NUMBER ONE   MAYDAY ISSUE 5/77   FIFTY CENTS

Photo: Melanie Nissen

CHAPTER 10

So Young & Beautiful

by John Doe

Black hair, brown faces, black hair, brown faces—beautiful, sweaty, Mexican teenagers swimming in a sea of white suburban kids.

It was summer 1978 when we first clocked a new gang of people coming to see X. Club 88 in July was where I remember it best, maybe w/ The Blasters. I've seen a picture w/ Pat Smear & Joan Jett up front and members of The Stains and The Brat surrounding them. Exene wore a blue, Chinese-style shirtdress & I was in a mesh shirt (my excuse? It was Los Angeles in July in a nearly airless club w/ 8ft ceilings). The audience was a broiling, oozing pool of primordial goo. Bill Bateman cut his hand on a cymbal early in The Blasters' set & bled all over his drums. Phil Alvin & I talked about getting a tank of oxygen the next time we played there.

Seeing this new contingent of teenagers from the east side made us feel legit, gave us a feeling that we could communicate to more than people we knew. Communicating to people outside of the Hollywood 200, everyone who had

been there from the beginning & probably played in at least three bands. Communicating to someone who probably heard too much Art Laboe, the Oldies Show on KRLA, because their parents were listening. Teenagers who answered the call to "new music" from a culture steeped in the '50s, where our heroes came from. In our minds these people had a direct connection to Ritchie Valens & the heart of Los Angeles. It was wishful thinking then, but it gave us confidence that this music of ours, this punk rock, wasn't just for one slice of the public; it could speak to everyone.

From the very beginning Latinos figured into the LA punk-rock scene. Alice Bag was another superwoman, lead singer & role model. Delphina owned the black lingerie & cropped black hair look well before it became a default. Tito Larriva, it was rumored, had been a child star in Mexico City & Chalo Quintana was a 17-year-old monster drummer who Tito plucked from the streets of El Paso. Brian Tristan, a frail kid who began as The Screamers' fan club president, ended up playing guitar for The Gun Club & The Cramps and could've given Peter Lorre a run for his money in the exotic looks department. Others made fanzines or fliers or just hung out. We knew their upbringing was vastly different from ours, but so were the teenage runaways who played in some other groups of the time. No one cared. They were travelers & had made a scattered journey to a crazy scene that welcomed all sorts of misfits. If you wanted to be part of a group that would be yelled at, have trash thrown at them from passing cars & were generally ridiculed, why would we care if you had olive skin?

But these kids from East LA, they were somehow different. They were more like normal citizens. What did we know? They seemed like another part of the growing audience, but

a much cooler part. Maybe they wore tight jeans & a skinny tie w/ a button-down shirt. They were individuals but looked like a group, like a band. They were roughly the same age & just wandered over the LA River to see what was happening on the west side. Like most of the audience, they didn't look like "punks." What set them apart was their unity and our desire to include something & someone exotic, to prove our scene wasn't just for disaffected suburban teens. Plus, they were all so young & beautiful.

It was probably Sid or Rudy Medina who introduced themselves first. They told us they had a band called The Brat & that we should come to one of the backyard parties they played. We had no idea what we were in for. Lincoln Heights, City Terrace, Boyle Heights could've been "south of the border" for our lack of experience, but it was thrilling. Exene & I felt we snuck into a rare land w/ great guides who cared about us and somehow thought we mattered. We were the only white faces there, the food was incredible & The Brat played w/ precision, passion & innocence. They had great culturally different songs & sounds that owed more than a little something to the songs they grew up on. Then, while the band roared through their set, someone squeezed off four or five rounds from a semiautomatic .45 into the air. An uncle quickly straightened out this overenthusiastic partygoer by hustling him out the back gate. It wasn't a cliché; it was just something that happened back then. This was a reality unlike what we had known and was all part of that bohemian lifestyle I moved across the country to find.

As '79 rolled around, we began to meet all manner of characters from Los Illegals, The Stains & Saccharine Trust & came to understand that their world was a world of many disciplines of art. Each group had their own demeanor &

style of music. Stains were a faster, scarier version of The Germs & some members would insist that you smoke angel dust w/ them. Los Illegals had a tight, well-crafted sound that was more new wave than punk. They sang more in Spanish than English & relied on their Latino roots to craft their sound. But The Brat were a blend of so many styles, had such great songs & looks, it still boggles my mind they didn't catch fire & blow us all away. They could've been a Latino version of Blondie & I believe that comparison was made at the time.

The deeper we dug, the more of a microcosm was revealed. A new club, The Vex, created a home for this wave of new music, partly due to Hollywood clubs' unwillingness to book another new branch of this unpredictable music. Richard Duardo & his art collective/screen print business, Hecho en Azatlan, would have a significant presence making beautiful art posters for important gigs. Truly independent labels like Fatima Records released LPs by The Plugz & The Brat using Dia de los Muertos–styled graphics, which I think was a first in pop culture.

This east-side culture folded into the blend w/ the original Hollywood scene & despite their difficulty getting booked, they found plenty of opportunities on the west side. It all might've been too little, too late. By the time The Brat, Los Illegals, etc. came onto the scene, it was already fracturing, but they planted a flag in the ground for all Latino rockers & paved the way for the Rock en Español movement years later.

CHAPTER 11

Punk-Rock Teenage Heaven

by Robert Lopez aka El Vez

In 1975 I was 15 years old. I had just left being fat, long haired, and bad skinned. I was born and raised in Chula Vista, a suburb of America's finest city, San Diego, California.

My family floated somewhere between middle and lower-middle class. Our diet included government cheese and something we called "poor people's chop suey" a few times a week. I attended Chula Vista High School in the later seventies. Surprisingly, compared to today's population, it didn't have many Latinos. It was mostly a surfer, stoner, sosch crowd. I didn't get high or play the sports ball, so I wasn't in any of those groups. I was not very popular.

I had always been a misfit. I cried very easily in elementary school. Didn't have many friends. By high school I was used to it. I was a very, very chubby kid who had found his nest of salt in Warhol, Dali, and the arts. I would spend my lunchtimes in the school library.

Looking back, I seemed to be an aware kid, at least that's what I remember. Insecure, for sure, but I would hope we all

were. I had knowledge of things other than just the school and its student body's curriculum. The year before I had gone to my first concert: Led Zeppelin. I much preferred my second concert: the New York Dolls. I read *Creem* and *Rock Scene* magazines. I was up on the latest bands, albeit through the writers' reviews: I had to use my imagination as to what the bands actually sounded like. On PBS television I watched *An American Family*, perhaps the first actual reality TV show. It was about a Southern California family who were about to implode by divorce. That is where I was introduced to Lance Loud and Kristian Hoffman (both of whom would go on to form the NYC-based punk band The Mumps). They too were Southern California guys who loved rock music and Warhol and knew that New York was the place to be. In 1975 they would be my first gay role models from watching television. They would become my friends that next year. I saw Iggy Pop smear peanut butter all over his shirtless body as he walked on the uplifted hands of people! PBS was pretty informative back then. These things, plus my older sister Rhoda, were my first exposures to punk rock. There was always something earlier that influenced punk—Iggy and the Stooges and the garage bands of the sixties that *Creem* magazine would write about, and so forth. The end of glitter rock had lots of foreshadowing to punk rock. These things served as a small but constant stream of "something else beside the norm" for me. I knew there was a whole different world out there after high school. I just didn't know yet what it held for me.

1976 I cut my hair very short in my parents' bathroom. I used my mom's scissors and caught the droppings into a brown paper bag—I was a tidy punk. I unevenly clipped down to maybe an inch all around. The back of my head

looked very chemotherapy. I was in a band called The Zeros, and we were on our way to play our first show outside our hometown. (Playing a quinceañera in Rosarito, a sleepy town south of Tijuana didn't count. That band was the Main St. Brats and had had only half of The Zeros.) This would be our first show in Los Angeles!

Now, we were a real band of like-minded Latino teenagers: me; Javier Escovedo, from the Main St. Brats; my cousin, Baba Chenelle; and his friend Hector Penalosa. Javier was the oldest at 18. Baba and I hovered at 16 and Hector was someplace in between. We had our own amps and guitars—mine bought from what I made from my paper route. I had bought a black Astoria Les Paul copy with three pickups, just like Ace Frehley, at Harper's Music Store in Chula Vista. We had our own original songs, plus a handful of covers from our favorites: The Velvet Underground, The Seeds, the New York Dolls, and The Standells. Javier borrowed his parents' brown Dodge Coronet station wagon with the modern cassette player, and we all piled in.

Jackie Ramirez from San Diego had a friend named Audrey who lived in Los Angeles. Audrey was dating this guy named Phast Phreddie, a writer for a magazine called *Back Door Man*. We had all seen it at the record store. Jackie had mailed him a C-30 cassette of one of our rehearsals with our songs: "Don't Push Me Around," "Wimp," "Hand Grenade Heart," "Main St. Brat," "Beat Your Heart Out." He liked it and asked us to be part of a show of new bands.

This was the infamous Orpheum show, across the street from Tower Records; the Whisky a Go Go was down the block. Perhaps the first punk-rock show in Hollywood—The Germs, The Zeros, and The Weirdos. Many of the audience would end up being my friends and neighbors. It was

The Germs' first show. They made a mess, were full of noise and great to see. To me that first show seemed more like performance art: How much could we get away with before someone told us to stop? We were all starving for something new, so it wasn't going to be any of us. Bobby Pyn (later to become Darby Crash) did the "Iggy Peanut Butter" I had seen on TV! The Weirdos were fantastic! Older than us, they had a more mature vision, sound, and look as well as great songs. They wore Jackson Pollock/Robert Rauschenberg–inspired outfits they made themselves of jumbled-together clothes that were splattered and spray painted, cobbled together with pins, staples, and tape, adding chains, bits of plastic from six-pack holders, and whatever else was about. Each outfit was different, but together they looked like a unit.

We were pretty tame in comparison. Straight-leg slacks and button-down shirts—no antics. Someone noted that we looked like the Jets from *West Side Story*. D. D. Faye said we looked like four young Sal Mineos, the actor from *Rebel Without a Cause*. She insisted we change our name to The Mineos. I think we mainly just looked down when we played that night. Our songs were short and fast or slow and short, a mix of the New York Dolls, The Velvet Underground. As I was still just sixteen, but now I see the KISS influence also. I think we played well.

Our songs were teenaged because we were teenagers. We were the youngest ones there that night. We were quiet and shy, which translates in having never been popular in school. These new people liked us and what we did. This was a new social experience!

Greg Shaw from Bomp! Records saw our show. He liked us! He asked if he could put out a 45 record of us on his

label. Of course we said yes! Javier drove us back to Chula Vista late that night. We were more than excited from what had just happened: playing on a stage in the big city in front of strangers—who liked us! And then being asked to put out a record by a guy we'd read about in magazines. This was punk teenage rock 'n' roll heaven!

We were back in high school the next morning. Before this, I had been an A and B student; I would receive my first D that year in US history—my first class of the day. Thus came my punk-rock education!

We quickly got labeled the Mexican Ramones. I loved The Ramones, so I didn't mind the title. But we thought our style was more New York Dolls and Velvet Underground; after all, we had guitar solos. Yeah, we were Mexicans—so what? It wasn't our calling card. Funny enough, that would become my raison d'être for my later performing—always a "Mexican" something.

Back then the California scene only existed in Holly-wood and San Francisco. There was nothing in San Diego; that's why we had to drive all the way up to LA. Javier did the driving—none of the rest of us had our driver's licenses yet. It was sort of a blessing to be *of* the scene but not *in* the scene. We were still in high school in Chula Vista. We would go to LA as often as we could or when the shows asked for us, but we were not constantly there. Perhaps that kept the best parts and the bad parts at a good distance. We could scheme and dream for the week and then be back with fresh eyes for the weekend.

Those early shows were pretty inspiring. I felt part of a movement, or something at least. Part of a music scene. It was a great feeling after years of misfitdom. Your friends and peers were in the audience, then performing onstage

after you. Or they were making posters or paintings. Gary Panter's angular, punky cubist art was a perfect companion for the times. There were writers like Claude Bessy and Craig Lee spouting opinion, making comparisons, or just talking trash. You would get a review in their fanzine and even in the major city newspapers. We even got to be on TV to promote our first single! (Sure helped that my dad worked at the local TV station in San Diego.) The always-great question of the morning TV show host would be: "What exactly is punk rock?"

These were great times to feed a developing teenage performer's mind. There were performance artists too! The Kipper Kids and Johanna Went—all the art forms I had read about in the school library, my friends and I were now doing.

I remember a rare underage drunk evening at the Masque (looking back, I rarely drank and wasn't having sex, which really seems like a missed teenage experience). This was later, after I had moved to Hollywood.

I had just seen Hal Negro and the Satin Tones, who ushered in the first wave of joke bands. The joke bands were pop-up groups who would quickly form to parody a certain current trend or comment or would form simply because they found matching orange tennis shoes at the Pic 'N' Save discount store. The Satin Tones were good, actually. Pat Delaney played saxophone and looked like a high school band sax player. They had a concept and a look. They were a piss-take on lounge music, way before its time, playing a cocktail classic in a punky style. Back then you could get the best matching horrible tuxedos for cheap at the La Brea Circus.

As they played, I was yelling for them to stop.

Trixie Plunger tried to console me as I was crying, "No, you don't understand! They are making a joke of us. They

are making fun of our scene! They are making fun of us!" I was actually crying. (And I am usually a happy drunk! Perhaps this was the last of my "and easy to make cry" from my elementary school days.) Now it seems sweet that it meant that much to me, to have respect for the scene. Funny that those cursed and hated joke bands would become the bread and butter for my later success.

My most romantic sixteen-year-old mind's eye paints it as a group of misfits joined together by a common love of the new music. We were trying to build something. We couldn't afford to exclude someone because they were a girl, a person of color, gay, or had long hair and flares. Sexism, racism, and homophobic ideas didn't come along until later, when the new music spanned so much wider than what it would narrow itself to—ahh, success!

We were like-minded outcasts. I may not have had friends in school, but here I made friends who spoke my language. In 1976 nobody at school knew of The Damned, The Clash, and the Sex Pistols. Here they did and could go back further musically! The bands I loved that got you labeled a freak to begin with—Bowie, Alice Cooper, and the New York Dolls—they loved them also! They knew the odd films too—*The Rocky Horror Picture Show*, *Un Chein Andalou*, *Salo*, *120 Days of Sodom*, and *Pink Flamingos*! Everyone knew who Warhol and Picasso were, and some even knew of the Dadaists. All the knowledge from my high school lunch library was blooming! All freaks were allowed, it seemed to me.

We didn't bond because you were the same color as me, the same gender as me, the same social class as me; we were trying to unite a scene of oddballs. It was hard enough to be an outcast—why would you not let somebody in if they would admit that they, too, were an oddball? Of course,

jerks and assholes were quickly shown the door and given the boot with a then-rare and hard-to-find Doc Martens Air Sole. If you look back at any of the pictures from the period, it was not a sea of camera-ready punks. There were kids with long hair and flares; there were regular, 1970s-looking folks tossed in with the mess. There was no need to specialize and subsect the Latino punks from the gay punks.

In 1976 and 1977 there was no East LA scene yet, but there were always Latinos. I remember the Latino punks Alice Bag, Delphina, X8, Brian Tristan, and Tito Larriva, amongst others. Being Latino never made much of a difference. We knew we couldn't bleach our hair like the other kids who would use the crazy color dyes. Black hair just turns this brassy orange kind of thing and doesn't take on color—Alice and my brother Guy had that a lot. It turns to a dried, dead-looking ocher, not a Bowie red or a natural ginger that goes well with bright pink clothes. It was a non-issue, no gathering "Oh, you are Latino too!" It didn't matter in the least. We came from a common background, but we were moving forward into the uncharted territory of the new music and scene. But we were growing up too. These were my first times far away from home without parents.

Once I remember someone asking a Latino if they liked Los Lobos in that early period. She said, "Naw, too beaner . . . " It made us chuckle. It didn't seem disrespectful or self-hating to be Latino punk and think that. We weren't ashamed to be Mexican or embarrassed of who we were; rather, we didn't want to be what you expected us to be. Perhaps stereotypes loomed louder back then: jocks, sosch, stoners, hippies, or beaners. We were a new social set. All the Mexican standards were in our Latino heads; we all were brought up with them. You would know them by heart, but

we didn't need to use that stuff. We were teenagers—well, The Zeros were. We didn't want to be our parents or our aunts and uncles. Their musical references—Vincente Fernandez, Eydie Gormé, Carlos Santana, or "Angel Baby"— was the old establishment. We wanted to be new!

It was 1977—"no Elvis, Beatles, or The Rolling Stones." So that for sure included Art Laboe and the Oldies. For The Plugz to take "La Bamba" and explode it seemed especially subversive, taking what you expected—Latinos playing "La Bamba"—and turning it on its head.

Los Lobos was ahead of the curve. They had been together longer. They were already into roots rock, including Mexican rhythms. Many of us—Alice Bag, Tito Larriva, Kid Congo, and myself as El Vez—would later mine our roots, embracing the music we heard as kids. But at that time, to forget your past and be now was the call of the day.

"No Elvis, Beatles, or The Rolling Stones." Indeed. I surely grin at the fact that I went on to be El Vez, the Mexican Elvis. Hector Penalosa went for the Baja Bugs, an all-Latino Beatles tribute, and Javier Escovedo's little brother Mario would do a yearly Christmas Eve show at the Casbah in San Diego based on The Rolling Stones.

We are new! What we are doing has never been done before. We are part of a change—at least in our own lives.

One should be allowed to think like this at 16. It is good for the soul, if somewhat bothersome for parents. I had friends my age and older who were recording 45s and LPs, making their artwork for posters, writing stories for fanzines, making—well, altering—their own clothes, playing in bands, doing performance art, being loud and disorderly. We were making ourselves known and heard, no longer hiding in the library during lunch.

One of my heroes of the scene was Tomata du Plenty. To me he was the man—funny, witty, irreverent, always trying new things but still rooted in vaudevillian showmanship and old-style Hollywood glamour (via the punk-shattered mirror). His life was his art onstage and off. He was an incredible front man to a groundbreaking, no guitar band, The Screamers. They were my favorite! They represented art, punk, sex, comedy, tragedy. And you could dance to it. They had the beat.

He was a magnet of personality. He knew everyone, and those he didn't know he named "Luigi," and they became instant friends. He would introduce people to other like-minded people.

He flirted with men and women, endeared himself to all. He made everyone seem like part of a party that was just about to start *now* because he had finally found you. The Screamers' parties at The Screamers' house (on Wilton Place), dubbed the Wilton Hilton, were the very best! A great old-Hollywood house painted flat black on the inside, maybe a chandelier hanging above the stairway with some great poster or found art on the wall. Fantastic music blaring—the latest punk single, to sixties garage, to Motown, to the soundtrack to *Suspiria* by Goblin. There was food and drink galore. Food was always a plus! I recall eating a lot of the Army ration crackers found at the Masque, the remnants of its past life being an air-raid bomb shelter. Being a former fat kid, I was still hooked on food. I think eating was a social relaxer to me in my early awkward days. Thanks to puberty, though, I could now eat like a horse—and did—and still stay slim.

The people at these parties were the greatest—gay, straight, black, white, bikers, rich kids and poor kids, lowriders, male

hustlers, young Hollywood actresses, drag queens, the soon-to-be famous, the used-to-be famous, hippies, and Wild Man Fischer standing in a corner singing about "Taggy Lee," plus the punk teens! All talking together, mixing ideas: "So what is this punk thing?" "You don't know about EST?" "No, video is the coming wave—it's going to change filmmaking." "Yeah, Frank Zappa used to live right down the street."

These were low-rent versions of the parties I had read about in the library, Truman Capote's black-and-white ball in New York, Gertrude Stein's salon in Paris—or at least a punk version of the Peter Sellers's film *The Party*. Here they served giant tin pans of Mama du Plenty's famous potato salad and containers of boozy punch. One time someone brought bags and bags of McDonald's hamburgers. Still eating government cheese at home, I remember being impressed with that luxury bounty.

These were the teenage high school house parties I never got invited to in Chula Vista. But in Hollywood I was part of the club.

The Zeros went on to record a second single with Bomp! Records, "Wild Weekend" b/w "Beat Your Heart Out." The front sleeve showed our pointy toed shoes—we would buy new old stock in Tijuana—and the back showed our home away from home, the infamous Plunger Pit. The Plunger Pit was a 1930s studio apartment behind a magazine stand/ adult bookstore known as Circus Books in West Hollywood. It was the after-party crash pad ruled by Trudi, Trixie, and Hellin, the members of the made-up band The Plungers, the answer to the constant plumbing problem at the abode. We toured up and down the coast but had no real direction for what we were doing, which seemed normal for a seventeen-year-old.

This is how I remember The Zeros breaking up. Javier was complaining that Hector was playing in too many different bands. (He was. He played with F-Word; Black Randy's side trip Mexican Randy, which I wish I had seen; and anyone else who needed a bass player. I thought it was great, like a jazz cat, playing with any gig just to play.) That seemed the main complaint, though there were others. And so we broke up. I don't remember an artist plea of "Let's stay together" or "We've come so far in such a short time." I suppose I was ready for a change. They re-formed the next week without me and then moved to San Francisco. I don't remember being too broken up about it.

During my early years in music I was pretty much a passenger, along for the ride. I don't think I added that much to projects. But watching and learning from other people put me in better control when I later took the driver's seat. I had graduated high school early that year and would be turning 18 by summer. And I knew where I was going.

A girl named Doris helped move me from Chula Vista to Hollywood. She was friends with that new group of kids recently arrived from Phoenix, Arizona. They got called The Cactus Heads—Don Bolles, David Wiley, Paul Cutler, and Rob Graves. They were great little bits of smarts and poison who would come to shake things up in little Hollywood. We stuffed Doris's blue Volkswagen Golf with all my possessions from home. After one last trip to my favorite thrift store in Chula Vista, Am Vets, we made the drive to Los Angeles. It was September 28, 1978. Pope John Paul I died that day. Pope Paul VI had just died thirty days earlier. I took these as good omens.

Jane Wiedlin had just moved out of the Canterbury. The Canterbury was the wonderful, terrible punk home, crash

pad, after-show party central, rehearsal space, four-story, collapsing 1920s apartment building right off Hollywood Boulevard, the avenue of the stars. She left me her apartment and mattress! I was set! She had painted the whole room white, with white enamel floors. She had left boxes of sixties fashion magazines, remains from her design school days. She was on her way to becoming a rock star. I had windows to the courtyard, where I could hear my friends yell to each other from their apartment windows, like in the New York movies! I would hear fights from different floors and people practicing their guitars over and over.

I got a job as a waiter at the Pizza Hut on Hollywood Boulevard. I got to serve beer and was only 18. Older men asked me whether I wanted a sugar daddy. I would feed my punk-rock friends free pizza and beer. Of course, I didn't have a car—I could walk to work! It was four blocks from the Canterbury, which was right across the street from the Masque. How much more punk-rock teenage heaven could I be in?

That winter Margot Go-Go and I went to New York City. She had just gotten kicked out of The Go-Go's, and their band's ascent seemed for sure: "Hey, I got kicked out of a band too, so let's go!" We got round-trip tickets for $99. It was the first time for both of us. This was before I HEART NY—the city was a wonderful bankrupt shell of its older, former self, a completely different world from what it is today. I remember going to a party way below SoHo, and the taxi driver told us, "You know, you won't be able to get a taxi back—nobody comes to this area at night."

I first stayed with Trixie Plunger, who had recently transplanted herself from Hollywood. Then I stayed in a midtown basement apartment with Chase Holiday. Before I

moved to Hollywood, I lived in her spacious hallway closet at the Canterbury, where I hung a black-and-white poster of Yoko playing golf. Chase worked at an amazing record store. I stole every Shaun Cassidy and Nino Rota soundtrack albums I could. I still have them all to this day.

I had my first beer at a bar in Saint Mark's Place, bought for me by Howie Pyro and The Blessed. You could drink at 18 then! 15, 17, and eighteen-year-olds in a bar, being served! This was truly a wonderful place.

I saw Teenage Jesus and the Jerks, The Contortions, The Cramps, and Johnny Thunders at all the spots—CBGBs, Max's Kansas City. I would go to Studio 54 to pick fights with Steve Rubell. I refused to dance (although I really wanted to)—I stuck to my punk-rock morals of that time. Then I would go to the Mudd Club and hang with Klaus Nomi and the kids of that time. It was the New York City of my Velvet Underground dreams back then. I was there for a few months. It was a great eye opener for an eighteen-year-old. New York was a much darker colder place than palm-tree-lined Southern California. It was my first actual cold, cold "winter"—but not of my discontent.

Then it was back to California, where things seemed different. I was becoming a jaded nineteen-year-old. I got an older boyfriend. Gorilla Rose, an art director/ideas man/lyricist of The Screamers, was moving out of his black room, where 1930s rose-patterned wallpaper peeked out at the ceiling's edge. I moved in. It was just west of La Brea near the Rock & Roll Ralphs—almost the suburbs compared to living right off Hollywood Boulevard. I would swim twice a day at the Hollywood YMCA and showered with Bruce Springsteen. I was the only one there who knew who he was. He asked me not to blow his cover, but I still got his

autograph for my friend Ruth. I think I worked at El Coyote, the cheap Mexican restaurant of choice, as a cashier. I was in a couple of bands, The Johnnies and another called Catholic Discipline.

The music scene then had seemed to take on a different format—harder, faster, shorter. Catholic Discipline headed in the opposite direction: longer, slower, scarier. I think we saw Catholic Discipline as a "postpunk" band. Claude Bessy, singer and editor and writer for *Slash* magazine, was our figurehead. I think he felt a little constrained with his editor duties at *Slash*, and here was a way for his words to leap off the page and onto the stage. Craig Lee, our drummer, was the music writer for *LA Weekly*. Perhaps that gave us our literary bent. He would give me notes on how I played my Farfisa Combo Compact—"Play spookier." Craig was afraid I didn't like Claude's wild-man antics—swinging his mic stand as a weapon to go with his verbal assaults. But, actually, I thought it was great. I was still pretty stoic in my demeanor in those days. I think I was sitting, waiting, and learning for my lead singer time.

Admittedly Penelope Spheeris came into the game pretty late. She started hanging out at our rehearsals before filming us for her movie, *The Decline of Western Civilization*. The scene had changed a lot by then, and not for the better, if you ask me. Clubs were shutting down because of the violence caused by people we didn't know, those new guys from Orange County. Punk had turned a corner. Less art and more machine, punk wasn't dead; it had just become something else.

CHAPTER 12

Starry Nights in East LA

by Teresa Covarrubias, with Tom DeSavia

Since the first wave of late '50s/'60s garage bands, LA Chicano culture has played a vital—if often overlooked—role in the evolution of American alternative music. Bands like The Champs and The Midnighters to Cannibal and the Headhunters released tunes that seeped into the world consciousness, their ethnic roots and inspirations most likely lost on most who they reached through the airwaves.

In 1976 East LA was a forgotten swath of neighborhoods directly east of a dilapidated downtown, across the LA River, and known primarily for gangs and poverty. Insulated from the city at large, those who didn't enjoy slow dancing, car clubs, arena rock, or copying the lyrics of bland FM radio hits in perfect script on PeeChee folders found growing up on the east side a rather lonely experience. During the summer of 1976 I discovered the whole punk aesthetic from British fanzines sent to me by my sister. I was also listening to Rodney's show on KROQ, and my musical tastes were

beginning to morph from Roxy Music and David Bowie to The Ramones, Blondie, The Jam, and The Clash.

Almost immediately the most striking to me were the women: Poly Styrene, Siouxie Sioux, The Slits—these really wild women. To me that was so encouraging. I grew up when rock 'n' roll was so much more of a male-dominated field, it was *all* about the guys. To see this whole wave of new music coming out with all these women was just amazing. That was what first got me to thinking, *Hey, I can do that too.*

There were these punk shows in Hollywood where, for two bucks, you'd see seven bands. That was so inspiring; it was almost like an open-mic environment: if you had something to say and you had some heart, the stage was yours. That was foreign back then. Up until then it always felt like you had to be a super-accomplished musician and have a *big* show to even get onstage. This was the exact opposite. This was totally inclusive.

I started checking out shows on the west side of town. I saw The Ramones, Siouxie, The Selecter, and Madness at the Whisky. On April 14, 1978, I saw The Jam at the Starwood, with The Weirdos and The Zeros opening. That was such a great show and would prove life altering for me. The place was packed: there were the local punk scene regulars—the forerunners, who had that leather, tattered, bobby-pin look down—as well as individuals from the east side, which surprised me.

I met Rudy (Medina) at that show. We were sweating as we pogoed right in the middle of that delirious crowd to those bands, and that very moment led us to the idea of putting a band together ourselves. That night The Brat was born.

The Brat was formed by me and the guitar team of Rudy and his nephew Sidney. We started by learning covers and

played gigs at high school dances and bars, and within a year, by 1979, we had all original music, but getting gigs on the west side was proving difficult. The golden age of the LA punk scene had seemingly come and gone, and the clubs were now booked solid with the local punk stars like Fear, The Weirdos, The Germs, and X. That openness and nurturing nature of the scene in 1977 and thereabouts was changing. That feeling of "C'mon everybody, you're all welcome" that drew us to that world was ending. It became obvious that unless you were really a part of that early scene or knew somebody who booked clubs, it was really hard to get gigs. So in that respect we felt sort of excluded. But that's a natural thing, right? You create a scene, and if you're not a part of that inner circle, you're kind of an outsider in a way.

I suppose this very lack of access is what really created the East LA scene.

There was a sense of the geography that a bunch of artists and musicians shared, and there was a healthy sort of competitiveness as well. Instead of simply struggling to break into the established LA punk world, we banded together, creating our own universe, maybe not even realizing what we were doing at the time. Together with Los Illegals, Odd Squad, The Undertakers, and a handful of others, we became equally as tethered around the whole East LA art scene, which was really vibrant. And growing.

Initially we played exclusively on the east side, mainly at backyard parties or car club events. Usually the band would play simply to give the DJs a break. We were entirely out of our element, and the reaction to us was mixed, though generally positive. I remember once playing a house gig up in the hills of City Terrace. The DJ stopped playing and the dancers cleared the floor, grabbed their beers, and sat

down to enjoy the cool evening sky. We started our set, and a couple of dudes ventured closer. As we played, a few more people started to join the crowd. Soon we had a small assemblage of live music lovers in front of us, moving to the music. We launched into one of our more frenetic tunes, and this one dude off to my right started flailing his arms about and howling with delight. All I remember seeing were these sparks of light, and our guitarist quickly got between me and this guy—he was shooting a gun into the air! It was so punk rock. After the gig I discovered that John and Exene had come around to check out the band and were outside the front of the house when they heard the shots and decided to call it a night.

House parties were always a big thing in East LA. Because there were so few outlets for us to play on the west side, it was almost like we had to create something for ourselves in the community. We played lots of these sorts of gigs. All the east side bands did. I think it was 1979 or so when we played our first real club, the Hong Kong Café. That gig was probably the first time we played to a more "punk" crowd. The place got hot, and the ceiling was so low that one jump onstage could cause a head injury. It was also around that time when the punk scene started to take hold in our own neighborhood, and it was obvious the shows needed to grow beyond the local backyards hosting them.

Opened by nun Sister Karen Boccalero in the early 1970s in Boyle Heights, Self Help Graphics & Art is a nonprofit arts center serving the Latino community of Los Angeles to this day. Focusing on visual and performance art, its importance to the early punk-rock scene cannot be overstated.

Our growth was really thanks to Self Help and Sister Karen and the whole mission of that center, which was all about

encouraging art and making art available to the community and bringing that community into that space. Before that it was really like a desert out there—there was really nothing cultural happening. It just happened to be at that moment when the whole punk scene—the whole new wave—was happening, and it sort of incorporated itself into the whole Self Help model. They had been doing that stuff for years with the arts—they had screen-printing classes and originated the whole Day of the Dead celebration in the very early '70s, well before it became usurped by mainstream culture. That history all happened there: the Day of the Dead, the Virgen de Guadalupe ceremonies, and on and on. I guess when the whole punk thing happened, Self Help ultimately became more open to the mainstream and less Chicano in a way, though we really didn't realize that at the time.

Willie Herrón, known before then for his work with the performance art group Asco, had started his own band, the aforementioned Los Illegals. Herrón had befriended Sister Karen, and she let them rehearse out of one of the art studios there at Self Help Graphics, later offering him the second floor of the space to start his own club. Eventually Joe "Vex" Suquette moved his namesake venue from a small space located in the basement of an apartment building on Alvarado Street into Self Help. This incarnation of The Vex was open from March to November of 1980 and hosted punk-rock shows twice a month. The first major event there was the infamous "Punk Rock Prom," which featured X as a headliner. That show almost single-handedly opened up the west side's awareness of East LA. The Vex was born, and instantly not only was it the only place to play on the east side, but it also quickly emerged as a go-to spot for bands from around LA, Orange County, and the San Fernando Valley.

The first real Vex show featured The Plugz, Los Illegals, The Undertakers, The Fenders, and The Brat. This gig proved to be instrumental to the whole East LA scene. Before, I'd always felt isolated, as if I were the only person this side of the LA River who liked punk music and art. But there I discovered that there were youngsters just like me. The stereotype of streets filled with cholos and lowriders had in some ways integrated into my thinking as well, so it rather surprised me to find so many others with the same sensibilities. Among the musicians was also an array of visual and performance artists. The collaboration between musicians and these artists was what made the East LA scene unique. Although there were others who were part of the LA/Hollywood punk scene of 1977, few if any really embraced their East LA roots. East LA was the place you ran away from to find others who shared your interests.

But The Vex was all about the geography (and 25 cent beers!). She dared the Hollywood punks to cross the river. She dared you to rethink your ideas of what East LA was all about. Sure, you had the stereotypes—the gangsters and the macho types—and I'm sure people got their cars broken into, but not any more or less than they did at Al's Bar or anywhere else. The range of talent went from the hardcore thrashings of The Stains—who represented the more nihilistic, Sex Pistol tradition—to The Odd Squad, who had a more pop sensibility. There was a core of bands—Los Lobos, Los Illegals, The Undertakers, The Odd Squad, The Stains, and us—who often played gigs together and basically became the ambassadors of the East LA scene.

For me, I think I really felt like there was something going on when the whole Vex scene was starting out. It was then when I got a sense that it wasn't just our band by itself

just doing this thing in East LA; it was kind of a networking that started taking place, not only between the band
but also among writers and artists and dancers. When that
scene came together—when The Vex started happening and
doing the first shows there—that's when I got a sense of
"Wow, this is really a scene and a community and we're
creating this space." That's when the lightbulb went on and
I realized that this was different and separate from what was
going on in Hollywood and the music scene there. We had
our own little camp.

The Vex became popular as a music venue, and west side
bands saw it as a cool place to play. The venue lasted for
a year or so before there was some disturbance and she
was thrashed by a couple of reckless hardcore fans—it was a
Black Flag gig, alongside some other Orange County punk
bands. That last show at The Vex—that Black Flag gig—
brought in the hardcore kids, including a few incendiary
hooligans who came in and thrashed Self Help. They tore
the place up. Self Help was largely an art community center,
and these guys broke into where they had the prints and
destroyed these works of art that had been archived there
for who knows how many years. It was such disrespect of
that place and our community. They broke windows and
smashed statues and other works of art. The damage was so
great that the club relocated to a new address. Even though
the "new" space remained open until 1983, it never regained the cultural importance of the Self Help location;
it was simply another venue. Ironically, after the demise of
The Vex, the east side had received enough press and attention that getting gigs was no longer impossible. We'd always hear about a few of these errant fools who were bent
on destruction in the Hollywood scene—usually high on

angel dust or some such thing–but until this, we had been "protected."

That new attitude that a segment of the new audience thought was "punk" wasn't about art and creating at that point; it was just "fuck everything." For me, that's the downside of what punk evolved into, this sort of nihilism. That was the end of Self Help as we knew it: people started hearing about it, and bands from the west side wanted to come play there because they saw it as a viable venue on the east side but had no respect for its roots or what it was about. That was the end of it. There goes the neighborhood.

We played some wonderful art openings, like Aztlan Multiples' print show at the Exploratorium at Cal State Los Angeles, which featured the master printing of Richard Duardo. Richard designed The Brat's EP cover and was an avid supporter of the scene. The show at the Los Angeles Photo Center was a typical ensemble of east side talent featuring photography by Harry Gamboa, poetry reading by Marisela Norte, and music by The Brat and The Odd Squad.

We played some really joyful gigs with Los Lobos at Madame Wong's East. Those gigs felt like wedding receptions, with lots of drinking and dancing on the tabletops. When the Brat EP came out and started getting played on KROQ, we opened for some pretty cool acts like Bauhaus, The Cramps, The Gun Club, Suburban Lawns, Adam Ant, and The Go-Go's.

I think it was 1982 or 1983 when the Roxy hosted an East LA night featuring The Brat, Los Illegals, The Undertakers, and The Clichés. We had moved west and were finally feeling a real acceptance from punk audiences all over the city. But we never lost sight of our roots, and the music continued to reflect that. But now the crowds were more integrated.

Although the overriding punk credo of disillusionment and rebellion ruled, a sense of community pride was steadfast. With that sense of pride in geography was a whole group of people that did not fit into the stereotypical idea of what people thought the East LA native was. Still today, you mention East LA, and people immediately think of gang culture. Thankfully—partly due to this time—those stereotypes are actually less monolithic. People see now that Chicanos are not just gangbangers, that they're so much more. Back then we definitely felt like we were representing to this whole segment of the population that doesn't really know us beyond what they see on television. That got fragmented though—when they moved The Vex to the new location, it had already changed. At that point it just became a venue that integrated the west side bands and the east side bands, which was great, but it lost that community thing that it had in the beginning.

With the scene starting to end and becoming fragmented and the internal support system falling away a bit, I definitely saw disruptive influences coming in. We all did. It was suddenly less about us supporting each other and more about dealing with outsiders coming in—outsiders who saw it as an opportunity for them, not opportunities for the art. The clichéd managers would come in and their best interest was not about the community and supporting it; they just saw opportunity for them to cash in on something that was happening at the moment.

I think there's always a certain competitiveness among people that leads to the deterioration of any support system. For us personally, we got involved with this terrible management situation that basically destroyed the band. It wasn't about what we were doing anymore but about them trying

to market us. They came in with all these ridiculous ideas and suggestions, all these stereotypes about what a Chicano band was, how we should present ourselves. We were young, but right from the get-go I knew it was a bad idea, and it became very decisive for our band. People wanted "success"—whatever that was—and striving for that proved a stake in the heart.

That was the "beginning of the end," as they say. The whole control of how we were going to present ourselves and what we were going to represent was basically given to this management team, these white dudes who came at the whole Chicano experience from what they had learned from the mainstream culture, which was all about lowriders and cholos.

There's this one day I will never forget—it was probably the saddest day of my musical life. We had done these demo tapes for Capitol Records and had been working on them for months. Our management wanted to finally present the music to the A&R people. Management had this bright idea—it was so embarrassing, and I kept telling them this was a bad idea, begging them not to go through with it. They got like five or six lowriders to pull up to the Capitol Tower, and the A&R people and some other folks from the label got in the cars and listened to the music while driving them around in these lowriders. That had *nothing* to do with us. It makes me cringe to this day.

I'm second-generation Mexican, which means my parents were born in the States, as was I. So I was much more assimilated than people who were first generation, obviously. For me, I came to the whole cultural thing kind of late; my parents brought me up affirming, "You're an American and you need to blend in." We celebrated American

holidays, trying to fit in. So I came into the whole music thing not necessarily to express my Chicana roots; it just sort of became that. A huge part of it was being involved in the whole Vex scene and meeting other people who were more inclined to bring their heritage in and represent the community. That inspired me. It really just started as expressing myself creatively. I was always writing poetry, but it wasn't Chicano. The influences came from the neighborhood, not my own house. My mom and dad grew up listening to big band music. We did not listen to any sort of Mexican music in our house. I came to that later, as a young adult.

In that little group there was a sense of purpose and commonality, like we were a part of a greater scene. I can't speak for the other bands who were part of the so-called East LA scene—The Stains, Violent Children. Their stuff was more hardcore, more thrashy. But for us there was a sense of camaraderie, more so from the bands centered on the art scene—the Vex/Self Help world.

I remember thinking I just wanted to be in a band. I always was a singer, but I wanted to write music and to sing with a band. I wanted to be onstage—that was the goal. It was simple. I wanted to perform for people. Getting signed and making a record wasn't in the plan at all; the goal was just to express oneself, to have a voice, and see what happened. Beyond that, there wasn't a lot of planning.

PUNK PROM

WITH X & HAL NEGRO & THE SATINTONES

AND THE STINGERS

& PUNK FASHIONS
CROWNING OF THE KING & QUEEN
VICIOUS DANCE CONTEST

SUNDAY MAY·11th

AT SELF HELP GRAPHICS
DADAFEST L·A·

Fig. 55.—Convection currents in air.

LAMP CHIMNEYS

A B

Advance tickets $5.00   door $6.00

Advance ticket sales only from SPARC, 685 Venice Blvd. 822-9540

SPONSORED BY THE SOCIAL AND PUBLIC ART RESOURCE CENTER

sponsored by the City of Los Angeles and CETA Title VI

3802 Brooklyn Ave.
Self Help Graphics

The Brat (from L-R):
Rudy Medina, Lou Soto,
Mark Stewart, Sid Medina,
Teresa Covarrubias

Henry Rollins of Black Flag

Black Flag's
first LA show
with Henry
Rollins, 1981

Jack Grisham of T.S.O.L

The Flesh Eaters, 1982, Chris D. with bassist Robyn Jameson

Minutemen on stage (from L-R): D. Boon, George Hurley, Mike Watt

Minutemen (from L-R): Mike Watt, D. Boon, George Hurley

Black Flag in front of Frederick's of Hollywood, 1979 (from L-R): Keith Morris, Jill Jordan, Greg Ginn, Trudi, Chuck Dukowski

Exene on stage at Masque with beer can

Germs (Darby & Pat) at Hong Kong Cafe, 1979

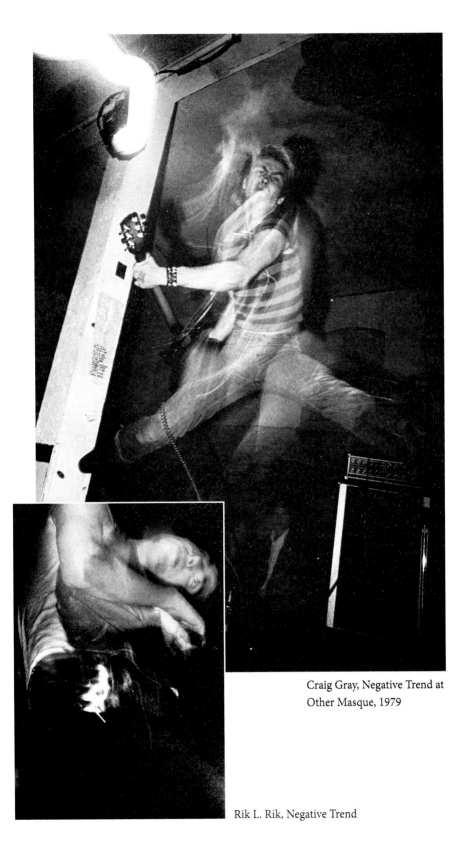

Craig Gray, Negative Trend at
Other Masque, 1979

Rik L. Rik, Negative Trend

The Wolves (biker-like gang created by X & crew) in a motel, San Diego, Easter 1980 (from L-R): Kit Maira (roadie), John Doe, Chuck Baron (roadie, standing), Top Jimmy, Exene, Dan O'Kane, Penny, Jill Jordan, Farrah Fawcett Minor, Mirielle Cervenka, Johnny O'Kane, Kelly O'Kane

Billy Zoom in Hollywood, 1981

Phil & Dave Alvin, The Blasters at The Palace, Los Angeles, 1982

Top Jimmy backstage at
the Whisky, 1981

X on the roof of their rehearsal space, Hollywood, 1981

X, Club 88, June 1979. Joan Jett and Pat Smear in audience.

X, Club 88, June 1979

Claude Bessy, from Billy and
Denise Zoom's wedding concert
at the Whisky, 1982

The Screamers on a bus bench, 1977 (from L-R): David Allen, K. K. Barrett, Tomata du Plenty, Tommy Gear, a little old lady, the photographer's shadow at bottom left

Joan Jett, Farrah Fawcet Minor, and K. K. Barrett at the Whisky, 1977

The Randettes, backstage at the Whisky, 1978 (from L-R): Sheila Edwards, Trudi, Trixie, Connie Clarksville, Spazz Attack, Alice Bag, Nickey Beat, Exene, K. K. Barrett

The Go-Go's, backstage at the Starwood, 1980 (from L-R): Jane Wiedlin, Gina Schock, Charlotte Caffey, Margot Olavarria, Belinda Carlisle

Exene and John Doe, X, Club 88, March 1980. Filming of first *Decline of Western Civilization*.

CHAPTER 13

Go West, Go West, Go West

by John Doe

It was like a drumbeat constantly in my head during all of 1976. Finally, the day after Halloween, I packed my 1970 International Travelall & headed toward California. The Doors said, "The West is the best, get here & we'll do the rest." Yeah. The idea & reality of California, Los Angeles & the West always had a mythic hold on me & I still believe it is the place of dreams. Nathanael West and Charles Bukowski captured the decaying, film noir quality of Los Angeles that I longed for & I was so desperate to leave the East Coast's chokehold.

In the early '70s John Waters was the closest thing Baltimore had to a celebrity. I'll admit that celebrity & fame was something I desired back then. All John's actors had the kind of fame & notoriety that seemed attainable. They hung out in the same bars we did. John could be found having an afternoon cocktail at Bertha's, a Fell's Point dive where I played for tips on Thursday nights. At the time I reasoned that if I could hang out w/ John Waters & see his actors in

many of the same places where we hung out, then fame may not be as elusive as all that. John was a more focused & better filmmaker than Andy Warhol & David Bowie wrote songs & hung out w/ him. We were just this close, but I was done with the East Coast.

By 1975 my parents lived in Brooklyn, so CBGBs & Max's Kansas City were available w/ a free place to stay. It was there I saw Talking Heads, The Heartbreakers, and flyers pasted on telephone poles for Blondie & Television. I saw a particularly memorable Talking Heads performance in which they finished the set w/ "Psycho Killer"; David B. tossed the guitar over his head & w/ a singularly, crazed glare, walked straight out of the bar, perhaps never to be seen again. That was another moment when I thought, *I can do that, and I want to do that.* Patti Smith's *Horses* had been out for a year, and it was clear that some great change in the stagnant music world was happening. It was equally clear that NYC was already locked up. The East Coast was cold, full of ghosts & people who said, "You'll never make it, so why try?"

By this point I had dropped out of George Washington University in 1972, installed aluminum siding, gutters & roofing for two years, played in a band that rarely got gigs, smoked a huge amount of weed & drank too much peppermint schnapps w/ beer chasers. Downtown Baltimore had an avant-garde theater called the Theater Project. Through a few live performances there, I was introduced to Antioch College and eventually Grace Cavaleri, a teacher who changed my life. Grace was a petite, dark-haired woman w/ a teenager's eyes & the most open smile I'd ever had directed toward me. Clearly my parents didn't want me to spend my life as a roofer, so they paid for me to enroll in Antioch College. Now I was living w/ a childhood friend and bandmate Jack

Chipman in a rural black community outside Baltimore, named Simpsonville. I was learning about modern poets & becoming a part of an incredibly vibrant poetry community in the Baltimore/DC area. During the private weekly poetry tutorials w/ Grace she always found the best passages or fragments of writing and showed us how truthful & possibly transcendent they were. She would often say, "I wish I had written that." At the same time she would gently & lovingly point out the sections that were "not so good," which, w/ some more thought & editing, could complement the beautiful breakthroughs of the better lines. It was here I first believed I could write something worth more than shoving in the bottom drawer of a hand-me-down dresser.

In April of 1976 Jack Chipman & I flew to Los Angeles, rented an AMC station wagon & stayed at a rundown motel near Vermont Ave. The minute I stepped out of the terminal into the jet-fueled air by LAX, the light & a sense of well-being came over me like a déjà vu homecoming. Jack & I had written some songs that we naively believed were good enough for someone to buy & record. We tore the page for music publishers from the Yellow Pages & began cold calling them from a phone booth outside our shitty motel. I guess the room didn't come w/ a phone. It's incredible to think that we got through to someone who allowed us to drop off a cassette tape w/ four of what we thought were our best songs. After a couple of days one rather elegant black producer/publisher met w/ us in person. We played Mr.—oh, I wish I could remember his name—our tape & a couple of more songs live, with Jack on piano & me singing. He told us that he would "buy" two of our songs for $500 apiece. We knew nothing about publishing but had copyrighted our songs w/ lead sheets through the Library of Congress.

Naturally we were ecstatic & figured that if we sold two or three songs a month, we'd have it made! I don't believe we ever signed or sealed that deal—the producer's phone was always mysteriously busy—but when we left California ten days later, we were certain we could "make it" in LA.

Six months later Jack & I were living in a two-bedroom house at Pacific & Dudley Court in Venice, Cal. It was two blocks from the beach. I think we paid a whopping $800 a month rent & the proximity to the water was comfortingly like Baltimore. Because I had run a mildly successful poetry reading series in Baltimore, I figured the quickest way to meet kindred spirits was to drop into the poetry world. Beyond Baroque, home of the venerated Venice Poetry Workshop, was a 20 min. walk through a not-so-dangerous part of Venice. They offered a workshop w/ Bill Mohr, Jack Grapes, Kate Braverman & James Krusoe. Later someone told me that Tom Waits and Bukowski had attended. A great person & poet Frances Smith, who was the mother of Buk's only kid, was a regular.

I believe the first Tuesday I went was also the first time a strange beauty w/ dark lipstick, bleach-splattered jeans, and dark red Egyptian-styled hair attended. This was the night Exene & I met. We were asked to make a list of poets/ writers we admired. She asked to look at my list because she didn't have many names on hers. When she did, she pointed out that I had written John Ashbery's name twice. I thanked my good luck that someone who cut such an eccentric figure wanted to hang out w/ poets and—*holy shit*—she was a poet too!

She worked at Beyond Baroque on a government jobs program teaching her a skill as a typesetter. Naturally I went to the poetry workshop every Tuesday night until I asked her

to go next door to the Comeback Inn for a drink. They featured bad, soft jazz before it was even a genre, and I found out her real name was Christine & she had changed it to a phonetic version of Xmas. We were both born in February & had Czech last names. So here I was, in a place where the beatniks first hung out in Calif., hanging out w/ a woman named Exene. Of course neither of us was aware how fateful this meeting was.

Quickly I found that she had recently moved here from Tallahassee, Florida, by selling her prized mint-green 1950 Cadillac. She had lived in Illinois, where I was born, had three sisters, and her mother had died when she was fourteen. She was just the kind of person I had moved to LA to meet. Exene was hanging out w/ scary Vietnam vets who would twirl her over their head at other dive bars while alternately calling her Mary Magdalene or the Easter Bunny. The first time I thought I had fallen in love w/ her, we were in her apt. above Beyond Baroque, sitting together in a broken-down chair, watching the street life on Venice Blvd. In that apt. there was a big old console TV that only got sound. One night we carried it down the stairs to the vacant lot next door. We threw bricks at the picture tube until it burst, which was much more difficult than we had thought it would be & only gave an unsatisfying, low-pitched *thuuunk* when it finally broke. It took another year of wooing & cajoling for her to agree to be my romantic partner as well as a lifelong friend, songwriting partner & often times soul mate.

In 1976 the place everyone looked to find a car, refrigerator, cat, room to rent, boyfriend, or musician was the *Recycler*. It came out every Thursday and was oftentimes sold out at the liquor store by Friday afternoon. How I wish

someone had saved the want ad that Billy Zoom & I placed that same week late in 1976.

Billy Zoom had his own rockabilly band & had worked w/ Gene Vincent & dozens of other bands. I knew "Be-Bop-A-Lula" & that was legit. He was tall & thin, with straw-blond hair & he spoke deliberately & had a 1953 Hudson Hornet in his driveway. Billy had fashioned a somewhat soundproof rehearsal room in the garage at his house on 6th & Van Ness. The house resembled the Munsters'. It was a once-grand, two-story Victorian in Hancock Park w/ mahogany wainscoting, built-in glass cabinets in the dining room, a study—which would become Exene & my bedroom—& three other bedrooms upstairs.

Billy lived there w/ his girlfriend, Kittra, who broke an acoustic guitar over his head just before he moved out. But Billy was able to keep the rehearsal space & his Hudson Hornet in the drive. This is where we first got to know each other by playing songs like "Honey Don't," "Bring It on Home," & "Promised Land." At first we played w/ Steve Allen, who later formed 20/20; Jimmy Nanos & drummer Blaze Henry. Billy had had some success w/ the Billy Zoom Band & there was a small but hearty rockabilly scene. For a number of reasons, mostly the coming wave of new music like The Ramones, etc., Billy was disillusioned w/ that scene. We learned that we were both born in February, grew up in the Midwest & hated jamming. We both loved rock 'n' roll songs & old R & B. Strange as it may sound, back then he was almost reticent to play leads. So after our first or second meeting, this prompted me to ask him & Kittra if we needed to look for a "lead guitarist." When I asked that at the Carl's Jr. around the corner, I remember Billy giving me the iciest, almost quizzical look & Kittra saying, "Oh no, you don't understand—Billy *is* the lead guitarist." OK then, that's

settled. Leaving one of our rehearsal sessions, I remember getting pulled over by LAPD & asked what I had been doing that night. After telling them that I had been playing music, they asked what kind, to which I responded, "You know, old stuff like Chuck Berry, Carl Perkins, Gene Vincent." They replied, "Like what?" Me: "'Be-Bop-A-Lula'?" They: "How about singing some of that for us?" So I start singing, and they: "Come over here to the squad car." Me: crapping my pants because everyone knew what bullies LAPD were. I walk over to the car & they thrust the loudspeaker mic into my hands & the next thing I knew I'm singing "Be-Bop-A-Lula" over the black & white's bullhorn. That must've been late Nov of '76. It's remarkable to think that within a few weeks of moving to LA, I had met someone I'd play music w/ for the next 37 years.

By mid-November my roommate Jack had returned to Balto several weeks beforehand to see his girlfriend & came back just to get his instruments but never again to live there. This was sad but ultimately extremely liberating. I was finally living on my own. I hadn't realized how much baggage the relationship contained, that I was shedding another layer of East Coast doubt & I began to move from one beach apartment to another ("every other week I need a new address"). I had a day job working at Brentano's bookstore at the corner of Wilshire & Rodeo (which is pronounced like the Spanish *rodéo* & I pronounced like a cowboy for the first week) on the bottom floor of the Beverly Wilshire Hotel, still the grande dame of LA hotels. There I saw Farrah Fawcett, Helen Reddy & actually helped Gloria Swanson find nutrition books—wow, a real movie star!

Christmas that year was very lonely. I was living hand-to-mouth, didn't have enough money to fly home & decided that if I'd moved to California, then I would stay through

the holidays. This was certainly a stubborn, self-sacrificing move, but it allowed me to be sad & feel put upon. Because I had met Exene in December & she didn't have a phone, I thought I'd walk to her apartment above Beyond Baroque on New Year's Eve. A block or two after I had turned onto W. Washington Blvd (now Abbott Kinney), four kids between 10–13 yrs old clustered around me w/ a cup & asked if I wanted a drink. As I bent my neck to sniff, a sharp thwack hit the top of my head & two of them grabbed me. They only weighed 85–100 lbs each, so I was able to shake one free, grab the other & begin punching. The third or fourth kid kept swinging his belt, buckle first, at my head as we all collapsed onto the sidewalk. I was reaching for another's leg when they all sort of disappeared or ran away. I suppose it was just too much trouble. Pulling myself to my feet, picking up a bracelet, I felt the top of my head & came back w/ a hand slick w/ blood. There was a bar a few doors down, so I made my way there. I came in the door & headed straight for the bathroom. There was my face in the mirror, w/ streams of blood coming down it. I remembered the woozy, bent faces of the drunken NYE patrons & their looks of horror as I passed by. Looking in the mirror, wet paper towels in my hand, I figured I was really on my own, living the bohemian life that I thought I would find in the land of dreams.

CHAPTER 14

The Stucco-Coated Killing Field

by Henry Rollins

I came to Los Angeles in the late summer of 1981, having joined the band Black Flag.

Before then I was well aware of the amazing music scene in Los Angeles but only through the records I mail ordered or managed to find in record stores in the Washington, DC, area where I was from.

This association was in many ways quite pure. I evaluated the bands solely from their recorded output. Some of the bands I was listening to included The Germs, X, The Weirdos, The Alley Cats, The Bags, Black Randy and the Metro Squad, The Middle Class, The Deadbeats, and others. Besides the singles, the *Yes L.A.* and *Tooth and Nail* compilation albums were useful to try to get an idea of what was happening.

These were incredible records. I remember buying The Weirdos' *Destroy All Music* 7" on Bomp! through the mail. I played it over and over. The song "Life of Crime," to this day,

A HAPPY PERSON

BLACK FLAG

THE SEMINAL
(hand-sewn)

GIRL TRAIL

Wasco Wildcats rule

DEC. 9 SUN. at "CUCKOO'S NEST"
with **X** 714 Placentia-Costa Mesa
18 and over

DEC 16 SUN. at "BLACKIE'S"
with **THE DILS** and **THE UPBEATS**
607 N. LA BREA 18 and over 9:00

DEC 21 FRI. at "the WHISKEY"
with **THE PLUGZ, ARTHUR J. AND THE
GOLDCUPS, GEZA X AND THE MOMMY
MEN, HAL NEGRO AND THE SATIN TONES,
THE BUSBOYS** - on the Sunset Strip

Sunday is Fun Day

Sleep, Sleep, Sleep.

Black Flag Flyer #21 ≡ Buy the Black Flag EP: $2 from SST Records, P.O. Box 1 Lawndale, Ca. 90260

R. "I'm looking out for #7" Pettibone
(the lucky ones get caught, maybe in time)

strikes me as a 140, and some second masterpiece. In fact, I can't find one Weirdos song that isn't great.

I do remember that all these records seemed to have one central theme running through them: danger. The Black Randy singles, all of them amazing, were scary. It occurred to me that Randy was a genius maniac who didn't have long to live. The song "Trouble at the Cup" laughs off life in favor of some huge, absolutely lethal darkness.

There was a seasoned adultness to the music that made me think that the bands were living fast, free of life expectancy, making the soundtrack for a scene that was going to tragically self-extinguish.

The first proof of that was when, in December 1980, I read that Darby Crash of The Germs had died. The Germs' singles and their one, full-length album, *G.I.*, was music from a different place. From then to now I have never heard anything like it. Crash's death, which I knew nothing about more than what scant information I was able to find, made sense. There was a haunting finality to the *G.I.* album. The nine-minute song that closes out the record, "Shut Down," is the sound of a cold, dark, solitary walk into the abyss. How could the band have followed up? What could Crash have done next other than die? As upsetting as it was, it all made some kind of Rimbaudian sense. Mind you, this is all being contemplated from thousands of miles away, having no contact or context from which to draw from.

So when I finally arrived in Los Angeles with a duffel bag and about $200, I immediately realized I was going to have to make some adjustments.

The differences between what I was raised in and what I entered into were profound and changed the way I thought about the world.

I came from a music scene that was small enough to fit into a small to medium-sized venue. There were a handful of bands and a few record stores. There wasn't much interest in this different music on local radio, and the local press largely ignored or insulted it.

Los Angeles, on the other hand was an independent music boomtown. There were bands all over and venues for them to play in. There would be multiple shows in the city on any given night, and every one of them would be packed. There was Rodney Bingenheimer and his longstanding show on KROQ, which was a great messenger for music and information.

It was, for me, an overload. Beyond the abundant music, youth culture in Los Angeles and the surrounding areas, at least in the music scene I found myself in was something else entirely, and I found myself all but totally unprepared to deal with it.

I fairly radiated naïveté. I was a walking billboard for it. I remember, weeks after arriving, stupidly asking a teenager why he wasn't in school. He thought that was hilarious and informed me that he dropped out somewhere in early high school and had run away to Los Angeles. Again, another wide-eyed question about where he would sleep that night, resulting in more laughter. I had been out of my all-boys prep-school uniform for a little over two years, but it might as well have been two minutes. It was in Los Angeles, in the second half of 1981, where I started to learn the ways of the world.

This world that I am telling you about existed almost completely disconnected from the "real" one of the citizens. With no exaggeration, I can tell you that I was surrounded

by people who did drugs (the kind that kill you), committed crimes of all kinds, perpetrated deeds of life-changing violence with a casualness that was truly terrifying. One time, sitting on a bench at Oki-Dog, where Fatburger is now, at Gardner and Santa Monica Blvd., I saw a man walk by, heading east on Santa Monica, seemingly oblivious to the loquacious din we were making. Two guys at a table near me stand up at the same time, peel off from the crowd, and fall in behind the guy. It was obvious they were going to roll him. It was the seeming ease and confidence with which they made their move that was troubling—they were not new at this. They returned awhile later, laughing. They had indeed robbed the guy. It was no big deal. Around that time I had heard that a young girl's body had been found at the site of Errol Flynn's mansion, a popular party spot. Apparently it was a suicide. Right after I heard that, a woman told me how she had scored the drugs the girl had used and actually helped her kill herself by getting her to drink a large quantity of milk to make sure she choked if she happened to vomit. She laughed as she said this. I am willing to bet that if you were to talk to other people who were in this scene at this time, they might have a story or two like this.

Although it never once appealed to me nor did I ever feel remotely a part of it, it was more than fascinating. If your parents ever warned you about the big bad world, I don't think they really had much idea of what they were talking about; they just wanted you to be careful and get through in one piece. What they thought they were speaking to with authority was quaint and anemic compared to where I was. Generationally they simply had nothing with which to compare.

What I noticed immediately upon arrival was the influence of "Hollywood" and the culture of Southern California in the Los Angeles punk scene. There was an aspect of glamour and understated confidence that was James Dean–esque. Many of the males worked on their rugged, heroic looks with almost aspiring-model earnestness, and the ubiquitous beauty of the females was more than just the observational hunger of my youth—these were really good-looking young people. Many of them seemed as ready for their close-up as they were to go to the next show. I am in no way trying to imply that these were lightweight scenesters, but the fact that so many of them were so cosmetically evolved gave the overall scene an attraction that could not be denied. I think this was one of the things that made the LAPD hate punks and assault them with regularity. It is also why this time period is so well documented by local photographers; it was an irresistibly photogenic happening that was going to be over almost as quickly as it started.

As far as I knew, this was a very insular scene. X had come to the East Coast to critical acclaim, and The Dickies had made it there as well but canceled their Washington, DC, show. Beyond that, all these bands existed in fanzines and cassettes of Rodney Bingenheimer's radio show, dull sounding and off pitch due to multiple duplications. From the outside it seemed like a scene that wasn't driven by ambition or financial gain but capturing the moment whenever possible. Just listening to live tapes from the legendary Masque Club, you can hear the reverie and minute-to-minute discovery, especially in the recordings of The Screamers.

When I arrived in the summer of 1981 I couldn't figure out if something new had taken the place of what had so

recently transpired and deconstructed, or if this was the moment before the next thing was about to happen.

One thing was undeniable: the level of drug abuse in the scene was toxic. The scene was teeming with danger and die-young vigor but seemed devoid of any motivation, purpose, or intellectual/artistic content. What I saw made me conclude that it was a scene full of beautiful young people trying to off themselves. I never thought myself any better, but my inability to understand things in a larger context alienated me almost completely.

The cultish isolation of Black Flag soon separated me geographically from the LA scene as we soon relocated to Redondo Beach, where the band had its roots.

It was only several miles down the 405, but it felt like we were a world away. Occasionally we would go into Hollywood to see a show and felt the "you're not from around here, are you, son?" sneer. I remember seeing members of these Masque-era bands at shows. For me it was being in the same room as the legends from my record collection. I met a few of them, but it didn't go very well, so I left them alone.

Black Flag founders Greg Ginn and Chuck Dukowski had a label called SST Records. They were ambitious and driven as any two people I have ever met. The label released not only Black Flag's recorded output, soon-to-be quite prolific, but also the work of other bands like The Minutemen and Saccharine Trust. They had no interest in remaining local; they were looking to get as far into the world as possible.

I can only speak for myself, but I thought our method was not to write some kind of hit but, through a rapid release schedule and relentless touring, to conquer by sheer ubiquity. This approach takes all you can give to it and is rife

with confusing, ironic twists. For me it made the concept of success, beyond a severely defined idea of artistic truth and unrestrained fury against any and all who sought to neutralize us, to be repellent. So if the goal is to do the work as you see fit, any slings and arrows that may come are as much a part of it as anything else.

Whether real or imagined, we considered ourselves in opposition to almost everything and everyone. The artwork on the album covers and flyers was specifically meant to upset and provoke. At times I thought we were so extreme, we didn't want to have an audience at all.

As a result of our actions, we existed in a world of high contrast. We were rarely considered less than in the extreme. We studiously sought to obliterate the middle ground.

Within a few months of joining Black Flag and moving to Los Angeles, I spent most of the year on the road on tours that lasted months. We would return to Southern California primarily to record so we could leave again. Although the stays were longer, California became a state that was one of many I frequented. In a strange way I became the quintessential American, meeting people from all over the country, month after month, year after year.

Between tours I would visit Los Angeles in a series of brief jump cuts. I would find out what happened to some of the people I had met when I first arrived. There were deaths from overdoses and suicides, stints of incarceration, and other bad news. I noticed that there seemed to be a lot of heroin going around. I found out that it was plentiful as it was potent and cheap. At that time, I had never heard of Hoover's COINTELPRO efforts, but it seemed obvious to me that these people had been targeted in a campaign to clean things up, perhaps for the upcoming Olympic Games.

I identify with Los Angeles through the filter of music. It's the city that was as immortalized and defined by The Doors' keyboard-driven, poetic nihilism and X's first album as any industry, innovation, or event.

I have often referred to Los Angeles as "the stucco-coated killing field," and in a way, that's true, but you have to live here to die here. That is to say, there are no babes in these woods.

CHAPTER 15

When It Came to Drugs

by John Doe

When it came to drugs, the possibilities were endless. There was a "war on drugs," but bikers still made crank the old-fashioned way, not w/ bullshit cold pills; acid could still have some actual LSD in it; East LA had a solid supply of heroin & MDA & you didn't get AIDS from sharing needles. As dedicated bohemians, it was practically our duty to seek & find the other side of consciousness & break the rules of society along the way.

Of course, the most available drugs were alcohol & tobacco & we couldn't get enough of them. Among our immediate group, Camel filters & Marlboros were king & queen. An occasional Winston smoker might come along. Some who imagined they were hardened criminals went for Camel straights or god-awful Gauloises (I'll admit to a brief fling w/ the French cigarette until I came to my senses) & for the less hardcore Marlboro Lights had recently come on the scene. A haze of light blue smoke filtered every room & gig where more than a few people gathered. It was common

to fill & empty ashtrays several times throughout the night, have giant tin cans, crush out the butts on the floor or find that you had two cigs burning at the same time. The menthol craze came later when Kool Filter Kings made us feel like we had something in common w/ the culture of South Central LA.

Where the beer came from is lost to history. But there was never a lack of it until the corner convenience/liquor store closed at 1:30 or 2 a.m. Los Angeles had any number of cheap & "relatively" good beers—Eastside, Brew 102, Lucky X Lager (which had rebus puzzles inside the bottle caps) or Mickey's Big Mouth. Everyone had a short but meaningful relationship w/ Mickey's (fortified but not as nasty as Colt 45, etc.), up until the morning after, when everything smelled like skunk. And cleaning up the almost-full, forgotten bottles made you run to the bathroom retching. Gin was popular for its psychedelic effect. The fast gin fizz—Nehi strawberry soda and Gordon's gin—invented by Farrah Fawcett Minor, broke more than a couple lamps, coffee tables, hearts & relationships. We had yet to discover all the great dive bars in LA since we were too broke & busy hanging out in each others' apartments or gigs.

Everyone wanted to go fast because everything around us was going fast. Stories of beatniks & Hells Angels staying up all night, inventing who knows what, fueled our desire to "break on through to the other side." We had made a deal to break free of all the societal bullshit that sitcoms & The Eagles had told us was reality. Cocaine was too bourgeoisie & expensive. Pot was for hippies. Vicks inhalers no longer contained Benzedrine, but Black Beauties or White Crosses could be crushed up & snorted if you took out the annoying time-released dark flecks. Though it wasn't very reliable,

biker crank came around often enough to push several nights into insanity. Driving to or from San Francisco didn't seem to take as long while you talked a mile a minute. In Venice, Cal, I remember Claude Bessy shooting me up w/ a tiny amount of high-grade speed & then I watched the entire world bend into slow motion just before launching into hyperdrive. I believe I played, very badly, w/ Top Jimmy that night & my jaw ached so bad the day after, I vowed no more shooting that shit—too much.

So there we all were, breaking the law, doing our duty as outlaws. What's a little heroin to really see what hardcore drug use is like? Insidious as always, King Heroin sneaked onto the scene while most people were having a wild time drinking, creating, partying & generally carrying on. Some of us older ones had seen the damage done, maybe tried it but never got serious about it. For those who didn't get sucked into the dark well of dreams, it was only a side trip. But more & more people disappeared into their apartments only to emerge skinnier & stranger. It was clear to most of us who had something they wanted to accomplish that heroin was nothing but an edge to peer over, smile, nod & climb back to the faster pace of what was really happening: a punk-rock revolution. But the unsuspecting, unlucky ones got swirled into a toilet bowl of nodding, floating & talking about what they were going to do tomorrow. It amazed me how some people continued as serious users & creative artists, but that was usually short-lived. People started dying, first in SF then in LA, and suddenly it was no longer about breaking loose to see the other side. They were full-blown addicts, truly outside the law & lost to the rest of us.

CHAPTER 16

Punk as a Young Adult

by Chris D.

Set with the task of writing this, I had to ask myself what *really* is punk rock? It seems to be something very different to different people, depending on whom you ask. To me it is doing your music, art, or writing exactly as prescribed by what feels right inside of you. Because it was and still is to some extent tied to youth or youthful feelings, many of the sentiments expressed are by way of channeling all sorts of unfocused anger through a prism—defiance of authority and the status quo. And, to paraphrase Joe Strummer, it is not accepting bullshit for an answer; it is about truth. Telling it as well as hearing it. For me, carrying over from pre-punk and proto-punk icons like Jim Morrison, David Bowie, Lou Reed, Patti Smith, and Iggy Pop, it is also about sexual politics, trying to determine what love between two people truly represents. John and Exene from X and Jeffrey Lee Pierce from The Gun Club were on a very similar wavelength. X's song "The World's a Mess (It's in My Kiss)"—just the title alone—is a perfect illustration of this.

FLESH EATERS

GUN CLUB

MARCH 1
SUNDAY
NINE PM
CATHAY
de
GRANDE
(SELMA + ARGYLE
$3.00

Since I started writing poetry before making music in my bands, The Flesh Eaters and Divine Horsemen, my focus was initially on the song lyrics. And poetry is how I got involved writing record and live reviews for *Slash* magazine, submitting poems for consideration. *Slash* did *not* do poetry. Philomena Winstanley, co-editor of *Slash* along with Claude "Kickboy" Bessy, liked the writing enough, though, to solicit record reviews from me. Thus my first, an appraisal of Iggy and the Stooges' "I Got a Right/Gimme Some Skin," appeared in the third issue, the one with Johnny Rotten on the cover. A plethora of reviews followed in subsequent issues, under my own name, Chris D., as well as a variety of pseudonyms, including Half-Cocked, Mr. OK, and Bob Clone. I met other *Slash*-ites in due course, opinionated (and often very funny) scribes like Allen "Basho Macko" McDonnell, Ranking Jeffrey Lee (aka Jeffrey Lee Pierce), Will Amato, and Pleasant Gehman.

During the summer of 1977 I'd succeeded in making a mess of my personal life, with my first marriage disintegrating due to chronic infidelity. I had just finished grad school, getting an MFA in communication arts (in screenwriting). Life should have been roiling with promising possibilities, but I, in retrospect, could not navigate into some filmmaking harbor. I was and still am socially inept—a perfect recipe for involvement in punk rock. Networking with fellow grad students or show business contacts made through college at Loyola Marymount University should have been a piece of cake. But there was no one I had met to whom I felt connected, at least in filmmaking circles. The new music scene was another story, however. Through my connection with *Slash* magazine, I was going out to punk-rock shows at places like the Masque and one-off shows at galleries and

lofts three or four nights a week, minimum. I was meeting like-minded people, many of whom were musicians themselves. My long-held second love, being in a rock group, was raising its unruly head.

Coincidentally I had just landed a job teaching English at a private high school on the border between Westchester and Inglewood near LAX. On weekends it was a synagogue school, but during the week it was rented out to a middle-aged couple who apparently held some kind of charter for private education. The principal, whom I admired for his tenacity in the face of overwhelming odds against him, was morbidly obese and, when I met him, was already paralyzed on his right side. I had my long locks of hair shorn, needing to do this for the job as well as figuring I'd fit in better with all the punk-rock kids inhabiting my night life.

Newly separated—yet again—from my first wife, I was living in an apartment on Venice Boulevard across from the old abandoned police station (or was it the defunct city hall?) John Carpenter had used a few years before as a location for his exploitation action tribute to director Howard Hawks, *Assault on Precinct 13*.

Living in the apartment was a mixed bag. I was afflicted with an upstairs neighbor who did not appreciate me playing at full volume on my 1970 vintage Spectrasonic solid-state stereo The Stooges' LPs *Funhouse* or *Raw Power* or miscellaneous singles I needed to review for *Slash*. I remember him calling my landlord at least twice rather than calling me first as I had requested.

I was convinced something awful had happened in the apartment in the past. It was 1950s (if not '40s) vintage and had a long catalogue of tenants tromping on its hardwood floors. Abetting the uneasiness was my separation from my

estranged spouse, which had left me with a Spartan collection of secondhand furniture: one large antique dining table, a red leather-upholstered easy chair, my stereo (in the living room), one basic double bed with no bedstead accoutrements (in the master bedroom), three cinderblock bookcases filled with vintage pulp crime and science fiction paperbacks, a crappy black-and-white TV, and a mattress on the floor (in the second "guest" room). I had at least two ghostly experiences while living there, one seemingly so genuine—waking up in the middle of the night feeling as if something invisible was latched onto my chest, trying to suck out my soul—that I, still to this day, feel it was the real thing. Then again, I was smoking a lot of pot as well as drinking heavily in those days, so I suppose this experience could have been self-generated.

Claude and Philomena lived on Speedway in Venice, and Allen "Basho Macko" McDonnell and his then-wife, Delphina, lived off Rose Avenue. Sometimes various combinations of us would share rides to shows in Hollywood.

I remember driving my 1969 Ford Falcon all the way down east on Venice Boulevard to La Brea, then north to where it split off onto Highland, homing in on the Masque on Cherokee in the basement of the Pussycat Theater on Hollywood Boulevard, homing in on it like a beacon of gravel-pitted, concrete-blocked, acne-scarred depravity.

At the time, a block south, on Selma Avenue (spanning east-west) was a notorious cruising area for gay hustlers. The Gold Cup on Las Palmas and Hollywood was a tiny coffee shop and covert hangout for "chicken hawks" (older men interested in young teen boys), immortalized in song by Black Randy and the Metro Squad and as a band name by Arthur J. and the Gold Cups.

Often I would drive drunk, with a pint of Kamchatka, Jack Daniel's, I.W. Harper, or a bottle of Pabst Blue Ribbon at my feet. It is a miracle I was never arrested for a DUI.

The first show I remember seeing at the Masque was The Bags and a short-lived combo called The Spastics. On subsequent nights I caught The Skulls, The Eyes, X (every time they played), The Dils, The Germs, The Screamers, The Weirdos, The Alley Cats (nearly every time they played), The Deadbeats, Arthur J. and the Gold Cups, The Zeros, so many others. My memories of these shows all blend together. They were fun, they were chaotic, they were exhilarating, and they were sometimes scary and sometimes boring. Though I was in the process of separating from my wife, Bonnie, she still accompanied me to some of these early shows. She shared my interest in the scene, but things were uneasy between us, and I had already met someone who would take her place as 1977 gave way to 1978.

I had started to take tentative steps trying to put a band together—I'm not sure when, I believe it was as early as that past summer. Our first rehearsal was at DJ Bonebrake's house out in the Valley. DJ was a friend of Joe Ramirez, as DJ was also drummer for The Eyes, and Joe, who was The Eyes' singer-guitarist, was also playing drums for me. John Richey was on bass, and Bob Grasso, a crazy jokester of a friend of mine from college, played guitar. Bob only lasted that first rehearsal, and soon Tito Larriva, who was starting his own band The Plugz, replaced him. The Masque had rehearsal rooms as well as their main performance area, and we started to rehearse there. It was ratty, cold, and ill lit. I don't remember the rooms having PAs, and if I'm not mistaken, I think I sang my vocals through an extra Fender Twin guitar amp.

On the job front, halfway through that autumn semester the principal, Mr. H, had another stroke and went into the hospital and died. He was a master disciplinarian, despite his infirmities, but when his wife took over, all hell broke loose. There were several borderline criminal kids in the school, and Mrs. H, wanting to be everyone's friend as opposed to an authority figure, let them get away with all kinds of outrageous shenanigans. I drew the line at letting the kids roll joints in class, and I gradually became known by a handful of them as the killjoy pariah. By the end of the first week of January 1978, I was history. My eleventh-grade class, composed of mostly A- and B-grade African American female students, was sad to see me go. But four or five of my male nemeses in the tenth grade threw rocks at my car as I made my final exit.

By that time The Flesh Eaters had already made their debut at the Masque on December 23, 1977, opening for The Dickies, The Nuns, and The Eyes. This was the last Masque show I went to with my wife.

The official nail in the coffin of my marriage was divorce papers in the mail, but before that a more potent declaration came with Bonnie's father arriving in a truck by himself to pick up the big double bed that technically belonged to them. Bonnie's father was a tall, rangy self-made millionaire, a poor guy with a gravelly voice from the Mississippi hill country who married a senator's daughter (really) but made his fortune while doing research at Lockheed, inventing on the side, with his business partner, one of the early versions of Krazy Glue. I was always grateful to him for not thrashing me within an inch of my life for the way I'd treated his daughter.

By this time I was a week or two away from moving to new digs in Hollywood on Fairfax between Willoughby and Waring.

When I finally arrived in Hollywood I was already on the first of many "outs" in my new relationship with Judith Bell (soon to become an artistic collaborator), which made it awkward, as she was close friends with the three gay tenants who shared two of the other apartments. The fourth apartment, the one right above me, was inhabited by a scary, very cranky Korean War vet everyone had nicknamed Lurch. Lurch was a handyman and seemed perpetually drunk. I was soon to torment Lurch—unintentionally—on a nearly daily basis with my stereo cranked high.

At first I had virtually no furniture except for the mattress on the floor in the bedroom and the stereo and red leather-upholstered easy chair in the living room. I remember falling asleep on the living room floor that first night there, cold winds howling outside down the narrow driveway alley (the apartment building was set back from the street, located behind a kitchen cabinets shop run by the landlord.) I was slightly drunk and in a funk, using my father's rolled up WW2 sleeping bag as a pillow while I drifted in and out of consciousness.

Judith and I were soon back on good terms, and we could be found at the Masque at least twice a week and sometimes at the house and rehearsals of our new friends, John and Exene, of the band X.

Judith also wrote for *Slash* mag, and I can best describe the newsprint tabloid as a unifying force, something that inspired people and spawned other homemade, Xeroxed fanzines (Judith and I even had a two-issue enterprise called the *Upsetter* that featured all kinds of detritus, including interviews with bands like The Germs, The Bags, The Dils, X, and irreverent graphics spoofing various trendy fashions and music styles popping up in the subterranean

subculture). I've mentioned Claude and Philly, who tended to the editorial content (i.e., verbiage) of *Slash* mag, but two other people, artist and graphic designer Steve Samiof and photographer Melanie Nissen, were responsible for the iconographic masthead and striking visuals, aided and abetted by soon-to-be-legendary artists like Gary Panter, best remembered for his back-page comic strip about the super, subhuman punk Jimbo as well as the *Slash* mag logo that replaced the beautifully executed initial dripping blood one after thirteen or so issues.

Melanie Nissen remembers, "Steve and I used to put the mag together, paste it up—this was before computers, of course—out of our dining room or bedroom, wherever we were living. Steve had seen some newspaper stories about what was going on in London and said, 'Hey, why don't we do a magazine about this?' It was never about money. So in the beginning it was just Steve and I and Claude and Philly." Were there ever any problems with the printer about content? "Oh, no. They didn't care. Who knows if they even really looked at it. We just found the cheapest place we could. It was way out in the Valley, kind of funky. But we were just happy to get it printed every month. You know, it was a really special time. There was no one around to tell us, 'You can't do that.' We were young and didn't have all that crap in our heads yet, you know? I think that was one of the most special things about it." Midway through *Slash* magazine's lifespan Steve and Melanie and Claude and Philly got to move into a real office on the southwest corner of Santa Monica and Fairfax.

This DIY spirit Melanie mentioned was crucial to the scene, and I don't think one can overestimate *Slash* magazine's ripple effect on, at first, dozens, then hundreds of

little mini-scenes on the punk front that carried on the torch to new, sometimes seemingly incongruous frontiers. There were other newsprint tabloids and magazines too, such as Bruce Kalberg's *No Mag* (with its emphasis on avant-garde art as well as punk), Hudley and Al's *Flipside* (with its egalitarian participation of band and audience members alike), Greg Shaw's *Bomp* magazine (with its catholic taste running the gamut from punk to power pop), and the pioneering *Back Door Man* (1975!) with such alumni as Don Waller, Phast Phreddie Patterson, and D. D. Faye, all making an impact along with *Slash*. Other mags like San Francisco's *Search and Destroy* and, from the East Coast, *New York Rocker* (edited by swell guy Andy Schwartz) and *Boston Rock* were also influential. Surprisingly, too, enormously significant UK rags like *Melody Maker*, *Sounds*, and *New Musical Express* could be found on many local Hollywood newsstands as well as at hip record stores, and they had their own collision of styles and tastes rubbing off on the local scene.

Slash was relatively successful, considering the competition it was up against on magazine racks, in record stores and newsstands across the country. Not that people got paid, but it always seemed that the magazine was able to secure advertising from various major record labels looking to hawk their "new wave" acts as well as the smaller indies who were promoting the "real thing," thus breaking even.

I started recording various versions of the initial Flesh Eaters songs at Randy Stodola of The Alley Cats' house down in Lomita. I believe it was in January 1978. He had a four-track recorder. It may have been low-tech, but Randy was a whiz with that four-track. Shortly after the first session of three songs, we lost guitarist Tito Larriva, who gravitated to devote his full time to his own band, The Plugz. Following

his departure, Stan Ridgway (later of Wall of Voodoo) joined the band for a couple of months. Finally, around the beginning of the summer, I was back to square one and, despairing of ever holding a semipermanent lineup together, I asked another local trio, The Fly Boys, who were a bit more pop flavored, if they'd join me for a limited time, backing me on a four-song 7" EP and doing a few shows. Thus, the first Flesh Eaters recordings, once again recorded at Randy's, were unleashed on my own label, Upsetter Records.

One of my most vivid memories I have is of how cold and windy it was on the autumn and winter nights of 1978. I had one of those bronchial coughs that wouldn't go away. Partially surviving on unemployment and the largesse of my parents, I was getting to devote most of my time to writing for *Slash* and making music. I got a job in the tape library of Century City's CBS Records HQ in late 1978 through a temp agency Judith worked for, and I toiled away in the salt mines of their master vault, carting around multitracks of artists like Barbra Streisand and Toto. I always resisted some of my friends' suggestions to toss a couple of magnets into select boxes of analog twenty-four-track tapes.

The year 1979 saw the genesis of *Tooth and Nail*, one of the first—if not *the* first—Los Angeles punk compilation LPs, along with Dangerhouse's *Yes L.A.* one-sided album. I must give credit to Judith for really being a prime moving force behind making *Tooth and Nail* happen. I can't remember who came up with the title for the compilation, but she secured the financing from Rocky Stevens, a gay Oklahoma millionaire who was a friend and loved punk rock. It's hard to believe we did the whole thing—the recording and mixing, the pressing and manufacturing—for so little. Still, no one made any money beyond breaking even. Of course,

looking back on it now, some of the recordings don't live up to the more polished productions coming out of London or even local labels Dangerhouse or Posh Boy. Selection of the bands was partly based on who were our friends and also who we felt deserved exposure and hadn't gotten their share yet. In a classic example of DIY self-interest, that included my current lineup of The Flesh Eaters. Originally X was also scheduled to be included, but after their experience with Dangerhouse, guitarist Billy Zoom nixed any more involvement with small indie labels, including us, choosing to wait for a bigger label to take notice. Exene stayed tangentially involved, codesigning the *Tooth and Nail* record labels with Judith. The Controllers, Middle Class, and The Germs were all Southern California bands, and Negative Trend and UXA were originally from San Francisco. Negative Trend was the only band with previously recorded material, and their inclusion was heavily influenced by the presence of their then new vocalist, Rik L Rik. I was a big fan of Rik's previous aggregation, F-Word.

By late 1979 I had a part-time job with *Slash* magazine at their new offices on Beverly and Martel, working as circulation manager in the downstairs storeroom. Current and back issues of *Slash* resided in organized heaps on the dirty linoleum floor. Upstairs, in addition to housing the new studio for laying out the templates for the tabloid's printing, Bob Biggs had taken over financial and creative control of the fledgling Slash Records. Slash had already released a single by The Plugz and a 7" EP by The Germs, and Slash's first album, *The Germs (G.I.)*, produced by Joan Jett, was about to be released.

I wound up my tenure at CBS Records' tape library around the same time. I remember giving a copy of The Flesh Eaters'

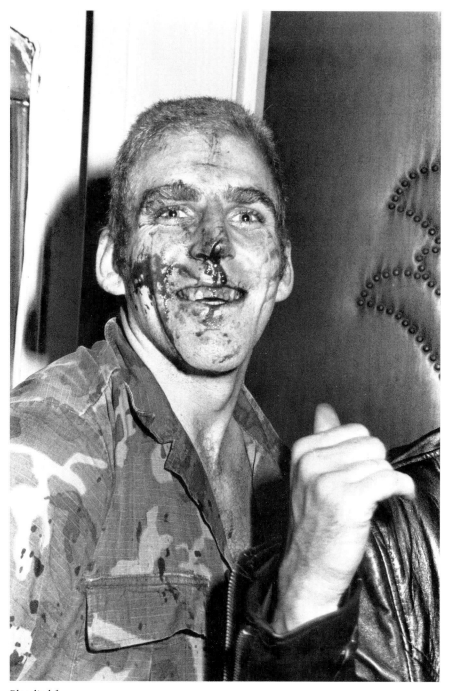

Bloodied fan

Top Jimmy and Luci Diehl wedding, 1981 (from L-R): Luci Diehl, John Pochna, Top Jimmy, Exene, Lydia Ortiz, Junco, unknown, Dig the Pig, Chris D., the rest all unknown, John Doe at lower right

The Alley Cats backstage (from L-R): John McCarthy, Dianne Chai, Randy Stodola

Gina Schock and Jane Wiedlin from The Go-Go's

Chris Morris and Phil Alvin at the Zero Zero

From L-R: David Hidalgo, unknown, Cesar Rosas, Michael Wilcox, unknown, Bruce Barf, Dave Alvin, Conrad Lozano

Hardcore Invasion

effrey Lee Pierce and Texacala Jones at the Whisky, 1981

Luci Diehl and Gerber

LAPD's finest

Darby and Exene, Slash Records rooftop

John Denney of The Weirdos meets LA's finest

The Zeros in another rented hall, 1979 (from L-R): Hector Penalosa, Javier
Escovedo

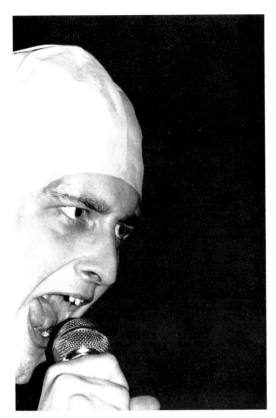

Black Randy at the Whisky

The Weirdos being shut down at Larchmont Hall, 1979 (from L-R): Dix Denney, Nickey Beat, Dave Trout, Cliff Roman (obscured from view), John Denney

Dinky and D. J. Bonebreak at the Starwood, 1980

LA Line-up, West Hollywood, 1977 (from L-R): unknown, Hellin Killer, Trudi, Pleasant Gehman, Bobby Pin, Nickey Beat, Alice Bag, Delphina, Lorna Doom, Pat Smear, Jena

Welcome to Los Angeles, 1977 (from L-R): John Doe, Rand McNally, Exene, Black Randy at the Palladium-Punk fashion show

The Zeros, San Francisco, 1977 (from L-R): Robert Lopez, Baba Chenelle, Hector Penalosa, Javier Escovedo, Hellin Killer

The Adolescents' Tony Cadena in his backyard in Fullerton, CA, 1982

Pat and Alice Bag at the Hong Kong Café, 1979

The Plugz (from L-R): Chalo Quintana, Tito Larriva, Tony Marsico

Circle Jerks at the Country Club in Reseda, CA, 1982 (from L-R): Keith Morris, Greg Hetson, Roger Rogerson

Tito Larriva of The Plugz at the East LA studio of graphic artist Richard Duardo, 1979

John and Exene post-show, Troubadour

EP to an A&R secretary I knew on the sixth floor, which was largely Epic Records label turf. She was nice and cool, but I honestly didn't think it was going to be her cup of tea. Then again, she was familiar with The Clash's *Give 'Em Enough Rope* and *London Calling*, both of them on Epic. I never did find out what she thought before I left. A weird memory from that job: at one point a few people in the building had tested positive for hepatitis B, and gamma globulin shots were pretty much mandated by a temporary medical station in the big boardroom off the downstairs lobby for everyone before leaving work for the day. Strange.

At *Slash*, down in the first-floor vault (or, once again, in less glamorous terminology, storeroom), I toiled going through the binder with the circulation sheets, a notebook with the accounts of every newsstand, record store, and bookstore that carried *Slash* magazine in the United States. I took out the required number of copies (usually five, ten, fifteen, at most twenty) of the current issue from the piled stacks, rolled them up, and wrapped them in plain brown paper. Once the orders were filled, the oblong parcels went flying out to their far-flung destinations on successive trips to the local post office on Beverly Boulevard and Spaulding. In the coming years those piled heaps of mags would gradually be replaced by columns of boxes of Slash Records releases (promotional copies and what-have-you). For a brief period—I think in 1982 or 1983—the storeroom, because it had a bathroom, even played host to a couple of band members of Aussie garage kings The Lipstick Killers, who took over my stockroom job once I'd been kicked upstairs.

No Questions Asked, the first Flesh Eaters album, was recorded in a real mix-and-match mode of personnel all through the beginning of 1980. Released on Upsetter Records

the same year, it was written up, along with *The Germs (G.I.)* LP, by Richard Meltzer in his infamous "blabbermouth lockjaw of the soul" review in the *Village Voice*. But *No Questions Asked* was dwarfed, as were so many other Los Angeles band releases at the time, by Slash Records' second album out, *Los Angeles*, X's debut LP. The production and material (already familiar to X's live audience) was startling not only in its competitive professionalism but also in its uncompromising attitude and lyrical imagery. One could hear distant echoes of other past California bands in the vocals and melodies (e.g., The Doors and Jefferson Airplane), yet it blazed new territory by incorporating the hard edge of the UK's Sex Pistols and The Clash as well as the chaotic, bourbon-fueled rockabilly swirl (on heavy metal steroids) of such artists as Billy Lee Riley, Hasil Adkins, and even Johnny Cash.

I don't remember the exact date, but somewhere in, I think, the spring of 1980, Bob Biggs hired me as his third employee at the record company, nominally an A&R rep for the label. There was always a creative tension between Biggs and I, and it gradually escalated through my term there, from 1980 through the last months in the spring of 1984. But I'm getting a bit ahead of myself. More on that later.

The magazine was still going, and as Steve and Melanie became less involved with the production side, I spent almost every other day running to the photography place over on the corner of Curson and Wilshire Blvd where they shot the halftones and line shots for our photographs and artwork that would end up in paste-up. You must remember this was before computers, before Photoshop and the advent of such futuristic inventions as JPEGs and desktop publishing.

In some respects I've felt the need to render everything here in this chapter in as chronological a fashion as possible, but I think with the remainder I'm going to have to break it up into a scattered mosaic jumping back and forth in time.

Slash magazine's days were numbered, what with the crush of the new record label and the diffusion of energy from contributors getting involved in various other creative endeavors. The last issue went out with a bang near the end of 1980, and it was the closest we got to a "slick" publication, with staples (instead of folded layers) and approximately twice as many pages. Judith and I were still reviewing singles, LPs, and live events, but we also conducted a mammoth interview with Hollywood maverick director Sam Fuller (*Pickup on South Street, Shock Corridor, The Naked Kiss*), who was just gearing up for release of one of his final films, a magnum opus about his military exploits in WW2 in the invasion of Sicily and, much farther north, liberation of a concentration camp, called *The Big Red One*. It was one of the longest and best interviews we had done for the mag.

Late in the year I began readying the material for a different kind of album as The Flesh Eaters' second LP. I was fortunate enough to corral friends John Doe and DJ Bonebrake of X, Dave Alvin and Bill Bateman from The Blasters, and Steve Berlin from Top Jimmy and the Rhythm Pigs (who would go on to join Los Lobos) into a lineup for an eight-song extravaganza, a mélange of seventies-style garage band punk, Link Wray–meets–Bo Diddley rhythm and blues, and African roots music. The lyrics were French symbolist-inspired mixed with voodoo-hoodoo/tragic country blended with imagery from transgressive cinema. The title, *A Minute to Pray, A Second to Die*, was also the moniker of a favorite spaghetti western from the sixties. Recorded in January of

1981, this was a prime example of the kind of fruitful creative DIY tension that was starting to rear its head between honcho Bob Biggs and me. Rather than bring out the unique effort on Slash, Bob decided to generate a subsidiary label called Ruby Records that would be primarily, though not exclusively, my province. *A Minute to Pray, A Second to Die* was released in the spring of 1981, right around the same time as X's second celebrated effort with Slash, *Wild Gift*. Things were moving fast with the labels, and many of the events, gigs, and releases tend to blur together in my memory, partly no doubt to a haze of incipient alcoholism.

The creative tension of working at Slash was a challenge and sometimes frustrating experience for someone like me who was and is, to this day, still a basically impatient person. Robin Weiss, Bob Biggs's secretary and Slash receptionist, and I were good friends with Jeffrey Lee Pierce and were fierce champions of the material he was starting to demo under the band name The Gun Club. It took months for Robin and I to whittle down Bob's resistance, playing for him the songs Jeffrey had already recorded with producer Tito Larriva to get him to agree to finance a second outing in the studio with me producing to complete a releasable LP. Finally, in the late summer of 1981, The Gun Club's debut album, *Fire of Love*, was unleashed to universal acclaim.

About the same time when *Fire of Love* was accumulating accolades, The Blasters were preparing their first phenomenal Slash record (they'd already had one LP, *American Music*, released by rockabilly label Rollin' Rock). Their newest album was so well received, it cracked *Time* magazine's Top Ten albums of 1981 and peaked at number thirty-six on *Billboard*'s charts. This was something unheard of for an indie punk-rock label, and along with X's success, it was a major

impetus in getting Slash Records picked up for distribution by Warner Brothers.

Simultaneously I was putting together a new lineup of The Flesh Eaters. This was going to be a slightly smaller unit and, as it turns out, have a bit different dynamic as far as composing the music. Don Kirk on guitar, Robyn Jameson on bass, Chris Wahl on drums, Steve Berlin on saxes (on the recordings only), Jill Jordan on backing vocals, and I recorded The Flesh Eaters' third album, *Forever Came Today*, on St. Valentine's Day in 1982. Once again we did the tracks at Quad Teck, engineered by Pat Burnette (whose father was country star Dorsey Burnette) on 6th Street, just two blocks west of Western Avenue. All of *The Germs (G.I.)*, all of *A Minute to Pray*, and roughly half of *Fire of Love* were also recorded there, and so was The Dream Syndicate's *Days of Wine and Roses* and Green on Red's *Gravity Talks*, both still to come in 1982 and 1983, respectively. The studio is now long gone.

Perhaps this is a good place to wind down my saga in some closing paragraphs.

Things were becoming increasingly clique-ish. A huge party thrown near the close of 1981 in Slash's upstairs lobby was the first scrawl of that writing on the wall. Or maybe it was just me being uptight. I remember having to throw Derf Scratch from Fear and John Belushi out of my office because I didn't appreciate them closing the door and snorting coke off my desk. There was a grassroots Hollywood-doing-music-business-as-usual vibe that was very gradually, almost imperceptibly creeping in—and I was intent on ignoring it as long as possible.

There were personal disappointments along the way during those years, nothing too big on its own, but the number of small setbacks at Slash had a cumulative effect on my morale.

Some of this, to be fair to Bob Biggs, was self-generated by my two-margarita-doubles-a-day for lunch. In general, I felt no one at the label—except for maybe friend and publicist Susan Clary (who had her office next to mine)—was on the same wavelength. Sometimes I felt we had our own little separate cabal there sequestered across the large entry hall. I increasingly had to fight for the bands I wanted to produce and release on subsidiary Ruby Records. My friends in X and The Blasters were constantly on tour. X decamped for a major label, Elektra. When it came to re-sign on either Slash or Ruby, both The Gun Club and The Dream Syndicate declined, opting for major label deals. It was nothing personal, but you know how that goes. Fear and Los Lobos came on board, but though I thought they were super-great, I didn't really connect in the same way with them on a personal level as I did with X and The Blasters. Other bands that I didn't care for, like The Violent Femmes, got signed. A group I really fought to get signed, Boston's The Neats, did not pass muster with Biggs. I was also having diverging inner conflicts between my ambitions at Slash and my vision for my band, The Flesh Eaters. Many times after returning from lunch, around three in the afternoon, I quietly closed the door to my office and lay my head down on the desk.

One thing, though, that changed all of us early on—a rite of passage, a coming of age, shedding any last vestiges of youthful illusion giving way to full-blown adulthood—happened in the spring of 1980. Exene's sister, Mirielle (aka Mary Katherine) and her husband, Gordon Stevenson, had come to town from New York City to promote and screen *Ecstatic Stigmatic*, an indie underground feature they had made. Gordon had written and directed it; Mirielle had starred. Mirielle and Gordon along with a number of other

mutual friends down from San Francisco were staying at my apartment on Fairfax while I temporarily moved in with Judith at her digs a couple of miles away on Beachwood just south of Melrose.

On Friday, April 11, I drove to work at Slash and arrived at about 10 a.m. I parked on the side street Martel, right outside the storeroom. No sooner had I stepped out onto the pavement then another car, going perhaps sixty miles an hour, missed me by literally inches and sheared off my door. They never stopped. I was so shaken, I had to go back to Judith's and chill out for an hour or two. Around noon we drove my car to a body shop on Gower across the street from Paramount Studios. Just as I was about to turn left into their parking lot, I realized a car coming in the opposite direction was driving faster than I'd thought, and I stopped to let it go by. The driver, however, thought I was going to follow through and, panicking, jumped her car up on the sidewalk, taking out a parking sign. What the fuck was going on?

The next day X was headlining at the Whisky, doing two sets. I don't remember the opening act. Steve Nieve, keyboardist for Elvis Costello's Attractions, and his wife, Fay Hart, good friends of Mirielle, were in town, having taken an apartment across from Paramount. The three of them—Mirielle, Steve, and Fay—had been doing their laundry earlier that night. They were supposed to meet Judith and me at Judith's place before we all went to the Whisky to see X. However, many minutes, then an hour ticked by. We hadn't heard from them, and it was getting late. You have to remember this was at least a good fifteen years before people had cell phones. So Judith and I left a note on the door and headed for the Whisky.

In between the first and second set we were upstairs, backstage with the band, when a couple of uniformed LAPD officers made their way through the punks who lined the hallway. We saw them speak to Exene, and she almost immediately slumped to the floor.

On the way to Judith's neighborhood Steve, Fay, and Mirielle were crossing on the green on the street of Willoughby at Vine when a drunk woman in a muscle car was barreling south on Vine and ran the red light, hitting the trio's Volkswagen, spinning it around, and turning it on its side. Steve and Fay both had broken bones, but Mirielle, sitting in the backseat, was killed instantly.

John and Exene, bereft though they were, decided to go on and do their second set. Judith and I left early, homing in on the supermarket, determined to buy up as much hard liquor as possible before the 2 a.m. cutoff for sales. We headed over to John and Exene's apartment (one half of a tiny duplex on Genesee, half a block north of Santa Monica Blvd) and waited for people to show up. That night everyone—and there were quite a few friends there—got blind drunk, staging an impromptu wake, trying unsuccessfully to obliterate our feelings and blunt the edges of a sharp, all-consuming grief. The night climaxed a couple of hours before dawn with several of the men chasing after an unbalanced, disgruntled next-door neighbor, and one or two of them ended up in jail overnight.

There were other deaths still to come—Darby Crash, Paul Zacha, Jules Bates, Robin Weiss, Jeffrey Lee, and so many more. But for me and, I think, many of us, this was the weekend that would stick with us like no other.

I've long swung back and forth between believing in astrology, fate, signs from God, but this was one of those

weekends that was a life-changer, shaking us all to the core, a demarcation point from youth to adult that seemed to be barely harboring us from some malevolent curse, and all of us who lived were somehow lucky we had come through it on the other side.

Growing up and becoming an adult, dealing with very real, inescapable things like death, that was a big part of punk rock too.

CLIMAX PRESENTS IN CONCERT

BLACK FLAG

WITH

FEAR

CIRCLE JERKS

CHINA WHITE

THE MINUTE MEN

THE REALITY OF EVIL

Advanced tickets available from Ticketron
Zed, Vinyl Fetish, Moby Disc.

WED. FEB. 11

STARDUST BALLROOM

5612 Sunset Blvd. $6 for more info call-462-1111

CHAPTER 17

Stuff Gets Twisted Up

by Mike Watt

I met d. boon some three or so years after coming to san pedro, ca, from norfolk, va, when he jumped out of a tree and landed on me in peck park, thinking I was a friend of his, nicknamed "eskimo"—I told him I wasn't eskimo, that I was someone who just moved from the navy housing to this proj that was just built next to the park. I told him I'd show him and, on our way walking there, he started reciting all these bits, really funny and trippy stuff. I thought, "man, this is the smartest dude in the world!" now I was only twelve years old and had never heard of george carlin—that's right, when the next day d. boon took me to his pad, a few blocks away in an older proj called "park western" (mine was called "park western estates"), he played me some of this comedian's act he had recorded from tv, and damn if those bits I thought he was making up on the spot yesterday were actually right from this man! after removing my palm from my forehead I realized this didn't matter cuz it was too late; I was way into him.

now, the reason I had to move from navy housing and, in fact, the reason I was in san pedro in the first place is cuz my pop was a sailor in the navy; he worked in the engine room as a machinist mate. california was a lot closer to viet-nam than virginia was, and that was the war that was going on then. in the service, families gotta move lots; as soon as "the orders" arrive you'd have, like, thirty days to reinvent your whole world. well, when my pop got transferred from the uss *long beach* to our first atomic-powered aircraft carrier, the uss *enterprise* (my pop worked in nuke engine rooms), the word came to move north to alameda and my ma said, "fuck that." so we stayed in pedro but had to leave the navy housing. trippy how 'pert-near right away of leaving there I would meet d. boon and then his family took me in like they did. his pop, danny, was like a second father to me—I mean all the tours my pop did in vietnam (yeah, they had "tours" too!) made for me hardly seeing him, but now it was even more that way. danny boon treated me like a son. d. boon's ma, too, was very kind to me. she was upfront about her thinking and didn't airbrush w/ words, but I liked that. it was her, too, who decided prolly one of the biggest decisions in my life: I would be on bass. yeah, she decided me and d. boon should be in a band and I would be on bass. hell, I didn't even know what a bass was. she played guitar when she was younger, so of course d. boon would be on guitar, but a band needs a bass, so that was for me. now, her thinking wasn't, I believe, cuz of careering but more like econo childcare or something. it was the early '70s, and there wasn't a lot of guns and stuff, but there was some fighting, so I think she wanted us to maybe be in the pad after school doing music and off the streets where we might get into trouble. hey, I was into it cuz I got to be w/

d. boon, that was good enough for me. thank you much, margie boon!

when I met d. boon, the only rock band he knew about was creedence clearwater revival—he knew nothing about cream, the who, steppenwolf, or t-rex cuz I think his pop was way into buck owens (even though danny boon was from nebraska, the boons had lived in bakersfield before coming to pedro), and that might've been a factor. but anyway, d. boon had all those first six ccr albums. they'd be laying on the hardwood floor w/out being in their jackets, grape juice and shit spilled all over them, and the econo record player needed, like, five quarters above the stylus to try and keep it from skipping. let's put it this way: it was hard to hear what the bassman was doing—hard for me anyway. hell, I can hear stu cook (ccr bassman) real good *now* but *then*, no way. actually, I was playing a cheap guitar from a pawn shop w/ only four strings on it, that's what I saw in the pictures on album covers—something like a guitar but w/ just four tuners. I really thought basses were guitars w/skinnier necks and two fewer strings! I didn't really comprehend that the word *bass* meant *lower*; what a dumbfuck I was. anyway, it stressed me so much not knowing what to play when we tried to copy ccr tunes, so looking at their album covers, I decided to wear shirts like their guitar/singerman john fogerty wore—flannels. I thought this was his kind of rock 'n' roll shirt and maybe if I wore shirts similar to his that d. boon still would like me, even w/ my inability to figure their bass parts out. d. boon had a big heart, though, and let me stumble through w/ whatever, and luckily we moved on to trying to learn tunes by the who and cream, where I could *definitely* hear the bass parts. a lot of the bass in rock coming from england had the bass way up and it helped much;

r & b stuff, too, like james jamerson and larry graham—that would have a big impact later now that I think of it. anyway, there was some u.s. rock like blue öyster cult and alice cooper, where I learned much too, but what really helped us both was a man who lived in his car named roy mendez-lopez. this guy gave lessons to d. boon out of chuck's sound of music in our town, a pad where they sold music stuff and albums too—it was like that in those days. roy was an incredible cat who was a very singular individual who built his own instruments, studied music constantly, and lived econo. he was way into prac and instilled that much in us, especially d. boon but me too. the way he brought it to us wasn't like the "b" word *burden* but more like the "o" word *opportunity*—to play for the love of it. it wasn't just talk: he lived his ideas out. he had an incredible impact on us.

I got my first real bass at fifteen. it was a kay that looked kind of like a gibson eb-3—kind of. I couldn't believe how big the fucking strings were. "no wonder there's only four of them," I was thinking. this bass had action like maybe william tell's bow—terrible and gave me much hurt—but eventually it did get my fingers stronger. damn, would they fucking hurt, but I wanted to be d. boon's bass player so I kept at it. the real problem I see looking back now was the culture or maybe I should say lack of culture when it came to composing your own stuff, using music as a form of expression. remember this is the era of arena rock—the first "concert" we went to was t-rex, and though we dug that and stuff like blue öyster cult (the band we saw live the most), it was nothing like the club gig culture we would find out about w/ the punk movement. actually we had never been to a club until our first punk gig. we graduated san pedro high school in 1976, which is right around when *creem* mag-

azine had these pictures and stories about "punk" stuff. we never did gigs, just played at the pad and then later in a garage near the junior high school w/ three other pedro guys and called ourselves the bright orange band even though we didn't have one original song (why have an original band name, why not cover that too?!). wait, we did have one gig when we were in tenth grade after a football game on a portable stage near the jetty at cabrillo beach. we were so terrible that everyone started throwing shit at us, and d. boon's pop drove his pickup right up to the stage so we could jump in and escape. some older guys had us borrow their stuff so we didn't lose anything except our spirit—that band was crushed. me and d. boon then started jamming w/ an old buddy named marc weiswasser at one of the barracks the army was renting out as they were closing down the lower reservation of fort macarthur (it's been dug out, w/ boat slips put in, and now is the cabrillo marina). of course we were copying songs, stuff like "dust in the wind" and "tie your mother down," w/ a singer-lady named erin we met one day when we stopped for a breather. outside this pad came walking by this guy w/ wild hair like in those punk pictures and what looked like a kotex around his neck. he told us there was a scene up in hollywood where people wrote their own songs. he said he was in one of the bands and we should check it out. d. boon and I did just that. we saw a band called the bags, and the first thing that fell out of my mouth w/out thinking when I saw them was to say to d. boon, "we can do that!" it was just a such a mindblow; it's hard for me to put how clearly *profound* this moment was. it's right up there w/ d. boon's ma putting me on bass.

we started going to as many punk gigs as we could. it was a trip how these cats weren't afraid. you could tell 'pert-near

all of them were just learning how to play, learning how to play in public, but it didn't matter cuz it seemed the main point was to express yourself any way you could. this is why we never felt punk was a style of music—that was up to each band. what it seemed to us was the movement was more about a state of mind. maybe some kind of funny karma, cuz I do think the hippie movement had lost its humor and the insights that come w/ that. remember, we were boys during the '60s w/ the civil rights and antiwar stuff and people taking issues into their own hands, and now in the '70s, arena rock seemed like the nuremberg rallies to me. I really wanted to start a band that was part of this movement w/ d. boon, but he told me to hold on. I got impatient and answered an ad in the *recycler*, where three people were looking for a fourth to make a band. they had prac in the drummer's pop's electric shop on santa monica boulevard, and I brought my bass and amp in my vw bug up from pedro (about thirty miles, we're the west part of the los angeles harbor) and jammed the stooges' "I wanna be your dog" for like three hours w/ them. they were very kind to me, nice people. I was so excited when I got home that I immediately told d. boon, and he told me, "ok, let's make a punk band." whoa, I didn't expect that—I never jammed w/ those people in hollywood again. this was the beginning of the reactionaries. d. boon picked that name from a list I had made up of all kinds of stupid shit, but he never wrote one song for the band. looking back, I think he did the band for me cuz he always had plans for another band in his mind; he just wanted to be ready for it. we never had a pad to play w/ a drummer, and this made it a blessing to find george hurley, who wanted to play drums after a bunch of years of surfing and even making surfboards. the shed where he

did that across from the high school is where we did prac. another high school friend, martin tamburovich, made us a quartet. this was the first time I ever wrote songs, and they were terrible. the other guys in the band had very big hearts to let me do that to them, to foist these feeble efforts. actually, I did write one song in secret as a teenager called "mr. bass king of outer space," where in the lyrics I blow away the rest of the band w/ a bass solo—obviously I was having inferiority issues, as discovering bass was like playing right field in little league, like where you put your 'tard friend in the band, that hierarchy shit that, happily, I didn't have to deal w/ so much w/ the punk movement cuz of a much more level playing field. everyone was learning, drummers and guitarists too. this band really didn't play that many gigs; most were a few times w/ the suburban lawns at their prac pad in long beach, but the first one was very important to us, big time. it was in pedro at a "teen post," which were these places set up for young people that a guy from a band called black flag, the bassman chuck dukowski, rented out for a gig. it was a trip how we got the gig. a band from england called the clash were finally playing so cal near the beginning of 1979, and we went to see them, bo diddley, and the dils at the santa monica civic center. in the parking lot were these dudes handing out flyers. the gig on the flyers was gonna be in pedro, and we couldn't believe this was gonna happen. when these guys handing out the flyers asked why (obviously they were in this band black flag), we told them that we lived in pedro. "you do?" they said, w/ us replying, "yeah, and besides that, we're the only punk band in pedro." they could not believe there was such a thing as a "pedro punk band" and asked us to open up. can you believe that shit? I think it was their third gig, but also on the

bill were two bands we saw a bunch up in hollywood, the alley cats and the plugz. right after us doing their first gig were the descendents, drummer billy just having broken his collarbone. the lapd (harbor division) actually had to lock everyone in the venue cuz the neighborhood, which was a kind of rough part of pedro, didn't have any idea of "this punk stuff," and one gig-goer w/ the words "white riot" on his jacket (the name of a tune by the clash) really got things boiling. man, that was a nightmare, but everyone made it out safe. after those gigs w/ the lawns, d. boon bailed, but he did find a replacement, a nice man named todd. however, I didn't wanna be in the band w/out d. boon, so it soon crumbled.

in january 1980 d. boon had just found an apartment in the alley between 19th and 20th. turns out joe baiza (originally from wilmington, the other part of the l.a. harbor) was living in the apartment downstairs. understand the old punk scene in late-'70s so cal was pretty tiny. you would see the same cats at the gigs week after week, and though you didn't really know these people, actually you kind of did. there really wasn't a "uniform" yet, and lots of folks from the old days were very individual about both their dress and their character—yeah, there were a lot of characters in those days, and I loved it. old punk was about people. if you fly over so cal, you think it's all one connected trip, but the reality is there's some very big-time balkanization, so we ain't in reality all that connected; it's all down to little neighborhoods. the movement for someone like me and d. boon transcended all that. we now had connections w/ folks who knew nothing about our pedro town, the only world I knew since virginia. and now I was meeting people from the valley, inland empire, orange county,

downtown, west side—even the beach towns. yeah it was funny how some people at the hollywood gigs thought anything south of ktown was "the beach" and that we were all kind of from the same tribe. the black flag guys from hermosa beach and us in pedro—actually the alley cats were from lomita but they never got the same kind of tag, but it was geography that brought us together unless you count flag having their third gig in pedro maybe—we're both by the water, but they're definitely beach and we're definitely harbor. gotta say that billy from the descendents was fishing for work as a teenager is pretty pedro, and he was there in redondo beach—things ain't ever black and white or simple like maybe people would like, but hey, that's the reality on the dealio. I will say the man who had and still does have much impact on me, second only to d. boon, is a man from hermosa beach named raymond pettibon. he's the first one to play john coltrane for me, learned me about all kinds of stuff. that's the thing about those days—the movement had lots of trippy people, but they were deep and intense about stuff. they just didn't fit in w/ the square-john world. the cats in the bands too—gigs were like people taking turns playing for each other. I never saw anything like it. the *slash* editor (zines were a big fabric of our scene) kickboy didn't mind a bit to talk w/ a total mook from pedro (me) about anything. you could rap to darby or pat or lorna or whoever from whichever band was playing. since I'm mentioning germs, don bolles could tell you tons about all kinds of esoteric music released and realized. I asked pat if he listened to anyone cuz I found him so original, and he told me he listened to queen! once at the hong kong café I was bourboned up and got darby to holler "pedro!" at the end of one of their gigs. I later wrote a tune about that called

"drove up from pedro." but anyway, the point is this whole bunch of people I kind of knew but kind of didn't (which means they had tons they could teach me) were incredibly profound for us, both me and d. boon. we found the movement very empowering, so when it came time to do the "real band," we were raring to go.

joe baiza later would tell me he heard all this stomping around when we were putting together the first batch of minutemen tunes—actually he thought we were dancing like crazy for hours at a time! see, there was no drummer, though d. boon had a plan: he'd met a welderman named frank tonche, and we'd work w/ him as soon as we both got our shit together. So we're up in his apartment, and of course we don't wanna make too much noise, so were using our electric guitar and bass w/out amplifiers. we're stomping on the deck to hold time—that's what joe baiza was hearing, the stomping but not the spiel (we'd whisper it) or the unplugged instruments. we didn't realize you could hear that stomping—we thought we were being so careful! anyway, like some of these cats at the gigs, we became friends just cuz we saw each other so much. I think it was easier to trust punk people in the old days cuz it was such a hated movement by so many, so many rock 'n' roll people especially—maybe more than square-johns! we painted on our clothes like richard hell (my first punk hero, a bassman who led his band!) and had them all wild, but then went back to high school clothes after so much hell from peckers—we decided to keep punk "up in the head" and not get added grief cuz of the clothes. gotta say, though, we loved the clothes, we really did, especially the unique and really wild stuff. oh well. at least we were gonna use music as expression and not compromise that a bit. it was

big decision time for us. I remember me and d. boon doing one of our many "thinking sessions" and deciding to divide the world up into two categories: flyers and gigs. everything that wasn't a gig was a flyer to get people to the gig. because punk gigs first and foremost for us were total mind-blows reacting to nuremberg rally arena rock, why not make that our focus? now, there was lots that was punk we found out about, such as making records, fanzines, and stuff like that, but our first focus was on gigs and, of course, jamming econo—remember we're from working people. but the good thing about the movement was that econo was ok and not something to be embarrassed about. the main mission was to find our voice and bring it to people at gigs.

one last thing I like to explain is our idea of what *econo* meant. of course we got it from the old ford econoline vans we did out-of-town gigs in; the first one we did, we borrowed black flag's. but what *econo* meant to us was not just finding what, at the time, might seem the least amount of coin. *econo* to us was finding the most bang for buck, look down the road at what we had to get done and find the way that made most sense—the "econo" way that guaranteed our autonomy and, at the same time, helped us work as many gigs as we could cuz that what's we loved doing. it was about not letting the lack of coin dictate to us what could and could not be done. of course, there's material stuff, and that's the reality on the dealio, but c'mon, we were from working families: we knew the score on that kind of scene, no prob! in this way we never had to "fake" our way, not one second, in the movement—like what popeye said, "I am what I am." hear hear. *econo* was not a slogan but a way of life for the minutemen, inspired by the movement. we got our first minutemen tunes together—oh, we got minutemen

for a name cuz d. boon picked it from a list again I made
for him. actually I had down "minute men," as we were way
tiny compared to an arena rock band, so *minute* as in very
small (pronounced *my-noot*). but d. boon liked the name
cuz he heard of some extremist kind of people using pa-
triotic stuff to shill, so he thought if we used words or a
name like that, then it would confuse things and give those
people maybe less power. I liked his reasoning. I have to say
we were very influenced by these gigs we were seeing up in
hollywood in the late '70s, bands like nervous gender and
screamers who didn't have a guitar (didn't need one!), as
well as records we'd get at zed of london in long beach. two
dollars for seven-inch singles of bands we'd never heard
(and never seen) like the pop group, wire, the fall, alternative television, cabaret voltaire, the lemon kittens, birthday
party—stuff like that. we'd buy them cuz of the band name,
cuz of the record art—just roll dice and take a chance. we'd
wait 'till we had time off from work and stuff (at this period
I was working three different low-paying jobs while putting
myself through college—I ended up w/ an electronics degree
I never used!) and then eat so we could hear these records
for the first time while frying our brains out. I would do this
on saturdays late when richard meltzer had his *hepcats from
hell* show on kpfk—that was a trip—as well as on the Fridays,
when I could, during *imaginary landscape* w/ carl stone on
the same station (great resource). d. boon and I really found
our minutemen voice actually and it big-time opened our
minds. we learned about the movements and connections
w/ older stuff like futurism, dadaism, and surrealism—all
this went into our idea of the band. definitely the shortness
of the tunes was a wire influence. and the pop group gave
us the confidence to put parliament-funkadelic w/ captain

beefheart—fuck, we could do whatever we wanted to: it was our band—let the freak flag fly!

something I was aware of then and still am now if not even more grateful for was the openness we had found in the movement, the fact that all these creative people had no prob letting me and d. boon take something that was so personal like making music together and letting us be part of their scene. as I already described, they'd let us interact as gig-goers w/ no prob, talking to us before/after they played, or just gig-goers themselves who weren't playing that night or whenever but didn't feel part of the mersh world so much, like us. I can't relate how big-time empowering this was to us, and in fact, I don't believe there would've been a minutemen w/out the movement that came out of hollywood in the later '70s. sure, there would've been the fact that two guys growing up in pedro shared making music as part of being together, but I don't ever think we would've been inspired to make a band, write songs, and do gigs/make records w/out the influence of the movement; I just don't, and I have to acknowledge that. the minutemen did not come out of a vacuum; they were a product of the movement. of course, a big tenet of this movement was no rubber-stamp cookie-cutter xerox shit (or like what raymond taught me emma goldman said: "no coercion"), so we weren't clones being pumped out of a shill machine, but it was the idea that we had permission to be all crazy regarding expression that we took to heart by seeing it firsthand as an example that propelled us, fucking corndogs, as we were looking for their voice.

we worked out our first batch of tunes w/ the welder-man frank tonche and did our first gig opening for black flag in the spring of 1980. we had still had the connect w/

them from a year before w/ the reactionaries at the teen post. man, it was a pants-shitter, but we did it. this was not the reactionaries; you could tell d. boon was involved at a whole other level. he was singing his songs (mine too) for the first time. it was very inspiring. d. boon called his lyrics "thinking out loud," and I dug that cuz in fact that's what we were doing. he also didn't like the hierarchy of where he saw rock 'n' roll going, the domination of the electric guitar, so he wanted to do something "political" w/ our band's makeup and decided to play really trebly like we learned from the r&b guys when we were younger. that way it opened it up for the bass and drums to come through more. d. boon said that real politics ain't really just using words, and he wanted to put into action some egalitarian ideas in our band structure. we did our second gig, and the drummerman said maybe that's enough for him, so when that gig ended, he left the band. now, at this gig was sst re-cords' greg ginn, and wouldn't you know it, but he asked us to be sst-002—he wanted us to make a record! luckily george hurley had left the band hey taxi!, which is who he had joined when the reactionaries were finished. georgie joined us and learned the tunes we wanted to record, and damn if in july we didn't do the whole *paranoid time* ep in one night, recorded and mixed. me and d. boon were very grateful to frank tonche for helping us get off the ground but also to george hurley for doing like he did also. two great drummermen helped us much, let me tell you.

we got closer w/ the black flag people. I started working there at sst in old downtown torrance and the minutemen started doing prac there. first I wound antenna tuner toroi-dal transformers (sst stood for "solid state transmitter"; it was not a record company at first), and then they had me

calling college stations to get the label's records played. they had me use the name "spaceman" so the stations wouldn't know I was one of the guys from one of the bands. we were harassed so *much* by the local police. flag had been dealing w/ this since the church (where they first practiced in hermosa beach), and we eventually got ran out. sst and black flag tried some deal w/ unicorn in hollywood, and we ended up practicing in long beach w/ nice cats in secret hate and outer circle, us sharing a space w/ them. of course, the label thing was a punk part of punk, so we did one called "new alliance records," and d. boon did a zine called the *prole* (he had me do a column called nitt's picks w/ record reviews!) d. boon also put on gigs in pedro at the star theatre, which he would rename the union and have the gigs start earlier for us cuz we had to work early the next day. we had just finished our second seven-inch (*joy*) and first twelve-inch (*the punch line*) and even started to do our own club gigs. we had been labeled a "violent sst band" and could not play the whisky or the roxy—the former we finally got to play cuz of fear and the latter cuz of x. I tell you, old punk was about people.

greg ginn did ham radio when he was younger, and, hence sst. I also think this gave him ideas about getting outside your locality, and by that, I mean touring. I once heard only the dils had a van in hollywood, though that might not be true. I do know black flag liked to tour and taught it to us. in early 1983 they took us through europe and the u.s. in what was our first big tour—and our first time in europe. we took a lot of hell. that wild and crazy late-'70s punk, where anything goes kind of got stomped out or at the least not tolerated. there were now a lot of "rules" to be correctly w/ the movement. what? we couldn't

believe this shit. now, I gotta say a lot of the people in the older days were older—it wasn't really a kid movement, maybe more like runaways—but by the early '80s a lot of the "folks who were first" were burning out and from the suburbs came younger and younger cats, like out of high school and younger. how many of the old hollywood bands had ladies in them? tons. later the movement had fewer and fewer, and that even went for the audience. my early take on the first influences of the movement was glitter and glam, which ladies always were strong in, even if it wasn't a huge scene. even the dancing changed from up-and-down pogo into side-to-side slamming—no more personal space, even if it was kind of vertical—things were definitely going horizontal, w/ fight after fight making what was called "the pit," and of course, the desired "background sound" to this was faster and faster, added to more of the same ol' same ol'. all that "no coercion" talk was over and "uniform" was very much in. I didn't totally get bummed cuz at least there was some scene, but damn if so much wasn't squandered like it was and all warped up. but hey, that's humans. hell, pat boone sold more copies of "tutti frutti" than little richard did, and how long ago was that? stuff gets twisted up, dumbed down w/ knuckleheads, and all the reasons involved for the movement getting started in the first place get forgot and stomped. damn.

in some ways the minutemen turned inward, recording "what makes a man start fires?" and then "buzz or howl under the influence of heat" (w/ the latter we made more than fifty dollars!). but I addressed some of this stuff w/ a tune like "fake contest," where some letter-writing thing in the *flipside* fanzine (letters from readers) was pitting us against t.s.o.l., which was crazy cuz I love jack, mike, and

ron. the next album we did was actually a double one cuz the huskers (hüsker dü) had come to town and did one, prompting us to write more tunes to turn our just-recorded single into two. it came w/in only a year and then left for the band, which though unknownst to us—I think it was our high point. I paid the eleven hundred dollars to do it myself, but damn if ethan james didn't mix the whole baby in one night! yep, forty-five tunes, but yeah, they were little ones. there's a song on it I wrote called "history lesson, part II" where I call out john doe from x's name, again trying to deal w/ this weird thing w/ no tolerance creeping into our movement, which was at times so frustrating. we did a big two-month tour for it, all minutemen—headlining all through the u.s., "the campaign trail 1984" tour. after this, though, georgie stopped writing words for the band. I always counted on him for that cuz it helped me be a little more original w/ my writing cuz I'd get into ruts, and both his and d. boon's words would help me bust out. but the next two recordings were missing his lyrics. musically I don't know how strong *project: mersh* and *3-way tie (for last)* were except for the d. boon tunes, which I really dig, but I definitely was in kind of a not-too-interesting place as far as my tunes when I look back at what we did. oh well. I think we were headed for a second wind anyway; we had some big plans coming up: a triple album w/ half of it live to fight the bootleggers! I was writing better too, being inspired by the first side band I ever had, dos w/ k.

our last tour turned out to be w/ these guys from georgia called rem. when we got asked, we had to buy one of their records to see what they sounded like. it was sure kind of them to have us aboard. when we met them it was easy to tell they knew about a lot of music, that they were deep

like dudes in the old days. the crew and the label w/ them, though, didn't dig us at all, and we got much disrespect. well, that's the way it goes—that's why we got in the movement in the first place! the four guys in the band, though, they were righteous. respect to them. the last tune I ever played w/ d. boon was w/ them in north carolina. it was us all doing television's "see no evil," and damn if me and d. boon weren't both on guitar, laughing at the whole trip. a few days or so after that tour ended, d. boon passed away in a van accident in arizona. our equipment was still aboard. I had just given d. boon some lyrics richard meltzer had written for us—ten of them. he was collaborating w/ us, doing singing and sax—a dream come true for us! I gave him those words and asked him to think of music for them. he was so red from fever; he had a flu. oh man, it's hard for me to write any more about this, but I will say the minutemen ended like it began: w/ d. boon. *big huge love* to him.

on bass, watt

CHAPTER 18

Unvarnished, Detailed, West Coast

by John Doe

Punk rock songs are not:

all screaming & yelling
3 chords (most Ramones songs are not)
2 minutes long
stupid lyrics w/ no leads
fast, loud & atonal

Punk rock songs are:
provocative
immediate
hook driven (title usually repeated many times)
specific
fast, slow & in between

Misconceptions about punk-rock songwriting are as wide & flat as the city of Los Angeles itself. Maybe it even begins

w/ the definition of punk rock. What it was & what it became are two vastly different things. Even by 1982 that definition had changed from anything that wasn't "old & in
the way" to "faster/louder." Provocative? Yes. Fast? Not necessarily. Simple? Yes. 3 chords? No. Not too serious? Definitely. Culturally significant? Always.

It's a small wonder that the Los Angeles basin didn't
partially lift off the ground w/ all the songwriting going
on between 1977 & '82—or maybe it did. Just as in NYC &
London, the differences between writers, bands & subjects
were spread all over the map. Blondie & The Ramones came
from the same minimalist pool, went to the beach, but
you would never be confused who it was when listening
to them. In Los Angeles the same went for Black Randy &
the Metro Squad, The Germs, The Weirdos, The Alley Cats,
Fear, The Dickies, The Go-Go's, The Plugz, etc. Blondie had
beauty, camp, melody & power. The Ramones had power,
camp, speed & minimalism. Black Randy had camp, humor,
funk & cynicism. The Alleym Cats had cynicism, technique
& beauty. Black Flag had power, violence & message. X had
poetry, power, ability & violence. All had similar traits but
w/ different emphasis on each part of the overall sound.
The binding element was that all were searching for something, something beyond that invisible line that had been
drawn between "then" & "now." You would never listen to
Black Flag & mistake them for The Weirdos, The Dickies, X,
or The Plugz. You may not even have known who it was,
but you would damn well find out.

We told real stories, exaggerated the facts, or just plain
made them up. We commented on a world that, to us, had
become unbelievably crass & stupid, a world that was just
recognizing the separation between rich & poor. We had been

told that the neutron bomb could be the end of us all, so The Weirdos wrote a song about it, using all the power without the destruction. We wanted to cut loose & have fun. This was a lesson learned from The Ramones, The Damned & Blondie & perhaps why Television or Patti Smith weren't as influential in LA. Devo knew how to poke fun & blaze a totally different trail. There was a fascination w/ mental illness because we all could identify w/ being abnormal. Maybe that's where jerking around while playing started? These were teenagers or recently post-teens who still had no idea what they were "going to do w/ their lives." Because we didn't think any of us would be around, creatively or otherwise, in 2 or 3 years, we certainly didn't take any of this shit seriously. But that didn't keep everyone from meaning every bit of what we played, sang, or said. These were songs that were simple enough for any musicians to hear & think, "I could write something like that." These were songs you could hear once, probably catch the title & possibly remember the next morning. These songs were meant to be played live, loud & sloppy. Having an actual record that someone could put on their turntable was still off in the distance for most of us.

I imagined early rock 'n' rollers with the same creative guts, cranking out the basics in sweaty clubs where underage drinking & carrying-on happened every night. The same probably went for early British Invasion, psychedelic, and garage bands as they figured out their individual sounds. They kept things uncomplicated but intuitive & real. Yes, there was the advance guard—MC5, The Stooges, The Modern Lovers, Velvet Underground, The Sonics—and they were heroes we could grasp. But more important to our small circle were the originators—Little Richard, Bo Diddley, Chuck Berry, Eddie Cochran, Wanda Jackson, Jerry Lee & every Sun

record, Big Joe Turner, & Fats Domino. Others looked up to
David Bowie, Roxy Music, New York Dolls & to most of us
in Hollywood that's why we accepted everyone's sexuality
& style, but that's another chapter.

Punk-rock songwriting brought songs back to "the
people" because Fleetwood Mac, The Moody Blues, The Eagles, The Beatles, etc. had gotten so full of themselves & full
of pompous art that no amount of "Get Back" could encourage an average guy/girl to believe they could start a band &
make songs that would communicate. Maybe it wasn't those
established groups' fault, but after so many years, so much
money, so many songs, so much insulation from reality,
such ridiculously long jams & trying to write the most general subject matter so that the maximum stadium size audience could "relate" to what you were "laying down, man," it
was just too much bullshit to still call it rock 'n' roll.

I wanted to tell stories about this city that filled my eyes
w/ decay & anonymity. A place where random violence
breathed in & out like the ocean. I didn't want to tell stories like Bob Dylan but like Bukowski (w/out the lurid sex
but a suggestion of it)—minimal, unvarnished, detailed
West Coast, filled w/ the kind of darkness The Doors and
Love had promised. We dug for images & sounds opposite
to what everyone in America thought of Los Angeles at the
time. Our melodies were simple & chord changes oftentimes
went one half step off of what was expected. We were contrary & always reached for something just left of center. But
at least we always had two verses & a chorus you could identify over the shitty sound system and the audience jumping all over each other. These were the first songs I'd written
that were actually any good. Exene was a partner, coconspir-
ator & if not the lyricist, then the catalyst. She would write

a line like "Johnny Hit & Run Pauline," tape it to the door & a few months later that story would come to me. Even though she'd never written a song, Exene could write lyrics on a page, top to bottom, as if the music was already there. All I had to do was match some music I'd been working on to the cadence of the words. Other pages were more impressionistic, scattered poems w/ whole pieces of songs waiting to be excavated & expanded on. Some of those scattershot poems became songs anyway. We didn't care about rhyming. We loved to set a scene that didn't follow a linear story & if we could poke fun at pop culture, even better. I still marvel at the trust she put in me to allow me that artistic freedom.

Billy, however, demanded that the music kept to his definition of rock 'n' roll. He kept us from getting too strung out on "arty shit" as he would call it. He loved The Ramones' "dumb lyrics" & wished we would write more like that. But as long as he could lay rockabilly riffs over my unconventional chord changes, he was happy. Our general contrary attitude, that rules were meant to be broken, and Billy's dogged refusal to include anything more than the basics & purity in his definition of what was & wasn't rock 'n' roll made X songs what they became.

As '79, '80, '81 rolled around, the cynicism got deeper, songs got faster & the music became more of a soundtrack for the audience to whirl around the dance floor. Those unfamiliar w/ punk rock will use this period to judge all punk-rock songs as crap. But dozens of new bands & their songs created their own version of what would overtake the first wave of LA punk & define what most people think of as punk rock.

Everyone had witnessed the new wave groups like The Knack and even the punk-rock party band The Dickies get

signed to major labels. It was clear that safer-sounding groups like The Pretenders, Elvis Costello, The Go-Go's, and Blondie could score airplay & hits w/ something the existing music business could wrap their corporate heads around. Punk rock need not apply.

Independent labels began to mirror the fierce spirit of the newer hardcore bands. SST and Alternative Tentacles provided diversity w/ even more contrary attitude but a lot less humor. The songs became more linear, more stream of consciousness, fewer hooks & more overall chaos & distortion. The sound of The Germs and Fear were templates for so many like The Stains (from East LA), T.S.O.L. (from the beach), or China White (from OC). But more eccentric groups like The Minutemen, The Crowd & Middle Class kept the crazy up front & still seemed to have a great time doing it. Black Flag went through several incarnations, became the flag bearer & w/ Henry Rollins began developing a nationwide underground network that allowed indie bands in the '80s to reap the rewards. Black Flag's original singer, Keith Morris, would form the Circle Jerks to continue his brand of fast, loud, hooky punk rock. And The Minutemen would distinguish themselves by releasing an epic double LP, *Double Nickels on the Dime*, displaying their mastery of jazz, beatnik & punk rock from San Pedro. In their own way they would all prove that hardcore bands encouraged their own kind of diversity & originality.

The song landscape was still vast like the S. California basin. Although it was on its way to becoming more codified & uniform, its branches were growing all over the United States & the world. Many are still discovering what came before & just how diverse it was & can be.

CHAPTER 19

The Almighty Song

by Charlotte Caffey

I felt like I was moving in slow motion, aware of every little detail, as I walked down the alley and descended the stairs into that basement. My senses were in overload—from the graffiti, to the sounds bouncing off of every surface, to the dog collars, safety pins, multicolored hair, crazy makeup, and wild clothing, to the toilets overflowing, to the feeling of the sticky walls and floors, to the nonventilated dense mixture of smells. The air would become so thick that with each breath, it tasted like a bong hit of piss, sweat, booze and drugs. It was 1977, and I was at the Masque. I knew that I had arrived at some sort of Mecca.

Somewhere between the blaze of the California sun and that basement of the Pussycat Theater on Hollywood Boulevard I became a songwriter. I had always been obsessed with songs. I came from a large Catholic family of thirteen kids. What I remember mostly about growing up was being in the midst of total chaos all the time. Also, I was never allowed to show or speak any of my emotions. So I started

Plugs · GO-GO's
Gears
AudioVidiot
FRI JAN. 4, 1980
9 pm
$3.50
BENEFIT
FOR THE
Margot
Defence
Fund
CLUB 88 PICO BL., WLA

AGED TWENTY-TWO IN JAILHOUSE ROCK' AND FORTY-TWO AT ONE OF HIS LAST STAGE APPEARANCES

listening to music via the radio—that was my refuge. That was my salvation. There were two pop stations, KHJ and KRLA. The earliest song I remember is "Hang Down Your Head Tom Dooley." I was five years old. And from then on, song after song, for as many hours of the day as I could, I would have my ear to the radio. In 1962 my grandfather took me to Wallichs Music City on the corner of Sunset and Vine and bought me one of my first singles, Brian Hyland's "Sealed with a Kiss." This song haunted me—I couldn't stop listening to it. I recently read that Frank Zappa used to work at Music City right around that time—I wonder whether he sold me that record? A few years later I saw my first concert: the Beatles. I sat there silent and riveted in a sea of thousands of screaming fans, my eyes fixed on the stage as I listened intently to the songs. Hearing the songs performed live was a whole other experience. That night, as I watched my beloved Beatles, a thought crossed my mind: "I want to do that when I grow up."

I started working at Woolworth's on Vermont and Hollywood Boulevard when I turned sixteen. The whole reason I wanted a job was so I could buy records. I had finally gotten my own bedroom and had saved up enough money to buy my very own record player at Zodys. My mom and dad got really mad that I had spent my money on the record player, but I didn't care. I started building my record collection with The Beatles and Led Zeppelin and added Neil Young, Joni Mitchell, the Stones, The Who, to name just a few. I'd buy as many as the amount of money that I had on hand. I would sit in my room by myself and listen to the records and stare at the album covers and read the lyrics. It was at this point when I first attempted to write songs. I had two older brothers who liked to torture me, so I had

to be really covert about my songwriting. I would go to the
garage where the piano was, press the soft pedal, and try to
play as quietly as I could. Melodies came very easily for me.
I started writing lyrics but was afraid to keep a notebook
for fear of being found out and mercilessly teased, so I kept
everything in my head.

My introduction to "art rock" and avant-garde music was
in high school. I attended Immaculate Heart High School
right in the middle of Hollywood. It is an all-girls Catholic
school. I had an English teacher named Mr. Vliet. His cousin
was Don Van Vliet, aka Captain Beefheart. One day he
brought in *Trout Mask Replica* to class and played a couple of
songs off this notorious record. I heard a whole different take
on songwriting in a matter of a few minutes. That album led
me to Frank Zappa and the Mothers of Invention, which seg-
ued into joining my first band, Manuel and the Gardeners.
I was seventeen and had just graduated high school when I
met this super-hyper guy name Joe Ramirez who asked me
to join his band. Manuel and the Gardeners was an early
progressive art-performance rock band. The lead singer, Mick,
had a hot plate that he used to fry women's underwear—live
onstage—and would run around in outlandish outfits. The
music was avant-garde with heady, surreal lyrics. We played
any and every show we could—a biker bar in Venice, a coffee
house at Pitzer College, and even a Mexican restaurant on
Hollywood Boulevard. I only played keyboards—I didn't sing
or write—but I got to experience the genius of Joe firsthand.
He was one of the smartest, funniest, most talented guys I
had ever met, and he would play an important role in my
early songwriting life. We bonded over albums like *Fragile* by
Yes, *Tyranny and Mutation* by Blue Öyster Cult, and too many
others to mention. And we became inseparable best friends.

All I wanted to do was play in a band and write songs, but my parents were hassling me about what my plans were now that I was out of high school. At the eleventh hour I decided to go to Immaculate Heart College, a small music and art school in LA. Sometimes they would have lunchtime concerts where I once saw Father Yod and the Source Family, who were way beyond avant-garde. During that time of my intense classical piano education I was listening to *Tapestry* (Carole King), *Aqualung* (Jethro Tull), *Led Zeppelin IV*, *Jesus Christ Superstar*, and the *Clockwork Orange* soundtrack, as the movie had just come out. One of my professors brought the soundtrack into class. He was *very* upset by the revolutionary use of the Moog synthesizer with Beethoven's legendary "Ode to Joy." I had just seen the movie and thought it was one of the most fucking brilliant things I'd ever seen. All the innovation in this soundtrack opened up my musical spectrum, and these influences showed up later in my songwriting. I graduated with a bachelor's of music degree.

I moved out of my parents house—FREEDOM! I had a job at a hospital and was able to get a cheap apartment and buy an old upright piano. I didn't have the threat of my brothers anymore, so I started writing down my songs. I told Joe that I had written a few songs. He wanted to hear them—I was horrified. I had never played anything for anybody. I sat down at the piano but couldn't bring myself to play. Joe saw the potential in me and proceeded to coax, prod, plead, and beg it out of me. Finally I got the courage and played him a song called "Oh Daddy-Oh." It was a demented beatnik love ballad. He absolutely loved it. That moment changed everything for me. Joe and I spent all of our spare time listening to records—*Radio City* by Big Star, Jonathan Richman and the Modern Lovers, Cheap Trick, The

Move. My whole songwriting world was opening up even more. Joe was my first songwriting collaborator. We wrote songs that were a mix of Joe's weirdo stuff and my pop melodies. It was a good combination. He wrote unconventional and outrageous lyrics and played his guitar, "Rosie," a Telecaster with a rosewood neck in open E tuning, which added to his unique style of writing.

We started a band called The Eyes with Don (DJ) Bonebrake in 1976. We met Don at a gig at one of the Immaculate Heart College shows where he was playing in a band called Rocktopus. He totally blew me and Joe away. I acquired my first bass, an electric blue Rickenbacker, even though I didn't know how to play it yet. I just started bashing away when the song started. I ended up breaking a lot of strings. We were going to tons of shows and seeing a lot of bands and were totally inspired. These were pre-punk bands that had finally made their way to the West Coast, paving the way for what was to come in the Hollywood punk scene. We saw Patti Smith, The Flaming Groovies, and Television. And in early 1977 Blondie opened for The Ramones at the Whisky. We stood right in front, watching The Ramones, getting our eardrums blown out by their Marshall stacks, and having the time of our lives. Something was unleashed inside of me that night.

The Eyes' songs had evolved into what I would call "prog-punk"—progressive punk. There were elements of punk but also more sophisticated chord changes and song structures. But as Joe and I were witnessing all this intense energy at live shows and listening to all these new bands, we had an idea. We decided to write an album in one hour: no editing, just pure, raw emotion—whatever came out of us. Well, it ended up taking us a couple of hours, but we wrote ten songs, including the manic "Kill Your Parents" and "Don't Talk to

Me," a favorite of young punkers even today. We played one of our first gigs at the Masque. It was ground zero for the small Hollywood punk scene and run by this crazy and lovable Scottish guy named Brendan Mullen (R.I.P.). There was a large room with a stage where the weekend punk shows took place, and there were also smaller rooms where bands would rehearse during the week. The stage was in the big cement room, so the sound from the amps, drums, and speakers bounced all over the place—it was a sonic train wreck. There were rivalries between different bands and drama between members of the same groups, all of which I pretty much ignored, but I was mesmerized by what people would do under the banner of self-expression. For instance, Bobby Pyn (Darby Crash) would smear peanut butter on himself onstage or Alice Bag and The Bags would wear paper bags over their heads when they performed . . . or just strutting down Hollywood Boulevard. I loved all of it!

It was pretty clear from our first show that The Eyes were an "out crowd." I looked like a full-on surfer chick, with waist-length blond hair, and Joe had a short afro. So right there we didn't fit in. But on the inside we were filled with latent teenage angst and untapped raw energy. One night I was at The Avengers' show at Larchmont Hall in Hancock Park, and it happened to be my birthday. I remember running into Pat Smear and Darby Crash (Bobby Pyn) of The Germs, and they asked me, "How old are you?" I told them that I had just turned twenty-two, and they said, "You're too old to be a punk!" I laughed at them because they were only a few years younger than me. I never hid my age—I really didn't care. But our outcast days came to an end one night when Joe kicked Darby in the head for heckling us during a set at the Masque. I guess Darby must have loved it, because after that we were no longer the "out crowd."

We played more shows at the Masque and got asked to play at the Whisky and the Starwood. But The Eyes were about to come to an end. Exene and John Doe asked DJ to join X. I was bummed and okay with this at the same time. I couldn't imagine the band without DJ, and I felt like Joe and I had taken this band as far as we could together. I also valued our friendship too much and knew in my gut I had to leave the band because we weren't getting along. And artistically Joe was going in one direction and I was moving in another. Oddly enough, one of the last shows Joe and I saw together was Edie and the Eggs, led by John Waters's superstar Edith Massey at the Nuart Theater in LA. Little did I know that the following year I would be in a band with the person that was drumming that night.

On April 14, 1978, I was sitting backstage at the Star-wood, writing a song list for our second set that night. The Eyes were third on the bill, opening for The Jam and The Dickies. As I was writing, two pairs of spiked heels walked up in front of me. I heard a voice say, "Hi, Charlotte . . . " I started looking up, past the ripped fishnet stockings, to a Hefty bag cinched at the waist and then to a head of bright purple hair. "I'm Belinda. Do you play lead guitar?" I lied and said, "Yes!" even though I had never played lead before. The other girl, Margot, was wearing a torn vintage dress and had pink-and-green hair and very heavy makeup. "We're starting an all-girl band and want to know if you'd like to join." "Okay," I said without a second thought. We exchanged phone numbers. And in that moment telling one teeny white lie changed my life forever.

I went to England with The Dickies (Leonard Phillips was my boyfriend) and missed The Go-Go's' first gig, which was at the Masque in May 1978. But when I got back we were able to get a rehearsal room at the Masque, which

we ended up sharing with X (and subsequently moved to another one that we shared with The Motels). The rooms were not soundproofed, so we could hear what every other band was playing and vice versa—we couldn't have cared less; it just added to the chaos and fun. Our first rehearsal together was classic. I had met Belinda and Margot at the Starwood, and then I met Jane Wiedlin, who was a super-smart, pixie-like girl, and our drummer, Elissa Bello, who was very intense. I was the only one who really knew how to plug the amps in and turn them on. This kind of helped break the ice. On the outside I was plugging in amps and joking around, but on the inside I felt so awkward. These girls were *in* the scene. Jane lived at the infamous punk-rock apartments, the Canterbury, and Belinda lived at the equally notorious Disgraceland just a few blocks away. They dressed really cool and were outrageous and funny as hell. I was thinking, "These girls are *real* punks. I *still* look like Marcia Brady."

I started learning songs that Belinda, Jane, and Margot were writing—"Robert Hilburn," "Blades," "Over Run," "Living at the Canterbury," "Party Pose." I loved these songs. They felt really rebellious and dark. They had heard "Don't Talk to Me," so when I said I had a song that needed to be finished, they wanted to hear it. Now I was really terrified because the song I decided to bring in was *so* pop and the lyrics were *so* boy-girl and the melody was very sixties. It was called "How Much More." Well, Belinda and Jane *loved* it. "How Much More" changed the direction of The Go-Go's. Shortly after this we learned a cover of "Walking in the Sand" by The Shangri-Las. We started out slow just like the original, then blasted into a full-on powerful punk version. We had fused our sixties influences with our punk rock—and we were on fire.

None of us were very proficient on our instruments and we sounded pretty horrible, but that didn't stop us. I had to covertly figure out how to play lead guitar. I just figured it was going to be easy because the strings were thinner than the bass strings and the guitar wasn't as heavy. Boy, was I wrong. I bought a red Fender Duo-Sonic guitar—I liked it because it was red. I started playing it at rehearsals, and my fingers were bleeding because the tiny steel strings were cutting into them. It was pure pain, but I kept playing. I also had no idea how to get a good sound on my amp. I kept turning the reverb up because I was trying to get a sustain for my guitar parts, and I inadvertently created a punk/surf hybrid that became my sound. This sound inspired many of the guitar lines that I wrote.

Belinda worked at a magazine publishing company that published things like *Guns and Ammo*. She booked gigs for the band and was writing lyrics as well while she was at work (that was some good multitasking!). She showed me "Skidmarks on My Heart" (lyrics). They were about her brother. I immediately fell in love with them and took them home to try to write them music. I was listening to a lot of Cheap Trick and Ramones at the time, so this was where my inspiration for the music for this song came from. Then I brought her an idea I was working on. I had come up with a rad surf-guitar intro riff, but I needed help finishing the song. Belinda finished the lyrics for "Beatnik Beach." Jane had also written a song with Don Bolles of The Germs called "London Boys," which quickly became a fan favorite. Joseph Fleury (R.I.P.), the manager of The Mumps (Lance Loud, Kristian Hoffman), showed me some lyrics and asked me to write the music. The song "Fashion Seekers" was born. These songs were staples in our early sets. In addition, there

were two songs Jane had written that just blew my brains apart—one she had written with *all* minor chords, which, in my music theory mind, was something you couldn't do (cannot remember the name of it), and the other was one of the band's favorites, "Fun with Ropes"—I didn't know you could stuff that many chords in one song.

Right around this time we had a personnel change. Jane met a girl named Gina Schock at a party. She was a wise-crackin' kick-ass drummer from blue-collar Baltimore. She told us that we had to rehearse at least five times a week. We followed her advice and became *so* much better live. Gina was the drummer for Edie and the Eggs, who I had seen the year before. The first time I met Gina she had a perm, avia-tor glasses, a baseball cap, and a pair of overalls—I suddenly didn't feel so bad looking like Marcia Brady!

There was a heck of a lot of songs being written in that one square block in Hollywood at that time. I didn't have any kind of rules for songwriting, and it didn't seem like anyone else did either. I don't recall actually being influ-enced by any songs per se from our little punk scene; it really was more about the *collective* energy, the visuals, the experimentations, and sonic assault that inspired me. I fed off of it. Don't get me wrong, there were some great songs, like X's "We're Desperate," "Lexicon Devil" by The Germs, "You're So Hideous" by The Dickies, The Screamers' "Peer Pressure," and "We Got the Neutron Bomb" by The Weirdos. But the songs that inspired me and knocked me on my ass were right in my own band.

The moment Jane finished "How Much More" we started a writing collaboration between us that was nothing less than magical. We discovered we had this sort of telepathic writing relationship. We had only known each other for a

short time, yet we were bringing in music and lyrics that just happened to fit perfectly with each other. We were collaborating but weren't in the same room. Jane and I wrote "He's So Strange" about a guy that we knew, but what we didn't know was that he was dating *both* of us behind our backs. We also wrote "Screaming," which was inspired by Tomata du Plenty. It opens with a frenetic guitar riff and ventures into raga rock–sounding verses with a surf-inspired chorus. At one point I had finished three songs that I was working on and knew that none of these were very good. But each song had one really good part. So I combined those three parts and came up with music I loved. Shortly after that Jane gave me a set of lyrics that were a cool twist on a love song and were just so beautiful and haunting. It just so happened that my music matched perfectly with her lyrics—it gave me the chills. The song was "Lust to Love."

"Lust to Love"

It used to be fun was in
The capture and kill
In another place and time
I did it all for thrills
Love me and I'll leave you
I told you at the start
I had no idea that you
Would tear my world apart
And you're the one to blame
I used to know my name
But I've lost control of the game
'Cause even though I set the rules
You've got me acting like a fool

When I see you I lose my cool
Lust to love
Was the last thing I was dreaming of
And now all I want is just to love
Lust turned to love

Every night consisted of one of three things: playing a show, rehearsing, or partying. I'm not sure if Jane and I deliberately set out to write an anthem-like song, but we did with "Tonite." She showed me a set of lyrics she had been working on, and I loved the idea because the words captured the feeling of exactly what we were doing every night. I had music for a verse I was working on that fit perfectly, and we finished the chorus together. I wrote a guitar intro that had a drone note in it—I think it was the first time I did this in one of our songs.

Not only was Jane a brilliant lyricist, but she also wrote amazing music. I remember how blown away I was when she brought in "Automatic." It was this really sparse, eerie love song. The riff that I came up with was very staccato-robotic to go along with the way the word "au-to-ma-tic" was pronounced in the lyric. The Go-Go's were really against doing a "ballad," and this was the closest thing we ever got to it.

Then one day she asked me to come over. She wanted to show me a new song she had written. I remember clear as day walking into her room in Agora Hills. She was sitting on the carpeted floor with an acoustic guitar and proceeded to play me a song called "Our Lips Are Sealed." It was incredible. Jane had had a mad love affair with Terry Hall, the lead singer of Madness. He had written her a letter, and Jane took some of what he had written and transformed it into

a masterpiece. The song was in a 3/4 (waltz) timing, and my only suggestion was that she try it in a more straight 4/4 beat. That is how we started rehearsing it, and I knew at that point that we had a hit song on our hands.

"Our Lips Are Sealed" was so great that it inspired me to come up with what would become one of the quintessential Go-Go riffs. I didn't know it at the time, but I was truly becoming a lead guitarist. I was learning that being a lead guitarist had little to do with noodling solos at breakneck speeds and everything to do with elevating the song with strong melodic riffs. I came up with melodies and runs that would uplift a song like George Harrison did with The Beatles. It was my natural instinct to play this way, coming from the era of classic pop I grew up in. I liked to write counterpoint melodies that wove in and out of the main melodies— this was a result of me learning about counterpoint from the hours spent playing the Bach inventions in college.

"Our Lips Are Sealed"

Can you hear them
They talk about us
Telling lies
Well, that's no surprise
Can you see them
See right through them
They have no shield
No secrets to reveal
It doesn't matter what they say
In the jealous games people play
Our lips are sealed
There's a weapon

That we must use
In our defense
Silence reveals
When you look at them
Look right through them
That's when they'll disappear
That's when we'll be feared
It doesn't matter what they say
In the jealous games people play
Our lips are sealed
Give no mind to what they say
It doesn't matter anyway
Our lips are sealed
Hush, my darling
Don't you cry
Quiet, angel
Forget their lies

I'm a natural collaborator, as it is one of my strengths. But in the case of "We Got the Beat," it was definitely an act of solitude. It was New Year's Day 1980, and I really wanted to write a beat-centric song. So I locked myself in my apartment, got as high as a kite, and listened to a ton of Motown while the annual *Twilight Zone* marathon played in the background on TV. I sat down a couple of times and tried to write something, but nothing happened. I gave up, did more drugs, and started watching TV. Around midnight this idea came to my mind. I scrambled to turn on my cassette player, and the entire song came to me in just a few minutes. I remember thinking, "Oh shit" because I believed I had just written a hit song. I still have that original cassette.

"We Got the Beat"

See the people walking down the street
Fall in line just watching all their feet
They don't know where they wanna go
But they're walking in time
They got the beat
They got the beat
They got the beat, yeah
They got the beat
See the kids just getting out of school
They can't wait to hang out and be cool
Hang around 'til quarter after twelve
That's when they fall in line
They got the beat
They got the beat
Kids got the beat, yeah
Kids got the beat
Go-go music really makes us dance
Do the pony puts us in a trance
Do the watusi just give us a chance
That's when we fall in line
'Cause we got the beat
We got the beat
We got the beat, yeah
We got it

"This Town" is the best song Jane and I ever wrote. When she showed me the lyrics, I knew I was looking at perfection. Instead of inviting the listener to join us, the lyrics sarcastically let the listener know that they will *never* be one of us. And "We're all dreamers, we're all whores" is hands-down one of my favorite lines of any of The Go-Go's' songs. The

music writing was a full collaboration. We wrote a darker-sounding verse that soars into a strangely uplifting anthemic chorus. I had the intro guitar part. Jane suggested that instead of a two-bar intro we make it longer into a four-bar intro. She came up with the idea of cutting the last bar in half, thereby making it a 2/4 bar rather than a 4/4 bar, and I started jumping up and down, saying, "Oh my God! We are prog-rock now!" We both laughed so hard, but let's just call it The Go-Go's version of progressive rock!

"This Town"

We all know the chosen toys
Of catty girls and pretty boys
Make up that face
Jump in the race
Life's a kick in this town
Life's a kick in this town
[Chorus:]
This town is our town
It is so glamorous
Bet you'd live here if you could
And be one of us
Change the lines that were said before
We're all dreamers, we're all whores
Discarded stars
Like worn out cars
Litter the streets of this town
Litter the streets of this town

Jane and I and the rest of the band knew we had really good songs. That is what kept pushing us forward through all of the obstacles we faced. We kept trying to find a record

deal, but no one would take a chance on us. They would say, "You're an all-girl band—we can't sign you!" even though we had great songs and continued to sell out every show. There was even an article in the *Los Angeles Times* about how we couldn't get a record deal.

After our performance opening for British supergroup Madness in early 1980, we were asked to join them on their next UK tour. We were beside ourselves. We figured out all the logistics and were on our way. Returning from that tour in July, we played the Starwood to an overcapacity sold-out crowd. Miles Copeland was there that night and also at our New Year's Eve run at the Whisky later that year, which included Kathy Valentine's debut as our new bass player. It was then that he offered us a record deal on his small independent label, I.R.S. Records. We started recording in April of 1981, and our record came out July of that summer. "Our Lips Are Sealed" was the first single released from the LP. I remember exactly where I was when I heard it on the radio for the first time. I was driving down Laurel Canyon and had to pull over because I burst out into tears of joy. "We Got the Beat" was the second single, which put us over the top and pushed our record to number one. And just as I had done when I was younger, I'd have my ear to the radio for as many hours as I could, listening to songs. But this time it was to the songs from my band, The Go-Go's.

CHAPTER 20

Sunglasses & Cool Cars

by John Doe

Cars, rock 'n' roll & sunglasses are inseparable. This is where Los Angeles tapped into something much darker & more dangerous than NYC's or London's punk rock. Young Hollywood movie stars' lives were cut short in car crashes. People got laid in backseats. You could escape to the desert or drive up the coast w/ the windows rolled down & blow out all those dark, sad thoughts that crushed you in the city.

In 1977 in Los Angeles you could drive w/out constant gridlock. Park pretty much anywhere. Because it was California & there was no rust to speak of, you could buy a drivable 1950s or '60s car for $500. Take it to East LA or Echo Park & get the seats completely redone for $200. And Billy Zoom might teach you how to fix them w/out making you feel like too much of a dummy. We would change oil, point & plugs, adjust the timing, replace brakes or transmissions & even convert a step-van/bread truck to a tour bus on the curb outside 1118 N. Genesee Ave. This was all part of the DIY movement & was also cheaper. It seemed

like Falcons (both Chris D. & Alice Bag), Delta 88s (Nickey
Beat), Sport Furys (Gil T), Coupe de Villes (Bill Bateman),
or even humble Dodge Darts were so available that anyone who didn't live at the Canterbury, walking distance
to the Masque & Hwd Blvd, could make them into their
own magic punk-rock carpet. These rides & the punishing
sunlight also provided everyone w/ plenty of opportunity
for wearing the '50s & '60s sunglasses so plentiful at many
thrift stores that weren't yet curated or picked over. Other
sunglass wearers, even silly new wave ones, were those who
took the most unreliable mass transit in any metropolitan
center, the LA bus system. Their reward for this sacrifice was
encountering the craziest of crazies in all of metro LA, great
material for songs or stories at parties.

All of this distance & freedom gave Los Angeles punk
rock more gasoline (leaded), exhaust fumes, rumble, muscle
& smoking tires than the punk rock that came before. New
York bands, as influential as they were on LA, had art galleries & London, who also spun our heads & inspired, had the
dole. But LA freeways, California auto culture & that freedom, that speed, the horizon w/ the windows rolled down
on warm nights connected us to Chuck Berry, The Doors,
Sun Records & Eddie.

CHAPTER 21

Descent

by Jack Grisham

I sleep with the light on. There was a moral code, unbeknownst to me, and I violated it, stepped over the line, and now the minute the sun goes down, the nightmares arise. Kicking an eye out is all good fun in your teens, but when the offending orb rolls into your thirties, forties, and fifties and hangs like blood-speckled gelatin from the ceiling, it gets real old. They didn't like us. They said we were violent, that we ruined their scene and brought in an element of muscle-headed beach thuggery. It hurt my feelings. I wasn't a thug. I was a gentleman. The cut of my coat was clean. The zippers on the back of my pants were eighteen-inch razor-sharp lines descending into silk-smooth lizard-skin boots—the spurs, polished silver. I guess if you wanted to dance all by yourselves, you shouldn't have played the music so loud. Your hard chords ran wicked along the edges of the freeways and stumbled onto our beaches—spoiled our suntanned Kashmir beliefs. To be honest, I could've done without your influence and your cold shoulder. I preferred

LIVE AT THE MASQUE

(an alternative rock and roll cabaret)

WITH **BAGS** IN SHOWCASE

FEATURING **EYES**

AND SPECIAL GUEST APOPLEXY **SPASTICS**

SATURDAY SEPT 10, 1977   9 PM
1655 N. CHEROKEE, HOLLYWOOD
(between Hollywood Blvd & Selma Ave, 2 blocks east of Highland)

the parties by the piers, the drunken cheerleaders getting ready to lose their virginity to some asshole they couldn't believe they'd slept with, but if you were a young punk from the beach and wanted to see The Germs, X, or The Bags, you had to drive into the city.

Los Angeles was a distance—a 1-Adam-12 see-the-woman through a mist of colored faces and filth. I hated it. The LA punks had a cooler-than-you vibe—although I wasn't sure how drug addiction and homelessness gave them the right to feel so superior. I stood at the edges and watched. The dancing, which the music press had dubbed "slamming," was nothing more than a polite art-school hop or pogo not meant to harm—more pose than pop. The boys from the beach brought life to the dance floor: tanned muscular bodies that were made to be hurt, suburban hybrid robots that thought bleeding was fun. The headlines read "Punk Rocker Carves Swastika in Baby's Forehead!" and we did our best to live up to the hype.

The first night I went to Los Angeles I wore black. I look good in it still. My grandmother said I looked like a storm trooper—handsome and serious. She said nothing about the swastika armband that adorned me. Why would she? Her politics ran, without apology, hard right—my politics, by contrast, were nonexistent. I didn't give a fuck about those who thought they were in charge. I was a kid living with my parents. I didn't vote, work, or pay taxes.

I greased what was left of my hair with a handful of brilliantine and jerked off thinking about the city—fantasizing about the rough punk girls, with their torn fishnets and their dirty Converse. There's something about chipped nails and a used-condom hairbow that turns me on. I've always been a fan of strong women—I'll fuck the weak ones, but I love being destroyed.

There were eight of us that first evening. A local crew who rolled close together for preservation. The punks in Hollywood lived inside walls—a circle of human-trafficked miscreants who let them pogo around the neighborhood without too much static. At the beach we stood out like dirty diapers on the sand—displeasing trash that the police and the concerned citizenry tried their best to remove. We had to travel in packs. Have you ever been hated and chased, stumbling frantically over lush green lawns as you were hounded by a mob? Have you ever been arrested, thrown into a holding cell with forty lice-ridden criminals who thought "punk" meant "faggot" and thought your split-colored mohawk looked like a great target for their cum? A punk in the suburbs was guilty by the sheer nature of his look. A dyed head was a black flag of piracy flown valiantly as you sailed down Main Street. When you slapped on your homemade Germs T-shirt, you were saying that you were willing to take a beating and that you were well aware that your trip to the liquor store to pimp beer and play a game of Pac-Man could go horribly south at any time. And when things did go down, no matter what your involvement, it was always your fault. Fuck. Those Hollywood punks should have printed a disclaimer on that *Yes L.A.* EP, one that read, "By listening to this music and believing these lyrics and adopting these fashions you acknowledge that you are willing to put yourself in danger and that at any time some blockheaded fuck might attempt to beat you senseless." Looking back, I find it amusing that those earlier punks considered us violent when their lives, their words, and their beliefs all influenced the way we behaved. It was their fault—not ours.

That first night made me a believer. I thought I'd been sucked into a family of those with like minds, sideways-torn

rebels whose willingness to take a beating mimicked my own. I was standing in an alley. The salt from that day's surf was still coating my skin. I was talking to a young man—maybe twenty-three or twenty-four. He was wearing a pair of leather pants and a jacket—no buttons, no badges, no bondage straps. Other than the words of sedition that spewed like aural cocaine from his mouth, he could have been a used-car salesman. The police pulled up—two black-and-whites—lights, no sirens. I started to walk away—cow-like behavior that'd been learned from the white teen kegger parties: when the man in blue arrived, you grumbled and made your way like a good hippie to the car. My alley companion laughed. He stood fast. He downed the last few gulps from his beer and then fired the bottle overhand, hurling glass-flashing anarchy into the face of one of the officers. I came in my pants. I wish you could feel what I felt—the satisfaction, the connection, the brotherhood. I was angry. I grew up with a father who was a military man. I had to salute him when he returned from work. I wanted people to hurt. I wanted to be big enough to grab the plastic cord from my father's hand and use it to tear his own skin. I wanted him to grovel on the ground, attempting to cover his ass and legs while I inflicted crisscrossing, bloody, raised welts across them. And here he was, the image of my father, wearing the dark blue uniform of the LA police, and he'd gone down on his knees bleeding before the Mickey's Big Mouthed assault of my new companion. I followed suit. I fired all I had. This was a now-declared war against anyone that wasn't with us.

There were punks that night who complained about our behavior. They cried over the closing of their club, the crackdown from the man. "They're ruining it for everybody,"

they whined. I was shocked. Could you imagine a group of freedom fighters crying because the tanks of their oppressors had bulldozed their clubhouse? Fucking bitches. I wanted to line them up against that alley wall and, one by one, deposit a hot-lead slug between their Gary Gilmore eyes. They seemed like police sympathizers to me. Not real. Losing the club was part of the deal—a war-torn casualty that gave credence to our struggles. It was "us against them." There was no safe ground, no "free zone." My violence was never directed at other punks—I thought we were family. My anger was directed at those who said we can't or we should not, and I had no problem with the oppressor's reflection of my hate bouncing back against me.

The first show I played was at the Fleetwood in Redondo Beach—my band, Vicious Circle, opened for The Middle Class and The Germs. I wore a straightjacket. It was hard to be on stage. I didn't like the exposure. I preferred to be in the crowd, immersed in the energy. My manners didn't match my look. I was afraid to move, to let go, to swing. I stood behind the microphone and squeezed the thin metal stand. The music started slow—a few bent guitar notes escaping from the tears in the speakers. The sound traveled across the stage and into my body, but like vein or lash or spleen, I was unconnected to its presence. It was buried. I screamed and lay upright—a verbal stiff fuck unwilling to wrap my legs around the crowd, but they defiled me. They slammed into each other. They fought. They hurt. They took whatever I was willing to give—anything I had—and then they moved on.

I was raised with rules—guidelines defined by our society: don't take what doesn't belong to you; keep your hands to yourself; honor your mother and your father; men sleep with women, boys with girls; and, above all, respect authority.

I was never comfortable there. I desired to be honorable, and I suppose in some fucked-up way this desire materialized toward my peers. But I was a creep, a deviant pretending to be civilized. Have you ever held your piss until your stomach cramps with the pain and then maybe just a squirt trickles out in your pants or panties and it feels good? But you know you can't let go, you can't wet yourself here, but then another squirt, and another feels good, and then more pain until you finally say fuck it and you release. I held in my desire to strike back until it hurt so bad that I had to let it go, and then after that first blast, the pain came again, so I released more, and then more, until the stream of my hate and my hurt cascaded onto those around me. It was the same with crime, with disrespect, and with sex. Action by action I released my willingness to be good, to be principled, and to be restrained. The next time I crawled onstage I was a cunt—a syphilitic whore willing to do any trick for the crowd. I was completely unbridled and unthinking. I had violated the instilled moral code—and there was no return.

People ask me about the music, what I liked about it, what my favorite bands were, but I don't know what to tell them. Yes, I saw X, The Germs, The Bags, and The Controllers. I played backyard parties with Black Flag and the Circle Jerks. I came from an area that spawned Social Distortion, The Adolescents, T.S.O.L., and The Crowd. I was part of a scene that has influenced millions with its style and its sound, but I really couldn't give a fuck. You might as well be asking me what color pants I wore when I threw my first Molotov cocktail or built my first bomb. The punk scene and the sound was just a bedspread that I fucked on; for me it was never about the music. It was about the pathway of letting go.

Now, if you wanted to ask me something, you could ask me about the backlash from the violence. You could ask me if I mind the night terrors and the inability to be close to another. You could ask me whether I could ever live vanilla when I had raped and slashed my way through the soft flesh of a rainbow. I apologize for nothing. I refuse to stand as some repentant fuck while the crimes of my past are read aloud in the court of post-punk history. I love waking up afraid, and although I no longer hold to those beliefs, I don't regret them.

CHAPTER 22

No Slow Songs Tonight: 1979–1982

by Dave Alvin

"**Those** of us who are about to die . . . salute you!"

With those words Lee Ving, the lead singer of the ferocious punk band Fear, raised a beer to us Blasters as he
stopped by our open dressing room door. We laughed ner-
vously, raised our beers, and saluted him back. Then he
walked down the long, smoky hallway and on up to the
stage of the gritty, old Olympic Auditorium just south of
downtown LA to face five thousand restless and agitated
punk kids. It was New Year's Eve 1981, and we were sharing
a bill with not just Fear but also the relentless noise-jazz-
punk of Saccharine Trust, the art-punk veterans Suburban
Lawns, and, most intense of all, the headliners were the
fierce, brilliant kings of hardcore, Black Flag.

There was no applause as Fear was announced, but in
those days there rarely was any applause at real hardcore
shows. This wasn't really a show for people who came to

HEY, HIGH SCHOOL GIRLS!!!

the

GEARS

MON. Aug 20ᵀᴴ
w/

X

PLUGZ

BLACK FLAG

- STAINS -

library benefit

C.S.O. building

CHICAGO + 1ˢᵀ
NEAR SOTO
E.L.A.

WED. Aug 22ᴺᴰ
w/ **Flyboys**

ADAPTORS

terminals

Hong Kong Cafe

425 GIN LING WAY

CHINATOWN
— X —

clap, cheer, and celebrate their musical heroes; it was more like a gathering of people alienated from polite consumer pop culture, who wanted to get fucked up past the point of feeling pain, ready and willing to beat each other into bloody pulps in the mosh pit or even attack the bands on-stage as a primitive initiation rite into an exclusive alternative society of pain. I couldn't help but hear the crazed roars, insane boos, and threatening catcalls of the audience upstairs echoing through the cavernous, cement halls of the underground backstage. Mr. Ving's first words to the audience were simple enough: "We're Fear. Fuck you!" This sent the crowd into a rage of even louder boos that quickly grew into throat-ripping shouts and booming death threats. Something ugly was going on up there or was just about to. Between the drunk, unruly crowd and the overzealous security guards, more than a few people were probably going to get the living shit kicked out of themselves that night.

Unlike the modern, clean LA sports venues like Dodger Stadium or the Fabulous Forum, the Olympic was a large, dingy concrete bunker built in the 1920s for the 1932 Olympics. Fifty years later, though, it had become a legendary, rundown bucket of blood. For decades it had been the historic home for such blue-collar sports as wrestling and roller derby, but the Olympic was especially famous for its boxing matches. It was a well-known fact among locals that the prizefights in the ring were often much tamer than the fights outside of the ring out in the crowd, and so it was now a perfect place for a night of drunken mindless violence and guaranteed teenage mayhem.

"No slow songs tonight," my brother Phil commanded as I wrote our set list. I agreed wholeheartedly. There would be no arguments between the Alvin brothers on this night.

I looked around the dressing room at bassist John Bazz, pianist Gene Taylor, and drummer Bill Bateman and announced, "All right. We open up with 'High School Confidential' and then don't stop playing even if someone gets killed." I smiled, but I was only half joking. Bill stared back at me with a blank-stone face and said, "Anybody fucks with me and I'll kick his fucking ass." Gene just laughed: "If any trouble starts, Bill, you're gonna have to kick three thousand crazy motherfuckers' asses. Good luck with that." "Hey, fuck you, Gene," Bill shot back. Then we drank more beer and prepared to die.

We'd been in similar surreal and borderline violent situations before, though. The front of my 1964 Fender Mustang guitar has many shards of glass permanently embedded in it from beer bottles thrown at us by pissed-off audience members at punk shows. These wounds were badges of honor to me back then. One is a long gash from a beer bottle thrown at me by a dissatisfied patron at an early 1980 show with the Angry Samoans at the Shark Club in San Diego, while another is an almost delicate spray of tiny brown glass fragments from a beer bottle hurled at the stage when we played with The Weirdos about a month later at West LA's Club 88. The deepest, most dramatic slash running across the front of my guitar was from when we opened in late 1979 for Orange County hardcore heroes The Crowd at the Cuckoo's Nest (a particularly vile former industrial Quonset hut turned punk-rock dive bar in Costa Mesa). The kid who threw that bottle had a pretty damn good arm and great aim, but I was just fast enough and lucky enough to see it coming, so I had a split second to raise my guitar in front of my face and deflect his projectile. Over thirty years later these lacerations are still visible on the front of my

long-retired Mustang, and yes, I still view them proudly as badges of honor.

You might be asking: How did this happen? How did The Blasters, a pompadoured blues/R&B/rockabilly band from sleepy old Downey, California, end up playing shows with the legendary LA punk groups? How did we wind up hanging out with, getting bombed with, becoming close friends with, and, in a small but meaningful way, being proudly linked with the glorious LA punk/new wave rock world of the late seventies and early eighties? It's not a bad question, really. The full answer is sort of complicated, but one simple reason was, despite all the anger, desperation, and alienation in the air, we really fucking loved it.

Growing up in the late sixties and early seventies, my brother and I were odd ducks among our teenage peers. We certainly heard the underground rock music of the time and enjoyed much of it, but we hated most of the Top Forty hits of that era. Listening to Jimi Hendrix, among other artists, helped us become aware of and deeply fascinated by older American music, especially the blues. Because so much of that music wasn't available anywhere at that time, we searched thrift stores and swap meets for hard-to-find old 78s and 45s. Soon we discovered music by more and more obscure artists as we were self-educating ourselves in not only the blues but also jazz, R&B, folk, country swing, rockabilly, and early rock 'n' roll. It wasn't too long before we learned that some of the older blues musicians lived and still performed relatively nearby, so we started sneaking into neighborhood bars to see them perform. Eventually we became underage regulars at a funky little club about twenty miles away in Los Angeles called the Ash Grove. It was a unique place that mixed blues and bluegrass with politics

and social consciousness. Even though I was only fifteen, I felt I'd found a second home among the Ash Grove's eclectic crowd of blues singers, hippies, folkies, artists, radicals, truck drivers, card sharks, and record collectors. When it closed down in 1973, I felt more than a little lost and searched for years afterward for some place, some social scene where I could feel that sense of community again.

By the late seventies all the future members of The Blasters were working day jobs and figuring that life had passed us by, but then we discovered that we were the same ages as the guys in The Clash and the Sex Pistols. So before we even thought of starting The Blasters, we began cautiously venturing from Downey and Long Beach up to Hollywood to see the local underground punk shows at the Masque, the Whisky, and the Elks Lodge, just to check out what all the buzz was about. We were completely blown away by the stunning variety of the first generation of LA punk bands we saw. Some bands, like The Weirdos and The Dickies, were loud guitar combos pounding out Ramones-influenced eight-note bar chords with clever, ironic lyrics. Some were hilarious pranksters like Black Randy, Arthur J. and the Gold Cups, or The Deadbeats. Some were full of angst and conceptual art dogma like the early techno squall of The Screamers, while the tough Plugz and The Bags sang Chicano street poetry and the very early, sweetly amateur Go-Go's played a noisier, sloppier punk/pop than their later million-record-selling slick hits would show.

Some bands, like The Germs, were highly literate with low musical skills, while others were highly literate with very high musical skills, like X, The Alley Cats, and The Nerves. Each of them had their own look, attitude, sound, and almost cult-like fans.

The groups and the audience who followed them were a wide cross-section of nonconformists, oddballs, rejects, and visionaries who couldn't fit in to mainstream society and had finally found a wild home in the developing punk scene. It was a unique community of people who'd come from Venice Beach and East LA, Beverly Hills and Highland Park, Torrance and Pacoima—poor, middle class, rich, the innocent, the guilty, loners, social butterflies, runaways, gays, students, poets, artists, actors, hustlers, bad musicians, great musicians, surfers, Anglophiles, Anglophobes, dealers, addicts, former glam rockers, former hard rockers, prostitutes, strippers, scam artists, older survivors of the sixties Sunset Strip era, whites, Chicanos, blacks, Asians, phony nihilists, wanna-be anarchists, pretend communists, progressives, apoliticals, and even a stray Republican or two, all united by this new music and the seemingly adventurous lifestyle that went with it. Even the mosh pits at the early punk shows were less about beating the shit out of somebody and more of a slightly rough physical expression of communal celebration of being with other misfits just like yourself who had somehow found each other. In 1979 I was a failed college student in my early twenties working as a cook, and after many years of feeling lost and confused about my future, I saw this inspiring—if a bit intimidating— scene and thought that maybe I belonged there as well, just like I had felt at the Ash Grove.

One reason The Blasters sort of fit in to this new scene was how we played our version of old roots music. Unlike most of the great but mellower blues bands making a living working the then-jumping beach-town bar circuit or the very talented country combos grinding out a living in the then-still-thriving California honky-tonks, The Blasters

played really fast and really loud. We happily and proudly bashed our tunes fast enough and loud enough to compete sonically with most of the cutting-edge groups on the LA scene. We didn't want the music we love to become a delicate and dusty museum piece. We sincerely felt—and I still do—that older American music could be as artistically challenging and viably contemporary as the latest disco and soft-rock hits on seventies and eighties Top Forty radio or whatever was the latest hip trend coming across the Atlantic from England. If that meant playing fast and loud, then so be it.

Phil and the other guys, because they were better, more experienced musicians than I was at the time, could easily play the blues slower, softer, and more traditionally than we did in The Blasters. They certainly could have gotten a technically better guitarist than me, but there was some sort of undeniably manic, energetic magic that occurred when the five of us played together that most roots-revival combos didn't have. It may have been because there were two close brothers in the group, but, as we'd all grown up together, listening to the same old records, going to the Ash Grove together, getting into and out of trouble together, we were actually five close brothers. When we started to play, the intensity came easily and naturally. With the veins in my brother's neck straining almost to the point of exploding as he sang and Bill Bateman pounding his drums as if he were trying to kill the damn things and bassist John Bazz pumping decades-old walking bass lines like they were brand new and pianist Gene Taylor hammering his piano like Vladimir Horowitz on methamphetamines, we were one tough, passionate, and more-than-a-little-insane orchestra who could proudly hold our own with anyone. When we hit the stage

I would go into a near-transcendental state from a primal
rush of playing music with the older guys who I'd grown
up admiring, cranking up the amps, bashing on my guitar,
drinking a lot of beer, jumping around the stage, sweating
through my clothes, making dumbbell musical mistakes,
and rushing the tempo as the band pushed the music, the
audience, and ourselves to the limit. I'd never been happier
in my life.

A big part of our band philosophy was that, despite being partial to playing with punk bands like X or raw local pop masters The Plimsouls, we would accept just about
any show playing with just about anyone, anywhere. We
believed American Music was for all Americans. We wanted
the scenesters at the Whisky or the Starwood to like us, but
we also wanted truck drivers at honky-tonks like the Palo-
mino Club or the shuffle-groovin' crowd at the Long Beach
Blues Festival to dig us as well. This attitude led to some
wonderful shows but also an absurdly bizarre gig or two.
In our effort to make a name for ourselves and win over
converts to our cause, we opened shows for an abnormally
wide variety of punk, power pop, and roots acts from late
1979 up to the 1981–1982 show with Black Flag. Besides X
and The Plimsouls, we also shared bills with The Cramps,
Asleep at the Wheel, The Go-Go's, Ray Campi and his Rockabilly Rebels, The Plugz, The Motels, The Weirdos, Wall of
Voodoo, The Ventures, Levi and the Rockats, Sir Douglas
Quintet, Split Enz, Rubber City Rebels, The Fabulous Thun-
derbirds, and The Boomtown Rats.

The strangest without a doubt was when we opened eight
arena shows for the monstrously popular rock band Queen
in the summer of 1980. Some of the members of Queen
had seen us playing a ridiculous gig at an old Hollywood

roller rink that had turned into a new-wave venue/pick-up
bar called Flippers. They liked what they saw and nicely
asked us to open their West Coast tour. We'd certainly heard
of Queen, so of course we said yes, but we had no idea how
hugely popular they were or how, let's say, vocally opinionated their fans were. We went from playing little two-
hundred-seat dive clubs to facing seventeen thousand angry
Queen fans in sports arenas who had no idea why some
pompadoured guys from Downey who bashed out old
three-chord American rock 'n' roll were opening for their
glamorous English heroes. Oddly enough, having seventeen
thousand pissed-off classic-rock fans booing and throwing
anything they could get their hands on at us did not deter
us in the least. If anything, it only strengthened our brotherly Blaster bond and our "us against the world" mentality.
From then on, whatever scorn five hundred punk kids in a
club could spew at us was nothing compared to the venom
of thousands of Queen fans. Well, at least I felt that way
until we were about to go up against five thousand riled-up
Black Flag fanatics.

It was very difficult at first, though, to overcome the prejudice many Hollywood club bookers and promoters had
against a rockabilly/blues band from Downey. We weren't
cute enough or well connected enough socially for most of
them to bother with. One woman who booked a legendary
Hollywood club flatly told me that if we weren't fucking
somebody famous, she would never give us a gig. Thankfully The Blasters' reputation and coolness profile was
helped immensely when LA scene heavyweights like John
Doe and Exene from X, Belinda Carlisle of The Go-Go's,
and Peter Case from The Plimsouls gave us opening slots at
their shows. Many other bands, plus nonmusicians yet hip

tastemakers like Pleasant Gehman and Anna Statman or enlightened club bookers like Mac at the Club 88, generously spread the news about us around town or gave us much-needed shows. After the initial period of struggling to get booked, we slowly started building enough local notoriety to get more and better gigs and then, eventually, to make enough money to quit our damn day jobs. Within a year of denying me a show, that club booker who was so interested in The Blasters' nonexistent sex life with celebrities was happily offering us shows at her club without asking any ridiculous personal questions.

Bands' willingness to help each other was one of the great attributes of the LA scene in those days. There certainly were petty feuds between bands for whatever personal reasons or between punk rockers versus new wavers or between bands who didn't have record deals against bands who did. Overall, though, most of the groups felt a sense of unity against the record labels that wouldn't sign us, the radio stations that wouldn't play us, the clubs that wouldn't book us, and the promoters that might rip us off.

My favorite example of this band solidarity was when we were scheduled to open for The Plimsouls at their sold-out show at the Cuckoo's Nest in 1980. I got into a heated, physical argument with some blockheaded security guys over whether I could bring a harmless bottle of milk into the club. They insisted I couldn't bring it inside. In my righteous and perhaps silly anger, I said, "Fuck you. Tell your fucking boss that we ain't playing your fucking club." Three security goons grabbed me and threw me and my bottle of milk out of the club. One of them said, "Big fucking deal, asshole. You're a fucking piece-of-shit opening act." When Peter Case heard this, he instantly declared, "Fuck the

Cuckoo's Nest. We ain't fucking playing unless The Blasters play." I was astonished by Peter's hard-line stance. I'd
only met Peter once before, but he knew and enforced the
unwritten code of the underground scene: don't fuck with
the bands. Within a few minutes the owner and the security
crew profusely apologized, and with my bottle of milk in
my hand, I proudly walked in and played the show.

As The Blasters made the transition into being a headlining act at the Starwood, Whisky, and Roxy, we tried to
return the favors shown us by giving opening slots to new
or unknown bands like Rank and File, The Gun Club, or
Phast Phreddie and Thee Precisions, bands we thought deserved attention. Some of those then-little-known opening
acts, like Los Lobos and Dwight Yoakam, would move on
to greater fame and success than we ever imagined for ourselves. We also gave gigs to some of our blues idols from our
Ash Grove days like Big Joe Turner and Roy Brown, or we
put together shows at Hollywood clubs where we would be
the back-up band for Big Joe, Bo Diddley, John Lee Hooker,
and Hank Ballard, exposing them to a brand-new audience.
It wasn't until much later, after venturing away from the
protective cocoon of the LA scene, when I sadly discovered
how cutthroat and self-serving many musicians/songwriters
out in the cold world of the music business actually were.

Despite the fact that we were now selling out the Whisky
for two or three nights in a row and had accumulated a
decent amount of good, original songs, no major label
was remotely interested in signing us. Eventually we signed
a recording contract with the local independent LA label
Slash Records. We owed some of Slash's interest in us
to our friends in X, who were also on the label and had
been prodding Slash's owners to give us a deal. Slash was

a spinoff of the groundbreaking punk music/art magazine of the same name and had already released, to unexpected commercial success, the seminal first Germs album as well as the first two masterpiece albums by X. This certainly sold me on being on the label, despite some trepidation from my brother and other Blasters. Plus, they had smart, passionate people working in their office, like the enlightened A&R staff of Mark Williams and Chris D. plus committed publicists like Susan Clary and Bill Bentley. It was also a nice bonus that their employees were also our friends. Over the next few years Slash (and its subsidiary, Ruby Records) gathered a remarkable stable of important bands, both local and national, like Los Lobos, The Violent Femmes, The Flesh Eaters, Fear, The Del Fuegos, The Gun Club, Rank and File, The Misfits, Dream Syndicate, and Green on Red. To say I was proud to be associated with Slash would be a major understatement.

Sadly our relationship with Slash was a mixed bag. On the plus side, Slash was a sympathetic environment that gave us more creative freedom than any major label ever would have given us. Unfortunately the two charming rascals who owned Slash were first-class purveyors of high-end cultural revolutionary sweet talk. At the time that sort of rebellious rhetoric meant an awful lot to me, though it certainly didn't mean quite as much to the other members of The Blasters. The depressing realization that, perhaps, the owners of Slash really weren't quite as interested in cultural revolution as much as the big money that can be made by telling people that they were interested in cultural revolution didn't become clear to me until much later. It seems to me the rascals at Slash also weren't terribly interested in accounting to us either. You live and you learn.

About a year before The Blasters signed with Slash I was invited by poet-songwriter Chris D. to be part of the latest lineup of his band, The Flesh Eaters. I'd gotten to know Chris a little through my friendship with John Doe and was honored but slightly intimidated when he asked. I felt I might not be good enough, but I quickly lost my initial sense of trepidation when Chris said that this new version of The Flesh Eaters would be a combination of members from X and The Blasters. Chris would be singing and John would be playing bass, DJ Bonebrake would be on marimba, timbales, and assorted percussive noisemakers while Steve Berlin would play various saxes and Bill Bateman would be the drummer. All I had to do was be the loud guitar player. All right, I thought, I can certainly do that.

Chris, who didn't play any instruments, had been driving around town, singing his new songs into a cheap cassette recorder he kept in his car. Chris gave me and John these rough tapes, and we divided the songs up between the two of us. We then separately figured out the chord changes and modulations of each song and devised loose arrangements to take to the band. As each musician added their own musical twists and Chris started singing his complex lyrics with his very distinctive voice, we were thrilled to discover that we had come up with a sound unlike any of the bands any of us had ever been in before.

Instead of X's razor-sharp punk or The Blasters' pounding roots rock, our one Flesh Eaters album, *A Minute to Pray, A Second to Die*, sounded like the murky soundtrack to a midnight voodoo ceremony being performed by junkies in an East Hollywood alley. It was a crazy blend of Catholic and Santeria liturgies, sixties garage rock, free jazz, swampy rhythm and blues, surrealist poetry, and zombie movies, but

somehow it all worked together. The album and the few live shows we played did confuse some folks back then. Some punks didn't like the slow, trance-like drones of certain songs, while some rockabilly purists didn't dig the modern jazz stuff, and even a few religious evangelists held the album cover up on TV and denounced us as evil Satanists doing the devil's work. However, we did have many passionate fans and admirers. The respected underground music scribe Byron Coley boldly stated that it was "the greatest rock album ever made." That might be going a bit too far, but many younger bands over the years, like Mudhoney, have been profuse in their praise of our album as a major stylistic influence. Not long after the album's release I read a very positive review of it in which the writer called the music of The Flesh Eaters "postpunk." I've never been quite sure what that term actually means, but it seems like as good a description as any other.

Whatever punk rock in Southern California was or wasn't by late 1981, it and the scene around it were changing quickly. Many of the older, initial LA punk scene makers were starting to stay away from the shows or moving off into different musical directions, from funk to western swing. Some of the original LA punk bands like The Go-Go's and X had signed major label deals and were spending as much time touring out of town as they were playing in LA. Many of the newer punk bands were less quirky and individualistic and more stereotypically what most folks thought of as punk. For The Blasters it was becoming apparent that, as we were then achieving a measure of local fame and headlining once-out-of-reach clubs like the Whisky, that our future ahead was one of hitting the highways to become roots-rock road warriors.

Violence at shows was now becoming commonplace, both inside and outside the clubs. High school kids who had just discovered punk rock were driving up to Hollywood from outlying towns just to get wasted, look for fights, and, as we used to say, fuck some shit up. They also became the arbiters of what was and what was not punk rock. This may have been the proper course of things or it may not have been. I certainly didn't know. I'm not a psychologist nor an anthropologist. I'm not sure what drove the LA punk scene to become a violent world with kids beating the fuck out of each other. Blame Reagan or a lack of spiritual direction or the lack of meaningful work. Blame drugs or alcohol. Blame The Eagles or disco music. Blame the boredom of the suburbs or shitty fast food diets. Certainly some of the shoving and fighting kids in the Black Flag Olympic crowd would end up in jail, while others would tragically die young due to one sad reason or another. Most would probably finish school, maybe join the Armed Services, then get jobs, buy houses, raise families, become regular solid citizens, paying taxes and mowing lawns. A lucky few, though, might leave the Olympic Auditorium inspired by the music they heard and walk into the new year of 1982 to start their own bands, playing whatever the hell kind of music they wanted, creating their own new scenes and their own new worlds.

When Fear ended their set it was our turn to face the ominous Olympic crowd. Lee Ving, who had just survived the onslaught, was laughing as he passed us in the narrow hallway that led to the stage: "Heads up, Blasters. They're throwing a lot of fucking shit out there tonight." Though I actually heard more than a few people clapping and cheering as we walked on the stage, the bulk of the crowded auditorium erupted into a cascade of boos and angry screams. Some big

guys were still fighting in the mosh pit, even though there wasn't any music to encourage it, and a few skinhead kids smashed against the front of the stage and screamed, "Rockabilly Sucks!" as they flipped us off. Bill glared at them and flipped them off as he stood behind his drum kit, taking a long pull from his beer bottle. John stood stiff and straight by his bass amp, ready for whatever nonsense might soon happen. Gene Taylor, built like a Sherman tank, stopped at the edge of the stage and stared down at the offenders, his beer bottle gripped menacingly in his fist, daring them to start something. They shut up. He took a long swig off his beer, walked to his piano, and sat down. My brother stepped up to his microphone and calmly yet proudly announced, "We're The Blasters from Downey, California."

As I walked onto the Olympic stage that night I had no idea what would happen with the crazed audience waiting for us. I had no idea what would happen in the coming years. I had no thought that I would ever leave my Blaster brothers or that there would be new scenes for me to be a part of, with different brilliant musicians to make glorious noise with. I had no thoughts of the different highways I'd soon be traveling on and no thoughts that I'd soon be mourning the deaths of friends, fellow musicians, and family members. All I thought at that moment was, "Yeah, we are the goddamn Blasters from goddamn Downey, California, and nobody is ever going to stop us from playing our goddamn music." Then I just turned up my guitar even louder, walked to the front of the stage, and faced the unruly audience as my brother confidently counted off "High School Confidential" at a tempo as fast as any punk song Fear had just played. There would be no slow songs tonight.

MAY GERMS 28

8 p.m. Memorial day

MIDDLE CLASS

*ÅLSÖ APPEARING: CYNICS & SCIENTISTS

EVERYONE IS SUSPECT

☆☆☆☆☆☆☆☆☆☆☆☆☆☆☆☆☆☆☆☆☆☆☆☆☆☆☆☆☆☆☆☆☆☆☆☆☆☆

BOBS' WESTERN DANCE CENTER
641 N. Euclid
ANAHEIM

$4.00

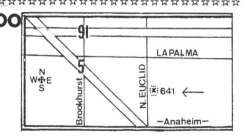

CHAPTER 23

How to Build a New World Then Tear It Down

by Kristine McKenna

The first generation of punk rock in Los Angeles? First, I have to tell you about the city at that time. Let's say our story begins in 1976—that's when the players in this particular drama started drifting into town from all corners of the country. It was the year I arrived in Los Angeles, and what did I find? In my memory it was like a ghost town. It seemed like there just weren't that many people around! You could sail down the freeways and pull up and park right in front of wherever it was you were going, and it felt spacious and quiet. You could do your thing in private, and the city would courteously ignore you. I loved it.

That world is gone now, and the locations and venues that gave shelter to LA's first punks, stretching from downtown LA to the beach, are mostly gone too. The Masque; the Starwood; the Anti-Club; the house where X lived at the corner of 6th and Van Ness; Licorice Pizza, across the street

from the Whisky (mercifully, the Whisky hasn't been de-
molished yet, but it seems kind of creepy now); Club 88;
the offices of *Slash* magazine on the second floor of an office building at the corner of Santa Monica Boulevard and
Fairfax; the second Masque, at the corner of Santa Monica
and Vine; the Stardust Ballroom; the Hong Kong Café; Madame Wong's; the Nickodell; Vinyl Fetish on Melrose; the
Atomic Café; and LACE, on Broadway, downtown. They're
gone, as is the Greyhound bus station on 5th Street in Santa
Monica, where Exene arrived from Florida on a rainy morning in 1976. John and Exene's house on Genesee, where
they birthed their fantastic song "In This House That I Call
Home" is still there, but I feel sad when I see it. A few weeks
ago I found myself winding across town through the city
streets, clogged with traffic, of course, and I passed some of
these absent landmarks and actually cried. It's not my city
anymore. But maybe that's how it works—cities belong to
the young and are transformed from one generation to the
next for use by the new breed. Good luck to them.

By the time the Sex Pistols released their first single, "God
Save the Queen," in May of 1977, the LA scene was already
percolating, so we found our way to the mountain without
a map. We weren't copying anybody else, and from the start
there were things that distinguished LA's punk scene from
the scenes in other cities. The first generation of LA punk
was literate and really smart, for starters, and each band had
its own sources of inspiration. Much of the punk that came
in its wake wasn't very smart at all, nor was it particularly
original. A tremendous amount of diversity coexisted under
the rubric of early LA punk too, and there was a surprising
degree of parity between men and women—it was not a sex-
ist scene, and women were treated as equals. Latinos and

gays were welcome too, as were old people: your tired, your poor, your huddled masses yearning to breathe free. Isn't that the way it's supposed to be? It was that way for a brief spot in time.

There was a period, from the mid- to late seventies, when punk existed, but the punk fashion industry had yet to co-opt it, so if you saw a punk-looking weirdo on the street, it probably was an authentic punk weirdo. There was no blue-print to work from, so dressing in an interesting way de-manded real imagination. People rose to the occasion too, taking personal style in any direction they chose. Everybody in the first generation of punk was a star, whether onstage and off—it really was a fascinating hodgepodge of people. You'd see a girl in a prim, secretarial-type cotton shirtwaist dress next to a dude with a mohawk, next to a girl dressed like a hooker. All kinds of people materialized, and anybody who'd gone to the trouble of showing up had a right to be there. It took a while for all this to start cooking, though, which brings me to the scourge known as social media. LA's first punk community took a while to get up to speed because things didn't "go viral" then. The jungle drum of word-of-mouth was how information got around, and mea-sured against the lightning speed information travels today, LA's first punk community coalesced at a glacial pace. Peo-ple had to physically be in rooms together and talk to one another to learn about things then, and that world was inti-mate and tactile and visceral in a way texting can never be.

I was a journalist covering the "new music" for various publications, and as such, I stood slightly apart. I wasn't one of the people getting drunk in an alley with misbegot-ten mascot Darby Crash—there was something genuinely mad about him, and frankly, he kind of scared me, which

I assume was his intention. I felt straight and responsible compared with members of the community who were truly living on the edge—and some of them really were—but I had my place in the scene, and people respected it, as I did theirs. It wasn't, however, a user-friendly crowd. This was, after all, a community of very young people, so there were feuds, misunderstandings, grudges, warring factions, and lots of dialectical discussion about who was and was not a "poseur." People tended to be a little gruff with one another, but if an outsider went on the attack? First-generation punks were fiercely loyal to the community in that case, and mainstream opposition only made the scene more cohesive.

A few names survived that time and achieved varying degrees of immortality, but so many amazing supporting players disappeared into the past. Every single one of them was a crucial thread in a shimmering tapestry, and in my mind the famous and the forgotten alike remain as pure and incorruptible as they were the first day I saw them. There was Rik L Rik, scuffling around barefoot, looking like he'd just hitchhiked into town from Appalachia; his manager, Posh Boy, a.k.a. Robbie Fields, in his cheap, shiny suit—Posh Boy always seemed to be selling something; fancy-dancing heart-throb Spazz Attack, who served as janitor at the Masque and lived there too, I think (a rather gruesome thought, as the place was filthy); rockabilly vixen Kitra; Belinda Carlisle, dressed in a billowing, belted, black Hefty bag, with bee-stung lips and baby fat that made her seem soft and sweet; Lee Ving, a stevedore who looked as though he could kick anybody's ass but was a lovely man and never would; K. K. and Trudi, who were like king and queen of the prom— there was something regal and dignified about them. And, of course, there was impresario Brendan Mullen. Equal parts

P. T. Barnum and the absentminded professor, Brendan always seemed to be in a kerfuffle of some sort. There were dozens more, and somehow they all hung together and created some beautiful things.

So why did it end? Where did it go? In retrospect it's obvious that LA's first generation of punk was an exotic flower meant to bloom for a short time; these things aren't supposed to last, and that's what makes them precious. The forces that brought about its demise are beginning to be clear to me now too. Darby Crash's death by OD, in December of 1980, has been cited as marking the end of something (an era? A life?), but the evaporation of the scene was more complicated than that. Cyndi Lauper (yes, I know—how did she get in here?) has a song called "Money Changes Everything," and it says a lot about what happened to LA's first generation of punk rock. It's easy to have ideals when there's little at stake, and it's very hard to say no to money. Poverty is tolerable, even romantic when you're young, but it gets wearing in fairly short order, and given the chance to leave it behind and live the high life? People just don't say no. This is America, after all, and temptation crept into LA's world of Baker Street irregulars. Some people got, others did not, and that bred animosity.

MTV invaded public consciousness in 1981, and that took everything down a notch too. It's almost impossible to make a three-minute video, conceived to promote a song and sell records, that doesn't reek of inauthenticity, and MTV made music stupider. Anything you see on television is harmless and familiar—we've been sucking our thumbs to television for decades—and mass culture has a terrifying ability to absorb and neutralize everything in its path. MTV did that to punk, to a degree. Revolutions need something

to kick against, and you can't rebel against somebody who's hugging you.

There were defections in the original tribe too. When X released its debut album, *Los Angeles*, on Slash Records in 1980, it was like the hometown team won the Super Bowl. But when The Go-Go's turned their backs on punk the following year, transformed themselves into harmless sorority-type chicks, and had a best-selling record with *Beauty and the Beat*, it was more a case of *what the fuck?* This really did seem like the beginning of some kind of end, and things began to sour right around then. Some punks retreated to depressing living rooms to shoot heroin, and we all know what that leads to: apathy and drool. Others returned to the "straight" world because they were able to. There were plenty of serious misfits who couldn't possibly function in mainstream society, though, and god knows what happened to them. They started falling away in the early eighties and simply vanished.

The official scribe for LA's first generation of punk, Claude Bessy, summed up the community nicely when he wrote, "We're just a pack of off the wall weirdoes with fringe leanings," in the pages of *Slash* magazine. There was lots of adrenaline churning around, yes, but mostly we were a ragged pack of kooky people in pursuit of genius and fun. This came to a screeching halt when Black Flag and the rest of the South Bay crew on SST Records came roaring onto the scene. Greg Ginn founded SST in 1978, but it wasn't until the early eighties that its ascendancy began, and when it did, it unleashed a furious wave of testosterone on the scene that was crushing. Women were the first to leave—there was no place for them in the world of hardcore punk; gays and sensitive artist types went next,

and the audience began to change. People who went to punk shows in the early days were respectful, they listened, and they were genuinely interested in the band onstage, even if they'd seen the same band four nights earlier. We knew we'd always see something new, partly because these were mostly not professional musicians, and nobody did the same show twice, because they weren't able to. Professionalism came later for some, but in the beginning the scene was truly experimental, and the audience was tolerant and supportive. With the arrival of hardcore, punk became a blood sport, and the mosh pit was colonized by sixteen-year-old boys with plaid flannel shirts tied around their waists, determined to transform themselves into human cannonballs. The entire scene became about one thing, aggression. Claude Bessy was long gone by then—he'd moved to England in 1980—but I imagine he would've found the whole thing boring because the undercurrent of humor that originally made punk so brilliant disappeared completely when hardcore took over.

So many members of this community are dead now—I won't recite the R.I.P. list of LA punk's first generation because it's too long and too sad. We're all like trees, and the leaves that are the people we love flutter to the ground one by one. Time is a brutal, devouring force, and until it's begun to do its handiwork, it's impossible to comprehend how very beautiful it is to be young, how privileged and innocent it is. You may think you know the score when you're twenty-four years old, but you never do, for the simple reason that you can't: life lobs curveballs that are unimaginable at twenty-four. We believed we were dangerous and subversive back in the day, but in fact, we were babies, yet to rub the fairy dust from our eyes. Time takes a heavy toll

on ideals, and looking back, it all seems unbearably idealistic and sweet.

So the scene is gone, and many of the people who created it are gone too, and I suppose that's how it's meant to be. Great art is immutable and eternal, though. I recently attended an X show where I watched young people—yes, they were young—crowding the lip of the stage, mouthing the words to "White Girl" and "Year One." The music continues to mean something to those who need it, and those who need it will continue to find it.

CHAPTER 24

My Only Friend, The End

by John Doe

No harsh screeching of wheels at dawn, no soft whimper-
ing late at night, no roaring wind as the sun went down or
moaning as the back door closed. None of these sounds
were heard at the close of the first LA punk-rock era somewhere in 1981 or '82. What was heard was quiet at the center of the music scene. A center that in 1977 through '79
was louder than hell w/ people running here & there &
back again. Now that center—which included art rock, hard
rock, punk rock, funk rock, performance art, roots rock &
all manner of rock that had influenced beginners & more
experienced—had moved off into different genres at the
fringe of the core.

It was quieter now, w/ loud pieces on the outside. The
rockabilly or roots scene & what was sadly named "cowpunk" had one audience where it was a bit safer, a place
where nonviolent or ethnic types didn't need to worry
about getting threatened or punched. The hardcore scene
pulled some of the other original Hollywood punk bands &

- X -

FEAR

HONG

KONG Cafe

THU. JULY 12

fans & hundreds of new people from the beach & San Fernando Valley into a swirling vortex. The truly adventurous art crowd went to downtown LA, found lofts & galleries, quieter roots music or experimental music bars & created more of an East Coast environment. By 1980 most of the core group of bands—The Weirdos, The Screamers, The Germs, Fear, The Go-Go's, F-Word, Rik L Rik, The Bags, The Alley Cats, The Plugz, The Skulls, The Nerves, The Dickies, The Deadbeats, Black Randy & the Metro Squad, The Controllers, The Gears, The Gun Club, The Flesh Eaters, Black Flag, the Circle Jerks, The Minutemen, Rhino 39, Catholic Discipline, The B People, The Eyes & a few I might have missed—had moved on, swapped members, or quit altogether. Each of these groups had an identity that may not have been completely original or different from each other but, as a whole, made up an incredibly diverse & broad style of music. And though they didn't always hang around w/ each other, they shared camaraderie in that they had been there at the beginning. That beginning may have been inspired by others, but it grew into something unique & extremely influential. There's no doubt that San Francisco & San Diego influenced & contributed a great deal to this stew of California punk rock.

We had ripped through what seemed to be so very much in such a very short time. Somehow people from all over the US had found each other in Hollywood, California, the land of fruits & nuts. Each arrival & story had uniqueness. There were few enough of us so that we all stood out in some way. We gravitated toward the kindred souls that could make a band. The Canterbury parties before & after the Masque or for no reason but to hang out, make noise, get drunk & argue about ideas were always on. It happened

late at night on the picnic tables outside Oki-Dog on Santa
Monica Blvd. It happened hungover at Duke's Coffee Shop
beside the Tropicana or at Peaches Records on Hollywood
Blvd or a corner pizza joint on Hollywood Blvd where we
competed for high scores on the Playboy pinball machine.
Sometimes it was only seven or eight people, sometimes
30 or 40. Everyone talked loud, smoked & drank & made
outrageous claims about what might happen & what they
might do. And somehow, through shitty jobs & asshole
bosses, we found time to rehearse & places to perform those
half-baked songs. Of that original "Hollywood 200," everyone did something, whether it was make a fanzine, front a
band, simply look outrageous, or all three. It took collaboration & will & maybe that's why even now those survivors
are proud & protective of that honor. By 1979 the Masque
had been harassed out of existence by the cops from a couple of different locations. Five or six private halls had had
their toilets or sinks ripped out by Black Randy or someone
too high, too emotionally damaged, or just too pissed off to
care. We had driven up & down the state to visit our rivals
San Francisco & San Diego because no other opportunities
existed in the middle of the state, or the country for that
matter. The Masque promoted two infamous benefit shows
at the Elks Lodge near downtown LA. One of them turned
into an all-out police riot, clubbing dazed punk rockers as
the cops stormed the building & the auditorium. More legit
clubs like the Starwood & Whisky a Go Go had allowed
some of us into their golden kingdom, where we didn't
have to bring our own PA systems, only to ban the more
adventurous for bad behavior. *Slash* magazine came & went
along w/ more than a few of its celebrities, but not before
it inspired hundreds to start their own band, fanzine, art

project, or at least take a stab at finding something to do that wasn't status quo. As *Slash* became a record company, some found a home for their music. But when the magazine closed & Claude Bessy moved to England, it seemed there were fewer times for those spontaneous gatherings. Some of the groups & individuals who seemed poised for greatness just faded, either from lack of ambition or maybe talent or possibly lack of attention from the music business that we all didn't care for in the first place. Maybe most of us *were* too weird & misfit for the world at large. Maybe it was a good thing we didn't do more than make a bonfire in Hollywood for a few years, then pass the torch to a version of punk rock that was more uniform & willing to sleep on anyone's floor, touring relentlessly under the SST or another DIY banner.

In 1978, after the Dangerhouse single "Adult Books" b/w "We're Desperate," X drove to & from New York to play only 3 shows (CBGBs, Max's Kansas City & Studio 54) because we didn't know of any other & there may not have been any other place to play in between. (Except one very sad pick-up "gig" w/ a broken-down Xmas tree—it was November—in Schwenksville, PA. Above the bar where we played for 20 or so people was an "apartment" where we could spend the night.) From '78 to '79 Club 88 & the Hong Kong Café opened & gave LA punk rock a more consistent home. Fear, The Germs, The Alley Cats, The Bags, The Go-Go's, etc. all worked out the missing pieces of their songs in these 150-capacity bars. LA's Chinatown, its broken-down courtyard, hokey wishing well, and Golden Pagoda Bar where we learned about the drink the scorpion became another hangout, a testing ground for punk rock. Seventy-five to a hundred punks hung around that courtyard every weekend

for a year or two. Madame Wong's welcomed the new wave bands. Blackie's in Santa Monica also let some of the roots bands make a racket. The Whisky & the Starwood finally re-opened its door to bands who could draw more than 100 people, but only after all these other venues proved that a movement was in their backyard. We thought that moving into legit clubs was what we wanted, but by walking into their world, we probably lost something in the bargain.

The *LA Times*, *LA Weekly* & *Los Angeles Reader* picked up on the new music & urged people to go out & find a style of music or band to love & they did. Now that the audience was bigger, they & the bands could afford to break off into genres & the bills where all manner of misfit bands playing together was becoming a thing of the past. Somehow amidst all this, Exene & I got married in Tijuana, where among the 25 friends who accompanied us, a couple of hotheads went to jail. Some local free newspaper ran a sensationalized account of the "crazed punk-rock wedding in TJ" & we were stung. A little more than a week later her sister was tragically killed in a car accident. Everything changed that night, though we didn't realize it all at once & we began to pull inward. Six months later we released our first LP, *Los Angeles*, & X began touring the US regularly. The Go-Go's finally got signed & released their debut. Then in December of 1980 Darby Crash ended his life at 22. We went on a US tour a week later. We weren't even around for the memorial & that hurt. For a few groups who had more ambition & opportunities, tours became longer & more frequent. There didn't seem to be the same people around when we returned. We all had grown tired of night-after-night parties & had seen the toll it took. We began to rely more on each other & a few close friends. We didn't go to the after-hours club

Zero Zero as much, a place where both The Germs and The Blasters could hang around w/ transvestites, artists, or other bands and desperate characters, a place where more than once I tried to talk Darby out of his final solution. By the end of '82 X had two critically acclaimed records on Slash & were about to sign w/ Elektra Records, the home of Love, MC5, The Stooges & The Doors. We were sure we were on our way, but we had left more behind than we knew.

Acknowledgments

JOHN DOE SPECIAL THANKS

Kristina Teegerstrom, Veronica, Elena & Amelia Nommensen, Kenneth F. Duchac, Gretchen B. Nommensen, Fred Duchac, Joelle Shallon, Alfred Harris, Michael Blake, Ray Manzarek, Grace Cavalieri, Michael Mogavero, Jack Chipman, Mike Rouse, Dave Alvin, Cynthia Wasserman, Dave Way, Viggo Mortensen

TOM DESAVIA SPECIAL THANKS

The DeSavias (Tony, Terry & Natalie), The Whites (Nicky, Corey, Ethan & Aaron), Cathy Kerr, Richard Edwards, Matt Messer, Joyce Caffey, Dave & Nicki Bassett, Matt Pincus, Carianne Marshall, Rob Guthrie, Frank Handy, Amanda Tufeld, Mitch Wolk, Rachel Jacobson, Ken Bethea, Murry Hammond, Rhett Miller, Philip Peeples, Eric Gorfain, Sam Phillips, Jenny Oppenheimer, John Vlautin, Lance Ummel, Jeff Boxer

JOHN DOE & TOM DESAVIA SPECIAL THANKS

John and Tom would like to thank all the authors and all the photographers who contributed to this project, our agent Lynn Jones Johnston of Lynn Johnston Literary, all at Perseus/Da Capo (especially Ben Schafer, Matty Goldberg, Maha Khalil, Kevin Hanover, Lissa Warren, Sean Maher, Justin Lovell, and Amber Morris), Richard Scheltinga and Christine Langianese from Kessler, Schneider & Co., Scott Sherratt

John Doe and Tom DeSavia would like to thank each other.

About the Authors

JOHN DOE

Born in Decatur, Illinois, John has lived in California for forty years. Graduated from Antioch College in Baltimore, Maryland, he remains a member of the band X, has made ten solo records & acted in over fifty films & television shows. He is the proud father of three daughters & currently lives with his sweetheart in Richmond, California.

TOM DESAVIA

A Los Angeles native, music industry veteran, and longtime record and music publishing A&R man, currently of SONGS Music Publishing, DeSavia started his career as a music journalist. He loves LA punk rock more than just about anything.

EXENE CERVENKA

Exene Cervenka is a member of both legendary LA punk band X and alt-country pioneers The Knitters. She has been writing songs, music, poetry, prose, and fiction since 1976. Her collages have

been exhibited in galleries and museums in LA, NY, Austin, Miami, and Copenhagen.

JANE WIEDLIN

Jane Wiedlin is a founding member of The Go-Go's. The band was the first-ever successful all-girl group to write their own songs and play their own instruments. Jane has released six albums of her own. Besides being a songwriter, guitarist, and singer, she is also a playwright, the world's first atheist minister (licensed to perform weddings), a comic book author, an actor, and an animal rights activist. She lives in Hawaii and San Francisco.

PLEASANT GEHMAN

Pleasant Gehman is a writer, dancer, actor, musician, and painter. She is the author of eight books, including *Showgirl Confidential: My Life Onstage, Backstage and on the Road* (2013) and *The Belly Dance Handbook* (2014). Her latest books *(Super) Natural Woman*, a memoir about her paranormal experiences, and *Journalista!*, a collection of her rock 'n' roll articles from 1977 to 1997, will be published by Punk Hostage Press in 2016. www.pleasantgehman.com

CHRIS MORRIS

Morris has been writing about music in Los Angeles since 1978. He was a senior writer at *Billboard* (1986–2004) and music editor at *The Hollywood Reporter* (2004–2006) and served as the music critic at the *Los Angeles Reader* (1978–1996) and *LA CityBeat* (2003–2008). Morris's writing has also appeared in the *Los Angeles Times*, *Rolling Stone*, and other national publications. His roots music radio show, *Watusi Rodeo*, aired on the legendary Indie 103.1 and Scion Radio. His book, *Los Lobos: Dream in Blue*, was published by the University of Texas Press in 2015.

HENRY ROLLINS

Born in Washington, DC, Henry Rollins moved to California in the summer of 1981. For over three decades Rollins made albums with Black Flag and The Rollins Band, wrote over twenty books, and performed in bands and on his own all over the world. He continues to write for magazines and newspapers, publish work on his imprint, 2.13.61 Publications, and speak to audiences in up to twenty countries a year.

CHRIS D.

Born in Riverside, California, Chris D. graduated from Loyola Marymount University, Los Angeles. Singer/songwriter for Divine Horsemen as well as for all incarnations of The Flesh Eaters, he is also a writer, actor, and teacher. He wrote record reviews for *Slash* magazine (mid-1977–1980), was an A&R man for Slash Records (1980–1984), and was a film programmer at the American Cine-matheque, Hollywood (1999–2009). His books include five novels, a short story collection, and two nonfiction film books.

MIKE WATT

son of a sailor, was born the year sputnik was launched. came from virginia as a boy and has lived in pedro town ever since. started the minutemen w/ d. boon after becoming involved with the punk movement. works bass and also paddles kayak in the los angeles harbor near his pad. got to learn for 125 months serving w/ the stooges. more information on him and other stuff is at the mikewatt.com website he runs himself.

ROBERT LOPEZ

Robert Lopez is an actor, comic, musician, and songwriter for stage musicals, theater, and film soundtracks (yes, that Robert Lopez).

He has been performing since a child in punk-rock music. He still performs with The Zeros and other music projects in the United States and Europe. He's most renowned for his over-twenty-five-year career as El Vez, the Mexican Elvis. Recording dozens of albums, he has toured all over the United States, Canada, Europe, Australia, and Japan. He has been presented on *Oprah* and *The Tonight Show*, and has even been a question on *Jeopardy!* He has had the honor of having his music and gold Mariachi suit displayed at the Smithsonian Institute in Washington, DC.

TERESA COVARRUBIAS

Teresa Covarrubias is a native of Los Angeles, California. Born and raised in Boyle Heights, she is a Chicana, educator, poet, and perpetual outsider. She was the lead singer and songwriter for The Brat and currently works as an elementary school teacher in East LA, where she shares her love of art, music, and lifelong learning with a rambunctious group of second graders.

CHARLOTTE CAFFEY

Charlotte was born and lives in Los Angeles and remains a member of The Go-Go's. She continues her intense passion for songwriting, composing for artists, and theater. She has been married to Jeff McDonald for twenty-three years. She is the fiercely proud parent of her twenty-one-year-old daughter, Astrid McDonald.

JACK GRISHAM

Jack Grisham currently lives in a haunted old schoolhouse with his wife and five kids. He writes. He tours. He refuses to play well with others. He is the vocalist for the punk band T.S.O.L.

DAVE ALVIN

Grammy Award–winning singer-songwriter Dave Alvin formed The Blasters with his brother, Phil, in 1979. After leaving that band in 1985 and playing guitar for X for two years, he has released multiple solo albums, including *King of California, Public Domain, Eleven Eleven*, and *Ashgrove*. He lives in California and on the national interstate highway system on his way to the next show.

KRISTINE MCKENNA

A native of Dayton, Ohio, Kristine McKenna moved to Los Angeles in 1976 and began writing about music for various publications. She's published two volumes of collected interviews and twelve books on different aspects of the West Coast counterculture between the years 1920 and 2001. She continues to live in Los Angeles.

CONTRIBUTING PHOTOGRAPHERS

Ed Colver	Gary Leonard
Frank Gargani	Melanie Nissen
Michael Hyatt	Rick Nyberg
Debbie Leavitt	Ruby Ray
Jenny Lens	Ann Summa

Permissions

Lyrics reprinted with permission:

"We're Desperate": Written by John Doe/Exene Cervenka. Published by Lockwood Valley Music. Administered by Pacific Electric Music/Grosso Modo (ASCAP).

"Living at the Canterbury": Written by Jane Wiedlin. Published by MGB Songs/Universal Music (ASCAP).

"Lust to Love": Written by Charlotte Caffey/Jane Wiedlin. Published by MGB Songs/Universal Music (ASCAP).

"Our Lips and Sealed": Written by Jane Wiedlin/Terry Hall. Published by MGB Songs/Universal Music (ASCAP)/Plangent Visions Music LTD (PRS).

"This Town": Written by Charlotte Caffey/Jane Wiedlin. Published by MGB Songs/Universal Music (ASCAP).

"We Got the Beat": Written by Charlotte Caffey. Published by MGB Songs/Universal Music (ASCAP).

Index

DATE DUE

GAYLORD

Designed by Trish Wilkinson
Set in 11.25-point Giovanni by The Perseus Books Group

Cataloging-in-Publication data for this book is available from the Library of Congress.
ISBN: 978-0-306-82408-1 (hardcover)
ISBN: 978-0-306-82409-8 (e-book)

Published by Da Capo Press
A Member of the Perseus Books Group
www.dacapopress.com

Da Capo Press books are available at special discounts for bulk purchases in the U.S. by corporations, institutions, and other organizations. For more information, please contact the Special Markets Department at the Perseus Books Group, 2300 Chestnut Street, Suite 200, Philadelphia, PA 19103, or call (800) 810-4145, ext. 5000, or e-mail special.markets @perseusbooks.com.

10 9 8 7 6 5 4 3 2 1

Under the Big Black Sun

a personal history of LA Punk

John Doe

with **Tom DeSavia and friends**

Da Capo Press
A Member of the Perseus Books Group

Under the Big Black Sun

are many and varied. Contemporary reasons can include the movement of refugees fleeing conflict zones, economic migrants hoping to make a better life somewhere else and environmental migration due to natural disasters. In addition there is what Michael Kimmelman has identified as 'middle-class' migrants – educated individuals in search of new experiences. [2] Whatever the reason, together, this influx equates to an estimated three million people moving to cities each week according to the International Organisation for Migration's (IOM) recent report. [3]

As a result, cities are becoming increasingly crowded, and every alley and rooftop is under greater pressure to perform with maximum effect. The financial and architectural impact of this squeeze on space is immense, so it is perhaps not surprising that many of the projects featured in *Mobitecture* are a direct effort to alleviate this tension. As the IOM report makes clear, 'strong population growth in cities poses a great deal of pressure on infrastructure, the environment and the social fabric of the city.' [4]

Homelessness

With urbanization a dominant challenge of the twenty-first century, works that address homelessness such as artist Winfried Baumann's, begin to suggest how mobile architecture can play a significant role in alleviating the lives of those seriously affected by urban crowding and rising costs of living. Baumann's works such as Portable Housing Space (page 93) and the I-H Cruiser (page 132) are moveable, practical, dignifying structures that offer thoughtful options for those with limited housing choices.

Privacy and protection for the homeless are also explored in Hwang Kim's project Cocoon (page 30). His use of cardboard to create a moveable shelter is an ingenious way to utilize a ubiquitous material that is readily, and often freely, available. By analyzing the shape and geometric possibilities of a single sheet of cardboard, and scoring a series of precise folding lines, a little like origami, Kim has created a structure that is carefully designed to provide a snug, albeit elemental, shelter. Mobile architecture with agency is similarly seen in the work of Gregory Kloehn, an exuberant designer who began his creative journey by exorcising his need to work with repurposed and reclaimed materials. His Homeless Homes Project (page 184) began as a folly but subsequently developed into a benevolent enterprise that has now resulted in more than forty-five little cabins on wheels that have been given away to homeless people. His cabins are weatherproof, able to be moved with ease and give a sense of ownership, pride and security to those who live in them.

Political Migration

The imperative needs of migrants who are forced to move as a result of political instability is also having an increasing impact both on cities and the way designers respond to these challenges. Our basic requirement for shelter – and the cost of human life when it is not provided – is portrayed all too clearly by the Syrian refugee crisis. This distressing prompt has become a catalyst for many designers. Recent projects in *Mobitecture* that respond to the refugee crisis include Angela Luna's seven-piece range of wearable garments called Crossing the Boundary (page 48), which addresses issues such as shelter, visibility and mobility. Conceived to balance a sharp street wear aesthetic with the practicalities of humanitarian assistance, her jackets contain all the essentials including options for tents, sleeping bags, baby carriers and even a flotation device.

Along similar lines, the brief for Wearable Habitation, a project by students at the Royal College of Art in London was shaped by the three basic needs of refugees – clothing, a place to sleep, and shelter (page 46). Using their design skills to make a difference, the folding 'suit' sits like a knee-length parka when unfolded and is formed of a tough breathable polyethylene material known as Tyvek. Its insulated body of Mylar – the 'space blanket'

more often seen protecting marathon runners – is intended to protect wearers against heat loss. The seams can be zipped up to form a sleeping bag and the tent is erected with kite rods inserted into seams, creating scaffolding that transforms the coat into a three-dimensional structure.

Environmental Migration

Alongside the turmoil that forces people to flee conflict zones, are the refugees who are stranded or displaced following environmental disasters. The evidence is clear: over the past twenty years the world has experienced a rapid increase in weather- and climate-related disasters, and for now, this effect is unlikely to reverse. [5] Mobile architecture offers unique solutions for such emergency situations. Lightweight, transportable, quickly erected, more stable than a tent, and often inexpensive to produce, 'mobitecture' offers functional, life-saving answers to the urgent need for shelter in the aftermath of natural disasters.

Designs conceived following the Japanese earthquake and tsunami of 2011, for example, highlight the potential for mobile architecture to offer critical aid in disaster zones. Architecture Global Aid, for instance, designed Origami Paper House (page 20) with lightweight, folding solutions built from cardboard. The specific choice of materials, and design specifications of these shelters accounts for the different effect of disasters in different parts of the world, such as the likelihood of a tsunami to accompany an earthquake in Japan.

Another compelling design response to the effect of our changing climate is Warka Water (page 44), which is easily assembled and moved, and offers essential life-giving support. Designed for use where water is scarce, such as in Ethiopia, the project enables water to be captured through a mesh and bamboo frame, which funnels rain, fog and dew down through the structure to provide several litres of water a day. Alert to the difficult topography that its users are likely to encounter, the whole unit can be packed down, rolled up and carried on a person's back.

Making the most of materials that are readily available is also highly relevant to design solutions for emergency zones. Recognising this, students at the Lebanese American University created a project nicknamed ECS-p1 (page 104). Using humble plastic crates and plastic cable ties that are stacked together to create a simple interlinked structure, the result provides dappled shade and a sense of place and enclosure. The structural rigidity of the crates allows the shelter to be self-supporting while additional boxes in and around the building serve as storage and seating.

Downsizing and Economizing

Away from the frontline of conflict zones and natural disasters, mobile architecture is gaining popularity as a way to downsize, highlighting a philosophical shift in society as well as economic advantages. The growing popularity of having a home on wheels is, arguably, a result of the rising gap between rich and poor. The shift towards mobile accommodation also addresses the environmental and social costs that come with occupying large buildings. With the amount of living space per person in the USA almost double what it was in 1973, and with the cost of purchasing a home rising steadily in relation to income, the need to find more viable ways to live is a pressing concern. [6]

As Oliver James points out, since the 1990s 'the desire for larger, more luxurious and better located houses' has been a central reason for the current residential pressure. [7] This has been intensified in recent decades by the voracious commercial appetite of property developers. For many, this combined pressure has resulted in the increasing impossibility of owning a home. Across the western world, and especially in cities, this trend is consistent.

Mobile housing solutions can offer a heartening alternative for those who refuse to join the ranks of Generation

Rent but for whom traditional home-ownership is unachievable. [8] Woody the Trailer (page 208) is one such instance. Designed and built by Americans Brian and Joni Buzarde, their cedar-clad house on wheels helped solve the dilemma, and gave the young couple an asset they could either continue to live in, or sell once they were more settled. This attitude underpins many people's choice to design, or move into, many of the tiny mobile homes featured in this book.

For university students, too, the idea of building or buying a small mobile home at the beginning of their tertiary education is gaining appeal. [9] Rather than spending money on renting flats or dorm rooms, living in a moveable dwelling means their costs are significantly reduced and, in addition, they gain a tangible asset to keep or sell after graduating. Though mobile homes may not address the broader challenge of financial inequality between generations, when compared to renting they offer comfortable, affordable, well-designed abodes that are both a home and an investment.

Activating Urban Spaces

Moveable architecture can also have a beneficial effect on shared public spaces. As a catalyst for activity, public structures that host events like markets or concerts draw people together to meet, talk, eat or just spend time. In

MOTOElastico's Bamdokkaebi Night Market (page 219) retractable zig-zagging orange canopies contribute to the vibrant street scene, sheltering vendors and their wares, and drawing visitors to the animated waterfront. The lightweight V-shaped metal frames are set on wheels and can simply be folded up and rolled away at the close of trade. The People's Canopy by People's Architecture Office (page 218) follows a similar logic – invigorating public places with its modular red canopies that move on dozens of unicycles. As well as creating a fascinating spectacle while in motion, once in place they form vast covered meeting spaces.

Refractor by Seattle Design Nerds (page 36) also acts as an urban space activator. Its nebulous form, composed of a combination of translucent and opaque plastic panels, revives the fun of inflatables. The large pillow-shaped bubble becomes a captivating space in which to play, and weighing so little it can be delivered almost anywhere by cart – swiftly reanimating underused urban spaces.

Related to these attention-grabbing and invigorating catalysts for public enjoyment are the itinerant service providers that improve our quality of life. A dental surgery in a truck saves on travel time and queues (page 232); a library and community space inside a bus with transformable interiors brings education to a broader audience (page 220); and a theatre in a train on the Ecuadorian coast offers its cultural programme to a wide audience (page 226). The social generosity of these mobile structures extends to recreational projects like the WA Sauna by goCstudio (page 265), which floats on Lake Union in Seattle. Continuing the city's long tradition of homes and cabins on the water, the project is the result of a Kickstarter campaign to build a floating sauna that bobs on the lake for everyone to enjoy.

Maximizing Abandoned Spaces

The nature of mobile architecture is also well suited to spaces that have been overlooked such as abandoned buildings and leftover pockets of land. In Hamburg's Eilbek Canal, a handful of floating homes have thrived as a result of the city's re-zoning regulations (page 254). With commendable foresight, in 2006 the local government allowed the Eilbek neighbourhood to be transformed from a neglected waterway to a residential zone. Following an open competition for houseboat designs, the winning entries were awarded berths on the urban waterway. Ranging in scale, materials and function, the eclectic suite of ten homes illustrates how floating accommodation can be contemporary and forward-looking, while also invigorating urban spaces. Opportunistic, too, are the parasite pop-ups that draw on their hosts –

usually, abandoned buildings – to provide a place for individual mobile units. Durable, private and providing a degree of security, solutions such as Light House designed by Bangkok studio All(zone) is an airy room contained within a polyethylene-coated metal grid (page 106). The lightweight structure is slotted into obsolete building sites, providing a place to sleep, study or work in overcrowded tropical cities such as the populous Thai capital. Emmy Polkamp's project, To Many Places (page 107), also reflects a rising interest in creating pleasant yet itinerant places to stay. Her hotel-tent concept can be deployed en masse or singly, creating nomadic hotel rooms that provide amenity while also breathing life and use back into the vacant host structure.

Middle-Class Migration

As Michael Kimmelman points out, those fortunate enough to be middle-class migrants are also on the move. They are educated, inquisitive and eager to experience life in a range of different places. For them, 'mobitecture' is an ideal fit – offering flexible spaces that dovetail with the increasingly global labour market and increasingly frequent changes in jobs and careers. Travelbox exemplifies this approach (page 114). Elegantly tailored to fit into an aluminium and timber box, Travelbox contains all the essentials for basic living: a bed, table, chair, shelving – and even a bicycle. With Travelbox, the architects, Juust, have created a solution for mobile living in which furniture can accompany each move, reducing both environmental and financial burdens.

In workplace environments, advances in technology, the digital economy and rising rates of self-employment also encourage middle-class migration. Identifying this trend, global design company IDEO's Work On Wheels concept (page 202) looks to the future with its self-driving flexible workspace vehicles that provide an office on the go. Rather than enduring a commute, the commuting workspace can come to you. Or rather than working in the city, Work on Wheels can be taken to the beach or the countryside. Complete with technologically and materially advanced systems for high-speed digital connections, projects such as IDEO's have the potential to transform the way, and where, we work.

Discovering the World

For all the people clamouring to reach the city, there are just as many for whom a break from its unrelenting pace is very welcome. Holidays that offer peace, isolation, an opportunity to connect with nature – and, increasingly, away from wi-fi – are becoming more and more popular. The Koleliba, for instance, was designed specifically to give its architect-owners relief from the crowded city (page 213). Set on top of a standard trailer, Koleliba makes the most of its limited size – extendable features such as an awning and terrace maximize outdoor leisure time.

The A–Z West Wagon Station Encampment in California, owned and run by American artist Andrea Zittel, offers a different kind of mobile outdoor experience. Part of her twenty-hectare (fifty-acre) property, the Wagon Stations are spartan steel and aluminium structures, dotted around the site and designed to offer visitors an immersive experience of the spectacular desert landscape (page 98). In Australia, the Wothahellizat Mk1 is a maverick mobile machine built by Rob Gray (page 230). Designed for spending up to three months in the outback, its muscular re-appropriation of an army truck includes robust aluminium chequerplate cladding and an outdoor deck, cantilevered high above reptiles, flash floods and other desert dangers. Brimming with opportunities to connect to the natural environment and offering adventure and freedom, these mobile dwellings challenge our habitual reference points for Recreational Vehicles (RVs) or camping equipment.

Travelling Light

Parallel to those projects that reflect the often confronting challenges many people face today, *Mobitecture* also includes travelling structures that are inspiring, playful and inventive. The Ice Huts captured in Richard Johnson's photo essays convey the idiosyncratic and often exuberant creativity evident in the hundreds of humble ice fishing shelters dotted across the frozen lakes of North America. Their owners have devised unique solutions to the challenge of staying warm during winter fishing expeditions. The results offer no end of variation – from a hut with skis attached, to one built on a sled (pages 248 and 249) but each illustrates the individual character of their owner-builders. Reinvention is the motivation behind Archive II, a work by David Garcia of MAP Architects who wanted to house a collection of books gathered over a lifetime (page 131). The rolling timber 'wheel' includes a reading seat and bookshelves in a neat circular form, embedded with hundreds of books. Archive II can simply be rolled to a different location, as and when the reader desires. The sometimes fleeting nature of 'mobitecture' resonates in Urban Campsite Amsterdam's idea to unite art and camping in a short-lived summer programme. Each year a series of artistic 'tents' are commissioned to transform a selected site in the city. Creative variety is paramount and ranges from the colourful Kite Cabin (page 50) and Goahti (page 72) to the ingenious expanding De Markies camper (page 146). In a similarly engaging way, Floating Cinema by Duggan Morris Architects (page 288) creates a lively, changeable space for community events that was commissioned by UP Projects to transform the waterways of east London. Part of a remit to produce engaging new work for public spaces, the barge travels along London's canal network, offering a range of programmes at different locations for a wide audience. The delight and entertainment that structures like these offer is perhaps more valuable than ever in the face of the weighty social and political concerns that colour our everyday existence.

In a surprising and sometimes bewildering array of forms, materials, colours, sizes and locations, *Mobitecture* demonstrates that architecture is very much on the move. Mobile structures in all their wonderful variety are celebrated here in a visual ode to life on the move. Ranging from quirky to sensible and from rustic to deluxe, from houseboats, huts, and tricked-out caravans, to disaster shelters, wearables, and futuristic prototypes, *Mobitecture* vividly demonstrates the exciting possibilities for life on the move.

Notes

Mobitecture is arranged in chapters, according to each project's primary means of mobility: from structures than can be carried by hand and on foot (Human), those that stack, fold, inflate and move by means other than wheels (No Wheels) to those on various numbers of wheels (One & Two Wheels, Three Wheels, Four Wheels and Five + Wheels), as well as those that move on snow and ice (Sleds +), or on lakes, rivers and oceans (Water).

At the top of each project can be found the name of the structure, the architect, designer, artist or maker, the country of origin or installation as well as the year in which the project was completed.

Below each project can be found the following additional information:
– The number of people that can be accommodated
– The means of mobility – by tractor, motorbike or shopping cart, for example (see the full range of mobility icons, opposite)
– The principal material palette from which each was built which includes such curiosities as mobile phone cases, plastic buttons, doormats, fluorescent tubes, traffic cones, zippers and umbrellas.

In rare cases where information is not available, a dash '—' takes the place of the information.

Key to Mobility Icons

 Hands

 Feet

 Pedals

 Caterpillar treads

 Bicycle

 Mobility scooter

 Car

 Truck

 Motorbike

 Onboard engine

 Skis

 Sled

 Horse / Donkey

 Camel

 Shopping cart

 Tractor

 Paddles / Oars

 Tugboat

 Helicopter

Human

No Wheels

One & Two Wheels

Three Wheels

Four Wheels

Five +
Wheels

Sleds +

Water

Bolt Half

Kama Jania

Finland

2015

Providing protection against lightning, this range of tents by Kama Jania was part of her graduate design thesis, which addressed common fears about lightening storms. Conceived for use on short trips, the Bolt Half is a compact tent for one to two people, composed of aluminium poles and connectors that offer robust shelter and give peace of mind during storms. Its bespoke locking mechanism creates a secure, easily assembled frame, with attached copper wiring that discharges electrical currents into the earth. Weighing just over one kilogram (two pounds) the design – insulated with Mylar and fully waterproof – is a trusted companion for solo hiking.

Human

Waterproof plastic, aluminium, PVC, Mylar

Octabar
Freeform
South Africa
2016

Designed to stretch out between poles, the Freeform tent is simple and flexible. A lightweight alternative to cumbersome marquees, the bold colours of the tent also evoke the Bedouin life. The canopy, a stable, long-lasting waterproof textile offers shade and promotes communal interaction. As the name suggests, the Freeform offers its owner scope to sculpt according to their needs, forming dynamic shapes with elastic ease. Varying in scale from large to small, the tents are ideal for a range of functions – including camping, social events and domestic living. Do not be misled by these effortlessly floating forms; the striking shelters are also strong and durable.

Waterproof two-way stretch polyester, poles, rope

Origami Paper House

Architecture Global Aid

Spain

2014

Part of a philanthropic enterprise to create emergency housing in Lorca, the Origami Paper Houses combine good sense with good design. These shelters, by Spanish-Japanese group Architecture Global Aid, are cheap and lightweight; sturdy alternatives to tents and ad hoc shelters. Easily carried by one person, the houses are suitable for short-to-medium-term occupation, particularly in areas under threat from earthquakes. They include hinged entry and window openings to control light and ventilation and, anticipating the likelihood of catastrophes, the houses are distributed ahead of time, thereby mitigating the aftermath of natural disasters.

Human

Cardboard

Yamaori Taniori Tent
Iyo Hasegawa
Japan
2011

Poetic and prudent, the Yamaori Taniori Tent series is a response to the massive earthquake that hit Japan's northeast in 2011. The origami technique creates a colourful, protective paper enclosure that is intended to 'rest and revive the senses'. A home for the displaced, the practical application of a traditional Japanese pastime is intended to lift the spirits with nostalgic reminders of childhood fun. Folded with heavier card to an A-frame or cubic form, the designs become semi-permanent. Like origami, the tents bring to mind moments of privacy and joy, overcoming conditions of crisis with a distinctly Japanese sensibility.

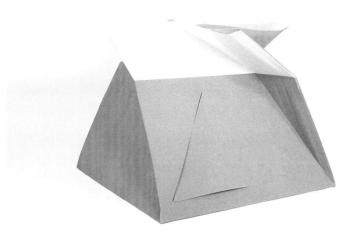

Kraft paper

The TeeZee (Pyramid Accordian Shelter)

Joseph Cabonce

Australia

2015

A far cry from the arguably clichéd origami paper crane, this human-scaled structure was designed as an efficient shelter that can be quickly erected at music festivals. Drawing on the traditional miura pattern technique discovered by Japanese astrophysicist Koryo Miura, the walls of the TeeZee, made from Corflute (a kind of corrugated plastic), gain strength as a result of their folded geometry. Weighing only fifteen kilograms (thirty-three pounds) when packaged, it is easily carried by a single person. Though originally designed to improve upon the inevitable aftermath of many festivals in which tents are discarded en-masse, it is also a highly effective solution for emergency housing relief.

Corflute

Umbrella House
Kengo Kuma
Italy
2008

Shielding people from both sun and storm, this temporary house is formed from repurposed umbrellas. The designer Kengo Kuma takes the humble umbrella – an item for solo use – and transforms it into a stunning enclosure to shelter a group of people. Waterproof zips, and the in-built spidery trusses of the umbrellas, provide all the architectural support Umbrella House needs. The structure is intended as a moveable pavilion; a playful temporary home for the curious, not to mention the ultimate protection for those who hate to get their hair and feet wet.

Umbrellas, waterproof zippers, timber base

Mikasi Tipi

Sascha Akkerman,
Flo Florian

Germany

2014

A contemporary take on the tipi, the Mikasi is Sascha Akkermann and Flo Florian's take on an age-old icon. Creating a playhouse for kids or a poetic adult retreat, Mikasi's scissor-like frames adjust in width and span. The lattice, hewn from ash, creates an airy space enveloped by a durable, semi-translucent skin of Tyvek (polyethylene fibre) that attaches with ease to the apex of the support. The hexagonal floor of the Mikasi is cushioned and slightly raised making it suitable for indoor or outdoor use. The three-part design is collapsible and compact: its lightweight form just rolls, folds and tucks beneath your arm.

Human

Ash framing, Tyvek, cushions

Walking Shelter

Sibling

Australia

2008

Designed as a one-off playful device that upacks from high-top shoes, the Walking Shelter is perhaps more coat than tent. For life on the move, this two-part, flight of fancy design is hiden in a mesh bag concealed within the heel of the shoe. The bulging nets contain a brightly coloured cloak that unfolds and zips up to form an instant raincoat. Instead of traditional tentpoles and strings, the wearer forms the human frame that gives the garment its shape. Its zipped window entrance evokes the traditional tent door, while the reflective silver lining gives a modicum of insulation.

Polyester, rope, plastic buckles

Bricks and Mortar

Field Candy

UK

Bringing weight to festival tents, this ironic print puts you ahead of the field. Its brickwork roof is entirely waterproof, cloaking a classic A-frame construction that gives room enough for two. With a fire retardant polyester skin that is also UV resistant, the print conceals a double-layered camping system, including a breathable inner with sewn-in groundsheet. High performance and suitable for year-round use, its easily assembled elasticated aluminium poles simply slot together to create a stronger, lighter system than its standard counterpart. Set up within minutes, the light-hearted design gives more time for play, and includes a zipped bag to take it away.

Human

Polyester, zipper, alluminum poles

Helix
Ootro Studio
Spain
2016

This spiky retreat-for-one is built from recycled cardboard and touches the earth lightly, conveying the designer's aim to promote connections between people and the environment. Formed from dozens of interlocking laser-cut pieces of card, the structure is lightweight and simple enough for a single person to carry and assemble. The habitable volumes are made by folding and securing tabs, without the need for tape or glue. Inside the interlocking space, small apertures give focused views of the landscape. Like a pinecone of polygons, its arresting shape captures attention and renders this everyday industrial by-product into a lyrical form with a timely vision.

Laser-cut cardboard

Wheelly

ZO-loft

Italy

2009

This clever solution for urban shelter is ready to roll. Tackling homelessness with smart design logic, the large aluminium wheel turns on rubber runners and is light enough to push along with the handle. Set down, the handle doubles as a brake, forming a sturdy basis for the integrated polyester tents that expand from either side of the structure into a three-metre-long (eleven-foot) tube. Large enough to recline in, and including a hanging bag for storing necessities, the sleeping tent is secured with an insulating rubber disc at one end, and the large bag on the other.

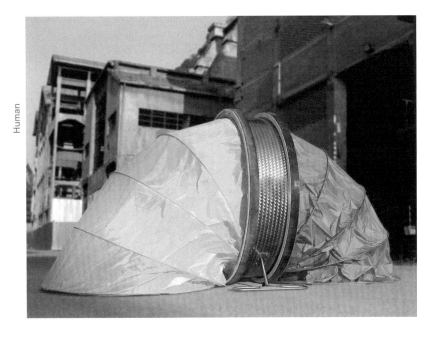

Metal wheel, rubber runners, polyester tents

Mollusc

Ru Hartwell

UK

2016

Doing away with pegs and soggy ground, the Mollusc is a reinvention of the humble tent. This unusual dome is designed as a portable, retractable hood that, when closed, provides a robust enclosure. Set on top of a circular base of heavy gauge PVC, the dome is held up by nine arched steel tubes that slot into the sturdy steel base. The waterproof cover is formed from marine grade acrylic, keeping rain, gales and hail at bay. Telescoping together, the Mollusc's frame can open or close in three seconds flat. Thus easily collapsed, and sized to fit in standard cars, the comfort and efficiency of the Mollusc Dome Tent leaves campers as happy as a clam.

Steel base, steel tubes, acrylic cover, PVC

Cocoon

Hwang Kim

Korea

2005

Like the protective homes spun by insects that give this structure its name, Cocoon is imagined as a shelter for the homeless. Part of Hwang Kim's thesis for his Royal College of Art MA degree, this elegant cardboard solution relies on carefully considered folds to shape the space needed for temporary shelter. Secured by tabs with plastic buttons, the enclosure is light, easily folded away and carried, and improves on the usual option of boxes or newspapers to protect the homeless against the elements. Kim's interest is in designs that consider the challenges of contemporary society, which this project achieves by addressing the rise in the number of homeless people.

Human

Pre-folded single ply cardboard, plastic buttons

DesertSeal

Andreas Vogler

Germany

2004

Devised to survive extreme arid terrain, the DesertSeal is an inflatable, reflective shell in which users can endure soaring temperatures in comfort. Designed according to the thermodynamics of such environments, where air at upper levels is cooler than that close to the sand, the tapered body includes an intake source at the apex, and an expelling fan at the base, both powered by a flexible band of solar cells. Lightweight and easily transported, its silver skin reflects piercing heat and contains a narrow space for rest, just over one metre (three feet) wide. Though developed on earth, this glistening hybrid might just have the potential to cater to human life on Mars.

Human

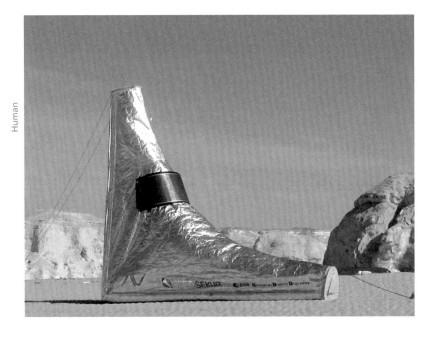

Polyethylene-coated fabric, electric fan, solar panel, nylon rope, zipper

Habitent

Lucy Orta

UK

1992

Somewhere between art, architecture and social protest, this habitable tent transforms bodies into buildings. Enveloped in a silvery aluminium shell akin to a survival blanket, this is a clever solution for modern nomads. This artwork by Lucy Orta explores a serious theme within its crisp, hooded cloak, bringing to mind issues of homelessness and refugee displacement. Telescopic armatures transform the piece from waterproof poncho to one-person tent, offering space for privacy and rest. Worn by the homeless in Paris and Munich, the work is described as 'operational aesthetics', and creates practical respite as well as compelling work of visual art.

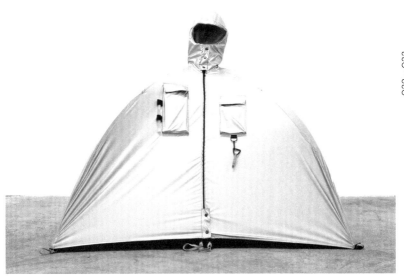

Aluminium-coated polyamide, polar fleece, telescopic
aluminium poles, whistle, lantern, compass

Cactaceae

X-Studio

Mexico

2013

Located near the Tropic of Cancer in Mexico, this shelter is designed as a place for introspection and peace. Inspired by the surrounding landscape, the small enclosure draws on the shape of local cactus flowers and the Mexican folk art tradition of *papel picado* – decorative sheets of perforated paper. Cut across its semi-transparent skin are hundreds of petals of various sizes. Its appearance changes with diurnal shifts: the decorative punctures allow dappled light to enter by day, while at night an internal light creates a gentle glow. The ten-sided curiosity can be easily carried to a new site – a lightweight lantern that is at one with its locale.

Human

Paper, timber

Chicken Coop

Valerie Vyvial

UK

2015

Part of Skip Garden, Chicken Coop is one of seven temporary structures designed for the King's Cross development site in London. The project is the brainchild of Global Generation, an organization that educates and inspires people about the importance of ecology. All seven works employ sustainable construction techniques and reclaimed materials. Formed of a bamboo frame joined by steel fixings, the coop for three chickens encloses a silver birch trunk reclaimed from nearby heathland. The cladding is made from panels of birch pierced by leaf-shaped patterns which transform the coop into a lantern at night.

Bamboo, birch panels, steel

Refractor

Seattle Design Nerds

USA

2015

The nebulous, globular Refractor is Seattle Design Nerds' answer to engaging the public and invigorating under-used urban areas. Delivered by cart and erected by hand, the installation is made from scavenged plastic and space blankets. Cut into standard triangles, the units join to form a contained building block. With a resilient base of layered cardboard, the varied skin of the inflatable form acts in distinct ways – its hazy plastic diffuses interior light while Mylar segments reflect the surroundings. Its conspicuous form attracts attention, becoming a captivating space for a range of public events.

Human

Plastic, cardboard, Mylar

Cocoon Tree
Glamping Technology
UK
—

The height of rustic dwelling, these lightweight bubbles – and their occupants – hang from tall trees. Assembled from aluminium framing and waterproof canvas, each Cocoon has twelve anchor points that secure to surrounding branches and trunks. Weighing less than 200 kilograms (150 pounds) this easily removable and ecological design fits a double bed inside. Sealed mosquito screens and controlled heating provide a temperate, bite-free vacation. Throwing camping a curveball, the Cocoon Tree is a memorable place to hang out.

Aluminium framing, stainless steel, waterproof canvas,
polyamide rope, metal nodes

Melina

David Shatz

Israel

2016

An accordion for accommodation, this backpack–tent by David Shatz is a thought-provoking addition to transient urban living. Addressing the need for safety and shelter in city locations, Shatz's expandable design is formed of a textile shell supported by ten steel frames. Giving stability when open and neatly contracting when closing, the concertinaed frame creates enough space for reclining as well as providing a sense of refuge from urban threats. Light enough to simply pack up and carry on the back, the Melina is ideal for a flaneur with fatigue. Shatz hopes this simple project will reclaim public space, giving a reassuring place in which to pause or linger.

Steel framing, nylon rope, canvas, denim

Basic House

Martín Azúa

Spain

1999

From golden square to blow-up quirky 'pad', Basic House is the hands down winner in lightweight housing. Activated by heat from sun or bodies, the foldable, inflatable home is almost immaterial. Created from fine metalized polyester, it expands to create a shelter for two people – and deflates to fit into the back pocket of your trousers. With a coating of gold on one side and silver on the other, its reversible form provides protection from both heat and cold respectively. Offering freedom from being tied down to a physical home, Basic House occupies very little space but gives a lot back.

Metalized polyester

Pop-Up Habitat

People's Architecture
Office

China

2011

Stirred by the rise in amateur photography in China – and the increasing obsession with selfies – the People's Architecture Office repurposed photographic panels to create playful pop-up spaces for rest or pause. Lightweight and strong, the modular, shiny structures are joined together with Velcro attachments. When assembled en masse they provide arresting shelters that deflect the light. Quickly erected, and equally easily collapsed, the accumulated panels act like units with which to create a range of spaces – from glittering canopies for *hutongs* – the narrow alleyways in traditional residential areas of a Chinese cities – to single-room huts.

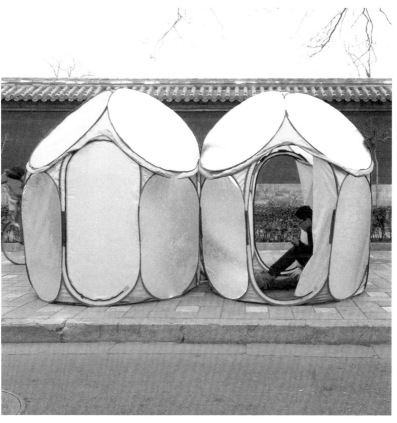

Fabric, spring steel rings, Velcro

Compact Shelter

Alastair Pryor

Australia

2014

Inspired by a wish to improve options for sheltering the homeless, this pop-up dwelling captured the attention of both investors and aid agencies who have since developed it for use in diaster zones. Its UV-stabilized polypropylene shell is durable, weather resistant and provides thermal insulation. A simple cubic form when erect, the Compact Shelter can be folded and flat-packed for easy transportation. Designed for a range of potential climates and scenarios, the shelter includes manually operable vents. Each unit houses two adults and two children in comfort and its modular form also allows for expansion with adjacent units to create a multi-room dwelling.

Human

UV-stablized polypropylene

paraSITE

Michael Rakowitz

USA

1998

The paraSITE project is a unique solution to homelessness, providing structures that are temporary and transportable, defiant and dignifying. As the project's name suggests, the various designs are parasitic interventions that rely on a host for volume and heat. The double-skinned polyethylene forms easily attach to exterior heating ventilation and air-conditioning ducts, which cause the bags to inflate. Though his protuberant forms are just a short-term answer they call attention to a perennial issue. As Rakowitz comments, the guerrilla homes are a lot more than hot air, they 'should disappear like the problem should – the real designers are the policymakers'.

Plastic bags, polyethylene tubing, metal hooks, tape

Warka Water 01

Architecture and
Vision
Ethiopa
2012

Warka Water is a life-giving device, designed to capture the most essential element on earth – water. Its tall cylindrical frame funnels water from rain, fog and dew, harvesting up to 100 litres (twenty-six gallons) each day. Using gravity, the mesh directs water down through the funnel, condensing into the tank at its base. Providing water for drinking or irrigation, the tower also encourages social interaction, with a detachable shade canopy providing shelter. Formed of mesh, rope and folding bamboo lattices, the tower references traditional Ethiopian basket-making techniques. Its lightweight modular construction allows for easy assembly and transportation.

Human

Bamboo, hemp, metal pins, bio-plastic, water tank

Flite +

Tentsile

USA

2016

An almost weightless tree tent that glides above ground, Flite + is the answer to getting above the fray. Using three sturdy polyester straps, the tent is designed to be attached to nearby tree trunks to provide a tensioned, habitable structure with a stable base. Threaded through with a continuous pole, the hovering home provides space for up to two. Its in-built mesh body protects against bugs and bites, while a removable rain fly allows for waterproof camping or open-air sleeping. Like a lightweight tree house, its distinctive frame is designed for maximum stability and minimum weight, packing down to a compact carry bag.

Anodized aluminium alloy, waterproof polyester, insect mesh, nylon-polyester composite floor

Wearable Habitation

Royal College of Art

UK

2016

From cloak to shelter, this collaborative project was initiated to respond to the Syrian refugee crisis in 2016. Developed according to established guidelines that reflect refugee experience, the Wearable Habitation transforms from clothing, to sleeping bag, to tent (as shown below). Constructed from Tyvek, a strong, synthetic material, the coats are insulated with Mylar and sealed with zips, and include a hood and internal pockets for small personal items. The design was created to withstand a migration of up to five weeks. Allowing for adaptive use, the garment's seams are strategically located to transform the coat into a small dwelling.

Human

Tyvek, Mylar

LYHTY

Erkko Aarti

Finland

2012

Seeking to reduce the doleful effect of long dark winter days in the far northern hemisphere, Erkko Aarti developed LYHTY as an enveloping alternative to existing Seasonal Affective Disorder (SAD) lamps. The faceted tent contrasts with the garish alternatives on the market, providing a glowing, enveloping refuge to rest and recharge. The construction is simple – an angular frame of welded steel pipes supports a diaphanous double skin, with lights embedded underneath. The LYHTY – *lyhty* is Finnish for lantern – is suitable for use indoors and out, and controlled by the inhabitant with a switch.

Steel pipe, fabric, LED lights

Tent 2

Angela Luna

USA

2016

Tent 2 is the second piece in Angela Luna's debut range of humanitarian fashion, collectively named 'Crossing the Boundary'. The convertible jacket and bag is a tent for two made from waterproof materials. This response – like all the pieces in Luna's collection – unites practicality with aesthetic polish. They offer realistic solutions that address issues of shelter, warmth, visibility and housing for refugees. The unisex garment is cut from durable high-tech fabric, forming a two-part (stylish) shelter. However, humanity, rather than hemlines, guides Luna's choice to address global issues through the mechanism of fashion.

Human

Polyester tarpaulin, nylon, plastic, zipper, reflective material

Kite Cabin

Frank Bloem

The Netherlands

2015

An annual affair, Urban Campsite Amsterdam offers a unique experience of public space. Here, on Centrumeiland, an artificial island near the city centre, the 2015 festival included Frank Bloem's Kite Cabin. The two-person accommodation is framed by an angular steel structure that creates both dwelling and tower, marked out by a yellow tent and flag. The sunny interior is secured by a robust plywood entrance and set beneath a transparent roof, which acts as a skylight and as an apparatus for controlling the kite. Publicly accessible and able to be booked online for short stays, the curious dwelling combines art, refuge, star-gazing and kite flying.

Human

Steel bracing, polyester, plywood, nylon rope

Portaledge

Black Diamond
Equipment

USA

2005

Defying gravity – and general logic – the Portaledge suspended tent offers a breezy bed for those who are feeling brave. Devised for daredevil climbers, the portable ledges give reprieve from long stints of rock climbing. Suspended from a single anchor point, the cloth and steel-tube frames are assembled with ease. These high-flying hammocks provide the essentials for the high life: a rain screen for surviving storms, hooks and clasps for holding kit, and a high ratio of space to weight for comfort and safety.

Steel framing, polyester tarpaulin, rope, zipper,
steel bolts

Piilo

Markus Michalski

Product Design

Germany

2011

Conceived as a retreat, the Piilo is a stylish abode. Engineered from eight slim screens and framed by carbon-fibre rods covered with translucent tensile fabric, the structure provides an elegant shelter. Transforming from a single stacked arch into a dome, Piilo expands in width from just a few centimetres, to almost two-and-a-half-metres (eight-feet). Like a vast gauzy fan, its double-ended panels are centrally pinned and hinge about each carefully crafted point. Lightweight, moveable and fastidiously constructed, the result is a honed hideaway for use indoors.

Human

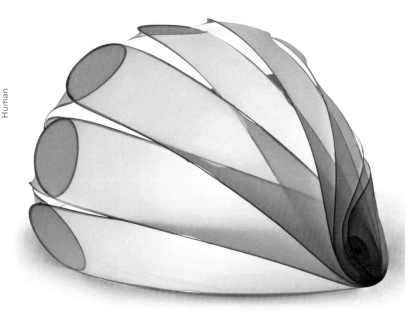

Carbon-fibre, elastic textile fabric

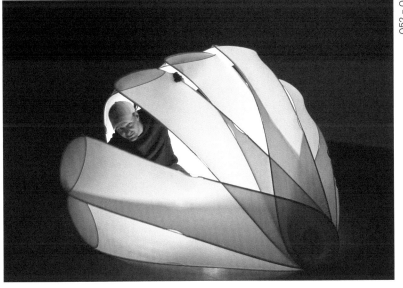

The Wedge

Heimplanet

Germany

2013

Allowing campers to spend less time pitching up and more time adventuring, the founders of Heimplanet bring their love of the great outdoors to The Wedge – a two-man tent with inflatable poles. Comprised of three connected air frames that can be erected with a single pump, The Wedge is speedy to inflate and easy to collapse. Weighing just over three kilograms (seven pounds) it's a light, practical companion for exploring the outdoors, with a highly waterproof shell that resists rain and dew. Outside, it captures attention for its azure skin; inside, it is filled with light, and includes helpful pockets for holding your kit.

Human

Inflatable thermoplastic urethane, high tensile polyester fabric

The Jello Pavilion

Cornell University

USA

2015

Resembling a larger-than-life bird's egg, The Jello Pavilion was designed by students at Cornell University and inspired by the fun inflatable structures that came of age in the 1970s. Its spherical form is made from over 100 sheets of plastic sheeting, seared together to create a hermetic volume which is inflated by a high-power fan. Inside, balloons fill the space, providing a joyful retreat from end-of-semester stress. Costing less than 300 US dollars to construct, and encouraging creative play, the Jello Pavilion is a fun reminder of the versatility of plastic.

Plastic panels, Velcro

| Glastonbury Solar |
| Concept Tent |
| Kaleidoscope and |
| Orange |
| UK |
| 2009 |

Amid the mud and mayhem of the Glastonbury music festival in England, this solar-powered tent is a warm welcome. An illuminated home for revelling campers, its tensile fabric body is embedded with photovoltaic threads. The design ensures maximum capture of sunlight with three adjustable solar panels at the crest of the dome. Collecting power for mobile devices by day, at night the panels reverse their role, transforming the tent into a luminous shell. Tired campers can even 'Glo-cate' their tents by text message. Though it doesn't solve the problem of lousy loos, this novel idea keeps campers covered as well as connected.

Photovoltaic fabric, solar threads, Plexiglas, plastic

roomoon

Hanging Tent
Company

UK

2014

The go-to globe tent, the roomoon is a clever tree-hung structure that's lightweight, portable, and provides a room with a view. The handcrafted sphere consists of stainless steel covered by a waterproof, high-strength canvas and a floor of light pine concealing storage space. Suspended by a customized hoist and stabilized by three internal polyethylene (Dyneema) slings, all the components are proportioned for practicality. Packed down, the floor becomes a handy holdall, and frames are designed to fit in standard-sized cars.

Stainless steel, water-resistant canvas, pine,
Dyneema slings

Human

No
Wheels

One & Two
Wheels

Three
Wheels

Four
Wheels

Five +
Wheels

Sleds +

Water

Bibliobeach

Matali Crasset

France

2013

The perfect seaside facility, this mobile library brings great books to the beach, offering more than 300 titles for visitors to browse. Alongside vendors of chairs, ice creams or snacks, the ingenious structure completes a perfect day out. Shading books and people alike, the library component is sheltered under a radiant orange canopy. Built of steel tube framing and tarpaulin the project includes three cantilevered alcoves lined with durable turquoise cushions to provide places to read while sunbathing. Continuing Crasset's interest in small structures, this lightweight and lyrical coastal project is suited to its surroundings, speaking of sun and summertime fun.

No Wheels

Steel tube, canvas, concrete weights

POP PUP

MOTOElastico
(Simone Carena and
Marco Bruno) with
VCUQatar
Morocco
2016

Part of an installation entitled TENTative Structures for the sixth Marrakech Biennale, this work by MOTOElastico reimagines the humble tent. A pop-up in fashion, its five-part structure adapts to the urban surroundings with a richly coloured enclosure held aloft by aluminium ladders. The piece recalls Morocco's rich palette with its use of bright Senegalese carpet sourced from a nearby souk. Giving much-needed cover, the carpet can be adjusted to give greater shade or create a more enclosed interior. The scaled-up tent is impactful and witty, using simple bold materials to render this archetype anew.

Carpet, steel bracing, aluminium ladders

Fold Flat Shelter

Form-al

Germany

2010

Addressing the growing need for simple homes for those who have none, the Fold Flat Shelter offers a tent-like alternative to sleeping rough. Formed of composite wall and roof panels, with a floor of composite plastic–metal honeycomb, the self-supporting design is based on the strength of its two intersecting pyramidal forms. The result is a structure with a square floor and an expandable roof. Provided flat-packed, with card packaging that transforms into furniture, the lightweight design is a potential solution for disaster relief housing. Unlike a tent, the shelter creates a stable, robust structure designed for semi-permanent or even permanent use.

No Wheels

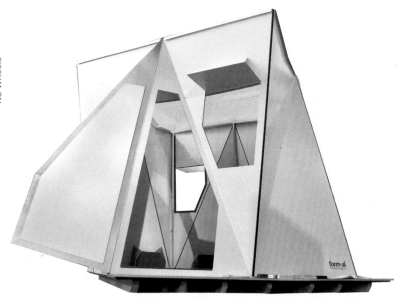

Dibond sheets, HeliPAN floor, acrylic glass, fibreglass

Y-BIO

Archinoma

Ukraine

2009

Designed for a windy coastal site near the Crimea, the Y-Bio modular camping structure was originally conceived as a way to test the endurance of the Archinoma-designed structural system. Drawing on the strength of pyramidal forms, the system uses multiple tetrahedral modules to create a 'stellated octahedron' – an eight-pointed star. Its sturdy, lightweight frame is then cloaked with translucent and opaque panels, or fabric slings, for the top of the structure. Housing a cafe, beach house and a place to relax, the low-environmental-impact tent can be expanded or contracted in size simply by changing the panel materials to vary its appearance and the desired function.

Steel framing, canvas, timber, steel staircase

Pneumad

Min | Day

USA

2014

The Pneumad draws on the principle of inflatable nomadic architecture first popularized in the 1960s. Originally designed as part of 'Truck-A-Tecture', an exhibition of mobile, technically progressive proposals, the design is a prototype for life on the move. A half-dome formed of hexagonal nylon tubes and Ripstop panels, Pneumad's airy space allows for different functions – from a solitary retreat to a place for small gatherings. Stored in a compact steel wagon complete with an air pump, the structure is easily erected and deflated. While the first version of the project is a simple experiment, in theory it can be multiplied to form more complex structures.

No Wheels

Nylon tubes, plastic, Ripstop

Caterpillar

Lambert Kamps

The Netherlands

2007

The Caterpillar is an itinerant, inflatable film theatre. Set up in parks and festivals to provide sheltered cover, the roving project commands attention with its pillowy red form. Built from PVC foil and shaped by steel cable connections, the double-walled skin becomes taut and supportive as it fills with air. Creating a comfortable environment for movies in hot or wet weather, the tunnel is strong enough to withstand wind and water. Its curious caterpillar 'feet' are stable as well as lightweight and unobtrusive. With a large screen at one end and room for up to thirty people, the nomadic caterpillar creates a memorable night out at the movies.

PVC, steel cables

Ecocapsule

Nice Architects

Slovakia

2008

Like a cosmic DeLorean, this adventurous little home is Nice Architects' answer to rising living costs and freedom of movement. Offering a comfortable, self-sufficient lifestyle, the Ecocapsule is designed to run off-grid and can accommodate two people. Built from an insulated fibreglass shell on an aluminium framework, the structure generates electricity through its integrated solar panels and a wind turbine. Inside, the pod includes a kitchen, living-dining and a sleeping space, as well as bathing facilities and a composting toilet. Light enough to rotate or push along on wheels, its gull-wing doors completes this sustainable prototype for the future.

No Wheels

Fibreglass, aluminium, plastic, Plexiglas, solar panels

ReActor

Alex Schweder,
Ward Shelley
USA
2016

Balanced on a concrete column, this artistic investigation is an
unstable residence for two. Connected by a central pivot, the entire
structure shifts depending on exterior forces and the movement and
weight of its inhabitants. Artists Alex Schweder and Ward Shelley
call the ever-changing structure 'Performance Architecture'. The
installation is clad in full-height glass walls, exposing the lives of the
collaborators during their five-day occupation. Requiring balancing
skills for everyday activities – and adjustment as the strucutre tilts
and spins with the wind – the relentless alterations give an entirely
new meaning to the modernist aphorism of 'a machine for living'.

Concrete, timber framing, glass, steel

La Matriz

Pontifical Catholic
University of Peru

Peru

2015

Recognizing the geophysical realities of Peru – and hence the risk of earthquakes – this shelter by Peruvian students is an innovative contribution to emergency relief. Based on a circular aluminium structure of self-supporting, large-scale mesh, the shelter is a light-weight, stable form. Transferring weight through its tapered metal frame, the project is clad with insulating foam and dozens of aluminium 'petals' that hook over the underlying mesh. Like a great foil hemisphere, doors or windows are created by simply removing petals. Packed down into a sturdy box and relatively lightweight, its dimensions are carefully chosen for easy delivery on land, sea or air.

No Wheels

Aluminium, insulation foam

Pillow Tent

Lambert Kamps

The Netherlands

2010

Fashioned from more than a hundred bulging airbags, this indoor–outdoor pop-up for festivals and events is easy to assemble and secure. Designed by artist–designer Lambert Kamps, the Pillow Tent can be illuminated at whim and secured by metal grommets along the outer edges. The scale and form of the project can be tailored to a variety of sizes depending on its use and purpose. The Pillow Tent can be used indoors or out, and can be customized with a woolly underside, to create a cozy space that evokes a child's cushion fort, and of course, pillow fights.

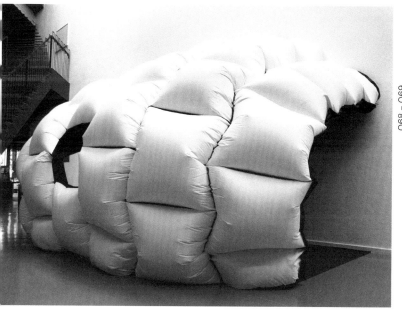

Plastic, metal grommets

D.E.M. Dream Excursion Module

Joachim Falser

Italy

2009

Marking the fortieth anniversary of the moon landings, this utopian dreaming machine is a three-part timber 'space ship' that encourages, as the title suggests, a journey into an alternate world of dreams. Its tripartite arrangement creates separate zones for sleeping and private reflection. When closed, the module is a solid timber fractal, raised on stout wooden feet. Split apart, the project reveals a series of pine-clad interiors. Designed for Falser's degree project, the Dream Excursion Module is built from Swiss stone pine. Inside, elastic cord has been fashioned into a storage rack. Positioned inside or outside D.E.M. brings new meaning to space exploration.

No Wheels

Pine wood, nails, elastic cord

Park Bench Bubble

Thor ter Kulve

UK

2014

Park Bench Bubble is Thor ter Kulve's take on contemporary urban life. Based on insights from time spent in Amsterdam and London, his project creates a public-private space that transforms a modest timber park bench into a solo inflatable retreat with a solar-powered USB charger. Though hardly luxurious, the seat provides a place to work from, while the cocoon forms an opaque barrier that is embedded beneath the timber seat and accessed through a zipped entry. Fashioned from scavenged materials, the project strips back the idea of 'home' to the essentials: something to power digital tools with, and protection against the elements.

Recycled timber, nylon, solar panel, USB charging station

Goahti

Victor Leurs

The Netherlands

2009

Based on the nomadic homes of the Sami – the indigenous people of Arctic Scandinavia – this vibrant tent by Victor Leurs reinterprets their traditional dwellings. His Goahti for the Urban Campsite Amsterdam is one of fourteen homes that form the heart of the camping festival. Its conical red form, which mimics the rustic timber panels of its vernacular predecessor, is held in place by nylon webbing that weaves through the structure top and bottom. Formed of fibreglass panels, the light, robust enclosure is easily erected and creates enough room for a double bed that basks in the reflected glow of its lustrous coloured interior.

No Wheels

Fibreglass, nylon webbing

Noah Emergency Capsule

Cosmo Power

Japan

2011

For those with enough cash, this emergency capsule caters to the elite. Like the Ark of its enduring namesake, the perky little pod is designed for hurricanes, quakes or tsunamis – a defiant globe that floats on water, is breathable, and shock-proof. Designed by Japanese engineers Cosmo Power, the capsule is brightly coloured to catch the attention of rescue teams. Its interior contains enough space for four adults with an in-built seat and lookout window. In less turbulent times the sunny survival pod serves a more playful purpose as a toy house for children.

Steel, aluminium, ceramic thermal lining, marine grade stainless steel, fibreglass

Digital Origami
Emergency Shelter
LAVA
Australia
2011

Created for an Australian exhibition exploring the design possibilities of emergency shelters, the Digital Origami Emergency Shelter fixes on an eroded pentagonal volume to create its amorphous, timber interior. Taking inspiration from the structure of a water molecule and prefabricated living capsules, the shelter is formed from milled sheets of plywood which are offset to give a louvred view in and out. With its arresting, curvaceous shape, the design highlights its individuality with green-painted edges and LED lights within, creating the impression of a glowing lantern from afar.

No Wheels

Plywood, LED lights

Kodomo no Kuni
Park Climbing Boxes
Anonymous
Japan
—

Part of Kodomo no Kuni or 'Children's Land' this project was commissioned for a vast urban nature reserve in Yokohama, Japan. Formed of stacked hexagonal prisms, built of sturdy frames and timber panels, the units are pierced by holes to assist with climbing and lifting. The structure is stacked three modules high with a variety of enclosed and open sides that create spaces to crawl inside. Creating an interlinked space to hide in and explore, the timber forms are strong yet lightweight and can be carried and assembled on site.

Timber, steel bracing

APoC

IK Studio and
Canadian
Homelessness
Research Network

Canada

2014

Offering a low-cost and respectful solution for the homeless, this project is a lightweight, modular shelter designed for ease of transport. Known as APoC (Architectural Prototype Capsule) its elliptical form is derived from the inexpensive and malleable laminated birch sheets, that are arranged in a double-layered cell secured with nuts and bolts. The prototype is also designed as a recreational space for parks and playgrounds in an attempt to reduce the social stigma of sleeping rough. With more than 200,000 homeless people in Canada, the APoC offers hope in the campaign for safe, affordable housing for those living on the streets.

No Wheels

Laminated birch, metal bolts

Unidome

James Towner-Coston
UK
2014

Inspired by the segmented structure of an orange, the Unidome creates a stable dome in which to camp, rest, party or play. Developed by James Towner-Coston, the timber-framed domes offer a lightweight unit that is easily assembled. Fabric and translucent finishes enclose the modules, which offer light, shade and privacy. Like a contemporary yurt, the design also includes a crown of clear thermoplastic polymer resin that brings in diffuse daylight and frames views of the sky. Completed by a striking gull-wing entry, the Unidome is a bright alternative for modular living systems.

Ash wood, coated fabric, timber, polyethylene

Ruup

Estonian Academy
of Arts
Estonia
2015

A forest respite that amplifies its natural surroundings, the Ruup project in Estonia's Võru county is a collaborative work by a group of architecture students. Like enormous megaphones, the three structures act as a foil to the art of quiet meditation. Constructed almost entirely from timber, the project is imagined as a 'forest library' that prompts people to pause and pay attention to the sounds of nature. Large enough to host a small huddle, and wide enough to lie in, the structures have hosted live music events, and have given shelter to hikers and campers. Their tapered conical shape allow them to be rolled to other forest locations.

No Wheels

Pine wood

Dom'Up
Bruno de Grunne,
Nicolas d'Ursel
Belgium
2015

The design of an arborist and architectural team, Dom'up is a suspended tree house shelter that harmonises with its surrounding. Rather than wrestling with branches, Dom'Up draws on the space between trees to capitalize on privacy, architectural support and woodland scenery. Including a UV-resistant double-skinned canvas shelter, tarpaulin roofing, a large terrace and generous interior, Dom'up provides space for two to four people. Its structural frame of galvanized steel and natural timber flooring creates a solid foundation for this ingenious uplifting hideaway.

Steel framing, canvas, tarpaulin, timber, rope, netting

Inflatable Gallery

Melissa Berry

USA

2009

Designed as a space for displaying artists' works at the El Cosmico festival in Texas, this prefabricated inflatable gallery is both lightweight and nomadic. Supported by a frame of PVC tubing, its body of three large plastic membranes is studded with a regular pattern of metal grommets. These give a quilted effect and reference the artist's hand-stitched works on display. Resourcefully built for around 150 US dollars, its attention-grabbing form is simply attached using plastic cable ties and duct tape – and easily erected within an afternoon. The billowing project gives shade from the unrelenting Texas sun during the day and creates an undulating, illuminated frame by night.

No Wheels

PVC tubing, plastic, metal grommets, duct tape, zip ties

Air Bridge

Lambert Kamps

The Netherlands

2001

One of several experiments with inflatable structures by the artist Lambert Kamps, this project tests the limits of a wide-span, inflated structure. Able to stretch across the varied widths of Amsterdam's canals, the flexible bridge is strong enough to support itself and the people crossing to and fro. Built from PVC foil and inflated with an air pump, the bridge is essentially a square, hollow traversable tube with three rows of porthole windows to provide views up and down the canal. Once inflated, the bridge transforms from a floppy plastic envelope to a stable, firm structure; not to mention a fun way to get to get around the city.

PVC, trampoline webbing, cord

Exo

Reaction

USA

2005

This tough home for four was developed in the aftermath of Hurricane Katrina and fulfils the basic need for shelter. Modest and structurally efficient, the Exo is more reassuring than a tent and more accessible than an RV – an ideal answer to disaster housing relief. Providing instant stable housing that is secure yet lightweight, the Exo was inspired by the stackable, durable, weightless, humble Styrofoam cup. The Exo can be transported by road, rail or air, and its two-part structure is light enough for several people to move by hand. The units simply slot into a base and latch down, and include fold-down beds or office desks as well as built-in electrical points.

No Wheels

Composite shell, plastic, sand, LED lights

Trampoline Tent

Atlantic Trampolines

UK

2005

For a bivouac with bounce, these tents can't be beat. Spanning two-and-a-half-metres (eight feet), the domes are designed to bridge across a trampoline, creating the ultimate summer pop-up. Supported by three arcs of collapsible metal tube and attached to the frame with brackets secured by Velcro, the covers provide a showerproof den or sleep-out. This model includes mesh windows and doors that zip tightly closed or can be toggled open, to provide the perfect camping combination: ventilation without bugs. Made from resilient and fireproof polyester, the collapsible domes turn trampolines into playhouses in the blink of an eye.

Steel framing, metal tubing, polyester, mesh

Rendez-vous avec la Vi(ll)e

Hans-Walter Müller

France

2014

Lightweight, moveable and full of air, this temporary structure creates an eye-catching feature overlooking Martin Luther King Park in Batignolles, Paris. Designed to house a three-day exhibition 'The Making of Batignolles', the inflatable pavilion created a waterproof, bright area enclosing maquettes, videos and prototypes that explain the future of the redevelopment of the Batignolles area. Spanning sixteen metres (fifty-three feet), the dome is set up between two stabilizing entry points. Secured around the perimeter, the project swiftly reaches its full height with the aid of an air pump, creating a pavilion with panoramic 360-degree views.

No Wheels

Plastic, plywood, rubber, metal

Skum

Bjarke Ingels Group (BIG)

Denmark

2016

Designed by the Danish practice BIG, Skum is an inflatable canopy of bubbles. Offering shelter for 170 revellers, the travelling summer pavilion is a fixture on the move, having been erected at Denmark's Roskilde Festival, Chart Art Fair and ARoS Aarhus Kunstmuseum. Skum (which is Danish for 'foam'), is inflated by two wind turbines and anchored by minimal guy ropes, and lit with inbuilt LED lights to create a glowing bubble-scape at night. This world, however, is fleeting. When the party is over, Skum swiftly deflates and is easily stored. Until the next party, that is.

Plastic, wind turbines, LED lights, ropes

Blob VB3

dmvA architecten
Belgium
2009

White, bright and providing respite, the Blob VB3 is Belgian studio dmvA's solution to bureaucratic planning restrictions that had repeatedly denied them permission for an office extension. This retreat defies convention and council objections, incorporating a kitchen, bedroom and bathroom in one space-age volume. Formed of timber framing plastered with polyester fill, the structure includes built-in storage niches to maximize the floor space. One end of the capsule hinges upward, creating a protected place to sit. Its dimensions correlate with standard trailer sizes, allowing it to move from place to place – a clever response to vexatious red tape.

No Wheels

Timber framing, plaster, polyester

Polaris M
MUD Projects
The Netherlands
2013

This innovative design was created for 'Urban Campsite', an experimental camping exhibition near Amsterdam. Its eclectic approach takes advantage of found objects that are reconfigured to form a comfortable camping shelter. Rather than adding further material to the urban landscape, MUD repurposed an old polyester silo. Turning the object on its side and connecting unusual Kermit-green steel legs, the design is quite removed from the original use of its components. Framed with a hinged glass entrance, its interior includes small bench seats and a wooden table, which complete the silo's transformation into a place to eat, sleep or rest.

No Wheels

Fibreglass, metal, wood, perspex, steel, polyester

OTIS – Optimal
Travelling
Independent Space

Green Mountain
College

USA

2014

The Optimal Traveling Independent Space (OTIS) is an alternative vision of the American Dream by sixteen Green Mountain College students. Designed to fit a standard trailer, its timber body includes an impressive array of facilities: a bed, desk, sink, wood-burning stove, toilet and rainwater collection. Low maintenance, mobile and economical, OTIS includes a 120-watt solar panel to power devices. Built using computer numeric controlled (CNC) machine fabrication, the design suggests less interest in ownership and greater emphasis on life experience. Tiny, self-sufficient and towed by car, OTIS provides plenty of inspiration for a sustainable nomadic existence.

Steel chassis, timber, glass, DuraVent stovepipe,
solar panel

Cozy Shelter

Lambert Kamps

Finland

2013

A creative variation on the idea of large inflatable structures, this coiled shelter defies its military appearance, as it name implies. Instead of using a wide-span carapace, Cozy Shelter is formed of a narrow tube that is inflated and then sealed. Secured by bright red straps with adjustable buckles, the self-sufficient structure builds on its own inherent strength and can be manipulated into different formations. Its pragmatic tawny, sandbag-like, military-style exterior contrasts with what's inside: a homely finish of checked wool blankets that line the interior and put the 'cozy' in the shelter's title.

No Wheels

Inflatable tubing, nautical fabric, blankets, webbing

City Aground

Mixuro Studio of
Architecture

Spain

2014

Made for Valencia's annual Fallas festival, a five-day celebration concluding with a ritual bonfire, the project unites cardboard and crowds. Constructed as an architectural effigy by the entire community, the geodesic dome is built from dozens of large triangles, each expressing the identities of different groups of makers and contributing to the overall structure. Placed on a pavement covered in sand, the modular, lightweight frame created a short-term place to play – filled with colour, and diurnal changes of shadow and light. At the festival's close, the dome was set alight to mark La Cremà – a citywide celebration expressed through flames and firecrackers.

ardboard, plywood, timber, metal screws

Corogami Hut

David Penner

Architect

Canada

2010

With Japanese precision and Canadian flair, this ice shelter appeared under cover of night. A rogue addition to the annual Warming Huts of Winnipeg competition, its uninvited presence left chilly skaters with a warm glow. Made from folded corrugated plastic sheets, its sturdy, lightweight form gives respite from bitter winds. Its beauty lies in its simplicity: just four folds create a stable structure and light-transmitting skin with ample internal space. Secured in the winter by watering the plywood feet to freeze them into solid blocks of ice, the bonds are released in the spring thaw. It can then be packed down to just 100 millimetres (four inches) in width.

Corrugated plastic, plywood, metal screws

Portable Housing Space

Winfried Baumann

Italy

2009

Observing the rise in the number of urban nomads, Germany-based artist Winfried Baumann created 'Building Life Systems', a series of solutions for homelessness which he has been working on since 2001. This interpretation, Portable Housing Space, involves stacked steel-mesh cages, which come complete with carrier bags and sleeping sacks. The cages provide a modicum of privacy and security and are the size of a narrow single bed. Elegant yet spare, they are reminiscent of similar solutions to desperate overcrowding in cities such as Hong Kong. Despite its finesse, the project is a disconcerting reminder of the challenges of being homeless.

Galvanized steel mesh, plywood, sleeping sacks

Firefly

Garrett Finney

USA

2014

Described as a 'camper and a tool box' the Firefly draws on designer Garrett Finney's experience at NASA. The result is a mobile recreational vehicle on legs that is strong, lightweight and compact. Firefly is designed to travel on the back of a trailer or pick-up truck, providing the essentials for temporary living. Inside, the steel-framed shell has just enough room for a folding double bed. Windows on all sides, and two large, hinged doors provide a fully immersive outdoor experience. A moveable yellow canopy, tethered by way of orange 'elbows', gives sun protection. Equipped with storage and water tanks, it might be the best bet yet for earth-bound adventures.

No Wheels

Aluminium, EPS foam

Mountain Research

General Design

Japan

2008

Part of the Kobayashi Residence, these brightly coloured North Face Dome Tents can be used year-round in this rustic weekend retreat. In the heart of the woods, and exposed to the weather, the domes offer both additional living space, and moveable camps. Housing up to eight people and engineered for base camp conditions, they are designed to endure extreme weather highs and lows. Drawing on Buckminster Fuller's 1950s geodesic invention, the domes are intrinsically strong. Rendered yolk-yellow, the two-metre models are elite equipment employed here for domestic bliss.

Nylon, aluminium

The Accordion
reCover Shelter
Matthew Malone,
Amanda Goldberg,
Jennifer Metcalf,
Grant Meacham
USA
2008

This accordion-like structure creates a swiftly erected shelter for four – a reminder of architectural agency in disaster situations. Constructed from polypropylene, the expanding form is designed as a first-response solution to homelessness and displacement. Easily transported by road, ship or air, the reCover Shelter is a temporary residence that provides an inexpensive, recyclable home in a hurry. Augmented by local materials for increased insulation and comfort, the single-unit shelters can be assembled in multiples, stretching out to accommodate larger family groups.

No Wheels

Polypropylene

Fantastic Trailer

Cheryl Baxter

USA

2012

Fleeting and fantastical, this installation is composed of five columns that lilt and sway from a customized trailer base. The mobile work combines sinuous tripartite fabric tubes with suspended industrial fans that extend from steel columns rooted in the trailer bed. Unfolded, the air movement stirs the columns, making the nylon dance and the organza glide around the human-scaled lightweight pockets. With seating fashioned from the trailer bed, the project encourages bystanders to stop and linger inside this surprising urban space. At dusk, the columns morph again, their integral LED lighting creating glowing lanterns that dance and jive in an arresting public spectacle.

Trailer base, Aluminet, Ripstop, fans, steel, AstroTurf

A–Z Wagon Station

Andrea Zittel

USA

2000

Part of Zittel's larger question of what we need to survive and prosper, and what we can live without, the Wagon Station Encampment occupies some of her A–Z West compound near the Joshua Tree National Park. The twelve steel and aluminium wagons designed by the artist offer spartan accommodation, and visitors can stay twice a year in exchange for an hour's labour each day. Set among the remarkable rock formations of the desert, the cabins offer a simple enclosure with just a mattress, clothing hooks and ventilation hatch. A transparent panel provides views to the sky and landscape. Lightweight, the pods are easily collapsed, moved and reassembled.

No Wheels

Steel bracing, plywood, Plexiglas, cotton

Bruuns Bazaar
Pop-Up Kiosk

Bureau Detours

Denmark

2011

This tiny kiosk built for clothing brand Bruuns Bazaar is conceived as a little shop with local appeal. Recalling the glamour of old luxury packing trunks, its industrial black shell conceals the new-season treasures within. The container has a plywood core with bespoke details to hang and stack the range, creating a refreshing retail environment for the Danish fashion favourite. From custom-made hangers and a folding till, to nooks that transform from storage to display, each item of the space is hewn from wood, creating a cozy timber-lined space. Warm and welcoming, its neon arrow points the way to an innovative retail experience.

No Wheels

Shipping container, plywood, flourescent lights

Graph

Rintala Eggertsson
Architects

China

2009

Created for the exhibition 'Crossing: Dialogues for Emergency Architecture' at the National Art Museum of China, Graph is a modular unit that offers stable, substantial homes in the face of disaster. The two design variations are formed of laminated wood, contained within a textile covering that provides insulation and waterproofing. The rectilinear compact form allows for easy transportation, and can be packed down into a slim kit-of-parts that can reach remote and challenging terrain. Graph addresses vital factors of human habitation in such situations: reassuring, robust, lightweight and low-cost – its simple forms promote recovery in both practical and emotional ways.

Laminated plywood, plastic tarpaulin

Mobile Little Room

Tian Yuan
and Xu Beiwen

China

2011

This tiny portable, modular room designed by graduate students of China's Nanjing Forestry University, is an inexpensive solution for an easily assembled and customizable place of one's own. Inside the chequer-board exterior, a bed of cartons and small drawers that integrate with the cladding shapes the humble interior. The availability of these materials contributes to its affordable price, costing only about three hundred US dollars to purchase. Arranged as a simple cubic prism the Mobile Little Room lives up to its name and can be rapidly disassembled or assembled within an hour.

No Wheels

Steel framing, timber, chipboard, plastic, Plexiglas

KODA

Kodasema

Estonia

2016

Acknowledging the importance of home and surroundings, KODA by Estonian design collective Kodasema is a moveable dwelling that can be assembled in a day. Free of foundations, the home is constructed with factory-made components. Framed by a full-height glazed panel set back within the cubic form, the project is intended to be adaptable in use – ideal as a summerhouse, a cafe, office space or workshop. The simple internal arrangement is an open-plan, insulated space. Roof-mounted solar panels provide off-grid living, and KODA accommodates a kitchen, bathroom, mezzanine loft and terrace into its tiny footprint.

Concrete, solar panels, glass

| Emergency Plastic |
| Crate Shelter |
| ECS-p1 |
| Lebanese American |
| University |
| Lebanon |
| 2014 |

Not a maths problem, but an architectural solution, ECS-p1 is a collaborative project by Lebanese American University students who created a temporary structure for emergency situations. Seizing everyday objects that are readily available and inexpensive, the project uses two ubiquitous components: plastic crates and cable ties. Floor, ceiling and all four walls are built from this basic interlinked structure, with non-supporting shutter crates having multiple uses as storage, seats and tables. Forming a simple interior that is dappled with light, this simple structure is a practical response in the face of natural disasters.

No Wheels

Plastic crates, plastic tie straps

Light House

All(zone)

USA

2015

A beacon for change, Light House addresses the problem of living costs in cities. Commissioned for the Chicago Architecture Biennial, the micro-dwelling is framed by a polyethylene-coated metal grid, which creates internal shelving and supports the cladding of nylon and fabric on a plywood base. Inside, live-work, sleep and dressing zones are formed from textiles of varying opacity, giving gradated levels of privacy. The prototypes are intended to be located in disused buildings in tropical cities, where the weather is mild and rents are high. Costing around nine-hundred US dollars, Light House is a clever nomadic solution that offers residents an affordable urban life.

No Wheels

Polyethylene-coated metal, nylon, polyester, plastic-laminated plywood

To Many Places

Emmy Polkamp

The Netherlands

2015

This peripatetic tent-hotel concept by Emmy Polkamp enlivens disused buildings with mobile shelters. Designed as a moveable, reuseable alternative for city hoppers, each To Many Places structure accommodates one or two people, and includes a bed and some storage space. The tents, each identified by a super-size number, are comprised of timber frames and pale canvas, and pack down into boxes that form the bed base. Accompanied by communal kitchens and social programmes, the project invigorates abandoned city buildings, opening them up to both campers and locals.

Plywood, canvas

Chiton

D'Milo Hallerberg

USA

2012

Like the armour of a mollusc, the Chiton is composed of an outershell providing protection and privacy in the Nevada Desert. Part of a swathe of inventive improvised dwellings at Burning Man, this offering by D'Milo Hallerberg makes ingenious use of telescoping tubing. Formed of two six-sided halves held with four stable feet, the Chiton is a visual treat. Marking out its territory with a distinctive serrated silhouette the interior is enclosed by stretched nylon cloth. Shielding against strong summer sunshine, sandstorms, and nosy revellers, the two-part module includes comfortable seats, creating a shady communal space for lounging and disco naps.

No Wheels

Plastic tubing, nylon

En-Fold

Woods Bagot

Australia

2013

This folding structure was commissioned as part of Australia's 'Emergency Shelter' exhibition, a fund-raising initiative that highlights the role of architecture in the aftermath of natural disasters. An elegant lean-to, it was developed by creasing sheets of A4 paper to create an inherently strong framework that uses minimal material for maximum use. With a concertina of folds giving shape to the translucent canopy, the modular 'skin-and-bones' shelter provides an expandable, self-supporting form. Its simple shape can be extended to create larger spaces. Collapsible and structurally efficient, the design also includes a simple L-shaped bench for internal seating.

Steel, paper

**Mobile Eco Second
Home**

Sanei Hopkins
Architects

UK

2008

Inspired by the discovery of an abandoned World War II stretcher, this small backyard pavilion suggests both economy and industry. Built as a moveable structure for a property in Suffolk and containing six stacked bunk beds, the space maximizes every nook and cranny. With bunk ends doubling as a ladder to reach the uppermost beds, this mobile sleeping structure is built from materials leftover from a play space: corrugated plastic, aluminium cladding and timber. Including detachable wheels that are affixed and removed by tilting the pavilion on its side, the shelter is light enough for two people to manoeuvre and can be towed greater distances by car.

No Wheels

Timber, corrugated plastic, corrugated aluminium, wheels

RDM (Rapid Deployment Module)

Visible Good

USA

2013

The Rapid Deployment Module suggests a new approach to emergency housing – and a viable alternative to the insecurities of tent life. Stable, modular, lightweight and easily transported, the units are formed of a high-strength plastic shell with windows, locking doors and a vented roof with solar shading. Assembled from a kit-of-parts it can be erected within an hour. The result is a substantial abode that is suitable for varied climatic conditions and remote locations. Its elevated adjustable legs discourage vermin from entering, avoid minor floods, and ensure it can settle on unstable terrain with ease – all essential considerations for disaster relief.

Steel bracing, plastic, Plexiglas, nylon rope, fabric

3D Printed House

3M FutureLAB

USA

2014

This ingenious refuge makes the seemingly futuristic idea of 3D printed architecture a reality. Developed by an urban design studio at the University of California, the 3D Printed House is made with industrial three-dimensional printers. Its carapace contains essential components for living – a kitchen, loft bed, a folding table and a folding toilet. The bespoke design allows every space to be utilized, including storage space under the floor. Produced in two halves from a sand-based plastic and custom-made glue, the house is imagined as an over-scaled piece of furniture that can be utilized both indoors or outside.

No Wheels

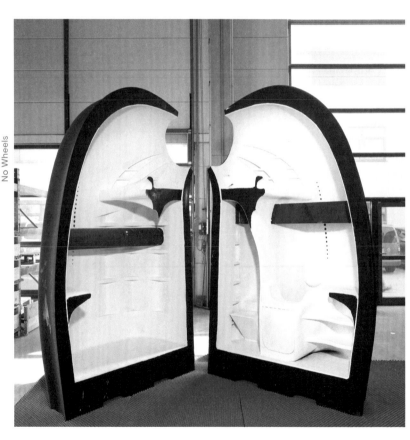

Plastic, glue

U-Dome

World Shelters

USA

2009

Creating transitional shelters for post-disaster regions, the U-Dome is a geodesic construction manufactured by the American non-profit organization World Shelters. The domes provide space for housing, medical clinics, relief agency centres or storage. Low cost and durable, the dwellings are formed of die-cut sheets of corrugated polypropylene that fold to create a fully sealed envelope. Weatherproof and waterproof, the homes include full-size doors and operable acrylic windows, allowing easy entry and good ventilation. Sealed with floors of plastic sheeting, the design is easily shipped and simply erected while its long-lasting materials offer ready reuse.

Corrugated polypropylene, Plexiglas, plastic

Travelbox

Juust

Germany

2015

This self-contained home for globetrotters offers an elegant solution for those on a budget and on the move. Developed by Stefan Juust, Travelbox enables users to transport home comforts quickly, safely and in style. Weighing just sixty kilograms (132 pounds) each element contained within the stainless steel and timber box unpacks to create a small furniture suite: a bed, table, chair and shelves. Rather than the wastage and cost of buying new things, Juust's design imagines life accompanied by a frame for living. Built of robust materials to endure shipping knocks, its trim kit-of-parts gives nomads a familiar environment wherever they are.

No Wheels

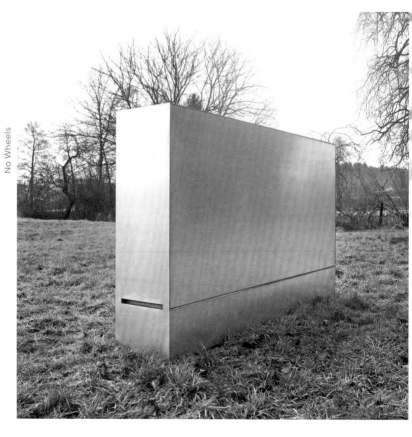

Timber framing, aluminium, bedding, table, bicycle, chairs

Human

No Wheels

One & Two Wheels

Three Wheels

Four
Wheels

Five +
Wheels

Sleds +

Water

Mobile Kitchen

Geneva University of
Art and Design
Switzerland
2013

Imagined as an alternative extension to a Modernist building,
the Mobile Kitchen is a moveable architectural solution that adds
useable space without impinging on existing elements. Referencing
the ingenious global variety of portable vernacular architecture,
the mobile module is built from a simple steel-framed structure set
on top of two bicycle wheels. Decorated with kitchen paraphernalia,
including cupboards, lighting and storage, the little unit provides basic
functions for home chefs. One of five identical frames that are adapted
to different uses, such as a book stand and a media centre, the Mobile
Kitchen is a spontaneous device that animates its surroundings.

Steel framing, plywood, plasterboard, wheels,
kitchenware

Pop-Up Caravan
Tas-ka
The Netherlands
2014

Part of the Hague's Design Quarter festival to celebrate Dutch design, this caravan by Tas-ka is one of many shops and exhibitions that pop up in unusual locations. Established by designers Jantien Baas and Hester Worst, Tas-ka is a Netherlands-based brand that has grown a reputation for delightful printed goods. This green-and-white camper offers a bright and temporary retail solution for displaying their wares, including cushions, books and posters. Pierced with unusual acrylic inserts that frame the items within, the modest, mobile structure gave Tas-Ka an ideal platform for the three-day event.

Steel chassis, aluminium, rubber, corrugated steel,
Plexiglas, chipboard

One of many creative interventions by the Dutch design collective N55, the Snail Shell System challenges sedentary living patterns. Made from a cylindrical polyethylene tank wrapped with rubber caterpillar tracks fashioned from doormats, the shell is simply rolled – or rowed in the case of a marine environment – into place, its tracks acting as buffers or steering aids. A hole in one side forms the entry to the Snail Shell, which is light enough to be moved by one person. A bilge pump, paddle and air intake are located beside the entrance, providing the means to remove excess water, navigate across lakes, rivers or seas, and be comfortably ventilated.

One & Two Wheels

Polyethylene, caterpillar tracks, Plexiglas, steel eyebolts, bilge pump, paddle, foam base

Caravan

Carwyn Lloyd Jones

UK

2015

A build-your-own getaway by Welsh carpenter Carwyn Lloyd Jones, this iridescent teardrop camper transforms what was a rundown second-hand trailer. The family retreat is compact, easy to tow and features a distinctive cladding system of 4,000 discarded CDs that give a dazzling fish-scale-inspired finish. Inside, the tiny space includes a kitchen, storage and retractable dining-sleeping space, as well as a homemade composting toilet – all built from off-cut timber. Completed for less than one thousand US dollars and built mostly from materials salvaged locally, the surprising finish of the sparkling home is its patterned floor fashioned from old vinyl records.

Trailer, timber, chipboard, CDs, vinyl records, glass

Bikamper

Topeak

UK

2005

For cycling fans who like to camp, the Bikamper is a sure-fire hit. Developed for carrying in bicycle panniers, the tiny nylon tent-bag weighs just under two kilograms (three-and-a-half pounds). When unfolded the simple three-sided structure utilizes the frame of the bike for structural support. Formed of Ripstop nylon covers with a similarly robust fly, the entrance is supported by the bike's handlebar. A detatched bike wheel holds up the tent's far end, with durable guy ropes to secure the whole ensemble. A simple, speedy shelter for a single person, the tent's compact dimensions and ingenious assembly make it an essential piece of equipment for life on the road.

One & Two Wheels

Ripstop nylon, taffeta nylon, bicycle, ropes, pegs

Fietscaravan

Bicycle Caravan

Project

The Netherlands

2014

Designed for cycling in the northern Dutch provinces, this sustainable, clever project is a hireable camper. Destined for life on the move, its curvaceous body gives improved aerodynamics with a lightweight timber construction to minimize its load. Towed behind a standard bicycle, the travelling companion includes space for one to sleep, integrated storage, and a kitchen-dining hatch to the rear. Equipped with insect screens for comfort, the interior is lit by a half-moon picture window and a wide access door. At the end of a long day on the road, its rooftop solar panel provides power to run lights or mobile devices.

Trailer, plywood, steel brace

Life Pod

| Michael R Weekes |
| USA |
| 2016 |

This faceted mobile module offers space for life on the go. The creation of engineer Michael R Weekes, Life Pod is a snug little unit framed by two geodesic domes at each end. The domes are connected by a ten-sided cylinder framed in sturdy timber. Clad with facets of plywood sheeting, the home is well insulated with thermoplastic foam. Despite its small internal space Life Pod is designed for two and carries a surprisingly comfortable range of amenities including a bathroom and sink. Offering relief from the compact interior, the Pod includes a generously proportioned door and two protected porthole windows.

One & Two Wheels

Trailer, timber framing, plywood, thermoplastic foam

Mehrzeller

Nonstandard

Austria

2013

An eclectic addition responding to the increased interest in nomadic living, this multicellular caravan offers customized interiors. Unlike the fixed arrangement that is common in its forebears, this camper is designed using a computer-generated 'Configurator' – a parametric equation that yields bespoke alterations. Mehrzeller's angular white exterior recalls a chamfered cloud on wheels, and is continued in the similarly slanted interior. With finishes and details determined by the owner, the lofty pale interior includes a generous kitchen, dining and living room, a niche for sleeping, as well as a bathroom – all enveloped in glossy exterior panels.

Steel chassis, plasterboard, chipboard, wheels, glass

The Classic American Dream Trailer

American Dream Trailers

USA

2013

Both a rowboat and a camper, The Classic American Dream Trailer is as tempting as apple pie. Produced by the Dahlmans, a husband-and-wife duo, this design revives a classic, retaining the latch-on roof-rowboat but updating the construction with a fibreglass body. Sitting on top of its robust steel chassis, the camper unit is custom-finished. Sleeping two adults, the camper has an in-built rear hatch for kitchen essentials. Each model includes a rowboat which can be fitted with a motor, oars and rowlocks, making this a safe and easy way to explore lakes and rivers.

Steel chassis, fibreglass, Plexiglas, plywood

My Carriage

Olaf Mooij

The Netherlands

2015

Olaf Mooij spent his childhood constructing imaginative forms from objects his parents had carefully saved in case of another war. My Carriage is a result of Mooij's experimental, thrifty approach, which is evident throughout his work. Serving as an artist's studio, the mobile unit is a medley of recycled found items – iron wagon wheels are paired with pneumatic tyres and a large fibreglass cylinder becomes a mini studio, kitted out with artist supplies, lights and workstation. Like a set piece from Mad Max, the eccentric appearance masks its purpose as a mobile 'refuge' in which artists can peacefully create.

One & Two Wheels

Fibreglass, steel chassis, aluminium, wheels, plywood, plastic

The Sauna Stoke 2.0

Mika Sivho

Canada

2016

Portable, warming and authentic – perhaps the only thing out of place with this Finnish craftsman's mobile sauna is the location – in British Columbia, Canada's westernmost province. Inspired by the saunas of his native country, Sivho decided to bring home a little closer by creating a wood-burning sauna on wheels. Created almost entirely by hand, each of his Sauna Stoke models is built from cedar and accommodates six adults, a stove and a porch for storing wood. Weighing just over 1,000 kilograms (2,500 pounds) and anchored to a sturdy trailer base, the design is made for towing, transporting the comfort, heat and banter of the sauna wherever Sivho chooses.

Steel trailer, aluminium, cedar, iron stove

The Wheel House

TMB Design Bristol for
Acroujou
UK
2008

Created by circus performers Acroujou, The Wheel House brings its story to life in the form of a rolling theatre set. Developed as a mobile backdrop for the street art consortium Without Walls, the acrobatic event by Jeni Barnard and Barney White narrates a post-apocalyptic tale. The performers occupy the moving stage, and the audience moves with them to follow the story as it unfolds. The Wheel House includes steampunk-themed elements of domestic architecture, including windows and doors, kitchen, table, bed and lawn. The over-scaled wheel unites these eclectic components and, together with the curious tale, spins a yarn of life turned upside down.

One & Two Wheels

Steel framing, plywood, canvas

Archive II
David Garcia
MAP Architects
Denmark
2005

Part of a design investigation into spaces and books, Archive II is a travelling library that gives access to a roving collection of books. David Garcia's structure answers the needs of individuals who wish to move their library. Housed in a large timber circle with deeply recessed edges, Archive II is the perfect solution. Evoking the ancient libraries of the Far East that visited courts and cities, Archive II is a miniature version operated by one person. While books can act as vehicles to transport the imagination, this library transports the imaginative source itself.

Plywood

I-H Cruiser

Winfried Baumann

Germany

2008

Part of a long-standing investigation by artist Winfried Baumann into shelter systems for the homeless, the I-H Cruiser, from his 'Instant House' collection, exemplifies his ingenious adaptations. Baumann's design replaces the all too ubiquitous cardboard and newspaper with sturdy aluminium framing and a reflective, quilted thermo-cover. His designs for instant housing often include additional tools such as a first aid kit, mirror, whistle and flashlight. Like the rest of the Instant House series, the I-H Cruiser is light enough for a lone owner to move. The extendable bed folds away, and the legs can be lifted up to wheel the structure to a new location.

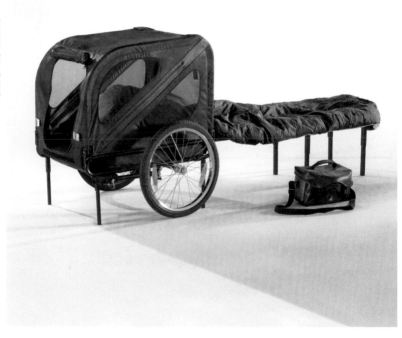

Aluminium framing, wheels, quilted thermo-fabric, mirror, whistle, flashlight

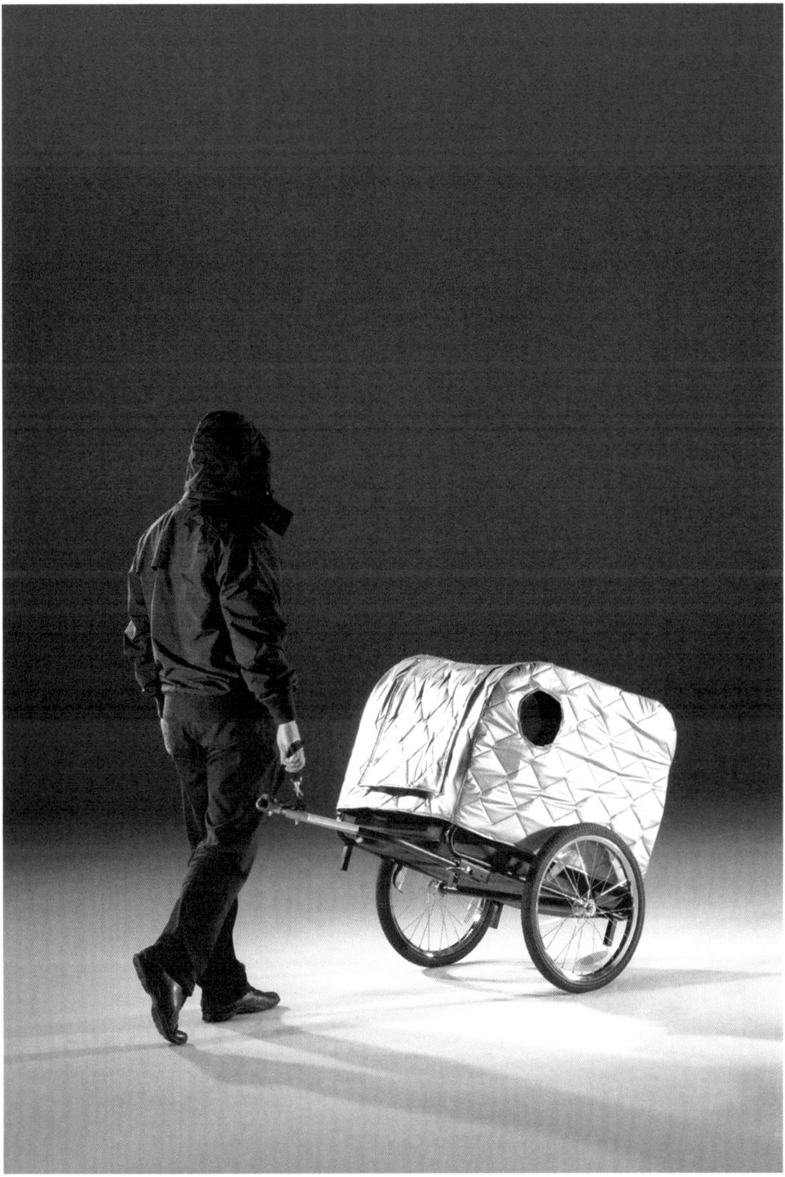

Foldavan

Wooden Widget

UK

2014

Rising to the challenge of designing a lightweight, foldable and pleasant camping vehicle, Wooden Widget developed the Foldavan. An expanding cycle-caravan, the Foldavan is small enough to be transported by bike and large enough to provide a comfortable resting place. Built from a simple frame of timber with a curvaceous upper framework, its shell is set on two sturdy wheels and enveloped by a lightweight textile canopy. When closed, the device is small enough to fit on car roof racks. Unfolded, the tiny van stretches to give a snug yet useable space for one.

Timber framing, steel chassis, PVC, bicycle wheels

Hütte Hut

Sprouting Sprocket
Studio

USA

2014

Making the idea of escapism a comfortable reality, the Hütte Hut is an elegant home-from-home that recalls the classic retro shape of the teardrop camper. Its marine plywood and Baltic birch body is entered through two broad doors that open along its length, while its form is completed by a cotton canvas top. Though tiny, the mobile structure sleeps two comfortably and includes several windows and minimal storage to enhance the sense of space. Weighing just 408 kilograms (900 pounds) its lightweight design is built from an aluminium space frame, which enables most light vehicles to take it on the road.

Trailer, aluminium framing, marine plywood, birch, canvas

Moving Space

Ohnmacht Flamm
Architekten
Germany
2000

Created by students at the University of Innsbruck and Ohnmacht Flamm Architekten, Moving Space uses slim sheets of plywood that can be rolled and rocked from the inside in order to travel from place to place. Enveloped by a curved form that was designed using three-dimensional digital analysis, the project is cut from flat timber sheets that fold together to create its stable, yet dynamic surfaces. With walls, roof and floor, as well as niches for sitting and reclining in, its two-person interior becomes an unconventional retreat. Simply by redistributing their weight, occupants can move and rotate the space for a truly off-the-wall experience.

One & Two Wheels

Plywood

Gidget Retro
Teardrop Camper
Gidget
Australia
2015

Adapting the aesthetic of classic retro campers, the Gidget updates the original with contemporary features. Its slide-out patented design gives twice the interior space of a traditional teardrop trailer. Inspired by the rise of sustainable living ideology, the Gidget creates a getaway that can be towed by an average car. The ecological intent continues inside, with timber-lined finishes sourced from sustainable sources. Delightful details, like tropical fabric curtains give it an authentic vintage feel. Boasting a queen-sized bed, pressurized water, LED lights and a solar panel, the trailer also includes a security alarm, entertainment console and a kitchen with integrated cooker.

Steel trailer, reinforced aluminium, fibreglass steel

Self-Lifting Mobility Project (S/LMP)
Mark Mack Architects
USA
2014

Part of the exhibition 'Truck-A-Tecture' at Kaneko in Omaha, the Self-Lifting Mobility Project (S/LMP) questions what nomadic architecture might look like. With a modest two-wheeled trailer that includes only the essentials for life on the move, the project pares life down to the basics. An adaptable mobile structure, the home has spaces to cook, sleep and work. Most striking is its scissor lift attachment, which creates an elevated sleep-work surface protected by a tensile canopy. The lower level includes seating and integrated storage, and, in an ironic gesture, a square of turf. The S/LMP packs down inside the tiny trailer, allowing for easy transportation.

Steel trailer, steel framing, plywood, plastic

Tiny Travelling Theatre

Aberrant Architecture

UK

2012

Inspired by historical records of a local coal merchant's home-made concert hall, this unusual mobile theatre provides a space for storytelling and entertaining. Part of London's Clerkenwell Design Festival, the Tiny Travelling Theatre reimagines a Victorian music hall, hosting a range of performances in its three-booth interior. Built from chipboard sheets painted red, its numerous chimneys are made from stacked coal scuttles. Each one sits above a skylight, with a large trumpeting funnel that channels sounds to those outside. Towed by a VW Camper Van throughout the weeklong event, the project revived the theatrics of its colourful predecessor.

Trailer, chipboard, glass, metal coal scuttles

Room-Room

Encore Heureux and
G Studio

China

2008

Imagined as an ally in the face of disaster, Room-Room is a design for reconstructing homes after catastrophic events. Commissioned for the National Art Museum Of China's exhibition 'Crossing: Dialogues for Emergency Architecture', the project restores critical conditions for human existence: a roof, a place of residence and a space for dignity. The go-anywhere solution is set on two wheels and can be towed by beast or bike. On the move it provides storage, while once set down, it gives a place to rest. For more permanent dwelling, the lightweight frame flips upside down, creating a sheltered place in which to settle.

One & Two Wheels

Aluminium framing, metal mesh, plastic, wheels

QTvan

Yannick Read for

Environmental

Transport Association

UK

2011

Designed to provide a camper for mobility scooter users, this tiny British van is the littlest of its kind. Small enough to be towed along the pavement, its narrow visage belies its convenience. Though diminutive, its tiny interior fits a single bed, as well as drinks cabinet, kettle and a large television. Its top speed is just ten kilometres (six miles) per hour, with a recommended range of up to ten miles (sixteen kilometres). Originally conceived to highlight the importance of mobility scooter safety (and breakdown insurance), the QTvan is a safe refuge for those stranded when their scooter breaks down.

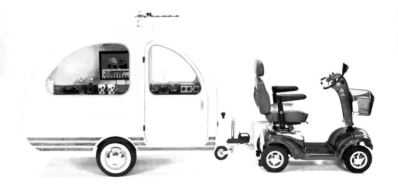

Aluminium, Plexiglas, solar panels, wheels

The Happier Camper

Derek Michael May

USA

2014

Inspired by a retro trailer, The Happier Camper offers a modern take on the classic without losing charisma. Modular and ultra-lightweight, these sturdy travel trailers are built from honeycomb fibreglass for maximum strength. Creating a broad and changeable room in which to camp, work or carry loads, the interiors are composed of small modules that allow for customization. From sinks to beds or tables, each module is scaled to fit, creating a Happier Camper shaped by its owner's needs. Like the bespoke interior, the contoured fibreglass shell is also chosen from one of seven vintage colours that span the colour spectrum.

Insulated fibreglass, stainless steel, solar panel, LED lights

MIU VI

Studio Orta

France

2002

Part of Studio Orta's investigation into aid for emergency situations, this construction is one of many Mobile Intervention Units (MIU) made by the studio. An itinerant vehicle for public use, its robust frame of steel includes a functional set of shelves large enough to sleep six. Paired with custom-made sleeping bags also designed by the studio, the hybrid trailer-bunk bed offers a practical place for people to rest as well as creating a clear social statement. As with other MIU works, such as the Nomad Hotel or OrtaWater, this variation is a poetic and conspicuous tool to highlight the essential needs of itinerant communities for shelter, food or water.

Steel chassis, steel framing, steel ladder, tarpaulin, aluminium

Bike Sauna

H3T Architects

Czech Republic

2012

Invigorating its environs – and those who sit within it – this nimble little sauna provides a spa on the move. Designed by Czech collective H3T Architects, the unconventional arrangement is a sweat-box towed by bike. Built of lightweight materials such as polycarbonate sheets and canvas, the timber-framed construction has space for six. Entered by a slit in the exterior elastic membrane, it includes a small wood-burning stove and classic wooden benches. While its mobile disposition means it can travel wherever its owners please, the Bike Sauna is designed to be used for social gatherings and to act as a distinctive device to transform unused public spaces.

Timber framing, polycarbonate sheet, canvas, bicycle, iron stove

Gypsy Junker

Derek Diedricksen

USA

2011

Just one of many homes that Derek Diedricksen has constructed, Gypsy Junker pushes the idea of tiny homes to the extreme. Taking discarded materials such as shipping pallets and household cabinets and re-fashioning them, Diedricksen uses his skills in carpentry as the basis for a growing business. While instructions for his buildings are available in his self-published books, Diedricksen's thrifty use of found materials means they are essentially one-offs. Gypsy Junker, for example, is fashioned from a pallet, wine bottles and corrugated plastic – with typically unusual additions of a cymbal for heat reflection and an exterior vent built from a frying pan base.

Timber, wine bottles, corrugated Plexiglas

De Markies

Böhtlingk Architectuur
The Netherlands
1985

Disguised inside a regular caravan shell, De Markies (the Awning) offers a wonderful camping surprise. Once settled in a chosen spot its two sides fold open, expanding the small interior to a light-filled haven that's three times its original size. With a central sturdy cabin for bathing, cooking, storage and eating, its two telescoping tent sides create large additional rooms. A tangerine-coloured textile encloses the private bedroom, providing enough space for four people to sleep. The facing side expands from its transparent cover to create an airy room for lounging in with far-reaching views. Catching attention for its ingenious solution, the project was the winner of Rotterdam's Public Design Prize.

Steel structure, plexiglass, nylon rope, polyster tarp, chipboard

Bicycle Teardrop Trailer

Matthew Hart Designs

Canada

—

The design of an innovative boat builder, this charming teardrop camper is a portable, aerodynamic dwelling that was towed by Matthew Hart's bicycle as he cycled across British Columbia. Built from bicycle wheels and fixed on top of a sturdy frame, the body is insulated with polystyrene and wrapped in thin-gauge aluminium sheets. The interior is lined with plywood and includes a folding table, a fridge, sleeping space and a cooker just big enough to brew coffee. The travelling home captured the attention of thousands of people along the way. Hart simply settled it down by parks, beaches or hill-tops to enjoy life on the move in prime real estate spots.

Aluminium, polystyrene insulation, plywood,
steel framing, bicycle wheels

The XS

So-Cal Teardrops

USA

2004

Once beloved by many, teardrop trailers have now generally been replaced by more modern recreational vehicles. This retro rendition revives an old favourite with contemporary appeal. Providing a compact, lightweight space to enjoy camping on the road, the aerodynamic trailers are framed in timber while their silvered exterior is the result of waterproof anodized aluminium sheeting. Creating a cozy sleeping space for two adults, the design includes a rear-hinged hatch that opens to reveal a fully equipped kitchen. Lined in birch plywood and customized for every owner, the range of finishes and accessories varies, but all share the same aerodynamic shape.

One & Two Wheels

Steel chassis, anodized aluminium, birch wood, aluminium, glass

560 Ultra Raindrop

Camp-Inn

USA

2002

Offering camping adventures in style and comfort, this shining model is the ultimate teardrop trailer experience. With its eye-catching aluminium exterior, the 560 Ultra Raindrop retains the appeal of its forebears with added amenities for modern life. The birch-lined interior contains a queen-sized bed and the kitchen includes stove, sink and running water. The camper is also wired for electricity and includes heating and cooling systems. Built by two engineers obsessed with teardrop campers, each Camp-Inn model is individually made. This extra-long version creates space for a convertible bunk-couch without losing the aerodynamic aesthetic for which teardrops are loved.

Trailer, aluminium, birch wood, insulation foam, glass

Exile

José Ángel Vincench

Cuba

2012

Part of the 11th Havana Biennial of art in Cuba, these letter-shaped mobile structures spell out the word E-X-I-L-E and are a public statement of the artist's intent. Set on modest steel trailers, the individual caravans are just big enough for one, though they stand uninhabited as a way of emphasizing the artwork's meaning. Representing isolated individuals who live outside their own countries, Exile confronts the idea of isolation, whether political or emotional. The work frames Vincench's wider artistic practice, in which dissent and exile are established themes.

Steel chassis, plasterboard, glass

Honda Spree,
Study of Temporary
Autonomy
Jay Nelson
USA
2006

An early foray into creative adaptive reuse, this Honda Scooter is an intriguing hybrid that brings together surfing and camping in one simple vehicle. The artist, Jay Nelson, who is also an avid surfer, works with what's available to construct his makeshift pieces. Called 'temporary autonomous structures' after the anarchic writings of Hakim Bey, the projects by Nelson are built for specific trips or events. Incorporating recycled materials for reduced environmental impact, this work is one of many that imbue an exploratory theme, while carrying quite a cargo.

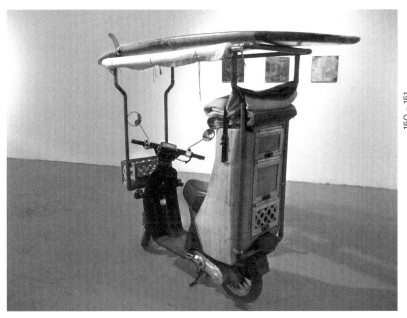

Honda motorbike, copper pipe, timber, canvas

Contemporary Shepherd's Hut

Thomas Alabaster

UK

2016

Inspired by childhood summers spent in a dilapidated shed at the bottom of his garden, this contemporary take on a rustic shepherd's hut by Thomas Alabaster allows its owners to be close to nature yet sheltered in a comfortable cabin-on-wheels. The elegant space includes a wood-burning stove and a generous gabled roof incised with high windows that flood the timber-clad interior with daylight. White-painted walls, strategically located windows and a built-in porch, complete the airy arrangement, which contrasts with the robust corrugated shell that encases it.

Corrugated galvanized steel, glass, pine, steel

Micro Camper

Wide Path Camper

Denmark

2014

Lightweight, compact and easily towed, this bicycle camper is a nimble option for life outdoors. Invented by Wide Path Camper, the mini-RV is a two-part design that opens and closes by rotating along its rear. At its full extent, the camper provides room for two adults to rest, as well as seating, storage and a folding table. Though built from a hard shell and thoroughly durable, its forty-five-kilogram (100-pound) load is eminently towable. When you're done with camping or picnics outdoors, the structure's hood hinges to almost half its length – and all that's left is to get on your bike.

Aluminium framing, fibreglass, plywood, polycarbonate

Pumba Trailer

Freedom Trailers

UK

2014

Hampered by the restrictions of transporting his two-man roof tent, the Freedom Trailer range is Dave Stephenson's inventive response. Providing fast set-up, as well as the ability to travel long distances, this sturdy trailer offers freedom and adventure. One of three models, the Pumba is a travelling workhorse, equipped for use on rough terrain and for long periods living off-the-grid. Its robust trailer shell includes a fridge-freezer, sixty litres (sixteen gallons) of water storage and solar panels for energy. On the roof, a hinged platform unfolds to reveal an elevated tent, accessed by ladder. A large suspended awning attaches underneath, providing room for beds and storage.

Trailer, steel framing, tent, solar panel, LED lights

GO!
Sylvan Sport
USA
2007

Based on the idea of 'one trailer for countless uses', GO! is an emphatic reason to get outdoors. Its robust steel trailer, consisting of welded aluminium framing, provides a compact base for the pop-up camper: an ultra-light model built by outdoor equipment makers, Kelty. Creating an elevated tent that sleeps two, the design includes comfortable mattresses and folding side panels to expand the bed base. The steel frame includes additional storage with an integrated secure locker, as well as an upper roof level for stowing bikes, boats and other equipment. A reliable packhorse, the design is also lightweight, making it easy for virtually all vehicles to tow.

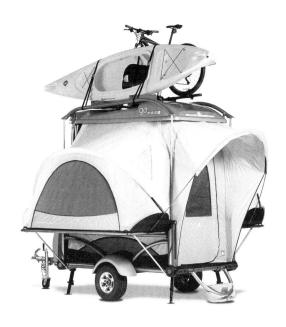

Steel chassis, aluminium framing, rubber wheels, nylon, chipboard

Sommer-Container
Markku Hedman
Finland
2002

Maximizing its size and the short Finnish summer, Sommer-Container is a portable one-room home for two. Designed for spending holidays in the woods, the small cabin can be transported into the forest on a standard towing trailer. Resembling a humble matchbox (though a giant in comparison), this wooden cabin is formed of two volumes: a pale cube, with a dark centre that slides in and out of the larger cube. This retractable feature allows the cabin to double in size. Containing a convertible seat-sleeper and built-in kitchenette, the container can easily be closed again and towed away in search of another idyllic spot.

Timber framing, polystyrene foam, plywood, acrylic glass

Terrapin
Casual Turtle
Campers
USA
2014

Set atop a standard trailer, this handcrafted home creates a distinctive woodsy feel for its owners wherever they roam. Inspired by retro trailers and the philosophy of less is more, the Terrapin combines vintage appeal with modern techniques. Portable and lightweight, it is designed for towing by most four-cylinder cars. Its most striking feature – the curved roof – increases the room inside the cabin, and makes it more aerodynamic. The cozy interior includes storage, a small counter and convertible bed–banquette, with windows on all sides and electrical power. Each Terrapin is handmade, allowing owners to create the camper of their dreams.

Steel trailer, Western red cedar, PVC, LED lights, glass

Cricket Trailer

Garrett Finney
and TAXA Outdoors

USA

2010

Conceived by Garrett Finney, a designer with NASA credentials, this space-saving module delivers maximum impact. Housed in an aerodynamic shell for efficient towing, the vehicle is somewhere between a tent and an RV. With its rigid shell and pop-up soft top, the unit provides sleeping space for two adults. Its tiny interior includes a bed, modest kitchen and integrated storage as well as generous space for grey and clean water. Though compact, the insides open up to the great outdoors with a wide entry door and windows. Additional features including solar panels and a bathroom allow for off-the-grid adventures whilst retaining a few creature comforts.

One & Two Wheels

Steel chassis, aluminium composite panels, polyester

Tiny Study Pod

Relax Shacks

USA

2014

Custom-made for a university professor, this tiny pod on wheels is the creation of Derek Diedricksen and employs his distinctive approach to using recycled materials. Big enough to sleep two and comfortable enough to work in, the project is largely built from reused timber, including a colourful rear wall of patchwork wooden offcuts and flooring retrieved from a 100-year-old house. Enclosed by a large translucent sheet of polycarbonate, the wall becomes a door by simply raising and propping it wide open. Offering ample access to the forest beyond, the door can be opened up or closed to give more peace for correcting student papers.

Timber, Tuftex, polyurethane beadboard, glass, plastic,

BeauEr 3X

Eric Beau

France

2010

A camper that slides out as well as rolls along, the BeauEr 3X expanding trailer delivers an interior space that is triple the size of its compressed state. Easily towed and a seriously spacious camper, the cylindrical-shaped BeauEr 3X is the ingenious creation of Eric Beau. Its telescopic sliding mechanism allows both ends to slide away from the central core, and provides enough space for a bathroom, kitchen, double bedroom and dining area. Able to be set up in an impressively quick twenty seconds by simply turning a key, the internal furniture automatically slips into position, ready for relaxation.

Steel chassis, polyester, aluminium, chipboard, plastic

Shelters

Joseph Griffiths

Australia

2012

This handmade, makeshift dwelling is one of three shelters in a series made by Joseph Griffiths for Melbourne's Next Wave Festival. In sharp contrast with its docklands surroundings of glass tower blocks, this rustic installation is constructed with detritus claimed from around the edges of the city. Inviting occupation, Griffiths' installations are both provocative and playful. For instance, this caravan-like piece reinterprets the popular leisure camper. Unlike a factory produced, expensive, off-the-rack counterpart, this intriguing urban camper is assembled by collage: marrying found materials of varied timbers, a trailer, a painted roof and a bulbous acrylic dome.

Trailer, timber, steel, rope, paint, Perspex, glass, tape, fabric, acrylic

Human

No Wheels

One & Two Wheels

Three Wheels

Four
Wheels

Five +
Wheels

Sleds +

Water

Camper Bike

Kevin Cyr

USA

2008

Powered by pedal, and large enough for one, the Camper Bike by artist Kevin Cyr is a delightful and intruiging mobile dwelling. The slim-line, time-worn camper contrasts with the ostentation and size of many contemporary RVs. Cyr, instead, embraces the signs of age; the rust, scratches and dents. The Camper Bike is formed from a tall, narrow shell mounted on a standard-issue Chinese tricycle. Now part of the Oxylane Art Foundation collection, the Camper Bike is more concept than camper – an artwork that comments on the differences between American and Chinese culture, where in the former people drive enormous vehicles and in the latter carry heavy loads on bikes.

Three Wheels

Tricycle, corrugated aluminium, Plexiglas, plywood, timber

Tricycle House

People's Architecture
Office + PIDO

China

2012

Addressing the reality of life in China, where individuals are not permitted to own land according to the laws of the prevailing socialist government, Tricycle House offers a roving alternative: a home on a tricycle frame. The house is built from scored translucent polypropylene panels that allow light in, ensuring the compact space feels pleasantly airy. The house contains all the essentials for off-the-grid life: sink, stove, bath, water tank, storage and furniture that can transform from a bed to a table, bench and countertop. Complementing the house is a Tricycle Garden that, along with Tricycle House, is imagined as a completely sustainable travelling dwelling.

Tricycle, folded polypropylene, wheels

Housetrike

Bas Sprakel

The Netherlands

2014

This unassuming ice cream cart performs a surprising double-act, turning from cycle-bound trolley to a bed built for one. Made by Dutch inventor Bas Sprakel, the project is intended for the homeless, nomads and campers, providing safe, waterproof accommodation that is more reliable than a tent. Instead of tubs of sorbet, its extendable interior offers a box-bedroom and the upper metal surface acts as a sturdy rooftop while portholes at the base bring light to the tiny interior. Locked from within for greater security, once you're refreshed and the room is retracted, the rooftop forms a table ideal for preparing camp-stove meals or making coffee.

Three Wheels

Tricycle, steel framing, coated timber

Bufalino

Cornelius Comanns

Germany

2010

A sturdy companion for solo journeys, this little camper is able to meet all of an individual's basic needs. Based on the three-wheeled Italian workhorse – Piaggio's Ape 50 van – this design is equally fuel-efficient and comparably robust. Conceived to give people a greater connection to their surroundings, its German designer, Cornelius Comanns describes it as a kind of base camp that can travel alongside you. With well-considered amenities, it includes a bed, a fridge, storage for goods and water, and areas for seating and cooking. Expressing the muscle of its mobster namesake, the Bufalino is modest in scale but not in might.

Steel chassis, plasterboard, plastic, aluminium, Plexiglas

Bao House

Dot Architects

China

2012

Quilted and mobile, the Bao House is a travelling cube with impact. Designed by Chinese architects Dot, the form is created by injecting spray polyurethane foam into a fabric and timber mould. Though normally concealed behind finished surfaces, the expanding foam is exposed here, an inside-out touch. Water resistant and thermally insulated, Bao House includes a sliding front wall that gives entry to the sleeping space. Meanwhile, overhead, light enters the room through a transparent polycarbonate panel, which also caters to stargazing at night. Meaning 'bulge' in Mandarin, Bao House lives up to its name – a billowy experiment for life on wheels.

Tricycle, spray polyurethane foam, fabric, timber, polycarbonate

Eyes Closed
DL Atelier
China
2012

Designed as a birthday present for their two-year-old son, this Chinese duo's travelling installation offers a creative view on the world. Sitting on a modified tricycle, its gouged foam interior is secured within a broad black frame. Filled with three-dimensional layers of black sponge ruptured with crevasses, Eyes Closed encourages tactile curiosity. As well as offering a space for childlike exploration, the mobile installation has been adapted to different uses. While their young boy and his friends play in the varied spaces inside, adults might make Eyes Closed live up to it's name and take a nap.

Tricycle, foam

Weekend

Carlos No

Portugal

2012

Dismayed at the inequitable nature of shantytown dwellings, this work by Carlos No draws attention to the improvised, unstable homes that are usually built from detritus by the poorest of the poor. Part of a larger series entitled Villa Bidão, Weekend develops No's concern with injustice. Built from discarded timber and other scavenged items, the mottled wooden tower-like form is mounted on top of a motor tricycle. In contrast with the relative luxury of many people's weekends, this vehicle serves to magnify the plight of those in poverty. Only large enough to stand up in, uncomfortable and fragile, the project is a thoughtful and unsettling provocation.

Three Wheels

Moto-tricycle, timber, PVC, glass, nylon

25 Pedra de Sal

Jacinta and Casimiro
Costa

Portugal

2007

Reusing cast-off kitchen storage units to form the base of their mobile baby care unit, designers and parents Jacinta and Casimiro Costa created 25 Pedra de Sal. The diminutive mobile unit reconfigures components from a child's bike and incorporates disused tubing, spare wheels, an acrylic sheet and an old car mirror. The combined result is a new brightly coloured crib that includes built-in storage for baby clothes, bedding and care products, as well as a nappy change drawer. Resourcefully designed and built by the Costas for their two children, the mobile unit is the coolest crib around.

Tricycle, repurposed kitchen unit, acrylic sheet, mirror

Ta đi Ôtô

Bureau A

Vietnam

2013

There's a lot to like about this tower-on-a-trike. A seven-storey performance space mounted on top of a tricycle, it provides a moveable structure for a variety of uses. Fashioned from a framework of blue-painted steel, the project includes a small roof, lights and a battery-powered fan. Commissioned by Ta đi Ôtô, a local bar and cultural centre in Hanoi, the wandering platform has hosted numerous events, including a street-food pop-up and art exhibitions. Constructed in a field near Hanoi, it was delivered to the city by old-fashioned pedal power. Drawing on local know-how and experience, the project is imbued with an authentic Vietnamese sensibility.

Three Wheels

Steel framing, tarpaulin, tricycle, wooden boards

Mobile Design Agency

Lava

China

2013

The charming Mobile Design Agency is made from a second-hand three-wheeled scooter, or *sanlunche* as it's known locally in China. The vehicle was used as Lava's roving studio for the duration of Beijing Design Week. The aim of the project was to offer advice to, and create logos for, small business owners in the Dashilan area. From fruiterers to barbers, Lava plied its trade, using bilingual questionnaires to determine each client's need and a brief. Allowing for greater interaction in the historic neighbourhood, the mobile agency gave local business people a sense of the value of Dutch design, as well as dispensing creative branding advice.

Three-wheeled scooter, steel, aluminium, Plexiglas

Parkcycle Swarm

N55

John Bela, Till Wolfer

The Netherlands

2013

Tricycle, park and social activism in one: the Parkcycle Swarm by Dutch collective N55 is a modular, moveable, instant park. Set on a three-wheeled base, a lightweight aluminium frame supports a mobile lawn and is strong enough to carry additional planters and even pets. A human-powered garden on wheels, the design is available for free online, encouraging social interaction and green-thinking. Imagined as a lawn for one user or a park for many, the 'DIY urban planning tool' enables citizens to reclaim public space. This bottom-up process to create green space means a park can be assembled whenever, wherever, by simply cycling the modules into place.

Tricycle, aluminium, plywood, AstroTurf

Supertramp

Lehman B

UK

2010

As part of an investigation into simpler ways of living, the Supertramp is a mobile living concept designed by Lehman B to be towed from place to place by tricycle. Enveloped in a pale canvas cover, loosely stretched over a steel frame, the small home on wheels anticipates an urban lifestyle where 'less is more' (a critique of the current norms). Access is through a large zippered door that gives way to a simple interior, complete with wood-burning stove, chimney, and enough room to sleep. This social and experimental project includes a large openable 'hatch' – a small 'window on the world' to encourage social interactions with passersby.

Tricycle, steel framing, canvas, plywood

| Wandering Home |
| Kacey Wong |
| Hong Kong |
| 2008 |

An interpretation of Hong Kong's rich and varied culture for the Venice Architecture Biennale, Wandering Home is an apposite response to the Hong Kong's rising living costs and the rapid escalation in the number of homeless people. Wong's tongue-in-cheek project addressed a serious problem while also becoming his temporary home during the exhibition. Set on top of the sort of sturdy tricycle often seen in China, Wandering Home's timber-framed body is finished with waterproof metal cladding, while the interior has space for a desk, a bed and storage. A potential solution for nomadic domesticity, its modest form underlines a growing urban concern.

Tricycle, steel chassis, aluminium, timber, glass

The DJ Trike 1.0

Jonathan S. Igharas

USA

2009

The culmination of Jonathan Igharas' graduate studies, The DJ Trike was initially inspired by his interest in different bicycles and tricycles around the world – from rickshaws in India to Vietnamese cyclos. The DJ Trike 1.0 is a popular fixture on the streets of New York City and was created by the Brooklyn-based designer to reclaim, activate and enhance public space. Drawing on its in-built pedal-powered sound system, Igharas simply parks his bike anywhere in the city and plays a set, inviting people to enjoy the impromptu entertainment. The inventive mobile structure is comprised of a tough, extendable DJ mixing board housed in a protective box, mounted onto a tricycle.

Tricycle framing, aluminium composite panels, steel, bamboo

Secret Operation 610
RAAAF
Studio Frank
Havermans
The Netherlands
2013

Spooky and stealthy in equal measure, Secret Operation 610 is an exercise in research and history. Cultivating the atmosphere of the Cold War and the aesthetics of military weaponry, this flightless vehicle was designed as a mobile research vehicle based at the now decommissioned Soesterberg Air Base. Providing space for up to ten visiting researchers, it travels slowly along the disused runway on caterpillar tracks. From afar, its blackened steel-armoured body, raised four-and-a-half metres (fifteen feet) off the ground with two large, wing-shaped legs, stands in stark contrast to the serene peace-time landscape.

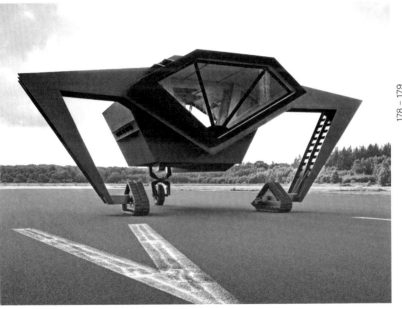

Steel, glass, caterpillar treads

Human

No
Wheels

One & Two
Wheels

Three
Wheels

Four
Wheels

Five +
Wheels

Sleds +

Water

The Collingwood Shepherd Hut	
Güte	
Canada	
2015	

Known as The Collingwood Shepherd Hut, this contemporary shepherd's wagon is worlds apart from its humble predecessor. Designed by Güte, Canadian specialists in hand-made wagons, the rounded cabin shape means the usual distinctions between walls, floor and ceiling are blurred, amplifying the sense of space in its tiny interior. Its shingled skin is perfect for keeping out the bleak wind and shedding ice and snow typical in chilly North American winters. Inside, the modest four-and-a-half-metre-long (fifteen-foot) wagon houses a wood-burning stove, timber bunk beds and a double bed that folds away to form a dining table and banquette seating.

Four Wheels

Steel chassis, plywood, galvanized metal, plywood, Western red ceder, glass

Tiny House

Walden Studio

The Netherlands

2016

This contemporary interpretation of a mobile, off-the-grid house is presented with clean simple volumes, inside and out. Designed by Walden Studio, specialists in compact, efficient homes, Tiny House features high ceilings and a large front deck. These attributes, in addition to the pale interior finishes and a generous window wall, increase the feeling of space. All of the available space is maximized: from the integrated storage hidden inside the stairs, to the corner sofa that transforms into a dining table. Clad in sustainably grown pine panels and with sheep's wool insulation, Tiny House is powered by three large solar panels that supply all the energy it needs.

Steel chassis, wood, plasterboard, aluminium, solar panel, glass

**Homeless Homes
Project**

Gregory Kloehn

USA

2014

This project brings new purpose to discarded waste found in urban dumpsters. Gregory Kloehn has applied his obsession with ad hoc structures to the issue of homelessness. Each hand-made home is ingenious and resourceful. His project up-cycles all manner of waste – from discarded white goods, and fish tanks to paint and timber pallets. Built at no cost, Kloehn's project creates unique homes, providing nomadic security in the concrete jungle. All units are lockable, mobile and raised off the ground, offering protection against theft, vermin, rain and urban-planning bureaucracy. Light enough to simply push along, these homes are playful, economic and impactful.

Four Wheels

Repurposed timber, plastic, fabric

Mobile Shop

How About Studio

UK

2016

Designed for London's Festival of Love, this pop-up shop sells sunblock and poolside accessories at the public fountain next door. Tiled in gradated shades of white and blue, with candy-pink rails and a miniature pool ladder, the cart is mounted on plastic wheels, allowing it to navigate through the crowds. Unattended, it is enclosed by stainless steel wings that fold down to protect the products on display. During business hours, its wings open up to create a shady canopy and revealing the glistening brass detailing of cupboards and drawers. This refreshing and cool design offers reprieve in the heat of this annual summer event.

Steel, tiles, wheels, aluminium

hOMe

Andrew and Gabriella
Morrison

USA

2013

Following the increasingly popular choice of having a small, affordable living space rather than a conventional domestic building, this home-on-wheels offers a contemporary take on a tiny house. The two-storey home is just twenty square metres (215 square feet) and includes all the essentials: kitchen, bathroom, dining-living-work space, bedroom and even a wood-fuelled stove. Hiding storage beneath the staircase and using simple finishes of timber floors and white walls, its crisp interior matches the simple exterior of timber cladding. Self-built and without the obligation of a mortgage or rent, 'hOMe' is a convincing alternative for domestic life.

Four Wheels

Trailer, timber, glass, steel

**Ice Fishing Hut #885
La Baie Des Ha! Ha!,
Quebec**
Anonymous
Canada
2016

Captured in Quebec as part of Richard Johnson's ongoing photography series 'Ice Huts', this tiny cabin on wheels features all the essentials to while away the freezing Canadian winter with a spot of ice fishing. Like the many other huts Johnson has photographed, this one indicates the character of its owner as much as the culture of fishing. This small timber hut for two in Quebec's Ha! Ha! Bay is a relatively sophisticated example compared with many ice fishing huts, and is mounted on wheels to aid retrieval before the ice thaws. Simply propped up on blocks to give temporary stability, it includes a wood-burning stove to fend off the cold.

Steel chassis, timber, corrugated metal, glass

AERO-Mobile

| Office of Mobile |
| Design |
| USA |
| 2015 |

The AERO-Mobile is part of Jennifer Siegal's ongoing interest in dynamic and ecologically sound structures. The project fuses mobility and prefabrication in a roving dwelling that can house a range of functions including exhibitions, start-up offices and retail sites. The space is elevated by a scissor lift and its internal volume can be increased by extending wings of panelled fabric. As with much of her work, the project is composed of recycled industrial materials, including a discarded aeronautical Unit Load Device (ULD) and textiles from sailboats. Portable and prefabricated, the AERO-Mobile is an uplifting experience.

Four Wheels

Truck, aluminium framing, nylon tarpaulin, aluminium

Future Wagon

Studiobird

Australia

2013

Australian architect Matthew Bird's Future Wagon employs found material and draws on precedents such as Wild West stagecoaches and gypsy wagons to imagine a nomadic home of the future. Constructed from a panoply of resources – steel wire mesh, skylight domes, multipurpose plumbing hose and steel pipes – the result is a lightweight, roaming home. Its striking diamond-shaped form, clad with cuttings of clear PVC carpet matting, is light enough for one person to manoeuvre. Seen from its bed made from blue garden hose, the rolling scenery outside the trolley provides ever-changing decor and liberation from the usual constraints of home ownership.

Steel framing, trolley wheels, clear PVC matting, cobweb brooms, shower curtain rings, steel wire mesh

The Rolling Shelter

Eduardo Lacroze

USA

2015

With a shopping cart at its heart, this rolling dwelling for the homeless is a modular house for one. The brainchild of architect Eduardo Lacroze, the shelter is easy to assemble, requiring only a screwdriver to put together. Made from collapsible panels the design features a folding side panel that creates space for a single bed and integrated Therm-a-Rest mattress. In transit the space compresses to sit above the trolley, with storage compartments that are accessible in either mode. The winner of an American Institute of Architects Small Project Practitioners Award, this temporary solution is a genuine attempt to address an endemic problem.

Four Wheels

Metal shopping cart, coated chipboard, galvanized bolts

Homelss Chateau

James Westwater

USA

2008

Part of a larger project called Plywood Chateaux, this version of James Westwater's mobile, modular, micro-architecture is just big enough for one. Devised after the 2007–08 financial crisis and ensuing questions about home ownership, the moveable shelter incorporates salvaged and recycled materials. A collage of reflective traffic signs, plywood, timber pallets and leftover building materials, the Homeless Chateau was intended for display in galleries to confront a privileged audience. Furnished with books, food and other everyday supplies, the chateau highlights the need for compassion towards the homeless.

Plywood, traffic signs, trolley wheels

Midget Bushtrekka

Kamp-Rite

USA

2012

Designed as a companion for cycle touring, this four-wheeled trailer-tent comes with all the bells and whistles that you might hope for. Its base structure provides waterproof storage and is the frame for an elevated tent. Made from a two-part folding platform the fully enclosed, elevated camp cot has a body of Ripstop nylon, with polyurethane coating for water resistance and insect screens to enable a peaceful night's sleep. Built from a frame of aluminium to reduce the load when towing, its name suggests its size – a tiny 120-litre (32-gallon) volume that gives just enough space for the essentials for a short camping trip.

Four Wheels

Trailer, aluminium framing, Ripstop nylon

EDAR Mobile Unit

EDAR – Everyone
Deserves a Roof

Project

USA

2007

An abbreviation for both the prototype and the non-profit organization 'Everyone Deserves a Roof', this mobile unit is the brainchild of EDAR founder, Peter Samuelson. The sturdy four-wheeled design has been developed into a viable, secure alternative for the rising number of homless people. Designed for sleeping and storage, the tent-like cover creates a secure enclsore. By day, the cover tucks into side cages and the sleeping base retracts, reverting to a compact, mobile cart. Complete with reflective strips, wheel locking devices, and a brake, this pragmatic structure expresses a commendable ideal: human dignity for all.

Metal trolley, mattress, waterproof canopy, mesh fabric

The Opera

Rob Vos

The Netherlands

2008

At the deluxe end of the 'life-under-canvas' spectrum, The Opera camper is a mobile holiday 'tent' that evokes the iconic sails of the Sydney Opera House. Doing away with messy poles, pegs and camp beds, The Opera offers the ultimate comforts of a home-away-from-home. Finished with teak floors, its interior includes electronically adjustable beds, in-built storage spaces, a top-loading fridge – and even a ceramic toilet. The exterior is equally well equipped, with an easily accessed baggage area and a collapsible kitchen for outdoor use. When packed up, the camper's compact dimensions make it easy to tow from place to place.

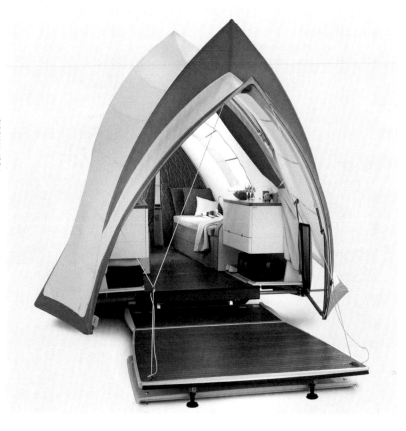

Metal chassis, polyester, teak, marine grade polyester, nylon rope, LED lights

Resulting from a fascination with mobility and automobiles, the Camper Kart by artist Kevin Cyr fashions a steel shopping trolley into an autonomous home. Its robust form renders it superior to many tent options and includes storage for food and tools, a retractable sleeping deck and a durable roof. Demounted, the trolley becomes navigable, with the wooden base, mattress and canvas packed away. To open, users simply turn the crank and raise the roof. An interesting experiment in mobile living, the project is also a social comment on the shopping trolley; a ubiquitous 1930s invention that has, for some, come to be associated with the urban homeless.

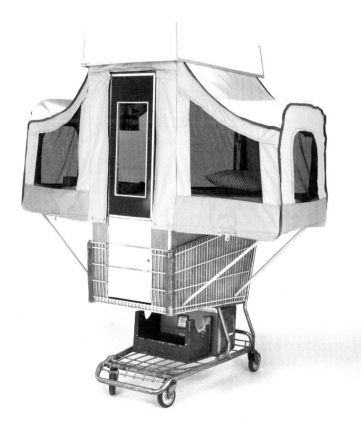

Steel shopping cart, chipboard, nylon, canvas

Homeless Vehicle	
Variant 3	
Krzysztof Wodiczko	
USA	
1988	

Not a gadget of artful homemaking but a critique of the 'symbolic, psychopolitical and economic operations of the city', Wodiczko's Homeless Vehicles are weighted with meaning. His range of metal units transform into spaces for sleeping and washing, with room for collected cans and plastic bags. Prototypes of the vehicles have been used by homeless people, and have also been displayed in art galleries as a social critique. Resembling a pimped-up supermarket trolley, the mesh panels and rubberized plastic are complemented by irregular-sized wheels and a striking metal half-cylinder body. Wodiczko's vision is a hard-nosed look at the reality of homelessness.

Four Wheels

Steel framing, polyster tarpaulin, plywood, rope, wheels, plastic

Toybox Tiny Home

Frank Henderson,
Paul Schultz

USA

2015

Standing out from its more sober neighbours, the Toybox Tiny Home brings to mind brightly coloured candy. Clad in an energy-efficient thermoplastic roof with cedar sidings and corrugated fibreglass panels, the cozy and carefully organized interior includes a plywood-lined kitchen, living space, a dining table-desk, as well as a sleeping loft. Conscious of the increasing demand for ecologically-sound camping, the colourful caravan includes options for solar panels or wind generators, and optional grey water-fed flower boxes, fulfilling the designer's aim to provide a home offering 'peace, simplicity, happiness and recreation'.

Steel chassis, cedar, fibreglass, plywood, glass

Tripbuddy

Bill Davis

UK

2012

A bold and aerodynamic alternative to standard caravans, Tripbuddy draws on computer-aided design techniques to create an optimum shape that lets you go with the flow. Unlike many of its competitors, it is formed of a complete moulded monocoque frame, which reduces drag when towing and negates leaks and drips in severe weather. Its compact interior is accessed via a rear hatch that opens up to the inbuilt catering, washing, and lounge-sleep zones, all finished in durable leather and teak. If two's company but three's a crowd, an integral awning expands the entry space, giving room for several small tents to be attached.

Four Wheels

Steel chassis, fibreglass, Plexiglas

Nebula

Andrew Maynard
Architects
Australia
2013

Commissioned by Arts Access Victoria for Art Day South (a collective of artists with cognitive disabilities), Nebula is a portable arts space with flexible programming that can become a gallery, workshop, seminar space or theatre. Large enough to admit up to sixteen artists, Nebula's distinctive colourful shell proudly introduces the work and artistic achievements into urban culture, rather than being limited to suburban fringe locations. The full expanse of the structure is revealed when Nebula's walls are folded out, becoming platforms that are enclosed by a concertinaed canopy of transparent, and brightly coloured, opaque plastic.

Aluminium, timber, plastic

Porta Palace

Daniel Venneman

The Netherlands

2015

This ecological and compact mobile home is a light, efficient option for life on the road. Porta Palace's design maximizes its tiny footprint, through the use of large picture windows above the kitchen and a multi-panelled glass entrance door which give the interior an impression of space. Inside, the mezzanine-level sleeping platform frees up floor space, and is accessed by an ingenious table that doubles as a stairs and storage area. Composed of bio-friendly elements, including pre-treated wood cladding and steel and glass elements that are one hundred per cent recyclable, the design allows for future solar panel additions, providing an entirely off-grid existence.

Four Wheels

Steel chassis, timber, steel, LED lighting

Golden Gate 2

Jay Nelson

USA

2014

An artist and avid surfer, each of Jay Nelson's mobile dwellings are hand-built, allowing him to learn new processes and ideas with each design. This second incarnation of his series 'Golden Gate', for example, is an architectural collage – a place for rest, for thought or for scoping out surf breaks. Built primarily of timber, its rounded form includes carefully located porthole windows, a gull-wing hatch and large windscreens at the front and back. A charming and eye-catching vehicle, Golden Gate 2 provides enough space for a bed, surfboard and the freedom to travel.

Steel framing, timber, plywood, Plexiglas, metal bolts

Work On Wheels

IDEO

USA

2014

Why travel to work when it can come to you? This pioneering idea underpins Work On Wheels (WOW) – a transparent, mobile workspace designed by global design consultancy IDEO. Powered by clean energy sources, the Work On Wheels concept anticipates the appeal and ease of working remotely. Its design provides a climate-regulated office space, with driverless controls that navigate by GPS. Inside the smart glass shields, there are flexible spaces for a vast range of trades, from dentists to dressmakers – or simply for those in need of a view. Forward-thinking and under further development, WOW may soon be rolling your way.

Four Wheels

Glass, plastic, steel, aluminium, wheels

Leaf House Version 2

Laird Herbert

Canada

2012

Faced with the cold Canadian climate and the need for a home that could accommodate a family of four, Laird Herbert's solution is the Leaf House. The custom-built, fully self-contained mobile home unites compact living with an appreciation for light, well-organized spaces made from quality materials. Its interior includes dining and kitchen areas, a compact bathroom and a tiny loft above the living space is big enough for a double bed. Leaf House is clad with cedar and corrugated steel, with spray foam insulation and triple-pane windows for thermal insulation. Its interior finishes of birch and cedar harmonize with the exterior, completing this trim mobile space.

Four Wheels

Steel chassis, cedar, corrugated steel, glass, plasterboard

The Emerald

Tiny Heirloom

USA

2015

Light-filled, spacious and full of charm, The Emerald lives up to its glowing moniker. Based in Oregon, Tiny Heirloom is a family-run business that specializes in high-quality homes on wheels. Never compromising, their tiny-living ethos is to downsize and upgrade: creating smaller spaces built from quality materials. This classic gabled version includes a granite-topped kitchen, bespoke built-in dining nook, a bathroom and sitting room, as well as extras like a washing machine and coat cupboard. Generously equipped, the white-painted timber walls give the home an airy spaciousness, its lofty reaches just tall enough to fit in a mezzanine bed and skylights.

Steel chassis, steel, cedar, glass

The Cowboy

Hummingbird Micro
Homes

Canada

2014

Riding into a town near you, The Cowboy is a tiny house on wheels that is a practical, efficient and affordable option for life on the move. Built by the Canadian-based Hummingbird Micro Homes, this model unites rustic charm with rigorous planning, and is designed to endure harsh northern winters. Its two-tone facade encloses a snug home, including kitchen, bathroom, a living-dining space and a sleeping loft. Clad in timber and corrugated steel, with pale timbered ceilings, its exterior is pierced by an abundance of windows. Set atop a double-axle trailer, this small but sturdy cowboy crib is all set for adventures at home on the range.

Four Wheels

Steel chassis, corrugated steel, timber, plasterboard, glass

Leaf House Version 3

Laird Herbert

Canada

2015

Based in Yukon, northwest Canada, Laird Herbert's tiny mobile homes combine contemporary vision with cold-climate construction smarts, creating modern homes that take the edge off winter. One of several models by the practice the Leaf House range champions simple amenities and green credentials. Version 3 includes two-tone open-joint cladding of reclaimed materials. Inside, natural, sustainable materials continue with a propane fireplace, bucket toilet and passive solar design. The spruce interior is finished with non-toxic materials such as birch plywood, giving this home on wheels serious ecological credentials.

Steel chassis, cedar, hardwood, drywall, spray foam insulation, glass

Woody the Trailer

Brian and Joni
Buzarde

USA

2012

With a limited budget, degrees in architecture and a nomadic lifestyle, Brian and Joni Buzarde began this project as an optimistic exercise in adventure. Nicknamed 'Woody', their trailer was the solution to having a home when they weren't yet sure where to settle. Instead of renting, they threw their savings into this mobile home: an angular cedar–clad camper that makes use of every available nook and cranny. Mounted on a customized trailer chassis, Woody includes all the essentials, as well as some creature comforts such as a wood-burning stove, bathtub, wardrobe and generous sliding glass doors that open onto the deck.

Four Wheels

Steel chassis, cedar, steel framing, Plexiglas, birch plywood

Moon Dragon House

Zyl Vardos
USA
2016

Like a fantastical fairy-tale cottage, this curvaceous one-bedroom home by Abel Zimmerman Zyl brings together his skills as an engineer and carpenter. One of many artistic tiny homes he has designed and built, the shingled skin and complex apertures of Moon Dragon display his appetite for custom-built works that are as sturdy as they are well organized. The living area amplifies the sense of space with its unified finish of timber cladding, surfaces and storage. Tiny staircase-boxes are a neat fix for storage, and lead to the upstairs bedroom. Complete with arched ceilings and picturesque windows, it's the perfect platform for adventuring in worlds real or imagined.

Steel chassis, plywood, glass, plastic, aluminium

ATLAS

Blake Dinkins,
Lance Cayko,
Alex Gore,
Sarah Schulz
USA
2015

Imbued with the idea that camping can be enhanced without losing connection to the environment, Atlas is an elegant getaway on wheels. Enclosed by a sturdy steel frame and with a large sliding glass entrance wall, the structure opens up via its hinged timber deck, to give ample room for relaxing in the great outdoors. Inside, timber finishes frame the kitchen, living room and mezzanine bed platform, while a brushed-steel door leads to the bathroom. The unit is self-sufficient and includes solar panels and a rainwater collector. Unlike its mythical namesake, Atlas relinquishes the weight of worldly trappings for a place that looks good and is great to live in.

Four Wheels

Trailer, steel framing, timber, glass, solar panels

Tiny Office

Ikke en Pind

Denmark

2016

Bringing freedom to the workplace, this mobile cabin addresses changing patterns in how and where people do business. Motivated by his need for on-site project management in different locations, Tiny Office is a year-round travelling solution, complete with desk, wood-burning stove and ample storage for stationery. Mounted on a trailer, the office can simply be towed to a new place to meet clients, collaborate with colleagues, or just make to get an inspiring change of scenery. Clad in timber panels, with a spare Scandinavian interior, each office is custom-built and its cost – around 12,500 US dollars – is comparable with commercial rental accommodation.

Trailer, timber panels, glass, plasterboard, stove

Try-on Truck

Spiegel Amhara
Workshop,

Mobile Office
Architects

USA

2015

An open-sided, mobile shop isn't the usual place to try on lingerie, but True&Co commissioned Spiegel Aihara Workshop and Mobile Office Architects to create just that: a nomadic fitting room for women to discover its internet-based range. Eye-catchingly exposed, yet cozy inside, the timber and steel store is arranged with public areas to browse and buy, and fitting rooms to the rear cloaked by a chequerboard of transparent and opaque glass panels. While giving privacy, the peek-a-boo design also offers a hint of voyeurism, not unlike the merchandise on offer. When it's time to move on, the truck's cantilevered niches simply unhinge and fold away.

Four Wheels

Steel chassis, timber, glass

Koleliba

Hristina Hristova

Bulgaria

2015

Seeking relief from holiday crowds, this tiny home, designed by architects Hristina Hristova, sits atop a standard trailer. Koleliba (the name is a neologism of the Bulgarian words for 'hut' and 'wheel') makes the most of its modest budget. The cabin rises to a standard room height and is lined with pale wooden finishes to increase the sense of space. Its timber-lined interior includes a kitchen, bathroom and integrated storage as well as a foldaway double bed. Framed by a large sliding glass door, the interior opens onto a porch with a removable wooden bench and a retractable canopy that extends the useable covered space.

Trailer chassis, steel framing, Bulgarian pine, glass, canvas, plywood

Vista
Escape Traveler
USA
2016

Is it a cabin? Is it a camper? With its robust timber structure, this tiny home defies easy categorization. Escape Traveler allows for one or two occupants to enjoy camping in comfort and, as its name suggests, the great appeal of Vista is the connection it offers to the great outdoors. Three large operable windows punctuate the living and sleeping areas, framing views outside. The interior is organized into dedicated areas for sleeping and living, with a small kitchen and bathroom and generous built-in storage. Finished with timber interiors, and clad with wood and Cor-ten steel, it provides a smart option for communing with nature.

Four Wheels

Trailer chassis, cedar, Cor-ten steel, glass

Filter Studio

Camera Buildings

Canada

2014

Bright, spacious and affordable, this little house on wheels is an inspiring option for those looking to downsize. Built to endure Vancouver's freezing winters, the modern, simple interior is matched by an equally pared-back facade. Built by tiny-home specialist John McFarlane, the project fulfils its owner's dream of a simpler life, with a home that offers a kitchen, living-dining space, bathroom and pull-out double bed. Its light-filled interior sets the mobile home apart, with full-height windows wrapping the main living space. Clad with timber slats for shade and privacy, this little house on wheels can easily be towed to new locations.

Steel, glass, timber, aluminium, plasterboard

Human

No Wheels

One & Two Wheels

Three Wheels

Four
Wheels

Five +
Wheels

Sleds +

Water

People's Canopy

People's Architecture
Office

UK

2015

The People's Canopy is a ten-wheeled contraption developed by Beijing-based People's Architecture Office. Designed to shelter a variety of events beneath its canopy, the project was originally conceived as a means of reinvigorating the lifeless urban centre of Preston in the UK. The canopy draws on the architect's experience of expandable canopies in southern China, which temporarily create spaces such as bars or restaurants – lively shared street spaces for community use. Like a red accordion, when fully open, each unit spans twelve metres (thirty-nine feet) and the units can be accumulated to form a continuous shelter, or contracted as required.

Metal framing, polyester, bicycle wheels

Bamdokkaebi Night Market

MOTOElastico
(Simone Carena and
Marco Bruno)

Korea

2016

Designed for use in Seoul's Bamdokkaebi Night Market, which only opens on weekend evenings, these vibrant moveable structures are collapsible and easy to store. Formed of a V-shaped metal frames that open and close like scissors, each frame is covered by orange PVC fabric. Composed of seventy modules in total, each unit creates a defined retail space while the open zigzag composition allows views through to the river beyond. Each bay is supported on pairs of wheels, which allow the units to move independently from one another. As in Korean folklore, this *dokkaebi* market is like its mythical namesake: a creature revealed at night but invisible by day.

Steel framing, PVC sheeting, wheels

A47 Mobile Library

Productora
Mexico
2012

Commissioned by the non-profit organization Alumnos47 Foundation, a cultural outreach and learning programme in Mexico, this stylish white truck is a library on the go. Known as A47, it carries precious cultural cargo in the form of approximately 1,500 books. In addition, A47 provides a platform for debates, discussions or performances. Its white, steel-mesh side panels can be fully opened, and its five-part hydraulic floor can be raised to create a tiered seating platform. With its eye-catching design, A47 invites casual browsing, discussions and participation in cultural programmes. When not in use, the project is simply secured by closing the shutters.

Five + Wheels

Truck, drilled sheet metal, hydraulic floor

**Mobile Art Shop
Kiosk: Flip**
MOTOElastico
(Simone Carena and
Marco Bruno)
Korea
2013

Flip kiosk for Seoul's Design Foundation is a candy-coloured concertinaed booth mounted on sturdy wheels. Part of the Mobile Art Shop held in the foundation's urban plaza, its zig-zagging form opens out to provide maximum display space. A contemporary interpretation of Korean folding screens, or *byung-poong,* that act as traditional room dividers, the bold yellow of the booth attracts attention. Catering for events, or the sale and promotion of design products, the kiosk is light enough for one person to easily move, but also includes a tow hitch to allow for transfer elsewhere by cart or car.

Five + Wheels

Chequerplate steel, MDF, wheels

Mobile Art Shop
Kiosk: Cone
MOTOElastico
(Simone Carena and
Marco Bruno)
Korea
2014

Commissioned by the Seoul Design Foundation this Mobile
Art Shop is one of a set of three strikingly original mobile kiosks.
Assembled in the outdoor spaces of Seoul's Dongdaemun Design
Plaza, the moveable units are used for various events and product
design vendors. This variation incorporates orange traffic cones
which, en masse, create a vibrant, spiky skin that is fixed to a waterproof substructure. When closed, the unit is entirely protected by
the spiky orange cones, creating a striking and easily recognizable
booth in the crowded urban precinct.

Steel structure, traffic cones, wheels

Rolling through a valley prone to floods, this herd of elevated huts replaces a campground of recreational vehicles. Designed as six holiday retreats for friends and family, the huts give simple respite in stylish boxes built on platforms of steel and wood. Their interiors are both comfortable and sparse, built from untreated and economical finishes such as cork and plywood. Though small, each hut includes a living room, bedroom, bathroom, wood-fired stove and a generous wrap-around deck to admire the view. These ingenious and idyllic huts are raised on wheels to protect them against wet weather and to avoid council red tape that forbids fixed structures.

Five + Wheels

Steel framing, glass, plywood, steel panels

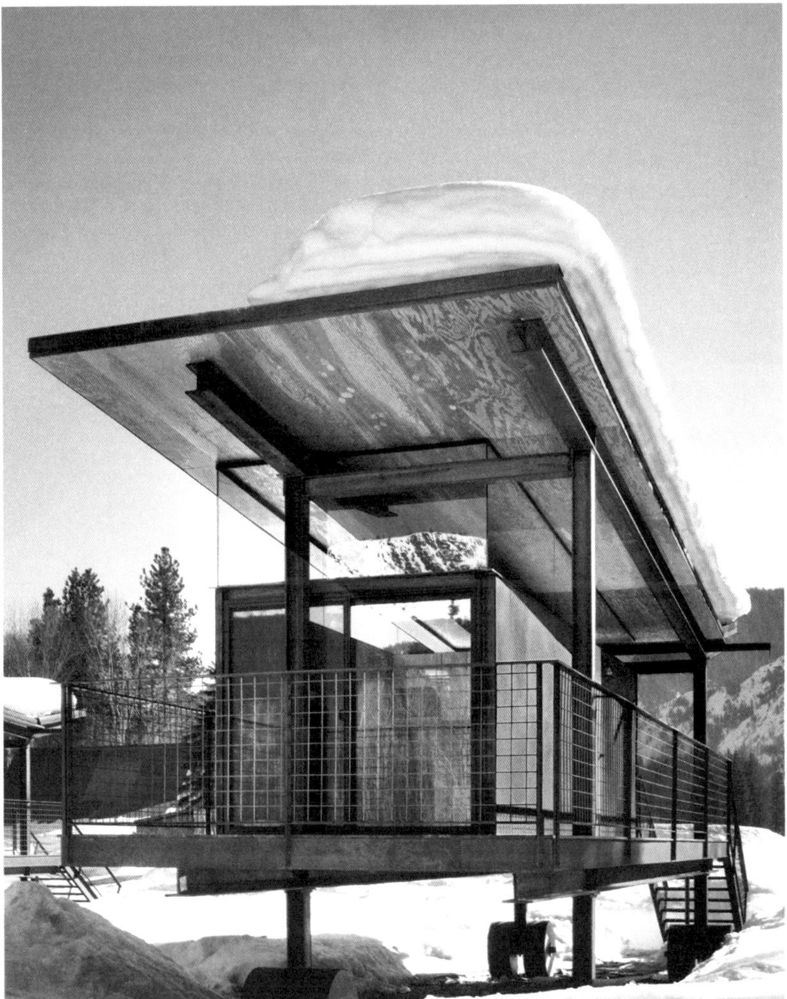

Vagón del Saber

Al Borde

Ecuador

2012

Distributing knowledge rather than freight, this reinterpretation of a classic railway car offers enlightenment on wheels. While retaining the glossy red livery of the original boxcar that it is adapted from, Vagón del Saber (or 'Knowledge Wagon') is a multi-use space that can accommodate up to eighty people in its small open-air theatre, or twenty in a semi-closed workspace. Easily reconfigured, its sides have been altered to include built-in seating and fold away stairs. A lightweight, retractable canopy gives protection against sun and rain. Like an itinerant teacher, Vagón del Saber engages with remote communities as it travels up and down Ecuador's coastal rail network.

Five + Wheels

Railcar, rubber, timber, canvas

More ecological – and definitely more memorable – than a delivery truck, this cargo bike suggests a radical alternative to fossil-fuel-powered vehicles. While philosophical about the difficulty of realising car-free cities, Nico Jungel's design prompts bystanders to consider how strong and sustainable cargo-cycles can be. As the largest version in the world, the 8rad² is carried on eight wheels that support a huge cargo tray. Steered and powered by two drivers, the 8rad² also has a solar-powered motor to assist if there is only one driver. This sturdy, versatile vehicle can also carry a timber-framed enclosure, transforming it from a beast of burden into a mobile home.

Steel chassis, timber framing, translucent plastic, bicycle parts

AMIE 1.0

Skidmore, Owings and
Merrill (SOM)

USA

2013

The 'Additive Manufacturing Integrated Energy' (AMIE), is a 3D printed shelter that tests the potential of renewable energy sources in both urban and remote locations. The project is housed in a high-tech white shell that has been designed to offer views out and allow light to stream in. Using the integrated photovoltaic panels on the roof, the structure shares its excess power wirelessly with an accompanying 3D-printed vehicle, which in turn stores a generator powered by gas. Together, the system represents the latent possibilities of efficient energy buildings and wireless energy technology.

Five + Wheels

Steel bracing, aluminium, monocrystalline photovoltaic solar panel, linoleum

Wothahellizat Mk1
Rob Gray
Australia
2001

Like an armadillo on wheels, Wothahellizat Mk1 is pitched as Australia's 'largest, weirdest and best-known motorhome'. The maverick moving house repurposes an army truck as a robust, go-anywhere home, clad in distinctive aluminium tread plate. Its hulking form belies the space and ingenuity within, with room for all basic living needs as well as two motor bikes, a substantial fresh water supply, three months' worth of food supplies and 'about 90 long-neck beer bottles'.
Not for the faint-hearted, the Wothahellizat Mk1 carves through much sand and dust, giving license for serious outback adventures of up to several months.

Truck body, aluminium tread plate, glass

Ovida by Getaway

Millenial Housing Lab

USA

2015

Investigating the viability and psychology of living in a tiny house, Getaway was founded by the Millennial Housing Lab, an initiative of Harvard students Jon Staff and Pete Davis. To test how effective and inviting a small space could be, they commissioned Ovida – a tiny get-away that is available for short breaks. Ovida focuses on quality materials and spatial economy. Offering creature comforts in the depths of the woods, it is clad in stained timber, with a similarly ligneous interior. Whether or not tiny homes will influence the mainstream remains to be seen, but Getaway's rentable dwellings near Boston and New York provide a taster of tiny home virtue.

Steel chassis, timber, glass

Studio Dental

Montalba Architects

USA

2014

Bringing the dentist's chair directly to you, Studio Dental effectively removes at least one excuse to delay a visit to the dentist. Designed by Montalba Architects a way to minimize the avoidance of dental treatment, this stylish studio-on-wheels includes a waiting room, a sterilization zone and two patient clinics. Compactly designed, the space is partitioned by timber panels milled with a decorative perforated pattern. Small cutouts high up in the ceiling bring light in while retaining privacy. Studio Dental's compelling, mobile solution might just ease the pain of trips to the dentist.

Five + Wheels

Steel chassis, metal, plasterboard, timber

Human

No
Wheels

One & Two
Wheels

Three
Wheels

Four
Wheels

Five +
Wheels

Sleds +

Water

Ski Haus

Richard Horden
Associates
Switzerland
1991

Not for the faint-hearted, the Ski Haus is a lightweight, nomadic retreat designed for remote mountain reaches, from Matterhorn to Mont Blanc and beyond. A altitudinous mobile home, it conquers Alpine landscapes, offering breath-taking views across snowy inclines. Easily transported by helicopter, it includes sturdy fasteners for airlifting to new locations, and four hexagonal feet to ensure safe and stable landings. Accommodating four, the self-sufficient, aluminium-shelled Ski Haus includes solar and wind turbines to generate energy. Inspired by the solace and serenity of the Swiss Alps, it's a high-tech shelter for skiers and climbers alike.

Sleds +

Aluminium framing, glass, solar turbine

The Mailroom

Timothy
Smith-Stewart,
Charles Spitzack

USA

2014

Described as a 'roving sanctuary', this immersive art installation on Minnesota's frozen White Bear Lake is a collector of stories and secrets. Clad in mirrored panels with a postbox-red front door, its reflective rectilinear form sits on top of a timber sledge. Inside, the walls taper in three dimensions to form a narrow central point of focus: a single timber desk where you can read handwritten letters by other visitors and scribe your own missives. Inviting visitors to become part of an ad hoc community sharing tales and experiences, the underlying idea of the project is to reveal the interconnectedness of everyone through stories lived and read.

Plywood, Mylar mirrors, timber

Solar Arc

Aaron Marx

USA

2011

This jaunty shelter was selected as part of the annual Art Shanty Projects programme, which transforms the frozen White Bear Lake region in Minnesota into an art residency and public event with dozens of shanties that draw the community together. Inspired by the hundreds of ice fishing huts stationed on the region's lakes during the frozen months, Solar Arc is a black polygonal structure mounted on a sled. From inside visitors can enjoy the passing patterns of light through the pierced ceiling panel while reclining on a large rope hammock.

Timber sledge, timber framing, plywood, tarpaulin, steel, netting

Ice Fishing Hut #711
Scugog Point
Anonymous
Canada
—

Part of Richard Johnson's 'Ice Hut Typologies' series documenting ice huts across Canada, this vibrant red example is an animated shelter for ice fishing. Beyond the necessity of the cabins to be weather resistant, transportable and have the ability to provide access to the ice, some include extra features, such as a wood-fired stove. Though they share basic similarities, Johnson's series captures the huts' idiosyncrasies, like this spray-on Elvis that adorns the humble facade of a hut at Scugog Point in Ontario. Set on a simple timber sled base to allow for an easy exit when the ice fishing season ends, the simple structure exemplifies architecture with everyday charm.

Wood, metal, glass

Rope Pavilion

Kevin Erickson

Canada

2012

Part of an annual competition for warming huts along the Assiniboine River in Winnipeg, this winning entry uses readily available materials to create a sculptural structure that gives protection from temperatures that can exceed minus forty degrees. Constructed on top of a sledge base from a frame of twelve vertical birch ribs wrapped with 128 layers of synthetic rope, the hut provides respite from the elements while allowing views in and out. Designed to withstand snow and wind loads, the rope is both the structure's bracing element as well as its exterior skin, with a woven effect created by the rope's undulating path through over 1,500 holes milled into the birch frame.

Sleds +

Rope, birch framing, steel screws, sledge platform

One Eye Folly
Donald Lawrence
Canada
2008

A folly on ice, this art installation is a strange boat-shed hybrid and part of the 'Ice Follies' exhibition on Ontario's Lake Nipissing. The One Eye Folly amalgam is comprised of a boat hull on a sledge, laden with a cabin of stamped tin tiles that form the textured roof. With two hatch-like windows, oars and an old shed door, the folly includes an aperture that allows light to enter, acting as a camera obscura. Recalling seaside entertainment during the Victorian era, the pinhole camera device reflects the frozen lake surface as well as distant views to other works included in the show.

Timber, rowboat, plastic, rope, stone, microphones, hydrophone, timber sledge

Nomad Sauna

Marco Casagrande

Norway

2012

Built in the bitter subarctic conditions of lake Røssvatnet in Norway, this sauna on skis was a collaborative project made by twenty students from the Survival Architecture Workshop under the direction of Marco Casagrande. The Nomad Sauna was conceived and built in response to challenging climatic conditions. The structure includes an external chimney and storage for fuel, while inside, it accommodates a platform for the small stove and a stepped seating area as well as an open ice-hole for chilly dips in the lake. In winter, it can be pushed across the frozen surface; in summer it reverts to a platform at the lake's swimming beach for local community use.

Sleds +

Timber, metal

Sound Booth

Barry Prophet

Canada

2010

Part of the WKP Kennedy Gallery's 'Ice Follies' exhibition in 2010, the Sound Booth is an acoustic sound art generator set up on frozen Lake Nipissing in Ontario's North Bay. Created by Barry Prophet, a composer, percussionist and sculptor, the two-piece installation comprises a fishing cabin, with a long resonator extending from one wall. The hut is a listening room for the sounds generated outside by a cylindrical music box made from pipe, threaded rod, steel bolts and repurposed stainless steel trays. When activated, the device makes a sound not unlike cracking ice. Sitting on a custom-built sledge, the project was towed to the site across the lake's icy surface.

Plywood, metal screws, timber sledge

The Starlight Room
Raniero Campigotto
Italy
2016

A lonely cabin for altitudinous camping, the Starlight Room is a remote glazed hut with the Dolomites as its dramatic backdrop. Set on skis, the insulated double room is available to rent. Built by local artisans with simple materials, its timber-framed structure is dominated by glass panels that give 180-degree views of the stunning snowy scenery. Serviced by Campigotto's nearby mountain lodge, visitors can enjoy delicious local food and wine in the peaceful setting at an altitude of 2,055 metres (6,742 feet). Far from the madding crowd and perfect for star-gazing, it can be reached by bike, snowmobile or snowshoe for an memorable isolated break.

Sleds +

Steel framing, timber, glass, skis

DW Sauna

Denizen Works

Finland

2011

Practical on the outside but cozy within, DW sauna is a contemporary take on the classic Scandinavian typology. Built on a timber sledge, this mobile structure is a solution that bypasses local bureaucratic planning rules that restrict the construction of permanent buildings. Built in the Finnish town of Åland, the modest structure is made from local timber and includes recycled windows and a pine-clad interior. On dry land, the sauna is temporarily anchored on concrete blocks but once the ice hardens it's pulled offshore. A toasty place to heat up before plunging into ice water, the hut is a triumph against both red tape and the climate.

Sleds +

Timber, stove, recycled glass, pine

Hut on Sleds

Crosson Architects

New Zealand

2012

This clever Hut on Sleds resolves the challenge of designing a moveable beachside getaway. Recalling the local 'bach' (a local term for holiday home) the timber cabin addresses the issue of soil erosion with large timber skis that enable the whole building to be moved by barge or tractor to stable ground. The double-height home includes a master bedroom, bunks, and kitchen, living and dining area as well as an upper deck. Framed by full-height doors and carefully placed windows, the holiday home can be opened to the elements via a dramatic folding timber wall.

Timber, Plexiglas, glass, steel

Ice Fishing Hut #680
Silver Lake,
Nova Scotia

Anonymous

Canada

2014

Drawn to documenting the 'crooked and textured' individuality of fishing huts in Canada's icy reaches, Toronto-based architectural photographer Richard Johnson captured this tiny shack in Nova Scotia. Ice huts, also known as ice shacks and fishing shanties, belong to a rich, varied and inventive building tradition in Canada. The size of a humble outhouse, this shelter for one is built with just enough room inside its aluminium-clad exterior for an entry and a strip of simple windows. When its owner chooses, it can be flipped onto its side, mounted on a pair of skis, and pulled along the ice to a livelier fishing spot.

Sleds +

Aluminium, Plexiglas, ropes, skis

Ice Fishing Hut #180
Lake Simcoe, Ontario

Anonymous

Canada

—

Richard Johnson photographed this little hut as a substitute portrait of its absent owner. The hut, on Lake Simcoe in Ontario, illustrates the spirit of someone on the move. Part of a long-standing tradition, this modest sanctuary, like hundreds dotted across Canada's frozen lakes, offers overnight accommodation for fishermen so they don't have to travel back and forth to their homes each day. This hut, with its in-built sledge, makes it particularly easy to move by a sole traveller. The humble weatherboard exterior encloses the essentials for fishing in temperatures that can reach minus forty degrees: a roof, four walls and a floor pierced with an ice-fishing hole.

Cast iron sledge, timber, glass, metal screws

Human

No Wheels

One & Two Wheels

Three Wheels

Four
Wheels

Five +
Wheels

Sleds +

Water

Waterwalk 1
Spatial Effects
The Netherlands
2005

This orange inflatable structure floats on water like a buoyant sugar cube. The work of Dutch collective Spatial Effects, a company specializing in creating memorable inflatables, this particular model lets people walk on water in an over-scaled transparent box. Strong enough to contain several people, Waterwalk is made from heavy gauge PVC. Its bonded external membrane is filled with air, to create a lightweight, breathable space, ready to roll. Accessed through an airtight zippered entry, the inflatables can be tailor-made to suit specific occasions. This vibrant version sports a flame-coloured surface – a fitting choice of hue for a nation of proud Oranje.

Water

PVC, zipper

Waterwalk 2
Spatial Effects
The Netherlands
2003

This rolling, transparent inflatable was commissioned to celebrate the centenary of St Petersburg's foundation. Traversing along the river Neva the spheres were a gesture to commemorate the eighteenth-century joint naval traditions of Holland and Russia. Originally inspired by 1960s experiments of walking on water with balloons, Waterwalk 2 has been finessed with durable PVC. Secured by hermetic zipper fastenings, the floating balls of air provide buoyancy for a limited amount of time. Wind and human effort propel the lightweight bubble forward, creating the miraculous sensation of walking (or cycling) on water.

PVC, zipper

House on Eilbekkanal

Rost Niderehe	
Architekten	
Germany	
2009	

One of ten boats commissioned for Hamburg's Eilbek Canal, this floating house is a harmonious addition to its waterside locale. Blending the comfort of a family home with the adventure of living on water, the result is a timber-clad floating dwelling. Providing a place to live and work, the house repeats the curved exterior motif throughout the interior. Linked by a central stairwell, the plan is divided into public and private zones: the upper floor accommodates the kitchen, living and dining areas, with bedrooms and sitting room below. While it creates a happy fit with its canal-side neighbours, should the need arise it can be towed elsewhere by tugboat.

Water

Timber, steel, plasterboard, glass

This floating design is the result of a brief to create a home that looks good, is lightweight and open to the elements. Conceived as a holiday home for an Australian sheep farmer and his extended family, architect Drew Heath was inspired by Japanese lanterns. Built principally from aluminium framing for lightness, Arkiboat is braced by three internal walls and a post at each corner. The simple timber interior continues the Japanese *shoji* aesthetic, with plywood sheets and a floor plan divided by sliding glazed screens. Surrounded on all sides by a timber deck, Arkiboat has seen a decade of use as an easy summer getaway.

Fibreglass, marine-grade aluminium, polyurethane-coated plywood, stainless steel

Zendome

Zenvision

Germany

2007

Combining the tensile strength of a geodesic dome with the freedom of life on water, this pavilion is a floating campsite. The triangulated dome structure was originally devised for various uses on land, but is just as suitable for water-borne use. Its lightweight, stable form with broad circular entrance includes both transparent and opaque panels to moderate shade and light. Constructed of galvanized powder-coated steel with a PVC-coated polyester membrane, this version of Zendome sits on a welded construction of steel with timber decking. Providing a space to drift about in, the relaxing retreat is ideally suited to short trips offshore.

Water

Stainless steel, PVC, timber

A–Z Habitable Island

Andrea Zittel for the
Indianapolis Museum
of Art

USA

2009

Located in the Virginia B. Fairbanks Art and Nature Park, this floating dome continues Andrea Zittel's exploration of what 'personal space' might mean. Measuring six metres in diameter (twenty feet), the island – an iconic symbol of autonomy, independence, isolation and fantasy – was used by the Indianapolis Museum of Art as an artist's retreat. Artists were invited to modify and customize the structure to suit their individual needs, though it's diminutive scale allows for only the most basic necessities of life. Made primarily from timber, fibreglass and foam, and only accessible by boat, Zittel's artwork questions what is essential for human existence.

Fibreglass, foam, timber

The Silver Fish

Flo Florian,
Sascha Akkermann
Germany
2009

The Silver Fish is a water-borne alternative to living cheek-by-jowl on land. The silver facade gives The Silver Fish its name and sets it apart from most riverboat homes. Coated in aluminium granulate panels to regulate seasonal temperature variation, the finish balances the desire for both a crisp silhouette and ecological credentials. Organized over two levels, with the kitchen, living and bathroom space on the lower floor, and bedroom above, the design also includes an AstroTurf roof terrace. The interior finishes in glossy white, as well as full-height windows enhance the sense of space and encourage greater connection to the passing landscape.

Water

Timber framing, reclaimed larch wood, aluminium, glass, plasterboard, cement, AstroTurf

Quaypad

Gillard Associates,
WaterSpace

UK

2008

Eschewing the mundane daily grind of a commute into the city, the Quaypad takes the working week to the water in an effort to put some inspiration into the nine-to-five day. Prefabricated locally, the interior includes desk and meeting areas framed by an expansive glazed wall. To the rear of the vessel an integrated ladder provides access to the upper deck which in turn offers an open space to relax in good weather, as well as housing a wind turbine for generating power. Despite Wales' reputation for grey days and drizzle, the floating office is perfectly suited for use in milder climates.

Glass reinforced plastic, toughened double glazing, stainless steel

Venice Biennale
Croatian Pavilion
Republic of Croatia
Ministry of Culture
Italy
2010

The work of a team of fourteen architects, the Croatian pavilion for the 2010 Venice Architecture Biennale took the form of a floating pavilion. Set on an existing barge, the structure is formed of more than forty layers of steel reinforcing rods (usually used to reinforce concrete). Each grid is welded in place, then each layer is cut with varying apertures. Weighing almost thirty tonnes (thirty-three tons), the resulting structure is an enormous diaphanous enclosure of rusted metal. Framing views out of the pavilion, and creating blurred views into it, the metal structure was assembled in the Kraljevica shipyard in Croatia and towed to Venice with a tugboat.

Water

Steel reinforcing bars, concrete barge

Antiroom II

Elena Chiavi,
Ahmad el Mad,
Matteo Goldoni

Malta

2015

The result of a 2015 European Architectural Student Assembly workshop led by Elena Chiavi, Ahmad El Mad and Matteo Goldoni, Antiroom II is a man-made island, accessible only by boat or by swimming from the shore. Formed of a circular timber structure created from twenty-eight small segments, the project is adorned with gauzy curtains that seem to effortlessly 'breathe' as the wind passes through them. Gently floating about in the Maltese waters of Valletta, Antiroom II is intended as a kind of primordial *stoa* – a classical portico that, in this case, acts as a stage for public enjoyment and defines a small inner pool amid the deep sea surrounding it.

Wood panels, mesh curtains

Free Floating

Marijn Beije Design

The Netherlands

2012

Designed as an eco-camping concept to attract younger Dutch audiences, this floating twin-hulled vessel is a compelling invitation. Constructed from responsibly-sourced timber, the sustainable retreat includes a bedroom, bathroom and rooftop deck – as well as a lofty crow's nest for bird watching. Providing space for up to four adults to sleep in fully glazed quarters, the little lodge is fitted with solar panels to power the LED lights. By day it offers a simple place for relaxation, with decks to sunbathe on. At night the buoyant craft gently rocks its guests to sleep.

Water

Timber, aluminium, glass, steel, solar panels

Creatura

Federico Forestiero,
Mark David Torrens

USA

2014

The result of the creative problem-solving ethos of Beam Camp's summer breaks for young people, Creatura is a floating structure built on a timber platform, its skeleton composed of wood and metal filled in with a variety of woven materials. Some exertion on the part of the campers is required to push the water wheel, while a captain in the crow's nest guides this water creature around the New Hampshire lake it was designed for. The structure is the result of the fundamental mission of Beam Camp, which is to focus on skill-building, collaborative challenges, responsibility and mentorship.

Timber, metal, recycled plastic

Flood House

Matthew Butcher

UK

2016

Floating on the flood-prone reaches of the Thames Estuary, this weather station is both a device and commentary, recording the effects of rising water levels over time and questioning the relationship between buildings and the environment. Designed to be towed from place to place, the nomadic project records seasonal and local conditions in the estuary. Its changing location, and the effect of tides on the structure highlight the effects of climate change and rising sea levels. Stranded on mudflats at low tide but otherwise buoyant, Flood House is a thought-provoking project that questions how static buildings might address the challenges of changing shorelines.

Water

Steel pontoon, timber weatherboards, plasterboard

Wa-Sauna

goCstudio

USA

2015

Designed for recreational use on Seattle's Lake Union, Wa-Sauna was inspired by its Nordic predecessors and funded with a Kickstarter campaign. Designed and built with the help of volunteers, the floating timber structure has a toasty interior to warm up in after dips in the lake. Secured on an aluminium frame beneath a deck of marine-grade plywood, its black wooden skin gives way to a pale interior of cedar. Like its Nordic equivalent, the project is a means for social gathering, inspired by the architects' wish to activate local waterways throughout the year.

Aluminium framing, marine-grade plywood, cedar, spruce, plastic barrels, stove

Floating Platform

N55

Denmark

2002

A democratic project by Danish collective N55, the Floating Platform comes with an assembly manual so that it can be built by anyone. Provided with a buoyant triangular pontoon with the strength to support a lightweight building, the structure is an adaptation of N55's modular space frame. Multiple small triangular aluminium panels, a steel lattice frame, a deck of plywood birch and polythene floatation tanks fit together to create the distinctive faceted structure. This model is the collective's silver Spaceframe building, which follows the same principles of low-cost, modular logic that features in all of their floating structures.

Water

Birch plywood, polythene tanks, aluminium, stainless steel

Floating Sauna

Rintala Eggertsson
Architects

Norway

2002

Drawing on the tradition of saunas in Finnish and Norwegian culture, this version takes the idea to the water. Floating on a fjord and only accessible by boat, the small timber structure offers a space to purify mind and body while enjoying the natural landscape. Set on a wooden platform, the spartan interior includes three timber benches and a wood-burning stove. Its envelope of transparent walls seals in the heat while offering views of the spectacular and remote scenery. To cool off, visitors simply plunge straight into the water from a cut-out in the base of the sauna. By night, with its gasoline lamps lit, the isolated sauna becomes a luminous lantern.

Timber, plastic sheeting, plastic drums, iron stove

Seattle Floating Home

Ninebark Studios

USA

2013

Resetting the standard for life on water, this generously sized home responds to its owner's wish for a floating house with maximum ecological credentials. Partially clad with locally milled, reclaimed cedar that forms an effective rain and privacy shield, the home is mounted on a nineteenth-century reclaimed log platform. Its lofty, bright interior includes a generous atrium space for living and dining, framed by a sweeping steel wall that rises to an angled roof with a viewing deck. Open to the Portage Bay setting, the project includes a lower timber-clad volume – tucked to one side for greater seclusion – that contains the bedroom, office and bathroom.

Water

Steel framing, Cor-Ten steel, glass, cedar

DublDom 1.26
DublDom
Russia
2015

Part of the Paluba Park Hotel on Russia's Zhabnya River, this floating cabin for up to six offers distinctive accommodation. Moored at the river's edge, the cabin, DublDom model 1.26, gives space for groups to relax right next to the water. Accessed from a jetty, the dark steel exterior is a contrasted with the naturally warm hues of untreated timber inside. A generous river-facing veranda forms an entrance lobby to the simple wooden interior, which contains sleeping space for four adults, a kitchen and dining area, and a folding children's bed. With modest cooking facilities that befit a camping experience, it is a charming alternative to a traditional hotel.

Timber framing, timber panels, corrugated steel, glass

Shelters

Joseph Griffiths

Australia

2012

One of three improvised structures, Joseph Griffiths' 'Shelters' series was commissioned as part of Melbourne's Next Wave arts festival. Built from scavenged building materials, this rendition is designed for time spent upon the water – its collaged, multi-textured exterior suggests a primitive raft fashioned from flotsam and jetsam. Including vivid archetypal flourishes such as fish netting, warning lights and buoys, the Shelter is a charmingly haphazard invention. Described by Griffiths as 'a sort of romantic initiative', the Shelters call to mind primeval dwellings, fashioned here, with anarchic flair.

Water

Rubber, timber, cardboard, fishing nets

Inusura

AODH Design

Ireland

2016

This floating pod uses materials salvaged from a derelict building and reinterprets them anew. Eoghan O'Broin's ad hoc vessel is inspired by his long-held fascination with the silence that abandoned building sites hold. Insura is intentionally small in an effort to replicate the isolation of these forgotten places. With a facade built primarily of timber set on a wooden pontoon, its envelope is pierced with a roof light and oversized acrylic porthole. Buoyed with bright blue plastic containers, the seaworthy project can be transported to different waterways by tractor. While its unusual form captures attention onshore, offshore, its diminutive scale offers a place for peace and silence.

Timber, Plexiglas, polyethyelene floats

Watervilla Omval

+31 Architects

The Netherlands

2010

Moored on the Amstel River, this sleek floating villa is one of several designs by +31 Architects that make the most of the proximity to water in the Netherlands. Part of the rising trend for floating homes in the countryside, this two-bedroom villa adopts a contemporary aesthetic and a large open-plan interior. The main living-kitchen space is at the water level, while the second bedroom, study and bathroom are housed below the waterline. A master bedroom sits off the broad split-level staircase, framed by large glass panels that bring light into the spaces downstairs. Decks adjacent to the living area offer an immediate connection to the natural environment.

Water

Aluminium, concrete, glass, plasterboard, wood

Neither rowboat nor caravan, Sealander is a novel concept by the eponymous German manufacturer that brings together the fun of being on water with the transportability of road travel. Constructed from a reinforced fibreglass-laminate hull, the craft has wheels for on-road use, while a waterproof galvanized zinc chassis enables it to be taken for a dip. It includes the usual necessities for comfortable camping: a cooker, built-in convertible seats and bed. Additional elements like a shower and toilet are also available. The design's compact size, light-weight and integral wheels mean launching is a breeze: simply park up, unhitch and roll Sealander into the water.

Reinforced fibreglass, acrylic panels, stainless steel, wheels

Inachus Floating Home

Sanitov Studio
UK
2012

In the face of London's lack of available building land, Inachus takes up residence on the Thames River. First moored at St Katherine Docks in the centre of the city, this floating home is a prototype for future settlements in the crowded capital. Envisioned as an elegant contemporary floating home, the two-storey design is a sleek affair. With living spaces at upper level and bedrooms and bathrooms below, the deluxe residence also features ecological credentials. Inachus features solar panels, a green roof and triple glazing – and even a green wall to improve air quality indoors.

Water

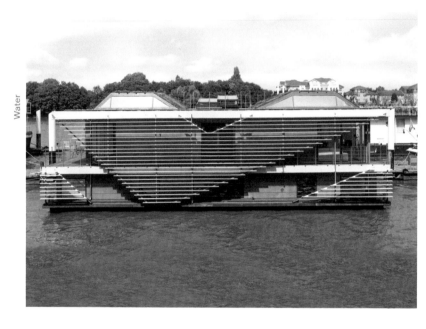

Concrete, timber, glass, solar panels, timber

One of One

Monoarchitekten

Germany

2009

Located in a former workers' quarter in central Hamburg, a new houseboat settlement on Eilbek Canal is the result of a citywide competition to revitalize urban waterways. Chosen as one of ten successful entries, One of One features a striking metallic armature. Designed with references to maritime craft and presenting a steely demeanour, the boat has a flexible, open-plan arrangement. Organized over two levels, it is spacious enough to accommodate a range of uses – from an office or a luxury apartment to a nightclub. The lower volume is partially separated by an oak staircase, with a sitting room on the upper level adjacent to the kitchen and bathrooms.

Steel, timber, aluminium plate, oak, glass

Freischwimmer

Tun Architektur

Germany

2009

Water

The Freischwimmer houseboat unites sophisticated urban sensibilities with domestic comforts. Part of an experimental zone for habitable waterways in Hamburg, Freischwimmer maximizes space with light-filled living areas that promote connection between living spaces and nature. The lower deck includes bedroom, bathroom and balconies, while the upper deck hosts the dining room, kitchen and a rooftop deck. The design shares the innovative spirit of other pilot projects in the city to revitalize urban waterways. Formed of two main volumes – the lower clad in larch, the upper in Cor-Ten steel – its top deck can be lifted off by crane to pass low-lying bridges.

Concrete, timber framing, Cor-Ten steel,
larch wood, glass

Houseboat on the
Eilbek Canal
Sprenger von der
Lippe
Germany
2010

Like its nautical neighbours, this houseboat on Hamburg's Eilbek Canal is one of a small handful of homes making the most of the revitalization of the city's waterways. A handsome addition to this inner-urban canal, this houseboat is a two-level home, with kitchen and dining spaces upstairs, and living, bedrooms and bathroom below. Extending the useable space, the upper level includes large timber decks and full-height windows provide opportunities for canal-gazing. Contrasting with its quiet residential location, the house's Cor-Ten steel finish recalls battered maritime structures, which are reinterpreted here with a robust contemporary approach.

Steel framing, timber, Cor-Ten steel, glass

Kaluga Floating Sauna	
Rintala Eggertsson Architects	
Czech Republic	
2008	

Part of the Festival of Landscape Objects in Russia, the Kaluga Floating Sauna is part of a suite of temporary structures for small groups of people to live in for short stays. Motivated by the increase in natural disasters, including recent flooding in the UK and Australia, these floating homes suggest an alternative, benevolent way to interact with nature. Borrowing from the culture of communal bathing in Scandinavia, the project includes a sauna – a place to warm up after cool dips in the Ugra River. Built from pine, and featuring a local pine tree growing on its roof, the Kaluga Floating Sauna is one of five pavilions that are set on small pontoons and linked by footbridges.

Water

Pine wood, plastic, glass, stove, timber

Jellyfish Barge

PNAT

Italy

2014

A greenhouse on the water, the Jellyfish Barge bucks the trend for intensive agricultural practices on land. Instead PNAT have designed a self-sufficient vessel designed for localized cultivation. A structure of timber and recycled plastic drums supports the greenhouse, which includes solar-powered units for desalinated clean water. A floating 'farm' for growing plants hydroponically, the prototype offers an alternative to unsustainable food production, cultivating produce that simply harnesses the power of water and the sun. Part of the PNAT collective's goal to draw on biomimetic processes, the barge uses nature as both a model and a co-worker.

Plastic drums, glass, timber

Set beside a nature reserve close to the busy urban redevelopment of London's King's Cross, this floating platform is a quiet retreat from which to view wildlife on Regent's Canal. Based on traditional Finnish shelters known as *laavus*, which are used for hunting and fishing, this design is an geometric variant and includes seating and spaces to shelter in. Clad in Cor-Ten steel with a timber interior, its finish fits with the formerly industrial surroundings as well as the passing canal boats. Giving respite from city life, and magical glimpses of local animals and birds, the project serves as an extension of the nature park along the waterways of central London.

Water

Cor-Ten steel, timber

Twin Blade

NIO Architects

The Netherlands

2010

Designed as a floating idyll, Twin Blade offers its inhabitants a perfect slice of life. Catering to the owners' different personalities, this asymmetrical floating home provides a variety of areas for different occupations. A 'sound cellar' space for the composer–musician nestles beneath the ground floor platform, while an 'image attic' for the visual artist is stationed at the top. United by a staircase that winds through the centre of the project, the two distinct studio spaces are linked by the bedroom, living and kitchen levels. Wrapped in sturdy steel cladding, the volume features expansive glazing, giving greater visual connection to the landscape in this house built for two.

Concrete, timber, steel, glass

The Wilcraft

Wilcraft Outdoors

USA

2006

From water to ice to land, the Wilcraft is an adventure vehicle designed to roll or float over all manner of terrain. Primarily designed as an ice fishing rig, its unusual form is also able to float due to its watertight hull of aluminium, retractable wheels and sealable fishing holes drilled in the hull. Sliding like a sled, or driving over slush, the two-person craft provides easy access to remote places. The Wilcraft's base is insulated to protect it from the cold and gives added buoyancy to assist the pneumatic wheels. In summer the Wilcraft sheds its icy skin, transforming into an efficient hunting vehicle.

Water

Aluminium, insulation, flotation tyres

Water Bed

Daniel Durnin

UK

2015

A response to the lack of affordable temporary lodgings in London, the Water Bed is an experimental structure that offers short stays in the capital. Essentially a convertible wooden boat-bicycle, the project is a miniature home on water, making use of the city's many canals and waterways as short-term places to camp out. The modest room for one is built on a boat hull and includes operable sidings of glass and canvas to embrace life outdoors and canal-side landscapes. With two wheels at the stern and a folding tow hitch to the bow, the boat can easily change setting by just floating with the downstream current or can be hauled elsewhere by bicycle.

Timber, bicycle wheels, plywood, canvas, Plexiglas

Water Chalet

Waterstudio

The Netherlands

2008

One of fifteen small dwellings designed for the small Dutch village of Jisp, these floating homes combine comfort and efficiency. Designed to maximize interior space, each chalet provides a basic living and dining area with kitchen, bathroom and double bedroom. The upper half of the wedge-shaped form creates a small attic loft for children or guests, and is filled with light from to the generously proportioned windows. Set on a concrete floating platform, the exterior timber cladding is designed to weather over time, in harmony with its natural setting. The timber construction is also lightweight, allowing the chalet to be hauled into place with the help of a towboat.

Water

Concrete, timber framing, aluminium, glass

Cotswolds House

Eco Floating Homes

UK

2013

Designed as a place to accommodate guests, this floating home on a Cotswolds lake creates a unique getaway for family and friends. Giving prime access to water and views, the two-bedroom dwelling is surrounded by a broad timber deck for relaxing outside in summer. Inside, a wood-burning stove allows for cozy winter living. Like all of the Eco Floating Homes, the project is sustainable, being built locally by hand using only materials with accredited ethical provenance. Commissioned individually and built to reflect each owner's preferences, this hideaway includes rustic recycled timber to create a sense of warmth and tiles in the interior for added character.

Timber, steel, plasterboard, glass

D-Type

Floating Homes

Germany

2012

Both a floating retreat and a well-equipped modern house, the Floating Homes concept offers the best of urban conveniences as well as access to nature. Built on a reinforced concrete pontoon, each interior is created to according to the owner's needs. This D-Type version is the most sizeable model, and includes a timber rooftop deck. With generous floor-to-ceiling windows, the interior is filled with daylight, offering greater connection to river life. Each open plan shell can be subdivided according to individual requirements, around a centrally located bathroom. Big enough to house four people, the family homes work just as well as inner-city pads, or countryside retreats.

Water

Concrete, timber, glass, aluminium

The Floating House

Jean-Marie Finot,
Denis Daversin,
Ronan and Erwan
Bouroullec
France
2006

A buoyant home for artists in residence at the National Centre of Printmaking and Printed Art in Chatou, this floating vessel provides an idyllic temporary retreat for creative minds. The low-slung structure recalls the shallow profile of traditional barges while the restricted material palette reflects the project's modest budget. Constructed from an aluminium framework and cladding, with external ribs of timber, the boat features outdoor decks, both fore and aft. Inside, simple finishes of timber and large window openings maximize views of the picturesque setting and provide a suitable place for creativity.

Aluminium, timber, glass

The Floating Cinema

Duggan Morris
Architects and
UP Projects
UK
2013

The Floating Cinema hosts screenings and events and serves to animate the waterways of East London. Duggan Morris's competition-winning design is inspired by classic narrow barges, which was constructed at the historic Turks Shipyard in Kent. This bespoke interpretation of the barge typology includes a semi-transparent volume for seating and the cinema screen. Glowing diamond-patterned panels announce The Floating Cinema's arrival like a welcome beacon. Bringing a pinch of movie magic and a dose of community spirit, the project's nomadic annual summer season sees it cruising the canals of East London.

Water

Steel, timber, Perspex

SeaSauna

Scheiwiller Svensson
Arkitektkontor
Sweden
2006

Embracing the Swedish tradition of ice-cold dips and saunas, this floating version takes the idea one step further. Rather than positioning the hut at the edge of a river or lake, the Sea Sauna floats upon the water. Designed for the designer's parents, the simple structure floats on a pontoon, housed in an envelope of solid wood with openings to the inspiring views. Its stained black exterior creates a sharp silhouette, in contrast with a warm untreated timber interior that accommodates a wood-fired stove and classic bench seating. The original model can be reproportioned to give three variations – small (for five people), medium (for ten) and a large version for fifteen.

Concrete, timber, glass

Seattle Floating Home

Vandeventer +
Carlander Architects

USA

2011

Building on the popularity of floating houses in Seattle, this luxurious version is moored on Lake Union. Commissioned by the client to build an 'upside down' house, the resulting design reflects this brief with bedrooms on the lower level and the living space above. This unusual arrangement maximizes light and views to the shared areas, which are open plan to emphasize the sense of space. Including terraces fore and aft, the upper level features a screen of narrow timber slats that echo the wooden finishes throughout. Downstairs, two bedrooms with en-suite bathrooms are screened from public view while the translucent glass entry provides light as well as privacy.

Water

Concrete, glass, teak, ceramic panels, terrazzo

San Francisco
Floating House
Robert Nebolon
USA
2013

This home is the happy result of Robert Nebolon's first floating design challenge and a radical lifestyle change for its owners. Priced out of the land-based property market, a houseboat in San Francisco's regenerating Mission Creek area was a viable alternative. Like the factories that once characterized the area, this boat features a saw-tooth roof, which creates a lofty and light-filled upper level for the open-plan living and dining room. On the lower level are bedrooms and services, while a basement level is used for games and another bedroom. Uniting each level is a staircase rendered in Golden Gate orange, a detail that is echoed in the entrance.

Concrete, steel, glass, timber

Floating Beach Hut 'Ted'

William Hardie

UK

2015

A repurposed iconic British beach hut, this charming cabin segues seamlessly between sand and sea. Its classic gabled form and colourful timber skin are small and light enough to stay afloat, providing space for four adults to cook, dine and sleep. The bright striped cladding wraps around a simple timber frame, which is set above an extendable floating deck with empty oil drums for floatation underneath. Inside, the open volume includes a mezzanine sleeping loft as well as two retractable, foldout sleep pods each side of the main room. Studded with tiny portholes and generous windows to the fore, the hut is a fun place to spend time out on the water.

Water

Timber, plastic, glass, rope, plasterboard

Paddling Home

Kacey Wong

Hong Kong

2009

Part of the Biennale of Urbanism and Architecture in Hong Kong and Shenzhen, this miniature floating structure is an urban intervention created by Kacey Wong. Developing his reputation for ironic cultural comment, Paddling Home is a diminutive reinterpretation of Hong Kong's ubiquitous apartment towers. Clad in dusty-pink tiles, a bay window and air-conditioning unit, as well as a stainless steel security gate, its typical Hong Kong features sit above a rudimentary barrel platform. The room floats precariously in the middle of Victoria Harbour, a reference to the myriad miniscule flats that are sold locally for crippling sums of money.

Tiles, sewage pipes, stainless steel, plastic barrels, glass, rubber tyres, AstroTurf

MetroShip

MetroPrefab

USA

—

This floating home offers the benefit of offshore living without the costs of land ownership. First imagined as an alternative to the designer's cramped living quarters, MetroShip slowly developed to become an airy, customizable house-on-water. Built on a fibreglass catamaran hull MetroShip is largely enclosed by semi-transparent panels, like Japanese *shoji* screens. Built from recycled glass sandwiched between an aluminium grid, the walls transmit daylight while also giving thermal protection. Combined with the generous ceiling height, lower deck storage and integrated kitchen and living space, this version provides plenty of natural light and picturesque views.

Water

Fibreglass, aluminium, thermal panels, steel, glass, wood

SayBoat
Milan Řidký
Czech Republic
2012

This elegant houseboat unites luxury and mobility. Built on a steel pontoon base, SayBoat is a home for all seasons. Taking up the majority of the vessel, the integrated kitchen-living-dining space creates one large elongated room finished with beech and stainless steel details. Above, a substantial master bedroom and study opens to an equally generous deck that houses a jacuzzi and enjoys wide-ranging views from all sides. The timber-clad structure is accented by rounded corners that soften the boat's geometry, while fine timber screens offer shade and privacy. Tough stainless steel decking and rails endure time and tide.

Timber, steel, glass, stainless steel

The Manta
Underwater Room
Mikael Genberg
Tanzania
2013

Facilitating the magic of under-water diving without clammy wetsuits, or weighty tanks, this private floating island offers guests a night below the water. Part of the Manta Resort off Tanzania's Pemba Island, the submerged holiday experience occurs in this luxury three-level floating suite. Floating above the Manta Reef, the timber structure includes a hardwood landing deck with lounge area and bathroom, and a roof deck above for sun bathing or stargazing. Below is the striking underwater experience – an underwater bedroom enclosed on all sides by windows that frame fabulous views of shoals of tropical fish, coral and sea creatures floating past.

Water

Timber, steel, glass

Archipelago Cinema

Buro Ole Scheeren
and Film on the Rocks
Yao Noi Foundation
Thailand
2012

As if holidaying on Thai beaches weren't idyllic enough, this project brings cinematic entertainment to the clear waters of the island of Yao Noi. The seating raft, as well as an enormous cinema screen of this tropical movie theatre are sheltered in a lagoon. Drawing on local techniques to make floating lobster farms, the simple wooden platforms are built as eight individual modules. Connected by a deck that includes a place for boats to tie up, the project is built from recycled materials and has space for around eighty people. The project also gives back to the local people: parts of the vessel were gifted to the Yao Noi community to create their own floating playground.

Timber, rubber straps, foam blocks

Floatwing

Friday

Portugal

2015

A sustainable vessel designed by a group from Portugal's University of Coimbra, Floatwing allows for spending time in far-flung lakes and rivers. It's modular design can vary in length from ten to eighteen metres (thirty-three to fifty-nine feet). Surrounded by glazed panels that slide back to access the deck, all models can be customized but include a compact bathroom and kitchen as standard. In addition to integrated solar panels, options such as a pellet stove and tanks for water and waste mean the boat can be fully equipped for up to a week away. Its ingenious components mean the boat is designed to be shipped internationally, fitting inside just two standard containers.

Water

Fibreglass, steel, Planitherm panels, pine wood, solar panels

Drijf in Lelystad

Attika Architekten

The Netherlands

2012

Attika Architekten were commissioned by eight families to create eight floating homes in the Dutch province of Lelystad. Shaped by the specific needs of each family, the dwellings come in a range of sizes, shapes and colours, displaying a great deal of variety and individuality where they are banked as a group on a broad causeway. With predominant hues of grey and white accented by individual patterns, the width of each home is identical in order to pass through the narrowest lock. Inside, the homes all include large decks, split level plans and generous window apertures, to maximize the space and give ready access to the water.

Concrete, timber, metal panels, glass

MFS II
NLÉ
Italy
2016

Part of the 'Waterfront Atlas' exhibition at the Venice Architecture Biennale, this is the second iteration of a floating school originally designed for Makoko Lagoon in Lagos, Nigeria. The timber A-framed structure is supported by large buoyant barrels of blue plastic. The three-storey project includes classrooms on its central level shielded by blue screens, with a playground below, and an open-air space above. Photovoltaic cells generate energy and systems for water collection mean the structure is partly self-sustainable. Representing an alternative approach to meet the effects of climate change, its simple floating form provides a vital structure for education.

Water

Timber, tarpaulin, plastic barrels

Walden Raft

Elise Morin,
Florent Albinet

France

2015

Referencing Henry David Thoreau's nineteenth-century treatise on life in the woods, the Walden Raft in France has a similarly environmental intent. Floating on a peaceful lake in a secluded region of the Auvergne, this Walden Raft follows the proportions of Thoreau's original cabin. Panels of acrylic sheet protect its spacious interior, which sits on a base of pine boards. Dispersed across the panels are short pine planks, their erratic patterned effect giving dappled shade within. Moved by a reel of cable fixed to the shore, the small buoyant vessel encourages a greater connection with the natural world.

Pine, acrylic glass, polyethylene floats, rope

End Notes

[1] Le Futurism, Le Figaro, Paris, 20 February, 1909

[2] Michael Kimmelman lecture, 'Boom Towns are Immigration Towns' at Cities in Migration, reSITE 2016 Conference, Prague, 2016

[3] International Organization for Migration, World Migration Report 2015. Migrants and Cities: New Partnerships to Manage Mobility, Printed in France by Imprimerie Courand et Associés, 2015, p.25

[4] As above, p.27

[5] Building Resilience to Natural Disasters: A Framework for Private Sector Engagement, World Economic Forum, The World Bank, United Nations International Strategy for Disaster Risk Reduction, Geneva, 2008, p.5

[6] According to recent US Census Bureau data, the square footage of living space per person in a new home has increased from 506.6 to 980.7 square feet using the median size home. See: https://www.aei.org/publication/todays-new-homes-are-1000-square-feet-larger-than-in-1973-and-the-living-space-per-person-has-doubled-over-last-40-years/ accessed 11 October 2016

[7] Oliver James, Affluenza: When Too Much is Never Enough, Vermilion: Random House Group, UK, 2007

[8] Shamubeel Eaqub and Selena Eaqub, Generation Rent: Rethinking New Zealand's Priorities, Bridget Williams Books, June 2015

[9] Melia Robinson, 'College Student Built a £10,000 Tiny Home Instead of Living in a Dorm', See: http://uk.businessinsider.com/college-student-builds-tiny-house-2016-1 accessed 10 October 2016

Picture Credits

+31ARCHITECTS 272
Aaron Leitz Photography
Aaron Squadroni 238
© ADAGP, Paris and DACS,
London 2016. Photo by
Philippe Piron 60
Adrian Lippmann 62
Ahmad El Mad 261
Alastair Pryor 42
Al Charest 206
Alex Kallenberger 236
Alex Mourant 57
Amir Sanei 110
Ankie Stam 284
Anouska Ricard 50
Antoine Espinasseau/Pavillon
de l'Arsenal 84
AtlanticTrampolines LTD 83
Attika Architekten 299
Aventoza 63
Ball and Albanese 231
Barry Prophet 243
Bas Sprakel 166
BeauEr 160
Benjamin Benschneider 290
Benjamin Rasmussen 208
Bernie Blackburn 218
BIG-Bjarke Ingels Group 85
Bill Davis 198
Boris Zuliani 172
Brian Gloud 240
Brian Reynolds 184
Brotherton-Lock 264
Bruce Damonte 212
Casagrande & Bjørnådal 242
Céline Laurière ©
Architecture and Vision 32
Chen Yan 168
Chris Pennings 270
Chris Wiebe 92
Christine Bree, Gidget Retro
Teardrop Camper 13
Cia Stiernstedt 289
Cornelius Comanns 167
Courtesy 2R Aventure 192
Courtesy Andrea Rosen
Gallery, New York and Sadie

Coles HQ, London. © Andrea
Zittel. Photo by Jessica
Eckert 257
Courtesy © Architecture and
Vision 44
Courtesy Arthobler Gallery,
Zurich, Switzerland. Photo by
Susana Dinis 170
Courtesy the artist and
Galerie Gabrielle Maubrie,
Paris 196
Courtesy Camp-Inn. Photo
by David Rossiter 149
Courtesy Charles Spitzack
237
Courtesy Cocoon Tree 37
Courtesy Gillard Associates
259
Courtesy EDAR.org 193
Courtesy IDEO, http://
automobility.ideo.com 202
Courtesy KANEKO. Photo by
Tom Kessler 188
Courtesy Lucy + Jorge Orta
© ADAGP, Paris and DACS,
London 2016. Photo by
Pierre Leguillon 33
Courtesy Lucy + Jorge Orta
© ADAGP, Paris and DACS,
London 2016. Photo by JJ
Crance 143
Courtesy MetroShip 294
Courtesy Michael Rakowitz
43
Courtesy Rintala Eggertsson
Architects 101, 267, 278
Courtesy of SOM © Oak
Ridge Natioanl Laboratory
228
Courtesy Studio Sascha
Akkermann 258
Courtesy taxaoutdoors.com
94, 158
Cyril Nottelet & Al Borde 226
Daici Ano 95
Danese 70
Daniel Durnin 283
Daniel Evans 126
Daniel Riera 40
Daniël Venneman 200

David A. Garcia 131
David Kahn 263
David McHugh/UNP 292
Derek Diedricksen 159
Deyan Tomov 213
DL ateler 169
Dominic French 285
Donald Lawrence 241
Dwightly 205
Dylan Euteneier 182
Dylan Gordan 201
Elmar Hahn 93, 132
Emmanuelle Bayart 118
Eric Hudiburg 89
Erik Jacobs 145
Erkko Aarti and Pyry
Kantonen 47
ETA 141
Featuring 72
Felicity Crawshaw 176
FieldCandy.com 28
Floating Homes GmbH 286
Florian Holzherr 112
Fotostudio Toelle 52
Frederik Vercruysse 86
Gabriella Morrison 186
GG Archard 185
Giacomo Pompanin 244
Greg Epperson/Shutterstock
51
© Gordian Overschmidt www.
zendome.com, 2007 256
H3T architekti 144
Hauke Dressler 254
Hipaholic 119
© Hwang Kim 30
Ian Ugarte 255
Igor Sapina 189
Iñaqui Carnicero 55
Iris Rijskamp 107
Itsuo Inouye AP/Press
Association Images 73
Ivan Juarez 34
Ivan Ovchinnikov 269
Iyo Hasegawa 21
Jacinta Costa & Carlos
Casimiro da Costa 171
Jack Hobhouse 288
Jan Kattein 35
Jesper Anhede © Genberg

Phaidon Press Limited
Regent's Wharf
All Saints Street
London N1 9PA

Phaidon Press Inc.
65 Bleecker Street
New York, NY 10012

phaidon.com

First published 2017
© 2017 Phaidon Press Limited

ISBN 978 0 7148 7349 7

A CIP catalogue record for this book is available
from the British Library.

Commissioning Editor: Virginia McLeod
Project Editor: Virginia McLeod
Editorial Assistant: Henry Martin

Picture Research: Annalaura Palma
Production Controller: Leonie Kelman

Design: StudioKanna

Printed in Romania